The Sacrificial Service
Gestures of Flesh and Spirit

Jonathan Grossman

תורת הקורבנות

The Sacrificial Service

Gestures of Flesh and Spirit

TRANSLATED BY

Sara Daniel

Maggid Books

The Sacrificial Service
Gestures of Flesh and Spirit

First English Edition, 2026

Maggid Books
An imprint of Koren Publishers Jerusalem Ltd.

POB 8531, New Milford, CT 06776-8531, USA
& POB 4044, Jerusalem 9104001, Israel
www.korenpub.com

The publication of this book was made possible
through the generous support of *The Jewish Book Trust.*

ISBN 978-1-59264-730-9, *hardcover*

Printed and bound in the United States

In loving memory of our fathers
and Saba and Zadie,

Noé Gidali z"l

Rabbi Jonas Hochman z"l

Barbara and Simcha Hochman
David and Ayelet Ellenbogen
Ariel and Amalia Hochman

In gratitude to

Rav Dr. Yoni Grossman

For his remarkable contributions to Torah study

Gail and Terry Novetsky

Contents

Foreword

> We shared sweet secrets as we walked along
> the crowd at the House of God. (Ps. 55:15)

It's no secret that the book of *Vayikra* – especially its opening section of sacrificial laws – is intimidating. Many are reluctant to delve too deeply into these chapters, usually for one of two main reasons. The first is that this section seems extremely technical and entirely based on elaborate detail. The second is that this detail is of little relevance today, and there are even certain reservations – sometimes emotional, sometimes moral – toward the idea of slaughtering animals and dashing their blood against the altar. The Talmud depicts with veneration the sheer quantities of blood that flowed while the Passover lambs were being slaughtered: "It is praiseworthy that the sons of Aaron walked in blood up to their ankles" (Pesaḥim 65b), but I am not convinced that this description sounds quite as venerable to the modern ear.

These two reservations pose a special challenge to those who wish to study these chapters. This book, however, is exempt from the second consideration, given that it explores the dissection of words, not animals. Its purpose is to understand the symbolic meaning of the sacrifices, not to gain any practical understanding of their execution. This book focuses on the intent and consciousness that accompanies these rituals, rather than the blood spilled upon the altar.

Dealing with the first issue – that is, breaking down the intimidating barrier of the difficult, complicated details of the sacrificial laws – is the main objective of this book. Throughout my analysis, my underlying thesis is that these apparently technical details in fact reflect or represent the fundamental, essential religious consciousness of the person who is offering a sacrifice to his or her Maker. The different laws relating to the sacrifices are a window to each offering and its particular meaning. to the various paths available to the person who wishes to approach the Sanctuary. The realm of the offerings momentarily pierces the mystery that veils the world of holiness; each pathway to God paved by the seeker driven by guilt or regret or longing for closeness offers a snatched glimpse of the elusive world of divine immanence.

It goes without saying that the works of many exegetes and scholars contributed to the analysis this book proposes, but two such works were my constant companions: R. David Zvi (Radatz) Hoffmann's commentary on Leviticus, with its sensitive, sharp dialogue between modern and traditional sources, and Prof. Jacob Milgrom's comprehensive, marvelous Anchor Bible commentary on Leviticus, whose breadth and importance cannot be overstated.

This book's sphere is largely based on *peshat*, but I did venture into Midrash Halakha and the premises of these midrashim. As will emerge throughout the book, many halakhic deliberations reflect different readings of the text, and halakhic rulings that initially seem far removed from *peshat* are actually addressing textual subtleties and disparities.

I first explored the material of this book in two courses I taught at Bar-Ilan University and Herzog College. At the end of 2016, a talented, diligent student by the name of Michael Israel approached me with a neat, thorough summary of every class. These notes were an indispensable basis for the reorganization of the material as a 2018–19 series of online lectures for the Israel Koschitzky Torat Har Etzion Virtual Beit Midrash. I am indebted to my teacher, R. Ezra Bick, *rosh yeshiva* of the

Virtual Beit Midrash, whose skill and guidance has broadened Torah horizons all over the world. This process also gifted me with an excellent editor, Binyamin Frankel, and I am grateful for his careful attention to every word and idea. Warm thanks are due to my friend and neighbor from Alon Shevut, R. Yitzchak Blau, who reviewed the first draft of this book and offered important, helpful insights that were incorporated into subsequent drafts.

This book was originally written in Hebrew (published by Maggid in 2021), and its English translation is dedicated to the memory of Esther Mann Snyder *z"l* by her devoted husband, Haim Shalom, and loving daughters, Lea Cohen and Sharona Adelman, and their families.

Esther was a devoted librarian and scholar who served as the director of Bar-Ilan University's Law Faculty Library for over thirty years. Raised in a rabbinical family in Boston, she deepened her connection to Jewish tradition by earning her bachelor's degree from Stern College. She later completed a Master's in Library Science at Columbia University and, specializing in legal bibliography, was invited to establish the law library at Bar-Ilan University, leading her to make aliya. Years of successfully running the library earned her recognition as an expert, and she was later asked to establish and plan law libraries for other academic institutions.

Alongside her professional achievements, she was a devoted mother who instilled in her children a love of learning and a strong commitment to Jewish values. Her dedication to knowledge, learning, and family guided her work and legacy. May her memory be a blessing.

Likewise, I thank the Hochman and Novetsky families for their support for the publication of this English edition.

I would like to express my gratitude to Sara Daniel for her professional and outstanding translation of the book. Her love for Torah study also enriched the discussions woven into the text, and I deeply appreciate her assistance.

Warm thanks are due to Koren/Maggid Publishers, who took on the publication of this book; to its head, Matthew Miller; to its CEO, Yehoshua Miller; to its Editorial Director, R. Reuven Ziegler, David Silverstein, Ita Olesker, Meira Mintz, and Debbie Ismailoff. Maggid's careful attention to each and every book they publish is not to be taken for granted.

With a heart bursting with love and gratitude, I wish to thank my dear mother, Rachel Grossman, and my wife Liora and our children, whose constant love and support have allowed me to pursue my studies, writing, dreams, and growth.

During the translation of this book, on the seventeenth of Adar 5784 (2024), my beloved father and mentor, Prof. Avraham Grossman of blessed memory passed away. His rare and noble personality touched everyone he met, and his imprint on my own study and work is ever-present. I hope that the study of this book will also be *le'ilui nishmato*.

Jonathan Grossman
Alon Shvut 2025

> "Israel's altar may not bring God to earth, but it enables man, through his worship, to reach heaven." (Milgrom, *Leviticus*, vol. 1, 251)

Introduction

FROM PRACTICE TO THEOLOGY

The book of Leviticus poses a special challenge. Not only are the sacrificial laws no longer relevant today, but at first glance, they seem so overly detailed that it is difficult to reconcile such technicality with any kind of spirituality; its problematic, daunting reputation seems all too justified. An impeccable example is R. Joseph ibn Kaspi's explanation of why he omits the book of Leviticus from his commentary on the Torah:

> All that this book includes was said from God to Moses in the month of Nisan, at the beginning of the second year after they left Egypt. It concerns mainly practical laws and little virtue; therefore it does not befit me to speak about the book at all.
> (*Mishneh Kesef*, part I, 155).

Because the book of Leviticus is almost wholly devoted to practical laws, R. Joseph ibn Kaspi writes that "it does not befit me to speak about the book at all." This is a bold, provocative statement, and he indeed devotes but a short paragraph to Leviticus before moving on to the book of Numbers. Others are far more subtle and write that the book of Leviticus is hardly relevant for the individual and speaks rather to a collective audience.[1]

From the outset, I should note my belief that this is a fundamental mistake; in truth, few books serve as a gateway to the religious world – and for communication between a person and their Maker – as the book of Leviticus does. It is this manual of technicalities that has the power to channel sanctity, unmediated. It focuses on holiness itself, not just on its historical or social implications.

This observation applies to the various sections of Leviticus, and it goes without saying that the book's second part – "The Book of Holiness" – expresses the idea of the centrality of holiness with pure, unadulterated clarity. Yet the same is true of the book's opening section of sacrificial laws. Its details are complex indeed, but they are not merely technical; rather, they should be perceived as vehicles for the expression of theological principles. The sacrificial laws are a looking glass for the spiritual experience that transpires in the House of God and the religious consciousness that can be manifested in God's presence. From this perspective, determining the difference between a burnt offering and a peace offering, or between both the latter and a grain offering, or between a grain offering of fine flour and a grain offering baked in the oven means determining the particular spiritual mindset that accompanies and is expressed through each process. Each offering has its own fingerprint, its own unique spiritual gesture.

The chapters of sacrificial law offer a smorgasbord of ritual expressions; furthermore, they detail precisely how to enact each different ritual. One who brings a sacrifice for the purpose of atonement obviously acts with different intent than one who seeks to express joy or thanksgiving. Moreover, the Torah does not merely offer one kind of freewill offering, but three different options – a burnt offering, a grain offering, and a peace offering – so that the person who elects to bring a sacrifice must ascertain precisely what he or she wishes to offer up to God. In order to go down this path, I wish to adopt Milgrom's premise:

1. Kasher, *Torah Shelema,* part 25, on *Parashat Vayikra,* vol. 1, 265–80.

"Obviously, the ritual complexities of Leviticus 1–16 make sense only as aspects of a symbolic system."[2]

There are several access points to the unique discourse that accompanies and characterizes each offering and its nature. Throughout our analysis, we will consistently note four such keys to each offering: its name, the details of its laws, the linguistic texture and design of its description, and any instances of the offering in biblical narrative. This analysis will illuminate the subtle differences between each kind of freewill offering; it will also help distinguish between the various obligatory offerings.

None of this dispels the notion that the sacrificial world truly transcends the sphere of the individual; sacrifices are indeed fundamentally linked to the Divine Presence in Israel. According to R. Judah HaLevi, the main purpose of sacrifices is to allow the Divine Presence to rest among Israel. This approach is particularly supported by the command for the regular burnt offering, which links the daily morning and afternoon offerings to the Divine Presence in the Sanctuary: "This shall be the regular burnt offering throughout your generations at the entrance of the Tent of Meeting before the Lord. There I will meet with you, there I will speak to you, and there I will meet with the Israelites. It will be sanctified by My glory" (Ex. 29:42–43). As we will see, this perspective is also expressed in the sacrificial laws of Leviticus, which supports the argument that sacrifices are not merely for the benefit of the individual's relationship with God, but for collective connection to the Divine as well. Thus, although this book is devoted to the analysis of specific offerings, it is still set against a broader theological backdrop: All sacrifices are ultimately channels of connection with the Divine.

RICH AND POOR; ISRAEL AND THE NATIONS

In the classic midrashic work Leviticus Rabba, obvious motifs are accompanied by two surprising recurring themes.[3] The first is special consideration for the poor. The Midrash seems particularly disposed toward the weakest layer of society and repeatedly emphasizes that they are just as welcome in God's presence as the higher, wealthier classes. This is

2. Milgrom, *Leviticus*, vol. 1, 440–43.
3. See Reizel, *Introduction to Midrashic Literature*, 130–32.

worth articulating when the topic at hand is sacrifices: When wealthy people are able to bring extravagant, expensive offerings to display their devotion to God, there is certainly a need to assuage fears that those who cannot afford such offerings are not worthy of God's service and blessing. In fact, the Torah itself is sensitive to this need: For various offerings, different sacrificial options are available for different budgets; there are no other biblical commandments for which this is the case. The Midrash is attuned to this sensitivity, and repeatedly emphasizes that God cares about the depth of a person's devotion, not their offering's monetary value. Here is one apt example:

> King Agrippa sought to sacrifice one thousand burnt offerings on one day. He sent for and said to the High Priest: "Let no man other than me bring an offering today." A poor person brought two turtledoves and said to the priest: "Sacrifice these." He said to him: "The king commanded me: Let no man other than me bring an offering today." He said to him: "My lord High Priest, each day I trap four [birds] and I sacrifice two and support myself from two. If you do not sacrifice them, you are cutting off my sustenance." He took them and sacrificed them.
>
> Agrippa had a vision in a dream that the offering of a poor person preceded his. He sent and said to the High Priest: "Did I not command you: Let no man other than me bring an offering today?"... [He repeated the story to him, and the king replied:] "What you did was right." (Leviticus Rabba 3:5)

A second recurring theme is the attitude toward the non-Jew and, more generally, the relationship between Israel and the nations. The Midrash underscores the disparity between Israel and the nations, as is already established in the work's opening chapter:

> What is the difference between prophets of Israel and prophets of the nations of the world? R. Ḥama bar Ḥanina and R. Yissakhar of Kefar Mandi. R. Ḥama bar Ḥanina said: The Holy One, blessed be He, appears to the nations of the world with only truncated speech, as it says: "God happened [*vayikkar*] upon Bilaam" (Num.

> 23:4). But [He communicates with] the prophets of Israel with complete speech, as it is stated: "He called [*vayikra*] to Moses." R. Yissakhar of Kefar Mandi said: So shall be their reward. "*Vayikkar*" is an expression of nothing other than impurity, as it says: "Who will not be pure due to a nocturnal emission [*mikre*]" (Deut. 23:11). But the prophets of Israel [receive prophecy] with an expression of sanctity, purity, and clarity, with an expression the angels use to laud the Holy One, as it says: "One called [*vekara*] to the other and said: [Holy, holy, holy is the Lord of hosts]" (Is. 6:3).... The Rabbis say: This can be likened to a king who had a wife and a concubine. When he would go to his wife, he would go in public, and when he would go to his concubine he would go in private. So too, the Holy One, blessed be He, appears to the nations of the world only at night, as it is stated: "God came to Avimelekh in a nocturnal dream" (Gen. 20:3).... But [God appears] to the prophets of Israel by day, as it is stated: "[The Lord appeared to him...] and he was sitting at the entrance of his tent in the heat of the day" (Gen. 18:1). (Leviticus Rabba 1:13)

At the outset, the midrashic author indicates the difference between divine revelation to Israel and to the nations: Israel's prophets are God's "wife," and the nations of the world are but God's concubines. This paradigm is repeated throughout the Midrash, which does display a complex attitude toward the nations; nonetheless, they are placed far below Israel. This is not the obvious choice. There are other possible models, such as that conveyed in Isaiah's prophecy of universal amity: "As for the foreigners who have come to join the Lord... I shall bring them to My holy mount, show them joy in My house of prayer. Their offerings and sacrifices are desired on My altar, for My House will be called a house of prayer for all peoples" (Is. 56:6–7).[4]

Even if it is not the obvious choice, the midrashic decision to underscore the disparity between Israel and the nations here is understandable

4. Marc Hirshman proposes that the disparity between Isaiah's prophecy and the midrash's tone is based on their respective historical contexts (Hirshman, *House of Prayer*).

in light of the fundamental challenge inherent in the sacrificial laws of Leviticus. In the ancient world, sacrifice was universal to all religious worship. *Encyclopaedia Hebraica* defines "*korban,*" "offering," as "one of the most common ritual acts in most world religions." Even the minor qualification, "most," which implies that a few religions (such as Buddhism) do not practice actual sacrifice, can be challenged given that they do offer up gifts as expressions of devotion and veneration, so that even if the religion does not officially recognize sacrifice as part of its ritual worship, the notion of sacrifice and "sacrificial models" are nonetheless given expression in the practical, popular sense.[5]

Ancient peoples offered sacrifices to their gods before Israel came into being, before the time of Abraham and Moses. This raises the question as to the nature of the sacrifices described in such depth and detail in the Torah and their relation to parallel acts of sacrifice in other religions. The author of the Midrash is well aware of this question, and therefore takes pains to point out that the superficial similarities to other nations' sacrifices do not reflect a fundamental similarity. Israel's sacrifices (and revelations) are inherently superior to those of other nations, and this is expressed in the Torah itself. These differences and similarities are beyond the scope of this book, but extensive studies have been devoted to the topic.[6] For now, I will note one fundamental difference – an idea that will continue to inform my entire analysis.

IS THE OFFERING "CONSUMED" BY THE ALTAR?

One fundamental principle of biblical sacrifices is that offerings are not cooked before they are offered up on the altar; rather, they are roasted

5. Werblowsky, "Sacrifice," 58–59.
6. See, for example, Tzvi Weinberg's dissertation *The Offering in Israel.* He notes in his conclusion that "the similarity between Israel's sacrificial laws and [the offerings of] the nations is most salient in details that are not significant enough to assume a fundamental similarity between them" (p. 186). Some scholars do believe that there are broader connections between the biblical sacrifice and the nations' sacrifices. On the theory of Canaanite influence on biblical sacrifice, see especially Gray, *Legacy of Canaan*; van den Branden, "Lévitique"; Dussaud, *Les Origines.* For theories of Mesopotamian influence, see Thompson, *Penitence and Sacrifice*; Leslie, *Canaanite Background.* Others claim that despite these similarities, the biblical offering has unique features that reflect its vast theological difference (Albright, *Archeology*).

by its fire. This idea is by no means obvious, as is evident from the story of Eli's sinful sons:

> This was how the priests would deal with the people: Whenever someone offered a sacrifice, the priest's boy would come along as the meat was boiling, a three-pronged fork in his hand. He would stab it into the cauldron, kettle, pot, or vat, and the priest would snatch whatever came up on the fork. This was how they treated every Israelite who came there to Shilo. Even before they burned off the fat, the priest's boy would come and say to the person who was sacrificing, "Hand over some meat to roast for the priest – he won't accept boiled meat from you, only raw." And if the man would say to him, "Let them first burn off the fat, then take as much as you want," he would reply, "No, hand it over at once – if not, I will take it by force." (I Sam. 2:13)[7]

The narrative's main point is that Eli's sons are not willing to wait until the meat has been offered on the altar before they take their priestly portion, but what is interesting for our purpose is that from the dialogue between the priest's boy and the sacrificing Israelites it can be understood that the sacrifices were usually boiled before they were offered on the altar.[8] Intriguingly, there is no mention of cooking the meat before it is offered in Leviticus; on the contrary, there is every indication that the meat should be offered while it is still raw, before it is fit for human

7. Unless otherwise indicated, all quotations of verses from the Tanakh are based on *The Koren Tanakh*, Magerman Edition (2021).
8. Some attempt to prove that this was Israelite practice based on the Gideon narrative: "Gideon went in and prepared a young goat and unleavened bread from an ephah of flour. He placed the meat in a basket and poured the broth into a pot. He brought it out to Him under the terebinth and served it" (Judges 6:19). The "broth" indicates that the meat was already cooked (Wellhausen, *Prolegomena*, 66). This is tenuous proof, however, given that Gideon was not sure whether his visitor was human or not, so he presumably prepared an "offering" that would be fit for human consumption as well.

consumption.[9] This is no trivial detail; it offers a glimpse into what made biblical sacrifices unique in the ancient world.

There is room to understand why the priests at Shiloh boiled the sacrificial meat before offering it on the altar; this improved the meat's texture and flavor and made it tastier, which would have resulted in a far superior gift to God.[10] Even so, according to biblical law, meat is not placed on the altar as food ready to eat, but as raw material. This reflects a central characteristic of the Israelite offering: Even if the altar "consumes" the offering, it is not considered God's food.[11] In contrast to the prevalent belief in ancient times that the gods subsisted on offerings from their worshippers and blessed those who served them food,[12]

9. It is no coincidence that the verb "cook" is used in conjunction with the Passover offering; whether tradition holds that it is cooked or roasted is a famous dispute. What is relevant for our purposes is that in Deuteronomy (16:7), it is presented as eaten by those who bring the offering ("You shall cook and eat it at the place that your Lord God will choose"). "Cooking" the meat – which implies stewing or boiling – makes it edible for human consumption.
10. On cooking the meat of offerings in ancient Chinese ritual, see Boileau, "Cooking and Sacrifice." He cites ancient texts that explicitly show that the sacrificial meat was cooked in water before being offered to the gods. On sacrificial preparation in ancient Egypt, see Weinberg, *Sacrifice in Israel*, 81–91. In Mesopotamia, some cuts of meat were cooked before being offered up, while others were offered raw (Weinberg, ibid., 99).
11. See especially De Vaux, *Ancient Israel*, vol. 2, 449–50. Anderson rejects this distinction between Israel and the nations and argues that there are biblical hints that offerings were indeed intended for God's consumption, based on phrases such as "the Lord's table" or "the Lord's bread" and the fact that offerings consisted of bread, oil, and wine, like a human meal (Anderson, *Sacrifices and Offerings*, vol. 2, 15). While the language sometimes does convey the sense that God "eats" the offerings, Milgrom argues that this is purely metaphoric (*Leviticus*, vol. 1, 44), and while the divine fire does "consume" the offerings, there is never any sense that God needs this food: "Were I to hunger, I would not tell you, for Mine is the world and all that fills it. Do I eat the flesh of bulls? Do I drink the blood of he-goats? Offer to God a thanksgiving sacrifice; pay your vows to the Most High" (Ps. 50:12–15). This is a clear distinction from other ancient religious cultures.
12. See many examples in Kaufmann, *Religion of Israel*, vol. 1, 398–403. On what differentiates biblical sacrifice from pagan sacrifice, he writes: "No convention has mythological basis: no conventions are explained by events in divine life or are related to any aspect of divine life... this cultic ritual is not rooted in divine life or in the nature of divine being, but in the person's relationship to God: reverence,

no such notion is evident in Leviticus, and there is no indication that the offering should be precooked. (The cooked grain offerings are an exception to this rule, and we will discuss them in the relevant chapter.)

The distinction between offerings in the Torah and in the rest of the ancient world is aptly reflected in the description of Noah's offerings after the Flood. The story of the Flood is also found in many extra-biblical traditions, the most famous being two Akkadian myths: *The Epic of Gilgamesh* and *Atra-Hasis*. A broader discussion of the biblical and Akkadian flood narratives is beyond the scope of this book;[13] what is relevant is a comparison of the heroes' offerings to the deity that saved them. The Babylonian flood myth, *Atra-Hasis*, describes: "He brought them out to the four winds and offered up a offering / he offered libation on the top of the mountain / he nourished the gods / burned incense of reed and cedar. The gods smelled the sweet savor, and swarmed like flies to the offering."[14] Desperately starving because they have wiped out most of the humans who feed them with sacrifices, the gods pounce on Atra-Hasis's offering.

Needless to say, there is no biblical account of God's hunger or thirst, nor any description of God needing any kind of food. In the parallel scene in Genesis, after Noah safely leaves the ark, "Noah built an altar to the Lord and, taking of each of the kinds of pure animals and pure birds, sacrificed burnt offerings on the altar. The Lord smelled the fragrant aroma and said in His heart, 'Never again will I curse the land because of man'" (Gen. 8:20–21). The similarity between the scenes underscores their difference: Both deities "smell" the offerings' savory aroma, but whereas this aroma stirs the Akkadian gods to fall upon the

---

sanctification, honor, love, joy, gratitude for God's kindness toward society and the individual – these are the ideals that sustain it, that give it meaning" (ibid., 532).

13. A more comprehensive comparison between the narratives reveals that the context of the biblical account is moral, whereas the Akkadian context is the selfish nature of the gods. See, for example, Grintz, *Genesis*, 42–45; Sarna, *Understanding Genesis*, 39–62; Frymer-Kensky, "Babylonian Flood"; Davidson, "Genesis Flood Narrative."
14. *Atra-Hasis*, Tablet III, lines 249–54; Shifra and Klein, *In Those Distant Days*, 127.

meat hungrily, the biblical God is merely inspired to bless Noah. He has no need to eat the meat on the altar.[15]

Perhaps all this is obvious to the modern reader raised with abstract monotheistic beliefs, but during the biblical era, this characterization of God was both a revelation and a revolution. Beyond the new perception of divinity, this scene portrays an entirely new concept of worship. An offering is not brought in order to provide God's needs, but rather to allow each of the worshippers to express themselves before their Maker, to approach Him and become close to Him. The offering is not accompanied by formulaic verbal content; this non-verbal content is its main objective. The living, evolving relationship between a person and God forms the basis for the sphere of action and interaction that constitutes every offering. The act of sacrifice is what tells the story, which is rooted in the experience of the sacrifice bringer, not in God's need for food. This is the premise that lies at the heart of this analysis of the sacrificial chapters of Leviticus.

15. See especially Sarna, *Understanding Genesis*, 53–56. Intriguingly, the "sweet savor" in the Babylonian version is from the incense, whereas in Genesis the meat itself has a delicious aroma. Some claim that the assumption is that Noah burns incense in Genesis as well, but this seems contrived: Roasting meat produces a mouthwatering aroma in itself. We will discuss this in the context of the addition of frankincense to the grain offering. Some argue that the Ancient Egyptians believed that gods were nourished by the scent of the offerings and not the actual flesh (see Weinberg, *Sacrifice in Israel*, 284).

Chapter 1

The Significance of Offerings

Before we delve into the actual text, I want to begin with a fundamental question: If the offering is not intended as food for God, then what *is* its purpose? What religious function do offerings serve?

The Rema, R. Moses Isserles, devoted a whole book to this question, *Torat HaOla,* in which he surveys different approaches to the nature and purpose of sacrifices. Also worthy of note is R. Menahem Kasher's extensive survey in his work *Torah Shelema,*[1] as well as Jacob Milgrom's commentary on Leviticus.[2] All three offer indispensable, largely accurate insight into the nature of biblical sacrifice. After a brief survey of these approaches, I will offer a fourth possibility, which I will adhere to throughout my own analysis.

1. Kasher, *Torah Shelema,* part 25, on *Parashat Vayikra,* vol. 1, 265–80.
2. Milgrom, *Leviticus,* vol. 1, 440–43.

1. A POLEMIC AGAINST PAGAN WORSHIP

One prominent approach, already firmly rooted in midrashic literature, perceives the sacrificial world as a necessary response to the pagan world of Israel's time. In ancient culture, ritual worship without sacrifice was unfathomable, much as a religion without prayer would be today. Thus, the Torah embraced and institutionalized this aspect of worship, but deliberately diverted it away from the idea that offerings were food for the gods or ritual safeguards from demons and evil spirits. This seems to be illustrated in the following midrash:

> R. Pinḥas said in the name of R. Levi: This is like a king's son who was coarse and used to eating impure carcasses. The king said: "This one will frequent my table, and on his own he will be restricted." So too, Israel eagerly served idols in Egypt and brought offerings to the satyrs, as it is stated: "They shall no longer slaughter their offerings to the satyrs [*se'irim*]" (Lev. 17:7). These satyrs are nothing other than demons, as it is stated: "They would slaughter to demons" (Deut. 32:17).... The Holy One, blessed be He, said: "At all times, let them sacrifice their offerings before me in the Tent of Meeting, and they will separate themselves from idol worship and will be saved." That is what is written: "Any man from the house of Israel." (Leviticus Rabba 22:8)

The quote from Leviticus 7:17 is mentioned in the context of the peace offering, but Rambam applies this theory to all offerings (see *Guide for the Perplexed*, III:32, 46). He proposes, for example, that the Torah commands the sacrifice of oxen and sheep because idol worshippers were careful not to sacrifice these animals. Another classic example of his theory concerns the prohibition of adding honey and the obligation to add salt:

> Because idol worshippers would never offer up unleavened bread, and because they would often offer up sweet things and season their offerings with honey, as mentioned above,[3] and because

3. He is referring to III:29.

> there is no mention of salt in any of their offerings, the Law therefore prohibited the offering of any leaven or honey and commanded to always add salt.[4]

This is a bold stance that assumes that all offerings are purely polemical and have no inherent value of their own; had oxen and sheep been the usual pagan sacrifices, the Torah would have prohibited the sacrifice of those animals. Famously, many challenge this reading as one that devalues the Torah's eternal nature; as Ramban sharply criticizes: "But these words are mere expressions, healing casually a severe wound and a great difficulty, and making the table of the Eternal polluted.... Far be it that they should have no other purpose and intention except the elimination of idolatrous opinions from the minds of fools!" (on Lev. 1:9). It is worth noting that Rambam himself claims elsewhere that the sacrificial world is too deep and profound to be fully understood: "All the offerings are considered statutes. The Sages said that the world continues to exist in merit of the sacrificial service" (*Mishneh Torah, Hilkhot Me'ila* 8:8).[5]

Although this approach might indeed be too limited to apply to the sacrificial world in general, it certainly has the power to illuminate specific details. It may well be that certain aspects are intended to differentiate biblical offerings from pagan offerings and to educate the people to a decidedly different sacrificial paradigm. The biblical sacrificial world is a silent revolution that pours new content into traditional ritual vessels. Robertson Smith points out three unique purposes that the biblical offering serves: It expresses partnership with God; it can be a gift; and it effects atonement.[6] The fact that he does not mention that these offer-

4. *Guide for the Perplexed*, III:46.
5. R. Tzadok of Lublin perceived this as the way the world was designed, not as a retrospective response; the concept of sacrificial service was a *tikkun* for the sin of the Golden Calf, because holiness and light and spiritual progress are achieved only in the wake of sin and darkness and failure (see *Likutei Maamarim, Derasha LeSiyum Shas* [Bnei Berak, 1973], 240).
6. Smith, *Lectures*. The various offerings are divided up among these roles: the peace offering shows partnership; the burnt offering is the ultimate gift; the purification and sin offerings provide atonement.

ings were believed to "feed God" or "drive away demons and evil spirits" shows the dramatically different nature of the Israelite sacrificial world.[7]

2. SUBSTITUTION OFFERING

Unlike the claim that sacrifices are purely polemical, one notable positive explanation is that the animals offered up to God are substitutions for the person offering the sacrifice. When people sin, they need something to offer up to God in place of their own selves, so they offer an animal instead. The ultimate model for this approach is the ram that replaces Isaac at the very last moment. After all, one of the leading objectives of that episode is to explain that animal sacrifices must replace human sacrifices – that the phrase "a burnt offering in place of his son" (Gen. 22:13) is no incidental detail, but the main point.[8] This implies that all burnt offerings are "in place" of people, especially given that the binding narrative describes how Abraham sanctifies Israel's future site of sacrifice through this act: "To this day, it is said: On the mountain of the Lord He will be seen" (22:14).

Ramban is a prominent proponent of this approach. Based on the requirement that the entire burnt offering must be consumed with fire – "The priest shall then burn it all on the altar as a burnt offering, an offering of fire" (Lev. 1:9) – he writes:

> This is a far more accurate reason for the offerings: Since man's deeds are accomplished through thought, speech, and action, God commanded that when man sins and brings an offering, he should lay his hands upon it to contrast with his sinful act. He should confess his sin verbally to contrast with his [evil] speech, and he should burn the innards and the kidneys [of the offering] in fire because they are the instruments of thought and desire in the human being. He should burn the legs [of the offering] since they correspond to the hands and feet of a person, which do all his work. He should sprinkle the blood upon the altar, which is

7. The great biblical scholar Yehezkel Kaufmann takes pains to prove this in his monumental work *The Religion of Israel.*
8. See further in Grossman, *Abraham,* 348–52.

> analogous to the blood in his body. All these acts are performed in order that when they are done, a person should realize that he has sinned against his God with his body and his soul, and that his own blood should really be spilled and his own body burned, were it not for the loving-kindness of the Creator, who took from him a substitute and a ransom, namely this offering, so that its blood should be in place of his blood, its life in place of his life, and that the chief limbs of the offering should be in place of the chief parts of his body. (Ramban on Lev. 1:9)

While Ramban's views are more complex than this comment, it is a convenient working example for discussion: He posits here that a sinner's own blood ought to be spilled, but an animal can be offered instead.

This idea is prevalent among modern scholars as well,[9] but it is insufficient in itself. First, it renders the act of sacrifice upon the altar as secondary, as it focuses upon the death of the animal – "that its blood should be in place of his blood, its life in place of his life" – whereas the biblical text seems to place utmost importance on the fact that the sacrifice is consumed by the fire of the altar. While the formulation can be adjusted to reflect this by explaining that it is the animal being sacrificed *to God* and not just its death that constitutes the substitutive act, this still seems unsatisfactory. The tone of the verses describing the peace offering does not seem to be one of "blood for blood."[10] Even the classic *ḥatat* – the purification offering – is not portrayed as an act of atonement, but as a means of purifying the Sanctuary; the element of substitution is less relevant. On the other hand, the requirement of laying hands upon the offering does create a sense of transferal. The animal is going to the altar on behalf of its owner; this aspect is in harmony with the theory of substitution.

---

9. See, for example, in Janowski, *Heilsgeschehen.*
10. R. Jacob ben Asher, Baal HaTurim, writes similarly of the peace offering: "The fat that covers the entrails – this comes to atone for the sin of ingratitude and rebellion: 'Jeshurun grew fat and kicked'…" (on Lev. 3:3). This is problematic, however, given that the peace offering is not an offering of atonement for sin.

3. MANIFESTING THE DIVINE PRESENCE

The most famous proponent of the third approach is R. Judah HaLevi (see *HaKuzari*, II:25–26). He believes that the purpose of offerings is to bring the Divine Presence into Israel's midst. When sacrifices are offered, the Sanctuary becomes a resting place for the Divine Presence. Perhaps this sounds somewhat tautological: "Why is there a need to offer sacrifices in the Sanctuary? In order for the Sanctuary to be a place where sacrifices are offered." Yet as we will see in our discussion of Leviticus 6–7, especially the law of the burnt offering, this is evident in the text itself.[11] At Mount Sinai, God's glory takes the form of a blazing, consuming fire (Ex. 24:17), and Israel's offerings upon the altar sustain this divine fire and keep it burning in their midst. We will return to this idea and its role in our discussion of the eighth day of consecration.

A related idea is that the purpose of offerings is to restore spiritual order. This approach is not formulated in terms of the Divine Presence, but it also holds that the world of holiness is inherently related to different levels of differentiation and order, and offerings serve to maintain this order and thus allow holiness to be an integral part of life in Israel.[12]

4. RELIGIOUS AND MORAL EXPRESSION

In addition to the central theories mentioned above, many other ideas have been suggested over the generations. I wish to focus on a specific aspect that I consider to be one of the main objectives of the sacrificial world, especially freewill offerings.

---

11. R. Judah HaLevi's general approach is to prefer straightforward, honest worship of God to sophisticated, philosophical views; he reiterates this in his discussion of sacrifices and the Sanctuary (see *HaKuzari*, II:26). For a discussion of his ambivalence toward philosophy, see, for example, Urbach, *Pillars of Jewish Thought*, vol. 1, 263–67. He also discusses R. Judah HaLevi's approach to sacrifices (275–76).
12. "Order, grading, and hierarchy are central organizing principles in the Levitical system. In this way the cult seeks to integrate all aspects of Israel's life and bring them under God's rule. Sacrifice plays a role in that enterprise by summing up and reflecting the values and hierarchies found in other areas of life. It also performs the essential task of restoring the order of things when it is compromised by fault of some kind. As such, it preserves and enhances Israel's life before God, which is constantly threatened by the disorder and death associated with impurity and sin" (Jenson, "Sacrificial System," 36).

After exploring various theories, Zvi Weinberg writes: "I believe it is correct to point to a single motive: The worshipper – individual or collective – seeks closeness to God, in order to receive His grace: (1) either because he has lost it (and thus offers a purification or guilt offering); (2) or to increase it (and thus offers a burnt, peace, or grain offering)."[13] I concur with this idea, but I wish to formulate it differently.

As background for the analysis below, it is worth mentioning the French Jewish sociologist David Émile Durkheim, who asserts that it is incorrect to analyze the religious world merely as a philosophical and theological system; rather, religious practices and rituals have their own weight. He points out that many believers testify that their religion is essentially expressed through the practice of normative actions, which is far more relevant in their daily lives than any religious philosophy. I wish to employ this premise in our attempt to perceive the practical act of offering sacrifices as a religious "social fact," albeit deviating from Durkheim's perception that ritual supersedes religious experience; with respect to the latter, I favor Rudolph Otto's belief that religious experience invokes great awe, wonder, and a sense of the beyond.

R. Yehoshua b. Levi claims that "prayers were established instead of daily offerings,"[14] and over the course of the talmudic passage, it emerges that even the opposing view (that prayers were established by the Patriarchs) agrees that the prayer times and orders were based on the sacrificial service.[15] This reveals a fundamental element of the sacrificial act. Offering a sacrifice is to be perceived as an act of expression, a non-verbal gesture. This gesture is a convention, and all participants are aware of its meaning. When a lover gets down on one knee and holds out a ring, his gesture expresses intense emotion, and his intentions

13. Weinberg, *Sacrifice in Israel*, 330.
14. Berakhot 26b.
15. The talmudic discussion continues: "According to R. Yosei b. R. Ḥanina, who instituted the additional prayer? It is not one of the prayers instituted by the forefathers. Rather, even according to R. Yosei b. R. Ḥanina, the prayers were instituted by the Patriarchs and the Sages based them on the laws of the offerings." Avraham Shammah pointed out to me that the capacity of prayer to replace offerings is already evident in Tanakh; see Ps. 141:2: "Accept my prayer like incense before You, my lifted hands like the evening offering"; Prov 15:8; and Solomon's prayer at the new Temple.

are clear; his girlfriend knows that she must respond to his proposal of marriage before he even utters a word. When the Sages identify the prayer service as a verbal substitute for the sacrificial service, they are essentially stating that offerings have always been a convention, a gesture that expresses a certain meaning, religious experience, or expectation.

The connection between offering and prayer may even have common linguistic roots. In biblical Hebrew, the root A-T-R means "pray" (in *kal* form) and "to accept a prayer" (in *hiphil* – see Genesis 25:21 for both forms). In Ugaritic and Arabic, however, the root A-T-R means "to slaughter," "to offer up," and some suggest that the biblical word also originally connoted some act of sacrifice or ritual to God in an expression of prayer.[16] Even if this is not the case, the different Semitic meanings point to a common semantic root.

Though the biblical offering is a gesture that conveys a concrete meaning, it is not accompanied by any official verbal formula – and this is revolutionary. Extant ritual texts show that ancient people placed great importance on the verbal formulations that accompanied ritual sacrifices. One striking example is the following Egyptian daily temple sacrifice. These are the instructions to the ministering priest:

> The beginning of the utterances of the sacred rites which are carried out for the House of Amon-re, King of the gods, in the course of every day by the major priest who is in his day's service.
>
> The Utterance for Striking the Fire. Words to be spoken: "Welcome, welcome in peace, O Eye of Horus,[17] who art glorious, unharmed, and youthful in peace! It shines forth like Re upon the horizon.... The Eye of Horus drives away enemies for Amon-Re, Lord of the Thrones of the Two Lands, wherever they may be. An offering which the king gives: I am pure"....

---

16. See further in Hamori, *Women's Divination*, 46. The most intriguing verse in this context is in Ezekiel: "Each man had his censer in his hand, and a dense (*atar*) cloud of incense was ascending" (8:11), although this root also appears in the literal sense of "prayer" in 35:13.
17. The incense smoke (and other offerings) is called "the Eye of Horus" in these texts.

> The Utterance for Breaking the Clay.[18] Words to be spoken: "The clay is broken; the cool waters are opened; the veins of Osiris are drawn. I have certainly not come to drive the god from his throne; I have come to put the god upon his throne. Thus,thou abidest upon thy great throne, O Amon-Re, Lord of the Thrones of the Two Lands. I am the one whom the gods inducted. An offering which the king gives: I am pure."[19]

This text continues with further ritual statements, but this excerpt suffices to convey the feel and tone of the Egyptian rite. In the Ancient Near East, the ritual text was of supreme importance, sometimes more so than the ritual itself. This should come as no surprise; after all, a gesture can be interpreted in various ways, but the verbal formula pinpoints its particular meaning. The act of breaking the clay is open to interpretation – until the priest declares that it represents the flow of the cool waters from the god's veins to the Nile. Just as the bridegroom betroths his bride with a binding legal verbal statement as he places a ring on her finger beneath the bridal canopy, it is the verbal statements that accompany ancient sacrificial rites that define the meaning and purpose of these rites.

Given the prominence of verbal formulas in most ancient cultures, their complete absence from the biblical sacrificial laws is striking. With the exception of the priestly confession during the Temple purification ritual on Yom Kippur, there are no other speeches associated with the regular sacrificial service. (The bringing of the first fruits and the tithe declaration merit separate discussion.) This is even more surprising in light of the Torah's reservations toward mystical or pagan perceptions of offerings; one might have expected more emphasis on the proper intentions than on practical rites.

Yehezkel Kaufmann aptly explains that the verbal formulas of pagan rituals were essentially spells and divinations – not prayers but incantations. He believes that due to a determination to prevent this kind of religious expression, the Torah omits any kind of speech that might

18. Breaking the clay seals the temple doors.
19. ANET, 325 (John Wilson's translation).

be mistaken for mystical incantations that have any bearing on reality. Worship of the God of Israel consists of actions, not words: "The priestly temple is the kingdom of silence."[20] Israel Knohl adds that this silence reflects an abstract concept of divinity: "Silence characterizes a person's stance before the sublime, mysterious divinity that dwells in the Sanctuary."[21]

Thus, the offering became a wordless expression of religious experience, a gesture never articulated in precise verbal form. Although the opposite might seem true at first glance, this is essentially a richer, more abstract form of communication than a verbal formulation.[22]

Moreover, unlike a verbal prayer, an offering is also a gift, something that is transferred from the worshipper to a Higher Authority. Moshe Halbertal points out that the two most prevalent terms for offerings in the Torah – "*korban*" and "*minḥa*" – are from the same semantic field. "*Korban*" is from the root K-R-B, meaning "to draw near"; "*minḥa*" comes from "*noḥ*," meaning "to place." When someone brings an offering, they "draw near" and "place" the offering before God. One does not merely "give" an offering to God; to "give" assumes acceptance.[23] The sacrificial terminology has profound significance: An offering is part of a dialogue; there is no guarantee that God will accept what the worshipper places before Him. This is not a theurgical pagan rite that forces some kind of procedure upon reality. It is a display of will – of both the worshipper and God.

It is no coincidence that the first instance of sacrifice in the Torah tells of both acceptance and rejection. Abel's offering is accepted; Cain's is not. Elsewhere, I propose that the fact that no explicit reason is given for Cain's rejection is part of the narrative objective: Cain's face falls not just because he is rejected, but because he doesn't understand why.[24] This communicates an important element of sacrifice: There is

20. *The Religion of Israel*, vol. 2, 476.
21. Knohl, *Biblical Beliefs*, 120. A turning point occurred when the Sages instituted that a shift of Israelites would recite the Act of Creation at the time of the priestly watch in Jerusalem (see Mishna Taanit 4:2).
22. See a similar direction in Wenham, "Theology."
23. Halbertal, *On Sacrifice*, 10.
24. For further reading, see my analysis in Grossman, *Creation*, 139–63.

no guarantee that an offering will be accepted; it depends on whether God finds the bringer worthy.[25] Ramban aptly notes that the name "God" does not appear in the context of the sacrificial world, but the particular Tetragrammaton (translated as "Lord") does.[26] The sacrifice bringer is not standing before the remote, eternal ruler of all worlds; rather, they are seeking an intimate encounter with the God of Israel, known by His personal name.

The offering signifies the living dialogue between the human and the Divine that transpires beside the altar. This transferal is regulated by clear, firm rules, which stem from the real concern that the offering might not be accepted. This is not merely because, in the words of Japanese author Haruki Murakami, "There's an essential order you have to follow in everything. It's a way of showing respect, following everything in the correct order,"[27] but because the detailed sacrificial laws serve to reassure the worshipper that they are doing all that they can to ascertain that "it be accepted on his behalf" (Lev. 1:4). As Halbertal neatly puts it: "The sacrificial ritual is a protocol that serves as a safeguard from the risk of rejection."[28]

The worshipper's mindset and fear of rejection is expressed in the blessing for the Temple service in the *Amida* prayer. Some read the main theme of this prayer as a request for the rebuilding of the Temple and renewal of its service, based on its conclusion: "May our eyes witness Your return to Zion in compassion. Blessed are You, Lord, who restores His Presence to Zion." Yet this blessing was apparently recited even when the Temple still stood (without its conclusion, of course):

---

25. The Sages were stringent about sacrificial flesh being flung, not placed; some even claim that this is why there was a space between the ramp and the altar (see Zevaḥim 62b; Rambam, *Hilkhot Beit HaBeḥira* 2:13). The Sages based this on the juxtaposition between the offering of the limbs and the dashing of the blood. The idea behind this concept may be to maintain a gap between the worshipper and the burning fire; in the end, the human cannot fully reach divine glory, and there will always be an unbridgeable gap.
26. Ramban on Lev. 1:9; see also his commentary on Gen. 7:1; Ex. 18:13.
27. Haruki Murakami, *Kafka on the Shore.*
28. Halbertal, *On Sacrifice,* 15. He argues that because humanity received animal sacrifice from God, this generated a cycle of gift-giving that the worshipper longs to be a part of (ibid., 11–12).

> The appointed priest said to [the priestly watch]: Recite a single blessing of the *Shema* blessings that accompany *Shema*. And they recited a blessing, and then they recited the Ten Commandments, *Shema*, *VeHaya im Shamoa*, and *VaYomer*. They then blessed the people with three blessings: True and Firm, and *the blessing of the Temple service*, and the Priestly Benediction. And on Shabbat, the new priestly watch would add one blessing recited by the outgoing priestly watch. (Mishna Tamid 5:1)[29]

The blessing of the Temple service was also recited by the High Priest at the end of the Torah reading on Yom Kippur (Mishna Yoma 7:1) and when the king blessed the people during *Hak'hel* (Mishna Sota 7:7). In the words of Yitz Landes: "These sources show that the Sages understood that the blessing of the Temple Service recited in the Temple was the same as the blessing in the *Amida* prayer. This shows that according to the Sages, there was liturgical continuity after the destruction of the Temple."[30]

If we omit the components of this blessing that were added after the Temple's destruction (about the restoration of the Temple service and the acceptance of prayer in place of offerings), this results in the following blessing (based on the prayer we recite today):[31]

---

29. Rambam discusses this in *Mishneh Torah* but replaces the priestly blessing with the blessing for peace (*Hilkhot Temidin UMusafin* 6:5). Yitz Landes suggests that this mishna's model of sacrifices accompanied by blessings and prayer was based on Aaron's blessing during the days of the Sanctuary consecration (Landes, *Development of Birkat HaAvoda*, 14–16).
30. Landes, *Development of Birkat HaAvoda*, 18.
31. There are two different formulas for the ancient blessing for the Temple service of different origins that developed in two different ways (see further in Landes, *Development of Birkat HaAvoda*, 51–96), but this does not affect our discussion. Ehrlich claims that the blessing "Find favor... and establish in Zion," which is one version, could have been recited when the Temple still stood, for it could be a prayer for the continual Divine Presence (Ehrlich, "Dwelling Place," 8–9). On the attempt by the *Geonim* and *Rishonim* to determine the original version of the blessing, see Landes, *Development of Birkat HaAvoda*, 11.

> Find favor, Lord our God, in Your people Israel, and accept in love and favor the fire offerings of Israel. May the service of Your people Israel always find favor with You.[32]

The repetition of the phrase "find favor" at the blessing's beginning, middle, and end creates an intense prayer for the acceptance of Israel's offering with love and favor. Ezra Fleischer surmises (based on ancient liturgical poems) that the blessing's original conclusion was: "Blessed are You…who finds favor with [Israel's] service."[33] Similar language is used in the Torah itself in a sacrificial context: "That it be accepted (*venirtza*) on his behalf" (Lev. 1:4).

This prayer reflects the fear of rejection and asks that God find favor and accept the worshipper's offering and their deeds in general, even beyond the Temple's bounds: "May the service of Your people Israel always find favor with You." In our own time, when the Temple has not yet been rebuilt and offerings have not yet been reinstated, we recite this blessing with yearning for the return of the Divine Presence and pray that our prayers will be accepted as if they were offerings.

In a certain sense, this blessing serves as the conclusion of the *Amida* prayer. Even without settling the broader dispute regarding when the *Amida* prayer was instituted (Elbogen and Heinemann argue that the prayer was already recited while the Temple still stood; Levine and Fleischer claim it was only instituted in Yavneh after the destruction), it is clear that from its inception, the *Amida* prayer had a precise order and number of blessings. David Henshke has shown that initially, the *Amida* prayer ended with *Modim*, the blessing of thanksgiving, followed by the priestly blessing; the blessing for peace and the conclusion are later additions.[34] This is evident from the description of the Rosh HaShana prayer:

32. If this blessing was indeed recited when the Temple still stood, this explains why we pray that God will find favor with the "fire offerings of Israel."
33. Fleischer, "Prayers," 245–52. Shulamit Elitzur also favors this version, as it forms an *inclusio*, with the conclusion echoing the beginning (Elitzur, "Early Benedictions," 27–28).
34. Henshke, "*Amida*," especially 362.

> The order of blessings: One recites *Avot* and *Gevurot*... then the blessing for the Temple service, and thanksgiving, and the priestly blessing – according to R. Yoḥanan b. Nuri. R. Akiva said to him.... One recites *Avot*, and *Gevurot*... and then the blessing for the Temple service, and thanksgiving, and the priestly blessing. (Mishna Rosh HaShana 4:5)

In this quote I have omitted the mishnaic debate regarding the order of the blessings for holiness and their accompanying shofar blasts in the *Amida* of Rosh HaShana, for what is relevant to our discussion is that both opinions hold that the *Amida* ends with the priestly blessing, and there is no mention of the blessing for peace.[35]

Henshke adds that this frames the priestly blessing at the end of the *Amida* as a kind of dialogue, as if God is responding to Israel's prayer with a blessing. This illuminates the *Amida* sequence further: If this prayer is essentially a list of requests that ends with a blessing of thanksgiving and then God's response, then the ultimate request before the thanksgiving conclusion is: "Find favor, Lord our God, in Your people Israel, and accept in love and favor the fire offerings of Israel." The entire *Amida* sequence builds up to this blessing because it is the key to Israel's dialogue with God: Only if God finds favor and accepts Israel's offering (and prayer) does the offering achieve its purpose. If not, then the offering is all in vain; no such dialogue takes place.

The world of offerings invites the worshipper to choose a certain path of interaction with God. The range of freewill offerings shows that there are various forms of religious expression, as we will discuss extensively below. The experience of offering a burnt offering is not the same as the experience of offering a peace offering; both are different from bringing a grain offering. All reflect different needs and channels of expression. Each offering is a different form of communication with God. The worshipper in the Temple barely opens his or her mouth; few offerings are accompanied by verbal prayers (first fruits and the tithe declaration are notable exceptions, and the only instances in Leviticus are the confession

35. Nonetheless, it is worth noting that the blessing *Sim Shalom* is a kind of request for the fulfillment of the priestly blessing, so it can be read as a kind of appendix to it.

pronounced in conjunction with a variable purification offering and during the Yom Kippur service). Expression in God's presence is through gesture that signifies a person's desire, intention, and mindset.

Similar to the institutionalized prayer service, wherein words were initially composed to express certain intentions that then served to guide the worshipper as to what intentions ought to be communicated to God, the sacrificial world is first and foremost a form of expression that was channeled into particular models that act as spiritual guides for the worshipper. Obligatory offerings are not voluntary forms of expression, but part of a broader system that requires and conducts a person's communication with God; they should be perceived as a form of religious expression that guides and encourages a person to take responsibility for their life and – as we will yet argue in the context of the variable purification offering – their failures as well. When someone sins, their sin will weigh down on them until it becomes too heavy to bear, but the purification and guilt offerings allow them to confess their sin and atone for it, to fix the damage done to the Divine Presence's manifestation in Israel and their own life as well.[36] Offerings facilitate a sincere, complex dialogue with God and provide reassurance that the worshipper has found favor with their Maker. It is for this reason that each offering has its own specific guidelines – each kind of offering conveys its own particular expression to God.

The opening of the sacrificial chapters is what invites this reading: "Speak to the Israelites. Say: When one of you brings an animal offering to the Lord" (Lev. 1:2). The sacrificial world does not begin with a commandment, but with an invitation: "When." If someone wishes to bring an offering to the Lord, they are welcome to do so, but in a certain way. We will soon argue that this formulation shows that offerings were common practice before these laws were given; indeed, worship in the ancient world was heavily based on sacrifice, and the Torah embraces this "social fact." By that, I do not wish to claim, as Rambam does, that

36. As mentioned, some modern scholars perceive offerings as rites that restore world order, because sin disrupts world harmony and sacrifices correct this imbalance. See, for example, Gorman, *Ideology*; Jenson, "Sacrificial System," 25–40. I do not believe that the sacrifices of *Parashat Vayikra* function on a cosmic level; perhaps there is more room to consider this in *Parashat Tzav*.

the Torah institutionalizes offerings only to combat problematic forms of worship; on the contrary, I believe that the Torah channels the deep human desire for connection and living dialogue with God by making full use of this form of expression. After all, Cain and Abel offer sacrifices without any divine command, as does Noah, and these offerings indeed lead to connection between the human and the Divine: "The Lord smelled the fragrant aroma and said in His heart, 'Never again will I curse the land because of man'" (Gen. 8:21). Thus, in addition to the polemical element pointed out by Rambam, the institutionalization of sacrifices is founded on an appreciation that the believer yearns to communicate with God, and the best way to do so is through the act of giving. A person is granted the privilege of giving to God, and in return, they receive God's favor and blessing.

Ultimately, all the aforementioned explanations illuminate different facets of the sacrificial world; there is room for them all. Rambam's approach does not contradict Ramban's. On the contrary, the idea that the Torah reshapes the world of sacrifice to combat pagan ideas of feeding the gods and driving away demons makes room for psychological theories of how the sacrificial world facilitates a deeper, truer form of connection with God. If the focus of offering sacrifices is indeed on the worshipper's psychological process, then Ramban's approach can be taken further, and offerings can be perceived as gifts offered up in the hope that they will be accepted, thus resulting in a living dialogue with God – a particular request, followed by a prayer for acceptance, followed by thanksgiving, followed by divine blessing.

All this, however, applies to the offerings described in the first chapters of Leviticus, in *Parashat Vayikra*. As we'll see, *Parashat Tzav* introduces a paradigm shift, when the text introduces the concept of the regular burnt offering and the altar fire that must never go out. The collective burnt offering and the ever-burning hearth transcend the sphere of the individual and reflect the Divine Presence within the camp, as per R. Judah HaLevi. The fire and smoke and blood of the sacrificial world and its silent yet vibrant gesture for divine favor is far greater than any one definition or another: "Turn it around and around, for everything is in it."

Chapter 2

Where Does the Book of Leviticus Begin?

It is not always simple to determine a book's starting point. Is the book of Leviticus a closed, independent unit? While there is general continuity between the five books of the Torah, whether Leviticus is a standalone work with its own beginning and conclusion is a complex question that touches upon the fundamental relationship between the books of Exodus and Leviticus.

The book of Leviticus opens with God summoning Moses to command him about sacrifices: "He called to Moses / and the Lord spoke to him / from the Tent of Meeting, saying" (1:1). This is a literal translation of the Hebrew, one that reflects the odd syntactic fact that the verse's subject, "the Lord," is mentioned only in the second part of the verse, whereas the entire book actually opens with the pronoun "He." This is a strange way to begin a new book; indeed, most translations simply read "The Lord called Moses. From the Tent of Meeting He spoke to him, saying."[1] This is how R. Saadia Gaon rephrases the verse in his commentary. These changes, however, only serve to emphasize the strangeness of the original language.

Moreover, why does God first "call" Moses before speaking to him, whereas elsewhere in the Torah, God's instructions to Moses begin: "God spoke to Moses, saying"? The Sages point out this "calling" as a lesson in courtesy:

> "He called to Moses and spoke" – Why did He call him before speaking? The Torah is teaching courtesy: A person should not speak to their friend before calling them. This supports R. Ḥanina's opinion, for R. Ḥanina said: A person should not speak to their friend before calling them. (Yoma 4b)

Why, though, does the book of Leviticus begin with God calling Moses? This midrash seems to assume that God consistently calls Moses before addressing him, even though this is only documented at the beginning of the sacrificial laws. As Rashi writes (based on Leviticus Rabba):

> All speeches, statements, and commandments are preceded by a "calling," a term of endearment used by the angels, as it says: "And they call to one another." But His revelation to the prophets of the nations is expressed with casual, impure language, as it says, "God met (*vayikkar*) Bilaam."

Rashi raises two intriguing aspects:

1. Firstly, Rashi indeed implies that God does not merely begin speaking to Moses as he is going about his day; rather, He summons him to the Tent of Meeting (either the one outside the camp – Ex. 33:7–11 – or that within the camp), and only then addresses him. This model is similar to God's first summoning

1. Some translations do attempt to maintain the Hebrew word order, such as "*Und er rief Mose, und der Herr redete zu ihm von der Stiftshütte aus und sprach*" (*German Scholachter Version*).

of Moses at the Burning Bush: "The Lord saw that he had turned aside to look, and God called to him from within the bush: 'Moses, Moses.' He answered, 'Here I am'" (Ex. 3:3–4); the *Sifra* Midrash already notes this similarity.[2]

2. Rashi's reading contrasts God's love for Israel with His attitude toward the nations. Some note that Rashi opens his commentary on each book with an emphasis on God's special love for Israel.[3] R. Mordechai Breuer perceives this as a fulfillment of his commentary on Numbers 8:13, which mentions the Israelites five times: "It says 'the Israelites' five times in a single verse, once for each of the five books of the Torah, to show His love (*ḥibbatan*) for them, as I saw in Genesis Rabba."[4] Rashi even uses the phrase "His love (*ḥibbatan*)" in his opening comment on Exodus and Numbers. This implies that Rashi indeed systematically emphasizes God's love for Israel at the beginning of each book, presumably to give them hope during the dark time of exile.[5] Rashi famously "felt great love for his people, identified with their suffering, and anticipated imminent redemption in the Land of Israel."[6] This great love moves him to quote midrashim that emphasize God's great love for them.[7]

In contrast to Rashi, however, the most straightforward reading is that Moses is "called" here because of the particular point in time. Not only does God's summoning emphasize the importance of the forthcoming sacrificial laws,[8] but the formulation and context serve an important literary purpose. A marvelous midrash links God's summoning of Moses

2. *Sifra*, under "Freewill Offerings." See also Leviticus Rabba 1:15.
3. Grossman, *Rashi*, 62–63; Breuer, *Pirkei Bereshit*, vol. 1, 26–32.
4. The above quote is from the Leipzig 1 Manuscript. Rashi refers to Genesis Rabba, but, as R. Breuer points out, the verse in Numbers 8:13 is in fact discussed in Leviticus Rabba 2:4.
5. See also Grossman, "Exile and Redemption."
6. Grossman, "Exile and Redemption," 265.
7. See especially Grossman, *Rashi*, 67–72.
8. Wenham, *Leviticus*, 49: "Sacrifice is the heart of Israel's worship, and therefore the regulations on sacrifice which are about to be announced are most important."

at the beginning of Leviticus with the Tabernacle's construction at the end of Exodus:

> "He called to Moses" – What precedes this matter? The *parasha* of the Tabernacle, "As the Lord commanded Moses." This is analogous to a king who commanded his servant and said to him: "Build me a palace." On each and every item that he built, he wrote the king's name. He built walls and wrote the king's name on them. He put up pillars and wrote the king's name on them.... Later, the king entered the palace, and he saw his name written on everything he saw. He said: "My servant accorded me all this honor, and I am inside and he is outside?" He called him so that he would enter into its innermost chambers. So too, when the Holy One, blessed be He, said to Moses: "Craft Me a Tabernacle," he wrote down "As the Lord commanded Moses" on everything he built. The Holy One, blessed be He, said: "Moses accorded Me all this honor, and I am inside and he is outside?" That is why it says: "He called to Moses." (Leviticus Rabba 1:7)

There is indeed a certain intimacy in God's "calling" to Moses; reading this as a divine reaction to Moses's efforts to build the Tabernacle creates an intricate dialogue between the end of Exodus and the beginning of Leviticus. Moreover, this illuminates the unusual syntax of Leviticus's opening verse. It begins with a pronoun, rather than with God's name, in order to emphasize the continuity between the two books, as Hizkuni explains: "It therefore says 'He called Moses' and not 'The Lord called to Moses,' because this clearly refers to the glory of God in the Tent of Meeting mentioned above" (on Lev. 1:1).

This also explains the purpose of God's summoning of Moses. The book of Exodus concludes:

> Then the cloud covered the Tent of Meeting, and the glory of the Lord filled the Tabernacle. Moses could not now enter the Tent of Meeting, because the cloud had settled on it, and the glory of the Lord filled the Tabernacle. In all the journeys of the Israelites, when the cloud rose from the Tabernacle, they would set out.

> But if the cloud did not lift, they did not move on; they waited until it had lifted. The Lord's cloud was over the Tabernacle by day, and fire was in it at night, in view of all the House of Israel through all their journeys. (Ex. 40:34–38)

Some are troubled by Moses's inability to enter the Tent of Meeting, such as Stuart:

> Moses could not enter the tent of meeting precisely because it was filled with God's glory. Why was this so? Had not Moses earlier entered right into the glory cloud at the top of Mount Sinai? Had he not been inside the little symbolic tent of meeting that served as a contact point between him and God until the tabernacle had been built, with God's glory descending upon the entrance just a few feet away?[9]

I will discuss his answer below, but the formulation of his question is problematic, given that the answer is presented at the very beginning of Leviticus, when God does invite Moses into the Tent of Meeting, just as he is called up to Mount Sinai. The statement that "Moses could not *now* enter the Tent of Meeting" is soon followed by God calling Moses and inviting him in. Several commentators indeed view the two chapters as one sequence, such as Ibn Ezra, who suggests that God invites Moses into the Holy of Holies itself, right where the cherubim stand:

> The reason that "He called Moses" follows "Moses could not enter" is that the Glory called him in to enter the Tent of Meeting, and there He spoke to him. The Glory was in front of the curtain and that was where Moses entered, for that it what is written, and that explains "He sees the Lord's form."

9. Stuart, *Exodus*, 792.

This reading is convincing.[10] Nor does it contradict the first explanation – it is no coincidence that Moses is invited inside the place where the Divine Presence dwells to hear about the sacrificial laws, if offerings are an expression of a person's connection with God.

Ramban also sees God's call to Moses as the solution to Moses's exclusion at the end of Exodus, and he takes this idea a step further: He points out the dialogue between these verses and God's call to Moses to enter the cloud of glory atop Mount Sinai:

> As Moses climbed the mountain, it was covered in a cloud. The glory of the Lord rested on Mount Sinai, and the cloud covered it for six days. On the seventh, He called to Moses from within the cloud. To the Israelites the appearance of the Lord's glory on the mountaintop was like a consuming fire. Moses entered the cloud and climbed the mountain, and he stayed there for forty days and forty nights. (Ex. 24:15–18)

These verses are easily connected to the end of Exodus and the beginning of Leviticus.[11] God dwells in a cloud of glory; initially Moses cannot enter; then God calls him. The common language points to an intentional connection:

Exodus 24–25	**Exodus 40–Leviticus 1**
The cloud covered the mountain	The cloud covered the Tent of Meeting
The Lord's glory rested on Mount Sinai	The Lord's glory filled the Tabernacle
The cloud covered it for six days	

10. The New English Translation Bible commentary notes: "The best explanation for the MT of Lev 1:1 arises from its function as a transition from Exod 40 to Lev 1. The first clause, 'And he (the Lord) called to Moses,' links v. 1 back to Exod 40:35, 'But Moses was not able to enter into the tent of meeting because the cloud had settled on it and the glory of the Lord had filled the tabernacle' (cf. J. Milgrom, *Leviticus* [AB], 1:134). Exod 40:36–38 is a parenthetical explanation of the ongoing function of the cloud in leading the people through the wilderness. Since Moses could not enter the tent of meeting, the Lord 'called' to him 'from' the tent of meeting."
11. See further in Shammah, "Two Objectives," 39–40.

On the seventh day, He called to Moses from within the cloud	He called to Moses
And the Lord spoke to Moses saying[12]	And the Lord spoke to him from the Tent of Meeting, saying

Based on this comparison, the phrase "The cloud covered it for six days" is essentially parallel to "Moses could not now enter the Tent of Meeting" (Ex. 40:35). Ramban emphasizes how this dialogue illuminates the Tabernacle's true purpose: It is a "miniature version of Mount Sinai that can be transported from place to place, to accompany the Israelites in their wanderings."[13] God's first revelation to Israel was at Mount Sinai; this was followed by His revelation to them in the Tabernacle (Lev. 9:24), and from there Israel and God made their way together to the Promised Land.

Ramban points out this parallel to discuss the Tabernacle's purpose, but it also serves to show how closely the beginning of Leviticus is tied to the end of Exodus. Moses's exclusion from the Tent of Meeting is mentioned at the end of Exodus, and his invitation to enter appears at the beginning of Leviticus. The connection between these passages is so strong, in fact, that it raises the question of why they are divided into two separate books. Why doesn't God's invitation to Moses serve as the end of Exodus, as the conclusion of the Tabernacle construction? The claim that the division is erroneous and that the two passages should be read as one is challenged by the final three verses of Exodus that appear after the description of Moses's exclusion from the Tent of Meeting:

> In all the journeys of the Israelites, when the cloud rose from the Tabernacle, they would set out. But if the cloud did not lift, they did not move on; they waited until it had lifted. The Lord's cloud was over the Tabernacle by day, and fire was in it at night, in view of all the House of Israel through all their journeys. (Ex. 40:36–38)

12. This is taken from the sequence there (Ex. 25:1), which introduces the instructions about the Tabernacle. There is room to debate whether it makes sense to include this in the parallel; I do so, as does Rendtorff, *Leviticus*, 22.
13. Cassuto, *Exodus*, 339.

These verses end the book of Exodus with focus on a different aspect of the Tabernacle: on its role as a guide to the Promised Land, which will be further developed in Numbers (9:15–23, which also describes the pillar of cloud). Thus, Moses's inability to enter the Tent of Meeting is not immediately followed by God's invitation; three verses come between them, hinting to another role of the Tabernacle. This creates the impression that the book of Exodus has two conclusions: The first mentions that Moses cannot enter the Tent of Meeting, and this thread continues with God's invitation to Moses at the beginning of Leviticus; the second describes the cloud's role in the Israelites' journey, and this thread continues with the description of Israel's departure from Sinai and their journey into the wilderness in Numbers 9.

This brings us back to our earlier question: Why isn't God's invitation to Moses extended at the end of Exodus, instead of postponed to the beginning of Leviticus, even though this invitation reads like a direct continuation of the penultimate verses of Exodus?

To go back to Stuart's answer to his own question about Moses's exclusion from the Tent of Meeting: "The answer is that the Tabernacle was now God's house and no one else's." Although Moses was in charge of building the Tabernacle and freely entered during its construction, once the house was completed and handed over to God, the builders no longer had permission to enter.[14] The fact that Moses has to wait for God's invitation to enter expresses that God is now Master of the House.

This explains why Moses is excluded at the end of Exodus while his admission is postponed until the beginning of Leviticus. It emerges that the Tabernacle has three different roles, which are discussed in three separate books. In the book of Exodus, the Tabernacle serves as the House of God: "They shall make Me a Sanctuary and I will dwell in their midst" (Ex. 25:8). Israel have the privilege of camping their tents around God's central tent, where the Divine Presence rests.[15]

This first role has two implications, which are discussed in two different books:

14. Stuart, *Exodus*, 792–93.

15. This perception also affects the two-chamber structure of the tent and the vessels within. See Grossman, "Wings Spread."

1. In Leviticus, the Sanctuary takes on a new role: "It is a positive commandment to make a house for the Lord where offerings can be offered up" (Rambam, *Hilkhot Beit HaBeḥira* 1:1). When the Divine Presence rests in God's house, it becomes a sacrificial center. Gifts to human kings are presented in their palaces; similarly, gifts to the King of kings are offered up in His dwelling place on earth. If Exodus establishes the Tabernacle as the House of God, then Leviticus establishes it as the house of God's worship. This is a new perspective of the Tent of Meeting, which barely appears in Exodus. Even the few offerings mentioned in Exodus are not sacrifices that reflect humans' desire to serve their Creator; rather, the offerings in Exodus serve to sanctify the Tabernacle and bring down the Divine Presence. This is especially evident in the commandment of the daily burnt offering (Ex. 29:38–45): "This shall be the regular burnt offering throughout your generations at the entrance of the Tent of Meeting before the Lord. There I will meet with you, there I will speak to you, and there I will meet with the Israelites. It will be sanctified by My glory. I will consecrate the Tent of Meeting and the altar. I will also consecrate Aaron and his sons to serve Me as priests. I will have My Presence dwell among the Israelites and I shall be their God." In his opening lecture on tractate Zevaḥim, R. Aharon Lichtenstein *zt"l* points out that the daily burnt offering in Exodus is part of the daily service in the Tabernacle – together with the lighting of the lamps, the incense, and the showbread – which expresses that the Tabernacle is "God's house."[16] In contrast, Leviticus presents a different aspect of the Tabernacle: It is the place where a person may serve God. Of course, this stems from it being God's house and the resting place of the Divine Presence – and indeed, there is a certain continuity between Exodus and Leviticus, as mentioned. These

16. Lichtenstein, *Zevaḥim*, 10–12.

are two related yet distinct aspects of the Tabernacle, just as Exodus and Leviticus are related yet distinct.[17]

2. The book of Numbers displays yet another facet of the Tabernacle: It is Israel's guide as they make their way through the wilderness. The rising and falling pillar of cloud informs Israel when to journey, when to make camp, and which way to go. This, of course, also stems from the Tabernacle being the resting place of the Divine Presence, for God leads Israel's way and is with them wherever they go. This aspect, mentioned briefly in Exodus, is developed further in Numbers, the book of Israel's journey through the wilderness.

Thus, the book of Exodus, which presents the Tabernacle as God's house, ends with two conclusions that emerge as two distinct roles of the Tabernacle. (1) God's call to Moses to enter the Tent of Meeting will demonstrate how those who seek God can meet Him and serve Him through the sacrificial laws of Leviticus. (2) The cloud that signifies the Divine Presence will lead the way for Israel's journey through the wilderness in Numbers.

This holds the key to understanding the purpose of the sacrificial laws. The offerings discussed in the first chapters of the book, *Parashat Vayikra,* express different ways for the worshipper to meet God in His house, where the Divine Spirit rests.

17. For a slightly different division, see Shammah, "Two Objectives." He claims that these roles are both introduced in Exodus (29 and 40) and expressed in Leviticus (6–7 and 1–5, respectively). Later on I will concur, in relation to the different natures of *Parashot Vayikra* and *Tzav.*

Chapter 3

Sacrificial Terms and Their Meaning

Before we consider the text, it is worth pointing out certain key terms and principles.

KORBAN – OFFERING

The term "*korban*" first appears in Leviticus (and appears elsewhere only in Numbers and twice in Ezekiel).[1] Offerings in earlier books are referred to differently: as "*minḥa*" (Gen. 4:3–5); "*ola*," "burnt offering" (e.g., Gen. 8:20); or "*zevaḥim*" (e.g., Gen. 46:1).[2] What does the word "*korban*" mean? In Modern Hebrew, the word is usually used in the sense

1. There is room to consider whether the descriptions in Nehemiah (10:35; 13:31) contain a unique form of the word based on Aramaic; see Fabry, "*Korban*," 153.
2. R. Avia Hacohen writes about the exclusive meaning of the verb "*lehakriv*," "to offer": "Giving to a person and the act of offering is not conveyed through the same word, and there should be a verbal differentiation between the two kinds of giving." The Septuagint uses the word "δῶρα," which also means "gift," in the usual sense, as in

of "sacrificing something important or precious," which focuses on the aspect of giving – on what we are prepared to sacrifice for a value we believe in. Even-Shoshan's definition emphasizes that sacrifice is for the sake of others: "Willingly giving up on something valuable for the good of others."[3] But more accurately, "others" can also refer to abstract values. People "sacrifice" their time and effort to achieve what is important to them.

In biblical Hebrew, however, "sacrifice" does not have such a general meaning, and the term refers specifically to a gift offered up to God.[4] Thus, the emphasis is on the receiving end: "When one of you brings an animal offering to the Lord" (Lev. 1:2). The worshipper transfers something that he or she owns to the altar, and God is the recipient. Even if the gift in question is not offered on the altar, it is still considered an "offering," especially if it is given as an atonement: "So we make an offering to the Lord of the gold articles each man found – anklets, bracelets, signet rings, earrings, and pendants – to make our atonement before the Lord" (Num. 31:50).

Is the word "*korban*" related to the word "*karov*," "close"? Bravman conducts an extensive study and concludes that the word "*korban*" is indeed derived from the concept of drawing close to God or the altar to offer a gift.[5] It therefore makes sense that the verbs "*hevi*" – "bring" (Lev. 4:23; Num. 5:15) or "*natan*" – "give" (Ezek. 20:28; see especially Judges 5:25)[6] are sometimes used instead of "*hikriv*." Thus, "offering" is a more accurate translation than "sacrifice,"[7] as "offer" is semantically related to drawing close. Thus, a *korban*, something that is "brought close," can be compared to other offerings whose name is related to a similar Hebrew verb: to a *tenufa*, which is something that is "waved"; or a *teruma*, which

---

the gifts Jacob sends to Esau in Genesis 32:19, or the gift Jacob's sons send to the "Egyptian ruler" (Joseph).

3. Even-Shoshan, *Dictionary*, "Korban," vol. 4, 1637.
4. For example, Kaddari, *Dictionary*, 963.
5. Bravman, *Studies in Semitic Languages*, 465–77.
6. Licht and Milgrom, "Sacrifice," 225.
7. Compare to the language of the eighth day of the Tabernacle consecration: "Moses said to Aaron, 'Approach the altar, prepare your purification offering and burnt offering'.... Aaron drew close to the altar" (Lev. 9:7–8).

is something that is "lifted up"; or *ketoret,* "incense," which is something that is "incensed," burned.

As we will soon see (in the discussion of the verb "*vehikrivu*"), Rashi and Ramban disagree regarding the relationship between the noun "*korban*" and the verb "*lekarev,*" but the idea that they are related reveals something profound about the nature of offerings. The worshipper is not actually "giving" an offering to God, but merely "offering" it up – holding it out, bringing it close. To offer up an offering does not automatically mean that God will accept it; the process is only complete when there is divine indication that the offering has been accepted. In other words, the biblical word "*korban*" distinguishes Israelite offerings from pagan sacrificial rites that are theurgical acts of imposition upon reality; a biblical offering is a dialogue, not a rite. As mentioned in our discussion of the purpose of offerings, this dialogue is a fundamental element of sacrificial consciousness. For this reason, the most the worshipper can do is extend their offering toward God in the hope that it will be accepted.

MALE AND FEMALE ANIMALS

The first offering mentioned in Leviticus is the burnt offering, and the first requirement is that the offering must be a male animal: "If the offering is a burnt offering from the herd, it must be a male animal without blemish" (1:9); the same applies to a burnt offering "from the flock" (1:10).[8] This is one of the most fascinating, inscrutable requirements of sacrificial law. On the one hand, the sex of the offering is clearly important: Whether one must bring a male or female animal (or either) is specified in every animal offering (but not bird offerings, which are also deviant in other aspects). On the other hand, there is no explanation as to why some offerings must be male while others must be female.

The data is complicated: The burnt offering must be from a male animal,[9] while a peace offering can be male or female. Most obligatory

8. One might expect the word "*shor*" to be used instead of "from the herd – a male," but perhaps the language is for the sake of a parallel with "male or female" with regard to the peace offering (as proposed by Rendtorff, *Leviticus,* 28).
9. While sacrificial law rules that burnt offerings must be male, in certain biblical narratives cows are offered up; see I Sam. 6:14. Rendtorff claims that David's offering

offerings must be male animals: The guilt offering must be a ram and three out of four purification offerings must be male (the anointed priest; the entire community; the leader), whereas the individual must bring a female goat as a purification offering.[10]

Some favor Philo's approach:

> The burnt offering must be male because the male is superior to the female, more suited for leadership and closer to the efficient cause, while the female is imperfect, subject, and more passive than active.[11]

Philo's premise is that the burnt offering must an animal of the superior sex, or, as Menachem Bula writes: "The reason seems to be that the burnt offering is the highest offering, as it is entirely given to God, except for the skin, which is for the ministering priest."[12] Bula supports this with a prophecy from Malachi, who points to the ram as the epitome of an ideal offering: "Cursed is the knave who has a ram in his flock but pledges and sacrifices a damaged animal to the Lord" (Mal. 1:14). Here, a fine male animal is contrasted with a blemished specimen.

Even if this seems consistent with the arguable claim that according to Tanakh, the male is superior to the female (a claim that requires extensive, intensive study to be substantiated), it is still difficult to adopt. The Torah requires that certain offerings be female (the individual purification offering), while others can be either male or female (the peace offering). It makes little sense to require an offering that is inherently inferior; if the male animal was indeed considered inherently superior, then surely every offering would have to be male, just as every offering must be without flaw or blemish.

On the other hand, it is difficult to adopt Milgrom's suggestion, which essentially makes the opposite claim: that the Torah shows consideration

---

from the threshing floor of Araunah is clearly female, as male oxen were not used (*Leviticus*, 29), but I do not find this convincing.

10. Ramban's proposed solution is difficult to understand; see his commentary on 3:1.
11. Philo, *Laws I*, part 200 (*Writings*, vol. 2, 273). Ibn Ezra also adopts this approach (on Lev. 1:3).
12. Bula, *Leviticus*, 10.

by demanding male animals, because female animals provide milk and bear young, so offering a male is less costly for the worshipper.[13] This too is problematic: If the idea is to show consideration for the worshipper, surely the most considerate option is to leave the choice up to them for all offerings, as is the case with the peace offering.

It seems that the answer is to adopt Philo's premise that the requirement has symbolic meaning, but to challenge the nature of this symbolism. The purification offering is the best way to determine this symbolic meaning, given that the sex of the offering changes according to the sinner's identity. As we will see later, in our discussion of chapter 4, the individual's purification offering has unique undertones of consolation and reconciliation. Compared to the offerings of the priest and the leader, the Torah shows subtle affection for the individual's offering, to the extent that the offering is said to have a "sweet savor." This is a strange expression to apply to an obligatory offering (and indeed, it is not mentioned in any other obligatory offering); below, we will suggest that it hints to the new sense of closeness and reconciliation regained after the alienation caused by sin. This, perhaps, implies that female offerings are brought as a sign of closeness to God, whereas offerings that symbolize reverence and religious devotion must be from male animals. As for the peace offering, as we will yet discuss, it is a display of full partnership between worshipper and God, to the extent that part of the offering is eaten by the worshipper as well. Therefore, the worshipper is able to choose whether to bring a male or female offering. In contrast, the burnt offering reflects the person's self-effacement before his or her Maker, and thus must be a male animal. This disparity between human and God is the religious experience expressed through most offerings, and accordingly, most offerings are male animals.

PRIESTS AND "PRIESTESSES"

In addition to the fact that most offerings are male animals, priests in the Israelite Sanctuary are also exclusively male. In the ancient world, this

---

13. Milgrom, *Leviticus*, vol. 1, 147; also Hyatt, *Exodus*, 247. The claim that female animals were more expensive in ancient times is not obvious; Rendtorff, for example, assumes the opposite (*Leviticus*, 29).

was unusual: In most other cultures, women had central ritual roles, especially in temples devoted to goddesses. Women were priestesses, dancers, and singers; in ancient Egypt, there were so many women in service that some temples had special harems to house them.[14] "Priestesses" are often mentioned in Ugaritic sources as well, by name and by the name of the goddesses they served.[15] Most famous of all are the cult prostitutes of Mesopotamia, who would perform ritual sexual acts in the temple of Inanna, the goddess of love.[16] In Egypt and Mesopotamia, the king traditionally appointed his daughter as high priestess. There are many more examples; suffice to say that the fact that Israelite priests were exclusively male is by no means obvious or typical of its time.

This is presumably related to the biblical sensitivity toward sexual purity. Ritual sexual worship was a fundamental part of the pagan priestesses' roles; the Sages already noted that Israel were drawn to idolatry largely due to sexual temptation. The absence of priestesses was tantamount to a declaration that there is no ritual sexual worship in the Israelite Temple. Practically, the world of sexuality and the impurity brought in its wake was carefully distanced from all that was sacred. Thus, while the Babylonian New Year was "consecrated" by the high priest's coupling with the high priestess in a public ritual inside the temple, the Israelite priests were prohibited from marrying a promiscuous woman (Lev. 21:7) and were commanded to take special care to ensure that their daughters behaved appropriately (Lev. 21:9). While pagan priests sometimes went naked as part of cultic rituals, the Israelite priests wore special linen trousers to ensure that they would never reveal their nakedness in the Sanctuary (Ex. 28:42–43).[17] All these laws served to distance any semblance of ritual sexual worship from the Israelite Temple.

14. Bergman, "Kohen," 62.
15. Ringgren, "Kohen," 65.
16. Ibid., 63.
17. Gershon Hepner posits that Nadav and Avihu's offense is that they entered the Sanctuary naked (Hepner, "The Naked Truth"). He claims that Philo suggests this, but Philo is speaking allegorically and considers Nadav and Avihu as positive figures.

TAMIM – WITHOUT BLEMISH

The second requirement of the sacrificial laws is that the animal must be "*tamim*" – whole, perfect, without flaw or blemish.[18] The most straightforward explanation is that the worshipper must honor God with a perfect offering, not some sickly specimen that was going to die anyway. As Malachi complains: "You offer defiled bread on My altar. Yet you say, 'How have we defiled You?' in saying the Lord's table is repugnant. When you offer a blind animal to be sacrificed, is this no evil? And when you offer the lame and the sick, is this no evil? Offer it if you will to your governor. Would he then accept you – let you lift your face to him?" (1:7–8). God's table should certainly not be any less dignified than the table of the human ruler whose subjects wish to appease him. Yet the requirement is not merely a question of appearance and aesthetics. Rather, it should be perceived as part of the sacrificial discourse; Malachi, too, insists on high-quality offerings as an expression of love and the covenant between Israel and God. Similarly, Gordon writes: "The formal worship was not important to our prophets in itself, but for its deep religious content; this content is the sense of deep reverence and profound belief in the God of Israel that is expressed through this worship."[19]

Some Sages understand that this was the problem with Cain's offering: "Cain brought the fruit of the land as an offering to God – of the waste. This can be likened to a corrupt tenant farmer who would eat the finest first fruits and bring the last of the crop as tribute to the king" (Genesis Rabba 22:5; see also Rashi on Gen. 4:3). I do not necessarily accept this reading of Genesis,[20] but it does imply that the quality of the offering is a measure of the worshipper's devotion and reverence. According to the Midrash, the world's first offering was rejected because of its inadequacy.

There is also room for a more fundamental rationale: An offering to God is only as strong as its life force. A weak, dying animal is not truly

18. The exception is bird offerings.
19. Gordon, *Malachi*, x.
20. It can also be seen the other way: Cain is the initiator, who understands that he must first offer of his fruits to God, while Abel imitates him; see further in Grossman, *Creation*, 145–55.

alive; it does not make for a worthy offering to the Living God. Moreover, an offering is not a true sacrifice if the worshipper is not sacrificing anything of real value. To bring an animal that would die anyway is not a true experience of giving something to God, because the worshipper will not feel any true sense of loss.

LIRTZONO

The concept of "*lirtzono*" in Leviticus 1:3 is the subject of much halakhic and exegetical debate. I will now outline one fundamental dispute that is crucial for my discussion throughout this book. There are various readings of the phrase "*lirtzono*." The first reads the term in the sense of "*ritzui*," to "please" or "appease" God:

> If the offering is a burnt offering from the herd, one must offer a male animal without blemish. The one making the offering shall bring it to the entrance to the Tent of Meeting before the Lord, *to please Him* (*lirtzono*).

R. Joseph Bekhor Shor understands the term this way: "*Lirtzono* – so that it will be pleasing to Him." The worshipper brings an offering in an attempt to please God. Accordingly, the next verse reads: "And he shall lay his hand upon the burnt offering's head *that it may be accepted* (*venirtza lo*), to atone for him" (1:4). Milgrom also understands the verse this way and perceives the phrase as part of the requirement for the burnt offering: If the worshipper brings a perfect, flawless offering, then it shall be accepted. He regards the word as a synonym for acceptance and conciliation (compare to Mal. 1:8).[21]

Another reading, however, seems more likely to me:

> If the offering is a burnt offering from the herd, one must offer a male animal without blemish. The one making the offering shall bring it to the entrance to the Tent of Meeting, *of his own will* (*lirtzono*) before the Lord.

21. Milgrom, *Leviticus*, vol. 1, 149; see also Wenham, *Leviticus*, 55–56; Rooker, *Leviticus*, 86–87.

Based on the talmudic discussion in Arakhin 21a, which argues that the word *lirtzono* means that the worshipper must offer the animal willingly, Rashi explains: "'Shall bring it' – this teaches that they force him. Can he bring it against his will? Hence it says 'of his own will.' How? They force him until he says that he wants to." Ibn Ezra also favors this approach: "He must bring it of his own will and not be forced." This reading is more convincing than the first because the term is also mentioned in the context of the variable offering and the peace offering (Lev. 19:5, 22:21, 29) – that is, only in conjunction with voluntary offerings, and not with the obligatory offerings a person must bring to atone for sin. Moreover, in verses that address the Israelites, the verb appears in the plural form, "*lirtzonekhem*" (Lev. 19:5; 22:29), which shows that it refers to the worshipper and not to God.[22] As Hizkuni points out: "*Lirtzono* – Because the offering is voluntary it says "*lirtzono*," but this is not stated about the rest of the offerings, which are sometimes obligatory" (on Lev. 1:3).

The word "*venirtza*" in the following verse does refer to *ritzui*, to pleasing God so that the offering will be accepted: "He shall lay his hand on the head of the burnt offering *that it be accepted* (*venirtza*) on his behalf, to make his atonement" (1:4), but this meaning should not be projected onto the same root in the previous verse.[23]

This teaches that bringing the offering willingly is a fundamental aspect of its nature. The phrase appears repeatedly in the context of freewill offerings, painting them as voluntary religious expressions that are not obligatory acts of atonement. This idea poses a challenge, however, in relation to the burnt offering, given that atonement is mentioned in the very next verse: "He shall lay his hand on the head of the burnt offering that it be accepted (*venirtza*) on his behalf, *to make his atonement*" (1:4). The relationship between "*lirtzono*," which expresses free will, and the apparent need for "atonement" is crucial for understanding the nature of the burnt offering, as we will discuss below.

22. Those who claim that the word means "to appease Him" suggest that the plural form also makes sense; see Barstad, "Ratza, Ratzon."

23. Similar wordplay can be found in Leviticus 19:5–8; 22:17–25.

LAYING THE HANDS

Laying the hands on the animal's head is a requirement in every individual offering, both freewill and obligatory (according to the Sages; we will discuss how the guilt offering is actually described in the text below). The Sages are correct to point out that this does not mean merely touching the animal's head, but involves actual leaning, as in the prophetic image: "Like a man who runs from a lion, then encounters a bear, then comes home, leans his hand (*vesamakh yado*) against the wall, and a snake bites him" (Amos 5:19).[24] This is how the action is depicted in the Talmud: "Anyone who places hands on the head of an offering must insert his head and most of his body into the courtyard. What is the reason? We require placing hands with all of his force" (Zevaḥim 33a). (For this reason, the leper cannot remain outside the courtyard and stick his hands inside to bring an offering.) This is an important distinction, as there are similar actions depicted elsewhere in the Torah (such as laying the hands upon someone's head to bestow a blessing, as in Genesis 48:8), but this is not the same.[25]

What purpose does this leaning serve? There are two main replies: Some argue that laying the hands shows ownership and demonstrates a certain affinity between the worshipper and the animal offering so that the slaughter of the animal is carried out truly in the worshipper's name.[26] Radatz Hoffmann states that the purpose of laying the hands is always to appoint the animal as the worshipper's emissary, so that it will be offered up to God in his or her name.[27] Others claim that the point of leaning on the animal is to express the symbolic transfer of something from the worshipper to the offering. This is especially apt when the offering is an atonement for a certain sin: The worshipper seeks to transfer the

---

24. Bula, *Leviticus,* 12.
25. See also Milgrom, *Leviticus,* vol. 1, 150.
26. For example, De Vaux, *Ancient Israel,* vol. 2, 416; Ringgren, *Israelite Religion,* 169. In the introduction to his commentary on Leviticus, Abarbanel writes more harshly that the offering is instead of the sinner himself. Some are even more extreme and perceive this as an act of identification that combines the human spirit with the offering's spirit (Dussaud, *Les Origines,* 72).
27. Hoffmann, *Leviticus,* vol. 1, 88–89.

offense to the offering.[28] This approach seems to be supported by the halakha that *viddui,* confession, is recited as the worshipper leans on the offering.[29] Some argue that both of the above are conveyed through the laying of the hands: "Laying the hands has dual significance: It renders the animal into an offering to God in the worshipper's place... when the worshipper recites the confession, the animal takes on his sins instead."[30]

There is another possibility: that the laying of the hands serves different purposes in different offerings. This was first suggested by Meir Paran, who interprets the expression "*lismokh al*" – "to lean on" – as "to appoint" or "to substitute," and the expression "*lismokh al rosh*" – "to lean on the head" – as the transferal of sin.[31] This is a problematic suggestion, however, given that the expression "to lean on the head" appears in the context of offerings that are not related to sin or atonement, such as those brought during the seven days of consecration (Ex. 29:10, 15, 19) and the peace offering (Lev. 3:2, 8).

I wish to adopt the reading that there are indeed two different kinds of laying the hands, but to suggest a different division, one related to how the hands should be laid. According to halakha, the worshipper must lay both hands upon the animal, as Ramban writes on Leviticus 1:4:

> "He shall lay his hand" – both hands, for we find: "Aaron and his sons shall lay their hands on the head of the bull" (Ex. 29:10), and: "Aaron and his sons shall lay their hands on the head of the ram" (29:15), and it is explained there: the hands of each individual, and this means both hands. In the case of the goat designed to be sent [to Azazel], it is expressly stated: "And Aaron shall lay both his hands upon the head of the live goat" (Lev. 16:21).

Ramban quotes two different instances – from the consecration ceremony and from the Yom Kippur service – to show that both hands must be laid. The first example is problematic, as it refers to Aaron and his

28. Volz, "Die Handauflegen."
29. Yoma 35b–36a.
30. Bula, *Leviticus,* 12.
31. Paran, "Laying the Hands."

sons, so even if everyone lays a single hand, "hands" would still appear in plural form.[32] Ramban is aware of this and therefore focuses his argument on the scapegoat, where the text explicitly says that "Aaron shall lay both his hands on the head of the live goat" (Lev. 16:21).[33]

However, this "proof" may in fact prove the opposite – that the Yom Kippur service is unique, whereas the usual practice was to lay a single hand upon the animal's head – as Ibn Ezra points out:

> "He shall lay his hand" – The plain meaning is that he should lay one hand, because the scapegoat is not like any other offering and therefore the text differentiates it. But when we found that the scribes rule that both hands are laid every time, we concur. (Ibn Ezra on Lev. 1:4)

Ibn Ezra notes that most instances of "laying the hand" are written in singular form, whereas the scapegoat is the exception, which implies that the usual practice is to lay just one hand. Ultimately, he concurs with halakha, but only due to rabbinic tradition. Pseudo-Jonathan is also of the opinion that the worshipper should lay just one hand – the right hand: "He shall lay his right hand heavily on the head of the offering so that it will be an atonement for him."

Perhaps this seems somewhat pedantic, but these subtleties may reflect different functions of this act within the sacrificial service. Ibn Ezra's reading raises the question of why both hands are mentioned in the context of the scapegoat offering, and I believe that the answer lies in the text itself. There, the purpose of laying the hands is explicitly mentioned:

> Aaron shall lay both his hands on the head of the live goat and confess over it all the Israelites' iniquities and rebellions, all of their sins, putting them on the head of the goat and then sending

---

32. Rendtorff writes similarly: *Leviticus*, 33.
33. It is intriguing that the MT has "*yadav*" without a *vav* rather than with a *vav*, the latter being the regular plural form. Perhaps this form hints to the usual way of laying the hands; I will suggest that the fact that the scapegoat procedure is done with two hands reveals that the usual act is done differently.

> it away into the wilderness.... The goat shall carry all their iniquities upon itself to a desolate place. (Lev. 16:21–22)

To transfer all of Israel's sins to the scapegoat, both hands are necessary for the task.[34] It is difficult to interpret the laying of the hand/s in a freewill offering in the same way; freewill offerings have nothing to do with sin. In these cases, the Torah uses the singular form, "hand," rather than "hands," because the purpose of leaning in these cases is to generate a connection between the worshipper and their offering.[35]

This may explain the surprising halakhic requirement that the High Priest must lay his hands on the Yom Kippur scapegoat twice: once to establish the regular sacrificial connection and once to transfer Israel's sins.[36]

Thus, both interpretations of this symbolic act hold true: Laying one hand generates a connection between worshipper and offering, and laying both hands serves to transfer something from the worshipper to the offering.[37] This distinction may also illuminate the scene in which Moses lays his hands on Joshua (Num. 27): God commands him to "lay your *hand* upon him" (v. 18), but he in fact "laid his *hands* upon him" (v. 23). Rashi explains: "He laid his hands – More generously than he was commanded. For God told him, 'Lay your hand,' but he used both hands, and he fashioned him like a vessel filled to overflowing, filling him fully and generously with his wisdom."

God tells Moses to lay his hand upon Joshua before he appoints him in front of all of Israel. Practically, however, Moses places both hands upon Joshua in Israel's sight as part of the appointment process; by doing

---

34. Ramban discusses the unique nature of the scapegoat (on Lev. 16:21); given how unique it is, it is not surprising that the act of laying the hands on it also serves a unique purpose.
35. See also Sansom, "Laying of the Hands." He is aware of this possibility but is inclined against it.
36. As some *Aḥaronim* conclude based on the pseudo-Rashba commentary on Menaḥot 92b. See: *Ḥiddushei HaGriz HaLevi* on Zevaḥim 40–41, where it is discussed whether the laying of the hands must be with full force or not.
37. Kidner also concludes that the sins were only transferred to the scapegoat, not to other offerings (Kidner, "Metaphor and Meaning").

so, he uses this symbolic act to fulfill God's command to "give over to him some of your majesty, so that the entire Israelite community will obey him" (Num. 27:20). Perhaps laying one hand is sufficient to establish Joshua as his successor, but Moses goes above and beyond God's word and lays both hands upon him with all Israel as witness. Just as the High Priest lays both hands upon the scapegoat's head to transfer all of Israel's sins to it before sending it out to the wilderness, Moses rests both hands upon Joshua to transfer all his wisdom and honor before sending him off to lead Israel into the Promised Land.

PRESENTING THE BLOOD

When we delve into the burnt offering, we will see that after laying the hands, the priests must perform the following steps:

> He shall have the bull *slaughtered* before the Lord.
> And Aaron's sons the priests shall *present* the blood,
> *Dashing* it against each side of the altar at the entrance to the Tent of Meeting.

The verb "present" – *vehikriv,* literally "bring close" – is not used in relation to any other offering; elsewhere, slaughter is immediately followed by dashing the blood (3:2; 4:25; 7:2). But given that the blood technically needs to be brought closer to the altar before it is dashed or poured out, this step presumably applies to all offerings, and for this reason I wish to include this in the preliminary discussion.

The Sages list four steps for dealing with the sacrificial blood: slaughter, collecting the blood in a basin, bringing it to the altar, and dashing it against the altar.[38] This verse, however, mentions just three: "slaughter… present… dash." Rashi explains: "Present – This is collecting the blood, which also implies bringing it." That is, the verb "present" includes two steps. Rashbam writes similarly: "Present – Receiving the blood and bringing it in order to dash it against the altar."

---

38. Sometimes in the Talmud there is a different order: "Four stages do not count for *piggul*: slaughtering, dashing the blood, collecting the blood, bringing the blood" (Menaḥot 14b).

Ramban, however, explains that "present" refers only to collecting the blood:

> "Present" means to collect the blood. For "*vehikrivu*" is not related to bringing the blood close ("*karov*") to the altar, but rather to "*korban*," "offering" – for turning the blood into an offering by collecting it and dashing it against the altar. Thus, He mentioned that the owner of the offerings brings it, lays hands on it, and slaughters it, and after the slaughtering He immediately mentioned the sons of Aaron. It thus follows that receiving the blood is in itself a priestly duty that may only be done by a qualified priest with proper vessels; and even more so that only a qualified priest may bring it to the altar and dash the blood. (Ramban on Lev. 1:5)

Ramban does not disagree with Rashi's definition that bringing the blood is part of the priestly service. Rather, he challenges the idea that the verb "*lehakriv*" – "to present" – refers to bringing the blood close, and argues instead that it is derived from the word "*korban*," "offering," and means to offer the blood upon the altar. The act of bringing the blood is implicit given that offerings are slaughtered to the north of the altar, whereas the blood must be dashed at the altar itself.[39] This dispute between Rashi and Ramban thus reflects a fundamental disagreement about the meaning of the verb "*lehakriv*."

Either way, it is worth mentioning the mishnaic laws about the act of bringing the blood. In the Midrash Halakha, it is usually considered as an integral part of the service; Rambam even rules that it is a necessary step: "The blood must be brought over by foot or it is not considered bringing; therefore, a High Priest who collects the blood, *stands in place*, and dashes it toward the altar *nullifies* the sacrifice" (Rambam, *Hilkhot Pesulei HaMukdashin* 1:23).[40] Yet in some talmudic discussions,

39. Similarly Weinberg, *Sacrifice in Israel*, 299.
40. Rambam holds that there must always be a bringing of the blood, even if the offering is slaughtered right next to the altar. Rashi and Tosafot disagree; see in depth in *Mishneh LaMelekh* and *Minḥat Ḥinnukh*, commandment 115:17.

whether this is so is questioned (see especially Eiruvin 104a; Pesaḥim 65b; Zevaḥim 35a).

As noted, "presenting" the blood is not explicitly mentioned in the context of other offerings, not even the burnt offering from the flock, which follows the laws of the burnt offering from the herd. Instead, the text moves directly from slaughtering to dashing the blood: "The one making the sacrifice shall have it slaughtered on the north side of the altar before the Lord, and Aaron's sons the priests shall dash its blood against each side of the altar" (Lev. 1:11). This implies that the in the biblical text, bringing the blood is considered a technical stage rather than a fundamental stage of the service in itself.[41] A non-priest cannot bring the blood to the altar, but only because it is considered the first step of dashing the blood.[42] This has many implications, largely pertaining to the halakhic status of bringing the blood, but most are beyond the scope of this discussion, and one example will suffice: Is there a law of bringing the blood in bird sacrifices, which are slaughtered on the altar itself? Some argue that the stage in which the blood seeps out of the bird until it reaches the altar wall is considered "bringing the blood,"[43] while others justifiably claim that because the bird is slaughtered upon the altar itself and there is no technical need to bring the blood from another place, the laws of bringing the blood are meaningless.[44]

In addition to the laws of bringing the blood, this discussion also has implications for understanding the textual requirement that the burnt offering from the flock must be slaughtered to the north of the altar. This is not mentioned in regard to the burnt offering from the herd. Does its

41. This is the basis of the debate surrounding whether the blessing should be made before bringing the blood. There is a blessing for each stage of the offering, but the ruling regarding bringing the blood is not clear. R. Aharon Cohen in *Avodat HaKorbanot* writes that there is a blessing (52), but some *Rishonim* disagree, such as Avudarham; see also Ariel, "Blessing of the Commandments." If it is indeed a technical stage, it is clear why there is no blessing for it.

42. I believe that those who claim that bringing the blood of holy of holy offerings requires the "north of the altar" – like the law of receiving the blood in these offerings – perceive the actions as related. See *Encyclopedia Talmudit*, "*Holakha*," vol. 8, 446.

43. Tosafot on Zevaḥim 15a, "*Ḥattat*."

44. See this debate in the *Encyclopedia Talmudit*, ibid.

absence imply that the latter can be slaughtered elsewhere, or is it merely a literary omission with no halakhic implications? The absence of mention of bringing the blood reinforces the notion that the place of slaughter is inherently related to the law of bringing the blood: Given that a burnt offering from the flock is slaughtered right next to the altar, there is no need to mention bringing the blood. In contrast, this is mentioned in regard to the burnt offering from the herd, which seems to imply that bulls are not necessarily offered right next to the altar.

VEHIKTIR – BURN?

One of the most important verbs in the sacrificial world is "*hiktir*." Some argue that this is the ultimate purpose of sacrifice; others merely point out the fact that this verb appears more than thirty-five times in Leviticus, and that every single offering ends with this verb, which describes the act of burning the offering upon the altar.

What, then, does "*hiktir*" mean? Most translations indeed use "burn" (KJV; NAB; NIB: NIV; NJB; RJS), but R. Ezra Bick is correct to point out that this is not strictly accurate.[45] In sacrificial law, the Torah distinguishes between offerings that are burned on the altar – "*muktarim*" – and those that are burned outside the camp, which are "*nisrafim*" (see 4:12, 21; 10:16; 16:27–28; Num. 19:5, 6, 8).

The Septuagint indeed distinguishes between a regular "burning" and specifically "burning upon the altar," but uses the regular verb for "offering": ἐπιθήσουσιν. Onkelos does not use the regular verb for "burning" either – the Aramaic "*veyoked*" – and instead has "*veyassek*" in Leviticus 1:9.

The verb "*hiktir*" is related to the noun "*kitor*," meaning "smoke"; as Rashi writes: "a pillar of smoke" (on Gen. 19:28). This links it to the verb "*lekatter*," meaning "to turn something into smoke,"[46] parallel to the Akkadian "*qatāru*," which has the same meaning. If so, then JPS's

45. Bick, "*Haktara*."

46. The Akkadian verb "*qataru*" means "to raise," and "to turn to smoke" in Akkadian D form (see the Akkadian Dictionary CAD, Q, 943–44). The Ugaritic "*qtr*" has another, more surprising meaning: a person's soul leaving his body. (See Averbeck, "K-T-R," 913.)

translation is more accurate than most: "And the priest shall turn the whole into smoke on the altar."[47] This, of course, recalls the incense, the *ketoret,* which is burnt to produce fragrant smoke; similarly, the animal flesh is turned to smoke upon the altar.[48]

This precise definition has dramatic implications for understanding the sacrificial process and purpose. The consistent use of the verb "*hiktir*" expresses that the whole point of offering a sacrifice is to transform flesh into smoke, to render something from flesh to spirit. In this new insubstantial state, the offering can rise up to heaven. The smoke of the burnt offering becomes a *re'aḥ niḥoaḥ,* a pleasing aroma or sweet savor to the Lord – a phrase that we will discuss in depth in context of the frankincense added to certain grain offerings.

The altar fire turns flesh into smoke, into spirit, which rises up to the heavens.

ISHEH – FIRE OFFERING

Many of the offerings end with the concluding formula: "An offering of fire, a sweet savor to the Lord." The meaning of "*isheh*" is the subject of a fascinating debate. The most prevalent reading among *Rishonim* is that *isheh* is derived from the altar fire – *esh/ isheh* – meaning "going up in flames"/"intended for fire"/"an offering that goes entirely or partially up in flames."[49]

Rashi (on Lev. 1:9), for example, writes: "*Isheh* – When it is slaughtered, it is designated for the fire. *Isheh* always means 'fire'"; or in Abarbanel's words (on Ex. 29): "These daily offerings of thanksgiving and praise will become a sweet savor when they are burned upon the altar and go up in smoke, and they will become an *isheh* to the Lord, that is, to be consumed by the altar fire."

Jacob Milgrom, however, claims that the word "*isheh*" is not related to "*esh,*" "fire," and prefers the term "food gift." He argues that the full phrase is in fact "*leḥem isheh*" (as in Lev. 3:11, 16; Num. 28:24) and that the

47. Similarly: "And the priest shall offer up in smoke all of it" (New American Standard Bible).
48. See also Milgrom, *Leviticus,* vol. 1, 160–61; he translates "turn into smoke."
49. Steinberg, *Biblical Dictionary,* 78.

abbreviated form "*isheh*" still refers to the full expression. He bases this on the similarity between "*isheh*" and the Ugaritic "*itt*," meaning "gift."[50]

My initial intuition is to accept the usual reading, given the obvious similarity between *isheh* and *esh*, but Milgrom aptly points out that certain offerings referred to as *isheh* never touch the altar fire, whereas others that are burned upon the altar are not referred to as such.

There are a number of offerings referred to as "*isheh*" that are not actually burned on the altar:

1. Wine libations: Milgrom points out that wine libations are not burned, but the Torah still calls them "*isheh*": "You shall also offer half a *hin* of wine as a libation; it is an ***isheh***, a sweet savor to the Lord" (Num. 15:10). Yet this is not convincing: Although wine libations are not actually burned on the altar, they are still brought to the altar and poured out in this place of divine fire and smoke.
2. The breast of the peace offering: "With his own hands he shall present the *ishei* of the Lord. He shall bring the animal's fat and breast so that the breast can be displayed, this way and that, as a wave offering before the Lord" (Lev. 7:30–31). This leads Milgrom to conclude that "*isheh*" cannot mean "fire offering," because the breast is not burned upon the altar but is given to the priest as a gift. Considering, however, that the breast is part of an offering that is partially burned upon the altar, the term here may focus on the fats that *are* burned as a fire offering, whereas the breast is just an appendix to the fire offering.
3. Milgrom's third example is the showbread, which is also called "*isheh*," even though the bread is actually eaten by the priests (Lev. 24:5–9). I would argue that this term refers to the frankincense that is burned on the altar in place of the bread itself, so that the bread is a symbolic fire offering.

---

50. Milgrom, *Leviticus*, vol. 1, 161–62. For further support of this claim and the idea that "*isheh laShem*" is a keyword in freewill offerings, see, Warning, *Literary Artistry*, 102–03. On the other hand, not all agree that the Ugaritic "*itt*" and "*isheh*" are related; see Dietrich and Loretz, "Ugaritisch."

As mentioned, Milgrom also supports his theory with the opposite claim: Some offerings are burned but are not called "*isheh*." He refers especially to the purification offering; this term is not mentioned throughout chapter 4, which is devoted to this offering. Its absence is even more salient when the purification offering is mentioned alongside other offerings that are referred to as "*isheh*":

1. The seven days of consecration: Both burnt offerings (Ex. 29:18) and peace offerings (v. 25) are referred to as "*isheh*," but the purification offering is not (v. 13).
2. The additional (*musaf*) offerings: The daily offering (Num. 28:6) and the daily afternoon offering (v. 8) are called "*isheh*," as are the additional burnt offerings on festivals (24), whereas the purification offering mentioned in the middle of these offerings, in the same chapter, is not (22).
3. Two ostensible exceptions to this rule in fact serve to support it. The individual purification offering: "He shall remove all its fat… the priest shall send it up in smoke upon the altar with the other *ishei* to the Lord. So shall the priest make atonement" (Lev. 4:35). The term "*ishei*" initially seems to refer to the purification offering as well, but a more careful reading reveals that it in fact applies to the other offerings upon the altar, but not to the purification offering itself.[51] The same is true of the variable purification offering (Lev. 5:12). According to Milgrom's theory, it is clear why a purification offering is not considered a "food gift," for it is an obligatory offering, not a gift.

This may also help shed light on the offerings brought in case of a communal error:

> If it is done unintentionally by the community, the entire community must offer one bull from the herd as a burnt offering, a sweet savor to the Lord, with its prescribed grain offering and

51. The same is true of the end of the peace offering description, "along with the burnt offering" (3:5), as we will discuss in context.

> libation, and one goat as a purification offering. The priest shall then make atonement for all the community of Israel and they will be forgiven, because it was an accidental failing, and because they brought their offering, a fire offering to the Lord *and the* purification offering for their error before the Lord. The community of Israel and the migrants living among them will all be forgiven, because all the people acted in error. (Num. 15:24–26)

Intriguingly, "their offering" refers to two separate offerings:

> a fire offering to the Lord /
> *and* the purification offering for their error before the Lord.

This could be a classic biblical parallelism, but the repetition could in fact distinguish between the nature of the burnt offering and the nature of the purification offering. As Rashi explains (based on the *Sifri*): "They brought their fire offering to the Lord – this is the burnt offering, which is called a burnt offering to the Lord; and 'their purification offering' – this is the goat." The *Siftei Hakhamim* rightly points out in his commentary on Rashi: "He explained that this is the bull of the burnt offering, which is called 'an *isheh* to the Lord,' to exclude the purification offering from this definition, for it is not an *isheh* to the Lord; only the burnt offering is an *isheh*."[52] Ibn Ezra and Ramban also adopt this reading, which clarifies that the text is careful not to define the purification offering as an *isheh*.

To conclude, whereas Milgrom's examples of offerings called "*isheh*" that are not actually burned on the altar can be refuted, his examples of offerings that are burned but are never referred to as "*isheh*" make his theory far more convincing. Nonetheless, it is still difficult to adopt, given that while purification offerings are never called "*isheh*," guilt

52. It is worth mentioning that even though the purification offering is placed on the altar before the burnt offering when they are offered together, here the burnt offering is first (as Rashi points out). Whatever the reason, the conclusion fits this order – first the burnt offering is mentioned and called "*isheh laShem*," then the text goes back to the purification offering.

offerings are (Lev. 7:5),[53] even though they cannot be considered "food gifts" any more than purification offerings. Moreover, the passage in Numbers 15 proves that all obligatory offerings except for purification offerings can be included in the category of "food gifts" – even though they are obligatory, and therefore not strictly gifts.

Thus, it makes sense to revert to the usual translation of "*isheh*" as "fire offering" – an offering designated for the altar fire. To do so, we must justify why this term is never applied to the purification offering. As we will show below, this seems to be related to the unique nature of the purification offering. While most offerings are brought as food that is consumed by the altar fire, the purification offering – *ḥattat* – serves to purify – *leḥatteh* – the altar. It is an offering that cleans, not feeds; its smoke does not rise up in a sweet savor to the Lord, so the term "*isheh*" is not applicable.

53. It could be argued that even though guilt offerings are for sin, they have a dimension of reconciliation and thus can be likened to freewill offerings, but this is somewhat contrived. Radatz Hoffmann claims that purification and guilt offerings are not called "*isheh*" (*Leviticus*, vol. 1, 104), although the term is mentioned with regard to guilt offerings; perhaps he is referring to the specific phrase "*isheh laShem*."

Chapter 4

Two Lists of Offerings

The sacrificial chapters of Leviticus are repeated in two separate lists, one after another: the list of sacrifices in *Parashat Vayikra* (chs. 1–5) and the list in *Parashat Tzav* (6–7). Both lists present the laws of the same offerings; no new offerings are introduced in the second list, although there are some new laws. As Rashbam writes: "All the offerings mentioned in *Parashat Vayikra* are repeated and their laws are completed" (on Lev. 6:2). But why aren't all the laws mentioned together, in a single list, instead of being divided into two repetitive lists?

Some *Rishonim* suggest that the first list discusses offerings in general, while the second details the particular laws for each offering and hints to its spiritual meaning: "After discussing the sacrifices, it then states the particular Torah about each one" (Sforno on Lev. 6:2). Sforno's use of the word "Torah" underscores the repetition of the word "Torah" in the second list: "This is the *Torah* of the burnt offering"; "This is the *Torah* of the grain offering," etc., which certainly hints to a deeper, broader exploration of each offering, rather than a general presentation of the sacrificial service.[1]

Yet this reading is problematic, given that many laws and particular details appear in the first list, not the second; nor are the sacrificial laws in *Parashat Tzav* significantly more detailed (with the exception of the guilt offering, which we will discuss below). How, then, can the division and repetition be justified?

The most striking difference between the two lists is that they discuss different stages of the offering. *Parashat Vayikra* describes the offering's journey from its arrival at the Tabernacle to its offering upon the altar; *Parashat Tzav* describes what happens from the altar until it is eaten by the priests or owners.[2] This is especially salient in relation to the burnt offering; since the priests do not eat any part of it, the description in the second list focuses on how it is "consumed by the altar" until the morning, when its remains are cleared away. That is, when the offering ends up entirely upon the altar, the description in the second list is much shorter, and focuses on the altar itself. This also explains why peace offerings are allocated so much room in the second list: Unlike other offerings, the person who offers up the peace offering partakes of its meat, thus leading to a depiction of how the sacrificial meat must be eaten, the fear of contamination, and other laws that are not relevant to the first list, whose descriptions end when each offering is placed upon the altar.

THE ADDRESSEE OF EACH LIST

Yet this does not suffice. As Ramban shows, the two lists have different addressees, and this showcases the nature and purpose of each one:

1. Above, I emphasized the distinction between offerings in general and particular laws that Sforno hints to. This can also be expressed differently: In the second list, the Torah hints to the inner significance of the various offerings, as R. Yehuda Copperman writes in his introduction to *Sforno*: "While *Parashat Vayikra* discusses types of offerings and their place in the general system of atonement and communion with God, *Parashat Tzav* discusses the inner nature of each offering" (Copperman, *Sforno*, vol. 2, XIX).
2. Marx, "Theology."

> It says in *Parashat Vayikra*: "Speak to the Israelites," for there it is commanded to bring offerings, and Israel are the ones to bring them. And here [i.e., *Parashat Tzav*], it says: "Command Aaron," for it speaks of carrying out the service, which is done by the priests. (Ramban on Lev. 6:2)

Parashat Vayikra turns to every individual: "When a person brings an offering to the Lord" (1:1), and explains how one should act if they wish to bring a burnt offering or a grain offering or if they must bring a purification offering. In contrast, *Parashat Tzav* addresses the priests and instructs them how to deal with the offerings people bring to the Tabernacle.

Note that Ramban also specifies that *Parashat Vayikra* describes how to "bring offerings," while *Parashat Tzav* speaks of "carrying out the service," which is similar to the aforementioned division. This also explains the sequence of the lists: A person brings an offering to the Tabernacle; the priests receive it and must follow the sacrificial guidelines for that particular offering. This is a simplistic overview (suffice it to say that the sacrificial laws are more detailed in *Vayikra* than *Tzav*), but it nonetheless serves as a solid basis for discussion.

The Midrash points out that in *Vayikra*, Aaron's sons are mentioned first, whereas in *Tzav*, Aaron is mentioned before his sons:

> From the beginning of the book until here, it is written: "The sons of Aaron, the priests, shall arrange"; "The sons of Aaron, the priests, shall sprinkle"; "The sons of Aaron shall place." Moses said before the Holy One, blessed be He: "The cistern is hated but its waters are beloved. You accorded honor to the trees because of their produce, as we learned there: All wood is fit for the arrangement except from the olive tree and from the vine, but to Aaron you do not accord honor due to his sons?" The Holy One, blessed be He, said to him: "As you live, for your sake I will draw him near. Moreover, I will render him primary and his sons ancillary: 'Command Aaron and his sons, saying.'" (Leviticus Rabba 7:1)

With the exception of the grain offerings, when Aaron is mentioned before his sons (2:3, 10), Aaron's sons precede him throughout *Vayikra*, but this changes in *Parashat Tzav* (6:13, 18; 7:31, 34–35).

The Midrash interprets this as a reversal made in Aaron's honor, but we can offer a different reading.[3] The expression "Aaron and his sons" creates a subtle sense of intimacy, as if Aaron and his family are standing next to Moses, listening to what God has to say about the sacrificial order. In contrast, "the sons of Aaron, the priests" focuses on legal and social status, singling the priests out from the Israelites. This is consistent with Ramban's reading: *Parashat Tzav* indeed focuses on the family that have been granted the privilege of serving in the Tabernacle – Aaron and his sons, who will teach their sons how to serve God for generations to come. *Parashat Vayikra*, in contrast, turns to everyone in Israel and offers everyone the opportunity to offer a sacrifice to God, while the priests are there to facilitate this service.

This distinction can be taken a step further and considered in relation to the order of the offerings in each list.

THE ORDER OF OFFERINGS IN EACH LIST

Whether or not there is significance to the order of the items that appear in any given list, the reader will encounter those items in that particular order. One might expect that grain offerings would be listed separately from animal offerings, as Rambam does: After discussing animal offerings, he turns to grain offerings, emphasizing that "grain offerings are also offerings" (*Hilkhot Maaseh HaKorbanot* 12:1). Rambam deviates from the biblical order, but his logical organization raises the question as to why the Torah does not present the sacrificial chapters in the same straightforward way that Rambam does.

---

3. The *Keli Yakar* explains that Aaron's sons are mentioned first in *Vayikra* because they did not need the atonement these offerings brought, as they had not sinned with the Golden Calf while Aaron had, but then Moses asked that Aaron be forgiven (on Lev. 6:2).

The First List

The first list (*Parashat Vayikra*) presents the offerings in the following order:

1. *Ola* – the burnt offering (ch. 1)
2. *Minḥa* – the grain offering (ch. 2)
3. *Zevaḥ shelamim* – the peace offering (ch. 3)
4. *Ḥattat* – the purification offering (ch. 4) + *Ḥattat oleh veyored* – the variable purification offering (5:1–4)
5. *Asham* – the guilt offering (5:14–26)

A cursory glance reveals that the list is arranged by the worshipper's motivation: The first three are freewill offerings, offered up voluntarily, and the last two are obligatory offerings that the Torah requires as atonement for sin.

This division is reflected through two different "speeches." God first "speaks" to Moses "from the Tent of Meeting" (1:1) about burnt, grain, and peace offerings; then, at the beginning of chapter 4, "The Lord spoke to Moses" again, this time about obligatory offerings. Accordingly, the *Sifra* Midrash refers to the first three chapters as "*dibbura denadava*" – "freewill speech," and to the second unit as "*dibbura deḥova*" – "obligatory speech," referring to God's two "speeches" to Moses.[4]

The Second List

The second list (*Parashat Tzav*) has a different order:

1. *Torat HaOla* – the law of the burnt offering (6:1–6)
2. *Torat HaMinḥa* – the law of the grain offering (6:7–11) + *Minḥat Ḥavittin* (6:12–16)
3. *Torat HaḤattat* – the law of the purification offering (6:17–23)
4. *Torat HaAsham* – the law of the guilt offering (7:1–7)

---

4. The *Sifra*'s present form, especially its division into chapters, is heavily redacted, to the point that it is difficult to determine its original division. See further in Naeh, "Structure and Division"; Raizel, *Introduction to Midrashim*, 61–64.

5. *Torat Zevaḥ HaShelamim* – the law of the peace offering (7:11–34, 36)

The difference between the lists is striking: In the second list, the peace offering appears last, resulting in the strange order of freewill-obligatory-freewill offerings. Thus,the giver's motivation clearly cannot be the criterion – but if not, what is? Moreover, how can we explain the general division and repetition of these chapters?

The different addressees of the two lists, as mentioned, moved Ramban to explain their different orders: The first indeed divides the offerings into freewill and obligatory offerings, whereas the second is arranged in descending order of holiness: "He wished to explain the laws of the most holy offerings together, since there is one law for them all…and only afterward He explains the law of those offerings which are less holy" (on Lev. 6:18). The Sages refer to the first group as "holy of holies" and to the second as "*kodashim kalim*" – entities that have lower or lesser holiness (similar to the firstborn offering, animal tithes, and other commandments not mentioned in these lists).[5]

These two orders correlate with the lists' respective addressees: The first list, which addresses the Israelite worshipper, is arranged according to what motivates them – why have they come to the Tabernacle? Coming freely to express praise or thanksgiving or coming out of obligation are two entirely different purposes, and the first list reflects this difference. The worshipper is less concerned about how the priests must deal with their offering – but this is precisely what governs the order of the second list. Whether the worshipper brings an offering freely or out of a sense of obligation, what matters to the priests is how to prepare, offer, and deal with the offering that has been entrusted for their service: what parts they must burn on the altar, where and when they may be eaten, and by whom.

Ramban's analysis is confirmed by the concluding verses of the "holy of holies" offerings, before the text goes on to discuss lesser offerings:

---

5. Other religions also had offerings of different levels of holiness, such as the Egyptians and Hittites; see Milgrom, *Cult and Conscience,* 41–43. We will discuss the Torah's new approach compared to other nations through the definition of "holy of holies."

> The guilt offering follows the same law as the purification offering: It belongs to the priest who makes atonement with it. The priest who offers any person's burnt offering shall keep the skin of the burnt offering that he has offered. Any grain offering baked in an oven or prepared in a pan or griddle also belongs to the priest who offers it, while every other grain offering, whether mixed with oil or dry, shall belong equally to all of Aaron's sons. (7:7–10)

These verses – which describe which priest receives which priestly portion – appear here, even though they could have been incorporated into the discussion of who receives the skin of the burnt offering at the beginning of the second list. The sense is that these verses serve as a summary and conclusion at the end of this first section of holy offerings.

To be more precise, which offerings are explicitly defined as "holy of holies"? One is the grain offering: "It shall not be baked with any leaven. I have given it as their portion of My fire offerings; it is holy of holies, like the purification offering and the guilt offering" (6:10). This extends the definition to the purification and guilt offerings as well, even though both are explicitly defined as "holy of holies" in context (6:18; 7:1).

Two offerings in the list are not defined as "holy of holies." The more obvious is the peace offering, which is indeed of lesser holiness, as is evident from its laws: It can be eaten by anyone pure, even non-priests and women, in any pure (not even holy) place. More surprising, however, is that this definition is not ascribed to the burnt offering – the first offering in both lists,[6] one that is entirely burned on the altar and is surely no less holy than a purification or grain offering.

The text also implies that from a halakhic perspective, the burnt offering is of utmost holiness, as one of the inferences from an offering being "holy of holies" is that it is slaughtered on the northern side of the altar, which is based on the law of the burnt offering. The purification offering, for example, "shall be slaughtered before the Lord at the place

6. I do not accept Watts's suggestion that both lists open with the burnt offering to show that the ideal offering is one that does not benefit the priests ("Sin and Guilt Offerings"). The priestly portions are not presented as problematic in other offerings; there is no reason to assume that the burnt offering differs from these.

where burnt offerings are slaughtered; it is holy of holies" (6:18). That is, because the purification offering is holy of holies, it must be slaughtered where the burnt offering is slaughtered. If so, this only amplifies the question: Why doesn't the Torah define the burnt offering as "holy of holies," when it is clearly of highest holiness?

In order to answer this question, we must consider when this definition appears and its implications for the laws of that particular offering. It turns out that it is mentioned in the context of where and when an offering may be eaten, and by whom: "Aaron and his sons shall eat what is left of it. It shall be eaten as unleavened bread in a holy place; in the courtyard of the Tent of Meeting shall they eat it. It shall not be baked with any leaven. I have given it as their portion of My fire offerings; it is holy of holies." This is the reference to the grain offering in 6:9–11; similar laws apply to the purification and guilt offerings (6:19–22; 7:6). Another law related to its status concerns the place of slaughter: "[It] shall be slaughtered before the Lord at the place where burnt offerings are slaughtered; it is holy of holies" (6:18; see also 7:1–2). As we will see below, the requirement to slaughter a holy offering in this particular place stems from concern that it will come into contact with something non-holy before it can be offered up. There is no such concern regarding offerings of lesser holiness, for they do not sanctify others (as we will discuss below).

Thus, two main laws derived from this special status are related to how the offering must be eaten, which explains why the burnt offering is not defined as such – no one consumes the burnt offering but the altar itself. In fact, designating the burnt offering as "holy of holies" might even lead to the mistaken conclusion that it can be eaten by male priests in a holy place, which is never the case. We will explore this further while discussing how an offering that is considered "holy of holies" transmits its holiness to others.

THE TIME AND PLACE OF THE TWO LISTS OF OFFERINGS

So far, we have explained the relationship between and different order of the two lists, based on Ramban's analysis. I now wish to go a step further, based on a brilliant idea of Radatz Hoffmann.[7]

Readers naturally read texts in the order in which they appear on the page; in this context, the second list is usually read after the first. However, there are good reasons to assume that the second list (in *Parashat Tzav*) was actually said to Moses before the first list (in *Parashat Vayikra*).

The time and place of the first list is easy to determine: "From the Tent of Meeting He spoke to him and said" (1:1). God gives these instructions to Moses after the Tabernacle consecration; as noted, this verse seems to be a direct continuation of the cloud of glory filling the Tabernacle as described at the end of Exodus. Sforno may be correct that the beginning of Leviticus took place on the same day that the cloud descended upon the Tabernacle:

> Our verse speaks of what occurred on the day when Moses had completed erecting the Tabernacle, for it was then that God's glory descended to sanctify the site as well as those performing their sacred duties in and around it. All of this is the execution of God's promise in Exodus 29:43–44: "And there I will meet with the Israelites and it shall be sanctified by My Presence... after this first day Moses could always enter the Sanctuary outside of the Holy of Holies, that is, up until the dividing curtain. (Sforno on Lev. 1:1)

What about the second list? No explicit information is provided about where and when it took place, but there is a hint in its conclusion:

> This, then, is the law for the burnt offering, the grain offering, the purification offering, the guilt offering, the ordination offering, and the peace offering, which the Lord commanded Moses at

7. See the introduction to his commentary on Leviticus, p. 17 and on.

> Mount Sinai when he commanded the Israelites to bring their offerings to the Lord, in the Wilderness of Sinai. (Lev. 7:37–38)

It is clear that this conclusion refers to the second list, for two reasons. First, the conclusion follows the same order as the offerings in the second list: "This is the law of the burnt offering/the grain offering/the purification offering/the guilt offering/[the ordination offering]/and the peace offering." Second, the phrase "this is the law of" – *zot torat* – characterizes the second list, not the first; every offering in the second list is introduced with "This is the law of the [x] offering."[8]

Surprisingly, the list of offerings in this conclusion includes "the ordination offering," which appears for the first time. How can a concluding list mention an offering that has not been discussed before?

There have been some claims that the ordination offering is actually referring to one of the offerings described in *Parashat Tzav*[9] – most likely a grain offering that priests were required to bring – but none are convincing, especially since it is not juxtaposed with the grain offering. Rather, it seems more likely that this refers to the special offering brought during the seven days of consecration, which Moses hears about in God's presence on Mount Sinai (in Ex. 29). This is indeed the prevalent reading, especially because it appears in the appropriate place: The ordination ram is a kind of peace offering, but one that must be eaten within a single day, so it makes sense to mention it in between the "holy of holies" offerings and the peace offerings. But if so, why does the ordination offering suddenly appear in the concluding list of offerings in *Parashat Tzav*?

The answer can be found at the end of the verse: "Which the Lord commanded Moses at Mount Sinai." It emerges that Moses hears about

---

8. See further in Shammah, "Two Objectives," 40–43.
9. As suggested, for example, by R. Meir Simcha HaKohen of Dvinsk, as well as modern scholars (such as Kuenen, *Origin and Composition*, 84; Snijders, "M-L-A," 303). The problem – as R. Meir Simcha himself points out – is that the offering is not juxtaposed with the grain offering. The Netziv suggests that the ordination offering refers to the thanksgiving offering, so it precedes the regular peace offering; Rabbeinu Bahya suggests that this does not refer just to the ordination ram, but to all offerings that were offered during the consecration week.

this second list of offerings while he is still upon Mount Sinai, when God also commands him to build the Tabernacle and to consecrate its vessels and priests during the seven days of consecration. The sudden mention of the ordination offering in the conclusion of the second list reveals where and when God conveyed it to Moses. As He was instructing him about the days of consecration (Ex. 29), He also transmitted the laws of offerings Moses would have to bring during this time: the burnt offering (Ex. 29:15–18); the grain offering (Ex. 26:2, 23); the purification offering (Ex. 29:10–14); and the ordination ram, whose laws are similar to the peace offering (Ex. 29:19–28). The sacrificial laws are not detailed in Exodus because the focus there is the Tabernacle and priestly consecration. Now, however, in these sacrificial chapters, the Torah includes the sacrificial laws that God transmitted to Moses at Mount Sinai.[10]

This reading is further supported by Rashbam's analysis of what the Torah means when it refers to the time "at Mount Sinai":[11]

> It says "at Mount Sinai" about all the commandments that were related during the first year, before the Tabernacle was built, whereas after the Tabernacle is built on the first of the month of the second year, it says "in the Wilderness of Sinai in the Tent of Meeting." (Rashbam on Num. 1:1)

Rashbam explains that commandments given "at Mount Sinai" were transmitted to Moses before the Tabernace was built, whereas commandments given after are conveyed "in the Wilderness of Sinai" or "in the Tent of Meeting." As soon as the Divine Presence settles in the Tabernacle, Mount Sinai loses its holiness. If so,[12] this supports the theory that the second list of offerings was transmitted to Moses before the

10. There is still room for the question why the ordination ram is included in the conclusion of the list. It should be taken into consideration that the next topic is the days of consecration, so mentioning this offering may generate a connection with the next unit. This is also related to this list's objective, as I will discuss below.
11. Some modern scholars also favor this approach. See Milgrom, *Leviticus*, vol. 1, 437–38.
12. Ramban disagrees with Rashbam's analysis; he believes that all the commandments were told to Moses at Sinai and some were repeated at the Tent of Meeting (see Ramban on Lev. 7:38).

first: The first was transmitted "from the Tent of Meeting" (1:1), whereas the second was conveyed "at Mount Sinai."

Note that the continuation of the verse might seem confusing when read according to Rashbam: "Which the Lord commanded Moses at *Mount Sinai* when he commanded the Israelites to bring their offerings to the Lord, in the *Wilderness of Sinai*" (7:38). The same verse mentions that Moses received the sacrificial commandments at Mount Sinai – before the Tabernacle – but ends with the phrase "Wilderness of Sinai," which implies that the Tabernacle already stood. One may, of course, disagree with Rashbam's definition (as Ramban does);[13] alternatively, the two phrases may draw a distinction between when Moses receives the commandments and when he conveys them to the people (as Radatz). Similarly, Avraham Shammah suggests that Moses is given the sacrificial laws at Mount Sinai, whereas "the Wilderness of Sinai" refers to where the Israelites will bring these offerings.[14]

We can also propose that this verse intentionally combines the two phrases, corresponding to the two sacrificial lists.[15] The first list opens at "the Tent of Meeting," after the Tabernacle's consecration; the second list was transmitted before the Tabernacle was built; and the concluding verses of the sacrificial chapters has two conclusions, in chiastic order: The first refers to the list in *Parashat Tzav* "at Mount Sinai" and the final words of the section refer to Israel bringing their offerings "in the Wilderness of Sinai."

This idea cannot prove the two lists' chronological order, but it does seem that the sacrificial laws of *Parashat Tzav* are transmitted to Moses while he is still on Mount Sinai, before the Tabernacle is built. Radatz Hoffmann brings further proof to support this theory; I will mention just one interesting comment of his. The waste disposal areas next to the altar and outside the camp are mentioned in the first list as if they are already familiar (1:16; 4:12), even though the laws of waste disposal

13. Ramban (on Lev. 7:38) holds that the complex conclusion hints that Moses was commanded about some offerings on Mount Sinai (ordination) and others at the Tent of Meeting.
14. Shammah, "Two Objectives," 41–42.
15. See also Milgrom, *Leviticus*, vol. 1, 438.

are only mentioned for the first time in chapter 6, in the second list. If the second list was indeed transmitted to Moses before the first, this explains the formulation in the first list.

WHY ARE THE LISTS IN REVERSE ORDER?

If so, why aren't the lists arranged in chronological order? I have already answered that the sacrificial chapters follow the proper order of bringing a sacrifice: *Parashat Vayikra* relates the laws of bringing an offering to the Tabernacle until it is offered upon the altar, while *Parashat Tzav* explains where, when, and by whom each offering may be eaten. Yet I wish to propose a more profound reading of these lists' arrangement.

There is a delicate tension between the priests and the Israelites throughout the book of Leviticus, which is also known as "*Torat HaKohanim*" – "The Law of the Priests." Much of the text seems to address the priests, who are ostensibly its protagonists. Yet a closer look reveals a more complex – perhaps even reverse – picture.

Beginning the book of Leviticus with the first list, which addresses the Israelite worshipper, rather than the second list, which mainly concerns the priests and their role in the sacrificial service, makes a crucial statement: The Tabernacle and the sacrificial world is for Israel, not the priesthood. The regular Israelite is not as holy as a priest and requires the priestly services in order to bring an offering, but the world of biblical sacrifice begins and ends with Israel's relationship with God: "When a person brings an offering to the Lord" (1:2). The opening act of the book of Leviticus is to invite the Israelites to stand before God and offer Him an offering.

The tension in Leviticus is encapsulated in a talmudic dispute (Berakhot 37b) regarding whether the *Sheheḥeyanu* blessing that accompanies a grain offering should be recited by the priest (as Tosafot hold) or by the Israelite worshipper (as Rashi). Rambam interprets that this refers to a grain offering brought from the new crop (after the two-loaves offering of Shavuot): "Whoever offers a grain offering from the new crop must first make the *Sheheḥeyanu* blessing" (*Hilkhot Temidin UMusafin* 7:18). Various commentators debate whether he is referring to the worshipper or to the priest; given the context, I believe that Rambam holds that the Israelite is the one who makes the blessing (as per Rashi). The

Israelite is the owner and bringer of the offering, the one who is rejoicing over his new crop; the priest is but his emissary.

Perhaps this seems obvious to the modern reader, but the truth is that in relation to Ancient Near Eastern worship, it is revolutionary. In Ancient Egyptian and Mesopotamian temples, priests were gatekeepers; only priests and scribes were literate, and the people did not have access to ritual texts. The Modern Hebrew expression "*ketav ḥartummim*," "hieroglyphics," or, literally, "the writing of magicians," idiomatically refers to illegible handwriting, but it reflects a deeper truth: In the ancient world, only the priests and mages were able to read ritual texts and serve in the temple. The word "*ḥartummim*" is related to the Ancient Egyptian word "*ḥry-tp*," meaning "the chief bearer of the ritual scrolls."[16] Only the priests were responsible for the temple service; when the Egyptian worshipper brought an offering, the priests would take it off of their hands and offer it to the gods. This was the usual ancient practice, as Yeivin writes:

> For this reason, a sect of priestly experts became responsible for cultic rituals, because most people were not able to perform them without prior preparation. This automatically led to most of the people's exclusion from active participation in cultic ritual, which then became concentrated in a place where only experts were allowed to serve, hidden from the sight of those whose ignorance of the correct ritual might be harmful, for it would ignite the wrath of the gods instead of appeasing them.[17]

The laws of the ancient temple were shrouded in secrecy, which rose up as a barrier between the people and holiness. In contrast, the book of Leviticus extends the sacrificial laws of the Temple to all of Israel: You all know exactly what the priests are doing on your behalf; the sacrificial laws are out there for all to see.

When viewed in relation to the ancient ritual world, this cannot be taken for granted, and not all experts on sacrificial law agree. Prof. Israel

16. Muller, "Ḥartum," 177.
17. Yeivin, "Tabernacle," 308.

Knohl, for example, argues that the first half of Leviticus (1–16) "was not written for the people ... it is priestly literature intended for priests. They are the ones who offer up offerings .... It is writing similar to that of Egyptian and Babylonian temples ... written by experts for experts ... secret esoteric literature that was forbidden to non-priests."[18]

Prof. Knohl is a leading scholar on Leviticus, and his contribution is valuable, but he is mistaken in this particular respect. The book of Leviticus opens with an address to the people of Israel, not to the priests: "Speak to the Israelites. Say: When one of you brings an offering to the Lord" (1:2), and this opening reflects the book's entire objective: to lay out the secrets of the Tabernacle before the eyes of all the people, inviting them to be active participants in its service. This is not "secret esoteric literature that was forbidden to non-priests"; on the contrary, it is open to all and taught to each and every child from a young age.

This illuminates why the book opens with the first list, which focuses on the Israelite's role in the sacrificial world rather than the priest's. This order signifies that although the Tabernacle is run by priests, its purpose is to enable the people's connection with God.

TWO SACRIFICIAL OBJECTIVES

This can be taken a step further. The relationship between the two lists also touches upon the fundamental meaning and purpose of the sacrificial service.[19] The first list addresses the individual who seeks closeness with God, inviting them to stand before God in His House. This, of course, focuses on the nature of that individual's offering to God, and whether they stand before God to seek forgiveness or to express praise. In contrast, the second list, which was given to Moses in the context of the Tabernacle consecration, is designed to bring the Divine Presence down to Israel, to facilitate revelation. The chief purpose of the offerings during the days of consecration was to sanctify the Tabernacle and its

18. Knohl, *How Was the Bible Born*, 53–55.

19. R. Eli Hadad suggests that the second list's connection to the days of consecration makes a statement about the role of offerings in general, a different role than the one presented in *Vayikra*, which, he holds, is that they are chiefly for atonement (Hadad, "*Piggul*"). I will propose a similar idea, formulated differently. See also Shammah, "Two Objectives."

priests; the Divine Presence can only rest in a sanctified place, and the way to achieve this was through offerings, which bring down the divine fire to the altar and keep it perpetually alight.[20] This is especially salient in the culmination of the consecration process on the eighth day, which is described in Leviticus 8–10. After the second list of sacrifices ends, "Moses said, 'This is what the Lord has commanded you to do so that the Lord's glory be revealed to you'" (Lev. 9:6). The purpose of offerings is to bring down the Divine Presence so that it may rest amidst the human presence. We will yet discuss the significance of this day, but for now, we can already draw a diagram with arrows pointing in two opposite directions: The first list concerns how a person stands before God; the second list focuses on divine revelation to the human. The two are not contradictory, of course; on the contrary, the ultimate purpose of sacrifice is to generate a perpetual dialogue between the two sides.

The difference between the two lists is also evident in their respective language. As R. Baruch Kehat notes, in *Parashat Vayikra* "the subject of the opening verses of the sacrificial laws is the worshipper: 'person,' 'when one brings,' etc. In contrast, the headings of the sacrificial laws in *Parashat Tzav* focus on the offerings: 'the law of the burnt offering,' 'the law of the grain offering,' etc."[21] Indeed, *Parashat Vayikra* focuses on the worshipper, while *Tzav* focuses on the offerings upon the altar.

This affords further insight into the order of these chapters. The first list is based on God's summoning of Moses to the Tent of Meeting (1:1); that is, once God dwells in His House, a person cannot stand before Him until God invites them to come. This is consistent with the tone of *Parashat Vayikra,* which explores how a person is invited to express himself before God. The second list, however, is juxtaposed with the days of the Tabernacle consecration; on the eighth day, the Divine Presence descends in a blaze of fire and consumes the offerings. The

20. This may be expressed in R. Shimon ben Tzemaḥ Duran's surprising counting of the offerings as a positive commandment based on the verse "The burnt offering shall remain on the altar hearth all night until the morning" (6:2), rather than basing the commandment on a direct command for an offering (*Zohar HaRakia,* positive commandment 51). Rambam does not count burning the offerings as an independent commandment, but as part of the commandment about offerings.
21. Kehat, "Sacrificial Laws," 71.

second list is related to this characterization of divine revelation as a force fueled by these offerings; that is why the two sections are side by side.[22] I have already noted that the sudden mention of the ordination offering in the second list's conclusion connects these two units, and it emerges that this connection is not merely technical: The second list is fundamentally related to divine revelation through the fire of the altar.[23] The analysis of the opening of the second list below will discuss how this has a bearing on how the offerings are eaten, which is a central topic in the second sacrificial list.

THE ORDER OF THE SECOND LIST BASED ON FREQUENCY

This brings us back to the order of the offerings in each list. Earlier, we favored Ramban's approach that each list is arranged according to its addressee: The list in *Vayikra*, which focuses on the worshipper, is based on the worshipper's different motivations for bringing an offering (freewill or obligatory), while *Tzav*'s list is arranged in order of the offerings' holiness (from "holy of holies" to offerings of lesser holiness). Another intriguing possibility, however, is Gordon Wenham's idea that the second list is arranged according to the frequency of each offering:[24]

- The first offering is the daily burnt offering, which was offered twice a day.
- The burnt offering was accompanied by the grain offering, which is mentioned next.
- This is followed by the purification offering, which was the most frequent method of atonement for sin; besides for individual purification offerings, it was offered up on festivals alongside the additional festival offerings.

---

22. See further in Kehat, "Sacrificial Laws," 72.
23. The dispute in Yoma regarding the reason that the High Priest must leave home seven days before Yom Kippur is interesting here: One approach is that it recalls the seven days before the Tabernacle consecration; the other is that it is based on the days leading up to the revelation at Sinai (see Yoma 3b).
24. Wenham, *Leviticus*, 118–19.

- The guilt offering was not offered systematically as the purification offering was, but given that it was an obligatory offering, it was presumably brought frequently.
- The final offering is the peace offering, which was not offered systematically; as a freewill offering, theoretically it may not have been offered up at all.

This proposition is worth mentioning even though I do not find it convincing; it suffices to mention the rams brought on Shavuot, which were peace offerings, to argue that according to this theory, peace offerings should be listed before guilt offerings. Nor does the Torah seem to be referring to the festival offerings in this context. Yet this idea still strikes a certain chord. The burnt offering and grain offering at the top of the list indeed seem to refer to the daily offerings that kept the altar fire perpetually alight. If the role of offerings in this section focuses on the Divine Presence, which remained in Israel's midst thanks to their offerings, then the idea of frequency and perpetuality being an organizing principle indeed rings true.

Chapter 5

"When One of You Brings an Offering"

THE STARTING POINT

> The Lord called to Moses. From the Tent of Meeting He spoke to him and said, "Speak to the Israelites. Say: When one of you brings an animal offering to the Lord, you may bring it either from the herd or from the flock." (Lev. 1:1–2)

The implicit drama of this opening is astonishing. The underlying premise of this verse is that a person wants to bring an offering to God, and now the text will institutionalize this desire by laying down the sacrificial laws. These chapters do not begin with any command or hint that bringing an offering is a proper thing to do; rather, the entire journey begins with the Divine yielding to human will: "This shows that offering sacrifices was already the way of the world, and there is no need to command it."[1] In the ancient world, sacrifice was a given; the verse reflects this fundamental form of religious expression. Humanity seeks

1. Ahuviah, *As Written*, 19.

to bring an offering to God, and the Torah sets out to legally define how this must be done.

Years ago, I heard Prof. Zwi Werblowsky, of blessed memory – an eminent scholar of religion – point out two common features of all ancient religions: shamanism (the act of communicating with the world beyond) and offerings. After fierce, lengthy debate, Werblowsky conceded that this rule did not apply to a certain esoteric branch of some ancient Chinese religion that did not, in fact, practice offerings, but this exception only serves to prove the rule that the human need to bring offerings is deeply rooted in the human religious experience.

Long before the Torah lays down the sacrificial laws in Leviticus, there are many stories of people who offer sacrifices, such as Cain and Abel (Gen. 4), Noah (Gen. 8), and many others before the sacrifices offered at the covenant at Sinai (Ex. 24). Moreover, some of these offerings share the names of offerings defined in Leviticus (such as "He sacrificed burnt offerings on the altar" – Gen. 8:20). Of special note are Jacob's "sacrifices to the God of his father Isaac" (Gen. 46:1). What does the expression "He offered up sacrifices" mean? The term "*zevaḥim*" may simply mean "animal sacrifices," as opposed to plant sacrifices,[2] but perhaps Ramban and Rabbeinu Bahya are correct that this term alludes to the peace offering. Did Jacob's family already know the difference between burnt offerings and peace offerings?[3]

This theory is useful in other scenes that mention both burnt offerings and peace offerings: "Then he sent young men of Israel, and they sacrificed bulls as burnt offerings and peace offerings to the Lord" (Ex. 24:5). Whoever these "young men" are,[4] they know the difference

2. This is the accepted modern reading; the Sages also use this term to mean animal sacrifices, as we will discuss in regard to peace offerings.
3. R. Tzadok of Lublin suggests that Jacob offers these peace offerings on the altar his father Isaac built (Gen. 26:25), not on the one Abraham built at Hebron (see *Peri Tzaddik* on *Vayigash* 4). This links Jacob's exile to Isaac's exile to Gerar in Genesis 26. See further in Grossman, *Jacob*, 114–18.
4. Onkelos translates that these young men are firstborns, as do many medieval commentators. Ramban suggests that they are called "young men" to distinguish them from the elders in that chapter and that this term conveys the sense that the entire people are involved in the Covenant at Sinai, from young to old. Moreover, this is in dialogue with Moses's demand that Pharaoh release "young and old" (Ex. 10:9).

between burnt offerings and peace offerings, and they offer up both kinds. Similarly, on the eve of the exodus from Egypt, Moses says to Pharaoh: "Then give us sacrifices and burnt offerings to present to the Lord our God" (Ex. 10:25); the distinction between the two kinds of offerings is evidently clear to both Moses and Pharaoh. It thus emerges that not only were offerings part of the ancient religious world long before the laws were recorded in Leviticus, but different kinds of offerings were common practice – at least burnt offerings and peace offerings, a basic distinction that was also made in other Ancient Near Eastern cultures (notably Ugaritic and Canaanite). I do not mean to say that the sacrificial laws of these cultures were identical to biblical laws. I am merely pointing out how integral offerings were to ancient religious life.

As I already noted in the introduction, although this practice was universal, the biblical sacrificial laws were notably distinct, as can be seen from the first biblical offering. Although there were different kinds of offerings, in the Ancient New Eastern world the most prevalent belief was that offerings bring an abundance of blessing: "The main purpose of cultic ritual in general and offerings in particular was to channel divine blessing for the good of the gods and the world."[5] This led to a surprisingly odd phenomenon: the idea that gods offered sacrifices to other gods.[6] If sacrifices were what made rain fall, then the gods themselves would offer sacrifices so that higher deities would send rain.

This is not the case with Cain and Abel. Without giving any explicit reason, God rejects Cain's offering and accepts Abel's. As mentioned in the introduction, this unexplained surprise is fundamental to the narrative's objective: It moves the reader to feel sympathy for Cain when his offering is rejected.[7] This biblical sacrificial debut dictates that it is God, and not the worshipper, who decides whether or not an offering is acceptable. Biblical offerings are not automatically accepted. A person

---

Elsewhere, I suggest that this phrase hints to the Binding of Isaac narrative, when a burnt offering is offered instead of Isaac himself (Grossman, "Binding of Isaac," and "Covenant at Sinai.").

5. Kaufmann, *The Religion of Israel,* vol. 1, 399.
6. Kaufmann brings many examples in *The Religion of Israel,* vol. 1, 409–15.
7. See further in Grossman, *Creation,* 141–55.

is invited to bring an offering and hope for blessing, but there are no guarantees; all depends on God's will.

The most famous biblical story of sacrifice is the Binding of Isaac. Abraham sanctifies the site of Israel's future offerings, and does so when he sacrifices a ram in place of his son.[8] Does this story teach anything about the Torah's perception of offerings in general? Are sacrifices always symbolic replacements for those who offer them up? As discussed in the introduction, there are various possible reasons for the sacrificial world, and the Binding of Isaac narrative may express one of them. Even if we must take care to avoid drawing general conclusions from the famous scene, it is still fascinating to explore the relationship it presents between obligatory and freewill offerings. I stated earlier that there are biblical instances of offerings long before the sacrificial laws are laid out in Leviticus, and they all seem to be freewill offerings. Cain chooses to offer a sacrifice to God, and Abel imitates him. After the Flood, Noah offers sacrifices to thank God of his own free will; although some read the divine command to bring extra "pure animals" into the ark as a hint that God expects offerings at the Flood's end (such as Rashi, Riva, and Rabbeinu Bahya),[9] this is not akin to an actual command.

Even in cases in which one might have expected the sacrifices to be brought by explicit command, it appears that they came purely from human initiative. Such is the case, for example, in the Sinai Covenant. It is possible that there was an earlier command to Moses not recorded in the text; however, on a straightforward reading, it seems that Moses himself sent the young men of the Israelites to offer freewill sacrifices: "He sent the young men of the Israelites, and they offered burnt offerings and sacrificed bulls as peace offerings to the Lord" (Exod 24:5). Before the description of the sacrifice, the Torah recounts God's revelation to Moses, commanding him to ascend to the top of the mountain, but nothing is mentioned there about building an altar or offering sacrifices.

8. For a broader discussion that offering the ram in Isaac's place is the main narrative objective, see Rosenson, "Concerning the Binding"; Grossman, *Abraham*, 348–52.
9. Radak (on Gen. 7:2) disagrees, arguing that fewer than seven of each kind would have been enough for a sacrifice; he suggests that the command is in order that Noah and his family would have plenty of pure animals so that they could eat their meat.

As noted, it would seem that these were voluntary offerings, grounded in human motivation.

Here too, Ibn Ezra finds a hint of a command in what God said at the conclusion of the revelation at Mount Sinai: "An altar of earth you shall make for Me, and you shall sacrifice on it your burnt offerings and your peace offerings" (Exod 20:21). But this is a forced reading. In the plain sense, the command after the Sinai revelation is a general, ongoing instruction concerning the regulations for building an altar. Indeed, the command there continues by specifying the animals to be brought upon the altar – "your sheep and your cattle" – while at Mount Sinai only bulls ("your cattle") are explicitly mentioned. In any case, even if Ibn Ezra is correct, this is at most an allusion, and it is difficult to regard this as a "mandatory" sacrifice

This brings us back to the Binding of Isaac, that monumental scene that sanctifies the site of Israel's future altar and Temple. Unlike the other instances we have just mentioned, the Binding narrative begins with God's explicit command to Abraham: "Take your son, your only one, the one whom you love – Isaac – and go to the land of Moriah. There, offer him up as a burnt offering on one of the mountains, the one that I will show you" (Gen. 22:2). From this perspective, Abraham's sacrifice is an obligatory offering. However, before we assert that this is an anomalous instance of obligatory sacrifice before Leviticus, we must read what happens after the angel prevents Abraham from slaughtering his son. There is no command to offer a sacrifice in Isaac's stead, but Abraham "happens" to notice that a ram is caught in a nearby thicket, and of his own free will, he decides to offer it up in Isaac's place: "Abraham looked up and saw a ram caught in a thicket by its horns. Abraham went, took hold of the ram, and offered it up as a burnt offering in place of his son. And Abraham named the place The Lord Will See" (Gen. 22:13–14). Just as Abraham decides to name the place, he also looks up, notices the ram, and decides to offer it on the waiting altar: "Abraham's agency is emphasized here: He notices it ('he looked up'), he goes to it ('he went'), and he offers it up ('and offered it up'). Abraham is acting with full intent, without any instruction, to replace the offering of his son with a ram."[10] The angel

10. Rosenson, "Concerning the Binding," 324.

could have theoretically commanded him to offer up the ram in Isaac's place – "Do not lift your hand against the boy; take this ram and offer it up in your son's place" – but this is not the case; the burnt offering is the product of Abraham's own initiative. Even if the ram's convenient appearance is no coincidence – as Radak notes, "This was a miraculous invitation from God"[11] – it is still an invitation, not an actual obligation.

Thus,the sacrificial world in the Torah indeed begins with the human desire to offer something up to the Creator. From this perspective, the book of Leviticus starts from the same place: "Speak to the Israelites. Say: *When* one of you brings an animal offering to the Lord."

The book of Leviticus opens with God's assumption that some of the people wish to offer sacrifices. The detailed laws that follow are all based on this premise: One who wishes to bring a burnt offering must do such-and-such; one who wishes to bring a grain offering must do such-and-such, and so on. This perspective reinforces Rambam's belief that the sacrificial laws aim to channel and regulate the natural human desire for tangible forms of worship. But other approaches can also assume that the desire to offer sacrifices to God is deeply rooted in the heart of the believer, a trivial human gesture that reaches out to the infinite of the Divine.

Before we move on from God's opening words to Moses (1:2), it is worth noting that the sacrificial chapters open with animal offerings: "When one of you brings an animal offering to the Lord, you may bring it either from the herd or from the flock." "Animal offering," it seems, refers to either "from the herd or from the flock." That is, this is a case of classic biblical *kelal uferat*, a general statement followed by detailed descriptions: "Animal offering: either from the herd or from the flock." And indeed, this opening statement is followed by the laws of the free-will animal offerings, with separate instructions for offerings from the herd and the flock. Two deviations, however, stand out.

---

11. Radak himself notes that the ram was roaming freely, without its shepherd: "This ram caught in the thicket was separated from the flock, and the shepherd did not notice." I am not convinced that this is what proves that it is an invitation so much as the fact that it appeared by Abraham's side.

The first is that there are not two but three options for a burnt offering:[12] from the herd, from the flock – and from the fowl: "If the offering for the Lord is to be a burnt offering of fowl" (1:14). This third offering is not mentioned in the heading. Secondly, even though the heading refers to animal offerings, which creates the expectation that all the animal offerings will be listed first, before grain offerings, a chapter about grain offerings of fine flour comes between the first chapter, which discusses burnt offerings, and the third chapter, which describes peace offerings. Below, we will attempt to explain these two deviations from God's opening words.

12. As elsewhere in the Torah, the general heading has the word "*ki*," "when," whereas the specific details that follow have "*im*," "either," which shows that this is a subcategory. We will discuss below how this distinction affects our understanding of the relationship between different offerings.

Chapter 6

The Burnt Offering (Leviticus 1): The Chance to Come Closer

THE NATURE AND ESSENCE OF THE BURNT OFFERING

What moves someone to bring a burnt offering? As mentioned, the burnt offering is a freewill offering that can be offered by anyone who so desires. I am not referring to the collective obligatory burnt offerings, of course (the daily burnt offering, additional festival offerings, etc.), although their meaning is related to that of the individual burnt offerings.

The question is not only what motivates someone to interrupt their daily routine in order to bring an offering, but why someone might specifically choose a burnt offering over two other freewill offerings: a grain or peace offering. What does a burnt offering express? How does it differ from what other freewill offerings signify? I believe that each of the freewill offerings conveys a different religious expression; otherwise, there would not be several options available to the worshipper.[1]

1. The challenge of understanding the nature of the burnt offering (and grain offering) moved Milgrom to write: "All that can be said by way of generalization is that sacrifices cover the gamut of the psychological, emotional, and religious needs of the

The most striking feature of the burnt offering is that it is entirely burnt up on the altar. This is evident in the traditional English term for "burnt offering," which is "holocaust," based on the ancient Greek words for *holos* = whole + *kaustos* = burnt (the Septuagint uses "*holocauston*"), a term that has understandably fallen out of use since it took on a new meaning following World War II. The priests do not receive any of its flesh, only its skin. Some claim that the name "*ola*," which literally means "go up," hints to its nature: "Something that entirely goes up in smoke is called '*ola*'" (R. Joseph Bekhor Shor on Lev. 1:3).[2] If so, this reflects the most important aspect of the offering's nature. In fact, how the offering is consumed seems to be the organizing principle of the three freewill offerings:

1. The burnt offering: The whole offering is entirely burnt upon the altar.
2. The grain offering: A handful is burnt on the altar; the rest is eaten by the priests.
3. The peace offering: Some is burnt on the altar; the rest is eaten by both owners and priests.

The extent of the worshippers' participation therefore seems to be inherent to the nature and meaning of each offering. In this first offering, the

---

people. We therefore seek the specific rationale that underlies *each* kind of sacrifice. Even with this limited aim in mind, the texts are not always helpful. However, hints gleaned from the terminology and the descriptions of the rites themselves will occasionally illuminate our path. The comprehensive rationales for the two sacrifices, the burnt and cereal offerings, remain unclear, whereas the three remaining sacrifices, the well-being, purification, and reparation offerings, can be satisfactorily explained" (Milgrom, "Priestly Source," 457).

2. Aharon Ehrlich challenges this reading with the claim that just as the purification and guilt offerings are named for the worshipper's action, the same ought to be true of the *ola* (Ehrlich, *Mikrâ ki-Pheschutô*, 209, based on Ibn Ezra). But this is not binding; offerings might be named for different reasons. Moreover, the purification offering – *ḥattat* – is named not for the worshipper's sin but for the purification – *ḥittui* – of the Tabernacle. The name "*ola*" is linked to the verb "*laalot*" – "to go up" – in many places (e.g., Gen. 22:2, Ex. 24:5, Josh. 8:31, and many others).

owners bring the animal and observe while it is being sacrificed, but do not take part in the process.

Although the entire animal is burned, sacrificial law dictates that it must not be offered up at once; it must first be divided into parts (this is also possibly due to technical reasons): "Then Aaron's sons the priests shall arrange the pieces of the sacrifice / with the head / and the suet" (1:8). The same is true of the burnt offering "from the flock": "The sacrifice shall be cut into pieces, including the head and the suet" (12). Why are the head and the fat/suet singled out both times?[3]

In the Talmud, it is proposed that the head and suet are mentioned separately because one might think that only pieces that are skinned are arranged on the altar:

> Why does it say: "The head and the suet"? Are the head and suet not included in "all the pieces"? Why are they singled out? This is because it says: "He shall skin the offering and cut it into pieces." One might have thought that this only refers to pieces that are skinned. How do we know that this includes the head, which was already partially severed by slaughter? From "With its head and its suet, and the priest shall arrange them." (Ḥullin 27a)

The Talmud points to a correlation between skinning the animal and placing its parts on the altar. Just as skinning was performed out of respect for the altar (because skin was considered unclean), dissecting and washing the parts before placing them on the altar was also an act of respect for the altar. Perhaps the talmudic discussion implies that the offering is considered worthy of the altar after it has been prepared and cut into pieces that are ready to serve.

I believe, however, that there is another explanation for the separate mention of the head and suet. Firstly, the head and suet are mentioned for different reasons. The suet is always offered up on the altar; its special mention here emphasizes that in addition to the suet that is always

3. Ibn Ezra disagrees with those who claim that *peder* is part of the body itself, given that there is clear distinction in Leviticus 8:20. Ramban claims that this refers to a specific kind of fat between the innards.

God's portion, in the case of the burnt offering the meat is offered up as well. But why does the Torah mention the head separately? If not for this specific mention, would the offering really be placed on the altar without its head? The description of Moses offering up the burnt offering during the week of the Tabernacle consecration, which also mentions the head separately, reinforces this question: "Moses cut the ram into pieces and sent the head, pieces, and suet up in smoke" (Lev. 8:20); "They presented him with the burnt offering in its pieces, with its head, and he sent them up in smoke upon the altar" (9:13). The emphasis on including the animal's head as part of the offering seems to imply that this was not always the case in the ancient sacrificial world. Herodotus describes an Ancient Egyptian sacrificial practice:

> After leading the marked beast to the altar where they will sacrifice it, they kindle a fire; then they pour wine on the altar over the offering and call upon the god; then they cut its throat, and having done so sever the head from the body. They flay the carcass of the victim, then invoke many curses on its head, which they carry away. Where there is a market, and Greek traders in it, the head is taken to the market and sold; where there are no Greeks, it is thrown into the river. The imprecation which they utter over the heads is that whatever ill threatens those who sacrifice, or the whole of Egypt, fall upon that head. In respect of the heads of sacrificed beasts and the libation of wine, the practice of all Egyptians is the same in all sacrifices; and from this ordinance no Egyptian will taste of the head of anything that had life.[4]

Herodotus documents that the Egyptians had a strong aversion to sacrificing the head upon the altar, or to consuming the heads of animals in general, fearing that the heads were saturated with curse. If this

4. Herodotus, *History*, book II, part 39. There is a similar, interesting division in the Babylonian New Year ceremony performed to exorcize demons from the temple: The priest takes a lamb and casts the body into the river and its head to the open field (see Linssen, *Uruk*, 230).

belief was prevalent across the ancient world,[5] it explains why the Torah emphasizes that the head *should* be offered up upon the altar as part of the burnt offering.

Moreover, the head's special status is especially relevant for bird offerings, wherein the head is burned on the altar separately (according to the *peshat*, even before the blood is dashed). Although the head is burned together with the rest of the carcass in animal offerings, its separate mention perhaps reflects that it still has special significance. Could this be related to the fact that the worshipper lays hands on the "head" of the animal (1:8)? Does the head somehow symbolize the worshipper?

In any case, the Torah emphasizes that the entire animal must be sacrificed upon the altar, albeit cut into pieces – meat, flesh, and even the head, which was considered a dangerous threat in some cultures. This entirety reflects the essence of the burnt offering – one of total sacrifice and submission to God's presence.

A further glimpse into the essence of the burnt offering is garnered through a surprising description of the burnt offering from the herd:

> If the offering is a burnt offering from the herd, one must offer a male animal without blemish. The one making the offering shall bring it to the entrance to the Tent of Meeting to be accepted on his behalf before the Lord; and, that it be accepted on his behalf, to make his atonement, he shall lay his hand on the head of the burnt offering. (1:3–4)

How is atonement relevant to a freewill offering? There is no mention of atonement in relation to grain or peace offerings; why does it appear with reference to burnt offerings? Rashi already comments on this curiosity, based on the *Sifra* Midrash:

5. It is difficult to reach unequivocal conclusions. Some rituals clearly offer up the animal's head, such as the aforementioned Babylonian New Year ceremony. On festival days in Tishrei the priest takes "the ox heart and the lamb head" and apparently burns it later on (see the text in Linssen, *Uruk*, 189–90); a similar ritual is enacted in honor of the goddess Ishtar (ibid., 241).

> That it be accepted on his behalf – [Atonement] for what? If [the offense] deserves being cut off, the death penalty, or lashes – then the appropriate punishment must apply. This must refer to [atonement for] failing to fulfill a positive commandment.

The Sages, and Rashi in their wake, reason that the burnt offering cannot atone for offenses whose penalty is decreed in the Torah, such as lashes or the death penalty, and that the burnt offering must therefore atone for offenses such as failing to fulfill a positive commandment or for violating a negative commandment that follows from a positive commandment, which does not warrant lashes. This implies that a burnt offering is not dissimilar to an obligatory offering. The ambiguity of its status is the subject of much halakhic debate, as the following example shows.

A rule regarding sacrifices dictates that if someone vows to bring a freewill offering but fails to do so, the *beit din* may seize the offering from their possession (Mishna Arakhin 5:6; Rambam, *Hilkhot Maaseh HaKorbanot* 14:17). According to the Mishna, however, the same is not true of purification or guilt offerings, because the offender is presumably interested in atonement, so it is not likely that they will fail to bring the required offering (as the Tosafot and Ramban rule based on Bava Batra 48a). If so, however, why does the *beit din* enforce a burnt offering? Shouldn't the offender be concerned about atonement as well? The *Rishonim* offer various explanations, all of which underscore the burnt offering's ambivalent nature that hovers between freewill and obligatory – in the worshipper's consciousness as well.[6] Rashi (on Arakhin 21a), for example, asserts: "Although the burnt offering atones for a missed positive commandment, it is not an obligatory offering, so it is not a regular atonement, and therefore they might postpone it – that is why it is enforced" .[7] This ambivalence continues later on in the same

6. R. Kasher suggests that the worshipper does not perceive it as atonement, yet it still atones (*Torah Shelema,* ch. 26, 172), although later on he tends toward the rabbinic position that it is a gift, not an act of atonement. It is clear that the Sages do not perceive the burnt offering as the same level of obligation as the guilt and purification offerings (see Mishna Zevaḥim 1:1, 4:6, and many more).
7. Some versions have "Although the peace offering atones for a missed positive commandment," but this is obviously a mistake, as peace offerings do not atone for a

talmudic discussion, where it is explained that the term "*lirtzono*" means that even when the person is forced to bring the required burnt offering, they must express that they actually want to do so in order to maintain the freewill aspect of the burnt offering's nature.[8]

R. Joseph Bekhor Shor also believes that the burnt offering atones for a formal offense:

> According to the *peshat*, when a person accidentally eats forbidden fat – they must bring a purification offering; if there is doubt – they must bring a variable guilt offering; when they believe they are eating permitted food but it is actually forbidden fat – the burnt offering atones for what they are unaware of. (Bekhor Shor on Lev. 1:4)

According to Bekhor Shor, a purification offering is brought for a known offense; a variable guilt offering atones for a doubt; and a burnt offering is brought for an unknown offense. If so, it is clear why the latter must be a freewill offering: Rather than being brought for a specific offense, it is more of a safeguard against sin that is committed unwittingly. Israel Knohl takes this to the extreme: "The most striking example of atonement and appeasement is the burnt offering."[9] The burnt offering is indeed frequently juxtaposed with the purification offering in contexts of atonement or purification. (All seven-day purification processes such as *zav* and *zava* require a burnt and purification offering on the eighth day, for example.) The burnt offering's connection to the world of atonement is also evident from the Yom Kippur service: "Then he

missed positive commandment; moreover, the rest of the sentence is suited to a feminine noun (burnt offerings are in feminine form, peace offerings are masculine).

8. My rabbi and teacher, R. Lichtenstein, proposes reading the talmudic dispute of whether one must offer up an animal pledged as a burnt offering when its owner has died: Because it has an aspect of atonement, it must be offered up (*Zevaḥim*, 162).
9. Knohl, "The Law of the Purification Offering," 6. Its association with atonement leads some to surmise that the name of the offering, "*ola*," is linked to "*avla*" – wrongdoing, sin; i.e., this offering atones for wrongdoing like the *ḥattat* (sin) and *asham* (guilt), names that pun at words associated with wrongdoing (Levine, *The World of the Bible*, 16); see also Is. 61:8; Job 5:16.

shall come out and offer his burnt offering and the burnt offering of the people, to make atonement for himself and for the people" (Lev. 16:24). If this atonement is indeed achieved through the burnt offering, then this verse specifically links the two.

Nonetheless, Knohl's formulation is too extreme. Even if the burnt offering is linked to atonement, its main purpose is to exude a "sweet savor to the Lord," which is a term associated with freewill offerings, as we will soon see. The burnt offering is first and foremost characterized by its context – as the first of the freewill offerings. Atonement is only a secondary characteristic.

Ramban perceives this aspect of atonement as more abstract and quotes a verse from Ezekiel that plays on two different senses of the word "*ola*": the thoughts that "come in" (*oleh*) to your mind and burnt offering:

> I have seen in the Aggada, in Leviticus Rabba: "R. Shimon b. Yoḥai taught: The burnt offering's sole purpose is to atone for sinful thoughts. Said R. Levi: It is a clear biblical text: "And the thoughts that come into your mind (*ha'oleh*) will never be"– *the ola* effects atonement for the thoughts that come into your mind. Similarly it says of Job: "And he offered burnt offerings according to the number of them all; for Job said, 'It may be that my sons have sinned and blasphemed God *in their hearts*. This proves that the burnt offering only comes to effect atonement for sinful thoughts of the heart." The reason that it serves this particular purpose is because it is a sin that no one recognizes except God; therefore, it is wholly burnt to God.

According to this approach, the burnt offering "atones" for sinful thoughts, not for a specific or concrete offense. If someone has doubts about whether God is just and then regrets such thoughts, for example, they can bring a burnt offering to achieve a sense of atonement. Given that such thoughts are not a concrete sin, they are neither obligated nor able to bring a regular sin offering. If so, the burnt offering serves to restore a person's spiritual and emotional connection with God.[10]

While the prevalent reading is that the name "*ola*" refers to the whole animal being burnt on the altar, Ramban's explanation hints to the motivation for offering it, as Ibn Ezra writes: "An offering that atones for 'thoughts that come (*oleh*) into your mind' is called an *ola*; similarly, offerings brought for sin (*ḥattat*) and guilt are called a purification and guilt offering" (on Lev. 1:4).

The connection between the burnt offering and atonement is indeed supported by various biblical sources. As Ramban mentions, Job brings a burnt offering to atone for his children's possible sinful thoughts.[11] An even more apt example is the communal sacrifice in Numbers:

> If it is done unintentionally by the community, the entire community must offer one bull from the herd as a burnt offering, a sweet savor to the Lord, with its prescribed grain offering and libation, and one goat as a purification offering. The priest shall then make atonement for all the community of Israel and they will be forgiven, because it was an accidental failing, and because they brought their sacrifice, a fire offering to the Lord and the purification offering for their error before the Lord. (Num. 15:24–25)

The burnt offering is mentioned along with the purification offering as part of the act of atonement.

Ramban's approach can be taken a step further to an even more abstract formulation wherein the burnt offering is linked to atonement conceptually but not legally. According to this approach, the burnt offering is not brought for specific sins, nor for sinful thoughts. Rather, it expresses a general desire for "atonement" before God. We tend to think of "atonement" in terms of the act of being cleansed from a particular

---

10. Rabbeinu Bahya usually favors Ramban; here is no exception. (See his commentary on Lev. 1:3.)

11. There is room to debate whether Job specifically offers up burnt offerings or whether "*olot*" here is a generic term for offerings. As stated, the term "*korban*" is unique to Leviticus and Numbers (and Ezekiel), whereas elsewhere "*olot*" is used in a general sense.

offense, but essentially, the verb "*kofer*"/"*kappara*" has a whole range of biblical meanings.[12] One such example can be found in the law of the half shekel:

> When you take the census of the Israelites, as you count, each must give *ransom* (*kofer*) for his life to the Lord, so that no plague strikes them when you count them.... The rich shall not give more, and the poor shall not give less, than this half shekel. It is an offering to the Lord to redeem your lives. Take this *redemption money* (*kesef hakippurim*) from the Israelites and assign it for the service of the Tent of Meeting. It shall be a remembrance for the Israelites before the Lord, to *redeem* (*lekhapper*) your lives. (Ex. 30:12–16)

The fact that the words "*kofer*," *kippurim*," and "*lekhapper*" are translated as "ransom" and "redeem" reflects a different aspect of the root K-P-R here, one that is not associated with sin and atonement. Here, rather, the word expresses basic human inadequacy in the face of the eternal Divine, certainly when each member of the camp is being singled out to determine its size.[13] Rendtorff proves this from the war against Midian, where the warriors who safely return from the battlefield offer gold to "redeem" themselves: "Your servants have counted the warriors in our charge; not one of us is missing. And so we make an offering to the Lord of the gold articles each man found... *to redeem ourselves* (*lekhapper al nafshoteinu*) before the Lord" (Num. 31:49–50).[14] There is no need to seek out a particular offense; their offering is the grateful expression of one whose life has been saved even though they do not feel worthy of this salvation.

If so, the person who brings a freewill burnt offering is not doing so to atone for a specific offense, yet they still seek redemption. The burnt

12. E.g., Lang, "K-P-R."
13. For an interpretation of this census as a military census, see Ibn Ezra in context. On how counting the people is dangerous and may result in a need for atonement, see Propp, *Exodus 19–40*, 534–38.
14. Rendtorff, *Leviticus*, 37.

offering is a fundamental religious expression of a basic sense of inadequacy, of the unbridgeable gap between the flawed, fleeting human and the immortal, perfect Divine. This recalls the end of the confession recited throughout Yom Kippur. After a long list of various sins and offenses, the confessor adds: "My God, before I was created I was unworthy; now that I have been created, it is as if I was never created." Beyond the list of actual mortal corruptions and regrets, the confessor feels that their very existence is not quite justified. They are not necessarily suffering, but they feel distant from God, and they seek His closeness; they seek redemption. The burnt offering is a statement that the person wants to stand before God despite their distance and disparity.[15]

The burnt offering is wholly burnt upon the altar. The worshipper does not partake of its meat. Even the priests do not receive a portion, because this offering is first and foremost an expression of the disparity between the human and the Divine, and human consumption represents convergence between the two, not acknowledgment of their difference. While this offering ultimately embodies a searching for renewed closeness, this can only be achieved through initial human effacement in the face of God's unreachable sublimity.

This explains why those who are not allowed in the Sanctuary due to some form of impurity must bring a burnt offering when this condition ends. Each time a person comes before God anew, they must express their desire to draw close to God's glory despite the unbridgeable chasm between them, despite the distance, despite human smallness and inadequacy.

This applies to all kinds of burnt offerings – from the herd, flock, or fowl. At the same time, each of these three variations has its own specific character, as we will now explore.

15. If so, the burnt offering is entirely a freewill one, despite its expression of atonement. This represents the same mindset as the prayer annexed to the chapters of the offerings recited before the morning prayers. The obligatory offerings are concluded with the prayer: "My it be Your will … if I was obliged to bring a purification offering, may this utterance be accepted before You as if I had offered up a purification offering." In contrast, freewill offerings are concluded with this prayer: "May it be Your will as if I had offered up a peace offering/a thanksgiving offering." The burnt offering has the latter conclusion, implying that it is freewill, not obligatory.

THE BURNT OFFERING FROM THE HERD

> If the offering is a burnt offering from the herd, one must offer a male animal without blemish. The one making the offering shall bring it to the entrance to the Tent of Meeting to be accepted on his behalf before the Lord; and, that it be accepted on his behalf, to make his atonement, he shall lay his hand on the head of the burnt offering and shall have the bull slaughtered before the Lord. And Aaron's sons the priests shall present the blood, dashing it against each side of the altar at the entrance to the Tent of Meeting. The burnt offering shall then be skinned and cut into pieces. The sons of Aaron the priest shall arrange wood on the fire they will have placed upon the altar. Then Aaron's sons the priests shall arrange the pieces of the sacrifice, with the head and the fat, upon the wood on the altar fire; the inner organs and legs shall first be washed with water. The priest shall then burn it all on the altar as a burnt offering, an offering of fire, a sweet savor to the Lord. (Lev. 1:3–9)

The first option is a "burnt offering from the herd," a young "bull." This is the largest offering and therefore merits first mention; in general, bulls are listed before sheep (see especially the consecration of the altar in Numbers 7 and the additional offerings in Numbers 28). Later, however, we will raise the possibility that there are more essential differences between the animals, which leads to a further reason why the bull is listed first.

The Hebrew phrase "*ben bakar*" – which literally means "the son of a bull" – rather than simply "*bakar*," "bull," implies that a young bull should be used. As Bekhor Shor writes (on Lev. 1:5): "A young bull – This means youth, for they must not bring one that is too old or sick, as in, 'Offer it to your governor if you will.'" On the other hand, the text specifies "young bull" rather than "*egel*," "calf" (as in Lev. 9:2); the Sages therefore define that a "young bull" is ideally two to three years old.[16]

16. R. Meir's opinion about the offering's age implies that he believes that older animals are not fitting for the altar's honor (Mishna Para 1:2).

A young animal is presumably more choice than an older animal. Abraham, the ideal host, runs to his herd to choose "a tender, choice young bull" for his guests (Gen. 18:7). This may also represent a young animal that is full of life, but more developed, independent, and valuable than a nursing calf.

It is not always the case that an offering must be from a young animal; the peace offering, for example, requires a "bull," not a "young bull" (Lev. 3:1). When the princes of each tribe bring offerings, their burnt offering is a "young bull" and their peace offerings are "bulls" (throughout Numbers 7). We cannot delve into this distinction before discussing the nature of peace offerings; for now, it suffices to note that an immature bull is a fitting offering for the worshipper who seeks to express their own inadequacy before their Maker. (Accordingly, the purification offering also requires a "young bull.") As we will yet see, unlike the burnt offering, the peace offering expresses a sense of mutual respect and covenant of love and joy, symbolized by the offering of a mature bull in its prime.[17]

In my discussion of sacrificial terms and their meanings (chapter 3), I have already noted certain elements mentioned in these verses. I would now like to explore certain complexities that revolve around the question of who actually offers up this sacrifice.

Worshipper or Priest?

Who is active at each stage of the sacrificial process? The offering is brought by the Israelite worshipper, while many stages are executed by the priests; thus, it is necessary to define their respective roles. As mentioned, *Parashat Vayikra* is addressed to the Israelites, so instructions such as "He shall lay his hands on the head of the burnt offering" refer to the worshipper unless specified otherwise. If so, the burnt offering ceremony is performed as follows (with the priests' actions in italics):

> If the offering is a burnt offering from the herd,
> one must offer a male animal without blemish.

17. The Torah does not always maintain this distinction and sometimes refers to the two sacrifices together. (See, for example, Num. 15:8–9.)

> The one making the offering shall bring it to the entrance to the
> Tent of Meeting to be accepted on his behalf before the Lord;
> and, that it be accepted on his behalf, to make his atonement,
> he shall lay his hand on the head of the burnt offering
> and shall have the bull slaughtered before the Lord.
> *And Aaron's sons the priests shall present the blood,*
> *dashing it against each side of the altar at the entrance to the Tent of Meeting.*
> The burnt offering shall then be skinned and cut into pieces.
> *The sons of Aaron the priest shall arrange wood on the fire they will have placed upon the altar.*
> *Then Aaron's sons the priests shall arrange the pieces of the sacrifice,*
> *with the head and the fat, upon the wood on the altar fire;*
> the inner organs and legs shall first be washed with water.
> *The priest shall then burn it all on the altar as a burnt offering.* (1:3–9)

It emerges that the worshipper and the priests are both active participants, taking turns to complete the burnt offering process even after the priests begin their actions. This is worth emphasizing because it sometimes seems that the worshippers have an active role only until the animal is slaughtered.[18] Yet the worshipper does not merely hand over the animal and leave all the work to the priests; rather, the labor is divided as follows:

The Worshipper	**The Priest**
Laying the hands	Dashing the blood
Slaughter	Arrange the wood and lighting the fire
Skinning the animal	Arranging the pieces on the altar
Cutting it to pieces	Burning the pieces on the altar
Washing the inner organs and legs	

18. I will soon mention the Septuagint, which also adopts this position, as does *Sefer HaḤinnukh.*

The biblical division of labor is maintained in halakha. As Ramban summarizes:

> The phrases "shall then be skinned" and "cut into pieces" refer to the owner of the offering, as does "shall lay" and "slaughter." For the skinning and cutting is not considered part of the service and can be performed by a non-priest. And this is why the text specifies "The sons of Aaron shall arrange" (7). And the legs can be washed by a non-priest, which is why it says "The inner organs and legs shall be washed with water" (9) by the owner, and then "The priest shall burn." (Ramban on Lev. 1:6)

This formulation seems to imply that the worshipper may perform the actions that are not actually considered part of the halakhic "service." Note that his language, "can be performed by a non-priest," implies that the worshipper *can* do these actions, but *may* leave them up to the priests. The biblical text, however, implies that the worshipper *must* do them, which concurs with the Zohar's reading: "It is written: 'He shall slaughter the young bull' – the non-priest, not the priest, as this is forbidden by law for the priest."[19]

According to the Zohar, not only "may" the non-priest slaughter the offering, but this is forbidden to the priest. Even if we do not adopt kabbalistic terminology, the biblical text might imply that ideally, the worshipper should execute as much of their offering as possible, but certain actions must be done by the priest instead.

Ramban's criterion for dividing the work between worshipper and priest is what is defined as "service," but a more specific delineation is that the worshipper takes care of the offering itself (slaughter, skinning, cutting, washing) and the priest deals with actions that involve the altar: dashing the blood against the altar; arranging the wood, lighting the fire. This distinction defines the priests' fundamental role in the sacrificial world. Non-priests may not approach the altar, for "the altar becomes holy of holies – and anything that touches it will become holy" (Ex.

19. Zohar, *Parashat Naso*, III:124a. See R. Kasher's discussion of this idea in *Torah Shelema*, XII, 147–48.

29:37). We will explore this further when discussing the meaning of the term "holy of holies" and "contagious holiness," but it is clear from this verse that only those defined as "holy" (i.e., priests) may approach the altar. Thus,the non-priest deals with the offering itself, but when the offering must come into contact with the altar, the priest must take over as the owner's emissary.

Intriguingly, the Septuagint finds it difficult to allow room for the worshipper and translates all verbs into plural form, as if they all refer to the priest.[20] Given that the translation retains the mentions of "Aaron's sons the priests" (which in the MT only serve to differentiate between who performs which actions), this is clearly an intentional change rather than indication of a different *Vorlage*. The idea that non-priests are expected to play such an active role in their offering, so close to the altar, is indeed surprising.[21]

Yet this division of labor between worshipper and priest applies in other offerings as well, which proves that this is inherent to the sacrificial experience. The peace offering has a similar division:

> The one bringing the offering shall lay his hand on its head
> and have it slaughtered at the entrance to the Tent of Meeting.
> *Aaron's sons the priests shall dash the blood against each side of the altar.*
> *A priest shall present of the peace offering a fire offering to the Lord…*

---

20. Philo's description is similar: "After that, one of the priests takes it and slaughters it" (*Laws II*, part 199; *Writings*, vol. 2, 273). R. Avia Hacohen told me that this seems to be the *Minḥat Ḥinnukh*'s stance as well: "…the priest dashes the blood and skins and cuts it up into parts" (mitzva 115). This is surprising, given that according to rabbinic literature, skinning and cutting may be performed by a non-priest (*Sifra*, Freewill Offerings, 5:4 – "Skinning and cutting may be performed by anyone"; Yoma 26b; Rambam, *Hilkhot Biat Mikdash* 9:6).
21. See further in Hacohen, *Leviticus*, 34–36; he believes that the Temple service is based on partnership between the priests and the rest of the people. As mentioned, I believe that this is more than mere partnership: The priest is performing the service on the worshipper's behalf; the worshipper would perform the entire ritual, but as they are not allowed to approach the altar, the priest performs those parts of the process for them instead.

> the two kidneys and the fat that is on them at the loins; and the diaphragm of the liver, he shall remove with the kidneys.
> *Aaron's sons shall send all these up in smoke upon the altar.* (3:2–5)

This has dramatic implications for the sacrificial practice. We have already seen that beginning with *Parashat Vayikra* and its focus on Israel's role, rather than with the more priest-centric *Parashat Tzav*, underscores that the Tabernacle and its offerings are designated for Israel, whereas the priests are servants that facilitate this service. The Israelite worshipper's surprisingly active participation in freewill offerings answers the talmudic question of whether priests are "people's agents" or "God's agents" (Nedarim 35b). The first list of sacrifices in Leviticus imply that they are Israel's agents, whose main role is to enable Israel to offer sacrifices. The worshipper performs as much of the sacrificial process as possible, and the priest only steps in because the worshipper is barred from approaching the altar.

If so, then the Zohar's aforementioned conclusion about slaughter can be extended to the entire process: The worshipper is commanded to do as much as possible, and the priest is forbidden to perform any tasks in their stead, for the world of sacrifice is intended for Israel, not the priesthood.

Dashing the Blood (1:5)

One of the most central acts that accompanies every animal offering is the dashing, sprinkling, or pouring of its blood upon the altar. The Sages perceived this as the main action that effects the worshipper's atonement. Moreover, the language of the text implies that the steps leading up to this act are essentially a preparation for presenting the blood to the altar: The animal must be slaughtered, its blood collected, and then brought to the altar all for the sake of "dashing it at each side of the altar."

Since the blood symbolizes the spirit (e.g., Deut. 12:23), this act is what pours the animal's essential life force onto the altar. But if so, then the place where the blood is dashed is surprising: Most commentators agree that "*al hamizbe'aḥ saviv*" – "dashing it against each side of the altar" – refers to the altar walls, not into the fire that burns upon it;

otherwise, the description "on each side/around" makes little sense.[22] But if the fire is what "consumes" the offering, then the blood does not actually reach the fire and is therefore not "consumed." Why isn't the blood thrown into the altar fire?

Some explain that the animal's flesh constitutes the main offering, while the blood is dashed against the wall to make sure that the worshipper or priest does not eat the blood, which is forbidden for human consumption. This seems unlikely, given the ceremonial centrality of the act. If its purpose were solely to remove it from the flesh, it would surely be disposed of, not dashed or sprinkled. Others suggest that the blood is not actually "offered" and that its purpose is to purify the altar.[23] This too is unconvincing – there is no mention of "purification" in the freewill offerings. Moreover, while this *is* the purpose of the blood of the purification offering, in that context the blood is "applied" (4:25), not "dashed," which differentiates this action from the dashing or sprinkling of the blood in other offerings.

Naphtali Meshel offers a surprising reading: that the phrase "*al hamizbe'aḥ saviv*" refers not to the walls, but to the top, where the fire burns. He argues that this is supported by the parallelism in Ezekiel: "These are the statutes pertaining to the altar on the day that it is fashioned: to bring burnt offerings *upon it* / and to sprinkle blood *upon it*" (Ezek. 43:18); and by the law in Deuteronomy: "Of your other sacrifices, the blood shall be poured out *on* the altar of the Lord your God, but you may eat the meat" (12:27). While these verses can be read differently, the account of Ahaz offering sacrifices upon the altar also implies that the blood is dashed upon the altar itself:

> When the king arrived from Damascus and saw the altar, he approached the altar and ascended it and offered up his burnt offering and his grain offering, poured out his libation, and dashed the blood of his peace offering upon the altar. (II Kings 16:12–13).

22. See, for example, Rendtorff, *Leviticus*, 52, and many others.
23. For a discussion of these and other approaches, see Knierim, *Text and Concept*, 56–57; Meshel, "Grammar of Sacrifice," 277.

The king ascends the actual altar and dashes the blood "upon" it. Based on this, Meshel reads Leviticus's "*saviv*" in the sense of "all over" the top of the altar, similarly to "They cut off his head and stripped off his armor and sent word *all over* (*saviv*) the land of the Philistines" (I Sam. 31:9).[24]

This reading is fascinating, but it does not solve the problem: Even if the blood is to be dashed "all around" the top of the altar, this still means that the blood is not directed at the fire itself.[25]

In fact, the order of the sacrificial service described here shows that the blood is dashed before the altar fire is actually lit; only two verses later do the priests arrange wood upon the altar fire (v. 7), which is presented as preparation for burning the flesh. Thus, there is no choice but to concede that the blood is not dashed into the "consuming" fire, unlike the flesh, which is consumed by the flames.[26] Some suggest that the fact that the blood is not directly consumed by the fire teaches Israel that they should not eat the blood either, as if to show that God Himself refrains from consuming blood and is satisfied with the flesh.[27] I too favor this approach, albeit in a different formulation.

In the context of the prohibition of offering sacrifices outside the Sanctuary, the prohibition of not consuming the blood and its rationale are also reiterated: "I will set My face against that person who eats blood and will sever him from his people, for the life of a creature is in

24. Meshel, "Grammar of Sacrifice." Avraham Shammah rightly notes that this is related to the halakhic question of whether there is slaughter upon the altar itself. The story of the Binding of Isaac suggests that this is so, given that Isaac is placed on the altar while he is still alive, although I do offer an alternative explanation elsewhere (see Grossman, *Avraham*, 318–19). Shammah also points out that the perception in Leviticus, that the blood and the flesh have different relations to the altar, differs from that in Deuteronomy, where they are the same.
25. Meshel once pointed out to me in conversation that he believes that the entire top of the altar was alight – that is, there was no space on top that wasn't alight. However, the laws of the bird offerings imply that the blood must reach the altar *wall* (1:15; 5:9), although in both of these verses the blood is "drained" and not "dashed."
26. R. Baruch Kehat suggested to me that the altar can "consume" the offering even without fire; the placement of the offering upon the altar is consumption enough. But since the "sweet savor" is only achieved through burning the offering, it seems that the blood serves one purpose and the burning of the flesh another.
27. Gane, "Ritual," 86–87.

its blood. I have given it to you to make atonement for your lives on the altar, for blood, which is bound up with life, atones" (Lev. 17:11). Because a creature's essence is its lifeblood, blood is dashed against the altar to symbolically atone for the Israelites' lives. Once again, this "atonement" is not necessarily atonement for formal sin so much as a symbolic expression of the flawed, inadequate nature of the human in the face of the Divine. To stand before God is to acknowledge the disparity between the worshipper and the Almighty. Dashing the animal's lifeblood is essentially an apology for this disparity: It is a mortal life "atoning" for the worshipper's own life.

This symbolic act of "atonement" is an essential part of every offering, even those that have nothing to do with wrongdoing, such as the peace offering. It is essentially a convention that expresses regret for the mere mortal's audacity in standing before the immortal Divine, an act of returning the offering's lifeblood to the Giver of Life.

While the flesh of the burnt offering turns to smoke and rises up, the blood is not consumed by the altar flames. What matters is the gesture of dashing the offering's vital essence toward the altar.

The Altar Fire (1:7)

The notion of the Israelite worshipper's centrality in the sacrificial world can help illuminate another curious stage of the process: the commandment to "place fire upon the altar" (1:7). The priests must place more wood "on the fire they will have placed upon the altar" so that the flames will not go out. This instruction implies that without this step, the priests will not be able to offer up the sacrifice, because the fire is not lit. However, *Parashat Tzav* describes that the altar fire burned continually and was never allowed to go out (6:2–6), "*esh tamid*." If the fire is perpetually burning, why is the priest commanded to light the fire in order to burn the burnt offering?

The Sages define the commandment in Leviticus 1:7 as the halakha of adding wood to the existing fire ("Even though fire would descend from Heaven, it is a mitzva to add wood to the man-made fire" – *Sifra*, Freewill Offerings, 5:10), but the contradiction still stands: Leviticus 1:7 still implies that the worshipper presents their burnt offering when the altar fire is not yet burning.

Avraham Shammah proposes that this can be understood through the relationship between *Parashat Vayikra* – which addresses the Israelite worshipper and perceives the sacrificial service as an act of religious expression – and *Parashat Tzav* – which addresses the priests and perceives the sacrificial service as the means of keeping the Divine Presence among Israel, as discussed. *Parashat Vayikra* introduces the altar fire as if it is ignited specially for each and every individual's sacrifice, as if divine fire descends to the altar for each specific, intimate encounter between each worshipper and God. We soon learn from *Parashat Tzav* that this is not the case – that there is a whole sacrificial system designed to keep the Divine Presence resting in the Sanctuary, including a perpetually burning fire upon the altar – but this fact is ignored in the first chapters of Leviticus.[28] The halakha to add wood before each offering thus reflects both *Vayikra* and *Tzav*: The flames continue burning through the merit of each new offering.

THE BURNT OFFERING FROM THE FLOCK

Why are there various options for a burnt offering? Are there fundamental differences between these options? Are they accompanied by different psychological or spiritual mindsets, or are they all variations on the burnt offering rite, with different options for different budgets? Even those who concur that the three different kinds of freewill offerings (burnt, grain, and peace) reflect three different religious expressions can easily reject the idea of a significant difference between offering a bull, ram, or bird.

Indeed, the prevalent exegetical approach is to perceive the difference between the three options as purely financial, given that bulls are more expensive than rams, which are more expensive than birds. (Some even argue that the grain offering that follows in Leviticus 2 is an even cheaper option for those who cannot afford birds; we will discuss this in context.)[29]

28. Shammah, "Two Objectives," 43. See also Kehat, "Sanctuary."
29. As I have already noted in the introduction, one main motif throughout Midrash Leviticus Rabba is that what matters is not the offering's cost but the worshipper's

This reading is certainly reasonable bearing in mind the variable purification offering, which explicitly takes a person's financial means into account. If so, there is no fundamental difference between a burnt offering from the herd or from the flock, and we wouldn't expect any significant differences between the sacrificial process of each option.

The problem with this reading, however, is that there are slight differences between them, and if this is still the case after the size of each animal is taken into account, this would imply that the differences between each option are not purely technical. The question is complicated indeed, and I hope to propose a cogent resolution, even if it cannot be proved beyond doubt. To compare the two animal burnt offerings:

From the Herd (1:3–9)	**From the Flock (1:10–13)**
If the offering is a burnt offering from the herd, one must offer a male animal without blemish. The one making the offering shall bring it to the entrance to the Tent of Meeting to be accepted on his behalf before the Lord; and, that it be accepted on his behalf, to make his atonement, he shall lay his hand on the head of the burnt offering	If the offering is a burnt offering from the flock, whether a sheep or a goat, one must offer a male without blemish.
and shall have the bull slaughtered before the Lord. And Aaron's sons the priests shall present the blood,	The one making the sacrifice shall have it slaughtered on the north side of the altar before the Lord,
dashing it against each side of the altar at the entrance to the Tent of Meeting.	and Aaron's sons the priests shall dash its blood against each side of the altar.
The burnt offering shall then be skinned and cut into pieces. The sons of Aaron the priest shall arrange wood on the fire they will have placed upon the altar.	The sacrifice shall be cut into pieces, including the head and the fat,
Then Aaron's sons the priests shall arrange the pieces of the sacrifice, with the head and the fat, upon the wood on the altar fire;	and the priest shall arrange these upon the wood on the altar fire,

intention; accordingly, one recurring motif is the value of the virtuous poor man's offering (e.g., Leviticus Rabba 3:2).

the inner organs and legs shall first be washed with water. The priest shall then burn it all on the altar	the inner organs and legs having been washed with water. The priest shall then offer it all, sending it up in smoke upon the altar
as a burnt offering, an offering of fire, a sweet savor to the Lord.	as a burnt offering, an offering of fire, a sweet savor to the Lord.

In general, the two processes are virtually identical. While the laying of the hands and the skinning are not mentioned in the second offering, this is probably a case of abbreviation; the Midrash Halakha on these verses, for example, assumes that they apply to the burnt offering from the flock as well and are omitted for brevity's sake (although Radatz Hoffmann disagrees). In fact, there seems to be proof that certain details in the first burnt offering also apply to the second. The Torah refers to the burnt offering in one of two ways throughout the process, and at first glance there is no evident logic for using one or the other:

> He shall lay his hand on the head of the *burnt offering*
> and shall have the *young bull* slaughtered before the Lord....
> The *burnt offering* shall then be skinned and cut into pieces.

Why does the worshipper skin and lay their hand on the "burnt offering," but have the "young bull" slaughtered? It emerges that components that are not mentioned again in the description of the burnt offering "from the flock" refer to the "burnt offering" – which can apply to the ram as well – whereas steps that are repeated specify the "young bull." Hands should be laid upon the head of all "burnt offerings"; all "burnt offerings" should be skinned, bull and ram alike.[30] This may explain Rashi's

30. The status of cutting the offering into pieces is more complex in this context, as there is no subject, neither "burnt offering" nor "young bull" – although the pronoun is feminine (*venittaḥ* **otah**), which points to "burnt offering." This would imply that the action applies to both bull and ram, yet the description of the burnt offering from the flock does repeat the act of cutting. Whether the cutting of bull and ram is identical is not clear: The text implies that the head and fat of the bull are not cut into pieces but are laid upon the altar whole (v. 6), whereas the ram's head and

commentary: "The burnt offering shall then be skinned – Why does it say 'the burnt offering'? So that this will apply to all burnt offerings, to be skinned and cut" (see also Abarbanel on Lev. 1, p. 23).

The Offerings' Introductions

Another hint that the laws of the burnt offering from the herd also apply to those from the flock can be gleaned from a comparison between all three headings:

> If his *burnt offering* is from the *herd,* one must offer a male animal without blemish. (v. 3)
>
> If his offering is *from the flock,* whether a sheep or a goat, the *burnt offering* must be a male without blemish. (v. 10)
>
> If it is to be *of fowl, his burnt offering,* one may offer doves or pigeons. (v. 14)

The burnt offering from the herd introduces the concept of "burnt offering" and then specifies the kind of animal, whereas the second and third options introduce the type of animal – "If from the flock" / "If it is to be of fowl" – before using the term "burnt offering." This implies that the opening paragraph is the default definition of the burnt offering that describes the whole process – a process that applies to all burnt offerings – whereas the two other options are possible variations.

---

fat do seem to be cut into pieces (v. 12). If this difference is intentional, it is clear why the process is repeated with the ram – but this raises the question of why the Torah does not use "young bull" in conjunction with cutting, instead of the feminine pronoun that refers to "burnt offering," although it is less definitive given that "burnt offering" is not the explicit subject. Abarbanel notes that "it says 'It should be cut into pieces' about the ram because otherwise we would have thought that this only applies to burnt offerings from the herd and not the flock" (see his commentary on Leviticus 1, p. 23).

Herd or Flock?

Given that the opening description is a full, comprehensive overview of the process, whereas the second two offer more compact variations, it is difficult to determine whether there are fundamental differences between a burnt offering from the herd and the flock. The young bull is slaughtered "before the Lord" (v. 5), whereas the ram is "slaughtered on the north side of the altar before the Lord" (v. 11). Both are "before the Lord," but "the north side of the altar" appears for the first time about the ram. Does this apply to both, or is it an actual halakhic difference?

The Sages rule that all details mentioned in the first description apply to the second. A more surprising rule, perhaps, is that the same is true vice versa (in the words of the *Sifra*: "'And if from the flock' – The extra *vav* means that they mean both").[31] If so, then all burnt offerings should be slaughtered on the north side of the altar. This reading is supported by the formulation of the individual and leaders' purification offerings (Lev. 4; see also 8:18; 7:2): "It shall be slaughtered in the place where burnt offerings are slaughtered before the Lord," which presumably applies to all burnt offerings, bulls and rams alike.

Unlike the Sages' reading, however, the biblical text indicates that the young bull can be slaughtered anywhere in the courtyard, which is all "before God." The fact that the description of the slaughter refers specifically to the "young bull," rather than the more general term, "burnt offering," suggests that the two variations are slaughtered differently.

Further support that there are substantial halakhic differences between the two is that the priests bring the young bull's blood to the altar (v. 5), a detail that is not mentioned about the ram slaughtered to the altar's north side (v. 11). The young bull's blood must be brought to the altar, since it can be slaughtered anywhere in the courtyard, whereas the blood of the ram, which is slaughtered right by the altar, is dashed immediately.[32]

Moreover, the distinction between the place of slaughter is also evident in the purification offering, where all offerings from the flock must

31. Rainey, "Sacrifice," 639.
32. This differs from Abarbanel's opinion that this is purely abbreviation and that collecting and bringing the blood are included in the act of dashing (on Lev. 1, p. 23).

be slaughtered to the altar's north (4:24, 29, 33), a detail that is absent from descriptions of purification offerings from the herd, which again, must be simply slaughtered "before the Lord" (4:4, 15).

Whether this has halakhic ramifications or not, why is slaughter at the northern side of the altar repeatedly associated with the flock but not the herd? Milgrom believes that this is technically related to the offerings' size: The larger, more aggressive bull should be slaughtered wherever the worshipper is able to do so, whereas the smaller, more docile ram should be led to the ideal spot, the altar's north side.[33] Milgrom adds that the north side is preferable for technical reasons (waste disposal is to the altar's east; the basin to the west; the ramp is south).[34] Yet neither claim is convincing; the practice of slaughtering oxen was and remains common, nor does it seem likely that the only reason for slaughtering to the north was that it had the most room.

Like a Ram to the Altar/Bovine Revelation

A more illuminating reading is that the place of slaughter reveals a fundamental difference between the two kinds of burnt offerings. I will start by presenting Radatz Hoffmann's theory; though I will not adopt it word for word, it advances the discussion. Radatz believes that the Torah's discussion of the burnt offering from the flock is referring to the daily burnt offering: "It is not too far-fetched to presume that the verses in Leviticus 11–13, which describe the burnt offering from the flock, were already mentioned at Mount Sinai after the instructions of the daily burnt offering."[35]

This is how he clarifies the disparities between the two kinds of animal burnt offerings: Laying the hands and appeasing God are relevant only for individuals' offerings, so they are not mentioned in the context of the burnt offering from the flock, whose main model is the communal daily burnt offering. Ultimately, even according to Radatz Hoffmann, the

---

33. Milgrom brings proof for his opinion: In the Second Temple, there were designated rings that marked where the animals were placed for slaughter.
34. Milgrom, *Leviticus*, vol. 1, 164.
35. Hoffmann, *Leviticus*, vol. 1
, 97.

laws in Leviticus 1 apply to individuals' offerings as well, but the model is in dialogue with the description of the communal daily burnt offering.

I believe that the connection Radatz points out between the burnt offering from the flock and the daily burnt offering is indeed valid, but it is a *result* of the deeper nature of the differences between bull and ram, rather than the *explanation* for the subtle distinction between the two kinds of burnt offering. These distinct natures are reflected in the different areas of the Tabernacle associated with each animal. An offering from the herd – burnt offering and all the rest – is associated with the Tent of Meeting, whereas offerings from the flock are linked to the altar. This division can be traced again and again through the sacrificial chapters.

First, in addition to the different slaughter sites, there is a subtle difference between where the blood of each animal is dashed. The blood from the young bull is dashed "against each side of the altar at the entrance to the Tent of Meeting" (1:5), whereas the ram's blood is dashed "against each side of the altar" (v. 11). In fact, the young bull is associated with the Tent of Meeting from the beginning of the process: "The one making the offering shall bring it to the entrance to the Tent of Meeting to be accepted on his behalf before the Lord" (v. 3). This place – "the entrance to the Tent of Meeting" – is not mentioned in relation to the burnt offering from the flock.

Another indication is the site of the peace offering's slaughter: The peace bull is slaughtered "at the entrance to the Tent of Meeting" (3:2), whereas the peace rams are slaughtered "before the Tent of Meeting" (3:8, 13). Whether the two locations refer to the same area is not entirely clear, but there is a subtle symbolic difference: "At the entrance to the Tent of Meeting" links the bull more closely to the Tent of Meeting than "before the Tent of Meeting" (which refers to the entire courtyard; cf. Num. 8:9–10).

The definition of the area as "the entrance to the Tent of Meeting" links the event to the revelation that takes place inside: "This shall be the regular burnt offering throughout your generations at the entrance of the Tent of Meeting before the Lord. There I will meet with you, there I will speak to you, and there I will meet with the Israelites" (Ex. 29:42). Some even suggest that the Tent of Meeting itself is a place of revelation for all of Israel, not just the priests (for example, during Korah's rebellion – Num. 18–19).[36] For our purposes, what matters is the literary impression this place evokes: The young bull is slaughtered next to the site of God's revelation inside the Sanctuary, and this association is absent from the offering from the flock.

The proposed division between herd and flock is found in obligatory offerings as well; in fact, it is even more explicit. There are two main groups of purification offerings: those brought by an anointed priest or the whole congregation (Lev. 4:3–21) and those brought by the leader or individual (4:22–35). The first is an "internal purification offering" – the blood is brought into the Tent of Meeting itself and sprinkled in front of the inner curtain – whereas the second is an "external purification offering," whose blood is sprinkled on the altar in the courtyard. Intriguingly, the first, "internal" offering is a young bull, whereas the second, "external" kind, associated with the altar, is from the flock (a male goat or ewe).[37]

It is unlikely that this pattern is coincidental. Based on their sacrificial associations, we may posit that the cow/calf/bull is related to the Divine Presence inside the Sanctuary, whereas the sheep is linked to the altar. The worshipper may choose whether to offer a sacrifice that faces the cloud of divine revelation inside the Tent of Meeting or one that is connected to the altar, to service of God, and to divine fire that consumes its offering.

The respective natures of these animal offerings are alluded to at the Sinai Revelation. In many cases, animals from both herd and flock are offered in large groups (on festivals, during the Temple consecration, and so on), which makes it difficult to determine the meaning of individual offerings. At the Sinai Revelation, however, offerings from the

36. Stollman, *Search of Lost Meaning*, 266–71.

37. The exception to this is the Yom Kippur scapegoat, which is from the flock, not the herd. I believe this is linked to something fundamental in the purification of the Sanctuary; delving deeper requires analysis of the Yom Kippur service in Leviticus 16, which is beyond the scope of this book. A general comment will suffice: Ibn Ezra is correct that the requirement "He shall then go out to the altar before the Lord and make its atonement" (Lev. 16:18) refers to the outer altar, not the inner incense altar, which shows that this is a unique model of internal and external purification, and for this reason the scapegoat is used. It may also be related to the mingling of its blood with the purification bull.

herd occupy a central place: "Then he sent young men of Israel, and they sacrificed bulls as burnt offerings and peace offerings to the Lord" (Ex. 24:5). This is a particularly interesting source, given that only bulls are mentioned for both burnt and peace offerings.[38] It is bulls that are offered at the most famous divine revelation in Israel's history.

This brings us back to Radatz's theory, which explains the differences between the first two kinds of burnt offering by linking the burnt offering from the flock to the daily burnt offering. The daily burnt offering is the first and last offering each day; thus, the sheep fundamentally symbolizes the altar. The burnt offering from the flock, therefore, is linked to the altar from the moment of its slaughter,[39] whereas the burnt offering from the herd is associated with God's presence and revelation at the Tent of Meeting.

Although this brings us to the world of *derash* barely tethered to the text, it is worth pointing out that this is also expressed through the distinction between the Shabbat and festival additional offerings. The festival offerings include a mix of burnt offerings from both herd and flock; on Shabbat, just two sheep and no bulls are added to the daily burnt offering.[40] This perhaps expresses that Shabbat is part of the regular Israelite week based on God's creation of the world,[41] whereas each festival marks a moment of God's revelation in the world and its momentous effect on history.[42]

If the reader will allow me to present another side issue, we can apply this theory to the difference between the wave offering – the *omer* – and

38. Ibn Ezra seems to believe that the bulls refer to the peace offerings, while Ramban believes that they were used for both peace and burnt offerings.
39. Yoel Elitzur writes that the northern side of the altar perhaps challenges the Ugaritic belief that the gods dwell upon the "northern mountain." The place of slaughter signifies that God dwells within the Sanctuary inside the Israelite camp and not upon the northern mountain revered by the ancient peoples (Elitzur, "Place," 173–76).
40. I am not relating to the purification offering that does not accompany the Shabbat offerings but does accompany the festival additional offerings; see R. Samson Raphael Hirsch's commentary on Numbers there.
41. See, e.g., Bazak, "*Ḥodesh BeḤodsho*."
42. This is similar to R. Joseph B. Soloveitchik's formulation: On festivals God comes to visit the Temple; on Shabbat God comes to visit in the person's own home (*Shiurim LeZekher Abba Mari z"l*, vol. 1, 80–83).

the two-loaf offering. Many question why the *omer* offering is accompanied by a lamb as a burnt offering: "On the day you display the sheaf this way and that, you shall offer a yearling sheep without blemish as a burnt offering to the Lord" (Lev. 23:12), whereas the two-bread offering is presented together with "seven unblemished yearling male lambs, one young bull, and two rams – these shall be a burnt offering for the Lord" (23:18). This may be related to the Torah's desire to characterize the *omer* as an individual offering rather than a collective offering (as we will discuss in the context of the first fruits offering),[43] but it may also be related to animal symbolism. The *omer* offering gives the people permission to eat from the year's new crop, whereas the two-bread offering allows the new grain to be used for sacramental purposes. That is, the new grain cannot be brought to the Sanctuary after the *omer* offering, so a bull is an inappropriate accompaniment. Fifty days later, however, when the two-bread offering renders the new crop fit for sacramental purposes, the sacrifice of a bull symbolizes that the grain can now be used in the place of divine revelation.

Thus,the two different options for an animal burnt offering are related to two different locations in the Tabernacle, which are two different focal points of religious consciousness: The Tent of Meeting is where the Divine Presence rests, and the altar is where humans offer sacrifices to God. The burnt offering from the herd directs the worshipper's gaze inside, to the Tent of Meeting; the burnt offering from the flock is entirely focused on the altar. Is there a reason that the bull signifies the Divine Presence resting in the Tent of Meeting, while the sheep represents the encounter between worshipper and God through the altar? One can often adopt Rambam's approach in *Guide for the Perplexed* (III:26): There is rhyme and reason for general principles, but in order to bring them down into a worldly resolution, at one point the signified is ultimately expressed through an arbitrary signifier.[44] The Torah wishes to

43. Compare Milgrom, *Leviticus*, vol. 3, 1986.

44. In his words there: "You must know that Divine Wisdom demanded it – or, if you prefer, say that circumstances made it necessary – that there should be parts [of His work] which have no certain object. And as regards the Law, it appears to be impossible that it should not include some matter of this kind. That it cannot be avoided may be seen from the following instance. You ask why must a lamb be

distinguish between two kinds of encounter – one through the Tent of Meeting and the other through the altar – and the distinction between these two kinds of encounter is more important than which kind of animal is used to symbolize which.

Nonetheless, based on the premise that revelation increases as we delve deeper into the Sanctuary, we can understand why the bull – more prized, more expensive, more important – represents the encounter with the internal divine, whereas the sheep – cheaper, smaller, more obtainable – is used for the external altar. In the ancient world, the bull was considered a symbol of glory, power, and even divinity (compare the sin of the Golden Calf).[45] Perhaps it is somewhat surprising that the Torah chooses the bull as the most important sacrificial animal, despite its importance in the pagan world. Ultimately, however, the bull or cow is associated with majesty and glory far more than the sheep. Moreover,, its importance for agriculture perhaps explains why it is linked to divine revelation, while the sheep represents human service.[46] R. Samson Raphael Hirsch points out the respective symbolism of these two animals:

> We have already shown ... that biblical animals symbolize human characteristics. The cow/bull/calf exemplifies the active, laboring worker of its master while the sheep/ram/goat epitomizes the creatures whose needs are provided by their shepherd. Thus,

---

sacrificed and not a ram? But the same question would be asked, why a ram had been commanded instead of a lamb, so long as one particular kind is required."

45. The bull is particularly notable in Ugarit, where the god El was represented as a bull; other gods were also associated with bovine imagery – see Curtis, "Bull." Many understand the sin of the Golden Calf as a fertility ritual (especially in light of Exodus 32:6); others perceive the calf as associated with war imagery, that the Israelites perceived it as a symbol of protection against their enemies (Janzen, "Character of the Calf").

46. Binyamin Frankel pointed out to me that Rambam describes the ancient veneration for the bull (*Guide for the Perplexed,* III:46) and that the Torah attempts to challenge this, even though there are still biblical echoes of this veneration (see also ibid., III:30).

> cattle and sheep represent two aspects of people's life: their actions and their fate.[47]

My friend, R. Itamar Eldar, develops this approach further: He suggests that the bull or ox is completely enslaved to its master; it is a pack animal, a plowing animal, one whose energies are entirely devoted to its master: "Even an ox knows its owner." The ox works for its master; it earns its keep; it subjects itself to its owner's will. In contrast, the sheep is led by its shepherd, but it does not work for him; on the contrary, to a great extent the sheep are the shepherd's master. The shepherd leads the flock from place to place, caring for its needs: "He lets me lie down in green pastures; He leads me beside still waters" (Ps. 23:2). The sheep relies upon the shepherd, but it does not work for him; it does not efface itself for its master's sake. R. Eldar proposes that these qualities are related to the religious experience that transpires in each location in the Sanctuary. The animal of self-effacement and servitude is linked to revelation and closeness through utter devotion. Only those who are prepared to pay dearly and devote valuable resources to their Maker are able to achieve the self-effacement of revelation. In contrast, sheep do not work for their owner and thus maintain certain autonomy, but they rely upon their master's care and trust that he will always shelter and provide for them.

THE BURNT OFFERING OF FOWL

Dove or Pigeon

When introducing the (surprising) world of the fowl burnt offering, the Torah deems two different species as suitable offerings: doves ("*tor*") and young pigeons ("*ben yona*"). The two are from the same family, *Columbidae*; the former is generally wild, the latter generally domesticated.[48] Given that the Torah refers to a "*ben yona*" but never to a "*ben*

47. R. Samson Raphael Hirsch on Lev. 1:3.
48. Translator's note: There is no actual taxonomic difference between doves and pigeons, of which there are over three hundred species. Many are referred to as both "pigeon" or "dove," such as one of the most common species, which is known as both "rock pigeon" and "rock dove." In common usage, the "pigeon" generally refers to larger species and the dove to smaller, more delicate birds. This is consistent with their very different literary connotations: The dove portrays a more romantic, beautiful

tor," the Sages concluded that one must bring a mature dove, but a young pigeon (Mishna Ḥullin 1:5). Why are doves the sacrificial bird of choice?

The prevalent approach is that these were the most common, most readily available birds, as Rambam writes in *Guide for the Perplexed*:

> Because most people cannot afford to sacrifice an animal, He also commanded an option of sacrifice from the most common, best, and most easily attainable birds in the land of Israel.[49]

Today we can indeed confirm that "during the biblical era, [pigeons] were already domesticated, and wild doves were widely found near human habitats."[50] Chickens were not yet domesticated at this time, so it makes sense that pigeons and doves were the Torah's default option for sacrifice.

Nonetheless, the advantages of using pigeons can be formulated with even more precision. Rambam implies that they were chosen for their being convenient, as they were "most easily attainable," but the reason for this is that they "were widely found near human habitats." The world's first domesticated bird, pigeons are the closest to the human world. While it can still spread its wings and fly, the pigeon has been part of the human world for millennia. As Philo states:

> Of the creatures which are fit to be offered as sacrifices, some are land animals, and some are such as fly through the air. Passing over, therefore, the infinite varieties of birds, God chose only two classes out of them all, the turtledove and the pigeon; because the pigeon is by nature the most gentle of all those birds which are domesticated and gregarious, and the turtledove the most friendly and domesticated of those which love solitude.[51]

---

image, whereas "pigeons" are often perceived in the western world as pests on wings. In the sacrificial context, we will use "dove" ("*tor*") for wild species and "pigeon" ("*yona*") for domestic species.

49. *Guide for the Perplexed*, III:46.
50. Amar, "Bird Sacrifice," 117.
51. Philo, *Laws* 1:162.

Perhaps Philo's analysis can be read as similar to Rambam's. I believe that it is no coincidence that he chooses to point out that they are the "most gentle," "the most friendly and domesticated" of all birds – that is, a natural part of the human household.

This has interesting implications for the nature of fowl burnt offerings. Only domesticated animals make suitable offerings, and the same holds true of bird sacrifices; the birds offered up must be familiar with the land and its inhabitants. Perhaps the Torah's fondness for the dove can be traced back to the Flood narrative, which subtly sketches out a certain intimate relationship between Noah and the dove.[52] The dove has a close, positive relationship with humans; for this reason, it serves as a fitting representative of them upon the altar.

Why Isn't the Bird Burnt Offering Mentioned in the Heading?

The inclusion of the bird burnt offering within this chapter is intriguing, given that the chapter's introduction fails to mention it: "When one of you brings an animal offering to the Lord, you may bring it either from the herd or from the flock" (Lev. 1:2). (The word for "animal" used here is "*behema*," which generally means mammals, excluding birds.) Not only does the first verse refer to the "animal offering," it even defines this "animal offering" as either from "the herd or the flock." Yet these first two options are followed by an unexpected third option: a burnt offering of fowl.[53]

Radatz Hoffmann suggests that the heading "from the herd or from the flock" applies to both the burnt offering and the peace offering. Given that the latter does not have a bird option, the heading refers only to the common denominator between them: animal offerings from the

52. See how this surprising association contributed to the objective of the Flood narrative in Grossman, *Creation*, 272–81.
53. Surprisingly, medieval commentators do not ask this question; perhaps the issue was clear to them. In contrast, modern commentators found this so difficult that they suggested that it was a later amendment to allow an option for the poor (Milgrom, *Leviticus*, vol. 1, 166–67, based on Leviticus Rabba 3:5). If so, however, the question is why the heading was not changed accordingly, especially given that the bird burnt offering is mentioned as an option for both the poor (12:8; 14:22) and for everyone (15:14–15; 15:29–30).

herd or from the flock. Yet this does not explain why the text doesn't use a more general word instead of "*behema*" (which specifically refers to mammals, especially livestock), such as "*nefesh ḥaya*"/"*ḥaya*," a more general word for "animal" that means "living things," or "*basar*," "flesh."

The sudden appearance of the bird burnt offering despite its absence from the heading only serves to prepare the ground for much bigger surprises about its laws. As we analyze these surprises, I will propose why the bird offering is not mentioned at the beginning of the chapter.

Birds and Animals

> If the offering for the Lord is to be a burnt offering of fowl, one may offer doves or young pigeons. The priest shall bring the offering to the altar, sever its neck, and burn it on the altar; its blood shall be drained against the altar wall: the priest shall remove the crop with its feathers and throw that to the east side of the altar, to the place where the ashes are gathered. Then he shall tear the bird open by its wings, without dividing it completely. The priest shall then send it up in smoke upon the altar, on the wood of the altar fire. It is a burnt offering, an offering of fire, a sweet savor to the Lord. (Lev. 1:14–17).

There are certain differences between this burnt offering and those from the herd and flock:

1. The worshippers bring their animal burnt offering and slaughter it; the priest only takes over to receive the blood and bring it to the altar. With a bird offering, the owners leave the scene at an earlier stage; it is the priest who severs its neck (which is parallel to slaughter). This is presumably related to the fact that birds are killed directly on the altar, so only the priest may perform this stage.[54]

---

54. Thus, according to the verses, Rambam is clearly correct that there is no "bringing" of the bird's blood (*Hilkhot Pesulei HaMukdashin* 13:5).

2. The soiled parts of the animal (the innards and legs) are first washed and then burnt on the altar with the rest of the animal (1:9, 13), whereas these parts of the bird are removed and discarded: "The priest shall remove the crop with its feathers and throw that to the east side of the altar, to the place where the ashes are gathered" (1:16). What "the crop with its feathers" means is a matter of dispute; according to Rashi this means the innards, including the crop and gizzards, whereas Ramban rules that it refers to the actual feathers, which should be pulled off together with the crop and gizzards. Either way, note that this means that part of the "*holo*-caust," a burnt offering that is supposed to be "entirely" given to God, is not actually offered up. This is reflected in the text, which states that the "priest shall then send it up in smoke upon the altar" (1:17) without using the word "all," unlike the animal burnt offering: "The priest shall then offer it *all*, sending it up in smoke upon the altar as a burnt offering" (1:9, 13). The fact that the animal parts are washed and then burned whereas the gizzards are discarded can be explained in one of two ways:

(a) This may be an immaterial technical difference. The gizzards are too difficult to clean, so they are better off discarded. The verb "*vehishlikh*," "throw" or "cast away," indeed connotes "the disposal of something worthless."[55]

(b) Alternatively, there may be a fundamental difference between the animal's innards and the bird's gizzard. R. Joseph Bekhor Shor, for example, explains that whereas animal innards can be eaten, "the gizzard is not even worthy of human consumption" (on 1:16). The Sages interpret this difference as a reflection of the bird's moral inferiority compared with the animal. Rabbeinu Bahya explains that the gizzard is not fit for consumption even after being rinsed because the bird, unlike the animal, is "nourished by stolen food," so the organ that digests this stolen food is not fit to be offered up.

55. Bula, *Leviticus*, 25. Compare to Ehrlich, *Mikrâ ki-Pheschutô*, 211. Note that there are a few instances in which the verb has positive associations (see Ps. 55:23).

3. An interesting difference that says much about the difference between birds and animals is that for some reason, the text does not mention that the bird must be "*tamim*," "without blemish." While the Sages do forbid the offering of a bird missing a limb,[56] there is no halakhic prohibition against offering up a bird with a minor deformity. One could theoretically argue that "*tamim*" is omitted for the sake of brevity, but given that this requirement is mentioned for all the rest of the animal offerings in these chapters, this particular omission does not seem coincidental.
4. One final difference worth mentioning is the absence of laying of the hands. The question is whether this is mere brevity (the same question applies to skinning the bird),[57] or whether there is no laying of the hands in bird offerings, which is the halakhic conclusion.[58] This is indeed strange; if there is need for this step for animal burnt offerings, why shouldn't there be the same need when offering a bird burnt offering? This could theoretically be explained as a technical issue due to the bird's smaller size – especially given that there is no laying of the hands in bird purification offerings either – but if the point of laying the hands is to create a certain connection between the person and their offering, why would this stage be omitted when a person offers up a bird?[59]

---

56. On whether a bird missing a limb is invalid due to the law of *mum* or a different law, see Rappaport, *Mikdash David*, 531–34. R. Aharon Lichtenstein proposes that a creature lacking a limb does not meet the definition of "bird," so it is invalid as an offering without reference to the question of *mum* (Lichtenstein, *Zevaḥim*, 368, n. 6).
57. The Sages teach that there is no skinning or cutting for bird offerings. Perhaps one might argue that cutting off the head separately is comparable to cutting. As for the bird's skin, there is a fascinating dispute in Tractate Shabbat (which also discusses whether tefillin can be written on bird skin) as to whether it is even considered skin (Shabbat 108a).
58. "Does the bird burnt offering require laying of the hands? The verse says 'burnt offering,' meaning all burnt offerings but the bird burnt offering" (*Sifra*, Freewill Offerings, 4:7).
59. Dillmann suggests that the bird's size does not exempt it from laying of the hands, but that this automatically occurs when the worshipper brings the bird in their hands,

These differences all point to the unique nature of the bird offering.[60]

R. Samson Raphael Hirsch's View of the Bird Offering

R. Samson Raphael Hirsch's creative analysis of the bird burnt offering is an excellent basis for further exploration. He finds this particular offering much more violent and aggressive than any other:

> The biblical bird is a metaphor for someone helpless, defenseless, persecuted, in dire straits… for this reason the bird offering is a particular expression of suffering… this illuminates the nature of the bird offering, which is an apt reflection of the suffering worshipper. We find that the bird burnt offering is a fitting expression for one whom God has condemned to a fate of suffering….
>
> Accordingly, each stage of the bird burnt offering is composed of acts of violence: severing the neck, draining the blood, removing the gizzard, tearing into two… while ritual slaughter is a careful, humane act, severing the neck – slitting the nape of the neck with a fingernail – is a coarse, violent act…. There is similar contrast between draining the [bird's] blood against the altar wall and collecting the [animal's] blood in a bowl; and between discarding the crop and gizzard and washing the innards and legs and then burning them upon the altar; and between tearing the bird by its wings and cutting the animal into its organic parts. The stages of offering a bird burnt offering are closely tied to the bird's symbolic meaning, which is the suffering of the defenseless….
>
> The bringer of the bird burnt offering is the "sufferer"; the one who wishes to grow close to God through ascent and progression.[61]

---

which makes it clear that it is brought in their name, on their behalf (Dillmann, *Leviticus*, 438).

60. Intriguingly, in Mishna Zevaḥim as well, there is a fundamental disparity between animal and bird offerings. The tractate opens with animal offerings (chapter 1) and discusses bird offerings only in chapter 6. Although the laws are identical, the arrangement of the Mishna separates them, revealing their different natures.
61. R. Samson Raphael Hirsch on Lev. 1:16.

R. Hirsch's connection between the bird burnt offering and the suffering worshipper certainly explains why there is no option to sacrifice a bird as a peace offering, which, as we will see, is an expression of joy and gratitude.

Draining the Blood of the Bird Offering

R. Hirsch's reading is intriguing, but it does not explain all the differences between the bird and animal burnt offerings. One salient difference is the lack of treatment of the bird's blood. The use of a passive verb, "Its blood shall be drained" (15), hints that this is merely a by-product of the process, rather than a ritual part of the priestly service: When the priest severs the bird's head, of course its blood drains out.

The lack of ritual treatment of the bird's blood also has bearing on the sacrificial sequence. In all animal offerings, the ritual treatment of the blood is mentioned before the offering is burnt to smoke upon the altar, but the bird offering appears in a different order:

> He shall sever its neck, and burn its head on the altar;
> its blood shall be drained against the altar wall:
> the priest shall remove the crop with its feathers and throw that to the east side of the altar, to the place where the ashes are gathered.
> Then he shall tear the bird open by its wings, without dividing it completely.
> The priest shall then send it up in smoke upon the altar.

The bird's head is burnt upon the altar before the blood is drained and the rest of the body is sacrificed. Rashi parses the order of this description carefully:

> "Severed," "burned," "drained." How can that be? When it is burnt to smoke, the blood has already drained out!... The plain meaning of the abbreviated text is that when the head is severed and burnt to smoke, the blood has already been drained. (Rashi on 1:15)

Rashi asks how this is technically possible: How can the head be drained of blood after it has already been burned up on the altar? He answers that the fact that the blood has already been drained before the head is burned is implicit in the verse and that this order serves to emphasize that the head and the body are offered up separately.

Siftei Ḥakhamim on both Rashi and Ramban, however, point out that this sacrificial sequence is surprising not for technical reasons, but for fundamental reasons: "The body parts are never offered up before the blood is taken out" (Ramban on 1:15), so why are the actions reported in the opposite order in this case? This surprising order is further underscored by the halakhic ruling that the blood must indeed be drained before the head is burned on the altar (see Mishna Zevaḥim 6:5). The use of the passive form for the blood's draining and the postponement of its mention until after the head is burned both serve to downplay the importance of the blood service within the bird burnt offering.

One suggestion is that the blood service is far less important because birds have much less blood than animals, as R. Bekhor Shor points out (on 1:15). But it may be that this apparent technicality in fact reveals the unique nature of the bird burnt offering and how it is integrated into this chapter.[62]

The two anomalies in this description – the fact that the priest is not commanded to dash its blood and the mention of the blood only after the head is burned – both reflect that the bird's blood is clearly a secondary part of this offering. This is surprising, given that there are two fundamental components to every animal offering: the sacrificial treatment of the blood and the parts of the animal being offered upon the altar. If one of these elements is lacking, what is the meaning of that offering? If "the blood is life," what significance is there to an animal offering that barely involves any blood?

62. The Mishna refers to bird offerings only after its discussion of all animal offerings (including those that are of lesser holiness, but before grain offerings), "because they have a kind of blood" (Zevaḥim 10:4). This is an intriguing expression – not because they "have blood," but "a kind of blood." Another reference that shows the liminal nature of bird blood is the law of blood accidentally brought into the Sanctuary. Only offerings with animal blood are rendered invalid, but grain offerings are not. There is a dispute, however, regarding what happens to bird offerings (Zevaḥim 92b).

The Sacrificial Status of Birds

If a bird offering is not merely a poor person's alternative to animal offerings, but rather a burnt offering with its own unique significance, what information can be gleaned from the fact that it is not mentioned at the beginning of the chapter?

The answer, I believe, can be traced back to the creation of birds in Genesis 1 and their place in the order of creation.

The phrase "And God said" appears ten times in Genesis 1, which is the source of the mishnaic statement that "the world was created with ten utterances" (Mishna Avot 5:1), but essentially, creation is manifested through only eight of the ten instances of this phrase in that chapter.[63] Each statement introduces a new aspect of reality, but there are two statements that introduce two, which of course shows a close correlation between the two creations effected through the same "And God said." For our purposes, I will focus on the creation of both birds and fish with a single "And God said" on the fifth day:

> And God said, "Let the water teem with swarms of living creatures, and let birds fly over the earth across the heavens' expanse." So God created the great sea creatures, and all the kinds of crawling, living things that swarm in the water, and all the kinds of winged, flying creatures. And God saw that it was good.
> God blessed them, saying: "Be fertile and multiply and fill the waters of the seas, and let flying creatures multiply on earth." (Gen. 1:20–22)

The bird's of the sky and the fish of the sea are created at the same time, with the same utterance. Note the repetition in all three components of their creation:

63. Because there are more "creations" (eight) than days (six), more than one thing must be created on two days, the third day and the sixth day. Creations created on the same day have a profound affinity. See further, for example, in Breuer, *Acts of Creation*.

- In the initial utterance: "Let the water teem with swarms of living creatures" / "and let birds fly over the earth."
- In the actual act of creation: "All the kinds of crawling, living things that teem in the water" / "and all kind of winged, flying creatures."
- In God's blessing of fertility: "Fill the waters of the seas" / "and let flying creatures multiply on earth."

This repetition underscores that there are two different acts of creation at once, which only exacerbates the question: Why are fish and birds created at the same time?

There are various theories that explore this question; elsewhere, I suggest that birds and fish move similarly through the "upper waters" (i.e., the sky) and the "lower waters."[64] There are other possibilities as well. Regardless, the fact that they are created on the same day, with the same utterance, links birds more closely to fish than to the animals that are created on the sixth day. This endows birds with a more complex status within reality: On the one hand, they are created together with the sea creatures on the fifth day; on the other, they are distinct from fish and they receive their own blessing of fertility: "Let flying creatures multiply on earth" (1:22).

This complex status has significant implications for the world of holiness. Before we delve into the status of birds, however, I will first point out that their ostensible twins – fish – have nothing to do with holiness. Fish are never brought as any kind of offering, nor are they ever considered "impure" (a status that implies some kind of connection with holiness).

The complete disconnect between fish and the altar is explored in the Midrash, which perceives certain representation of water creatures in the form of salt. About the phrase "a covenant of salt," Rashi writes (on Lev. 2:13): "For there was a covenant made with salt since the six days of Creation: The lower waters were promised that they would be offered

64. Grossman, *Creation*, 40–41.

on the altar, through salt and through the water libations of Sukkot." In lieu of fish, salt is offered upon the altar (and water itself, on Sukkot).[65]

Two factors seem to explain why fish are not part of the sacrificial service. First, they do not share the same sphere as people do, and holiness is inherently tied to human experience and reality, so creatures who live in water cannot represent human life. Second, in biblical thought, life is associated with breath; the fact that fish do not breathe air as people do means that fish are not strictly considered "living creatures."[66] Coupled with the fact that fish have a completely different blood system, fish are considered a different, lower life form.

This perception has implications that go beyond the sacrificial world: According to halakha, fish do not have to be killed by ritual slaughter (*Tur, Yoreh De'ah* 14), nor is there any prohibition against eating fish blood. The topic goes beyond the scope of this discussion; relevant for our purposes is that according to halakha, fish are not strictly considered "living creatures." If so, what about birds? Does their etiological connection to fish have any bearing on their status in the world of holiness?

This can be explored through comparing the halakhic statuses of birds and fish. The laws of Leviticus 11 imply that birds, like fish, do not cause impurity:[67] Unclean land animals,[68] creeping things, and the carcasses of pure animals render one who touches them unclean, but there is no mention that birds or fish do the same.[69] Impurity, it seems, stems from contact with loss of life, but only creatures created on the sixth day are

---

65. Milgrom suggests that fish were never part of the sacred world because they were not in wide use in Israelite culture (*Leviticus,* vol I, 660), but this is unconvincing, especially given that the Torah does discuss kosher and non-kosher fish (Lev. 11).
66. Whitekettle, "Fish."
67. The structure of this chapter is worthy of further exploration; see especially Wenham, *Leviticus,* 164–65 (he also points out the connection to Genesis 1); Warning, "Terminologische Verknüpfungen."
68. Rashi and Rashbam argue about the division of verses in this chapter, but this dispute has no bearing on our discussion.
69. The Sages taught that birds that are not killed in the proper way do render the throat impure, but this is a unique element in the world of impurity; the *Aḥaronim* debate whether this kind of impurity is related to contact impurity or impure eating (see the *Ḥiddushei Gra, Hilkhot Avot HaTumot* 3:3; *Minḥat Ḥinnukh,* mitzva 161; *Ḥatam Sofer, Oraḥ Ḥayim* 102; Wolf, "Pure Bird Carcass").

considered "living creatures"; those created on the fifth day seem to have a different status.[70]

At the same time, the fact that the Torah mandates that some birds and fish may be eaten and others may not implies that even though fish and birds are not considered living creatures, they still have "flesh."

It is thus somewhat surprising that birds are part of the sacrificial world even though fish are not, and this liminal status is reflected in the unique nature of the bird burnt offering. The bird burnt offering has flesh but no blood; the worshipper offers up a creature that moves across the earth like a living creature, but – from a biblical perspective – this winged being is hardly considered "alive."[71] For this reason, perhaps, whether it is male or female, pigeon or dove, is not important, even from a halakhic perspective.[72]

This is the most fundamental difference between animal burnt offerings and bird burnt offerings. Of course, some bird blood happens to drain upon the altar when it is slaughtered, but this blood is almost meaningless – it is not part of the sacrificial service as animal blood is. The central ritual component is the bird's flesh. As mentioned, unlike the animal burnt offering, the bird's head is first burnt upon the altar, and the blood is mentioned only as an afterthought. The bird burnt offering is a gift of flesh, not of life (although the bird purification offering is more complex, as we will discuss in context). The fact that the bird's blood is not significant within the sacrificial process is not due to the technical reason that a bird has much less blood than an animal; it is inherent to the offering's nature.

---

70. Birds also have a different status from animals when it comes to mixing meat and milk; some *Tanna'im* hold that the two may be eaten together because birds, like fish, are a lower life form than animals and may therefore be eaten with milk ("Fish and locusts may be eaten with milk" – *Tur, Yoreh De'ah* 87).

71. This is also evident in the bird variable offering. See below for my discussion of Ibn Ezra's explanation that one bird is brought as a purification offering and the other as an alternative to offering up animal flesh.

72. This is also true regarding the individual's purification offering, which must be a female animal, but can also be a male or female bird. Their sex is of little consequence because birds are a lower life form; thus, according to R. Eliezer, birds that are androgynous or *tumtum* (neither sex) can still be brought as offerings (Yevamot 83b; see also *Sifra,* Freewill Offerings, 18:2).

The fact that a bird is not truly considered "living" also explains why a bird's neck is severed instead of the bird being slaughtered; moreover, it illuminates the absence of the laying of the hands. Even the Midrash Halakha rules that all burnt offerings include laying of the hands, except for bird burnt offerings (*Sifra*, Freewill Offerings, 4:7). Just as the grain offering does not include laying of the hands because it does not represent a life (as it comes from grain, not an animal), the same is true of the bird burnt offering! Laying of the hands is profoundly linked to the worshipper's representation via their offering, but neither grain nor bird offering is equivalent to human life; they are lower life forms, not "living creatures" created on the sixth day.

This definition also explains why a verb other than *shaḥat*, "slaughter," is used for the killing of birds. The verb "*malak*" – which means severing the bird's nape rather than its throat, as in classic ritual slaughter – is not, as R. Samson Raphael Hirsch explains, symbolic of violence.[73] Rather, it expresses how killing a bird is far more technical because it is not truly alive.[74] Just as a fish can be eaten without ritual slaughter, a bird offering does not require the usual ritual slaughter necessary for the offering of an animal, a "living creature." A more provocative formulation, perhaps, is that just as there is no need to slaughter a grain offering, there is no need to actually slaughter a bird as one must slaughter an animal; it suffices to merely sever its neck before burning its head upon the altar.[75] Accordingly, it comes as little surprise that although one must wash a garment that has been accidentally sprayed with the blood of a purification offering, there is no need – according to the Midrash Halakha – to wash a garment that has been sprayed with the blood of a bird purification offering.[76]

---

73. R. Hirsch also posits that the use of an alternative verb to "*shaḥat*," in this case "*malak*," recalls how a different verb is used to describe the breaking of a calf's neck when a murder victim is found in between two towns (Deut. 21). There, the verb "*araf*" is used – also to distinguish this killing from the usual "slaughter." See further in Grossman, "Egla Arufa."
74. In halakha, killing animals not through ritual slaughter makes them unfit for offering.
75. On *melika*, "severing the neck," as an easier, more technical method than slaughter, see Zevaḥim 69b.
76. Rambam, *Hilkhot Maaseh HaKorbanot*, 8:2.

This further underscores the liminal nature of the bird offering. Fish are not offered as sacrifices at all and can be eaten regardless of their manner of death; animals must be killed by full ritual slaughter, and dealing with their blood is part of the sacrificial service. Birds, however, are somewhere in between, and their liminality is aptly expressed in a talmudic discussion of the laws of slaughter:

> With regard to what law is an animal equal to a bird and a bird to an animal? The verse comes to say to you: Just as an animal [avoids the impurity of being an unslaughtered carcass] through slaughter, so too, a bird [avoids the impurity of being an unslaughtered carcass] through slaughter.... Bar Kappara teaches that the verse states: "This is the law of the animal, and of the bird, and of every living creature that moves in the waters, and of every creature that swarms upon the earth". The verse situated the bird between the animal and the fish.... Fitness for consumption of animals, which were created from the dry land, is accomplished through cutting two *simanim*, the gullet and the windpipe. Fitness for consumption of fish, which were created from the water, is accomplished with nothing [as no slaughter is required]. Fitness for consumption of birds, which were created from mud [*harekak*], is accomplished through cutting one *siman*. (Ḥullin 27b)

This encapsulates the entire discussion: The Sages recognize the bird's liminal nature; as Bar Kappara marvelously expresses: "The verse situated the bird between the animal and the fish"![77]

This, perhaps, illuminates why the biblical introduction to freewill offerings fails to mention the bird burnt offering. It is not an ideal option not due to its low cost, as many explain, but rather because it is a lower life form. A more fitting offering is an animal that represents the worshipper, an animal the worshipper can lay hands on and offer in place of his

77. See also Genesis Rabba's discussion of slaughtering fish, where Jacob of Nevorai Village announces that fish require ritual slaughter, and R. Haggai replies, "Come here to be flogged" (Genesis Rabba 7:2).

or her own life. For some reason, the Torah offers the option of bringing this lower life form to the altar. Perhaps it is indeed due to the fact that many cannot afford to offer up an animal.[78] But perhaps it allows for the expression of a certain religious mindset, one that involves the body, the flesh, but not life itself. After all, the next option in the list of freewill offerings is the grain offering, which – as we'll discuss below – does not represent a person's actual life, but rather their needs. Thus, the transition from animal to bird to grain reflects the gradual transition from offering up life itself upon the altar, to an offering of flesh from a lower life form, to a plant offering that does not represent any kind of life at all.

The introduction to freewill offerings focuses on living creatures, animals with life and blood enough to dash against the altar. The bird burnt offering is added in as an offering of mere flesh, somewhere in between an animal and a grain offering; it does not merit inclusion in the chapter heading.

This concludes our discussion of the three types of burnt offering: the burnt offering from the herd, which is juxtaposed with the Tent of Meeting; the burnt offering from the flock, which turns toward the altar; and the burnt offering of fowl, which is flesh without life blood sacrificed upon the altar. All three variations share a core meaning: When someone feels distant from their Creator, they may seek closeness and approach Him through a burnt offering despite their awareness of their unworthy, flawed existence.

> To God, a broken spirit is an offering;
> a crushed and broken heart, God, You will not spurn. (Ps. 51:19)

78. See, for example, Dillmann, *Leviticus*, 438, and many others. This idea is reinforced by the fact that other offerings are also related to the worshipper's financial situation (Lev. 5:7; 12:8; 14:21–22), where those who cannot afford to bring an animal offering may bring a bird.

Chapter 7

The Grain Offering (Leviticus 2): The Necessities of Life

THE NATURE AND ESSENCE OF THE GRAIN OFFERING

The simple, most accepted approach is that the name "*minḥa*" refers to a specific offering, parallel to "*ola*" (burnt offering) or "*zevaḥ shelamim*" (peace offering). This might seem obvious to most readers, but Rambam actually interprets the name "*minḥa*" differently. In *Mishneh Torah,* he writes:

> The *menaḥot* are a kind of offering; there are *menaḥot* brought as independent offerings and *menaḥot* brought as accompanying libations – both public and individual. (*Hilkhot Maaseh HaKorbanot* 12:1)

Rambam points out that there are independent *minḥa* offerings – which is the subject of this chapter – and there are *menaḥot* that are accompanying libations to animal offerings. But the most surprising aspect is his opening words: "The *menaḥot* are a kind of offering." Why is this definition necessary? Rambam does not introduce each kind of offering with the phrase "The *olot* are a kind of offering"; "The *asham* is a kind of offering." Why does he state this in regard to *menaḥot*?

Rambam's perception of *menaḥot* can be derived from a different halakha, in which he is defining the different kinds of *menaḥot*. One such definition is "*minḥat ḥoteh*":

> There are nine kinds of *menaḥot* brought by the individual, all of which are offered upon the altar. What are they? *Minḥat ḥoteh* is brought by the poor person who cannot afford to bring a purification offering. (*Hilkhot Maaseh HaKorbanot* 12:5)

Rambam then lists the other eight kinds; this first kind suffices for our purposes. His decision to include the *minḥat ḥoteh* in this list is surprising, given that (as we will see in our discussion of Leviticus 5) it is not considered a freewill offering but an obligatory purification offering brought by a poor sinner who cannot afford to bring an animal offering. While its laws are similar to the law of the freewill grain offering (as the text states: "It is *like* a grain offering for the priest" – 5:13), it is not actually a freewill grain offering.[1]

If so, why does Rambam include this offering of fine flour in the list of *menaḥot*? The Sages indeed use similar language,[2] and Rambam is presumably using the same terminology,[3] yet even so, it is surprising to include the poor person's purification offering in the list of freewill offerings.

It seems that Rambam is not using the term "*minḥa*" as the name of a specific offering, such as "*ola*"; rather, he is defining it as any kind of grain offering, freewill or obligatory. This is almost explicit in the next

1. This is the straightforward reading, as we will discuss below. Based on Rashi's commentary on Zevaḥim 63b, it emerges that one may bring fine flour instead of a goat; the text thus changes the offering from a purification to a grain offering. If Rashi is referring to different kinds of sacrifices and not just what they consist of, then he perceives the change of offering differently from my interpretation.
2. See, for example, Mishna Menaḥot 1:1; Menaḥot 59a–b.
3. "If he cannot afford a bird he brings a tenth of an ephah of fine flour, which is called a purification grain offering" (*Hilkhot Shegagot* 10:4).

halakha: "All offerings, whether animal or bird or grain – it is a positive commandment to bring them to the Chosen House" (*Hilkhot Maaseh HaKorbanot* 18:1). Rambam does not list the offerings by name, but rather by the three kinds of offerings that are burnt upon the altar: animal, bird, and grain. This formulation also implies that he defines "*minḥa*" as any kind of grain offering and not as the name of a specific offering.

While this definition is surprising, the biblical word "*minḥa*" admittedly means "gift" before it is used in the sense of "grain offering." It first appears when Cain and Abel bring the world's first offerings: "Time passed, and Cain brought fruit of the land as an *offering* (*minḥa*) to the Lord. Abel too brought of the fat portions from the firstborn of his flock. The Lord looked favorably on Abel and his *offering*, but upon Cain and his *offering* He did not look with favor" (Gen. 4:3–4). In this scene, "*minḥa*" is a general term that refers to both grain and animal offering.[4] Rambam uses the term in a more specific sense – meaning any kind of offering that consists of flour[5] – but it is certainly justified to use "*minḥa*" as a more general term than the name of a specific offering.

If we adopt the Sages' and Rambam's reading, then the term "*minḥa*" is metonymical; it is named for one particular quality: what it consists of. The name "*minḥa*" testifies that it is a grain offering. (I will suggest below that the way it is offered up reflects the offering's name as well.) If so, we must explore the significance of the transition from animal offering to grain offering, which will illuminate the offering's nature and essence.

Yet the most prevalent reading is that the name "*minḥa*" refers to a specific freewill grain offering, as described in Leviticus 2: "When one brings a grain offering (*korban minḥa*) to the Lord" (2:1). Later on, the

---

4. Alfred Marx begins his extensive study of the grain offering with this point; he adds that the word is not always used in a religious context (Marx, "Minḥa," 1–5). See also his discussion of instances that may be either a grain offering or an offering in general (ibid., 5–12).
5. If the meaning of "all grain offerings, either mixed with oil or dry" (Lev. 7:10) indeed refers to the purification offering as well, then this is already an instance of an obligatory offering being referred to as a "*minḥa*." The Ugaritic term "*manaḥat*" may mean "cereal," which is consistent with Rambam's reading. In a text translated and published by Dahood (in Fisher, *Ugarit*, 32), it says: "… 1800 heavy jars of cereal (=*d.mnḥt*)."

Torah refers to the offering as "*minḥa*" alone, without the word "*korban*" (e.g., 2:6).

Where does the word come from? There is a linguistic dispute as to whether it is derived from the word "*lehaniaḥ*," "to place," or "*lehanḥot*," "to lead."[6] Either way, the main theme of this sacrifice is its conveyance to God, as when Jacob takes care to send gifts to Esau before their reunion: "They are a *gift* (*minḥa*) sent to my lord Esau" (Gen. 32:19), and as Joseph's brothers bring a gift to the Egyptian ruler who then reveals his identity as their long-lost brother Joseph: "The men took this gift ... they prepared the gift before Joseph came at noon .... Joseph came inside and they brought him the gift they had brought inside to his home" (Gen. 43:15–26).

Some suggest that the meaning of the term "*minḥa*" changed with time, that it meant a general "gift" in ancient times.[7] Either way, this meaning may have bearing on the nature of the offering with this same name. This brings us back to what a *minḥa* consists of: the staple of the human diet. We will discuss this extensively below, but it is already worth noting that just as a tribute to an earthly king consists of part of his subjects' crops ("He offered the tribute to King Eglon of Moab" – Judges 3:17), the person who brings a *minḥa* to their God offers up part of their sustenance.

Therefore, whether we adopt Rambam's reading that the name "*minḥa*" refers to any grain offering or the more prevalent reading that it means a specific kind of grain offering (as defined in Leviticus 2), the name still refers to what the offerings consists of: not an animal but grain, the staple of the human diet, the flour used to make one's daily bread.

The Grain Offering's Place in the Text

The laws of the grain offering (Lev. 2) follow the laws of the burnt offering (Lev. 1) and precede the laws of the peace offering (Lev. 3). The chapter can be divided into three main sections: *minḥat hasolet*, the fine flour offering (vv. 1–3); cooked grain offerings, flour that is either

---

6. See Radak's debate in *Sefer HaShorashim*, "M-N-Ḥ"; Rashbam on Lev. 2:1; Weinfeld, "Afternoon Prayer," 407–10; Fabry, "Minḥa," 407–10.
7. Fabry, "Minḥa," 412–15.

baked or prepared on a griddle or pan (vv. 4–10); and *minḥat bikkurim,* a grain offering of first produce (vv. 14–16). From this perspective, the structure of Leviticus 2 is similar to chapters 1 and 3, given that there are also three kinds of burnt offering (herd, flock, and fowl) and three kinds of peace offering (bull, sheep, and goat).[8] Yet even so, it is strange that a chapter describing grain offerings interrupts the sequence of free-will animal offerings.

The unit's surprising placement thus serves as the most direct pathway to the meaning and essence of this offering. The opening chapter of Leviticus begins: "When a person brings an animal offering to the Lord" (1:2) – yet the grain offering suddenly appears, even though it is not an animal offering, and interrupts the sequence of burnt and peace offerings. Even if the grain offering's inclusion in this list can somehow be justified, its placement between the two animal offerings is strange.

Note that the Torah does not hide the fact that the grain offering interrupts this sequence; on the contrary, its use of opening words emphasizes this interruption. In biblical Hebrew, a new section typically begins with the word "*ki*," "When/If," whereas "*im*," "Whether/If," serves as a secondary heading. A good example of this model can be found in the laws in *Parashat Mishpatim* in Exodus: "*If* (*ki*) you buy a Hebrew slave, he shall serve for six years, but in the seventh he shall go forth free, without paying anything. *If* (*im*) he came alone, he shall leave alone. *But if* (*im*) he was a married man, his wife shall leave with him. *If* (*im*) his master gave him a wife..." (Ex. 21:2–4). Each new law in this section begins with "*ki*," whereas the details of each law start with "*im*."[9]

This model can also be found in the sacrificial laws of Leviticus. The laws of animal offerings are introduced with the heading "*ki*" and each secondary option starts with "*im*":

> *When* (*ki*) one of you brings an animal offering to the Lord...

8. See further in Luciani, "Structure et Théologie."
9. In relation to this style in *Parashat Mishpatim,* see Cassuto, *Exodus,* 186–87. On the general structure of *Mishpatim* in light of the aforementioned rule, see Herzog Bible Center, *Genesis and Exodus,* 74–75. A broad survey of the use of "*ki*" as a heading can be found in Meyer, "The Particle *Ki.*"

> *If* (*im*) the offering is a burnt offering from the herd…
> *If* (*im*) the offering is a burnt offering from the flock…
> *If* (*im*) the offering for the Lord is to be a burnt offering of fowl…

Given that the chapter of peace offerings introduces a new kind of animal offering, we would expect the chapter to open with the word "*ki*," yet surprisingly, the beginning of Leviticus 3 continues with the word "*im*":

> *And if* one's sacrifice is a peace offering and brought from the herd…
> *And if* one's offering is a peace offering from the flock…
> *And if* the sacrifice is a goat…

This implies that this new kind of animal offering is referring back to the original "*ki*" introduction to animal offerings at the beginning of Leviticus; the conjunctive *vav*, "and if," emphasizes this further. Thus, the first chapter of Leviticus introduces freewill animal offerings with the word "*ki*," and burnt and peace offerings are each subcategories that begin with the word "*im*."

This makes the interpolation of grain offerings in Leviticus 2 all the more surprising, especially given that the grain offering is not presented as a subcategory of animal offerings – it begins with the word ***ki***! "*When* (*ki*) one brings a grain offering to the Lord" (Lev. 2:1). Why does the grain offering interrupt the sequence of animal offerings?[10]

Ralbag proposes that the laws of the grain offering are juxtaposed with the burnt offering because in the Temple service, the grain offerings were usually offered up in conjunction with burnt offerings as a libation.[11] There are several problems with this suggestion. First, this kind of grain offering has nothing to do with animal burnt offerings; they are an independent freewill offering.[12] Second, grain offering libations also

10. This is Abarbanel's ninth question, but his answer is very strange: that at a later stage, the redactor added this chapter, not noticing that it was interrupting the sequence of animal offerings. This is unconvincing; it makes far more sense that this sequence is intentional.
11. Some modern scholars assume the same, such as Wenham, *Leviticus*, 67.
12. Dillmann, *Leviticus*, 439.

accompany peace offerings, so it is difficult to justify this specific placement; by the same logic, the chapter would have been just as accurately placed after the section about peace offerings.

Nonetheless, Ralbag does seem to be correct that this juxtaposition reflects a certain affinity between the burnt offering and the grain offering, which is evident in other places as well. First, on the eighth day of the Tabernacle consecration, these two offerings are also juxtaposed:

> Then he brought close the people's offering. He took the goat of the people's purification offering, slaughtered it, and prepared it as a purification offering like the first. He presented the burnt offering and sacrificed it in the prescribed way. He then presented the grain offering, took a handful from it, and sent this portion up in smoke upon the altar, with the morning's burnt offering. He slaughtered the ox and the ram: the people's peace sacrifice. Aaron's sons presented him with the blood, and he dashed it against each side of the altar. (Lev. 9:15–18)

The order of offerings on this day is: purification, burnt, grain, and peace. This is no surprise; it is in line with the usual order of biblical offerings.[13] But for some reason, after the grain offering is mentioned, the verse refers back to the burnt offering: "with the morning's burnt offering." This implies that the two offerings are so closely linked that the burnt offering is not considered complete until the grain offering has also been offered up.[14] This reading is further reinforced by the continuation of this chapter: "Then Aaron raised his hands to the people and blessed

---

13. The importance the Torah places on the sacrificial order is salient; it is evident, for example, in the order of the offerings the Nazirite must bring at the end of his process. They are mentioned in this order: burnt, purification, peace, with the basket of matzot (Num. 6:14–15), but they are offered in this order: purification, burnt, peace, with the basket of matzot (6:16–17). The Sages teach that the purification offering is always offered before the burnt offering (Zevaḥim 90a). See further in Milgrom, *Leviticus*, vol. 1, 488–89.
14. Note that the grain offering is mentioned after the peace offering (9:4), but in the description of the sacrificial order, the grain offering is juxtaposed with the burnt offering, and the peace offering is mentioned last.

them. And, having presented the purification offering, the burnt offering, and the peace sacrifice, he stepped down" (9:22). For some reason, the verse omits the grain offering that he also offered up. Some surmise that the handful of grain is too insignificant to worth mentioning,[15] but it seems more likely that in this context, the grain offering is presented as part of the burnt offering and is therefore not mentioned separately.

A second example can be found after the tribes of Reuben, Gad, and half of Manasseh reassure the rest of the Israelites that the altar that they have built is not for actual sacrifice:

> O Lord, God of gods! O Lord, God of gods! He knows, and Israel shall know. If we rebelled or broke faith with the Lord, do not save us today! If we had built an altar to turn away from the Lord, *to offer up burnt offerings and grain offerings, or to prepare peace offerings upon it* – then the Lord would seek us out. No – we were moved by concern that one day, your children will say to our children, "What have you to do with the Lord, God of Israel?" (Josh. 22:22–24)

The speakers inadvertently divide up the sacrifices into two parallel groups: burnt offerings and grain offerings/peace offerings. These three could have been mentioned in three separate phrases or all at once, yet the Israelites intuitively use this division. Moreover, they use two separate verbs – to "offer up" (*lehaalot*) burnt and grain offerings, and to "prepare" (*laasot*) peace offerings – which reflect the respective sacrificial process of each kind of offerings: The burnt and grain offerings are "offered up," burnt so that they rise up to the heavens, while the peace offering is prepared differently. This distinction is found elsewhere. One such example is: "Then the priest *shall prepare the purification offering* to make atonement for the one to be purified of his defilement. Then he shall slaughter the burnt offering. *The priest shall offer the burnt offering and the grain offering* on the altar" (Lev. 14:19–20).

Thirdly, and for our purposes most important of all, Radatz Hoffmann points out a halakhic connection between the burnt and grain offerings.

15. Milgrom, *Leviticus*, vol. 1, 588.

Undoubtedly, the most unique, definitive characteristic of the burnt offering is that it is entirely burnt upon the altar. This is the only offering that is wholly given to God; as discussed, this is also expressed in the name "*ola*," which reflects how the entire offering rises up to God.

Ostensibly, this is not the case with the grain offering, of which only a handful is burned upon the altar, while the rest is given to the priests. Yet this may not be quite so straightforward: The laws of the grain offering in *Parashat Tzav* mention a unique grain offering that the High Priest must offer up daily. We will yet discuss this particular offering. For now, it is worth pointing out its surprising description: "The priest among Aaron's sons who is anointed to succeed him shall prepare it; it is the Lord's perpetual share, to be sent up in smoke in its entirety. Any grain offering from a priest shall be wholly burned; it shall not be eaten" (Lev. 6:15). If so, a grain offering offered by a priest can be considered a kind of burnt offering.

Why the priest may not eat of his own grain offering is irrelevant to this discussion; what matters here is that when other offerings – which are usually divided up between the altar and the priests – may not be eaten by the priests for some reason, the portion that should have been theirs is burned outside the camp, not offered up on the altar! For example, the purification offering is usually divided between the altar and the priests (the innards are burned and the priests receive the rest of the meat), but during the Tabernacle consecration, the priests do not eat Aaron's purification offering, and these parts are burned outside the camp instead (Lev. 10:12–20). The same is true of purification offerings brought for unintentional sin (4:1–21).[16] In contrast, however, the priest's grain offering is wholly burnt upon the altar.

16. The similarities between the internal purification offerings and the priests' grain offering are misleading. Wenham writes: "A similar principle underlies the rules about the purification offerings. When the priest brought one, the whole animal was burned, but when a layman brought a purification offering the priest could eat some of the flesh. Similarly, cereal offerings donated by laypeople could be eaten by the priests, but when the priest offered one for himself, it had to be burnt in its entirety" (Wenham, *Leviticus*, 121–22). Yet these are two entirely different kind of "burnings."

Based on the difference between the grain offering, which when not eaten by the priest is burned upon the altar, and the purification offering, which when not eaten is burned outside the camp, Radatz Hoffmann argues that until the sacrificial laws were conveyed to Moses at the Tent of Meeting, grain offerings were wholly burnt upon the altar, just like a burnt offering.[17] Even if this cannot be proved historically, Radatz Hoffmann is correct that there is a profound affinity between the grain and burnt offering. What does this mean?

It seems that the priests acquire their portions via one of two different paths: The first is when a worshipper designates their entire offering for the altar, but for whatever reason, the priests are still allowed to take a portion from the altar; the second is when the worshipper brings an offering with the intent to share it between the altar and the priests. Thus, when an offering is wholly intended for the altar, if the priests do not take their share, it is simply burned upon the altar with the rest of the offering. If, however, the priests are supposed to receive their share directly from the worshipper, then, when they do not take it, it must be burnt outside the camp; the worshipper cannot eat it because they are a non-priest, but neither is it intended for the altar.

It emerges that in the case of the grain offering, the worshipper designates the entire offering for the altar – similar to the burnt offering – while the priests are allowed to reserve a portion of it for themselves.[18] This is actually stated explicitly in *Parashat Tzav*, when the priests are forbidden to bake this portion as leaven bread: "It shall not be baked with any leaven. I have given it as their portion of My fire offerings" (Lev. 6:10). God explains that He is sharing a portion of the offering intended for Him; this is not said of any other offering. Because the entire offering is originally designated for God, when the priest does not receive his portion, it is simply burnt on the altar with the rest of the offering.[19]

---

17. Hoffmann, *Leviticus*, vol. 1, 104.
18. See also Heike, "Priestly Leadership," 5.1, although I believe that his interpretation of the priestly status based on the grain offering is incorrect.
19. It may be that this is consistent with the Sages' interpretation that the priest's grain offering is burnt at once. According to R. Shimon (Mishna Menaḥot 7:1), even though the priest's grain offering is entirely burnt on the altar, the priest should still

This idea is supported further by the language of the text: The priestly portion of the grain offering is called the "*notar*," the "remains" (2:2–3),[20] while the potion burned upon the altar is called the "remembrance," which recalls the entire offering,[21] and implies that what "remains" is what is left of the whole.[22] The term "remains" appears elsewhere, but always refers to the grain offering (2:10; 6:9; 10:12). In other offerings, the priestly portion is not referred to as the "remains." As mentioned, there are two distinct paths to the priestly portion: In other offerings, the priest receives his portion directly from the worshipper.

This language seems to be related to the unique method of offering up the grain offering. Unlike animal sacrifices, the entire portion is laid upon the altar before it is divided up between the altar and the priests: "You shall bring the grain offering made in one of these ways to the Lord, presenting it to the priest, who will bring it to the altar. The priest shall lift a remembrance from the grain offering and send it up in smoke upon the altar.... What is left of this grain offering shall belong to Aaron and his sons" (2:8–10). If the aforementioned view that the name "*minḥa*" is derived from the word "to place" or "to lead, to bring" is correct, then

---

take a separate handful; if so, the handful was taken before the offering was offered upon the altar. He may read the sacrificial process differently.

20. Eberhart claims that it is the priest who takes the handful (and that this is the part defined as "the remainder"), while the rest is offered up the altar (Eberhart, "Burning Rite," 488). It is indeed difficult to determine from the text which part is which, especially as there is certain logic that most should be burned on the altar. However, given that the handful is added to the frankincense, it makes more sense that the handful is the part burned upon the altar.
21. The accepted understanding of "remembrance" is that it is a part that represents ("recalls") the whole. Haran surmises whether the word might mean "the perfumed part" given that the root Z-KH-R is associated elsewhere with frankincense (Is. 66:3) and the smell of wine (Song. 1:4).
22. Or an appendix of the whole, such as "the diaphragm of the liver" (Ex. 29:22, and elsewhere). It makes sense that "*notar*" is sometimes parallel with "*she'erit*" (Is. 44:17–19; Jer. 39:9; Mic. 5:2). The root Y-T-R is found in all Semitic languages. In Akkadian, it is associated with economic and mathematical content; in Amorite and Ugaritic texts, it means "excellence" or "superiority," especially in names (this seems to be the meaning of "Jethro," Moses's father-in-law).

this unique stage of placing the offering upon the altar before dividing it up is especially apt.[23]

There are varying views as to who is responsible for the act of presenting the grain offering to the altar. Ramban writes that the priest is the one who presents it to the altar, whereas according to the Tosafot, it is the worshipper.[24] R. Mosheh Lichtenstein notes that according to *Parashat Vayikra*, it seems that the worshipper brings the offering to the altar and the priest joins the process only when he scoops out a handful of flour, whereas according to *Parashat Tzav*, the priest also presents the offering to the altar: "This is the law of the grain offering. Aaron's sons shall bring these before the Lord in front of the altar" (6:7).[25]

In *Parashat Tzav*, the priest indeed seems to be the one who presents the offering, whereas the text in *Vayikra* is far more ambivalent: "You shall bring the grain offering made in one of these ways to the Lord, presenting it to the priest, and bring it to the altar" (2:8). Whether it is the worshipper or the priest who must "bring it to the altar" is not clear; while the use of third person implies that it is the priest, the next verse then mentions the priest again: "The priest shall lift a remembrance from the grain offering," which suggests, as Tosafot do, that the worshipper is the one who actually presents the offering to the altar.

If the worshipper is indeed the one who presents the grain offering to the altar, then the following idea is even more striking (although it remains valid even if, as Ramban says, the priest presents the offering): When the grain offering is presented to the altar, the entire offering is transferred from the worshipper's ownership to the altar. Only after this transferral is the offering divided up between the altar and the priests. If so, the priests only receive their portion after it has been consecrated with the holiness of the altar.

It seems that the Sages seek to emphasize this in the Midrash Halakha: "I might think that only the fistful alone required 'touching.' Whence

23. See n. 5 above.

24. Ramban on Lev. 2:2; Tosafot on Megilla 20b, "*likemitza*." Modern scholarship holds that the priest is the one who presents the offering to the altar (e.g., Marx, "Minḥa," 74).

25. Lichtenstein, *Torat HaKorbanot*, 125.

would I derive that the entire meal offering is intended? It is therefore, written: 'And you shall bring the meal offering'" (*Sifra,* Freewill Offerings, 11:1). The idea raised by the midrashic author – that only the handful should be offered upon the altar – expresses the premise that only what will be burned upon the altar ought to be presented to the altar, but that premise is rejected. The entire grain offering is presented to the altar, even though only a handful of it is burned.[26]

It thus emerges that the grain offering is essentially a burnt offering, presented entirely to the altar; in certain cases, it is even burned in its entirety as well.

I wish to conclude this characterization of the grain offering as similar to the burnt offering by noting that the grain offering is the only offering whose eating is discussed in *Parashat Vayikra*. The first chapters of Leviticus describe the sacrificial process until the offering reaches the altar, whereas the laws of their consumption are only discussed from chapter 6 and on – with the exception of the grain offering. Moreover, the grain offering is referred to as "holy of holies" in *Parashat Vayikra* (2:3, 10), whereas the sanctity of all other offerings is discussed only in *Parashat Tzav*.[27]

These two anomalies are obviously related: The sanctity of each offering must be defined in order to determine which offerings may be eaten, and by whom. The laws of eating are not discussed in the first list of *Vayikra,* so there is no need to consider the sanctity of each offering. Given, however, that *Parashat Vayikra* does describe how the grain offering is eaten, it is necessary to define its level of sanctity, and the two are indeed juxtaposed: "What remains of the grain offering shall belong to Aaron and his sons; it is holy of holies among the fire offerings to the Lord" (2:3, 10).

---

26. This seems to be the rule of which offerings are presented: Those that ought to be entirely burned but are not are presented, while those which are supposed to be shared with the priests (such as the two-loaf offering and the showbread) in the first place are not (see R. Shimon's opinion in the *Sifra*, Freewill Offerings, 13:6).
27. Based on these deviations, Hadad concludes that the grain offering is not an original part of Leviticus conveyed to Moses at the Tent of Meeting and was added at the writing stage (Hadad, "Piggul," 124).

The laws of the priestly consumption of the grain offering are already mentioned in *Parashat Vayikra* due to their unique nature: Eating the grain offering is considered an integral part of the *sacrificial* process, and it therefore makes sense to include it in the first sacrificial list, which is devoted to the sacrificial process.[28] In a certain sense, the priests' consumption is almost a form of apology; the worshipper brought the offering to the altar, but the priests receive a portion from the altar itself, "from the fire offerings of the Lord" (2:3). From the worshipper's perspective, the entire offering is for the altar; from God's perspective, the priests are invited to partake in it, and their portion is considered a "holy of holies."[29] It emerges that the grain offering is described immediately after the burnt offering because from the worshipper's perspective, they are both offered up to God in their entirety – even though, practically, God invites the priests to partake of the grain offering.[30]

What, then, is the meaning of this connection? There are two possible approaches. Although the first is more widely accepted by commentators, I believe that the second direction seems more likely.

The Grain Offering as a Poor Person's Burnt Offering

Abarbanel (and many modern scholars) perceives the grain offering as a burnt offering for people who cannot afford bulls, sheep, or even birds:

---

28. This does not contradict the mishna that allows disfigured priests to eat of the offerings, although they cannot offer up these sacrifices (Zevaḥim 12:1). It is conceivable that grain offerings differ from animal offerings; as we will discuss below, there is a difference between them in these contexts as well.
29. As mentioned, the phrase "fire offerings of the Lord" is unique to grain offerings; it appears together with the part of the peace offerings that is waved with the fat. See our discussion below, in the context of the waving of the peace offering.
30. As mentioned, Radatz Hoffmann (and Milgrom) believes that the grain offering was initially burned entirely, like a burnt offering, but this evolved with time. This is reflected in the verb K-T-R, "burn to smoke," associated with the grain offering in some contexts. Haran also argues that some sources imply that the grain offering is burned (I Kings 18:29, 36; II Kings 3:20; Is. 57:6; 66:3; Jer. 14:12). In Judges, Samson's parents offer a grain offering that is entirely burned, as does Gideon (see further in Haran, "Minḥa"). Others, however, propose the opposite: that the grain offering was once eaten at a festive meal, like the peace offering, but then came to be given to the priests (Noth, *Leviticus*, 22; Elliger, *Leviticus*, 44).

> The grain offerings are mentioned before peace offerings for two reasons: to arrange the burnt offerings in order...because the grain offering is counted among them, so that the bull burnt offering, which is the best, is mentioned first, then the sheep burnt offering that follows it, and then the bird burnt offering, for an animal offering is superior to a plant offering. But the peace offering is not a burnt offering, so it is mentioned after that. (Abarbanel on Lev. 2:1)

Needless to say, Abarbanel's analysis clarifies the affinity between the burnt offering and the grain offering: Not only are they connected, they are essentially one and the same! They have different names because one is an animal offering and the other from plants, but that is the only significant difference between them.

Abarbanel's premise is that the grain offering is an option for the poor; given that a poor person unable to afford a sheep or even bird for a variable purification offering may use fine flour (5:11–13), Abarbanel applies the same hierarchy to the burnt offering.

This theory is widely accepted,[31] and its roots can be traced to rabbinic literature. As Rashi writes:

> When someone (*nefesh*) offers – The only freewill offering that says "*nefesh*" [which literally means "soul"] is the grain offering. Who usually offers up a freewill grain offering? The Holy One says, "I am accepting it as if they had offered up their very soul." (Rashi on Lev. 2:1)[32]

While, as mentioned, this reading certainly explains the affinity between the burnt and grain offerings, and commentators ascribe various details to the grain offering's association with the poor, this theory is

31. See, for example, Rambam, *Guide for the Perplexed,* III:46, and Hoffmann, *Leviticus,* vol. 1, 103–05; Leibowitz, *Leviticus,* 41–43.

32. This midrashic approach is problematic; the word "*nefesh*" is not unique to the grain offering, as it also appears several times in the purification and guilt offerings. While Rashi does specify that it is unique among freewill offerings, each of the three freewill offerings has its own different opening.

nonetheless problematic. Technically, it is difficult to assert that the Torah is presenting the grain offering as a variation of the burnt offering, because the passage opens with the word "*ki*" rather than "*im*." As explained, the former is used for a new category and the latter for a subcategory. Once again, the general introduction to animal offerings at the beginning of Leviticus begins: "When (*ki*) someone brings an animal offering to the Lord," and the peace offering in Leviticus 3 opens with "If (*im*) one's sacrifice is a peace offering," which makes it a subcategory of the freewill animal offerings introduced in Leviticus 1. If the grain offering were indeed a subcategory of burnt offerings, it should have been introduced with "*im*," not "*ki*."

Moreover, there is a more fundamental problem with the idea of presenting the grain offering as a poor man's burnt offering: It is not as budget friendly as one might imagine. As Menachem Bula points out, the grain offering requires both oil and frankincense:[33] "This means that the freewill grain offering is more expensive than a bird burnt offering, given that bird burnt offerings are from doves or pigeons, which can be hunted or raised cheaply, whereas a grain offering is a considerable amount of flour – a whole day's worth of food – and must include frankincense, which is costly indeed."[34]

Burnt Offering, Grain Offering, Peace Offering

Given that the Torah introduces the grain offering with a new, independent heading, it makes more sense to regard it as a separate offering despite its similarity to the burnt offering. While there are spiritual and psychological similarities between the accompanying mindset for the two offerings, they are still rooted in two different spheres. The worshipper submits both the burnt offering and the grain offering to the altar to be burnt whole as a symbol of utter, total devotion to God. While the bringer of the peace offering comes to share a meal with God, the

33. This is especially true of frankincense; apparently it barely grew in the Land of Israel, and had to be imported (see Is. 6:20). See the survey in Kam and L. Kwun-Cheung, "Incense Burning."

34. Bula, *Leviticus*, 29. This is not true of the purification grain offering – which the Torah explicitly presents as cheaper than a bird offering – as it does not contain oil or frankincense.

bringer of the grain offering submits their offering to the altar without partaking of it.

Even so, the burnt offering is an animal and the grain offering is from grain, and this generates different religious discourses. The nature of the message the grain offering conveys can be traced to its place in the text. The order of the freewill offerings as presented in *Parashat Vayikra* reveals their deeper nature: The sacrificial chapters begin with the burnt offering and conclude with the peace offering. The burnt offering is offered up when someone feels distant from their God and seeks closeness. The total submission to the altar expresses their total effacement before the great, ineffable God; they bow before their Maker as a reflection of their fleeting, insubstantial existence. In contrast, as we will yet see, the peace offering is a covenant of peace and friendship with God.

This brings us to the nature of the grain offering, which is presented in between these two different expressions to God. The grain offering is not merely a variation of the burnt offering; it expresses something similar, yet it is also in dialogue with the peace offering that follows. It emerges from the religious experience of the burnt offering, yet it has the power to propel the worshipper toward the mindset of the peace offering. As we will see, the worshipper is able to choose which kind of grain offering to bring – one more aligned with the burnt offering or with the peace offering.

THE DIFFERENCE BETWEEN THE BURNT OFFERING AND THE GRAIN OFFERING

For further clarification, we will first point out the difference between the burnt and the grain offering. The first and most obvious difference is that the burnt offering is an animal offering, whereas the grain offering is plant matter: wheat ground to fine flour.[35] Commentators who perceive the grain offering as a variation of the burnt offering are effectively

35. As proposed by Weinfeld, based on the Akkadian *siltu* (Weinfeld, "Afternoon Prayer," 79); see also the talmudic discussion in Shabbat 74b, where R. Menashe uses the same root (*desaleit siltei*) in the sense of "cutting up something very finely."

overlooking this difference, which is, in fact, the key to the fundamental distinction between them.[36]

An animal offering brings life to the altar; a grain offering brings food. This is a fundamental difference: To bring a life to the altar expresses something about life itself, whereas bringing food to the altar is a statement about sustenance. Perhaps this is also reflected through the different epithets for the worshipper: Animal offerings open with "When a person (*adam*) brings an animal offering" (1:2), whereas grain offerings begin: "When someone (*nefesh*) brings a grain offering" (2:1).[37] I would like to propose the following idea cautiously, given that the term "*nefesh*" is also associated with obligatory animal offerings. However, if we may draw a distinction between freewill and obligatory offerings, we can posit that the biblical term "*nefesh*" is often associated with the craving for food. For example: "When you say, 'I shall eat some meat,' because you (*nafshekha*) have the urge to eat it, you may eat meat whenever you desire it.... These you may eat within your towns whenever you wish (*nafshekha*)" (Deut. 12:20–21); "Spend the money on whatever you (*nafshekha*) choose: cattle, sheep, wine, strong drink, or whatever else you (*nafshekha*) like" (Deut. 14:26). There are even more surprising expressions that imply that food is what activates the *nefesh*, such as: "Then make me delicious food, prepared in the way that I love, and bring it to me to eat so that *my soul* (*nafshi*) may bless you before I die" (Gen. 27:4); or the juxtaposition of food and soul that seems intentional, such as: "Whenever you desire (*nafshekha*), you may slaughter and eat meat in any of your towns, according to the blessing that the Lord your God gives you" (Deut. 12:15).[38]

---

36. Menachem Haran proposes that small altars found in different sites across the land (that many believe are incense altars) were in fact used for grain offerings (Haran, "Incense Altars"; Haran, "Altar-ed States").

37. Out of all the books in the Torah, the word "*nefesh*" appears the most in Leviticus (60 times), although it appears even more in Isaiah (62 times) and Psalms (144!); see the full statistics in Seabass, "Nefesh," 502.

38. This also seems to be related to the references to the Levite who joins the service in the Sanctuary (Deut. 18:6–8): "He may do so whenever he wishes (*bekhol avvat nafsho*)... they shall have equal portions to eat." The Levite seems to be motivated by the promise of food, which perhaps is related to the Levite's lack of actual land (Deut. 18:1).

It is generally accepted that the concrete meaning of "*nefesh*" is "throat," "maw," or "gullet." This is implied through the various verses. For example: "And so – Sheol spreads herself (*nafshah*) wide / her mouth gapes wide without limit" (Is. 5:14); "We are (*nafshenu*) dragged down to the dust / our bellies pressed to the earth" (Ps. 44:26).[39] The craving *nefesh* craves to be sated with food.

These connotations may well affect the epithets chosen for each offering: Animal offerings open with "*adam*," "person," which hints to existence itself, to humanity (*adam*) being created from the earth (*adama*), whereas the grain offering uses "*nefesh*" to express that people need food in order to exist. The bringer of the animal offering is declaring that life itself, their very existence, belongs to their Maker – that is why they are offering a life upon the altar. In contrast, the bringer of the grain offering is not making a declaration about life itself, but rather about the source of their sustenance and needs. One who brings a day's worth of bread to the Sanctuary and anoints it with oil[40] is thereby declaring that they know the source of their livelihood; they realize that everything comes from the true King of the world. It is likely that a grain offering is also a prayer for livelihood, a prayer that one's daily bread will be constant and plentiful. This may be why the law that salt must be added to every offering is mentioned in the context of the grain offering and extended to all other offerings (2:13): Adding salt emphasizes the edible aspect of each offering (see further below). The lack of laying of the hands also supports the reading that animal offerings represent the worshipper, who must lay their hands upon the animal, whereas there is no need to do so with grain offerings, which represent a person's food and not the actual person.

This idea is also expressed through the amount of fine flour that constitutes the grain offering. The amount is not specified in this chapter,

39. See Seebass, "Nefesh," 504. Wolff claims that the *nefesh* is the outer neck, not the throat, when discussing the difference between "*nefesh*" and "*ruaḥ*" (Wolff, *Anthropology*, 14), but the more accepted reading is "throat."

40. Oil symbolizes wealth; Radatz Hoffmann believes that the addition of frankincense also symbolizes "one's satisfaction with God's leadership and providence and joy in one's lot" (*Leviticus*, vol. 1, 105). Below I will propose another way to read the meaning of frankincense.

but the Sages teach that the freewill offering – like other grain offerings whose amount is specified in the biblical text – comprises a tenth of an ephah (approximately two liters).[41] This amount first appears in the context of the manna: "Each of you gather as much as you need, an omer for every person; each take enough for all the people in your tent.... An omer is a tenth of an ephah" (Ex. 16:16, 36). Each person must gather an omer – that is, a tenth of an ephah – per day for each member of their household. Rashi connects this measurement to the laws of the grain offering: "This is the measurement for *ḥalla* and grain offerings" (on Ex. 16:36).[42]

In light of this, R. Samson Raphael Hirsch perceives the omer as the biblical daily portion of bread, the amount of food a person needs each day.[43] If so, when a person brings a grain offering, they are effectively offering up a day's worth of bread, a symbolic gift for a day of the existence God has granted them.

This leads to the conclusion that when a person brings a burnt offering, they are declaring that their life belongs to God; when they bring a grain offering, they are declaring that their daily bread and all their needs are a gift from God.[44] Perhaps this explains why, as Abarbanel believes, poor people are likely to bring this offering: as an expression of their struggle to put bread on the table and as a prayer for abundance. But it may well be that this was also a popular choice for wealthy people who

---

41. Biblical measurements are of volume, not weight (Rambam on Mishna Teharot 3:4). On the logic of this principle, see Benish, *Middot*, 194–96. The ephah is about twenty-four liters (according to R. Haim Naeh) or forty-three liters (according to Ḥazon Ish). Intriguingly, some modern scholars argue that it changed over time: Before the Exile it was about ten liters, but became about thirty-six liters afterward (Fuller, "Ephah"). R. Eliyahu of Lublin suggests that it is one oven's worth of baked goods; hence the name "*eifa*." In general, the grain offering is mentioned with reference to the ephah measurement (see Ezek. 46:14: "Offer a grain offering each morning, a sixth of an ephah").
42. Compare to R. Samson Raphael Hirsch on Ex. 16:16, 36; Hoffmann, *Leviticus*, vol. 1, 105. There is a profound affinity between the manna and the grain offering; see further in Grossman, "Manna and Passover."
43. In his commentary on Ex. 16:16, 36, Radatz Hoffmann summarizes: "The poor person who offers up his daily bread to the altar dedicated his capital and soul to God."
44. For further study, see Sabato, "Freewill Offerings," especially 22; Grossman, "Minḥa."

wished to offer thanks for God's gift of abundance. The grain offering can be both prayer for the future and grateful acknowledgment of the past and present: "For all is from You, and we have given You what is but Yours" (I Chr. 29:14).

This brings us to the grain offering's addition of oil, which is emphasized in the context of the cooked grain offerings but is required in all freewill grain offerings, including the basic offering of fine flour. Oil is a biblical symbol of wealth and material pleasure: "From Asher will come the oil for food, and he will proffer kingly delights" (Gen. 49:20); "Where once there was mourning – oil of joy" (Is. 61:3); "Your God has anointed you with oil of bliss" (Ps. 45:8). Oil is associated with joy and abundance; thus, a mourner may not use oil. For this reason, when Joab asks the woman of Tekoa to disguise herself as a mourner, he says: "Now pretend you are mourning: don mourning garb, do not anoint yourself with oil, and act like a woman who has been mourning the dead for a long time" (II Sam. 14:2).

These connotations would be surprising if the grain offering were indeed a poor person's burnt offering. Oil, with its associations of wealth and pleasure, makes it an unlikely candidate for a poor person's offering. One might claim that the addition of oil is a prayer for wealth, but it is more likely that it represents a person's daily needs. The worshipper offers up a portion of their daily bread and laces it with a symbol of richness and earthly pleasure.

THE FINE FLOUR OFFERING AND THE COOKED GRAIN OFFERINGS

Until now, we have discussed grain offerings in general, but Leviticus 2 essentially presents two different models of grain offerings that, although obviously related, symbolize two different forms of religious expression, which are conveyed through the halakhic and literary differences between the two variations.

The general introduction to the grain offering, "When one brings a grain offering to the Lord" (2:1), is followed by four different kinds of grain offering:

1. The fine flour offering

2. The baked grain offering
3. The grain offering prepared on a griddle
4. The grain offering prepared in a pan[45]

The verses list the laws of the grain offering twice through the presentation of two different models of grain offering. The first description details the fine flour offering, and the second instance describes the laws of the three kinds of cooked grain offerings, which undergo an additional process that makes them edible:

The Fine Flour Grain Offering (2:1–3)	Cooked Grain Offerings (2:4–10)
When one brings a grain offering to the Lord, it shall be of *fine flour*. The one who brings the sacrifice shall pour oil over it, then place incense upon it,	When you bring a grain offering *baked in an oven,* it shall be of fine flour: unleavened loaves mixed with oil or unleavened wafers spread with oil. If your offering is grain *prepared on a griddle,* it shall be of fine flour mixed with oil, and unleavened. Crumble it into pieces and pour oil over it; this is a grain offering. If your offering is grain *prepared in a pan,* it shall be of fine flour in oil.
and bring it to Aaron's sons, the priests.	You shall bring the grain offering made in one of these ways to the Lord, presenting it to the priest, *who will bring it to the altar.*
From this, the priest shall scoop out a handful of its fine flour and oil, together with all its incense,	The priest shall lift a remembrance from the grain offering
and send this remembrance up in smoke upon the altar as an offering of fire, a sweet savor to the Lord.	and send it up in smoke upon the altar as an offering of fire, a sweet savor to the Lord.

45. The fifth grain offering is listed as an appendix at the end of the chapter; we will discuss it further in context.

What is left of the grain offering shall belong to Aaron and his sons; it is holy of holies among the fire offerings to the Lord.	What is left of this grain offering shall belong to Aaron and his sons; it is holy of holies among the fire offerings to the Lord.

That there are two distinct models is evident through the repetition of the sacrificial process. The basic fine flour offering is described first; this is followed by a description of the cooked grain offering (8–10). The repetition is especially evident through the formulaic phrases "an offering of fire, a sweet savor to the Lord" and "It is holy of holies among the fire offerings to the Lord" (3, 10). As Abarbanel points out: "It says, 'What is left of the grain offering shall belong to Aaron and his sons,' twice, even though once would have been enough."[46] The double statement points to two distinct models.

Were the Torah's objective to point out that there are various types of grain offering, we would have expected a list of various possibilities, followed by a description of the sacrificial process itself: "This is how the cooked grain offerings are presented: The three types are listed, followed by the process." The fact that the fine flour offering and its sacrificial process are presented separately proves that there are two distinct models; we will soon show that the halakhic differences between them are a reflection of their different natures.

In order to describe these differences, I will first list the halakhic and subtle linguistic differences between them.

1. The Raw and the Cooked

The most obvious difference between the two models is that the fine flour offering is offered up as a raw dough.[47] While the cooked grain offerings are also made of fine flour, they first undergo some kind of process:

1. "When you bring a grain offering baked in an oven, it shall be of fine flour: unleavened loaves mixed with oil [and/or] unleavened wafers spread with oil." What is the relationship between

46. In his commentary on Leviticus, question 11 at the beginning of *Parashat Vayikra*.
47. See the description of its preparation in Rambam, *Hilkhot Maaseh HaKorbanot* 13:5.

"unleavened loaves mixed with oil" and "unleavened wafers spread with oil"? One option is that one must bring one of each: one loaf and one wafer.[48] The Sages, however, interpret the *vav* between them as "or": One may bring either loaves or wafers.[49] As Rashi explains: "If one pledged to bring a baked grain offering, the text teaches that one may bring either loaves or wafers; the loaves are mixed with oil and the wafers are spread with oil."

2. The second option is to fry the grain offering: "If your offering is grain prepared on a griddle, it shall be of fine flour mixed with oil, and unleavened. Crumble it into pieces and pour oil over it; this is a grain offering." When the grain offering is fried before it is presented to the altar, it must be crumbled into pieces after being fried.
3. The third option is "grain prepared in a *marḥeshet*." The Sages discuss what the word "*marḥeshet*" means:

   > What is the difference between a griddle and a "*marḥeshet*"? The *marḥeshet* has a lid [i.e, it is a pot] and the griddle does not – this is R. Yossi HaGelili's opinion. R. Ḥananya b. Gamliel says: A *marḥeshet* is deep and what is prepared in it is soft; a griddle is shallow and what is prepared in it is crisp. (*Sifra*, Freewill Offerings, 12:7)

   According to R. Yossi, the *marḥeshet* is a pot with a lid; R. Ḥananya holds that it is essentially a kind of deep fryer. The second option seems more likely (this is Rashi's preference), especially given the description in *Parashat Tzav*: "Any grain offering baked in the oven or prepared *in* a *marḥeshet* or *on* a griddle" (7:9). One fries *on* a griddle, but deep-fries *in* a pot.[50] Either way, pre-

48. Wafer means thin, as seen in the description of the thin cows in Pharaoh's dream (Gen. 41:19) and the Akkadian root (*raqāqu*). Kaddari (Dictionary, 1032) prefers the comparison with Syrian ("thin," "delicate") or Arabic ("a thin cake eaten by farmers").
49. Both possibilities are found in the tannaitic dispute as to whether one may bring a mixture of loaves and wafers (R. Shimon) or only one kind at a time (the Sages, which became the halakhic ruling). See Menaḥot 63a–b.
50. Shadal on Lev. 2:7, 396.

paring the offering in a *marḥeshet* yields a specific result, either because the offering is covered with a lid or deep-fried in a pot.

The fact that a grain offering can be offered up when ready to eat is related to its nature. As discussed, this offering is related to food, sustenance, and livelihood; it makes sense for someone to offer up what they actually eat.[51] Therein lies the difference between the two kinds of grain offering: The cooked grain offering is cooked (which is unique among all offerings, both grain and animal), whereas the fine flour offering is raw.

2. Oil

The second difference between the two kinds of grain offering is the amount of oil used. The fine flour offering requires a drizzling of oil (2:1), which suggests that the amount is merely symbolic;[52] Moses "drizzles" oil upon Aaron's forehead to anoint him (Ex. 29:7), which is surely a minor, symbolic amount. (The Sages agree that Moses did not actually "pour" oil on Aaron's forehead; rather, he dabbed him with oil in the shape of an X.) The same verb generally points to a symbolic amount (see especially Gen. 28:18; 35:14). In contrast, cooked grain offerings mention oil again and again; as pointed out in the *Sifra* (Freewill Offerings, 10), all three kinds use a significant amount of oil in their dough: Baked offerings are either mixed or spread with oil;[53] oil is added to offerings fried on a griddle twice – in their dough and after it is crumbled – while Rashi holds that oil is added three times (!); and offerings prepared in a pan are actually deep-fried in oil.

51. It is interesting that the peace offering – which is the closest offering to a human meal – is not offered up ready to eat. It is also worth noting that, surprisingly, the cooked grain offerings are edible, given that this was one of the most striking differences between biblical and pagan sacrifices: Other nations believed that offerings were actually food for the gods, but this was strictly challenged by the Torah.

52. An interesting study of the meaning of the verb "*latzeket*" can be considered through the difference between Exodus 29:12 and Leviticus 8:15; I will discuss this in the context of the days of consecration.

53. Menaḥot 74b–75a. A different opinion is that each wafer must be entirely spread with oil.

3. Frankincense

Unlike oil, which features significantly in cooked grain offerings, frankincense is mentioned only in regard to the raw fine flour offering. The Sages teach that all grain offerings must include incense; this is supported by the description in *Parashat Tzav*, which draws no distinction between the different kinds of grain offering: "The priest shall lift a handful of the fine flour and oil from the grain offering, and all the incense on it, and send this remembrance up in smoke upon the altar" (6:8). In fact, even before the frankincense is mentioned there, the offering is presented to the altar (6:7), a detail that in *Parashat Vayikra* is mentioned only in regard to the cooked grain offerings. This justifies the Sages' statement that all laws of the fine flour offered should be applied to the cooked grain offerings. But even if so, the question still stands as to why in *Parashat Vayikra*, the incense is mentioned only in relation to the fine flour offering (and why the law of presentation is mentioned only in relation to the cooked grain offerings, as we will discuss below).[54]

The Sages' approach is favored by some modern scholars, such as Baruch Levine: "Frankincense is not mentioned in this grain offering for brevity's sake, but later on in the chapter (v. 9), the method of offering is clarified through the mention of the token portion, whose main component is frankincense."[55] However, I believe that he is incorrect on two counts: The description is not aiming at brevity, nor does the "token portion," the remembrance, necessarily contain frankincense. In relation to the fine flour offering, it is stated: "From this, the priest shall scoop out a handful of its fine flour and oil, together with *all its incense*" (2:2), whereas in the cooked grain offerings, "the priest shall lift a remembrance from the grain offering and send it up in smoke upon the altar" (2:9), with no mention of incense. The different verb might

54. The extent of the importance of dividing the grain offerings into categories – *Parashat Vayikra* divides them, whereas *Parashat Tzav* refers to the general "law of grain offerings" – is discussed in depth in Menaḥot 3b, where the Sages debate whether the grain offering is valid if the priest treated it as one kind of grain offering while the worshipper intended it as a different kind.

55. Levine, *The World of the Bible*, 22; also Weinberg, *Sacrifice in Israel*, 304: "All grain offerings include frankincense except for the *sota* grain offering and the purification grain offering."

also point to the absence of incense: The priest "scoops out" a handful of fine flour, whereas he "lifts" up a piece of the cooked grain offering. He "scoops out" a handful to make sure that the mixture contains incense as well, but when there is no incense, he simply "lifts" a piece of cooked grain offering.

Moreover, the "grain offering of first produce" listed after the cooked grain offerings (2:15–16) does include incense. Thus, incense is mentioned in the grain offerings described before and after the cooked grain offerings, which supports the idea that they do not include incense.

Nor is Levine's assumption that the "remembrance" necessarily includes incense convincing: While the fine flour offering's handful does include incense, the actual word, "*azkara*," has nothing to do with incense; it merely refers to the part burned upon the altar.[56] All grain offerings offer up a "remembrance" upon the altar, whether they contain incense or not, including the purification offering of grain (5:12) and the wayward wife's grain offering (Num. 5:26).[57]

There is therefore reason to explore the addition of incense as the symbolic difference between the two models of grain offering.

4. Presentation to the Altar

I have already mentioned that grain offerings are governed by a unique law of presentation to the altar: Before the priest takes a handful, the grain offering is "presented" to the altar in its entirety, which serves to sanctify the entire offering. This is a key step, given that most of the offering is not actually burned upon the altar; instead, the altar "gives" the priests most of its offering. For some reason, however, the law of presentation is only mentioned as part of the cooked grain offering, but not as part of the fine flour offering.

---

56. On understanding the term "*azkaratah*," "remembrance," see Rendtorff, *Leviticus*, 100–01; Hartley, *Leviticus*, 30. I tend to agree with De Vaux that the handful is a metonym – i.e., "remembrance" – of the entire offering (De Vaux, *Ancient Israel*, vol. 2, 422).

57. In relation to the showbread, in contrast, the remembrance is the frankincense; this may be why Levine suggests that this is the main part of the remembrance. However, the showbread is not burned on the altar, because it is leaven; I will discuss this further below.

As mentioned, the Sages teach that the law of presentation applies to the fine flour offering as well, as in *Parashat Tzav* the law applies to all grain offerings. In the words of the *Sifra*: "'And he shall present it to the altar' – How do we know that this applies to all grain offerings? From the phrase 'and the grain offering'" (*Sifra*, Freewill Offerings, 11:1). If so, however, why isn't this law included in the fine flour offering in the first place?[58]

5. Who Takes the Handful?

As we saw in relation to the burnt offering, the text tends to use third person singular to refer to the worshipper: "*He shall lay* his hand on the head of the burnt offering / *and shall have* the bull slaughtered before the Lord." In contrast, the third person plural is used to refer to the priests: "The sons of Aaron the priest *shall arrange* wood on the fire *they* will have placed upon the altar. / Then Aaron's sons the priests *shall arrange* the pieces of the sacrifice." I am mentioning this here in relation to the determination of who takes a handful of flour as the grain offering: Is it the worshipper (in a parallel action to the slaughter of their own burnt offering) or the priest?

For cooked grain offerings, the answer is clear; after presenting the offering to the altar, it is the priest who lifts a piece for the altar: "The priest shall lift a remembrance from the grain offering and send it up in smoke upon the altar" (2:9). Regarding the fine flour offering, however, the language is ambiguous:

> When one brings a grain offering to the Lord, it shall be of fine flour. The one who brings the sacrifice *shall pour* oil over it, then *place* incense upon it, *and bring it* to Aaron's sons, the priests. From this, *he shall scoop out* a handful of its fine flour and oil, together with all its incense, *and the priest shall send this*

58. Ramban's approach is based on the absence of any mention of the law of presentation in the text. He explains that unlike the Sages' opinion as quoted in Rashi, the priest's service begins with the act of presentation, but since it is not mentioned in relation to the first fine flour offering, the Sages state that the priest begins his service only from "the handful and on."

> *remembrance up in smoke* upon the altar as an offering of fire, a sweet savor to the Lord. (2:1–2)

The worshipper must "pour" oil over the offering, "place" incense upon it, and "bring it" to the priests. The priests are mentioned in the plural form, but the next action is in the singular form, "He shall scoop out," which implies that it is the worshipper who scoops out a handful. Moreover, the next action is explicitly attributed to the priest: "The priest shall send [it] up in smoke," which also seems to indicate that the previous action is ascribed to the worshipper. On the other hand, the act of scooping appears right after the worshipper brings the offering to the priests, which indicates that the priests take over at this point. As Shadal writes:

> There is no doubt that the priest is the one who takes a handful… it does not say "The priest scoops out" because it says "He shall scoop out a handful and the priest shall send it up in smoke," joining the two actions together, for he sends it up in smoke right after he scoops out a handful.[59]

Both possible readings are evident in various translations. Some assume that the priest is the one who takes a handful: "He shall bring it to Aaron's sons, the priests. From this, the priest shall scoop out a handful of its fine flour and oil."[60] Other translations assume it is the worshipper: "He must then bring it to the sons of Aaron, the priest, and must take a handful of the flour and oil."[61]

Jacob Milgrom inadvertently points out the verse's ambiguity: "[The priest] shall scoop out therefrom a handful," and comments: "[The priest]: moved up from 2b for clarity."[62] His translation unequivocally makes the priest the subject, but it is no coincidence that he has to change the order "for clarity," because the Hebrew is unclear.[63] Thus,while the

59. In his commentary on Lev. 2:2, 396.

60. *The Koren Tanakh.*

61. Wenham, *Leviticus,* 66.

62. Milgrom, *Leviticus,* vol. 1, 181.

63. Some ignore the ambiguity in the verse but note a similar ambiguity about the law of presentation mentioned in the context of cooked grain offerings (Wenham,

priest is clearly the one who takes a handful of the cooked grain offering, it may be that the bringer of the fine flour offering is the one who scoops out a handful, which he then gives to the priest to burn upon the altar.

6. Second Person/Third Person

The final difference I wish to point out touches upon the use of second and third person in the two models of grain offering. In the fine flour offering the worshipper is referred to in third person: "The one who brings the sacrifice shall pour oil over it…." In the cooked grain offering, however, the second person is used: "When *you* bring a grain offering baked in an oven, it shall be of fine flour."[64] This difference is of special significance given that the third person is used in the whole sacrificial section, with the exception of the text relating to the cooked grain offerings, which is the only place that the worshipper is referred to in the second person. R. Meir Simcha of Dvinsk perceives this as the text's concern that the worshipper will accidentally bring a leavened offering:

> Notice that all of *Parashat Vayikra* is written in third person… The fine flour offering, which is just fine flour and oil and cannot become leaven is written in third person. But grain offerings baked in an oven or prepared in a griddle or pan, which are prepared like bread and may become leaven, are written in second person: "You shall not make them with leaven," for the prohibition is against anyone causing the offering to become leaven – both priest and non-priest – and therefore the second person is used to emphasize the prohibition. (*Meshekh Ḥokhma* on Lev. 2:4)

I will soon propose a different explanation, but the *Meshekh Ḥokhma* is certainly correct to point out that the use of the second person is unique within the sacrificial chapters. This also helps draw a distinction between the two models of grain offering, a distinction which is

---

Leviticus, 68, n. 2). There is indeed room for debate there as well.

64. Note that the description of the priest's actions revert to the third person; I will discuss this below.

not merely stylistic, but halakhic as well. Do these differences have an underlying root, and do they point to a fundamental difference between the two models?

THE COOKED GRAIN OFFERING

Second Person

The ostensibly technical use of the second person in cooked grain offerings is a convenient starting point; it may well reflect the worshipper's significant agency in this particular offering.

Ready to Eat

The first aspect that reveals the worshipper's significant agency in this offering is the fact that they are able to determine how to prepare the grain offering – whether to bake it in an oven or fry it on a griddle or in a pot. The text does not discuss why one might bring a baked grain offering rather than a fried one. Although commentators make various suggestions about the reasons why one might bring one or the other,[65] the biblical text seems to present this as the worshipper's choice. Why would someone bring a baked offering, rather than a fried one? The reason may be banal enough: It may simply be a matter of personal taste. If someone likes baked goods, they will offer up baked goods; if one is fond of fried food, they may choose to offer up their favorite griddle cakes to God.

The fine flour offering, however, leaves no room for personal preference: It is offered up on the altar as a raw dough of flour, oil, and incense. In this sense, the fine flour offering is comparable to animal offerings. People offer up the animal's raw flesh upon the altar; they do not choose whether to stew it or fry it. The raw material is prepared upon the altar, whose fire consumes it. This is an important aspect of sacrificial theology, although others have different perspectives. Alfred Marx, for example, writes that the Israelites' offerings consisted of:

65. The Netziv discusses the four options in relation to four of the ancient "humors" (on Lev. 2:1). See R. Samson Raphael Hirsch's commentary for a different angle.

> "the main product of their agriculture or their livestock. These are brought to him... ready to be prepared for a meal... to be baked into bread, or roasted. This points to the fact that the offerings are considered meals which are either presented solely to God (whole offering) or shared among God, the priests, and the offerer (well-being offering). As is expressly stated in connection with the latter offering, the part burnt upon the altar is God's food.[66]

I believe that this is a fundamentally incorrect interpretation of biblical sacrifices. In my introduction, I have already pointed out that while offerings are indeed edible, they are not presented as food for God; on the contrary, in contrast to prevalent ancient beliefs, the Israelites do not believe that God has any need of food, nor does God's existence depend on their sacrifices. The flesh is not skinned and washed in order to make it edible, but for aesthetic reasons, just as it is forbidden to bring a deformed or sick animal as an offering out of respect for the altar. The only offering made of prepared, ready-to-eat food is the cooked grain offering. This does not change the general biblical paradigm of offerings. The worshipper does not offer ready-to-eat food because it is food for God; rather, the cooked grain offering reflects people's desire to share their food with the One who provides their daily bread.

Where Is the Grain Offering Prepared?

The second unique aspect of the cooked grain offering is that the worshipper brings the offering to the Sanctuary only after it has been prepared. This topic is more complex and subject to dispute, but this seems to be the plain meaning of the text. Rashi writes that the griddle (*maḥavat*) is "a vessel that was in the Sanctuary," thus revealing his opinion that the grain offering was actually prepared in the Sanctuary, and Ramban and the Sages concur. This makes sense, given that it would be problematic to assume that all cooked grain offerings have been prepared in proper purity and holiness. Yet the *peshat* of the text implies that the worshipper prepares the grain offering at home: "You shall bring the grain offering made in one of these ways to the Lord, presenting it to the priest, who

66. Marx, "Theology," 112.

will bring it to the altar" (2:8). The grain offering is brought to the priest only after it has been cooked. Abarbanel reads this verse thus:

> The worshipper brings his grain offering when it has already been baked.... "Made in one of these ways" refers to the three kinds of cooked grain offering, which is brought after the worshipper has prepared it at home; they then bring them to the priest with oil and incense. (Abarbanel on 2:1)[67]

The image that comes to mind – and may the reader forgive my obvious romanticization – is of a person preparing food for their family at home, feeling blessed at the sheer abundance of grain and thus inspired to bring an extra portion to the Sanctuary to thank God for this abundance. The father, fond of baked goods, is moved to bring a portion of baked grain to be offered upon the altar; the mother, delighted with her fresh batch of fried delicacies, is excited to bring a portion of fried grain to the Sanctuary; the son and daughter beg to bring a portion of their favorite griddle cakes to present to the altar. This scene, albeit sentimentalized, captures the essence of the cooked grain offering, which invites the worshipper to bring their favorite food as an offering to God. The impression that this offering is prepared at home reinforces the sense of sharing and cooperation between human and God. This, of course, differs from the usual sacrificial experience.

This also explains why the description of the cooked grain offering refers to the worshipper in the second person instead of the usual third. Speaking as if directly to the worshipper creates a sense of intimacy and friendship, a more mutual relationship with God. The cooked grain offering brings the worshipper to the Sanctuary with an offering suited to their own taste, brought from their own house to God's house.

The Law of Presentation

The requirement to present the grain offering to the altar before scooping out a handful is somewhat elusive and can be read in different ways. I have already noted that this step serves to transfer the offering from

67. Eg., Rainey, "Sacrifice," 641, and others.

the worshipper's ownership to the altar, and that it is especially necessary for grain offerings, which are essentially offered up in their entirety but in practice are only partially burned upon the altar. I now wish to address the surprising fact that this law is mentioned only in conjunction with cooked grain offerings.

This can be perceived as a counterpoint to the worshipper's surprising agency in this particular offering. Given that the grain is cooked in the worshipper's own house, according to their own personal preference, there is a need to present it to the altar to emphasize its transferral from earthly to heavenly possession. The worshipper is a much less active participant in the fine flour offering, so there is no need for a ceremony to mark its transferral, as expressed by Hizkuni:

> "Presenting it to the priest" – In the Sanctuary. When unprocessed fine flour is brought, there is no need to present it to the altar, for it was obviously brought for the sake of Heaven. But cooked grain that has been prepared in the oven, griddle, or pan must first be presented to the altar, to show that it was brought especially for the altar, and so that it does not seem like the person prepared the meal for himself and then sent a portion of it to his friend. (Hizkuni on 2:2)

Hizkuni boldly declares that unlike the Sages' opinion, there is no need to present the fine flour offering; that it is a law exclusive to cooked grain offerings. He explains that since the cooked grain offering might seem like something a person made for themselves and decided to give a portion of it to God,[68] the law of presentation establishes that the offering is being transferred to the altar and no longer belongs to the worshipper. The raw fine flour offering is not edible; in this sense, it is similar to animal offerings, which are obviously brought especially for sacrificial purposes. However, cooked grain offerings must first be

68. This proves that Hizkuni – like Abarbanel – assumes that the worshipper prepares the cooked grain offering in their own home. If it were prepared in the Sanctuary, there would be no such concern.

presented to the altar to signify that they are not merely leftovers from a person's own meal.

The Handful

This explanation also illuminates a further disparity between the two models of grain offering. As mentioned, the text explicitly notes that the priest is the one who offers up a handful of cooked grain offerings (2:9), whereas the description of the fine flour offering is ambiguous. In light of the law of presentation in cooked grain offerings, it is clearly the priest who scoops up a handful, for the offering has already been consecrated to the altar; thus, only the priest is able to deal with what has been consecrated. However, as it is not specified that the fine flour offering must be presented to the altar, the grain is not yet holy, and the specified handful should be scooped out by the worshipper. Once again, the "scooping out" of fine flour is akin to the worshipper's slaughter of the animal offering, because the animal has not yet been consecrated.

"Oil and Incense Gladden the Heart" (Prov. 27:9)

Oil

The aforementioned fundamental difference between the two models of grain offerings clarifies the rest of the disparities between them, namely, concerning oil and incense.

As mentioned, oil is a central ingredient in cooked grain offerings. The explanation that oil is part of most baked or fried goods and is therefore part of the offering is not sufficient, because the offerings incorporate oil twice, both before and after their preparation, both in the dough and drizzled on top of the cooked product. One rabbinic opinion is that this second addition is a symbolic "x" drizzled on top:

> All the cooked meal offerings require three additions of oil: pouring, mixing, and placement of oil into the vessel prior to their preparation... Loaves are mixed with oil; as stated by Rebbe. And the Rabbis say: It is with fine flour that one mixes the oil. Although the loaves require mixing of flour with oil, wafers do not require mixing, but rather a smearing of oil on them after baking.

> How does one smear oil on them? In the shape of an X, and the rest of the oil is eaten by the priests. (Mishna Menaḥot 6:3)

This approach presents a surprising interpretation of what "smearing" the wafers with oil means: It is not related to food preparation, but rather to the offering's consecration. The wafers are anointed with oil as priests are: "The Sages taught: Kings are anointed with oil smeared in the shape of a crown, and priests with the shape of the letter *chi* (X)" (Keritot 5b; Horayot 12a).

The question why priests are anointed with oil in the shape of an X is complex. For our purposes, R. Kasher's explanation is sufficient: In the book of Ezekiel, the prophet is told to mark the foreheads of all the people worthy of salvation with a "*tav*" (9:4). R. Kasher explains that the ancient *tav* resembled the letter X and that the priests anointed for the Temple service were marked with this letter, just like those who were worthy of being saved from Jerusalem's destruction.[69]

Whether or not we accept R. Kasher's theory, anointing the grain offerings with oil in the shape of an X symbolizes their consecration to the altar. That the grain offering is anointed with oil as the priests are anointed is presumably based on the term *meshiḥa*, "anointing" – "unleavened wafers spread/anointed (*meshuḥim*) with oil" (2:4) – given that the verb "to anoint" usually refers to the consecration of people or vessels.[70]

If so, there is a striking dialogue between the description of the High Priest's consecration: "Take the anointing oil, *pour it on his head, and anoint him*" (Ex. 29:7), and the anointing of the grain offering prepared on a griddle: "Crumble it into pieces and *pour oil over it – this is a grain*

69. Kasher, *Torah Shelema*, vol. 25, 194–97. He also suggests that the phrase "a kind of X" rules out the actual shape of the crucifix, which the Sages wished to prevent. Milgrom, in contrast, proposes that they actually used to pour the oil in the shape of a cross, but stopped this when the crucifix became a Christian symbol (Milgrom, *Leviticus*, vol. 1, 184).

70. The first act of anointing with oil in the Torah is Jacob pouring oil on the rock as a monument (Gen. 28:18; 35:14). It is interesting that oil was used for anointing, given its centrality in the Ancient Egyptians' worship, particularly in their burial rites (see Krüger, "Salbungsrituale"). The Torah is not consistent in what aspects of pagan ritual are excluded from biblical worship.

offering" (2:6). Thus, the expression "It is a grain offering" is charged with full significance: Pouring oil over the pieces transforms them into a "grain offering" and consecrates them to the altar as a priest is consecrated.

Before we consider an alternative reading, it is worth noting that this theory leaves room for distinguishing between different types of grain offering based on the verb used for the addition of oil to each offering, which perhaps points to different paths of consecration: The baked grain offering is "anointed with oil," while oil is "poured over" the grain offering prepared on a griddle.

As mentioned, both of these verbs are used in the description of anointing the High Priest: "Take the anointing oil, *pour it on his head, and anoint him*" (Ex. 29:7), whereas they are split up between two different kinds of cooked grain offering.[71]

If so, the addition of oil in cooked grain offerings seems to be part of the law of presentation, which is only mentioned in relation to cooked grain offerings: It is the offerings that have been prepared in the worshipper's home that require consecration. This shift from the worshipper's ownership to the altar's is achieved through presentation to the altar and consecration with oil.

The consecrative nature of oil in this context does not negate other aforementioned biblical associations such as wealth, pleasure, and abundance; in ancient times, oil was widely used by the wealthy for both food and cosmetic purposes.[72] This terminologyis appropriate for God-given abundance represented by the grain offering – particularly the cooked grain offerings.

Before we go on to discuss the addition of incense, we can already state that cooked grain offerings invite the worshipper's active, personal participation in the sacrificial process. This kind of involvement is not consistent with the total self-effacement that characterizes the bringing of the burnt offering. The sense that a person must offer up a sacrifice

71. The Sages take care to extend the law of pouring to all grain offerings except for the baked grain offering (Menaḥot 75a).

72. See Amos's cynical description of Israel's upper class: "You who dismiss the day of evil but embrace violent rule, who lie on beds of ivory, lounge upon your couches, feasting on the choicest of sheep... who anoint yourselves with the finest of oils, but are not heartsick over Joseph's ruin" (Amos 6:4–6).

to have the audacity to approach their God is vastly different from the sense of mutuality and partnership expressed through the cooked grain offerings. While they do not indicate the extent of mutuality represented by the peace offering (wherein the worshippers actually partake of their own offering), the shift from burnt offering to grain offering changes the trajectory from awe and fear to religious joy that reaches a climax with the peace offering.[73]

Frankincense

As noted, one of the differences between the fine flour offering and the cooked grain offerings is that the addition of incense is mentioned only in conjunction with the fine flour offering. This is surprising, given that if frankincense indeed symbolizes satisfaction and pleasure, it would be an apt addition to the oil-rich cooked grain offerings that express the worshipper's satisfaction and delight in God.

Understanding the law of incense poses a special challenge. There is no mention of incense in animal offerings, which implies that the addition of incense is restricted to grain offerings. However, the poor person's purification grain offering does not contain incense (Lev. 5:11), nor does the wayward wife's grain offering (Num. 5:15), which indicates that it is only added to freewill offerings. Once again, there is no mention of incense in cooked grain offerings, but it is added to the grain offering of first produce at the end of the chapter (2:15–16). Why is it added to grain offerings, but only certain ones?[74]

Milgrom explains that additions to grain offerings should ideally be kept to a minimum, given that (in his opinion) they are largely sacrificial options for the poor. However, he claims, frankincense must be added to the freewill offering in order to distinguish it from the purification grain offering, which is only fine flour.[75]

73. Compare to Marx's beautiful analysis: "Theology," 114.

74. It is worth noting that frankincense, or at least some kind of incense, was used in pagan worship in Egypt and other places as well (see the survey of Watts, *Leviticus*, 238–39; Vinci, *Incense*, 14–21; Nielsen, *Incense*, 25–33); yet it still had a central role in biblical worship.

75. Milgrom, *Leviticus*, vol. 1, 183, 198–99.

This explanation is not convincing. Firstly, the purification grain offering is already distinct from the freewill grain offering because it does not contain oil, so why is there a need for further distinction? More important, however, is that according to Milgrom's explanation, frankincense is a purely technical marker without any intrinsic meaning. This is unlikely, given that it appears in other contexts and is even offered up as an offering in its own right upon the altar.[76] One example is Isaiah's prophecy, which is also the *haftara* for *Parashat Vayikra*:

> You did not bring Me the lamb of your offering; / it was not Me your sacrifice honored;
> I did not enslave you to My gifts / or weary you with frankincense.
> You did not pay silver for calamus for Me / or slake My thirst with fat of the sacrifice,
> yet you enslaved Me to your iniquity / and wearied Me with your sins. (Is. 43:23–24)[77]

Similarly, Jeremiah asks on God's behalf: "For what purpose do I need frankincense brought from Sheba or choice cane from some distant land? Your burnt offerings are not desirable, nor do I find pleasure in your sacrifices" (Jer. 6:20; see also 17:26; 41:5).[78] Frankincense has a significant, central role in the sacrificial world; its presence is unlikely to be merely technical.

R. Baruch Kehat remarked to me (in a private conversation) that frankincense is not added to cooked grain offerings because the main idea is to offer them to the altar in the same way as they are served at the

76. The Sages also hold that one may offer frankincense alone as an independent offering (*Sifra*, Freewill Offerings 8:3).
77. Commentators are divided as to whether this refers to the frankincense of the incense (Radak) or of the grain offerings (*Metzudat David*), but either way, frankincense is presented as an individual offering.
78. In the final source, the worshippers, "shaven of beard, clothing torn, scratched in grief," are clearly mourning the destroyed Temple, so why are they bringing incense? Some (like Radak) claim that they did not know about it when they set out but only found out when they were on their way; others (such as Rashi) explain they hoped to worship at the site anyway. After all, this is how the Second Temple began – with an altar, before the actual Temple was built.

table. Were frankincense used as a spice, it would be a fitting addition to cooked grain offerings, but since it is never served at the table, it is not used when the cooked grain offering is served to the altar.

The disadvantage of this theory is that it only explains why frankincense is not used in cooked grain offerings, not why it *is* added to the fine flour offering. Why is it used in the first place? After all, it is never added to animal offerings. Why is it part of the fine flour offering?

The more logical path is to determine why frankincense is added; then, based on this explanation, we will attempt to understand why it is omitted from cooked grain offerings. I will first present three proposed theories, followed by an additional idea:

1. As a vehicle for consecration: Frankincense is the only item offered up on the altar that is not edible (unlike animals, grain, oil, and salt). While oil becomes part of the grain offering itself, the frankincense remains distinct from the flour-oil mixture.[79] Thus, some conclude that the frankincense is not actually part of the grain offering, but rather serves a distinct purpose: to consecrate the grain offering to God. When the offering serves as atonement, it already has a defined purpose and there is no need for any consecration, but freewill offerings must be connected to the sphere of sanctity. Those who favor this theory liken the addition of frankincense to the laying of the hands in the burnt offering.[80] I find this idea questionable, especially as the problem remains: Why is the addition of frankincense an acceptable substitution for the worshipper laying hands upon an animal offering in a symbolic act of transferral?
2. Mitigating the smell of the offerings: Similarly to Rambam's position that incense was burned to mitigate the unpleasant odors

79. Rendtorff surmises that frankincense was not added to the actual grain because the priests eat the remainder, and frankincense is not edible (Rendtorff, *Leviticus*, 98). He also adds that the amount (which is not specified) must be small, given that only a handful of grain is offered up (ibid., 97–98). Nonetheless, there are no amounts given for any of the ingredients at all in the biblical text – not even how much grain must be offered.

80. Budd, *Leviticus*, 58.

of animal slaughter, blood and flesh (*Guide for the Perplexed,* III:45), some propose that the addition of frankincense serves the same purpose.[81] While frankincense is indeed used for its smell, as will emerge below, it makes little sense that the addition is mandated in grain offerings rather than animal offerings. Indeed,proponents of this theory are compelled to add that the priests would also scatter fragrant leaves on the altar to improve the smell,[82] an unlikely embellishment which has no basis in the text.

3. Smoke production: Others suggest that the addition of frankincense increases the smoke: "The frankincense is added to increase the amount of smoke produced by the offering, thus rendering the burning rite more impressive."[83] This explanation does justify the addition of frankincense to grain offerings rather than animal offerings, which produce far more smoke, yet the choice of this specific ingredient seems unlikely: Other plants are known for their smoke-raising properties, such as *Leptadenia pyrotechnica,*[84] but frankincense is not among them.
4. "A Sweet Savor": The most likely reason for the addition of frankincense seems to be related to its most obvious feature: its scent. Unlike the second suggestion, which links its use to the mitigation of unpleasant odors, I believe that its significance should be formulated differently.

Frankincense is celebrated throughout Tanakh for its fragrance: "Perfumed with myrrh and frankincense more fragrant than all the merchants' powders" (Song. 3:6; see also 4:6, 14, and many others). It is one of the most important ingredients in the ritual incense: "The Lord said to Moses, 'Take sweet spices: stacte, onycha, galbanum, and equal measures of frankincense and make them into incense'" (Ex. 30:34). The

81. Watts, *Leviticus,* 242.
82. Haran, "Uses of Incense," 113.
83. Eberhart, "Burning Rite," 113.
84. The Sages saw utmost importance in the addition of a smoke-raising herb; this issue was even the basis of a harsh dispute between the Sadducees and Pharisees. See Luria, "Maaleh Ashan."

formulation implies that the amount of frankincense is equal to all the other ingredients put together (this is Rashbam's reading); if so, "frankincense is not merely one of the spices, but the main ingredient of the incense."[85] This is presumably the reason that frankincense is used: to add fragrance to the grain offering.

This is even more likely given that scent is considered a key aspect of the sacrificial world. When Noah brings sacrifices to God after the Flood, "the Lord smelled the fragrant aroma and said in His heart, 'Never again will I curse the land because of man'" (Gen. 8:21).[86] Reconciliation between the human and the Divine is expressed through the smell of Noah's offerings. In curses and prophetic reproach, too, scent is instrumental: "I will turn your cities into ruins and make your sanctuaries desolate. I will not savor your sweet savors" (Lev. 26:31); "I have hated, I have loathed your holiday sacrifices, and I will not take in the scent of your festival offerings" (Amos 5:21). R. Tzadok of Lublin concludes his book *Tzidkat HaTzaddik* thus: "The secret of all offerings lies in none but their scent."

The phrase "*re'aḥ niḥoaḥ*," "pleasing aroma" or "sweet savor," is a key term in the sacrificial chapters, and producing this aroma seems to be the ultimate purpose of offerings. To be precise, the term "sweet savor" is a key term in freewill offerings; it does not feature in obligatory offerings brought for atonement (with one exception: the individual purification offering – 4:31 – which will be discussed below). Freewill offerings express closeness and conciliation (as do communal offerings like the daily burnt offering and additional offerings on festivals).[87]

This brings us to the next stage: What is the nature of this "sweet savor"? Onkelos reads this metaphorically: "An offering is received with favor before God." Rashi, too, attempts to avoid the personification of

85. Cassuto, *Exodus*, 280.
86. As discussed in the introduction, these verses are sometimes described as the most extreme instance of God's personification in Tanakh. Even so, when compared with parallel accounts from other Ancient Near Eastern cultures, the disparity between the gods who "need" the people's offerings and God's enjoyment of their scent is clear; as Sarna notes, the Torah clarifies that God doesn't actually *need* Noah's offerings (Sarna, *Understanding Genesis*, 54).
87. Compare to Abarbanel's question on Lev. 6:7.

God: "A sweet savor – It is gratifying for Me that I spoke and My will was carried out" (on Num. 28:8).[88] However, even if the language is metaphorical, it is still rooted in reality. Roasting raw meat upon the fire produces a rich, mouthwatering, aroma. Noah's animal offering yields a "sweet savor."[89] It makes sense that "parts that are roasted before they are placed upon the altar do not produce a sweet savor" (Rambam, *Hilkhot Maaseh HaKorbanot* 6:4), for it is roasting that creates this delicious smell; burning meat that has already been cooked produces a burning smell.

But if roasting meat is what produces this delicious smell, then how can a "sweet savor" be achieved with freewill grain offerings? The smell of burning flour mixed with oil cannot be considered a "sweet savor." This, then, is why frankincense is added to the fine flour offering – to give the offering the requisite "sweet savor."[90] This explains why frankincense is part of grain offerings but not animal offerings, where the "sweet savor" is produced by the aroma of the roasting meat. Moreover, this idea is supported by the biblical specification that frankincense should not be added to the poor person's purification offering (Lev. 5:11),[91] whose purpose is to achieve atonement, not to produce a "sweet savor." It is also understandably absent from the wayward wife's offering. Just as there is no mention of a "sweet savor" in regard to the animal and bird

88. The commentators' concern about personification based on this phrase is also expressed by R. Saadia Gaon and Rambam. See further in Marwil, "A Soothing Savor."
89. The delicious smell of meat is also referred to in other ancient cultures; see the Egyptian threat against the gods that they will no longer enjoy the smell of meat (*ANET*, 327) and the Aramean instructions how to offer sacrifices to the gods: "Set the offerings upon the fire… send forth a sheep, make an abundant good smell to Baal" (as translated by Richard Steiner in Hallo, *Context of Scripture*, 314).
90. This understanding of the purpose of the incense illuminates Rambam's explanation that "the handful and frankincense are like the blood and the offered parts of the sacrifice" (on Mishna Menaḥot 1:3).
91. Kellerman argues that frankincense is not added to the poor person's purification offering because its cost might deter the poor person from bringing an offering (Kellerman, "Frankincense," 445), but I believe that frankincense is simply not relevant to a purification offering, whose purpose is atonement.

purification offerings, frankincense is not added to grain purification offerings either.

The Absence of Frankincense from Cooked Grain Offerings

If frankincense is added to produce a "sweet savor," why isn't it mentioned in cooked grain offerings? The answer is that baked and fried grain offerings, browned in the cooking process, produce a "sweet savor" of their own,[92] so there is no need for the addition of frankincense.[93]

This apparently technical difference reflects the fundamental difference between the different kinds of grain offerings: Cooked grain offerings are ready to eat and inherently appealing, whereas the fine flour offering consists of raw ingredients that do not have a naturally pleasing aroma. Flour is used to make food, but it is not yet food. To employ anthropologist Claude Lévi-Strauss's terminology, we might say that the fine flour offering represents the "raw" – the wild and natural – whereas the *cooked* grain offerings represent culture and civilization.

This may also illuminate the law of "presenting" the cooked grain offering to the altar: Because the cooking process creates its own "sweet savor," the priest immediately serves it up to the altar before this aroma dissipates, so it will not be lost during the sacrificial process.

To conclude this discussion, it is worth noting that there is one kind of baked grain offering that nonetheless does contain frankincense – the showbread: "Lay pure incense on each stack, as a remembrance for the bread, as a fire offering to the Lord" (Lev. 24:7). Even the dispute as to precisely where the incense is laid so that it will serve as a "remembrance"[94]

92. While leaven bread smells even more delicious, the baking or frying of unleavened dough still produces a good enough smell for sacrificial purposes. See further in Grossman, "Frankincense."

93. Weinfeld believes that the phrase "sweet savor" derives from the libations that accompany all offerings (Weinfeld, "Afternoon Prayer"; "Minḥa"), but this is not convincing.

94. See further in Noordtzij, *Leviticus*, 243; Milgrom, *Leviticus*, vol. 2, 2098; Hartley, *Leviticus*, 401.

raises the question: What is the relationship between the frankincense and the showbread?[95]

Essentially, however, the showbread is no exception to the aforementioned rules established in Leviticus 2. Even though baked loaves produce their own "sweet savor," frankincense is necessary here because the leaven showbread could not be offered up upon the altar to convey this aroma to God. Thus, in this case, the frankincense is burned in place of the showbread itself.[96] There is reason to question whether the frankincense that accompanied the showbread was actually offered up on the inner incense altar instead of the outer sacrificial altar.[97] The unique specification for "pure frankincense" in this context perhaps encourages this reading, even though the "sweet savor" is usually associated with the outer sacrificial altar, as in the phrase "fire offering to the Lord."[98]

In conclusion, the purpose of frankincense is to produce a "sweet savor to the Lord" in offerings that do not produce this sweet savor on their own.

BURNT OFFERING – GRAIN OFFERING – PEACE OFFERING

The above analysis of the two models of grain offering invites further exploration of the order of freewill offerings in *Parashat Vayikra*. As mentioned, burnt and peace offerings represent two different religious mindsets. The burnt offering conveys sacrifice, self-effacement, and the sense of human inadequacy in the face of the eternal Divine; a way to seek closeness when one is feeling distant. In contrast, as we will see below, the peace offering is a way to reach out to God from a place of joy and celebration. The exaltation of the peace offering is vastly different from the apologetic supplication of the burnt offering.

95. See further in Rendtorff, *Studien*, 185–87. Note that he expresses a different opinion in his commentary on Leviticus (*Leviticus*, 100).
96. Some argue that this was a polemic to prevent the anthropomorphizing of God; incense replaced bread so that it would not seem like God needs the offering of food (Gayne, "Bread of the Presence"). Even if this is correct, however, note that the showbread is not actually offered on the altar anyway.
97. Milgrom, *Leviticus*, vol. 2, 2098.
98. As rightly pointed out by Knobel, *Leviticus*, 554.

The grain offering is situated between these two offerings. Given that it consists of grain, whereas the burnt and peace offerings are animal offerings, chapter 2 seems to have been positioned between Leviticus 1 and 3. From a psychological perspective, however, the grain offering is set in its rightful place.

We saw that there are two kinds of grain offering. The first is the fine flour offering, which is fundamentally similar to the burnt offering in that the entire offering is consecrated to the altar (even if the altar then allocates part of this offering to the priests afterward). The bringer of the fine flour offering humbly offers up their daily bread to the One who provides them with all their needs; they are submissive, like the bringer of the burnt offering. Thereafter, however, the Torah moves on to cooked grain offerings. Although they are also considered grain offerings, the unique use of the second person expresses the personal nature of these offerings. It is up to the bringer to decide how the grain offering should be cooked, based on their personal preference. They are not bringing raw material and passing it on to the priests; rather, they are preparing the offering themselves. From this perspective, the cooked grain offering is closer in nature to the peace offering that follows.

Yet the grain offering is not merely a technical bridge from the burnt offering to the peace offering; it is a conceptual bridge that facilitates this transition. I wish to tentatively propose that it is the focus on one's everyday material needs, rather than contemplating life itself, that allows the worshipper to bridge the unfathomable gap between the flawed ephemeral human and the perfect eternal Divine. Focus on the source of one's sustenance and livelihood averts any sense of estrangement from God, for it is God who provides His creations with their needs. It is God who enables and desires the human's life and existence.

Thus, there are two kinds of freewill animal offerings: One expresses the human's sense of alienation and distance from God, while the other expresses the friendship and love between them. In parallel, there are also two respective models of grain offering that are in dialogue with the two kinds of freewill animal offering.

"APPENDIXES": LEAVEN, HONEY, SALT

Two "appendixes" are added after the description of the cooked grain offerings: the prohibitions against leaven grain offerings and the addition of honey, and the obligation to add salt to every offering. These are followed by a discussion of the *minḥat bikkurim,* the grain offering of first produce. The prohibition against leaven also touches upon the laws of what the priests may eat. As mentioned, the cooked grain offering is like a portion of food, so details like leaven or salt, which are usually included in the context of the laws of eating offerings, are also relevant here, because it is as if the altar is receiving a portion of food from the worshipper.

The Prohibition Against Leaven and Honey

> No grain offering that you bring to the Lord shall be made with leaven, for no leaven or honey may be used in a fire offering to the Lord, sent up in smoke. You may bring them as offerings of first produce to the Lord, but they may not be offered on the altar as a sweet savor. (2:11–12)

Ancient peoples – especially the Egyptians and Hittites – offered up leaven bread upon the altar. The Hittite daily offering was served with bread and wine.[99] In this context, the ancient Israelite custom was unique. The biblical placement of this prohibition after the laws of the cooked grain offerings is appropriate, given that they raise the most concern of contamination of the altar with leaven. Even though these offerings symbolize food, they are brought as unleavened offerings, not as foods in their usual leavened form. Yet, if these verses are read along with the verses in *Parashat Tzav,* then they are relevant to the fine flour offering as well, for even the portion given to the priests may not be baked as leaven loaves: "It shall not be baked with any leaven. I have given it as their portion of My fire offerings" (6:10).

The Midrash Halakha also clarifies that the remaining portion may not be baked as leaven (*Sifra,* Freewill Offerings, 12:1). The verse is

99. Weinberg, *Sacrifice in Israel,* 113.

ambiguous: "No grain offering that you bring to the Lord shall be made with leaven, for no leaven or honey may be used in a fire offering to the Lord, sent up in smoke" (2:11). This could mean that only the remembrance burned upon the altar must not contain leaven. In fact, there is a general impression that everything burned upon the altar must not contain leaven, but that this does not necessarily apply to the portion given to the priests: "No grain offering that you bring to the Lord shall be made with leaven."[100] Yet the *Sifra* establishes that this is not the case, emphasizing that this prohibition applies to the priestly portion as well. This is, after all, explicitly stated in *Parashat Tzav*: "It shall not be baked with any leaven. I have given it as their portion of My fire offerings" (6:10). Because their portion comes from the altar, it is included in the prohibition against using leaven.[101]

It is worth pointing out that even in offerings that are accompanied by loaves of leavened bread (such as those that accompany the peace offering or the two-loaf offering), the bread itself is not offered up upon the altar, which remains leaven-free all year long. The prohibition against honey is perhaps similar: Nothing sweet, including first fruits, is actually offered up upon the altar; first fruits are merely waved and given to the priest, but "they may not be offered upon the altar" (2:12).

Before we delve into a discussion about these prohibitions, I wish to first define what "honey" actually means. On the one hand, there are several reasons to assume that this refers to regular honey made by bees, which was used to sweeten dough and help it rise. More importantly, however, bee honey was used in pagan sacrifice,[102] so the biblical prohibition may have been instituted in order to challenge this practice.

Another possible reading, however, is that this verse refers to honeyed fruits. This is likely given that the next verse discusses the offerings of

100. This also clarifies why the command addresses the priests in the plural form (as noted by Ramban and Milgrom, *Leviticus*, vol. 1, 188), as they are the ones who burn the offering upon the altar.

101. On the debate whether the priest's portion of meat also requires salt, see Kasher, *Torah Shelema*, vol. 25, 312–15.

102. Hoffner, "ob"; Rooker, *Leviticus*, 98.

first produce, which are not actually offered up upon the altar; they are merely waved and given to the priests (Deut. 26).[103]

Some extend this prohibition to mean anything sweet. The Netziv, for example, argues that the Torah rejects adding any kind of sweetener to offerings; he is correct that honey is sometimes used as a generic term for sweetness (e.g., Prov. 24:13). In contrast, Rashbam restricts this prohibition solely to dates: "The fruits of the date palm are called 'honey.'" In Chronicles, dates are indeed referred to by the word "honey" (II Chr. 31:5).[104] Nonetheless, the most likely reading – which is also the most accepted – is that this prohibition includes all sweet, juicy fruits: "All sweet fruits are called 'honey'" (Rashi on 2:11). What does this sweetness represent?

This brings us to the prohibition against adding leaven or honey to offerings. Why are honey and leaven mentioned together? There are three possible explanations:

1. The two prohibitions are completely separate, but they are mentioned together for technical reasons. If the prohibition against adding honey is indeed a separate issue, it makes sense to extend it to include its addition to the incense mixture, as Bar Kappara indeed does in the *baraita* of *Pittum HaKetoret*: "Were they to have added a dab of honey, no one would have been able to resist its scent. So why did they not mix any honey into it? Because it says in the Torah: No leaven or honey may be used in a fire offering to the Lord." This is also clear to Ramban, who challenges Rashi's interpretation that *nataf*, one of the ingredients of the incense, was a mixture called "theriac" (see Rashi on Ex. 30:34), and writes: "Heaven forbid that there should be in the incense the flesh of forbidden animals and reptiles, leaven and honey, for it is written: 'No leaven or honey may be used in a

103. Similarly, *Siftei Ḥakhamim*. For linguistic evidence from other Semitic languages that biblical honey refers to fruit nectar, see Milgrom, *Leviticus*, vol. 1, 189.

104. Ibn Ezra (on Lev. 2:11) writes: "Many say that it means date honey, including in the phrase 'a land flowing with milk and honey,' and this is proven in the book of Ezra." He is presumably referring to the aforementioned verse from Chronicles.

fire offering to the Lord'" (Ramban on Ex. 30:34). Ramban also applies this prohibition to the addition of honey to the incense. If honey represents something negative, it makes sense that what may not be added to the outer altar should not be added to the inner incense altar as well.[105] Abarbanel notes that the Torah takes care to prohibit the use of fruit honey, given that four of the Seven Species are already used in the grain offering (wheat, barley, grapes, olive oil): "Thus,we might have thought that it was fitting to offer up the remaining of the Seven Species" (figs, dates, and pomegranates).

2. Honey and leaven might be two different forms of the same problematic issue. Rambam, for example, argues that both honey and leaven were widely used in pagan sacrifice, so the Torah forbids both these elements. An even more striking example of this approach is the Tosafot's claim that both honey and leaven are forbidden because neither of them is a suitable accompaniment to salt, which must be added to every offering. The sweetness of honey overrides its saltiness, and fermentation is inhibited by salt. This may be read on a more symbolic level: Both leaven and honey represent a negative quality forbidden by the Torah.
3. The connection between honey and leaven may be an even deeper one, to the extent that the prohibitions against them are considered as the same prohibition and for the same reasons. Ibn Ezra asserts that a grain offering may become fermented by the addition of either leaven or honey. If so, then the prohibition against honey is simply part of the prohibition against using leaven upon the altar.[106] According to this approach, the description of the "grain offering of first produce" refers only to the Shavuot two-loaf offering, not to *bikkurim*, the first fruits; this verse is concerned with the prohibition against leaven upon

105. Of course, even if there is an inherent connection between the prohibitions against honey and leaven, Ramban can still extend the relevant prohibition to the incense, even if leaven is not relevant. Nevertheless, the fact that one prohibition is expanded but not the other emphasizes this divergence.
106. Rambam defines the prohibitions against leaven and honey as a single law (*Hilkhot Issurei HaMizbe'aḥ* 5:1); however, Raavad and Ramban disagree.

> the altar, not with bringing fruits to the Sanctuary. The word "*attem*," "them," in the verse must refer to the aforementioned grain offerings,[107] so that the verse actually reads: "No grain offering that you bring to the Lord may be made with leaven, [except for] the offerings of first produce, [but even those] may not be offered on the altar for a sweet savor."

Although it is difficult to decide between these readings, Ibn Ezra's is most consistent with the context, given that the topic at hand is grain offerings, and one more kind is mentioned after the prohibition against leaven. Thus, the relevant discussion is of leaven, which is relevant to grain offerings made of dough, rather than honey, which is less relevant in context.

THE PROHIBITION AGAINST LEAVEN

Why is it forbidden to offer leaven upon the altar? Animal offerings must be from healthy, unblemished animals; similarly, perhaps, we might expect that grain offerings should be the best, most delicious, round, and golden of loaves. There are several theories as to why this is not the case:

1. Against idolatry: Rambam (*Guide for the Perplexed,* III:46) perceives the prohibition against leaven as a polemic against ancient pagan offerings of leaven bread – often served with honey, but not salt. This is reflected in Ezekiel's harsh prophecy against the people who used God's gift of abundance for idolatry: "The food I had given you – the fine flour, oil, and honey I fed you – you set before them as a sweet savor" (Ezek. 16:19). There is also evidence in Egyptian, Babylonian, and Ugaritic texts that honey was added to offerings. Honey was considered "the tears of the Egyptian god Ra," often offered up with grain and butter.[108] While the nations offered up sweet, delectable loaves as food for the gods, the biblical unleavened, unsweetened matzot can be regarded as a statement that God does not actually eat Israel's

107. Milgrom, *Leviticus*, vol. 1, 190.

108. See Hartley, *Leviticus*, 33; Caquot, "Devash," 130.

offerings. This also explains why the prohibition against offering leaven and honey are mentioned together.[109]

2. Transformation of the Raw Material: Various scholars claim that the prohibition is based on the fundamental change of the raw material. Adding leaven or honey to fine flour alters the nature of the raw material to a completely different state. According to this approach, matza and bread are two definitively different products; fermentation changes the former to the latter.[110]

   This may be the basis of Rabbeinu Bahya's kabbalistic explanation that leaven and honey hint to leaven being *middat hadin*, the attribute of strict justice: "*Because their nature changes* they are kept away from the altar" (on Lev. 2:11). He begins by explaining that offerings are offered up in the name of the Tetragrammaton rather than to the name "God," which represents strict justice, and because leaven represents this attribute, it is not brought to the altar (see also Ramban on 2:11).

   The Netziv also favors this approach, although he emphasizes the human intervention that brings about this change: "Given that leaven is added by people to change the nature of creation through human manipulation, the text warns that whoever wishes to come closer to God should keep human intervention to a minimum" (*Haamek Davar* on Lev. 2:11).

3. The Symbolism of Leaven: A third approach attempts to define the biblical associations of leaven. Rabbeinu Bahya, for example, explains:

   > Were there no evil inclination then there would be no sin nor any need for offerings. Leaven and honey are both symbols of the evil inclination... this is why they are both kept

109. In the "Ashur Temple," for example, these were the instructions to the priests: "The confectioners must take one *se'a* of honey, five liters of oil, and four *se'a* of sesame. The bakers must take ten *ḥomer* of yeast for the bread, and five *ḥomer* of wheat for the 'Kaduto bread'" (Nissinen, *Prophets*, 166). Intriguingly, even though Mesopotamian texts show that milk was also added to grain offerings (see Nissinen, *Prophets*, 176), the Torah does not forbid this.

110. Wenham's suggestion that only dead things may be offered upon the altar, but leaven is a living organism (Wenham, *Leviticus*, 71), is not convincing.

> away from the altar, for it does not make sense to have two opposites at once [i.e, the cause of sin and atonement for sin simultaneously], like someone immersing for purity while they hold something unclean in their hand.[111]
>
> R. Yoel Bin-Nun perceives leaven as the symbol of someone confident and satisfied who is at the end of a complete process. Therefore, he explains, leaven is sometimes appropriate: The thanksgiving offering or the two-loaf offering on the fiftieth day of the Omer, for example, celebrate the end of a process. But someone who stands before the altar is usually at the beginning or in the middle of a process, with some way to go.[112] Similarly, others suggest that leaven represents decay and death. Fermentation, after all, is a certain kind of rotting; at its peak, fermentation makes the bread tastier, but the raw material is in a state of decay, which is incompatible with the *tikkun* and life represented by the altar.[113]
>
> The historical aspect of leaven's symbolism is also relevant: The Ancient Egyptians were the inventors of leavened bread, so that bread is associated with Egypt, whereas the Torah sees "the exodus from Egypt" as an alternative culture.[114]

All the above readings have their advantages, nor are they contradictory. Given that certain offerings do have leaven (even if it is not actually offered up on the altar), the argument that leaven is inherently negative is problematic. In any case, leaven is not offered upon the altar, because it represents bread made for humans, not for God. The Shavuot two-loaf offering places special emphasis on the human, personal nature of the offering: "You shall bring two loaves *from your dwellings*" (Lev. 23:17). Leaven is not inherently bad, but it is inherently human. After all,

111. See also R. Yaakov bar Asher: "Because the evil inclination is like leaven. For this reason it also warns against honey, for the evil inclination seems as sweet as honey" (*Baal HaTurim* on Lev. 2:11).
112. Bin-Nun, "Ḥametz and Matza."
113. Bailey, *Leviticus*, 53.
114. Some also apply this to the prohibition against leaven on Passover; see Cohen, "*Hesed* and *Hamets.*"

bread is a symbol of human culture: "Bread is also an expression of the existence of developed culture ... the preparation of bread requires the use of special equipment, time for kneading, rising, and fermentation."[115] Sanctity is above human change and fermentation; for one week a year, Israel cleans their home from all leaven, creating a kind of sacred space.[116] Usually, however, leaven is simply a part of life – human life in the human sphere, but not when it comes to interaction with the eternal, unchanging sacred.

The Requirement to Add Salt

I have already noted that the additional laws at the end of Leviticus 2 are first and foremost related to the grain offering, even though they apply to other offerings as well. Does the requirement to add salt apply to all offerings or just the grain offering?

> You shall season all your grain offerings with salt; do not omit from your grain offering the salt of your covenant with God. You shall offer salt with all your offerings. (2:13)

Unlike the prohibition against adding leaven or honey, this is a requirement to add something to the grain offering – salt. As mentioned, the Tosafot point out that leaven and honey may not be added because they counter the effects of salt. I will shortly propose a different reading, but it is still worth pointing out that the Tosafot's interpretation revolves around the importance of adding salt to an offering.

While the prohibition against adding leaven or honey is expressed in the plural form – which suggests that it is primarily intended for the priests – the language of this commandment seems to address the individual worshipper. This is consistent with the fact that the prohibition against leaven and honey focuses upon the altar, the domain of the

115. As expressed by Motti Benmelech ("Baked"). It is generally assumed that bread was invented in Egypt; Benmelech views these verses as proof that they kept their recipe secret (which is why Potiphar does not allow Joseph to be responsible for "the bread he ate") and that bread is a symbol of Egyptian identity – in contrast to matza, which Benmelech defines as "anti-civilizational."

116. See further in Grossman, "Mannah and Passover."

priests, whereas salt is an important part of the offering's preparation, which, as discussed, is up to the individual.[117]

Given that the instruction to add salt only appears here, after both models of grain offering, it seems to be relevant to both. Why isn't it mentioned as part of the preparation for either kind of grain offering, together with the addition of oil, for example? It seems that salt is inherently an addition to the grain offering; while oil is an integral part of the grain offering, salt is a separate component. This certainly supports the theory that this law applies to all offerings, not just grain offerings.

The law of salt is presented in two stages. First: "You shall season all your grain offerings with salt." Then this law is extended to all offerings: "You shall offer salt with all your offerings." Rashi explains: "All your offerings – burnt offerings from animal and bird, and the portions of all sacrifices that are offered up on the altar." Ezekiel 43:24 also mandates that salt must be added to all burnt offerings.[118] However, there is room to debate whether this reading is necessary; one possibility is that this law applies only to grain offerings, and that the phrase "all your offerings" is a repetition of the law of grain offerings.[119]

Intriguingly, even though the Sages rule that salt must be added to all offerings, there is still a certain disparity between the level of obligation that applies to grain offerings and that of all other offerings:

> One who brings an offering without any salt is liable for lashes, as it says: "Do not omit from your grain offering the salt of your covenant with God." Even though he is liable for lashes, the offering is still valid and accepted, except in the case of the grain offering. (Rambam, *Hilkhot Issurei HaMizbe'aḥ* 5:12)

117. Unlike the above, the *Sifra* declares that "the salt is from the communal fund" (Freewill Offerings, 14:5), which is incompatible with the idea that salt is defined as part of the offering itself, for if so the worshipper should also pay for the salt; see further below.
118. See further in Kosman, "Salt," 28–29.
119. As proposed, for example, by Hartley, *Leviticus*, 32.

Although salt is a necessary addition to every offering, the lack of salt renders only grain offerings invalid. Ramban lists three possible explanations for this:

> [Rambam says] that the reason for salt is because [idol worshippers] will never use salt on their offerings. But it may be because it is not respectful for God's bread to be tasteless, without salt, as in "Offer that, if you will, to your governor" (Mal. 1:8) – for that reason there is no need to salt the [altar] wood or blood, for they are not edible (Menaḥot 20a). Or it may be that there is another reason that is hidden from us. (Ramban on 2:11)

Ramban first cites Rambam's explanation that this law is a polemic against pagan sacrifices, which never included salt.[120] We will discuss his second suggestion below. His third theory, that there is some kind of mystical explanation for adding salt, invites a more symbolic reading (he himself hints to its meaning in the next verses).[121] The key to understanding its possible symbolism can be found in the mysterious expression "You shall not omit (*tashbit*) the salt of your covenant with God." There are two striking aspects of this verse. The first is the verb "omit," *tashbit*. Not only is it obligatory to add salt to offerings, it must not be omitted. The only other instance of this form of the verb is found in relation to removing all leaven before Passover: "By the first day you shall have removed (*tashbitu*) leaven from your houses" (Ex. 12:15). This certainly generates a connection between the two different prohibitions regarding leaven; it also recalls the Tosafot's theory that the prohibition against leaven is profoundly linked to the addition of salt.

An even more surprising phrase is the "covenant of salt," especially when compared to the other instances of the word "covenant" in the Torah, such as the Rainbow Covenant, the Covenant Between the Pieces,

120. Today, we do know of the use of salt in pagan ritual, as shown by Latham, *Salt*, 29–42. Kosman proposes that Rambam's interpretation is derived from the Greek philosopher and historian Plutarch (Kosman, "Salt," 37–38).

121. On other symbolic associations of salt (Philo, Netziv, *Sefat Emet*, and more), see Kosman, "Salt."

the Covenant of Circumcision, the Sinai Covenant, and the covenant of Shabbat. What does "a covenant of salt" mean?

Ramban writes:

> The reason for this is because salt is derived from water, and it is through the power of the sun which shines upon it that it becomes salt. Now the nature of water is that it soaks into the earth and makes it bring forth and bud; but after it becomes salt it destroys every place and burns it, "nothing planted, nothing sprouting." Since a covenant is inclusive of all attributes, water and fire come into it...just like salt which seasons all foods and helps to preserve them, but destroys them when they are over-saturated with it. Thus,salt is like the covenant. (Ramban on Lev. 2:13)

According to Ramban, salt represents the convergence of water and sun/fire. A small amount of this potent substance adds flavor to food, but too much salt is ruinous. This quality thus represents the power of the covenant. This reading is supported by the two other biblical instances of this phrase, neither of which has anything to do with actual salt:

1. The covenant of priesthood given to Aaron and his descendants: "All the sacred gifts that the Israelites raise up to the Lord I give to you, your sons, and your daughters as an everlasting statute. It is an everlasting covenant of salt before the Lord, for you and for your descendants" (Num. 18:19).
2. The covenant of kingship given to David: "You certainly know that the Lord, God of Israel, gave kingship over Israel to David forever, to him and his sons as a covenant of salt" (II Chr. 13:5).

Ramban also mentions these verses and perceives them as an extension of the law of salt in Leviticus: Because the addition of salt to offerings is viewed as an expression of covenant, salt itself is a symbol of covenant. I wish to formulate this similarly: Salt represents eternity, stability, and permanence. A "covenant of salt" is thus a permanent, eternal covenant with God. The covenants of priesthood and kingship are both described with the word "*olam*," "eternal" or "forever." Salt never spoils. Note that there is emphasis on *God giving* both covenants: of priesthood and kingship. A "covenant of salt" is therefore an eternal covenant with God.

This brings us back to the requirement of adding salt to offerings and allows us to construe it as a concrete expression of an eternal covenant. The sacrificial world gives physical expression to metaphysical concepts: Every single offering must have a sprinkling of God's eternal covenant with Israel. Moreover, this explains the prohibition: "Do not omit from your grain offering the salt of your covenant with God." This everlasting covenant must be perpetuated through every sacrifice. Since the priests' portion of the grain offering is given to them directly from the altar, this symbolic association is especially apt in this context.[122]

If salt is more than just a flavor enhancer – if it is, indeed, a symbol of the covenant – this also explains why the Sages rule that salt must also be added to the bowls of frankincense that accompany the show-bread (Menaḥot 20a), even though they are not edible. Because they are offered upon the altar, they must also commemorate the covenant. This illuminates a further halakha: Although the biblical text implies that the worshipper is the one who must add salt to their grain offering, the Sages teach that this salt is funded by the public. The *Sifra* debates who must fund this salt and eventually concludes that it indeed comes from public funds (*Sifra*, Freewill Offerings, 14:5–6). If salt were added merely to improve the offering's flavor, the worshipper responsible for baking or frying the grain would also be responsible for its taste. Given, however, that salt symbolizes the covenant of God's perpetual glory resting in the Sanctuary, it is fitting that this symbol should be funded by the public to emphasize that God's presence rests among the united, collective people of Israel.[123]

As mentioned, however, there is room to question whether salt must be added to all offerings or just grain offerings. Although the Sages extend this to all offerings, it still remains questionable why the

122. See especially in Seebass, "Berit." He believes that the verses in Numbers reveal the true meaning of the phrase, which is a gift of food from God to the priests. I agree that these are the correct connotations, but it is not the phrase's primary meaning.

123. See also Marcus, "Salt." He points out additional halakhot that are clarified through the fundamental question of whether the purpose of salt is to represent God's covenant or to improve the offerings' flavor.

symbol of Israel's eternal bond with God is associated with grain offerings in particular.

Baruch Levine suggests that the requisite addition of salt is mentioned in the least obvious context. Salt is obviously added to animal offerings (to help remove the blood, as in the laws of koshering meat), but one might think that there is no need to do so in grain offerings. For this reason, the Torah states this law in regard to grain offerings.[124]

A more straightforward reading, however, is the opposite: Adding salt makes the most (and not the least) sense in grain offerings. Out of all possible suggestions, Ramban's second explanation is the most likely explanation of the law's *context*.

Ramban's second explanation (which we omitted earlier) is that the addition of salt renders the offering worthy of eating. Food is almost always seasoned with salt;[125] so too, offerings are only fit for the altar after they have been salted (Ibn Ezra and Rambam write similarly).[126] Unlike frankincense, salt is an essential part of food and eating; this explanation is implied from salt's most obvious association.

This brings us to a surprising connection between the ostensibly mundane idea of what makes food delicious and the eternal, divine concept of "the salt of your covenant with God."[127] Salt is added to offerings for the simple reason pointed out by Ramban: It makes food "good enough to eat" and, therefore, to offer upon the altar. Yet given the unchanging, stable nature of salt, the Torah utilizes this seemingly mundane law and charges it with the intensity of Israel's eternal covenant with God. This connection is not purely aesthetic or superficial: The simple act of preparing a grain offering and seasoning it to taste is an act of love, an

124. Levine, *Leviticus*, 13.

125. The addition of salt to food is so significant that the word "salad" is derived from "salt." In the ancient world, vegetables were often salted and preserved. Other testament to its importance is that Roman soldiers were sometimes paid with salt – hence the word "salary."

126. Rambam in *Sefer HaMitzvot*, negative commandment 99.

127. Ehrlich claims that the phrase "the salt of your covenant with God" refers to the unique, paradoxical nature of salt: "Its actual flavor is bad, but it improves the flavor of everything it is added to, and who is wise enough to understand this?" It is in this way that he reads the verse: "Salt – who has a covenant with your God – shall not be omitted from your grain offering" (Ehrlich, *Mikrâ ki-Pheschutô*, 212).

act of closeness, an act that declares, like someone preparing food for their family or friends, that they want to bring delight and pleasure to the one they are feeding. Thus,these associations of love and closeness are surprisingly, profoundly poured into the covenantal language and symbolism associated with salt. Salt's ordinary purpose is to improve flavor and add savor, but here it is utilized as a vehicle for the eternal covenant reflected through the sacrificial world, by the offering a person brings to God.

Ramban's second explanation emphasizes the grain offering's profound connection to food. As I discussed at the beginning of this chapter, unlike animal offerings, the grain offering represents a person's basic, daily needs; the livelihood God grants them; the sustenance they offer up to the altar in acknowledgment, appreciation, and prayer for continual provision. The addition of salt – which, according to Ramban, serves to improve the grain offering's flavor – underscores the nature of this offering: "Who can stomach unsalted food?!" (Job 6:6).

It is no coincidence that the grain offering comprises different ingredients (grain, oil, salt, and frankincense), whereas animal offerings are only flesh (unless we adopt the reading that all offerings must include salt). An animal offering is a pure, straightforward, simple offering that represents life itself, while the multi-ingredient grain offering represents the various, more complex needs of humanity.

THE OFFERING OF FIRST PRODUCE (*MINḤAT BIKKURIM*)

> If you bring a grain offering of first produce to the Lord,
> it shall be brought as soon as it ripens on the stalk. Barley roasted in fire, crushed from fresh kernels; thus shall you bring the grain offering of first produce.
> You shall put oil and incense on it; it is a grain offering.
> The priest shall send its remembrance up in smoke – some of the crushed new grain and oil together with all of the incense – as a fire offering to the Lord. (Lev. 2:14–16)

For some reason, after the appendixes to the grain offerings – the prohibition against leaven and the requirement to add salt – another kind of grain offering is introduced (*im*). This is referred to as "the grain offering of first produce," and it differs from the aforementioned grain offerings in several respects. The main difference is that other grain offerings are from wheat, whereas this is from barley.[128] The reason for this is that barley ripens before wheat, and this is a grain offering of "first produce."[129] This results in a further difference: The new grain is crushed, not ground into fine flour.

Opinions differ as to the meaning of the expression "first produce."[130] There are various offerings of "first produce" (first fruits, firstborn animals, firstborn sons). Moreover, Leviticus 23 explores the first of the wheat crop in depth: the waving of the *omer* and the two-loaf offering fifty days later. What, then, is the difference between this "grain offering of first produce" and the more familiar *bikkurim* later on in Leviticus? There are two completely polarized readings of these verses.

The Sages read these verses as the *omer* grain offering.[131] Indeed, Leviticus 23 does not instruct what must be done with the grain after it has been waved:

> Speak to the Israelites. Say: When you come to the land that I am giving you and reap its harvest, bring the first sheaf of your harvest to the priest. He shall wave the sheaf this way and that

128. See *Sifra*, Freewill Offerings, 13:4, and Rashi there. Only this offering and the *sota* grain offering are from barley; all others are of wheat. Moreover, only these two offerings are both waved and offered to the altar (Rambam, *Hilkhot Maaseh Ha-Korbanot* 12:6). The rest of the laws of this grain offering are presumably the same as for all other grain offerings (as per Rambam, *Hilkhot Temidin UMusafin* 7:12).
129. The text emphasizes the unique aspect of this offering through an *inclusio*: "If you offer a grain offering of first produce / offer your grain offering of first produce," which emphasizes the unique content: "Roasted by fire, crushed from fresh kernels."
130. My student, Asaf Steinberger, pointed out to me that the semantic purpose of the word "*bikkurim*" here is not clear. "The *morning* grain offering" (Ex. 29:41) refers to *when* it is offered; "the grain offering *prepared in a pan*" obviously refers to *how* it is prepared. What does "*minḥat bikkurim*" mean here? Is it offered during the time of the *bikkurim*? Is it brought from the first of the produce? Is it prepared the same way as *bikkurim* are?
131. *Sifra*, Freewill Offerings, 13:4; see also Mishna Menaḥot 10:4. Flavius Josephus also explained accordingly in *Antiquities of the Jews*, 3:10:5

> before the Lord for your acceptance; on the day after the day of rest the priest shall wave it. On the day you wave the sheaf this way and that, you shall offer a yearling sheep without blemish as a burnt offering to the Lord. Its grain offering shall be two-tenths of an ephah of fine flour mixed with oil, a fire offering for the Lord, a sweet savor; and its libation shall be a quarter of a *hin* of wine. (Lev. 23:10–13)

According to the Sages, Leviticus 2 completes the picture: The text describes how the *omer* must be roasted, crushed, and mixed with oil and then frankincense before a portion is removed and burned upon the altar as "a remembrance." This "grain offering of first produce" is an obligatory communal offering, and for some reason its laws are divided into two separate sections.[132]

Rashi also favors this reading: "If you bring – *When* you bring. "*Im*" is used in the sense of "*ki*," for this is not optional; it discusses the *omer* offering, which is obligatory" (on Lev. 2:14).[133] Given that this refers to the *omer* offering, the opening word "*im*," which usually means "if," means "when" here, because the *omer* offering is obligatory.[134] Rashbam is even more straightforward: "When you offer the *omer* offering."

Identifying this as the *omer* offering has broad implications. First and foremost, without the description in Leviticus 2, one may assume that the *omer* offering is waved but not actually offered up upon the altar. This is certainly feasible; not all offerings are actually burned upon the altar: The priest waves part of the peace offering and then keeps it as his own portion; for the Nazirite offering, "the priest shall take the boiled foreleg of the ram, one unleavened loaf from the basket, and one unleavened wafer, and place them on the hands of the Nazirite.... The priest shall wave them as a wave offering before the Lord" (Num. 6:19–20). He thus receives these offerings as a gift without placing them, and they never

132. Besides the *omer*, there are only two public grain offerings: the two-loaf offering on Shavuot and the showbread. Neither are offered up on the altar, presumably because they are leaven. (The Sages hold that they are not leaven, but this does not seem to be the case in the biblical text.)

133. Compare to what he says in the *Rashi Responsa*, section 251.

134. This is also expressed by Rabbeinu Tam, who is quoted in the Tosafot on Gittin 90a.

go near the altar. Aaron waves the actual priests as part of the consecration service (Num. 8:11). Most pertinent of all is the two-loaf offering of Leviticus 23, which is waved and not burned.[135] According to the Sages, however, part of the *omer* is offered upon the altar after being waved (Mishna Menaḥot 10:4).

Ibn Ezra, however, disagrees with this reading:

> Many say that the word "*im*" indicates an obligation, but I believe that there is no need for this explanation, for there is an obligation to bring the first of the grain and not the first grain. One who wishes to bring a meal offering from the first grain as a freewill offering may do so. (Ibn Ezra on 2:14)

Ibn Ezra believes that this grain offering is not the *omer* but a freewill offering, like the rest of the offerings in the chapter: the (optional) first grain of the individual farmer's crop, not the official, communal offering. The Netziv also favors this reading, even though he usually concurs with the halakhic midrash.[136]

If so, it remains to determine the law of the *omer* in Leviticus 23, which, as mentioned, does not discuss what to do with the *omer* after it has been waved. The prevalent explanation is that its law is identical to

135. Many commentators who do not agree with the Sages do believe that according to Leviticus 23, the *omer* is waved but not offered up. Michael Kochman, for example, writes: "The *omer* in our chapter is waved in a purely symbolic ceremony" (*Leviticus*, 163).

136. The *okimta* (specific case in which this law is relevant) that the Netziv explains is not convincing (he posits that this offering would actually be relevant if the Israelites in the desert would somehow have an *omer* of grain from the land of Israel). Nonetheless, his explanation still implies that this offering is voluntary, not obligatory. Shadal also perceives it as voluntary. This is also the prevalent reading in modern exegesis – see, for example, Haran, "Minḥa," 27; Licht, "Omer," 302; Paran, *Leviticus*, 23. Milgrom is the exception: He writes that the Sages may be correct in identifying this offering with the obligatory *omer* offering (Milgrom, *Leviticus*, vol. 1, 193), although he holds that Leviticus 2 is responding to Leviticus 23 (Milgrom, *Cultic Theology*, 148).

that of the two-loaf offering (Lev. 23:17–20), which is indeed waved and then given to the priest without any portion being burned upon the altar.[137]

There are therefore two points of dispute between the two readings: According to the Sages, this is an obligatory communal offering; according to Ibn Ezra, it is a voluntary individual offering.

On an initial view, the Sages' reading seems unlikely, for three main reasons:

1. The offering's opening phrase is "If (*im*) you offer," which implies choice. Rashi claims that this should be read as a chronological description – "*When* you offer" – but this seems unlikely, given that it is used in the sense of "if" throughout the first two chapters.[138] As R. Baruch Kehat adds, this is especially unlikely given that, as noted, the words "*ki/im*" are used to distinguish between categories and subcategories throughout these chapters.[139]
2. The offering's context implies that it is an individual offering, given that Leviticus's first chapters are entirely devoted to individual offerings[140] and that there is no textual hint that this indeed refers to the elaborate communal ritual that takes place "after seven complete weeks."
3. The use of the second person and its association with cooked grain offerings further reinforces Ibn Ezra's reading that this applies to the individual, not to the community.

Nonetheless, there are certain textual markers that support the Sages' reading. Radatz Hoffmann notes several affinities between this offering

137. Licht even proposes that the *omer* is waved and then returned to its owners, not offered up to a higher authority (to the priests or the altar); see Licht, *Festivals of Israel*, 156.

138. Here, Ramban's reading seems more likely. He adopts the Sages' reading that this is an obligatory offering, yet reads "*im*" in the sense of "when." He explains that each "*im*" in the chapter simply lists the laws of each new offering; thus, whether the offering is freewill or obligatory cannot be determined based on this word.

139. Kehat, "Bikkurim Offering," 4–6.

140. A separate discussion is required for the purification offering brought for a communal offense, which is not a communal offering in the usual sense of the term and therefore does not contradict the aforementioned rule.

and the *omer* offering. One point that warrants special attention is the similar language: "If you bring a grain offering of first produce to the Lord, it shall be brought as soon as it ripens (*karmel*) on the stalk. Roasted (*kalui*) in fire, crushed from fresh kernels" (2:14); "Until that day, until you bring this sacrifice to your God, you shall eat no bread or *roasted grain* (*kali*) or *ripe grain* (*karmel*)" (23:14). The *omer* is presumably brought from the produce that may not be used until the grain offering of first produce mentioned in Leviticus 2 is offered up.[141]

Essentially, the strange duplication between Leviticus 2 and 23 created by Ibn Ezra's reading serves to support the Sages' reading. Why would an individual need to bring his or her own offering of first produce, given the centrality of the communal offering of the fiftieth day? Would it occur to anyone to offer a daily burnt offering in addition to the communal daily burnt offering?

Above all, the structure of Leviticus 2 shows that the grain offering of first produce is not just another option in the list of grain offerings; it has its own special status. The laws of the individual grain offering have already been listed twice – separately for the fine flour offering and the cooked grain offering – and these are followed by general laws that apply to all grain offerings, so the offering of first produce is framed as a later addition. While these general laws certainly apply to the offering of first produce, the new introduction with its mention of God's name (2:14), which generally appears at the beginning of each new section (2:1), suggests that this is a new kind of grain offering, not just another variety of individual freewill offering.

Moreover, the literary design hints that something is missing in this section and should be completed elsewhere. There are two notable anomalies. The first is the text's silence about what is done with what remains of the grain offering:

141. Hoffmann, *Leviticus*, vol. 1, 113.

Fine Flour Offering	Cooked Grain Offering	Offering of First Produce
From this, the priest shall scoop out a handful of its fine flour and oil, together with all its incense, and send this remembrance up in smoke upon the altar as an offering of fire, a sweet savor to the Lord.	The priest shall lift a remembrance from the grain offering and send it up in smoke upon the altar as an offering of fire, a sweet savor to the Lord.	The priest shall send its remembrance up in smoke – some of the crushed new grain and oil together with all of the incense – as a fire offering to the Lord.
What remains of the grain offering shall belong to Aaron and his sons; it is holy of holies among the fire offerings to the Lord.	What remains of this grain offering shall belong to Aaron and his sons; it is holy of holies among the fire offerings to the Lord.	

A remembrance is burnt upon the altar, but what of the remains of the offering of first produce? The continuation is clearly lacking, but it does not appear here.

The second anomaly that encourages the Sages' reading is the absence of the phrase "a sweet savor to the Lord." Even though this offering contains incense, whose purpose is to raise "a sweet savor," the phrase is missing; this indicates that the offering in question is obligatory rather than voluntary.[142]

Thus, there is textual support for both readings, which, perhaps, allows us to hold the stick at both ends. Why is this offering listed separately at the end of the chapter? If it indeed refers to the *omer* offering, why doesn't it appear together with the description of the first part of the sacrificial process in Leviticus 23?[143] The answer, perhaps, is essen-

142. This does not serve as irrefutable proof, given that communal offerings sometimes include this phrase regarding obligatory offerings. Nonetheless, it supports the proposed reading that this offering is essentially a freewill individual offering from a thematic perspective.

143. Bula proposes that the law of this offering is similar to the laws of the freewill or vow fulfillment grain offerings, so it is first mentioned here (Bula, *Leviticus*, 41). Even if this explains why the offering is included here, it does not adequately explain its unique style of commandment, characteristic of a freewill offering.

tially and fundamentally that the grain offering of first produce ought to be an individual offering, just like the offering of first fruits described in Deuteronomy 26.

The farmer's first grain, however, is tied to a far more elaborate national ritual: the counting of the Omer, which begins and ends at a particular holy time. This count transcends the subjective, individual experience. But before the laws of the waving ritual are depicted in a national context in Leviticus 23, the laws of the remembrance for the altar are brought in Leviticus 2, in the second person – in the context of the individual freewill grain offerings – to express how each individual farmer ought to experience the communal offering of the *omer* on the fiftieth day. Although the offering is communal and linked to the national experience, the farmers must express their own individual gratitude for the renewal of their personal crop and sustenance in God's presence.

This complex idea is mirrored in Leviticus 23, which also hints to the individualistic aspects of this communal offering. First of all, there is no explicit statement that this is a communal offering,[144] and this ambiguity is certainly intentional. In addition, the individual, voluntary nature of this offering is hinted at through the surprising phrase "He shall wave the sheaf this way and that *at your will* (*lirtzonkhem*) before the Lord" (Lev. 23:11). As discussed in the context of Leviticus 1:3, this phrase may refer to God's acceptance or the human choice to offer up a sacrifice. In fact, the Sages use it as the source of the law that all offerings must be offered up freely.[145]

144. Kochman, *Leviticus*, 164. He prefers the reading that this an obligatory commandment for the individual. As I already noted, it can even be proposed that not only does the text discuss the individual's obligation, but after the priest waves the offering, the *omer* is returned to its owners (see Licht above). It is worth noting that in the parallel verses in Deuteronomy 16:9–12, both readings are possible.

145. Therefore, even if he is forced into it, he must say, "I want this": "Those who owe purification or guilt offerings – the court does not repossess their property; those who owe burnt and peace offerings – the court does repossess their property, even though they do not achieve atonement until they bring it of their own volition, as it says: 'Of his volition' – that is, they force him until he says 'I want this'" (Mishna Arakhin 5:6).

Given that this phrase expresses the worshipper's free will,[146] it is obvious why it does not appear in conjunction with obligatory offerings. If so, however, why it is mentioned in the context of the *omer* offering in Leviticus 23, which is a communal obligation?[147] This reflects the true essence of the *omer* offering: Fundamentally, it is brought as if by each and every individual farmer in Israel of their own free will.

This tension may have a bearing on the nature of the counting of the Omer. The Midrash Halakha specifies that each individual must count the Omer: "You shall count for yourselves (*usefartem lakhem*) – each individual."[148] This is certainly not obvious; the *Shemitta* cycle, for example, is not a mitzva for the individual, but a collective count, as the *Sifra* explains: "You shall count (*vesafarta lekha*) – in the *beit din*."[149] Ironically, the use of the plural form for the Omer teaches that it is a mitzva incumbent upon each individual, whereas the singular form of counting the *Shemitta* and Jubilee cycle refers to a collective obligation, not an individual one.

Given the collective obligatory nature of the *omer* offering, it is not at all obvious that counting the Omer is an obligation for the individual. The other extreme would be if counting the Omer were an individual mitzva leading up to an individual grain offering of first produce: Each farmer would begin counting as soon as the first of their grain begins to ripen (just as each person counts the days of their uncleanliness based on their own impure discharge, as described in Deuteronomy 16, for

146. Similarly, Malbim (on Lev. 1:3) and others. Some disagree; Onkelos's translation implies that this refers to God's favor, not a person's will, and many medieval and even modern commentators interpret thus. See this dispute in Hoffmann, *Leviticus*, vol. 1, 86–87.

147. Ibn Ezra indeed argues, based on this verse, that the word "*lirtzonekhem*" must refer to God's will, as it cannot mean human volition since this is an obligatory offering. However, we have discussed otherwise.

148. *Sifra, Emor,* 12:1; Menaḥot 65b.

149. *Sifra, Behar,* 2:1; see also Ramban on Lev. 23:15, who debates whether the *beit din* must make a blessing when counting. In this context, Ramban considers the Omer count in relation to communal counts such as the *Shemitta* cycle as well as personal counts such as the *zav* (impure discharge) counts. See also the Tosafot (on Ketubot 72a, s.v. "*vesafera*"), who rule that the *beit din* does make a blessing on counting the *Shemitta* cycle.

example). The Sages' ruling thus reflects a certain ambivalence: Everyone must count for himself, but everyone counts at the same time.[150] This also reflects the tension between each farmer's individual experience and the collective offering brought fifty days later in an expression of both personal and collective gratitude.[151]

Intriguingly, the Sages emphasize how individual farmers work together to harvest the *omer:*

> How would they perform [the *omer* harvest]?
> Emissaries of the court would go out on Passover Eve and arrange the barley into sheaves while the stalks were still attached to the ground, so that it would be convenient to reap them. All the people of the nearby towns would assemble there, so that it would be harvested with great fanfare.
> Once it grew dark, the [court emissary] says to [those assembled]: Did the sun set? They say: Yes.
> Did the sun set? They say: Yes.
> He says: Shall I reap the sheaves with this sickle? They say: Yes.
> He says: With this sickle? They say: Yes…
> …He says: Shall I cut the sheaves? They say: Cut.
> He says: Shall I cut the sheaves? And they say to him: Cut.
> He asks three times with regard to each and every matter, and they say to him: Yes, yes, yes. (Mishna Menaḥot 10:3)

The Mishna immediately explains this ritual: "It is because of the Boethusians [a sect similar to the Sadducees, who deny the value of the Oral Law], who say that the *omer* is not harvested after the festival."

150. Compare to R. Eliezer's identification of "the day after Shabbat" with the day after Yom Tov in Menaḥot 65a, which is repeated by R. Yehuda b. Beteira later on in the same discussion.

151. R. Lichtenstein perceives the *ḥazan*'s counting of the Omer in the synagogue as a fulfillment of the collective aspect of the Omer count. See further in Helfgot, *Holidays and Blessings*, 79–86. He proposes that the Omer count has two purposes: a count that connects the waving of the *omer* and the two-loaf offering (which is incumbent upon the individual) and a count that generates the sanctity of Shavuot (which is incumbent upon the community). This aptly concurs with my own analysis.

However, there may be much greater significance to the "great fanfare" of the whole event: This fanfare drew a great crowd of people and made them all part of the ritual.[152] This seems to be R. Shimon's approach, as quoted in the *Sifra*:

> R. Shimon says: "And if you offer a meal offering of first produce to the Lord" – This meal offering is mandatory. I might think it is voluntary; it is therefore written: "And you shall bring the *omer*, the first [grain] of your harvest to the priest" (Lev. 23:10) – it is mandatory.
>
> If so, why is it written: "If [you offer]"?[153] To teach: If you bring it willingly, I shall account it to you as if you brought it as a gift; and if you do not bring it willingly, I shall account it to you as having brought it for your personal needs only [i.e., to allow you to eat the new grain].[154]

The grain offering of first produce is somewhat of a chameleon. Although the *omer* offering is ultimately an obligatory, communal offering, it initially appears in the context of freewill individual offerings, and this reflects its deeper, dual nature. In this way, it is representative of both the individual farmer's personal gratitude to God for the annual harvest that sustains each family in Israel, as well as the national process intrinsically linked to the count from Passover to Shavuot, from the waving of the *omer* to the waving of the two-loaf offering. In a certain sense, it is even a microcosm of the first three sacrificial chapters, for the post-Passover *omer* offering is accompanied by a single sheep as a burnt offering, whereas the Shavuot two-loaf offering is offered along

152. Yitzhak Baer claims that the words of the Mishna can be read in light of Philo's description of "a festive national gathering for the purpose of religious worship" (Baer, *Studies*, 461–62). He even adds: "The *omer* harvest service in Israel during the Second Temple period is one of the purest, holiest rituals that can be found in the history of religion and human belief in general" (470).

153. This midrash reads differently than Rashi ("*ve'im*" in the sense of obligation), but emphasizes that within the obligatory framework, the text seeks to create a voluntary feel.

154. *Sifra*, Freewill Offerings, 13:3.

with a burnt offering and a generous peace offering in a lavish celebration of the new harvest.

> May He recall all your grain offerings and accept your burnt offerings – Selah.
> May He give you your heart's desire and ensure that all your plans succeed. (Ps. 20:4–5)

Chapter 8

The Peace Offering (Leviticus 3): A Covenant of Friendship

THE NATURE AND ESSENCE OF THE *ZEVAḤ SHELAMIM*

Many offerings have names with reasonably clear meanings, but this is not the case with *zevaḥ shelamim* (Lev. 3:1). Its full name consists of two words, *"zevaḥ"* and "*shelamim*," and there are different opinions regarding the relationship between them. Some modern scholars suggest that the two words represent two different offerings, which were then merged for various reasons under one name in Leviticus 3. The leading proponent of this approach is Rendtorff,[1] who argues that "*zevaḥ*" refers to an individual's freewill offering, in which the bringer partakes of the meat, whereas *"shelamim"* is a communal celebration that is not eaten, but rather offered up as a burnt offering, like the sheep offered on Shavuot.[2]

1. Rendtorff, *Geschichte des Opfers*; see a variation in Myhre, "Måltidsofferet."
2. The Sages taught that the end of the verse, "The priest shall wave them this way and that with the bread of the first produce as a wave offering before the Lord together with the two sheep; *they shall be holy to the Lord and belong to the priest*" (Lev. 23:20),

However, this suggestion is not convincing; some "*shelamim*" are not communal celebrations, such as the Nazirite's *shelamim* offering (Num. 6:13–21) and various individual libations referred to as "*shelamim*" (Num. 15:8). This theory is also problematic given that some *shelamim* are eaten, such as following the sin of the Golden Calf: "The next day, they rose early and sacrificed burnt offerings and brought peace offerings. The people sat down to eat and drink" (Ex. 32:6). Although one may argue that this scene does not constitute proof, the feast following the covenant on the Plains of Moab should: "You shall also sacrifice peace offerings (*shelamim*) and eat them there, rejoicing before the Lord your God" (Deut. 27:7).

Nor is the theory that *shelamim* are offered whole, like burnt offerings, convincing from a semantic perspective. Different verbs are used for burnt offerings (*lehaalot*) and peace offerings (*laasot*). For example, "Then Solomon awoke – it had all been a dream! When he came to Jerusalem... he *offered up* (*vayaal*) burnt offerings and *presented* (*vayaas*) peace offerings, and he held a feast for all his servants" (I Kings 3:15; see also Ex. 32:6; Deut. 27:7; Josh. 8:31). This implies that *shelamim* were prepared differently from burnt offerings.[3]

While this theory is not convincing, it is worth mentioning because it does attempt to address the offering's compound name and its meaning.

"*Zevaḥ*"

The component "*zevaḥ*" indicates that eating the offering is inherent to its nature. Consistent with the basic distinction between the two lists of offerings, the eating of the peace offering is discussed only in *Parashat Tzav*. But the word "*zevaḥ*" links this offering to eating from the outset.

In the language of the Sages, "*zevaḥ*" means "animal offering"; it is first used as a generic name for animal offerings in Tanakh (as in Ex. 20:21 and many others). Some claim that in contrast to the verbs "*shaḥat*"

---

refers to the sheep and not just the bread, and therefore the male priests eat their meat (Mishna Zevaḥim 5:5). Rendtorff's understanding is that the priest receives only the bread, whereas the sheep become a burnt offering. According to the Sages, the sheep are not eaten by the worshippers who bring them, but by the priests, who represent the "holy."

3. Milgrom, *Leviticus*, vol. 1, 217.

and "*tavaḥ*," which largely refer to non-ritual animal slaughter, the verb "*zavaḥ*" is only used in a ritual context.[4] This distinction is not accurate, however: The word "*zevaḥ*" essentially means "meal" or "feast," not necessarily in a ritual context. The definition of the word "*zevaḥ*" is "a meal in which meat that has been slaughtered for a festive occasion is served,"[5] not necessarily a holy meal.[6] For example, Jacob prepares a feast for his family: "Jacob slaughtered a *zevaḥ* on the hill and invited his kinsmen to break bread" (Gen. 31:54). If this had been an actual offering, there would have presumably been mention of an altar (as is described soon after, when Jacob reaches Shechem – 33:20). Rather, this seems to be a family, not sacred, feast, as Radak explains: "He made a meal and feast in which they ate together before they parted ways, to commemorate their pact" (on Gen. 31:54). Sharing the flesh of the same animal in a shared meal is a powerful symbol of a covenant.[7] Another striking example is when Elisha becomes Elijah's attendant: "He turned back from him and took the pair of oxen; he *slaughtered* them (*vayizbaḥehu*), and, using the oxen gear, he boiled their meat and gave it out to the people to eat" (I Kings 19:21). The narrative does not present this slaughter as an offering to God, but as a feast in honor of his appointment as Elijah's attendant. In other places, it is even more obvious that the "*zevaḥ*" refers to a non-sacred meal, such as: "Better dry bread with tranquility than a house full of feasts (*zivḥei*) with contention" (Prov. 17:1; see also Zeph. 1:7–8).

It comes as no surprise that the verb root Z-B-Ḥ is profoundly associated with the *zevaḥ shelamim* offering. At the Sinai covenant, for example: "Then he sent young men of Israel, and they offered up bulls as burnt offerings and *sacrificed* (*vayizbeḥu*) peace offerings to the Lord" (Ex. 24:5); or at the covenant at the Moab Plains: "Of uncut stones you shall build the altar of the Lord your God. On it, offer burnt offerings to the Lord your God. You shall also *sacrifice* (*vezavaḥta*) peace offerings

4. Rainey, "Sacrifice," 639.
5. Licht, "Zevaḥ," 901.
6. As written by Levine, *In the Presence of the Lord,* 115–17. See also Milgrom, *Leviticus,* vol. 1, 218.
7. See Licht, "Zevaḥ," 901–02. This is Robertson-Smith's premise – adopted by many others – and he himself adds that this is also the purpose of the peace offering. I will soon present a variation of this theory.

and eat them there, rejoicing before the Lord your God" (Deut. 27:6–7; see also Josh. 8:31).

Ibn Ezra, however, rejects this association with surprising vitriol:

> I saw a heretic, may his bones be crushed, arguing against the Sages of the Talmud for saying: "Which was the place appointed for the sacrifices?" (Zevaḥim 5:1). The heretic claimed that he only found the Torah using the term "sacrifice" (*zevaḥ*) in association with the peace offering.... Now I showed this heretic that what he said was incorrect. Scripture here states "on that *sacrifice* your burnt offerings and peace offerings." He then admitted that he sinned in contradicting people eminently greater than any who lived in all the generations that came after them. (Ibn Ezra on Ex. 20:21)

Ibn Ezra offers a convincing argument. After the Covenant at Sinai, God commands Israel: "Make for Me an altar of earth and on that *sacrifice* (*vezavaḥta*) your burnt offerings and peace offerings, your sheep and your cattle" (Ex. 20:21). There, the verb "*vezavaḥta*" refers to both burnt and peace offerings. Nonetheless, there is an undeniable affinity between the verb and the offering; the above example is certainly outweighed by dozens of instances of the verb root Z-B-Ḥ referring exclusively to the peace offering. Ibn Ezra himself explains that Exodus 20:21 is anomalous because the laws of the altar listed after the Covenant at Sinai refer especially to the altar Moses built there, as described in Exodus 24 – which, as mentioned, does maintain a distinction between "offering burnt offerings" and "sacrificing peace offerings" (24:5).

This exception, in fact, serves to illustrate the nature of peace offerings. Occasionally in biblical narrative, a single verb comes before a list of nouns despite its suitability for just one of the nouns.[8] A famous example is "Every one of the people saw the thunder and lightning and the sound

8. This phenomenon occurs in other Semitic languages. See Moreshet, "Predicate." A similar, more common phenomenon is when the gender and form of a verb is suited to the first character in a list (e.g., a female, singular form of a verb applies to a male character mentioned together with a female character – see Num. 12:1).

of the ram's horn and the smoke-covered mountain" (Ex. 20:15). The verb "saw" is appropriate for the "lightning" and the "mountain," but not the "thunder" or the "sound of the ram's horn," yet even so, only one verb is used. The same is true of Exodus 20:21; the verb "*vezavaḥta*" is more appropriate for peace offerings, but is still used here for burnt offerings.

Nevertheless, the question of why this occurs here still stands. Though a thorough analysis of this passage exceeds the scope of this discussion, I will point out that these verses convey a strong sense of friendship and closeness with God. This verse ends: "Wherever I cause My name to be invoked, I will come to you and I will bless you" (Ex. 20:21). Although the covenant took place at Sinai, God is not limited geographically; He promises to "come" to wherever His name is invoked. The use of the first and second person – "I will come to you" (compare God's words to Moses on the eve of the Sinai revelation: "Behold I am coming to You in a cloud – Ex. 19:9) – create a sense of intimacy, of a personal relationship with God. To evoke this intimacy, the verb usually associated with the peace offering dominates the entire verse. As we will shortly see, in contrast to the burnt offering that showcases human limitation in the face of the Divine, peace offerings, which are essentially a shared meal, are an expression of intimacy and friendship with God.

"Shelamim"

The full name of the offering is "*zevaḥ shelamim,*" not just "*shelamim*" or "*zevaḥ,*" although it is sometimes referred to by just one component: "They rose early the next day and offered up burnt offerings and presented *shelamim* and the people sat to eat and drink" (Ex. 32:6); or: "Present your burnt offerings – the meat and the blood – on the altar of the Lord your God. The blood of your peace offerings (*zevaḥekha*) shall be poured out on the altar of the Lord your God, but you may eat the meat" (Deut. 32:6). In such cases, the partial name should be perceived as an abbreviation of the full name.

The offering's full meaning is based on the sum of its names: *zevaḥ* + *shelamim*. There are four main approaches as to the meaning of the component *shelamim*:[9]

1. Rashbam (and Hizkuni) understands *shelamim* in the sense of *tashlum*, repayment, fulfillment, as in repaying oaths. This implies that the *shelamim* is first and foremost an offering brought following an oath to bring a sacrifice. According to Rashbam, a *shelamim* offering is more appropriate for oath fulfillment than a burnt offering. When someone swears, "If You, God, rescue me from this predicament, I will bring You an offering," they are necessarily pledging a peace offering. We will yet see (in the context of the peace offering discussed in *Parashat Tzav*) that the Torah also distinguishes between two kinds of peace offering – thanksgiving offerings and offerings brought for vow fulfillment – which indeed shows that the peace offering is associated with vow fulfillment. This reveals an ingenious wordplay in Psalms 56:13: "I must fulfill my vow to You, God / I will repay (*ashallem*) thank offerings (*todot*) to You." The verb "repay," "*ashallem*," refers to oath fulfillment, but the phrase "*ashallem todot*" is a play on the name of the thanksgiving offering "*shalmei toda*."[10]
2. Ramban has a different approach: "*Shelamim* – meaning 'fulfilling all my will' (Is. 44:28), or 'whole stones' (Deut. 27:6)." Ramban's chosen quotations imply that he reads "*shelamim*" in the sense of "complete," "whole." According to this reading, the offering's name means "complete meal." This may be the basis of a different wordplay tucked into Solomon's prayer when the Temple is completed: "'May your hearts be fully (*shalem*) with the Lord our God, following His laws and keeping His commandments, as

9. As shown by Kiuchi ("Translating *selamîm*"), the confusion surrounding the offering's name is reflected in the variety of translations: "well-being sacrifice" (JPS; NRSV); "a shared offering" (REB); "fellowship offering" (NIV); or, as I will use here, "peace offering" (RSV, Koren Tanakh translation).
10. Compare Wenham, *Leviticus*, 78.

today.' And the king, together with all of Israel, offered sacrifices before the Lord; *Solomon (Shlomo) sacrificed the peace offerings (zivḥei shelamim) he offered* to the Lord" (1 Kings 8:61–63).[11] Solomon's very name may be in dialogue with his prayer and offerings.[12]

3. Baruch Levine offers a completely different reading: that "*shelamim*" is derived from the Akkadian "*šalmu*" – meaning "gift."[13] This suggestion casts a fascinating light on this offering: One freewill animal offering is named for being completely burned on the altar, "*ola*" – meaning "holocaust" – and the other for its nature as a gift (similar to the grain offering's Hebrew name, "*minḥa,*" which also means "gift"). The experience of giving underlies every offering, but it is manifest in various degrees. If "*shelamim*" means "gift," then this is the offering's essence, its deeper nature: "To You I will offer a freewill sacrifice; I will praise Your name, Lord, for it is good" (Ps. 54:8).
4. The most straightforward reading and the most common explanation among *Rishonim* (which is already hinted in the *Sifra* and is also prevalent in modern scholarship) is that "*shelamim*" is derived from the word "*shalom,*" "peace."

   But what peace does this refer to? Peace with whom? Rashi (based on the *Sifra*) explains that the meat is shared between all the participants: "Peace between the altar, priests, and worshippers." The peace offering expresses (and perhaps causes?) harmony between the altar that "receives" its share of the fats, the priests who receive the breast and thigh, and the worshipper, who receives the rest of the meat. A more immediate understanding, however, is that this offering expresses peace and harmony between worshipper and God. In biblical Hebrew, "peace" has a similar meaning to "covenant." It

11. Levine, *In the Presence of the Lord,* 35. He prefers the reading that "*shelamim*" comes from "peace" ("*shalom*"), but the word "*shalem*" ("whole") in Solomon's description refers to perfection.
12. I thank Binyamin Frankel for this observation.
13. Levine, *In the Presence of the Lord,* 19.

> expresses conciliation, friendship, and closeness. An apt illustration is the phrase "covenant of peace" that God uses in reference to Phineas: "Therefore, say this: I grant him My covenant of peace" (Num. 25:12); or Ezekiel's prophecy: "I will make a covenant of peace with them; it will be an everlasting covenant with them" (37:26). Malachi's description of the priest, "True teaching was in his mouth, no sin from his lips; he walked with Me in peace and uprightness and returned many from iniquity" (Mal. 2:6), shows that "peace" is not just refraining from a negative relationship with God, but an actively positive relationship of love, friendship, and integrity.

In summary, the name "*zevaḥ shelamim,*" "peace offering," reflects its nature: It is a covenant, an expression of peace between worshipper and God that conveys love and generosity. It is worth noting that in ancient times (and, effectively, to this day), sharing a meal was part of the covenant ceremony.[14] When Avimelekh forms a covenant with Isaac, he repeatedly emphasizes that he has come to form a covenant of peace (Gen. 26:28–31), whereupon "Isaac made them a feast" (26:30). This covenantal feast is performed with every peace offering. Rashbam is correct that vow fulfillment peace offerings are brought after a person has been saved from a life-threatening situation in which they swore to bring an offering if they survive, but the nature of the peace offering focuses on the bringer's gratitude and desire to form a covenant with the God who saved them. In the words of the aforementioned psalmist: "To You I will offer a freewill sacrifice; I will praise Your name, Lord, for it is good, for He has saved me from all danger; my eyes have seen my enemies' downfall" (Ps. 54:8–9).

As noted above, the offering's consumption is not mentioned in *Parashat Vayikra,* which again teaches about the dichotomy between the two lists of offerings as well as the dialogue between them. The two lists are not independent; they express two complementary aspects of biblical offerings. Even in regard to the peace offering, whose eating is

14. Vibreg, "Symbols of Law," 70–76.

an inherent, significant part of its meaning, the laws of its division and eating are postponed to *Parashat Tzav*.

The nature of the peace offering as a covenantal feast is supported by two different aspects: its appearance in biblical narrative and the fact that the worshipper receives a significant portion of the offering. Here are several examples of the peace offering as it appears in the Bible:

1. At Mount Sinai, the "young men" of Israel offer peace offerings as part of the elaborate pre-covenantal ceremony (Ex. 24:5).[15] Later on, they "eat and drink," and the straightforward reading is that they eat the peace offering, as Ibn Ezra explains (on 24:11).
2. Peace offerings are mentioned at the blessing and curse ceremony at Mount Gerizim and Mount Ebal. Moses commands Israel: "You shall also sacrifice peace offerings there and rejoice before the Lord your God" (Deut. 27:7), which they indeed fulfill after they enter the land (Josh. 8:30–31).[16] Here, too, peace offerings accompany a covenant with God.
3. When Saul is appointed as king, "All the people went to Gilgal and they crowned Saul king there at Gilgal before the Lord. They sacrificed peace offerings before the Lord, and Saul rejoiced greatly along with all the men of Israel" (I Sam. 11:15). This episode is especially relevant for our purposes, as it underscores the connection between the peace offering, God's presence, and great rejoicing.
4. The connection between the peace offering and joy is obvious to the Sages, who point out that the festival peace offerings are "joy offerings." While the spirit of the pilgrimage to the Temple is expressed through the burnt offerings, "*olat hare'iya*," the joy and celebration of the festivals demands expression through peace offerings:

15. It is interesting that in the covenant ceremony itself, Israel offer both peace and burnt offerings; in other words, the religious experience can encompass these seemingly contradictory states of yearning, alienation, reverence, and desire. Perhaps this ambivalence is inherent to the immanence of a covenant with God.
16. It is difficult to determine whether the joy mentioned in Moses's commandment is intentionally omitted from the commandment's execution in Joshua.

> Israel are commanded to fulfill three positive commandments at each of the three festivals of pilgrimage: Pilgrimage, as it says: "Three times a year, all your males shall appear before the Lord"; celebration, as it says, "Celebrate before the Lord"; and rejoicing, as it says, "You shall rejoice on your festival".... This festive joy refers to offering peace offerings in addition to the festival offerings; they are called "festive joyous peace offerings" (*shalmei simḥat ḥagiga*), as it says: "You shall also offer peace offerings and eat them there." (Rambam, *Hilkhot Ḥagiga* 1:1)

These examples show that the peace offering is an expression of the joyous fulfillment of a covenant with God. As mentioned, this will presumably be reflected in its laws. For now, it suffices to mention that the worshippers partake in the eating of this offering; in fact, they eat most of the animal. This is a bold idea: A person brings an offering to God, and in response, God invites them to share the offering as if they are sharing a meal. Even if it is God who sits at the head of the table with the worshipper as His guest, the idea of a shared meal – as if God and the worshipper are friends – is still revolutionary.[17] Needless to say, the joyous overtones of the peace offering are far removed from the trepidation that accompanies the burnt offering.

---

17. Given the prohibition against eating meat in the wilderness era (other than offerings), many perceive the peace offering as a way to allow the consumption of meat. Milgrom, for example, writes:

 > The main function of the well-being offering is to provide meat for the table. Assumed is that nonsacrificial slaughter is illegitimate ... and that whenever an Israelite craved meat he would first have to offer his cattle, sheep, or goat.... Such an occasion perforce was rare, for only kings and aristocrats could afford the depletion of their flocks. For the commoner, the occasion had to be a celebration – and because the meat was probably too much for the nuclear family, it had to be a household or even a clan celebration – hence the joyous character of the sacrifice. (Milgrom, *Leviticus*, vol I, 221)

 I believe that this is a misrepresentation of the true meaning: Eating the meat is not the purpose of the sacrifice, but rather one of its laws. Leviticus 17 indeed presents the peace offering as a solution for those who wish to eat meat, but this is a secondary use of the offering, not its main purpose.

Beyond the idea that the worshipper partakes of the meat, other laws of the peace offering further reflect its nature, especially the time allotted for its consumption (two days) and the accompanying bread, as we will discuss in the context of the laws in *Parashat Tzav*.

In order to further explore this nature, we will consider how it is expressed through its two different forms: the peace offering from the herd and from the flock.

THE PEACE OFFERING FROM THE HERD

Like the burnt offering, the peace offering may come from the herd or the flock, most of the laws are identical, and the peace offering from the herd is mentioned first:

> If one's sacrifice is a peace offering, and brought from the herd, whether male or female, the animal one offers before the Lord must be without blemish. The one bringing the offering shall lay his hand on its head and have it slaughtered at the entrance to the Tent of Meeting. Aaron's sons the priests shall dash the blood against each side of the altar. A priest shall present of the peace offering a fire offering to the Lord: the fat that covers the entrails and all the fat surrounding them; the two kidneys and the fat that is on them at the loins; and the diaphragm of the liver, which should be removed with the kidneys. Aaron's sons shall send all these up in smoke upon the altar, along with the burnt offering on the wood on the altar fire – a fire offering, a sweet savor to the Lord. (Lev. 3:1–5)

"Whether Male or Female"

That the offering must be without blemish is obvious. More surprising is that the animal may be either male or female. Burnt offerings must be male; why is the bringer of the peace offering given a choice?

The first hint to the answer may be in the formulation. The option to bring male or female is not a positive law so much as the absence of a limitation: "Whether male or female." While this can be read differently, the sense is that the animal's sex is insignificant; what matters is that it is without blemish.[18]

One likely explanation is that since the worshipper will partake of the meat, they are allowed to bring an animal based on their personal preference: Some prefer the meat of a male animal, while others prefer the taste of the cow to that of a bull.[19] A further development of this idea is that the worshipper's ability to choose is no coincidence; they are active participants in this offering of cooperation, covenant, and friendship from the start, and they may choose what animal to bring, similar to the ability to choose what kind of cooked grain offering to bring.

Hizkuni favors this approach, albeit in a different context. When attempting to explain why there is no mention of the washing of the peace offering's parts, he links this to the worshipper's involvement: "The washing of the insides and the thighs is not mentioned in peace offerings because the worshippers take part, and each one may deal with their portion as they wish" (on Lev. 3:3). A simpler phrasing may be that because these parts are not offered on the altar, they do not require washing (unlike the parts of the burnt offering, which are all burnt on the altar and therefore require washing). This reading is also consistent with the idea that the worshipper's significant, active participation has a bearing on the laws of the peace offering.

Laying of the Hands

The first action the worshipper must do after bringing the animal to the Sanctuary is to "lay his hand on its head" (3:2). We have already discussed this law in the context of burnt offerings; several scholars discuss whether the laying of the hands has a different significance in the context of the peace offering. Some argue that the act of laying the hands is worded differently. In other offerings, the text mentions the name of the offering or animal: "He shall lay his hand on the head of

18. As pointed out by Dillmann (*Leviticus*, 450), when biblical narrative specifies whether the animal offered as a peace offering is male or female, it is always male (Ex. 24:5; 29:19; Num 6:14; 7:88), and there is no evidence of a female being offered, despite the law. This implies that there is a preference for a male, but the person is still able to choose.
19. Milgrom, *Leviticus*, vol. 1, 204.

the *burnt offering*" (1:4); "He shall lay his hand on the head of the bull" (4:4; see also 4:15, 24, 29). In contrast, a more general term is used for the peace offering: "He shall lay his hand on the head of his offering." Given that the same term is used for the peace offering from the flock (3:2; 8:13), this formulation seems intentional. Some suggest that there is no actual need for laying of the hands in a peace offering, as there is no sin to transfer to the animal, but hands are still laid as a gesture for the sake of ceremony.[20] Although interesting, this proposition does not stand up to scrutiny; the idea that laying of the hands transfers the worshippers' sin to the animal is imprecise, at least in regard to individual offerings (as opposed to the laying of the hands upon the scapegoat on Yom Kippur). Laying of the hands creates an affinity between the worshipper and their offering; there is no reason that this should not be part of the peace offering.

If so, however, why does the text deviate from its usual formulation? Perhaps it is linked to another deviation: "Whether male or female." When bringing a peace offering, the worshipper determines the animal and its sex; accordingly, the Torah uses a more general term that reflects this: "His offering."

Kidneys and Fat

Unlike the burnt offering, only the fats, the kidneys, and the "diaphragm of the liver" (which the Sages refer to as "*eimurim*") of the peace offering are burned upon the altar. Which fats? The language of the text clearly implies that these are layers of fat that protect the organs ("the fat that *covers* the entrails and all the fat *surrounding* them; the two kidneys and the fat *that is on them* at the loins"). Rashi explains R. Akiva's description in Ḥullin 49b as a layer of fat – suet – that covers the inner organs like a garment, which has a thin coating that peels off easily. The difference between suet and other fats is that suet is a separate layer that covers the organs, whereas muscle fat is mixed into the flesh itself.

Besides the suet, the kidneys are also burned upon the altar. To what do the kidneys owe this honor? The burning of the kidneys can be understood in one of two basic ways. It may be a technicality, given that

20. Koch, *Die Priesterschrift*, 51–52.

they are not easily extricated from the fat, as implied in the text itself: "The two kidneys and the fat that is on them" (v. 4). This may similarly be why the diaphragm of the liver is also offered up: "The diaphragm of the liver, which should be removed with the kidneys." Perhaps it is difficult to separate them cleanly, and these parts are therefore all offered together. If so, this explains why the kidneys – unlike the suet – may be eaten. They do not inherently belong to the altar, while the suet does; they are offered up only because of the suet attached to them.

A different approach is that the kidneys are offered up for symbolic reasons. If so, why are they the designated organ? Perhaps Ibn Ezra hints to an explanation when he defines the word "*kelayot*": "'*Kelayot*' are so called because they are the source of lust and sex. The word '*kelayot*' is related to the word '*kaleta*' ('pine') in 'My soul yearns, yea, even pines' (Ps. 84:3)" (Ibn Ezra on Lev. 3:4; similarly, Ex. 29:13). Does Ibn Ezra believe that the kidneys represent yearning and desire and therefore make a fitting sacrifice? His explanation seems to be based on wordplay, indicating a semantic rather than deeply symbolic reading.

An alternative symbolic meaning is implied in a midrash about Abraham:

> His father did not teach him, he had no teacher; how did he learn Torah? The Holy One, blessed be He, instilled within him two kidneys that served as two teachers, which filled him with wisdom. (Genesis Rabba 61)

Elsewhere, the Sages liken the kidneys to advisors (see Berakhot 61a; Leviticus Rabba 4:4; *Midrash Mishlei* 12:20).[21] Indeed, various biblical verses reflect the perception that wisdom and morality – essentially, a person's conscience – are based in the kidneys: "I will bless the Lord who has guided me; even at night, *my conscience* (*kilyotai*) stirs me" (Ps. 16:7). They also appear in parallel to the heart: "The Lord of Hosts is a righteous judge; He discerns both mind (*kelayot*) and heart" (Jer. 11:20; see also 17:10). Moreover, this is further supported if we adopt

21. See further in Steinberg, "Kelayot," 118–24.

the medieval view that the word "*tuḥot*" also means "kidneys."[22] Further verses from Job and Psalms also support this symbolism.[23] Rashi also reads the phrase "*leummat he'atze yesirenna*" (Lev. 3:9) as referring to just above the kidneys, explaining that *atze* is derived from the Hebrew word for "counsel."[24]

It may be that the kidneys' physiological purpose – to remove waste by filtering the blood – made them an apt symbol of distinguishing between good and evil on a moral and spiritual level as well.[25] Another possibility is that "since it is an inner, hidden organ wrapped up in a membrane and a layer of suet, the kidneys are considered the root of deep yearning."[26] If so, then the worshipper is symbolically laying his or her innermost longings upon the altar and offering them up high.

In any case, in the ancient world, one of the most important organs in terms of spiritual discourse was the liver, which has a place of honor in Mesopotamian divination. Perhaps the fact that the kidneys – and *not* the liver – were offered up on the Israelite altar is a subtle polemic against pagan worship, especially since "the diaphragm of the liver" but not the liver itself is also burned to God. The kidneys are offered up while the adjacent liver is pointedly ignored.[27]

---

22. The word "*betuḥot*" literally means the covered, hidden place. The idea that it refers specifically to the kidneys is based on the fact that they are covered in membranes and fat (see Ibn Ezra on Ps. 51:8). Modern research tends to perceive the word in the sense of something covered, dark, and hidden, based on the Psalms 51 parallelism with the word "*satum*," "closed up" (see Schunk, "Tuaḥ," 319).
23. See Job 38:36; Ps. 51:8. Some read the word as a bird's name (see Kaddari, *Dictionary*, 378); Greenstein (*Job*, 170) interprets it specifically as "ibex." The parallelism in that verse supports this reading; if so, it is not relevant to our discussion.
24. There is no clear biblical distinction between *ḥokhma*, wisdom, and *mussar*, morality; both are elements of the human's inner world.
25. Of course, given that the ancient world was not aware of the kidneys' true biological function (Aristotle thought they served no real purpose – see Steinberg, "Kelayot," 112–14), it is problematic to base a symbolic function on a biological one. After all, connotations are based on popular understanding, not scientific facts.
26. Leibowitz, "Kilya," 854.
27. See a similar theory in Hartley, *Leviticus*, 40.

"Aaron's sons shall send all these up in smoke upon the altar, along with the burnt offering on the wood on the altar fire – a fire offering, a sweet savor to the Lord"

The most fascinating verse here is the description of the sacrificial order. The *eimurim* (the portions to be burnt) of the peace offering are laid upon the parts of the burnt offering upon the altar, which are laid upon the wood, which is laid upon the fire. Out of the whole list, the most surprising element is the burnt offering. Why is it suddenly mentioned? One might attempt to read the word "*ola*" as an abbreviation of the phrase "*mizbaḥ ha'ola*," the burnt offering altar (as in 4:10), but the context does not support this: The burnt offering is "laid upon the wood," not the altar itself.

Some suggest reading the preposition "*al*" as "with,"[28] but this too is unlikely, given that the other two instances in the verse clearly mean "on." Why does a burnt offering upon the altar await the bringer of the peace offering?

The fundamental question, of course, is which burnt offering this refers to. The Sages and most medieval commentators explain that this is the daily burnt offering, which is always offered first and is therefore always already upon the altar when the rest of the offerings are offered up (see, for example, Pesaḥim 58b). Burning a lamb takes hours; it may well be that other offerings are actually laid on top of the daily burnt offering pieces upon the altar. This reading is supported by the description of the eighth day of the Tabernacle consecration: "He then presented the grain offering, took a handful from it, and sent this portion up in smoke upon the altar, with the morning's burnt offering" (Lev. 9:17). If "the morning's burnt offering" were mentioned along with the eighth day's special burnt offering, it would emphasize that the daily burnt offering was offered up regularly, regardless of the occasion. But why is the grain offering mentioned "along with the morning's burnt offering"? This presumably shows that all offerings are connected to the daily burnt offering, not just other burnt or other animal offerings. Common sense also

28. As suggested by Milgrom, *Leviticus*, vol. 1, 208. The more common direction – among *Rishonim* as well – is the position adopted above.

supports this reading. It would not be economically feasible to require that each peace offering must be preceded by a burnt offering.[29]

On the other hand, the sudden appearance of the daily burnt offering – which has not yet been mentioned in these chapters – is surprising. Although it does appear in Exodus 29 (vv. 38–43), the fact that it has not yet been mentioned in Leviticus means that the identity of the burnt offering in this section is not obvious.

Either way, why does a burnt offering appear in the context of the peace offering? The burnt offering is not mentioned in the description of the grain offering, for example, even though the daily grain offering follows the daily burnt offering.

Notably, a similar description appears in regard to the ram of ordination, which is also a kind of peace offering: "Then take them from their hands and burn them on the altar *with the burnt offering,* for a sweet savor before the Lord" (Ex. 29:25). Moreover, this is repeated when Moses fulfills the above instruction: "Then Moses took [the *eimurim*] from their hands and burnt them upon the altar with the burnt offering" (Lev. 8:28). That is, the Torah repeatedly emphasizes the connection of the peace offering to the burnt offering.

This affinity has both halakhic and symbolic connotations. The former may suggest that this allows one to offer different kinds of offerings upon the altar at once. Perhaps it even implies that the altar is the place where offerings are consumed by the fire of God's revelation, which is ignited and perpetuated by the fire of the daily burnt offering, the *esh tamid*. Hence, all offerings are enabled by the daily burnt offering.

Essentially, the overlapping blood rituals ("dashing the blood all around," or, in the language of the Sages, "two which are four") already hints that these offerings are complementary, not contradictory. Some claim that dashing the blood of the peace offering actually has an aspect of atonement: The sheer audacity of standing before God constitutes an offense that the blood then atones for.[30] If so, the peace offering shares this aspect with the burnt offering, and it is symbolized by their common blood rituals. Yet this seems far-fetched within the sacrificial chapters

29. Watts, "OLAH," 131.

30. Kiuchi, "Peace Offering," 28.

(even if it is more convincing in Leviticus 17); it is no coincidence that the term "*kappara,*" "atonement," is applied in relation to the burnt offering but not the peace offering. Nonetheless, the identical blood rituals present the two offerings as complementary religious experiences.[31]

In a more spiritual-symbolic formulation, the fact that the burnt offering is the first on the list of offerings is not merely technical. It is the most fundamental and eminent of offerings; the religious expression of utter submission before God is the spiritual basis and precedence for all other forms of religious expression. That the fats of the peace offering melt into the flesh of the burnt offering is no mere technicality, as focus on the halakhic perspective might imply; it is an absolute prerequisite. The notion of friendship and partnership between human and God is only feasible when based on an acceptance of the unbridgeable gap between worshipper and Maker.

This may also explain why all biblical lists of offerings end with peace offerings, such as the eighth day of the Tabernacle consecration (Lev. 9:18), the offerings of the fiftieth day (Lev. 23:19), the altar consecration (Num. 7), libation laws (Num. 15:3–8), and many others. The arrangement of these lists reflects their various levels of holiness, which in itself is related to the accompanying religious mindset of the person bringing the offering. The peace offering's delicate gesture to the Divine can only be conveyed through the vector of the burnt offering.

This brings us to the peace offering from the flock and whether the difference between the two is merely financial or more fundamental.

THE PEACE OFFERING FROM THE FLOCK

The description of the peace offering from the flock is divided into two and repeats the process for both ram and goat. The only halakhic difference between them is that the ram has a fatty "broad tail" that the goat lacks, but for the sake of this slight difference, the entire process is repeated. There do not seem to be any fundamental differences between the offerings, and the repetition may be purely structural: The burnt

31. As mentioned, burnt and peace offerings are often sacrificed together in biblical narrative: See the Sinai Covenant (Ex. 24:5); the covenant at the Plains of Moab (Deut. 27:6–7); bringing the Ark to Jerusalem (II Sam. 6:17); and others.

offering has three variations (bull, sheep, bird), so the peace offering adheres to the same model, offering two kinds of offerings from the flock instead of a bird offering. As mentioned, the grain offering also has three different options: the fine flour offering/cooked grain offering/first produce. Thus, the three freewill offerings follow a cohesive pattern.[32]

Nonetheless, in the context of the purification offering, we will reexamine the relationship between ram and goat and the difference between their ritual purposes; this, in turn, will explain why the almost identical sacrificial processes are repeated.

> If one's offering is a peace offering from the flock, whether male or female, it must be without blemish. If one brings a sheep as his offering, he shall present it before the Lord. He shall lay his hand on the head of the offering and have it slaughtered at the entrance to the Tent of Meeting. Aaron's sons the priests shall dash its blood against each side of the altar. The priest shall present the fat from the peace offering as a fire offering to the Lord: the whole broad tail, removed close to the backbone; the fat that covers the entrails and all the fat surrounding them; the two kidneys and the fat that is on them at the loins; and the diaphragm of the liver, which should be removed with the kidneys. The priest shall send these up in smoke upon the altar: foodstuffs – a fire offering to the Lord.
>
> If the sacrifice is a goat, the one bringing it shall present it before the Lord. He shall lay his hand on the head of the offering and have it slaughtered at the entrance to the Tent of Meeting. Aaron's sons the priests shall dash its blood against each side of the altar. The priest shall present of the offering a fire offering to the Lord: the fat that covers the entrails and all the fat surrounding

32. See especially Luciani, "Structure et théologie." This repetitive structure raises the obvious question: Why aren't there bird peace offerings? Perhaps the bird does not provide enough meat for a proper meal; we have already explained that they have little blood/life force, which affects the sacrificial process. In ancient times, the birds used for sacrifice had much less meat than today's domesticated chicken, goose, or turkey, and could not provide the feast that is the essence of the peace offering (compare Avnery, "Sin Offerings," 29, n. 2).

> them; the two kidneys and the fat that is on them at the loins; and the diaphragm of the liver, which should be removed with the kidneys. The priest shall send these up in smoke upon the altar: foodstuffs – a fire offering for a sweet savor to the Lord. All the fatty parts belong to the Lord. (Lev. 3:6–16).

Is there any essential difference between a peace offering from the herd and the flock, as there is regarding the burnt offering, or, in this case, is the difference purely financial?

The first evident difference seems to be technical. The blood dashed in the peace offering from the herd is referred to without any kind of pronoun: "Aaron's sons the priests shall dash *the blood* against each side of the altar" (3:2), whereas regarding the peace offering from the flock: "Aaron's sons the priests shall dash *its blood*" (3:8, 13). Given its repetition, this possessive suffix seems intentional. Moreover,, the same difference is found in the descriptions of the burnt offering:

- The burnt offering from the herd: "They shall dash the blood" (1:5).
- The burnt offering from the flock: "Aaron's sons the priests shall dash *its blood*" (1:11).

Radatz Hoffmann seems to be correct that this stems from the animals' respective size: Bulls have much more blood, so only some of the blood is dashed, whereas all of the sheep or goat's blood is needed in order to reach all around the altar – hence, "*its* blood."[33] As discussed, the bull's vast amount of blood reflects "how much life" its sacrifice brings to the altar.

Additionally, the differences between burnt offerings from the flock and herd also apply to the peace offering: Both ram and goat are slaughtered "before the Tent of Meeting," in the direction of the altar, whereas bulls are slaughtered "at the entrance to the Tent of Meeting," facing inward. Without repeating the previous discussion, I will note that there are various indications that "at the entrance to the Tent of Meeting" links

---

33. Hoffmann, *Leviticus*, vol I, 119. He ascribed this to Abarbanel.

the Tabernacle courtyard to the Tent of Meeting's inner chamber; this is the significance of the "entrance" or "opening." This is evident, for example, in the description of the daily burnt offering: "This shall be the regular burnt offering throughout your generations at the entrance of the Tent of Meeting before the Lord" (Ex. 29:42).

The main difference between peace offerings from the herd and flock is expressed in the conclusions of each description. In the peace offering from the herd, it is emphasized that its fats must be burned on top of the burnt offering's fats: "Aaron's sons shall send all these up in smoke upon the altar, along with the burnt offering on the wood on the altar fire – *a fire offering, a sweet savor* to the Lord." In contrast, the description of the ram ends thus: "The priest shall send these up in smoke upon the altar: *foodstuffs – a fire offering* to the Lord"; and the goat: "*Foodstuffs – a fire offering for a sweet savor* to the Lord."

The peace offering from the flock introduces a new sacrificial term, "*leḥem isheh*" : "foodstuffs – a fire offering." Referring to the offering as the altar's food is bold, in light of the biblical reservations about characterizing offerings as food for God. This surprising term is presumably related to the unique nature of the peace offering as a covenantal feast. When the worshippers also partake of their offering, even the altar's portion is referred to as "food," which emphasizes the bond between human and God.[34] If so, however, why is this term introduced only in the context of peace offerings from the flock, not the herd?

The Midrash explains that "foodstuffs" is not mentioned in peace offerings from the herd, "sweet savor" is not mentioned about the ram peace offering, and "to the Lord" does not appear in the goat peace offering, but all three phrases apply to all three offerings (*Sifra*, Freewill Offerings, 14:10). While it is arguable as to whether "to the Lord" does in fact appear in the context of the goat, the midrash's main point is that bull peace offerings are also considered "foodstuffs," even if this is not explicitly mentioned.

34. There is room to debate whether the additional offering on Passover is called "*leḥem*": "In the same way you shall offer daily for seven days the *foodstuffs* of a fire offering, a sweet savor to the Lord" (Num. 28:24).

In contrast, this can be perceived as an intentional omission, perhaps linked to the mention of burnt offerings, which are the antithesis of "foodstuffs." "*Leḥem*," "food," is the opposite of the burnt offering, which is a gesture that recognizes the infinite chasm between human and God. Peace offerings from the herd are festive, joyous celebrations, but they are offered up "along with the burnt offering." In peace offerings from the flock, in contrast, there is no mention of the burnt offering; they are entirely "foodstuffs."

I present this next model with some hesitation, as I do not wish to venture too deeply into the realm of *derash*. If the conclusion of each description indeed reveals each sacrifice's deeper nature – and the difference between herd and flock – perhaps it is worth reexamining the difference between sheep and goat. Previously, we theorized that this repetition is for the sake of the three-part model of freewill offerings; this pattern notwithstanding, perhaps the difference between sheep and goat is significant in itself.

The sheep peace offering is called "foodstuffs" (3:11), but it is not said to produce a "sweet savor." In contrast, the goat peace offering is "foodstuffs – a fire offering for a sweet savor to the Lord" (3:16). If this is intentional, it generates a fascinating gradation: Bull peace offerings are not "foodstuffs," and their *eimurim* are offered on top of the burnt offering. Sheep peace offerings are considered "foodstuffs" for the altar, but they do not produce a sweet savor. Only goat peace offerings manage to create the ideal synthesis of "foodstuffs" and "sweet savor." In order to support this theory, further comparison between the various kinds of peace offerings is necessary, but I do not detect substantial differences in this chapter. As mentioned, I will come back to this theory in light of the various kinds of purification offerings, where there are further hints to the animals' symbolism.

To conclude the present discussion of peace offerings, I wish to note a marvelous midrash:

> "If one's sacrifice is a peace offering (*shelamim*)":
> R. Yehuda says: Whoever brings *shelamim* brings *shalom* (peace) to the world.

> This tells me only of *shelamim*. Whence do I derive a thanksgiving offering [as bringing peace]? I include it, for it is a variety of *shelamim*.
> And whence do I derive a burnt offering? I include it, for it is brought to fulfill a vow and as a gift.
> And whence do I derive [offerings of] the firstborn, the tithe, and the Passover? I include them [as bringing peace], for they are not brought for sin.
> And whence do I derive a sin offering and a guilt offering? From [the extra word] "sacrifice."
> And whence do I derive [offerings of] fowl, meal offerings, wine, frankincense, and wood? From "if one's sacrifice is a peace offering" – so that all who bring a peace offering bring peace to the world. (*Sifra*, Freewill Offerings, 15:1)

The midrash opens with R. Yehuda's statement that *shelamim* bring peace to the world. This is, of course, based on the offering's name. Yet the midrash continues and explains how all offerings actually bring peace to the world. He begins with freewill offerings, then all offerings that are not brought for atonement; then he justifies how even offerings that are brought for atonement still bring peace. In fact, everything that has to do with offerings, such as grain offerings, libations, frankincense, and even the wood that keeps the altar fire burning, all bring peace to the world.

Based on R. Yehuda's logic, what makes peace offerings unique? If everything sacrificial brings peace, how are peace offerings special, and why are they even called peace offerings? The midrashic paradox culminates with its end: "So that all who bring a peace offering bring peace to the world." This surprising conclusion moved R. Kasher to emend the midrash: "So that all who bring *an offering* bring peace to the world,"[35] which indeed makes the whole midrashic reasoning more logical. But even if we adopt this emendation, the midrash is still puzzling: Peace offerings are so named because of their particular capacity to bring peace. Why does the midrash attempt to explain how all offerings share this specific quality?

35. Kasher, *Torah Shelema*, vol. 25, 116.

The answer is that the midrash extends this quality to all other offerings through the biblical description of peace offerings. When explaining how a burnt offering also brings peace, the midrash still cites the verses about the peace offering, not the burnt offering; when referring to the purification and guilt offerings, the narrative explains how the description of the peace offering also applies to these other offerings. In other words, all other offerings bring peace through an aspect of similarity to the peace offering. Just as all offerings begin with an aspect of apology for the audacity to dare stand before God – for all offerings are mentioned only after the burnt offering – all offerings end with an aspect of closeness and partnership with God, which the peace offering likewise celebrates. The very fact that a person chooses to enter God's dwelling place, to stand before Him and offer sacrifices, ultimately brings closeness and reconciliation. Even the sinner who seeks atonement chooses to seek God, not to hide from Him. We will explore this further through the individual's purification offering.

> Enter His gates with thanksgiving /His courts with praise / thank Him and bless His name,
> for the Lord is good; His loving-kindness is forever / His faithfulness for all generations. (Ps. 100:4–5)

To summarize the unit of freewill offerings, I will reiterate that the order of sacrifices reflects a subtle axis of evolving religious mindset and expression. The list opens with the burnt offering from the herd, with a mindset of absolute reverence and submission before God. The next offering is the burnt offering from the flock, which also expresses reverence and effacement, but not by the very standing before God's presence so much as standing before the altar – that is, through worship. The grain offering also expresses a gradual transition from the fine flour offering, which is essentially similar to the burnt offering, to the cooked grain offering, which represents the worshipper's personal preferences and connection to God. Accordingly, the cooked grain offering is related in the second person, as if God is addressing the individual personally. Finally, the peace offering begins with the offering from the herd, which is explicitly linked to the burnt offering, while the peace offering from the flock is defined as "foodstuffs," which fully expresses the covenant of friendship and love between worshipper and God.

Both animal offerings begin with an offering from the herd and continue with the flock, opening with pure reverence for God and gradually evolving into a place of covenant and joyful closeness.

Chapter 9

The Purification Offering (Leviticus 4): Impurity and Purification

The second section of the first sacrificial list opens with the purification offering. The first section discusses freewill offerings; this section introduces obligatory offerings and accordingly opens with a new divine commandment: "The Lord spoke to Moses: 'Tell the Israelites...'" (4:1–2). Obligatory offerings are accompanied by a completely different spiritual mindset: From now on, the question is not what the worshipper seeks to express before God, but how each offering atones for sin, how the various obligatory offerings console and reconcile between sinner and God – and between a person and their own roaring conscience.

IF A PERSON SINS UNINTENTIONALLY

When is one obligated to bring a purification offering? The chapter's opening verse clarifies this:

> The Lord spoke to Moses: "Tell the Israelites: If a person sins unintentionally with regard to any of the Lord's commands, doing what should not be done; any transgression." (Lev. 4:1–2)

The chapter lists four different kinds of sinner whose offenses all meet two criteria: The sinner *unintentionally* committed a *forbidden* act. If someone fails to fulfill a positive commandment, the penalty is not a purification offering, nor is one obligated to bring a purification offering if they intentionally violated a prohibition.

The Sages impose further limitations. They rule that a purification offering is brought only in a case in which an intentional violation would incur *karet* or execution – that is, for a serious offense. Lighter offenses incur lashes, not a purification offering. This is based on a parallel discussion of purification offerings in the book of Numbers:

> If it is an individual who sins inadvertently, he shall offer a year-old female goat as a purification offering. The priest shall make atonement before the Lord for the person who sinned inadvertently, to atone for his sin, and he will be forgiven. There shall be one law for one who inadvertently commits a sin, whether he is a native-born Israelite or a migrant living among them. However, if a person commits a sin [i.e., intentionally], whether he is native born or a migrant, he reviles the Lord and shall be severed from the people. (Num. 15:27–30)

These verses imply that there is a difference between the penalties for intentional and unintentional sin. An inadvertent sin requires a purification offering, but after committing a "high-handed" offense, the offender "shall be severed from the people" – the punishment of *karet*. This invites a fundamental question: Why does an unintentional offense require an offering, whereas the intentional sinner is exempt? Shouldn't the opposite be true?

Ramban's introduction to the purification offering further exacerbates the question:

> Since the process of thinking is centered in the soul, and it is the soul which commits the error, Scripture mentions here "*nefesh*" (soul). The reason for the offerings for the erring soul is that all sins [even if committed unwittingly] produce a particular "stain" and blemish upon the soul, but the soul is only worthy of acceptance by its Creator when it is pure of all sin. Were it not so, then all the fools of the world would be worthy to come before Him. Therefore, the erring soul brings an offering in order to become worthy of approaching God, its Bestower. This is why Scripture mentions here "*nefesh*" (soul). (Ramban on Lev. 4:2)

Ramban is troubled by the use of the word "*nefesh*" in this context and suggests that the soul is damaged by sin. In order to purify the soul of this blemish, the sinner must bring a purification offering. But isn't the intentional sinner's soul in even more dire need of purification than the inadvertent sinner?

I believe that this question reflects the nature of the biblical audience. The text's premise is that the natural inclination of the congregation of Israel is to be faithful to their covenant with God. In the event that they lapse into sin, their conscience haunts them, and even inadvertent offense affects the manifestation of the Divine Presence in Israel. This is the purpose of the purification offering: The erring soul is invited to the Sanctuary to atone for their deed.

The text further assumes that there will always be intentional sinners, but these are far more marginal. The punishment of the man gathering wood in the wilderness (Num. 15) implies that his sin was intentional, but the description of this incident proves how startingly rare such an occasion is: The entire congregation brings the case to Moses for judgment, and the offender is stoned to death.

This reading is supported by the presentation and context of the purification offering in Numbers 15. The sequence begins with a description of communal unintentional sin, followed by an individual's unintentional sin, and finally an incident concerning an individual's intentional transgression. Why is there no mention of the communal intentional transgression? R. Yoel Bin-Nun, based on Ramban's commentary, proposes reading this as the impossibility of characterizing an entire congregation as willful sinners. If the lack of mitzva fulfillment is part of the collective culture, it must be some kind of collective error or misconception.[1]

A different formulation repeats the aforementioned idea that the Torah assumes that the people of Israel are faithful to their covenant with God, so while mistakes happen – even on a collective level – intentional sinners will always remain marginal to God's congregation. Thus, the Torah offers a solution for accidental sin, which causes such torment for the accidental sinner, whose conscience gives them no rest. The Torah offers a path of atonement that ultimately leads the sinner back to God.

THE NATURE AND ESSENCE OF THE PURIFICATION OFFERING

Leviticus 4 describes two different kinds of purification offering: internal purification offerings, whose blood is brought into the Tent of Meeting and sprinkled before the curtain (in the event of the anointed priest's sin or communal sin), and external purification offerings, whose blood is applied to the horns of the altar (when a leader or individual sins). This is a fundamental distinction in this chapter that informs the following discussion.

The unique blood rituals of this offering serve as the window to understanding its nature. The special status of the purification offering blood is more salient in internal purification offerings, given that the blood is sprinkled inside the actual Sanctuary. Instead of the altar, the blood reaches the floor in front of the curtain and the horns of the incense altar (where incense, not animals, are offered up). This surprising process indicates that this is not a typical offering, and the blood ritual requires a different explanation.

The blood ritual of the external purification offerings also deviates from that of burnt, peace, and guilt offerings. While it does reach the regular sacrifice altar, instead of "dashing" (*zarak*), the priest "applies" (*natan* – literally, "gives") the blood to the horns of the altar (4:25, 30).[2] This different verb has halakhic ramifications: The Sages rule that

1. Bin-Nun, "Unintentional Congregation."
2. The verb "*natan*," "apply," generates a further difference: In the purification offering, the priest "takes" of its blood, a verb which is absent in other offerings when the

in offerings whose blood is "dashed," the priest must dash the blood twice, once across each diagonal of the altar, so that the blood reaches all four of the altar walls ("two applications that are four"), whereas in the purification offering, when the blood is "applied," the priest must apply the blood four times, once on each altar horn.[3] The priest must collect the blood in a bowl, ascend the eastern ramp, turn right, stand at the southeastern corner, dip his finger in the blood, and apply it to that horn; he then does the same at the northeastern horn, the northwestern horn, and finally the southwestern horn. All these actions hinge upon the biblical change in verb for the blood ritual.

Before we delve into the significance of this blood ritual, we must first consider the name of the offering: What does the name "*ḥattat*" mean? Many commentators explain that the word is derived from "*ḥet*," "sin." Ramban, for example, writes:

> Now it has not been explained why the name of one offering is "a sin offering" and the other "a guilt offering," since they both come to effect atonement for sin.... It appears to me that the term "*asham*" denotes some serious deeds for which the person who did it deserves to be *shameim* (ruined) and destroyed because of it. This is similar to the expressions "*Haashimeim* (destroy them), O God; the pastures of the wilderness waste away," "*Te'sham Shomron* (Samaria shall be laid waste), for she has rebelled against her God," and "We are *asheimim*," which means "We are being punished." The word "*ḥattat*" (sin) denotes something which has turned aside off the way, as in the declaration "Every one could sling stones at a hair-breadth and not *yaḥti* (miss)." (Ramban on Lev. 5:15)

blood is dashed.

3. The horns of the altar are its four elevated corners (horned altars were excavated in Megiddo and Beersheba). Horns are a biblical and ancient symbol of might and power (see I Sam. 2:1, II Sam. 22:3, Jer. 48:25, Zech. 2:4, and more). Milgrom rightly notes that cutting off its horns was violation of the entire altar, as seen in Amos 3:14 (Milgrom, *Leviticus*, vol. 1, 236). To purify its horns was to purify its power and its entirety.

Ramban explains that a *ḥattat* is a lesser offense than an *asham*, given that the word for "sin," "*ḥet*," is derived from the word "miss," which implies that someone has merely gone astray, whereas "*asham*" implies that the sinner deserves destruction. His explanation also illuminates the nature of the *asham*, the guilt offering; for our purposes, what is relevant is the connection he draws between the "*ḥattat*" and "*ḥet*," "sin." This reading is reflected in translations that use "sin offering," and it is certainly supported by wordplay such as "If it is the anointed priest who *sins* (*yeḥeta*), bringing guilt upon his people, he shall bring an unblemished young bull to the Lord as a *ḥattat* for the *sin* he has committed" (Lev. 4:3).

Others propose a different direction, reading "*ḥattat*" as derived from "*ḥittui*," "purification."[4] This reading is already proposed by R. Saadia Gaon and is adopted by Shadal, among many others: "But it is called a '*ḥattat*' because it purifies the altar walls ... as in, 'Purify me with hyssop' (Ps. 51:9); that is why it is called '*ḥattat*,' not because it is brought for sin."[5]

Yehezkel Kaufmann writes similarly:

> If we consider the *ḥattat*, we see that its main purpose is to purify impurity or that it is rooted to the realm of the impure. It purifies and sanctifies vessels (Lev. 16:16; 18–20, 33), and not just vessels that have been used for sacred purposes, but also vessels that have not been used and therefore could not have been used in any sin (Ex. 29:36–37).[6]

This approach is developed further by Jacob Milgrom[7] and adopted by others who prove that the root of "*ḥattat*" is "*ḥittui*."[8] One such proof

4. Even if there is a common linguistic root, given that "*ḥet*," "sin," is a flaw and "*ḥittui*," "purification," is removing flaws (see Kaddari, *Dictionary*, 289), these are two different, even opposite, meanings.
5. Shadal on Leviticus 4:3, p. 397.
6. Kaufmann, *The Religion of Israel*, vol. 1, 567.
7. Milgrom, *Leviticus*, vol. 1, 253, and on.
8. See further in Kiuchi, "*Purification Offering*." I believe that this explanation is more convincing than that of Marx, who perceives it as an offering that marks a change of status (Marx, "Sacrifice de Reparation"). Milgrom rightly challenges this view by pointing out that it has nothing to do with the name "*ḥattat*." Not all accept the view that the *ḥattat*'s main purpose is purification; see Nihan, "Blood Disposal."

can be found in the description of the red heifer ritual: "Meanwhile, one who is pure shall gather up the ashes of the cow and place them outside the camp in a pure place. And they shall be kept by the Israelite community for the water of lustration, *as a purification offering (ḥattat)*" (Num. 19:9). In what sense is this mixture a "*ḥattat*"? If the word is understood as being derived from "sin," then it makes no sense in this context; rather, it must mean that the mixture serves to cleanse the impure of their impurity, as Rashi says: "It literally means purification."[9]

I too favor this interpretation; hence the use of the translation "purification offering,"[10] which casts the offering in an entirely different light. In order to understand the need for purification, we'll begin with a brief discussion of the Torah's attitude toward impurity.

IMPURITY IN THE TORAH

In halakhic thought, there is no prohibition against becoming impure. On the contrary, impurity is sometimes considered a worthy state, such as after childbirth or when burying one's dead. Although not a negative state in itself, impurity has halakhic implications: In a state of impurity, one may not come into contact with anything sacred. As long as someone does not want or need to enter the Sanctuary or eat sanctified food, however, they can remain in a state of impurity indefinitely.[11] Today, we are all in a perpetual state of ritual impurity from contact with the dead – *tumat met* – and because there is no Temple, this does not adversely affect our lives. This is true from a halakhic perspective, but is this conveyed similarly in the biblical text? Is being impure an inherently neutral or negative state?[12]

9. Compare also to Rashi's explanation of the bull of purification on the seventh day of consecration (on Ex. 29:36).
10. Wenham, who favors this reading, explains that there are other offerings for sin, while this one clearly focuses on purification. Wenham, *Leviticus,* 88–89.
11. See, for example, Rambam, *Sefer HaMitzvot,* positive commandment 109.
12. R. Aharon Lichtenstein (*Taharot,* 9–14) writes that the Sages indeed debate whether impurity itself is problematic even when there is no contact with holiness. See also Wright, "Spectrum"; Cohen, *Impurity and Purity*; Breuer, "Impurity"; Noam, *Qumran,* 27–22.

A fascinating article by Yochanan Breuer shows that the Torah does, in fact, perceive becoming impure as problematic. His analysis begins with a law regarding the variable purification offering:

> Or a person sins through touching an impure thing – the carcass of an impure beast, or a carcass of impure livestock, or the carcass of an impure creeping creature – and it escapes his notice, and while impure, he incurs guilt; or sins by touching human impurity of any kind that makes him impure, and it escapes his notice, but later he realizes his guilt.... (Lev. 5:1–3)

The law is referring to someone who became impure but then forgot about it: "While impure, he incurs guilt." The Midrash Halakha explains that he has incurred guilt because he entered the Sanctuary while impure, as Rashi notes: "Incurs guilt – by eating *kodesh* or coming to the Sanctuary." This is a necessary addition because the state of impurity does not incur guilt in itself, according to halakha. The fact is, however, that the biblical text does not mention eating *kodesh* or coming to the Sanctuary while impure, which seems to imply that merely being impure *is* problematic.

Another similar passage is the prohibition against eating certain animals because they are impure: "You may not eat the flesh of these animals or touch their carcasses; they are impure for you" (Lev. 11:8). Reading this verse literally implies that it is forbidden to touch these animals' carcasses because they are impure. Here, too, Rashi, based on the Midrash Halakha, explains that this refers to a prohibition against contact between impure and sacred:

> "You shall not touch their carcasses" – Are Israel indeed warned against touching their carcasses? It is written: "Say to the priests, etc." – priests are warned against it, but Israel are not. You may draw the conclusion that since Israel may touch a human corpse but priests may not, all the more so that this also applies to touching animal carcasses. When it says, "You shall not touch," [this means that a person must refrain from touching impure

> carcasses] before making pilgrimage on festivals. (Rashi on Lev. 11:8, MS Leipzig 1)

He explains that this prohibition only refers to touching impure carcasses before making pilgrimage to visit the Sanctuary and partake in the offerings; most of the time, there is no prohibition against touching carcasses. Rashi's formulation – "Are Israel indeed warned against touching their carcasses?!" – shows that there is a significant disparity between the implications of the biblical text and actual halakha.

Another example will clarify this even further:

> Anyone, native born or migrant, who eats an animal that has died of itself or been torn by beasts shall wash his clothes, immerse in water, and remain impure until evening; then he shall be purified. If he does not wash or immerse his body, he shall bear his guilt. (Lev. 17:15–16)

Here, too, the expression "He shall bear his guilt" shows that a person who eats an impure carcass and does not purify himself transgresses halakha. Once again, Rashi adds the Sages' qualifications: "He shall bear his guilt – If he eats holy sacrifices or enters the Sanctuary, he incurs punishment for this like all other cases of uncleanliness."

It is no coincidence that in all these instances, the Sages, cited here by Rashi, explain that this state of impurity incurs guilt only when the impure person comes into contact with holiness. Yet these qualifications are not present in the biblical text itself, which suggests that the Torah perceives the state of impurity as something inherently negative. The biblical text implies that it *is* forbidden to touch an impure carcass; that one who forgets about their state of impurity must bring an offering when they remember; that if one eats an impure carcass, they must then purify themselves – or bear their guilt!

The Torah cannot forbid people to enter a state of impurity; it is not always a matter of choice. It cannot be a sin to menstruate or give birth or bury the dead. A more likely objective is that the Torah does not wish for people to remain in a state of impurity when they have the option to purify themselves.[13] An accurate formulation, perhaps, is that "immersing as soon as possible is a mitzva";[14] the Torah wishes to keep the state of impurity to an absolute minimum, even when there is no imminent contact with holiness.

This is further clarified through the description of the Sanctuary's purification on Yom Kippur:

> In this way, he shall make atonement for the Sanctuary – from the impurity of the Israelites, from their rebellions and all their sins. And he shall do the same for the Tent of Meeting, which is with them in the midst of their impurity. (Lev. 16:16)

The Sanctuary itself must be purified from the people's impurity and sins. This seems to be a general purification that atones for the entire camp, not just for those who visited the Sanctuary in a state of impurity. The impurity of everyday life has the power to threaten the Sanctuary's purity; without regular purification, it cannot be a dwelling place for the Divine Presence. Human impurity and sin have a bearing on the sacred place in the center of the camp even when they do not venture inside. The Divine Presence rests among Israel even "in the midst of their impurity," but once a year, there must be a "deep clean," an absolute decontamination of impurity and sin.

This is also evident in the law of the red heifer:

> Whoever touches the dead body of any person shall be impure for seven days. He must purify himself with the water on the third and seventh days to become pure. If he does not purify himself on the third and seventh days, he will not be pure. Whoever touches a corpse of a person who has died, and fails to purify himself, defiles the Lord's Tabernacle. He shall be severed from Israel because, since the water of lustration was not sprinkled on

13. Büchler, *Studies in Sin*, 246–69; Wright, "Spectrum."

14. E.g., Nidda 30a. The tannaitic concept that timely immersion is considered a mitzva assumes that one must become pure as soon as possible. (See further in *Encyclopedia Biblica*, "Tevila," vol. 18.)

> him, he remains impure; his impurity is still with him.... Anyone who becomes impure and fails to purify himself shall be severed from the assembly, for he has defiled the Lord's Sanctuary. Since water of lustration was not sprinkled on him, he is impure. (Num. 19:11–20)

The verses do not state that the impure person is defiling the Lord's Sanctuary *by entering it*. The mere fact that a person remains in a state of impurity defiles the Sanctuary and severs that impure person from his people!

What emerges from these passages is that the Divine Presence resting in Israel means that the people must strive to keep impurity to an absolute minimum throughout the camp, not just in the Sanctuary itself. This is explicitly stated in the mitzva of sending the impure outside the camp:

> Then the Lord spoke to Moses: Command the Israelites to send away from the camp anyone who has an impure blight, or has had a discharge, or anyone made impure by contact with the dead. Male or female, you must send them away – send them away outside the camp, so that they do not defile their camp, in the midst of which I dwell. (Num. 5 1–3)

Here, too, the Sages qualify this commandment, based on other sources in which the impure remain inside their homes; they explain that only those with *tzaraat* (skin blight) must leave the actual camp. Yet the *peshat* of the above commandment is that anyone with a high degree of impurity must leave the camp.

Why do the Sages consistently reduce and limit the prohibition against impurity to actual contact with holiness? There are two possible directions. This might reflect the Sages' attempt to reduce the concept of impurity from an abstract, mystical, destructive force to a technical state that has few if any halakhic implications.[15] While the Sages' conception is more complex, and some *Tanna'im* do perceive impurity itself as

15. See especially Urbach, *The Sages*, 83–84; 329–30; Neusner, *The Idea of Purity*.

something more tangible,[16] we can nonetheless conclude that according to the Sages, it is not forbidden to be in a state of impurity.

Alternatively, the Sages' position might stem from their desire to extend these laws to the Temple and not just the Sanctuary. Once Israel leave the wilderness and settle in the land, the definition of "camp" undergoes a dramatic shift. When all of Israel are neatly arranged around the Sanctuary, the state of purity must remain very high in order to allow the Divine Presence to rest in the camp. Once the various tribes settle in their respective portions, much further away from the Temple, purity within "the camp" has completely different definitions. From now on, the area around the Temple becomes the "camp" that must remain pure, as Rambam writes:

> There were three camps in the wilderness: the camp of Israel, made of four camps; the Levite camp, of which it says "They shall camp around the Sanctuary"; and the camp of the Divine Presence, which is from the entrance to the Tent of Meeting courtyard inward. For generations after, the area from the entrance to Jerusalem up to the Temple Mount is equivalent to the camp of Israel; from the entrance to the Temple Mount until the entrance to the courtyard, the Nikkanor Gate, is parallel to the Levite camp, and the entrance to the courtyard inward is parallel to the camp of the Divine Presence. (*Hilkhot Beit HaBeḥira* 7:11)

Thus, in the wilderness, the state of impurity was ideally kept to an absolute minimum because it was the resting place of the Divine Presence; each member of the camp was required to purify themselves as soon as possible. This illuminates the significance of the purification offering: It purifies all the blemishes that contaminate God's resting place. Both impurity and sin are contaminating, and sins must be purified to enable a state of holiness within the camp worthy of the Divine Presence.

The individual purification offering in Leviticus appears in three main contexts:

---

16. See Noam, *Qumran*, 220–318.

1. During the seven days of consecration of the Tabernacle and the purification of its vessels, it is the purification offering through which the altar is purified: "Each day, offer a bull as a purification offering for atonement. Purify the altar by making atonement for it, and consecrate it by anointing it. For seven days, make atonement for the altar and consecrate it, so that the altar becomes holy of holies – and anything that touches it will become holy" (Ex. 29:36). Note the precise language: The purification offering purifies but does not consecrate. It is the anointing that consecrates, but purification is necessary before consecration is possible. (See further below in the discussion of the days of consecration.)
2. An unintentional sin: "If a person sins unintentionally with regard to any of the Lord's commands, doing what should not be done; any transgression" (Lev. 4:2). Any unintentional transgression of a negative commandment requires a purification offering. As mentioned, based on parallel verses in Numbers, the Sages state that this is only true of major transgressions. However, this initial formulation implies that a purification offering is required for every accidental transgression of a negative commandment.
3. After severe impurity of at least seven days (after a *zav* discharge or a Nazirite who has become impure), a person must bring a purification offering in order to become pure. After being cleansed of their impurity and counting seven days, they must bring a purification offering (alongside a burnt offering) on the eighth day.

Because a purification offering purifies from impurity, it is an obvious ritual when purification is required, such as when the altar is being purified for use, and following purification after childbirth, discharge, or *tzaraat*. Those who assume that the *ḥattat* is derived from "sin" must ask why a woman must bring a *ḥattat* after childbirth, but it is obvious why she must bring a *purification* offering: She has been impure for a long time[17] A more logical question, in fact, is not why a new mother must bring a purification offering, but why the inadvertent sinner must. What does sin have to do with purification of the Sanctuary?

This can be linked to the aforementioned verse about Yom Kippur in which the priest purifies the Sanctuary "from the impurity of the Israelites, from their rebellions and all their sins." The Sanctuary must be cleansed not only from impurity, but from contamination from sins and rebellions, which also taint the purity of the Sanctuary. In the words of Wenham: "Sin not only angers God and deprives him of his due, it also makes his sanctuary unclean. A holy God cannot dwell amid uncleanness."[18]

Every sin generates impurity that threatens to prevent the Divine Presence from resting amidst Israel. The purification offering purifies God's resting place and allows the Divine Presence to continue dwelling among Israel. To reiterate this last point: The blood of the purification offering does not purify the sinner, but the Sanctuary whose sanctity has been compromised by sin. Thus, the purification offering does not atone for the sinner or distinguish between sinner and sin. Rather, its purpose is to purify the *altar*, which thereby has the power to atone for the person who threatened its sanctity.[19]

In this context, it is worth mentioning why the phrase "fire offering to the Lord" is mentioned in conjunction with all offerings except for the purification offering. Is the latter not intended for the altar's fire? While some of its flesh is indeed consumed by the altar's flames, its main purpose is unique among sacrifices: It does not feed the altar, but rather purifies it and cleans it of its contamination. That is why the purification offering is not named "a fire offering to the Lord."

---

17. Tirzah Mitcham challenges this reading by claiming that the Sages link sin and impurity (T. Mitcham, "Suggestion of Linguistic Explanation in the Law of the Days of Purity and Impurity for the Birthing Mother of a Female," *Shenaton LeMikra ULeḤeker HaMikra HaKadum* 11).
18. Wenham, *Leviticus*, 89.
19. Milgrom reiterates this. See especially "Rite of Passage"; "Ḥattat"; "Two Kinds." See also Kiuchi's discussion of how the purification offering helps the sinner stop hiding from God and enables him to expose himself before God anew (Kiuchi, *Hatta and Hattat*).

CIRCLES OF PURIFICATION

If the purpose of the purification offering is to purify the Sanctuary, we can sketch out three circles of purification:[20]

1. The courtyard with its outer altar
2. The Sanctuary with its golden altar
3. The Holy of Holies with its Ark and cherubim

The greater the damage to the Sanctuary, the deeper the need for purification. An individual's sin causes relatively little damage, and so in that case only the outer altar requires purification (by applying blood to its four corners). This is an "external purification offering."

Two kinds of inadvertent sin require deeper, "internal" purification: (1) the anointed priest's (i.e., the High Priest's) sin and (2) communal sin. We will yet explore the nature of these sins and their consequences below; for now it suffices to point out that they require an "internal" offering, with blood sprinkled in front of the curtain covering the Ark and around the incense altar, while the rest is poured out at the base of the burnt offering altar where the perpetual flame burns.[21] Both internal and external purification offerings serve to purify; the difference is only the extent of purification required.[22]

Beyond these two circles, the deepest, innermost purification ritual takes place once a year, "deep cleaning" the entire House of God. On Yom Kippur, the High Priest brings the blood of the purification offering inside to the Holy of Holies. He does not stop in front of the curtain that separates him and the cherubim; he goes into the place where the cherubim are and begins sprinkling blood right there, in the very heart of the Sanctuary. I wish to emphasize that this act of sprinkling serves to cleanse and purify; it is incorrect to claim (as Gese does) that

---

20. Milgrom, "Ḥattat," 6.
21. Above, I adopt Milgrom's formulation; below, in the context of "sprinkle," I will argue that this is an action that throws the blood in a direction the priest cannot go. Thus, sprinkling blood toward the curtain is not just cleansing the Sanctuary, but is an expression of wishing to purify the Holy of Holies as well.
22. Milgrom, "Two Kinds." He disagrees with both Kaufmann and Baruch Levine, who argue that they are of a different nature.

this blood represents Israel in a symbolic meeting between the bringer of the sacrifice and God enthroned upon the cherubim.[23] Yom Kippur certainly expresses a rare encounter between human and God, but the blood sprinkled in the Holy of Holies does not represent Israel; its purpose is to cleanse the innermost chamber from Israel's impurity and sin.

The unique purpose of the purification offering's blood explains the use of a different verb for the blood ritual – "*natan*," "apply," instead of "*zarak*," "dash." The latter is used for the blood of offerings that is dashed all around the outer altar as a gift to God while their flesh is burned upon that same altar. In contrast, the blood of the purification offering serves to purify; it is applied to the inner and outer surfaces to cleanse, not as an offering.[24]

It now remains to clarify why some offenses require cleansing of the inner sanctuary, while in other cases only the outer altar needs purification.

INTERNAL AND EXTERNAL PURIFICATION OFFERINGS

Leviticus 4 is divided into four sections, and its structure differs from the chapters of freewill offerings. Burnt, grain, and peace offerings are categorized according to offering type: whether the offering is from the herd or flock (or bird); or fine flour, cooked grain, and first produce. In contrast, purification offerings are divided based on the identity of the sacrifice bringer: the anointed priest (vv. 3–12), the entire community (vv. 13–21), the leader (vv. 22–26), or the individual (vv. 27–35). Only the individual's offering has two different options (goat or sheep).

This difference reveals much about the nature of the purification offering. The identity of the sinner, who brings the offering, affects the type of offering and process required. It emerges that not all are equal in the eyes of the law: Whether the sinner is an individual, a leader, or a priest results in a different level of damage to the holiness of the Sanctuary.

While there are four different sinners listed in the chapter, the main division is between the first two and the second two: Offenses by the

23. Gese, *Zur biblischen Theologie*, 99–95.

24. Kaufmann explains that the purification offering began not as the result of sin but as a kind of agency (*The Religion of Israel*, vol. 1, 569).

anointed priest and the entire community of Israel require internal purification, whereas offenses by the leader or the individual require external purification. This distinction is expressed through a change in the opening word:

- "*If* (*im*) it is the anointed priest who sins" (4:3)
- "*If* (*im*) it is the entire community of Israel" (v. 13)
- "*When* (*asher*) a leader sins unintentionally" (v. 22)
- "*If* (*im*) an individual" (v. 27)

The first, second, and fourth case open with "If"; only the leader's offering begins with "When." There is no substantial difference between "If" and "When" here – as Rabbeinu Bahya writes: "*Asher* means the same as *im*" – but the change nonetheless conveys the shift to a new section. Rashi writes that the word "*asher*" expresses appreciation for the leader who is willing to admit his mistakes: "Fortunate (*ashrei*) is the generation whose leader takes care to bring atonement for his mistakes." A more straightforward reading is that the different word alerts the reader that this is the beginning of a new section and type of offering.

Besides the different blood rituals for internal and external purification offerings, there are two other notable differences:

1. The type of offering: Internal purification offerings are bulls, whereas external ones are from the flock (a he-goat for the leader and a she-goat or ewe for the individual). One theory is that a bull is a larger sacrifice for a more grave offense; however, as shown earlier, the difference between bull and sheep is not merely their size and expense. The different animals correlate with different parts of the Sanctuary. Bulls are associated with the inner Sanctuary, while sheep are linked to the outer altar.[25]

---

25. Abarbanel links this to the sin of the Golden Calf: The first offering recalls Aaron's part in the sin, and the second the people's fault; this explains why they both offer bulls. Yet it is not convincing that every future sin a priest commits is linked to that first sin.

2. Internal purification offerings are not eaten at all; the meat that is not offered on the altar is burned outside the camp (4:12). In contrast, the priests receive portions of the external purification offerings. The latter law is not mentioned in the first list in *Vayikra*, but it is noted in the complementary list in *Tzav* (6:19–22). There, after the priests' portion of the external purification offering is mentioned, the text emphasizes that no part of the internal purification offering is eaten at all (6:23).[26] We will analyze this below; for now, it suffices to point out the anomalous law of the internal purification offering being burned outside the camp instead of eaten by the priests.

These differences show that the two kinds of purification offering are almost two different types of offering, except for the fact that both of them serve to purify the Sanctuary from accidental sin. What is the reason for the difference between the two kinds of offering? Why is the anointed priest's offering grouped together with communal sin, and the leader's sin with the individual's?

Intriguingly, the Midrash Halakha indeed debates whether the High Priest is closer to the entire community or the leader (*Sifra*, Obligatory Offerings 2:1–4). Why is the High Priest grouped with the entire community?

One possibility is that both the High Priest and the people of Israel have been singled out for a higher level of holiness. Hizkuni, for example, suggests that the level of holiness of the High Priest and the collective Chosen People makes the blood of their atonement holier (so it is offered in a holier place) and the stench of their sin much more offensive (so the flesh must be burned outside the camp). By contrast, the offenses of regular leaders and individuals are less severe and can thus be offered on the regular altar, with the regular portions for the priests. However, I believe that a more specific feature explains the division between the two models.

---

26. This is the most straightforward reading there. Rashi understands this as referring to the external purification offering whose blood is accidentally sprinkled inside.

The text relating to the High Priest's sin uses a unique phrase: "If it is the anointed priest who sins, *bringing guilt* upon his people" (4:3). The *Rishonim* explain this phrase in three different ways:

1. The Sages extrapolate halakhic implications from this phrase, explaining that both the entire community and the High Priest are required to bring a purification offering only under specific circumstances (when they received the wrong information and also acted in error). This is Rashi's interpretation, for example.
2. Rashbam cites the above and then adds that the High Priest is responsible for the masses, since the priests' highest responsibility is to teach Torah; if the High Priest errs, the entire community will be misled. Abarbanel takes this a step further and explains that this refers to a case in which the High Priest actually gives the people incorrect instruction, so that they also err. Either way, according to this reading, the expression "bringing guilt upon the people" refers to accidentally misleading the people so that they all commit accidental sin; hence the severity of the High Priest's error.[27]
3. Rashi and Sforno offer a simple explanation: "When the High Priest sins, it is the people's fault, because they are dependent on him to atone and pray for them, but now he has been impaired" (Rashi on 4:3). The High Priest's offense is more severe not because he is liable to mislead the people to sin, but because he is their representative to God who prays on their behalf, and when he sins his agency is compromised. Sforno explains that if the High Priest himself errs, this certainly reflects badly on the people he represents. In the words of Philo: "The true high priest, not the one incorrectly called so, has no participation in sin; and if ever he stumble, this will happen to him, not for his own sake, but for the common errors of the nation."[28]

27. Also Milgrom, *Leviticus,* vol. 1, 232.
28. Philo, *Laws I,* part 200 (*Writings,* vol. 2, 273). See also Wenham, *Leviticus,* 97.

Even if this latter explanation sounds far removed from the literal meaning, it is actually supported in the text. The phrase "bringing guilt upon the people" replaces a different phrase found in the other three cases in the chapter: "Thus,incurring guilt" (13, 22, 27). This phrase is absent from the description of the High Priest's error, as if to say that instead of the High Priest incurring guilt for his own error, it is the people who are at fault, not the priest himself.

Casting the priest's guilt on the people instead is evident through two other aspects that are absent from the description of the High Priest's purification offering. First, the other three sinners all become aware of their sin: "When the sin that [the community] committed becomes known" (v. 14); "When the sin that [the leader] has committed becomes known to him" (v. 23); "When the sin that [the individual] has committed becomes known to him" (v. 28). For some reason, this is absent from the High Priest's error. Milgrom suggests that "there is no choice but to infer that these things are taken for granted (*Keter Torah*). Because the High Priest performs most of his rituals in the privacy of the tent-shrine, only he can inform himself of his error. And once discovered, it is inconceivable that he would not feel remorse."[29] Yet given that this omission is not the only difference, this seems to be significant, not a case of mere brevity.

The second omission in the High Priest's error is even more surprising. Each description in the chapter ends with a statement of forgiveness: "So shall the priest make atonement for him/them, and he/they shall be forgiven," (vv. 20, 26, 31, 35). Yet there is no such statement in the case of the High Priest. Ramban is troubled by this omission:

> The purification offering of the High Priest does not mention "So shall the priest make atonement for him, and he shall be forgiven," as in the case of the community, leader, or individual. Perhaps due to the stature of his position, he shall not achieve complete atonement or forgiveness until he prays and pleads to God, for he is like an angel of the Lord's hosts and he must be utterly clean and pure handed. (Ramban on Lev. 4:2)

29. Milgrom, *Leviticus*, vol. 1, 232.

According to Ramban, a mere offering does not suffice; in order to attain forgiveness, he must pray. Yet this suggestion is problematic, as there is no mention at all of prayer in this context.

Abarbanel proposes a different theory, which is consistent with his reading of the phrase "bringing guilt upon the people." Based on his explanation that the High Priest "brought guilt upon the people" by accidentally leading the people to inadvertent sin, it can be understood that the High Priest cannot achieve full atonement until the people have also brought a communal purification offering. Therefore, the clause "So shall the priest make atonement for the people, and they shall be forgiven" (20) applies to the High Priest as well, and thus concludes both the internal purification offerings.[30] This is a fascinating, creative reading, but it is still problematic: Given that the laws of the communal purification offering are written out separately as an entirely different case, it seems unlikely that its conclusion should suddenly apply to both of them.

I believe that Abarbanel is correct that the High Priest cannot achieve full atonement because he misled the people, but rather than positing that the communal offering's conclusion applies to him as well, the withholding of his forgiveness should be read as an intentional literary device. It is not, as Milgrom suggests, a case of brevity,[31] given that both these elements are listed in all three other cases. Rather, it seems to be the result of "bringing guilt on the people," as Sforno explains:

> Therefore, it does not say "thus incurring guilt" about him as with all the other sinners. For the phrase anticipates repentance, but that is not up to the High Priest, for he is not responsible for the sin at all; it happened to him because of the people's guilt.

The High Priest, the people's religious representative, is a kind of litmus test for the people's spiritual state, as if he is the portrait locked in the attic of Dorian Gray.[32] Therefore, he is not truly guilty, nor can he

---

30. Abarbanel on Lev. 4, p. 32.
31. Milgrom, *Leviticus*, vol. 1, 232.
32. Milgrom's general theology about the sacrificial world is what he refers to as the "Priestly Picture of Dorian Gray" – when an individual sins, the damage it causes

recognize his guilt or achieve atonement for it, for his error is not really his own but a reflection of the people's state.

If so, Abarbanel's theory can be revisited: Once the people achieve forgiveness and atonement, their representative – the High Priest – does as well. The High Priest's error is essentially a kind of communal error. This, of course, does not exempt him from responsibility; on the contrary, as the people's representative, he must strive for perfection, for if he errs he brings the entire generation down with him as well.

This clarifies why the High Priest's purification offering is grouped together with the community's. Communal sins require internal purification offerings; individual sins require lesser, external offerings. While there is still a difference between the leader's sin and the regular individual's, the leader is not considered the people's representative to God in the same sense that the High Priest is; his sin is less damaging to the Sanctuary.

In summary, the individual's sin does affect the Sanctuary's holiness, but to a lesser degree than a communal error, which requires an internal purification offering. Once a year, the High Priest brings the blood of the purification offering to the Holy of Holies and deep cleans the entire Sanctuary from the inside out, starting from the deepest, holiest place.

This brings us to the analysis of the various purification offerings.

THE HIGH PRIEST'S PURIFICATION OFFERING

The first case is the purification offering of the "anointed priest," the High Priest:

> If it is the anointed priest who sins, bringing guilt upon his people, he shall bring an unblemished young bull to the Lord as a purification offering for the sin he has committed. He shall bring the bull before the Lord at the entrance to the Tent of Meeting, lay his hand upon the bull's head, and slaughter the bull before the Lord.

---

cannot be perceived on his person, but it affects the Sanctuary or altar, which requires a purification offering (Milgrom, *Leviticus*, vol. 1, 49; Milgrom, "Dorian Gray"). This is even more salient with the High Priest's purification offering – not against the Sanctuary, but against the entire people through the High Priest.

> The anointed priest shall take some of the bull's blood and bring it into the Tent of Meeting. The priest shall dip his finger into the blood and sprinkle of it seven times before the Lord in front of the Sanctuary's inner curtain. Then the priest shall apply some of the blood to the horns of the altar of fragrant incense, which is in the Tent of Meeting before the Lord. The rest of the bull's blood he shall pour out at the base of the altar of burnt offerings, at the entrance to the Tent of Meeting. He shall remove all the fat from the bull of the purification offering: the fat that covers the entrails and all the fat surrounding them; the two kidneys and the fat that is on them at the loins; and the diaphragm of the liver, which should be removed with the kidneys, just as it is removed from the ox of the peace offering. The priest shall send these up in smoke upon the altar of burnt offerings. But the bull's skin and all its flesh, together with its head, legs, entrails, and dung – all the rest of the bull – he shall take to a ritually pure place outside the camp, to the ash heap, and burn upon a wood fire; at the ash heap it shall be burned. (Lev. 4:3–12)

Like all other offerings, the purification offering must be "unblemished" (*tamim*). An obligatory offering must be just as worthy as a freewill offering; a sickly or dying animal is not appropriate for the Sanctuary. Like freewill animal offerings, the purification offering also includes laying of the hands and ritual slaughter. It is interesting to note that here, too, the worshipper must lay his "hand" – not "hands" – which implies that this is not an act of transferring sin from sinner to offering, but rather of generating an affinity between them, which has the same purpose as the laying of the hands in freewill offerings.

The Blood Ritual

As mentioned, what distinguishes the purification from previous offerings is the unique blood ritual. In this case, the bull's blood is brought to the Sanctuary and used for purification in two stages:

1. The priest first stands before the curtain (while he is still standing in the Sanctuary – he does not go inside the Holy of Holies). He

dips his finger in the blood and sprinkles the blood seven times in front of the curtain. (The Sages explain that it must not touch the actual curtain.)[33] How does the act of "sprinkling" differ from "dashing" and "applying" the blood? What is its significance in the sacrificial world? Some scholars surmise that this serves to consecrate the blood itself before it can be used for purification of the incense altar,[34] but this does not make sense: Why should there be a need to consecrate the blood of an animal that has already been consecrated? The blood has already been consecrated; now it is being used for purification.

I believe that the law of the red heifer can illuminate the present discussion: "Elazar the priest shall take some of its blood with his finger and sprinkle it seven times toward the front of the Tent of Meeting" (Num. 19:4). The priest is too far to apply the blood with his finger; instead, he sprinkles the blood in the desired direction. The same seems to be true of the High Priest's sprinkling of the blood toward the cherubim on Yom Kippur (Lev. 16:14–16); they are too holy to be touched, so he sprinkles the blood toward them instead.[35] Sprinkling the blood is a substitute for actual contact.[36]

2. After sprinkling the blood, the priest starts to make his way outward. On his way out, he stops at the incense altar and applies the blood to the horns of the altar. This is not a gift to God; the incense altar is not for offerings, as a verse explicitly warns: "Offer no unauthorized incense upon it, or any burnt offering, grain offering, or libation" (Ex. 30:9). The blood is not an offering, but

33. The number seven suggests a re-creation, a resetting to a state of primordial purity. Regarding whether each seven sprinklings are one action each or seven small actions, see the talmudic discussion of whether the priest must wash his hands in between sprinklings (Menaḥot 7b).

34. Vriezen, "*Hizza*," who suggests that when aimed at people or objects, the point of sprinkling is to purify, but when aimed before the Lord (4:6) or inside the Sanctuary (16:14), the point is to sanctify the blood itself.

35. This recalls the custom of praying toward Jerusalem, which expresses the desire to pray in the House of God.

36. See also Kurtz, *Sacrificial Worship*, 216–17.

a purification agent. This act serves as purification of the entire Sanctuary; the first sprinkling in front of the curtain expresses the priest's desire to purify the Ark and cherubim inside, while applying blood to the horns of the incense altar reflects purification of the entire *Kodesh* (Sanctuary).

Why is the blood sprinkled on the incense altar, of all places? This seems to be related to its nature and placement. The incense altar is associated with the Divine Presence's manifestation in the Tabernacle. The incense and its fragrant smoke-screen is what makes it possible for the priests to serve alongside the Divine Presence.[37] This is especially salient in God's commandment to Moses: "Put it in front of the screen that veils the Ark of the Testimony, in front of the cover above the Ark, where I will meet with you" (Ex. 30:6). The altar's connection to the Ark of the Testimony is even more striking on the eve of the Tabernacle's consecration, which makes no mention of the curtain that separates between it and the Ark: "Put the golden incense altar in front of the Ark of the Testimony" (Ex. 40:5). This is also evident in the layout of the Tabernacle and its vessels: The candelabra and the table are laid out along the horizontal axis (see Ex. 26:25), while the Ark and cherubim and the incense altar are laid out along the vertical axis, which is the relevant axis for the present discussion. In this sense, the internal purification offering ritual concerns the two places that are directly linked to divine revelation: Blood is sprinkled in front of the curtain of the Ark and cherubim; then blood is applied to the incense altar whose smoke enables divine revelation. The purifying smoke then diffuses throughout the entire Sanctuary.

3. An additional stage follows the two main stages of the blood ritual: "The rest of the bull's blood he shall pour out at the base of the altar of burnt offerings, at the entrance to the Tent of Meeting" (4:7). "Pour out" is another new verb; it does not appear in the

37. For a more complex presentation of the purpose of incense, especially on Yom Kippur, see Stav, *Beyond the Curtain*, 189–208; and see below, in the discussion of Nadav and Avihu on the eighth day of consecration.

burnt or peace offering ritual, and it seems to refer to treatment of the leftover blood and not part of the actual blood service.[38] In the words of the Mishna: "The leftover blood was poured on the western base of the outer altar. If he did not do so, this did not disqualify" (Zevaḥim 5:1). The main part of the blood ritual has already been carried out, but much blood remains, so it is poured out at the base of the outer altar.[39] Note that no blood reaches the horns of the outer altar, where the blood of most other offerings is dashed. (Compare to the variable bird purification offering: "The rest of the blood shall be drained out at its base" – 5:9.[40])

Offering Up the *Eimurim*

Intriguingly, the parts of the purification offering burned on the altar are the same parts that are offered up from the peace offering. The text even explicitly notes this:

> He shall remove all the fat from the bull of the purification offering: the fat that covers the entrails and all the fat surrounding them; the two kidneys and the fat that is on them at the loins; and the diaphragm of the liver, which should be removed with the kidneys, just as it is removed from the ox of the peace offering. (4:8–10)

38. This seems to be the meaning of the *Sifra* here: "'Pour' – and not 'drip'; 'pour' and not 'sprinkle'; 'pour' and not dash" (*Sifra*, Obligatory Offerings, 3:12). That is, the verb "pour" implies that all necessary rituals have been done and this is pouring out the leftovers. On whether it is considered part of the actual ritual, see Soloveitchik, *Yom HaKippurim*, 113–16.
39. This may inform the *Aḥaronim*'s dispute as to whether the extra blood must be contained in a service vessel; in any case, failure to do this step does not make the offering invalid, as is evident from the Mishna in Zevaḥim 5 and the ruling that blood spattered on clothing does not require washing, as its level of holiness decreases after the main blood ritual is carried out.
40. The verb used for bird blood is "*yimatzeh*," "drained," instead of "poured out" because there is so little blood. The *Rishonim* debate whether this applies to the leftover blood of all offerings or just to the purification offering. See further in Kasher, *Torah Shelema*, vol. 7, 211.

This reference to the peace offering may be merely technical, clarifying that it is the same exact procedure, but even the text displays awareness that such similarity between two very different offerings is surprising. The peace offering is a joyous affirmation of the covenant with God; the purification offering is a remedial ritual following sin. How can the surprising similarity between them be understood?

Rashi (based on the Sages) explains thus:

> To link it to peace offerings: Just as the peace offering had to be designated for the specific purpose of a peace offering, so too, this sacrifice had to be designated for its specific purpose, and just as peace offerings [bring] peace to the world, so too, this sacrifice [brings] peace to the world. (Rashi on Lev. 4:10)

The first explanation, "for the specific purpose," refers to halakhic nuances that are beyond the scope of this discussion.[41] His second comment, however, is surprising: Does a purification offering, brought after accidental sin, really bring peace to the world? A deliberate connection between a freewill offering and an obligatory offering hints that reconciliation and even friendship between sinner and God is possible through the flesh of the purification offering.

The main ritual focus on the purification offering is on its blood. Blood is what achieves purification of the Sanctuary and resultant atonement, not flesh. In fact, its flesh – at least according to the biblical language – recalls the love and friendship of the peace offering. Once the blood has served its purpose, the flesh of the offering can rise up to heaven in a column of smoke and reconciliation. This is reflected in the conclusion of the individual's purification offering: "The priest shall send it up in smoke upon the altar as a sweet savor to the Lord. So shall the priest make atonement for that person, and he will be forgiven" (4:31). Mention of the "sweet savor" is yet another surprise; this phrase is generally associated with freewill offerings, whose purpose is not to achieve atonement but to produce a "sweet savor." This rule has one exception:

---

41. This is discussed at length in Tractates Zevaḥim and Menaḥot; see Mishna Zevaḥim 1:1; Menaḥot 1:1.

the individual's purification offering. We will explore this below; for now, I mention this in dialogue with the purification offering's sudden reference to the peace offering. Ultimately, even obligatory offerings can have the power to bring peace to the world.

Burning the Flesh Outside the Camp

For some reason, the priests do not eat the remaining meat of the purification offering. The meat is burned outside the camp instead:

> But the bull's skin and all its flesh, together with its head, legs, entrails, and dung – all the rest of the bull – he shall take to a ritually pure place outside the camp, to the ash heap, and burn upon a wood fire; at the ash heap it shall be burned. (4:11–12)

Why don't the priests receive their share of the flesh of internal purification offerings?

There is no mention of what happens to the flesh of external purification offerings in *Parashat Vayikra*; that the priests receive a share is only revealed in *Parashat Tzav*. This generates a fascinating tension: On the one hand, there is no description of eating any offering in *Parashat Vayikra* (with the exception of the grain offering). Even when there is great expectation, the Torah remains silent – the anticipated laws are revealed only in *Parashat Tzav*. On the other hand, this suspense creates an obvious dialogue between the two sacrificial lists. While the text in *Parashat Vayikra* is silent regarding the flesh of external purification offerings, it is "aware" that the parallel text in *Parashat Tzav* will come and fill in the gaps.

How can the burning of the internal purification offering outside the camp be understood? We must first understand how the priestly share of the purification meat is perceived. As mentioned, this is discussed in *Parashat Tzav*, but given its implication for the topic at hand, we will jump ahead to the later chapter.

Yehezkel Kaufmann suggests that eating the flesh of the purification offering "eliminates meat charged with dangerous force."[42] When the

42. Kaufmann, *The Religion of Israel*, vol. 1, 568.

blood purifies the impurity, the flesh absorbs it. Such negative, dangerous impurity cannot be offered upon the altar, so the priests eat it instead. While the external purification offering purges a moderate amount of impurity that can still be eaten by the priests, the internal purification offering becomes so dangerous that there is no choice but to burn it outside the camp. This is an intriguing concept, but it seems unlikely that the Torah would command the priests to consume flesh that has absorbed such impurity;[43] on the contrary – the Torah is especially stringent about the priests' purity.

R. Kasher proposes a completely different idea. He perceives the priests' eating of the purification offering as similar to the talmudic statement: "One who wishes to pour libations of wine over the altar should fill the throats of Torah scholars with wine" (Yoma 71a). R. Kasher explains: "When a Torah scholar eats in holiness and purity, with his thoughts devoted to the Supreme Light, then his eating is considered an offering and his table an altar."[44] This idea is based on the text: The Torah presents the priests eating their share as the continuation of the offering – upon their table instead of the altar. This explains why a priest who offers his own sacrifice cannot receive a priestly share, for he is cast in the role of sacrifice bringer, not ministering priest. In a certain sense, the priests are the biblical answer to the problem of divine anthropomorphism. If offerings are indeed what allow the Divine Presence to rest in the Sanctuary (as is especially evident in the second sacrificial list), then the priests serve as God's agents to eat the gifts of food offered by Israel. As mentioned repeatedly, according to the Torah, God does not need Israel's offerings. The priests receive God's share instead.

The difference between internal and external purification offerings can be explained through this paradigm: When the priests themselves are part of the congregation in need of atonement (either the High Priest or the entire community), they cannot eat of the offering, as priests normally do.[45] This is similar to Ibn Ezra's reading: "The priests eat of the leader's purification offering as written, but the High Priest does not

43. As claimed by Milgrom, "Two Kinds."

44. Kasher, *Torah Shelema*, vol. 7, 279.

45. See also Watts, *Leviticus*, 338.

eat of his own purification offering" (on Lev. 4:23). He cannot eat of his own offering; nor can he eat of the communal offering because he is part of the community. This explains why Aaron and his sons do not eat the purification offering on the eighth day of consecration after the death of Nadav and Avihu (Lev. 10:16–20), as we will discuss in context.

How Is the Burning of the Flesh Perceived?

> But the bull's skin and all its flesh, together with its head, legs, entrails, and dung – all the rest of the bull – (v. 11)
> he shall take to a ritually pure place outside the camp, to the ash heap, and burn upon a wood fire; at the ash heap it shall be burned (v. 12).

The burning of the purification offering's flesh can be perceived as "waste disposal" for the part of the animal that cannot be used. The priests cannot eat of the offering that atones for them, and the altar cannot accept parts of the animal that are not considered *eimurim*. Burning is the default option for disposing of consecrated flesh that may not be eaten. (Meat that is left over after the allotted time is also burned, as we will discuss below.)

A closer look at these verses, however, reveals that burning the flesh is not a simple matter of waste disposal. The strangest detail in this verse is the requirement to take the flesh to "a ritually pure place." If burning the flesh is merely waste disposal, why must the place be ritually pure? While it is possible to claim that the Torah wishes to prevent any holiness spreading from consecrated flesh, the continuation of the verse shows that this requirement is even more significant: "All the rest of the bull he shall take to a ritually pure place outside the camp, to the ash heap, and burn upon a wood fire; *at the ash heap it shall be burned*." The beginning of the second sacrificial list (6:3–4) describes how the altar ashes must be cleared away each morning and brought outside the camp;[46] this is what is known as "the ash heap." This is where the internal purification

46. According to the Sages, the ashes are not cleared outside the camp every morning; we will discuss this in context.

offering is burned. According to some of the Sages, the purification is supposed to be burned directly on top of the ashes, and if there are no ashes at the site, the priest must wait until more ashes are brought (*Sifra*, Obligatory Offerings, 5:1).[47] This is Ibn Ezra's reading as well: "It must be burned at the place where the altar ashes are." That is, the verse is not merely describing the place, but hinting that this heap of altar ashes is a kind of substitution for the altar itself. Moreover, the verse also mentions that the flesh must be burned "upon a wood fire," which recalls the wood laid upon the altar itself. Thus, these verses conjure up the scene of a kind of imitation of the altar.

This reading results in several surprising halakhic ramifications. The *Sifra* debates whether the wood used for burning must be altar-grade wood. While the conclusion is that any kind of wood may be used, the fact that the Sages even question whether the wood must be fit for use upon the altar hints to the nature of this act. This is further reinforced by the *Sifra*'s ruling that the flesh must be cut into pieces like the burnt offering before it is burned (Obligatory Offerings 5:1–2; see also Zevaḥim 50a).

This law demonstrates that this burning is considered an alternative form of ritual sacrifice, not merely waste disposal but the continuation of the sacrificial service.[48] There is the official altar at the heart of the Tabernacle at the heart of the camp, where only priests may walk. But there is another place outside the camp where the altar ashes are brought, a kind of parallel, unofficial, unauthorized altar, and it is there that the flesh of the purification offering that may not be eaten is burned.

THE ENTIRE COMMUNITY'S PURIFICATION OFFERING

This offering has already been discussed in relation to the High Priest's offering: Because it is a communal offering it is an internal purification offering whose blood is sprinkled inside the Sanctuary and whose flesh

47. Some learn from this verse that even if there are no ashes there, the bull can still be burned; what matters is the location (Pesaḥim 75b; Rashi on Lev. 4:12).
48. From a completely different direction, some scholars conclude that the priests have a share in all purification offerings, and burning the internal offerings is the adoption of the burnt offering ritual (Yanovsky, "Atonement," 236–38). Kiuchi rejects this (*Purification Offering*, 131–32). According to our reading, Yanovsky's reading has some merit, even if not on the diachronic level.

is burned outside the camp. Yet there are still subtle differences between the two internal purification offerings:

> If it is the entire community of Israel that commits an unintentional sin, the congregation unwittingly violating one of the Lord's commands, doing what must not be done, when the sin that they committed becomes known, the community shall bring a young bull as a purification offering, presenting it before the Tent of Meeting. The community elders shall lay their hands on the bull's head before the Lord and, before the Lord, the bull shall be slaughtered. The anointed priest shall take some of the bull's blood into the Tent of Meeting. The priest shall dip his finger into the blood and sprinkle it seven times before the Lord in front of the curtain. Then he shall apply some of the blood to the horns of the altar before the Lord in the Tent of Meeting, and pour out all the rest at the base of the altar of burnt offerings, at the entrance to the Tent of Meeting. Then he shall remove all its fat and send it up in smoke upon the altar. He shall do the same with this bull as he does with the bull of his purification offering; he shall do the same with this. So shall the priest make atonement for the people, and they shall be forgiven. The priest shall then take the bull outside the camp and burn it just as he burns the first bull. This is the community's purification offering. (4:13–21)

Some claim that the High Priest must offer up his own purification offering, while the communal purification offering may be performed by any priest.[49] This is unconvincing, however, given that the text specifically refers to the "anointed priest": "The anointed priest shall take some of the bull's blood into the Tent of Meeting."

The (slight) difference between the two offerings is in the description of where the blood is sprinkled. The blood of the communal offering must be sprinkled "seven times before the Lord in front of the curtain" (v. 17), whereas the blood of the High Priest's offering is sprinkled "seven

49. As proposed by R. Soloveitchik based on Rambam (Soloveitchik, *Yom HaKippurim*, 109–10).

times before the Lord in front of the Sanctuary's inner curtain" (v. 6). While it refers to the same place, Rashi still ascribes significance to this difference in description:[50]

> But above, Scripture says, "in front of the Sanctuary's inner curtain." This may be compared to a king against whom a province revolted. If only a minority rebels, his cabinet remains intact. If the entire country rebels, however, his cabinet does not remain intact. Here, too, when the High Priest sinned, the name of holiness was still attached to the Sanctuary. When they all sin, God forbid, the holiness is gone. (Rashi on 4:17)

Beyond Rashi's actual explanation, two further insights can be gleaned from his reading. Firstly, it implies that a person's sin threatens the dwelling of the Divine Presence and thus harms the Sanctuary itself, not just the sinner. This is consistent with the view that the purification offering heals the damage caused by sin. Secondly – and this is far from obvious – Rashi clearly thinks that the communal purification offering incorporates a higher level of severity than the High Priest's offering. He likens the latter to a minor rebellion and the former to a serious rebellion – so serious that it is as if the curtain is stripped of its association with the holy Sanctuary.

On the other hand, another difference leads Rashi to the opposite conclusion. The text's description of the *eimurim* burnt upon the altar in the communal offering is much briefer than the description of the High Priest's *eimurim*. Rashi argues that this is significant, not a technical abbreviation:

> Although Scripture here does not explicitly mention the diaphragm and the two kidneys, they are derived from "He shall do to the bull just as he did [to the bull (sacrificed) as a sin offering]." Now why are these details not specified here? The school of Rabbi Yishmael taught: This can be compared to a king who

50. The *Sifra* also notes this difference and emphasizes that it is a literary difference without halakhic ramifications (*Sifra*, Obligatory Offerings, 6:4).

> was furious with his beloved friend, but shortened [the account of] his offense, because of his affection for him. (Rashi on Lev. 4:19, based on Zevaḥim 41a)

The Torah uses a shorter description so as not to focus on Israel's offense.[51] This, however, implies that the Torah does not spare discussion of the High Priest's offense – perhaps because there is greater anger at his failing. If so, this generates a subtle contradiction with Rashi's earlier comment: When the High Priest sins, the curtain is still associated with holiness, but when Israel sins, the curtain is stripped of its holy association! Which sin is considered more offensive?

Essentially, there is no real contradiction between these two observations. On the one hand, a communal sin is obviously more offensive than the High Priest's sin. On the other hand, the order of offerings does not seem coincidental. Sforno claims that the purification offerings are listed according to frequency, from the rarest to the most common. It is unlikely that Israel's spiritual representative will sin or that the Sanhedrin will accidentally lead the entire nation astray, but as for leaders, "it does happen that they err," and as for individuals, "it frequently happens that one of the people sins." A more likely theory, however, is that the chapter lists purification offerings from the most to least severe. For the High Priest – Israel's holiest figure – to sin is severe, followed by communal sin. A leader's offense is worse than a regular individual's sin, but it is not so harsh as to require an internal purification of the Sanctuary.

THE LEADER'S PURIFICATION OFFERING

The leader's offense sees a shift from internal to external purification offerings:

> When a leader sins unintentionally with regard to any of the Lord his God's commands, doing what must not be done and thus incurring guilt, when the sin that he has committed is made

51. R. Eitan Sandorfi cites a similar statement from the Yerushalmi (Taanit 8a). It seems likely that the correct reading is that "*nasi*" here refers to the High Priest (Sandorfi, "Sin Offering").

> known to him, he shall bring an unblemished male goat as his offering. He shall lay his hand upon the goat's head, and it shall be slaughtered in the place where burnt offerings are slaughtered before the Lord. It is a purification offering. The priest shall take some of the blood from the purification offering with his finger, and apply it to the horns of the altar of burnt offerings. The rest of the blood he shall pour out at the base of the altar of burnt offerings. He shall send up all its fat in smoke upon the altar, like the fat of the peace offerings. So shall the priest make atonement for that leader for his sin, and he will be forgiven. (4:22–26)

As mentioned, opening the description with "When" (*asher*) rather than "If" (*im*) reflects the transition from internal to external purification offerings. Rashi notes the connotations of the word "*asher*": "Fortunate (*ashrei*) is the generation whose leader takes care to bring atonement for his mistakes."[52] Sforno supports his theory that the offerings are listed in ascending order of frequency by explaining that the word "*asher*" hints to the inevitability of mistakes and offenses in leadership: It is a case of "when," not "if."

Although Sforno makes a compelling case, the most likely explanation is that the word marks the transition between the two pairs of offerings.[53] This also explains the addition that follows the slaughter of the leader's offering, "It is a purification offering," which does not appear in other offerings. Perhaps the text wishes to clarify that even though its laws differ from the first two cases (beginning with its slaughter), it is still a purification offering that purifies and grants atonement.

Another anomaly at the beginning of the description is the mention of "his God": "When a leader sins unintentionally with regard to any of the Lord his God's commands." The phrase "his God" is not mentioned in any of the other three cases. Ramban aptly notes: "The reason for 'the Lord his God' is to say that even though he is the king and leader and has no fear of any other person, he must still fear the Lord his God, for He is the Master of all masters." The text emphasizes that the leader

---

52. See also Radatz Hoffmann, Leviticus, vol. 1, 132–33.
53. See also Milgrom, *Leviticus*, vol. 1, 246.

has sinned against God in order to point out to the reader – and to all leaders – that even the leader of the people must answer to a Higher Authority and take responsibility for his mistakes.

What Does "Leader" Mean?

Until now, our assumption is that a "leader," "*nasi*," holds some kind of leadership position. But what kind of leader does this refer to?[54] The biblical term has two different meanings. One is in the sense of "royalty," as in: "David My servant shall be their prince for eternity" (Ezek. 37:25); the more common use is the head of a tribe or community: "All the leaders of the community came and reported this to Moses" (Ex. 16:22), or "Chief of the leaders of the Levites was Elazar son of Aaron the priest" (Num. 3:32). It is not always possible to determine what kind of leader "*nasi*" refers to based on context: "Do not curse a judge, and do not deride a leader of your people" (Ex. 22:27).[55]

What kind of leader is our chapter referring to? The Sages read it as "king,"[56] but Ibn Ezra's understanding is favored by many modern scholars:

> The words are inverted. Our verse should be read as if written, "When the sinner is the ruler." It is connected to that which is written above, that is, "And if the whole congregation of Israel" (v. 13). Our verse, as it were, states: And if the one who sins is the ruler of a tribe or the ruler of a father's house.

Ibn Ezra's interpretation focuses on the word order, but he also incidentally explains that leader means "the ruler of a tribe or the ruler of a father's house."[57]

---

54. The word "*nasi*" is from the verb root "*nasa*," "lifted/raised up" (see further in Niehr, "Nasi"). The question is which "raised up" rank this refers to here.
55. Classic commentators such as Ibn Ezra, Rashbam, and Ramban assume this refers to a king. See further in Speiser, "Nasi."
56. Hoffmann, *Leviticus*, vol. 1, 133. R. Samson Raphael Hirsch and Ramban write similarly.
57. Most modern scholars adopt Ibn Ezra's approach. See the summary in Hartley, *Leviticus*, 66.

This is more convincing for two reasons. Firstly, the biblical term "*nasi*" usually refers to the ruler of a tribe or community;[58] it is therefore the more obvious reading.[59] Secondly, and more importantly, we have already pointed out that the chapter is concerned with the question of collective versus individual sin. The chapter opens with the case of the High Priest, followed by the sin of the entire community. Ibn Ezra's reading results in a logical sequence: The next case is a leader, who is responsible for a larger group or clan, followed by the case of the individual.

While the leader's case is considered an individual and not collective offense, his error may be dangerous for his clan or tribe, which explains why his offering differs slightly from that of the individual. Whereas the individual brings a she-goat, the leader must bring a he-goat. This is the only case in which this particular animal is offered up by one person. Other offerings of he-goats are communal offerings: the people's offering on the eighth day of consecration (Lev. 9:3); the communal scapegoat on Yom Kipper (16:5); the tribe leaders' offering (Num. 7); and, especially, as an additional (*musaf*) offering on festivals sacrificed alongside the burnt offering: "One he-goat for a purification offering" (Num. 28–29), among others. Thus,the leader's purification offering is somewhat liminal – between the communal bull and the individual's she-goat.

The Blood Ritual and the Burning of the Meat

Unlike the blood ritual in internal purification offerings, the he-goat's blood is not brought inside the Sanctuary; only the regular outer altar requires purification in this case. Beyond this significant difference, there are other, subtler differences between the two models of purification offering.

The first difference is the place of slaughter. The two bulls of internal purification are brought to the entrance of the Tent of Meeting and slaughtered there "before the Lord." There is no mention of the Tent of

58. It makes more sense to explain the aforementioned verse, "You shall not curse a leader" (Ex. 22:27) as referring to a tribal head, not a king, as there is no human royalty in Exodus, although Ibn Ezra reads otherwise (on Ex. 22:27).

59. The fact that there were clan leaders in each tribe in addition to the heads of tribes is evident, for example, in the description of Elazar: "Chief of the leaders of the Levites was Elazar son of Aaron the priest" (Num. 3:32).

Meeting in external purification offerings; rather, they are slaughtered "in the place where burnt offerings are slaughtered."

According to the Sages, these linguistic differences have no halakhic expression; the laying of the hands takes place to the north of the altar in both internal and external offerings, and all purification offerings are slaughtered there. Yet the biblical description has clear differences.

This is a further reflection of the difference between offerings from the herd and flock, as discussed in the context of burnt and peace offerings. There, too, the bull burnt offering is brought to the entrance of the Tent of Meeting and slaughtered "before the Lord" (1:5), whereas the sheep is slaughtered "on the north side of the altar before the Lord" (1:11). Once again, the sheep is associated with the altar, and the bull with the Tent of Meeting.

This fundamental difference between offerings from the herd and flock lines up neatly with the division between internal and external purification offerings. The blood of bulls is brought inside the Sanctuary and the blood of goats is applied to the outer altar.

While the place of slaughter is explicitly linked to burnt offerings, the list of *eimurim* is linked to the peace offering: "He shall send up all its fat in smoke upon the altar, like the fat of the peace offerings" (4:26). This effectively spares the need to record the full list of fats and organs. However, given that this is a purification offering, it would have made more sense to refer to the High Priest's purification offering, where the *eimurim* are described in full detail and are also the same as those of the peace offering. Why is the leader's he-goat compared to a completely different offering, instead of the bull of the same offering?

It may be that the Torah prefers to compare the leader's purification offering to a different offering from the flock, instead of to the same kind of offering that comprises a bull. Another possibility, however, is that here, too, the Torah intentionally seeks to link the purification offering to the peace offering in order to infuse the scene with the sweet savor of reconciliation and friendship. The blood ritual focuses on purification and atonement, which allows the sacrifice of *eimurim* to represent a renewal of love and closeness to God. This idea continues with the last offering in the chapter – the individual's purification offering.

THE INDIVIDUAL'S PURIFICATION OFFERING

> If an individual among the people sins unintentionally with regard to any of the Lord's commands, doing what should not be done and thus incurring guilt, when the sin he has committed is made known to him, he shall bring an unblemished female goat as his offering to atone for the sin that he committed. He shall lay his hand on the head of the purification offering, and it shall be slaughtered in the same place as the burnt offerings. The priest shall take some of its blood with his finger, and apply it to the horns of the altar of burnt offerings. The rest of the blood he shall pour out at the base of the altar. The priest shall remove all its fat, just as the fat is removed from a peace offering, and send it up in smoke upon the altar as a sweet savor to the Lord. So shall the priest make atonement for that person, and he will be forgiven. (Lev. 4:27–31)

An individual who sins may choose whether to offer up an ewe or she-goat; the Torah allows the sinner to bring either, as long as it is a female animal from the flock. This element of choice recalls the peace offering, which may be a male or female animal, and thus hints to the possibility of reconciliation and closeness.

The stipulation that the animal must be female is unique in the sacrificial world. With the exception of the peace offering, which may be either male or female, all other offerings are from male animals. The individual's purification offering is the only instance in which the Torah specifies that the animal must be female.[60]

---

60. Another difference between the individual's and previous purification offerings is how the altar at whose base the remains of the blood is poured out is referred to. In internal offerings the blood is poured "at the base of the burnt offering altar at the entrance to the Tent of Meeting." In the leader's offering, it is "the burnt offering altar," but in the individual's offering, it is just "the altar." Warning concludes that this is an intentional pattern (*Literary Artistry*, 147–48). The Talmud explains that the superfluous "burnt offering" shows that the blood of the burnt offering should only be dashed at sides of the altar that have a base, but not on the baseless eastern and southern sides (Pesaḥim 65a).

Commentators offer a range of explanations for this anomaly, but none are satisfactory. Milgrom offers the technical explanation that commoners can only afford to keep one male for breeding, while the rest of his flock is female, whereas leaders probably keep several males and can therefore spare one.[61]

Not without hesitation, I wish to tentatively tread in a different direction by linking this to another anomalous feature of the individual purification offering. The she-goat offering concludes: "The priest shall send it up in smoke upon the altar as a sweet savor to the Lord. So shall the priest make atonement for that person, and he will be forgiven" (4:31). Surprisingly, the fats of the purification offering produce a "sweet savor," a phrase associated with freewill or communal offerings (such as the daily burnt offering and the festival additional offerings). The appearance of this phrase supports the aforementioned idea that after the blood of the purification offering purifies, its flesh being burned upon the altar brings reconciliation and renewed closeness.[62]

Why, then, is the individual offering the only one said to produce this sweet savor? Radatz Hoffmann extends this effect to all purification offerings, arguing that it is mentioned only in the last offering for the sake of brevity,[63] but I favor Shadal's reading that it intentionally only appears regarding the individual offering.[64] Perhaps the sudden reference to a "sweet savor" can be likened to the revelation of the Thirteen Attributes of Mercy after the sin of the Golden Calf, which, as Ramban explains, creates a special intimacy even greater than the Sinai revelation: "The glory revealed at the last revelation is greater than the first time" (on Ex. 34:3). The apology and forgiveness that follows the alienation of sin can bring even more closeness than existed before.

This can be said of all purification offerings, yet the "sweet savor" appears only in the context of the individual offering, perhaps because

61. Milgrom, *Leviticus*, vol. 1, 252.
62. This idea is further supported in the discussion of the bird purification offering (5:7), in an attempt to explain why a bird burnt offering is offered alongside the purification offering; see below.
63. Hoffmann, *Leviticus*, vol. 1, 137–38. (He writes that he is following Naftali Hertz Wiesel's reading.)
64. Shadal on Lev. 4:35, 398.

the individual's offense is the least severe and most easily leads to reconciliation and love. Perhaps this explains why a female animal is required. The female of the species is associated more closely with love, tenderness, and motherly compassion. This may be what Ibn Ezra alludes to in his commentary: "A female she-goat – For his status is lower than that of the leader [who brings a male]" (on Lev. 4:28).[65]

It's All a Matter of Taste – Sheep or Goat?

The Torah offers two different options for the individual purification offering – ewe or she-goat. Yet instead of presenting the choice in the opening verse (as it does for the burnt offering from the flock: "If the offering is a burnt offering from the flock, whether a sheep or a goat" – 1:10), each option and its sacrificial process is laid out in a separate paragraph. This can perhaps be justified by the purification offering's similarity to the peace offering, where the sheep and goat offerings are also presented separately, given that the sheep has a fatty tail that the goat does not, as pointed out by R. Haim ben Attar.

Yet the list of *eimurim* is not included in either the ewe or she-goat purification offering, so why does the Torah repeat the entire process for the sake of one detail that is not even mentioned in the text? Does this repetition suggest that there is a fundamental difference between a she-goat and ewe or that one of the two is a better option? The question of affordability is more relevant to freewill offerings. In the ancient world, it seems that goats were more expensive than sheep, as emerges from Hittite law: "The price of three goats is two *shekel* of silver; the price of two sheep is one *shekel* of silver."[66] Yet the purification offering is obligatory, so the price of the animal seems less relevant.

Perhaps the symbolic world of associations can shed more light on this question. We will begin the discussion with a story presented in

65. R. Meir Simcha of Dvinsk notes that in other offerings, the word "*tamim,*" "without blemish," appears after the animal's sex, yet in the individual's purification offering, "*temima,*" "without blemish," appears first (*Meshekh Ḥokhma* on Lev. 4:28). He notes that this has halakhic ramifications. This raises the question as to whether the anomalous case of the requirement that the animal be female is a kind of compromise, and the requirement of *temimut* therefore comes first.

66. Goetze, "The Hittite Laws," clause 179, 196.

the Babylonian Talmud at the end of Tractate *Keritot*, which may shed light on this dilemma:

> Open the gates and expel Yissakhar from the village of Barkai, as he honors himself and desecrates items consecrated to Heaven. What would he do to deserve such a reputation? He would wrap silk [*shira'ei*] over his hands and perform the Temple service, as he was unwilling to dirty his hands.
>
> What ultimately happened to Yissakhar from the village of Barkai? King Yannai and the queen were sitting and discussing food. The king said that goat meat is better food than lamb meat, and the queen said lamb meat is the better food. They said: Let us ask Yissakhar from the village of Barkai, as he is the High Priest and is familiar with the various dishes. They asked him, and he said to them: If goat meat were better, it would be sacrificed as the daily offering. The fact that the daily offering is lamb proves that its meat is preferable to that of goat. As he spoke, he gesticulated with his hand. The king said to his attendants: Since he gesticulated with his hand, sever his right hand. Yissakhar bribed the official to sever his left hand instead. The king heard that Yissakhar had deceived him, and said: Let the official sever his right hand as well.
>
> R. Yosef said: Blessed is the Merciful One, who took retribution on Yissakhar of the village of Barkai. R. Ashi said: Did [Yissakhar] not study that which we learned in the Mishna: Lambs precede goats in almost every place in the Torah where they are both mentioned. One might have thought that it is due to the fact that sheep are more select than goats. Therefore, the verse states: "And he shall bring for his offering a goat" (Lev. 4:28), after which it is written: "And if he bring a lamb as his offering for a sin offering" (Lev. 4:32), *which teaches that both of them are equal.* Ravina said: Yissakhar did not even read the Torah, as it is written with regard to the peace offering: "If he sacrifices a lamb" (Lev. 3:7), and it further states: "If a goat is his offering" (Lev. 3:12). These verses indicate that one is permitted to bring

> whichever animal he wishes, and there is no preference. (Keritot 28b; see also Pesaḥim 57a–b)

The final story in Tractate Keritot describes King Yannai's heated argument with his wife the queen (presumably Salome Alexandra) as to whether lamb or kid meat is superior. They decide to ask a professional: the High Priest Yissakhar from the village of Barkai, a finicky character who is loath to get his hands dirty. He explains that lamb meat is clearly superior, as lambs are used for the daily burnt offering. His answer and exaggerated hand gestures infuriate the king, who decrees that his hand must be cut off for his insolence.

The Sages declare that this priest deserved his ill fate, given that he was clearly not versed in the mishnaic or even biblical verses that show that goats and sheep make offerings of equal caliber. Yet this passage underscores the tension beneath this question: On the one hand, sheep are always mentioned before goats (see Ex. 12:5; Lev. 1:10, 17:3, 22:27; Num. 15:11, 18:17).[67] On the other hand, the goat purification offering precedes the sheep purification offering and, as R. Ashi points out, there does not seem to be any preference between a sheep (3:7) or goat peace offering (3:12).

The truth is that the maligned High Priest Yissakhar's position seems perfectly reasonable: Lambs are clearly the offering of choice. The daily burnt offering is the definitive offering, the sacrifice that opens and concludes the sacrificial service each day. Moreover, seven lambs are offered up on each festival; new mothers and those recovered from skin blight (*tzaraat*) must also bring lambs for burnt and purification offerings; the *omer* offering must be accompanied by a lamb burnt offering; and the list goes on.

On the other hand, there is significance in the fact that the Talmud reaches the conclusion that sheep and goats are equally worthy offerings based on the purification offering. R. Ashi refers to the peace offering,

---

67. According to halakha, if the priest has a goat and a sheep purification offering in line, he first offers up the sheep (Rambam, *Hilkhot Temidin UMusafin* 9:9). However, this is due to the greater amount of *eimurim* in the sheep, and it is difficult to base any principles on what may be a technical reason.

which can be either sheep or goat, but his idea is less convincing, because sheep are mentioned before goats in this context. Yet the goat purification offering is mentioned before its ovine counterpart; moreover, the first option is mentioned without any indication that there is a second option for the individual: "If an individual among the people sins unintentionally… he shall bring an unblemished female goat as his offering." The second option comes as a complete surprise.

Some argue that the goat is mentioned first so that it appears in parallel to the leader's goat offering.[68] This reading is possible; a broader perspective, however, suggests that the goat's precedence is related to the deeper affinity between the goat and the purification offering.

While lambs are offered as burnt offerings on festivals, festivals also require a purification offering – which is always a goat. Thus, while burnt and peace offerings are generally sheep, the animal of choice for the purification offering is the goat.

This is also salient in the tribal leaders' offerings. Let us examine as an example the offerings of the leader of the tribe of Judah:

> One silver bowl… one young bull, one ram, and *one yearling sheep for a burnt offering; one goat for a purification offering*; and for the peace sacrifice two oxen, five rams, five male goats, and five yearling sheep. This was the offering of Naḥshon son of Aminadav.

The animal used for the purification offering is a goat. Most famous of all is the Yom Kippur scapegoat, one of a pair of goats of which one is sacrificed as the people's purification offering while the other is sent to Azazel.

Why is the sheep the animal of choice for burnt and peace offerings, while the goat is the definitive purification offering?[69] Malbim explains that this is related to the process of repentance as symbolically expressed through the goat:

68. Milgrom, *Leviticus*, vol. 1, 252.

69. Rambam offers two historical-literary reasons for preferring a goat for a purification offering: The word "*se'irim*" reminds the worshippers of their sin of idolatry; or it serves as a *tikkun* for the sale of Joseph, whose robe was dipped in goat blood (*Guide for the Perplexed*, III:46).

> The precedence of goat to sheep here can be explained through the passage in Tractate Sota 32b: When bringing a she-goat for a purification offering, it is clearly not a burnt offering, and therefore the sinner is shamed, but when bringing an ewe this is not the case, as the tail hides its genitals... According to this, it is better to bring a she-goat, for if one is shamed for his sin, all his offenses are forgiven. (Malbim on 4:32)

Malbim explains that one who brings a goat for a purification offering is not attempting to hide their sin, unlike one who brings a sheep, because the difference between male and female goats is obvious, whereas male and female sheep look alike because their broad tail hides their sex. Therefore, a goat is the preferable option for a purification offering, for it represents the person's self-awareness, acknowledgment of their sin, and readiness to undergo a process of repentance.

A more symbolic reading is also possible, one that distinguishes between the associations of each animal. The sheep is the classic flock animal – fully domesticated, grazing with its flock. Its owners benefit from its thick wool and rich meat. It is no coincidence that the Torah allots its fatty tail to the altar as the choicest, fattest piece of meat. While it is true that the goat also has an important place in the ancient household, largely for its milk (although sheep's milk is richer than goat's milk), goat meat is not as choice as lamb or mutton, and in biblical times, clothing was more commonly made from sheep wool than goat wool.

The goat, in contrast, is more wild and free. More resilient than the sheep, easier to raise under harsher conditions, and far more agile, the goat easily moves over hilly, rocky terrain. Goats are wily, strong, and sturdy creatures,[70] able to survive in nature (some suggest that the word "*ez*," "goat," is related to the word "*oz*," "strength");[71] its hide makes durable tents (see Ex. 26:7; Song. 1:5). Compared to the sturdy, agile goat, sheep are passive, helpless, and utterly dependent on their shepherd; a common biblical metaphor likens Israel to a flock gone astray (Is. 53:6;

70. Vancil, "Goat," 1040.
71. Vancil, ibid. This is not necessarily convincing, given that the root of "*oz*" is A-Z-Z, while goat, "*ez*," is probably A-N-Z (Kaddari, *Dictionary*, 786).

Ps. 119:166).[72] The susceptibility of sheep is expressed in a talmudic passage that discusses various coddling treatments that prevent the ewes from catching cold after being shorn and help rid them of worms: "After shearing, they soak a swatch of wool in oil and place it on the animal's forehead so that it will not catch cold.... Rav Ḥisda said to him: You are treating the sheep like Mar Ukva." Such treatments befit a human, not an animal! The sheep's delicate nature casts it as a symbol of vulnerability that needs – in the words of the Talmud – *raḥamim*, mercy.[73]

This brings us back to Malbim's approach. The bold, aggressive goat is a more fitting image for the penitent worshipper who must overcome their shame and admit their sin. The resilient goat is able to bear their guilt more than the meek, passive sheep. The purification offering serves to cleanse and purge the altar of its impurity; this is best achieved through the blood of a bold, strong animal that can survive grim conditions and overcome the harshest of circumstances. In contrast, the total submission of the burnt offering and the rich feast of friendship conveyed through the peace offering are better symbolized through the passive, indulgent meat of the meek, pampered sheep.

If so, it is clear why the goat is the first option for the individual's purification offering. It cannot be proven that this is the preferable option, but the fact that the option of bringing a sheep is listed only after the full sacrificial process of the goat hints that the first option is the most fitting – especially given that the phrase "sweet savor to the Lord" is only mentioned in reference to the goat purification offering, not the sheep.[74] Both options serve to purify the altar and achieve atonement, but the difference does not seem coincidental: It is the brash audacity of the goat that results in purification, atonement, reconciliation, and a sweet savor to the Lord.

---

72. Vancil, "Sheep, Shepherd," 1190.
73. I do not know if any conclusion can be drawn from the following, but perhaps the Akkadian word "*ḫānû*," meaning "fat," which is used in the phrase "fat sheep," is related to the Hebrew word "*ḥana*," meaning "encamped," dwelling on the land in peace and security.
74. Similarly, in the peace offering, the term "sweet savor" applies to the goat offering (3:16) but not the sheep offering (3:11).

Wash me well of my guilt; purify me of my sin,
for I am aware of my transgression, and my sin is ever before me. (Ps. 51:4–5)

Chapter 10

The Variable Offering (Leviticus 5:1–13): The Failure to Act

PURIFICATION OR GUILT OFFERING?

Understanding the nature of the variable offering, known to the Sages as "*oleh veyored*," poses one of the greatest challenges in the sacrificial world. At first glance, it is unclear why the Torah offers three different options for the same offense; according to most opinions, there are no comparable purification or guilt offerings.

Its placement further adds to the quandary: Does it conclude the section of purification offerings, introduce the section of guilt offerings, or is it in a category of its own? Some modern commentators refer to it as a modified or partial purification offering, which implies that it is an appendix to the purification offering.

A first reading seems to connect it to the guilt offering, the "*asham*," a word that appears repeatedly: "While impure, he incurs guilt" (5:2); "He realizes his guilt" (5:3); "When he realizes his guilt" (5:5); and especially,

"He shall bring as his guilt offering to the Lord" (5:6). The verb "he shall bring" suggests that this is a concrete offering, not just a feeling of guilt.[1]

The solid connection to the guilt offering is explored in the Midrash Halakha on these verses, which attempts to explain what a person must do when they set aside money for a variable offering and have some left over:

> "His guilt offering" is written here and elsewhere (Lev. 5:19): ("It is a guilt offering; a guilt offering, a guilt offering to the Lord.") Just as with his guilt offering there, its surplus monies are used for a donative offering, so with his guilt offering here, its surplus monies are used for a donative offering. (*Sifra*, Obligatory Offerings, 10:3)

The actual content of this midrash is irrelevant to our discussion; what matters is the connection between the variable offering and the laws of the guilt offering based on the word "*asham*." There are certainly elements that are common to both, which is clearly recognized by the biblical chapter divider, who devotes Leviticus 4 to the purification offering and groups the variable offering together with the guilt offering in Leviticus 5.[2]

However, the variable offering seems to fit the criteria of a purification offering. The word "guilt," "*asham*," also appears repeatedly in the context of the purification offering (4:22; 4:27); the term is indeed appropriate in the context of any offense, regardless of the offering or penance it requires.[3] We will later discuss why "guilt" is the name for

1. See Meshel, "Grammar of Sacrifice."
2. Some refer to the variable offering as "the variable guilt offering" (see Wolfson, *Emunat Ittekha*; HaCohen, *Yehuda Yaaleh, Parashat Vayetze*; Nolland, "Reparation"). This is also implied by R. Zvi Yehuda Kook, who cites a verbal offense and vow as an example of a sin that requires a guilt offering (*R. Z. Y. Kook's Lectures*, series 11, 13). Radatz Hoffmann mentions others who consider it a guilt offering, as does HaCohen, *Sanctuary*, 40. Naphtali Meshel offers a complex view that it is both purification and guilt offering in one ("Grammar of Sacrifice").
3. Radatz Hoffmann phrases this differently: "All sinners are also guilty to God; he pays off his dues with a purification offering and is thus saved from punishment" (*Leviticus*, vol. 1, 143).

the guilt offering, but guilt itself is certainly associated with all obligatory offerings.[4]

There is decisive proof that the variable offering is defined as a purification offering. First and foremost, this is how the actual text refers to it: "He shall confess the sin he has committed, and bring the amends of his guilt (*ashamo*) to the Lord for the sin he has committed: a female sheep or goat *as a purification offering*" (Lev. 5:5–6). Why, then, does the text first refer to a guilt offering, "the amends of his guilt (*ashamo*)"?[5] That "*ashamo*" means "his offering" is proven from the parallel verse in which the poor person "shall bring *his offering* (*korbano*) for the sin he has committed" (5:11). Thus,"*ashamo*" means "his offering," whereas all three options of variable offering are defined as "purification offerings" in the text: The bird offering: "Then he shall sprinkle some of the blood of *the purification offering* against the side of the altar" (5:9); and the fine flour offering: "And send it up in smoke upon the altar with the Lord's fire offerings. *It is a purification offering*" (5:12). Those who consider it a guilt offering have trouble explaining this repeated phrase, as exemplified by Gordon's feeble comment: "Purification offering – This means guilt offering."[6]

Further indication that this refers to the purification offering lies in the type of animal offered up: a female goat or sheep. Guilt offerings are from male animals, so the fact that the variable offering is from a female animal clearly links it to the individual's purification offering. Moreover, the text does not specify how to offer up the animal; the phrase "as a purification offering" informs the reader that the laws of the purification offering apply to the variable offering as well. The text lists only the sacrificial process of the bird and grain variable offerings, because the option of bird or grain purification offerings was not listed previously.

It is also worth noting that the guilt offering begins with a new divine commandment, "The Lord spoke to Moses, saying" (5:14), which

4. As Milgrom repeatedly emphasizes; see especially *Cult and Conscience,* 3–12.
5. Elliger, *Leviticus,* 78; see also Kellerman, "Asham," 432–33.
6. Gordon, *Leviticus,* 21–22.

strongly indicates that the guilt offering begins a new category, whereas the variable offering is appended to the purification section.[7]

Yet the use of the word "*ashamo*," which anticipates the section that follows, is no coincidence. Certain features indeed recall the guilt offering, and its purpose is similar, as we will soon see. Thus, even if the variable offering is technically a purification offering, it also serves as a transitional offering to the next section.

Classifying the variable offering as a purification offering has broad halakhic implications, especially for the blood ritual.

ARE ALL PURIFICATION OFFERINGS VARIABLE?

Before we consider what is common to offenses that require a variable offering, we must consider whether a poor person has the option of offering a bird or grain offering for all accidental sins – that is, whether the offenses listed in 5:1–5 are just examples of cases that require a variable offering. Abarbanel, for example, writes that whereas the High Priest or leader can obviously afford to bring an animal, a poor individual may bring a bird or grain offering for any offense that requires a purification offering.[8] Most modern scholars favor this view as well.[9] If so, however, why does the Torah cite these three particular offenses as examples of sins that require a variable offering?

Ibn Ezra (and others) also believes that a poor person can bring a bird or grain offering for any accidental sin and that these three offenses are listed because they are the only ones that require confession. While we will yet discuss the meaning of confession, the idea that these three offenses are just examples is still problematic, especially given the clause "When he realizes the guilt he has incurred *in one of these ways*" (5:5), which is repeated at the end: "Thus,shall the priest make atonement for that person for whichever *one of these sins* he has committed" (5:13). It is these three sins that require a variable offering, not any accidental sin.

7. It is thus inaccurate to state that the variable offering is "neither purification nor guilt offering," as Zvi Weinberg proposes in "Purification and Guilt Offerings," 529.
8. Abarbanel, *Introduction to Leviticus*, 17.
9. For example, De Vaux, *Ancient Israel*, vol. 2, 419–21; Rendtorff, *Studien zur Geschichte des Opfers*, 207–10; Rainey, "Sacrifice," 640; Wenham, *Leviticus*, 100.

In contrast to Ibn Ezra, who argues that the phrase "one of these" refers to the need for confession, the phrase seems to specify in which cases a variable offering is brought. This is supported by Milgrom's observation that "the relative *ki* that begins chap. 5 is the sign of a new case and thus cannot continue 4:27–35, where *ve'im* is used twice."[10] That is, perhaps the bird and grain offerings could be perceived as a possible option for all accidental sins if the opening word were "*im*," but it cannot be, as the opening word is "*ki*." Moreover, as we will soon see, one of the three cases that requires a variable offering is an intentional sin (failing to testify), so how can it serve as an example of an accidental sin?

The Common Denominator Between the Three Cases

The logical conclusion is that bringing a bird or grain offering instead of a sheep or goat is only a possibility in the three cases mentioned at the beginning of chapter 5.[11] Why is one allowed to bring a cheaper alternative after these particular offenses?

The question is whether these options are provided because the offenses in question are considered more or less severe. Theoretically, it can be argued both ways: The offenses are less severe and therefore a lesser, more affordable version of purification offering is effective; alternatively, the offenses are so severe that purification must be achieved as soon as possible, so a more affordable version of purification offering is available to facilitate urgent, immediate purification.[12] The latter reading is perhaps supported by the fact that one of the cases is not accidental but deliberate sin (when someone fails to testify), which is obviously more severe than accidental offenses that require a regular purification offering.

10. Milgrom, *Leviticus*, vol. 1, 308.
11. Spiro argues that these three cases are in fact one offense – the result of one failing to speak up and remind his friend that he has become impure/violated his vow/failed to testify. See Spiro, "Sharing of Information." But this is a problematic argument, especially given the use of "or" and "one of these," which suggests different cases. We will adhere to the usual reading that these are three distinct offenses. See also Kiuchi, *Purification Offering* 23–24.
12. Compare to the *Sifra*: "R. Yehuda says that a mitzva is best performed at the proper time, so it is better for them to bring a tenth of an ephah immediately rather than wait until they become wealthy enough to bring an ewe or goat" (*Sifra,* Obligatory Offerings, 19:1).

But, the most prevalent reading is that the variable offering is a leniency for the sinner. As Ramban explains:

> Scripture has been lenient toward these sinners by allowing them to bring an offering of either higher or lower value. It is possible that the reason for the leniency with regard to the offering in the case of oaths is because the punishment is not *karet*, excision. In the case of defilement of the Sanctuary and the holy food [He mitigated the obligation of the offering] because the person who did it erred whilst engaged in performing a religious duty, for the priest who eats the holy food or enters into the Sanctuary to prostrate himself or to bring an offering is engaged in performing a religious duty, and his intention is toward Heaven. Therefore, even though he sinned on account of having forgotten his state of uncleanness, Scripture gave him more ways of atonement. (Ramban on Lev. 5:7)

Ramban's interpretation that "Scripture is lenient toward these sinners" demands explanation, especially given that the first offense of the three is in fact a deliberate sin of failing to testify against a friend (or, according to the Sages, giving false testimony).[13] Ramban explains that because these offenses are not punishable by *karet*, there is room for leniency; whereas other offenses that require a purification offering would deserve *karet* if they were done on purpose, this is not the case with the first and third of the three cases that require a variable offering. He offers a surprising reading of the second case: In his opinion, someone impure who comes into contact with holiness deserves a lesser punishment because he "is engaged in performing a religious duty, and his intention is for the sake of Heaven."[14] When an offense is committed during holy worship, in God's presence, there is more room for leniency and forgiveness.

---

13. See *Daat Zekenim* on Lev. 5:1.
14. Ramban's term, "mistaken while performing a mitzva," is a halakhic term that implies that when one means to do a mitzva but makes a mistake, he is exempt from bringing an offering. Some read this to mean that one is exempt from a purification offering but not a variable offering (see Grodzinski, *Ahiezer* III:83), but it seems

While I do favor Ramban's basic direction that these three offenses are less severe, I find his rationalizations unconvincing. First of all, giving three different explanations is itself problematic; there ought to be a common denominator to them all. Moreover, his reasons can be applied to other offenses that do not result in *karet* either; why doesn't the option of a variable offering apply to them?

The *Daat Zekenim* of the Tosafot commentators suggests a common denominator for the three offenses: Because the offenders do not derive enjoyment from these transgressions – unlike those who eat blood or suet, who eat on Yom Kippur, who perform forbidden work on Shabbat, or have forbidden relations – they may bring a variable offering.[15] Most negative commandments prevent people from enjoying a particular pleasure; violating them therefore requires a purification offering. These three offenses, in contrast, do not result in any enjoyment, so a variable offering can atone for them. The advantage of this reading is that it suggests a common denominator. The problem is that "enjoyment" is difficult to define. Does someone who accidentally transgresses Shabbat necessary "enjoy" this violation? Does someone who slaughters consecrated animals outside the Sanctuary "enjoy" the results of this transgression? In fact – as we will soon see below – someone who fails to testify against his friend (which requires a variable offering) does so as the result of a certain laziness, which can actually be perceived as a kind of "enjoyment."

Our goal, therefore, is to determine the common denominator of the three offenses that require a variable offering and explain why their penalty is more lenient. A further, related challenge is to explain why these offenses also require confession: "When he realizes the guilt he has incurred in any of these ways, he shall confess the sin he has committed" (5:5). For some reason, the variable offering must be accompanied by confession. While the Sages extend this requirement to all purification offerings,[16] it is significant that confession is mentioned in the context of the variable offering.

---

more likely that R. Kanievsky is correct that Ramban is presenting this as the biblical text's rationale, not as a legal discussion (*Kehillot Yaakov, Nedarim,* n. 2).

15. See *Daat Zekenim* on Lev. 5:7.
16. *Sifri, Naso,* 2; see also Ramban on Lev. 5:5–6.

The first step on the way to determining this common denominator is to articulate a precise definition of these offenses. It emerges that there is a significant disparity between the Sages' reading of the first two offenses and a *peshat* reading of the biblical text. The Sages explain that the first case concerns someone who has been sworn to give testimony (Rashi: "They adjured him by oath, to the effect that if he knew anything regarding the matter, that he would testify for him"), yet he fails to testify; the second case is someone who came into contact with holiness despite their impurity (Rashi: "After becoming impure he ate sanctified food or entered the Sanctuary"); and the third concerns someone who swears to do harm or good to himself (Rashi: "Such as, 'I will eat' but he does not eat, or 'I will sleep' but does not sleep"), but later forgets his oath and violates it. I will now discuss the straightforward, literal meaning of these biblical verses.

The First Case: Failing to Testify

> If a person sins by failing to testify after hearing a public adjuration to do so: if he knows or has seen something, yet does not speak up, and thus bears his guilt. (Lev. 5:1)

This clearly describes someone who has certain information but fails to testify ("yet does not speak up"). But what is the meaning of the word "*ala*" – "public adjuration"? The term literally means "curse," as Ibn Ezra explains: "The text refers to this succinctly [through the word "*ala*"], warning that the witness must testify, for if not a punishment from God is upon him to bear his guilt."

Ibn Ezra explains that this *ala* is the public announcement of someone who has been wronged and declares that any witnesses must come forward for the sake of justice, and if they fail to do so, a curse will be upon them. The Midrash presents a similar reading: "Reuben stole from Simeon, and Levi knew of it. [Reuben] said to Levi: Do not publicize this and I will give you half. The next day, the cantor proclaims at the synagogue: Who stole from Simeon? Levi is there, but he does not come forward" (Leviticus Rabba 6:2). According to this reading, if someone has information but does not come forward even after a "public adjuration," they must offer a variable offering.[17] Ibn Ezra cites the story of Micah's Image as an example: Micah's mother notices her money has been stolen, so she publicly curses the thief. Her son, who is the one who stole her money, immediately returns it (Judges 17:1–2). This incident is an example of the custom to curse the wrongdoer in order to encourage witnesses or even the offender to come forward.[18] This implies that the case in Leviticus 5:1 does not refer to a legal vow, as the Sages read, but rather to a cultural phenomenon.

A person may fail to come forward for various reasons. Perhaps they are complicit to the crime ("He who shares with a thief hates himself; he will hear the *ala* but not testify" – Prov. 29:24); perhaps they do not wish to hurt their guilty friend.[19] But I assume that the most common reason is explained by the Mishna: "Lest you say, 'Why do we need this trouble?' as it says: 'And he knows or has seen something but does not speak up'" (Sanhedrin 4:5). That is, the witness dreads having to waste time and go through tiresome investigations and bureaucracy, so they choose to remain silent.[20]

The biblical mandate to come forward and testify is in fascinating tension with Ancient Near Eastern warnings to avoid getting mixed up in court business. Milgrom quotes several Egyptian and Mesopotamian sources:

> Do not frequent a law court, / Do not loiter where there is a dispute,
> For in the dispute they will have you as a testifier...

17. See also Bava Kama 55b: "For four things a person is exempt from human justice but is held culpable by Heaven.... One who knows testimony about his friend but does not come forth." This duty is based on the verse, "Do not stand by when your neighbor's life is in danger" – see the *Sifra* there.
18. Some suggest that she issues a curse at the outset, as a deterrent against theft (Rabinovitz, *Blessing*, 373), although this does not seem likely based on the order in the text. In medieval times, halting the prayer service in order to express rage for an injustice was an accepted custom (Grossman, "Postponing Prayer"); see also Barur, *Blessing*, 455.
19. Philo, *Laws* II, 26–28 (*Writings*, vol. 3, 28).
20. Ramban views the duty to give testimony as a kindness a person must show toward another.

> When confronted with a dispute, go your own way / pay no attention to it.[21]

In striking contrast, according to *Parashat Vayikra,* someone who fails to come forward to testify and later regrets their laziness must bring a purification offering, but if they cannot afford a sheep or goat they may bring a cheaper offering. It must be emphasized that this is the only offense that requires a purification or variable offering that is a deliberate, rather than accidental, sin. The usual phrase that conveys accidental sin – "it escapes his notice" – does not appear in this case.[22]

The Second Case: Failing to Become Pure

The second case concerns someone who becomes impure but "it escapes his notice." There seem to be two distinct versions of this offense:

- Or sins through touching an impure thing – the carcass of an impure beast, or a carcass of impure livestock, or the carcass of an impure creeping creature – and it escapes his notice, and while impure, he incurs guilt;
- Or sins by touching human impurity of any kind that makes him impure, and it escapes his notice, but later he realizes his guilt.

There are three different surprising aspects here. The first is the distinction between impurity caused by animal and human impurity. Regardless of how one becomes impure, they must stay away from holiness; either way, they must become pure. Yet each kind concludes with its own expression of impurity: "While impure, he incurs guilt" / "Later, he realizes his guilt."

21. Milgrom, *Leviticus,* vol. 1, 294–95; he points out similar sayings in Egyptian wisdom literature.

22. "These bring the same offering for a deliberate offense as for an accidental offense… For taking a false oath of testimony" (Mishna Keritot 2:2). This is also the accepted reading among commentators. Nonetheless, Yanovsky argues that these are all cases of offenses that were not strictly deliberate but rather instances of lack of responsibility (Yanovsky, "Atonement," 255).

The second surprise is in the emphasis that the impurity comes from impure animals, those that may not be eaten. Even though the carcass of a pure animal that has not been slaughtered according to halakha also contaminates, the biblical text repeatedly emphasizes that impurity comes from impure animals (with the impurity coming from the animals themselves, not the carcass, as is clear from the gender of the adjective "impure").

The third surprise is that the description focuses on impurity that comes from contact: "Touching an impure thing…touching human impurity of any kind."

I will begin with the third observation, whose solution seems to be pragmatic. It is unlikely that someone is liable to forget their impurity when it comes from bodily emissions: skin blight (*tzaraat*) or menstruation. If any of these people forget they are impure, they also need to bring a variable offering, but the more likely case is someone who became impure through contact with something impure.[23]

The other two points illuminate much about how impurity was perceived in the ancient world. Based on the mandate that only animals that may not be eaten cause impurity, Ehrlich (mistakenly) concludes that pure animals do not cause impurity, no matter how they died.[24] Halakha rules otherwise (see Lev. 11:39), but the biblical text does imply that there are different degrees of impurity, as conveyed by the differentiation between the impurity of impure animals (Lev. 11:24–28) and that of pure animals that may be eaten (11:39–40).

Moreover, the emphasis that some purity laws only pertain to impurity caused by impure animals is also noted in the context of eating the peace offering: "When anyone touches any impure thing – human impurity, or an impure animal, or any impure, detested creature – and then eats flesh from the Lord's peace sacrifice, that person shall be severed from his people" (Lev. 7:21). This formulation also implies that someone who touches a dead pure animal and then eats from the peace offering

23. It is interesting to note that despite this pragmatic explanation, these three cases involve three different senses: (1) hearing; (2) touching; (3) speaking.

24. Ehrlich, *Mikrâ ki-Pheschutô*, 214.

will not deserve *karet*. Even when not ritually slaughtered, pure animals impart less impurity.

The biblical distinction between impurity caused by contact with animal and human impurity shows that the states of purity and impurity are not absolute binaries but rather form a continuum. One may be in a state of low impurity or a state of high, extreme impurity. Some kinds of impurity pass within a day; others linger for a full week. Ultimately, all kinds of impurity require a variable offering, but the division itself shows that even if one might think that just one kind requires a variable offering, any kind of impurity does.[25]

Why must a person who becomes impure bring an offering? Rashi explains that this is the case when someone impure comes into contact with holiness. Ramban notes that this is a necessary addition because becoming impure is not a prohibition in itself. However, as we have already discussed in the context of the purification offering, the Torah attempts to reduce the state of impurity to an absolute minimum, especially during the wilderness years, when the Tabernacle travels along with Israel at the heart of the camp.[26] Impurity in the camp defiles God's dwelling place: "Anyone who becomes impure and fails to purify himself shall be severed from the assembly, for he has defiled the Lord's Sanctuary" (Num. 19:20).

Therefore, someone who is impure and does not rush to purify himself as soon as possible – whether they are aware of their impurity or even if they forgot – is harming the Divine Presence's dwelling in the camp, and they must bring a variable offering as soon as they become pure. To be sure, the offender is not culpable for becoming impure (this state is rarely preventable, and sometimes performing a necessary mitzva contaminates, such as burying the dead). A person is held accountable only when they do not purify themselves as soon as possible and their forgetfulness increases defiling impurity in the camp.

---

25. It makes sense that touching impure animals is less severe than bodily impurities, but it can be argued that the verses are surprising in both directions: Both kinds of impurity require the same variable offering, whereas one might think that bodily impurity requires a purification offering or whereas impurity from animals would require no offering at all.

26. Wright, "Spectrum"; Breuer, "Impurity"; Noam, "Purity Laws."

The Third Case: Failing to Fulfill an Oath

> ...or sins by making a verbal oath to do something, bad or good – whatever one might carelessly swear – and it escapes his attention, but later he realizes his guilt. (Lev. 5:4)

The third case concerns someone who violates an oath they made. Whether a person swears to do something difficult or positive for himself, they must fulfill the pledge they swore in God's name.[27] By the time of the Sages, making oaths was discouraged and therefore rare, but the biblical text does not seem to express disapproval of oath making in itself.[28] In other places, in fact, swearing in God's name is considered an affirmation of one's belief in God: "It is the Lord your God you must revere, Him you must serve, and only by His name that you must swear" (Deut. 6:13); or "Revere the Lord your God and worship Him. Hold fast to Him and swear by His name" (Deut. 10:20).[29] Swearing an oath is not a problem, but failing to fulfill this oath is.

Note the emphasis on the person's "verbal oath" – "*bittui sefatayim*," literally "the lips' utterance." If one's commitment is merely expressed in their thoughts, without any verbal statement, then its lack of fulfillment does not require a variable offering. Only a verbal statement is binding, as Rashi writes (based on the *Sifra*): "Not in their heart."[30] The binding nature of verbal statements is evident in other biblical passages, such as this exchange between Jephthah and his daughter: "'I have gone and opened up my mouth to the Lord, and I cannot go back.' 'O, Father,' she

27. The word pair *lehara/leheivtiv* (to do bad/to do good) appears elsewhere (Jer. 4:22; Zech. 8:14–15). Its use here demonstrates that what matters is not the content of the oath but whether it is fulfilled.
28. See, for example, Halevi, *Oaths*.
29. However, see Rashi and Ramban.
30. According to the Babylonian Talmud this is only true of oaths that have nothing to do with the Sanctuary, whereas the thought to pledge an offering is binding (Shevuot 26b), while Shmuel's opinion in the Jerusalem Talmud is the opposite: For an offering, one must make a verbal declaration for it to be binding (Terumot 83:4). The *Aḥaronim* discuss this in relation to charity: The Vilna Gaon rules that one who promises to give charity must do so even if the promise was not a verbal declaration.

said to him, 'if you opened your mouth up to the Lord, do to me whatever it was that came out of your mouth'" (Judges 11:35–36).

A legal formulation is that a verbal statement represents a fully formed, conscious commitment. Swearing an oath is not a fleeting thought; it means that a person is fully committed to the idea. We will soon see how the use of God's name is central to the requirement of bringing an offering if the oath in God's name is not fulfilled; thus, a verbal utterance that includes God's name is a key component here.

The Common Denominator: Desecrating God's Name Through Omission

What all three offenses seem to have in common is a problematic passivity. Someone *fails* to come forward for testimony; someone *fails* to purify themselves on time; someone *fails* to keep their oath. This inactivity is what results in the need for a variable offering. Regular, active offenses – committing a forbidden act – require a regular purification offering. A variable offering is brought for an omission that leads to the commission of an offense.[31]

When a person has a certain responsibility – social responsibility to ensure that justice prevails (giving testimony), spiritual responsibility to maintain the camp's holiness, personal responsibility – but then fails to act responsibly, they must bring a variable offering.

The rationale behind the nature of the variable offering is that it is unjust to punish someone who has not committed an active offense. The *beit din* does not exact penalties for failure to fulfill positive commandments. Although some mishnaic and talmudic Sages argue for a penalty of lashes for a *lav she'ein bo maaseh* – a transgression that does

31. It is true that in the third case, one may transgress his oath by doing a certain action he swore not to do. Yet this too is inherently an omission, as they did not fulfill what they swore to fulfill.

not entail any actual action[32] – this is a minority opinion, and the majority rules otherwise.[33]

The unease of forcing someone to take responsibility is a fascinating legal discussion even today. For example, Israeli Supreme Court Justice Prof. Yitzchak Englard comments on tort law:

> Traditional halakha rules that one should not be held liable for omission, unless there is a prior relationship that imposes an obligation on a person to act. This is what reality dictates, given that the general public cannot be held accountable for general damage that may occur. It must be remembered that imposing an obligation to act for the sake of others is necessarily a violation of a person's freedom. In Jewish tradition, as in some legal methods, there is an exception regarding the case of saving a life. A recently legislated law's purpose is to fulfill an idea from Jewish tradition, namely, "Do not stand by when your neighbor's life is in danger."[34]

The problematic transition from tort to criminal law in the context of omission is widely discussed.[35] The premise of such discussions is that it is far more difficult to convict someone for a criminal omission – a failure to act – than for a forbidden act: "Negligence is an offense by omission, and proper legal policy dictates that it be kept to a minimum in criminal law."[36]

When a person has a *responsibility* toward someone else or is in a place of authority (a parent, a teacher), modern Israeli law has one notable

32. This is R. Yehuda's position in Makkot 4b, and seemingly also that of Resh Lakish in Pesaḥim 63b and Makkot 16a. Tosafot discuss the problematic aspects of this in Bava Metzia 90b, s.v. "Resh Lakish."
33. As Rambam states (*Hilkhot Sanhedrin* 18:1–2): "Lashes are for prohibitions that have an action, such as eating meat and milk together or wearing *shaatnez*, but a prohibition that does not have an action, such as gossiping or taking revenge or bearing a grudge, does not warrant lashes."
34. Hadassah Medical Association Hadassah Ein Kerem v. Ofra Gilad, PD 59(2) 516 (1995).
35. The three fundamental aspects of transition from tort to criminal law in the context of omission can be found in an article by Statman, "Thou Shalt Not Stand Against."
36. From FHCrimA 2974/99 Ohana v. State of Israel.

exception, as mentioned by Englard: the law of "Do not stand by when your neighbor's life is in danger." Unsurprisingly, the legislation of this law generated deliberation as to whether the court is able to punish someone for failing to meet what was expected of them. Knesset member R. Hanan Porat declared the following when proposing this law:

> This proposal has a certain audacity. But it joins other recent proposals that proclaim: Sometimes a person commits an offense not by doing a bad deed, but through inertia, omission. In extreme cases, such as someone who must disclose and report if they see abuse of the vulnerable; or someone who sees their friend in distress and fails to offer help; or other extreme cases when someone should act but fails to do so – this is a transgression of "Do not stand by when your neighbor's life is in danger."[37]

It is no coincidence that the only situation of culpable inactivity concerns serious harm to someone's life; under less severe circumstances, the legislator generally refrains from punishing a lack of action. Punishment is for active offenses; a lack of action is not punishable to the same degree.

There are obviously differences between legal questions and underlying biblical values that shape the sacrificial world. I do not perceive the variable offering as a punishment; this is supported by the fact that the offering is almost always brought after an accidental offense,[38] and "atonement" is a more fitting term than "punishment." Nonetheless, the same principle applies: In both worlds, concrete consequences usually follow active offenses, not the failure to act.

A good example that clarifies this is the Sages' ruling regarding the blasphemer. Even though a blasphemer receives the punishment of *karet,* if he blasphemed accidentally, he is exempt from bringing a purification offering, because "he did not perform an action" (Keritot 1:2). The Sages do not regard speech as an action, so the accidental blasphemer

---

37. R. Hanan Porat as the head of the committee for an Israeli constitution, "The Proposal of the Punishment Law (Amendment 47) – Do Not Stand By When Your Neighbor's Life Is in Danger," 1995.
38. See Mishna Keritot 2:2.

is exempt from bringing a purification offering. The same is true of one who accidentally misses the Passover offering or does not perform circumcision on time, even though doing so intentionally deserves *karet.*

The next step is to extend the discussion from punishment to actual damage. Bringing a purification offering is a response to the damage that accidental sin causes to the Sanctuary. A variable offering, however, is brought as a response to the lack of action, to an offense by omission. As we will soon see, this also causes – albeit indirectly – certain damage to the Divine Presence's dwelling in the Sanctuary.

Given that lack of action causes less damage, if the offender cannot afford to buy an animal, they may bring a cheaper offering – even one that does not contain blood, as we will discuss below.[39]

This of course raises the question: How can there be an obligation for offenses that are essentially the failure to act? How can a person owe an offering for their passivity? A court of law is not usually authorized to impose an obligation on the basis of a person's passivity. What makes the variable offering an exception?[40]

This brings us to the main problem that characterizes all three cases: This lack of action causes the desecration of God's name and adversely affects the dwelling of the Divine Presence in the midst of Israel.

This is obvious in regard to the first case – someone who fails to come forward to testify after he hears a public adjuration in God's name. Whether this adjuration is an individual's (Rashi) or a general proclamation (Ibn Ezra), God's name is desecrated when the witness fails to come forward. A similar desecration occurs when a person fails to fulfill an oath they swore in God's name. Finally, when someone does not purify themselves in time, this compromises the Divine Presence's

---

39. This is also Milgrom's approach; as mentioned, many modern scholars favor Abarbanel's interpretaton that this applies to all purification offerings, so there is no need to find a common denominator between these three cases.

40. As mentioned, the Sages perceive the burnt offering as atonement for failure to perform a positive commandment (*Sifra,* Freewill Offerings, 4:8), but it is fundamentally a freewill offering.

dwelling in Israel's midst. In all three cases, a person's failure to act compromises sanctity in Israel.[41]

Before we consider the implications of this understanding, I wish to point out the stylistic differences between the formulations of the ending of each case:

1. The failure to testify – "Yet does not speak up, and thus bears his guilt." (5:1)
2. The failure to purify oneself from contact with an impure animal – "It escapes his notice, and while impure, he incurs guilt." (v. 2)
3. The failure to purify oneself from human impurity – "It escapes his notice, but later he realizes his guilt." (v. 3)
4. The failure to fulfill an oath – "It escapes his notice, but later he realizes his guilt in any of these ways." (v. 4)

These slight differences reveal two interesting issues. Firstly, as noted, the first case does not say, "It escapes his notice," because this is not a case of accidental sin. The phrase "incurs guilt" is ambiguous. Sometimes it refers to forgiveness and atonement (such as in Ex. 34:7); elsewhere it refers to a sinner bearing his guilt (Lev. 17:16).[42] Here, it is the latter: If one fails to come forward to testify, he must bear his guilt.[43] Even so, the damage to the Sanctuary's sanctity is less severe than in cases of accidental sin that are active offenses.

Furthermore, the third case's conclusion serves to group the three cases together: "He realizes his guilt, in any of these ways."[44] In all three,

41. See the Netziv's explanation that the long formulation of the phrase (5:6) reflects how the person seeks atonement for the first stage of their deliberate or almost deliberate sin.
42. Kaddari, *Dictionary*, 732. The most accepted reading is that its meaning depends on context; Baruch Schwartz claims that both meanings are derived from the concept of "*masa*," "burden" (Schwartz, "Nosei avon").
43. Surprisingly, this phrase also appears in the context of the variable guilt offering (5:17), which raises the question of why the text is so stringent regarding someone who did not necessarily sin.
44. For a different reading that this concludes only the third case, see Netziv; also Goldenberg, *Biblical Exegesis*, 12.

the offender is guilty because they remained passive, and all three require a variable offering.

Viddui That Defines Sin

This explains the requirement of *viddui* (ostensibly "confession) that must accompany the variable offering: "When he realizes the guilt he has incurred in any of these ways, he shall confess the sin he has committed" (Lev. 5:5).

Given that the variable offering is appended to the purification offering, it is surprising that *viddui* is first mentioned here and not in any cases of the purification offering. The Sages extend this obligation to all purification offerings as well (Rambam, *Hilkhot Teshuva* 1:1), yet this does not explain why confession is not mentioned until the variable offering.

Some argue that it is first mentioned here because a regular purification offering does not actually require confession (see Ibn Ezra on Lev. 5:4). Yet this also exacerbates the question: Why is confession required for these less severe offenses and not for active offenses that require a purification offering?[45]

Ramban makes a surprising suggestion: Confession is not required in all three cases, but only in the first one, which is a deliberate sin. This is why confession is mentioned here and in the context of a guilt offering for theft in the book of Numbers: There is no need for confession of an accidental sin; only when someone has deliberately committed a sin are they able to express regret. To state that one is sorry for their poor, foolish decision has the power to redefine intentional sin as an accidental sin, and thus to achieve atonement.[46] This is a bold proposition, but it

---

45. I believe that this is related to the Sages' attempt to focus on the spiritual and psychological aspect of the sacrificial process. This is apparent through Rambam's recommendation for "confession" even for the peace offering (*Hilkhot Maaseh HaKorbanot* 3:15), that there should always be a verbal accompaniment that defines its purpose. This is not found in the biblical text itself, where the actual act of sacrifice expresses the symbolic meaning instead of words. In fact, some suggest that the lack of words is one of the most salient characteristics of the biblical offering (Kaufmann, *Religion of Israel*, vol. 2, 476). We have already pointed out that Knohl perceives this as a reflection of the abstract nature of divinity: "The priestly temple is the kingdom of silence" (*Biblical Beliefs*, 120).
46. As expressed by Milgrom, *Leviticus*, vol. 1, 301; see also p. 374.

is difficult to read the text as meaning this: "When he realizes the guilt he has incurred *in any of these ways*, he shall confess the sin he has committed." Confession is a requirement in all three cases.

What purpose, then, does confession serve, and why is it introduced with the variable offering?

Halakhic literature draws a profound connection between *viddui* and the laying of the hands: One is supposed to confess while laying the hands (Yoma 36a).[47] However, *viddui* also appears independently, not in the context of the sacrificial service (Lev. 26:40; Dan. 9:4; Ezra 10:6; Neh. 9:3), which suggests that it has a specific purpose, as does the confession we still recite today, especially on Yom Kippur. Here, *viddui* is mentioned unrelated to the laying of the hands, and even before mention of the offering itself.[48]

While generally understood as "confession," the root may be associated with the meaning Y-D-H, meaning "to cast away," like the Akkadian verb "*nadû*." This reading aligns particularly well with the High Priest's actions with the scapegoat on Yom Kippur: "Aaron shall lay both his hands on the head of the live goat and *confess/cast* over it all the Israelites' iniquities and rebellions, all of their sins, putting them on the head of the goat and then sending it away into the wilderness" (Lev. 16:21).

Either way, in the case of the variable offering, the offender is the one who does the act of *viddui*. This is worth emphasizing, given that some scholars show that confession was a ritual act in other Ancient Near Eastern religions (especially the Hittites), but the priest usually pronounced confession on the sinner's behalf.[49] In the Torah, the sin-

---

47. *Aḥaronim* argue as to whether *viddui* was recited when the hands were upon the offering's head (R. Y. Kimhi, *Avodat Yisrael*) or immediately after (*Encyclopedia Talmudit*, "*Viddui*," vol. 11, 420). The two are so closely linked that Rambam debates whether one must repeat *viddui* if it was not recited during the laying of the hands (*Maaseh HaKorbanot*, 36). See also Wasser, "Laying of the Hands."
48. It makes sense that the Torah does not repeat the law of the laying of the hands after it is detailed in the burnt offering; it is one of the laws that the Torah does not repeat, such as the requirement that every offering be "*tamim*," "without blemish." Ramban explains thus; see also Sandorfi, "Variable Offering."
49. Milgrom, *Leviticus*, vol. 1, 302.

ner confesses; this is inherently related to the nature and purpose of this confession.

The act of confession indeed conveys a request for forgiveness and the acceptance of responsibility; from this perspective, it is appropriate for all offerings brought on account of sin. Why is there a particular need for confession for a passive offense of omission? For regular offenses, the need for atonement is clear, but when bringing a variable offering, the worshipper is essentially stating: "I have come because I failed to act." In order to clarify the ritual process, the worshipper must actively define their lack of action as a sin and accept their responsibility for their failure to take action.

He Must Bring *Ashamo* to the Lord

The need for *viddui* is also related to the term "*asham*," "guilt," that appears repeatedly (five times!) in the context of the variable offering. We have already asserted that the variable offering is a form of purification offering, not a guilt offering, so the multiple repetitions of the word "guilt" demands explanation.

The term "*asham*" is a multivalent, metonymic term in biblical Hebrew.[50] Sometimes it expresses imminent punishment, as Abimelech accuses Isaac: "'What is this you have done to us?' said Abimelech. 'One of the people might have slept with your wife, and you would have brought *guilt* upon us" (Gen. 26:10).[51] Sometimes it expresses the acceptance of responsibility for one's action: "We are *guilty, guilty* because of what we did to our brother. We saw his suffering when he pleaded with us but we did not listen" (Gen. 42:21). It is even used as a term for "compensation": "If you are sending the Ark of Israel's God back, do not send it empty-handed; be sure to *recompense* Him with a guilt offering. Only then will you be cured" (I Sam. 6:3).

Thus,it poses a challenge to understand the term in a sacrificial context; not all the instances necessarily share the same meaning. The

---

50. Kaddari, *Dictionary*, 75–76. Milgrom devotes an entire book to the guilt offering and discusses this at length in the first chapter: Milgrom, *Cult and Conscience*.
51. Compare Ps. 34:21–22; perhaps also Jer. 51:5; Ps. 68:22.

distinctions are reflected in Onkelos's translation of 5:5, where he translates both "*asham*" and "*ḥata*" using the same root, Ḥ-V-B.

While the precise distinction between "*asham*" and "*ḥattat*" is elusive, there are two approaches worth pointing out. Most discussions devoted to this question revolve around the relationship between the guilt and purification offerings, but it is also possible to clarify the difference between the terms in their semantic context. Nearly a century ago, Schötz proposed that guilt offerings are brought for sins against God or the desecration of His name, whereas purification offerings are for breaking the law and committing offenses.[52] We will yet discuss the nature of the guilt offering, but Schötz's definition certainly clarifies why the term "*asham*" is a keyword in the description of the variable offering. Guilt is the justification for the obligation to bring an offering for the failure to act. Although omission does not usually require punishment or atonement, when there is guilt there is desecration of God's name.

A second direction points to an inherent link between "guilt" and *viddui*: "When he realizes the guilt he has incurred in any of these ways, he shall confess the sin he has committed" (5:5). It is the sense of guilt that moves the sinner to confession. Sometimes this sense of guilt is the result of actively breaking the law (as in usual purification offerings); sometimes, however, a person feels guilty for their negligent passivity. This sense of guilt is central to the significance of the variable offering. Although they have not committed any active offense, their sense of guilt at their inactivity is what moves them to confession.

THE WEALTHY PERSON'S OPTION: A FEMALE SHEEP OR GOAT

The Torah first presents the sinner with the option of bringing the usual purification offering; the phrase "as a purification offering" proves that the variable offering is essentially a version of the purification offering. Even so, the slightly different formulation offers a glimpse into the unique nature of this particular offering.

Like the individual's purification offering, the sinner has a choice of offering "a female sheep or goat as a purification offering" (5:6). Unlike

52. Schötz, "Schuld- und Sündopfer," 32–34.

the original option, however, here the sheep is listed before the goat. This subtle change of order is no coincidence. As discussed, a sheep is the preferable choice for freewill offerings, whereas the goat is the preferable purification offering. If so, why is the sheep listed first in the variable offering? R. Simcha Meir of Dvinsk offers a fascinating explanation:[53] When offering up the *eimurim* is the main purpose of the offering, a sheep is preferable because of the fatty tail portion sent up in smoke upon the altar, but when the blood ritual is the most important part of the offering, a goat is preferable (because it also atones for idolatry).

I wish to formulate this reading differently. Offenses that require a variable offering do not directly damage the Sanctuary as active offenses do. Thus, the offering's ritual center of gravity shifts from the blood ritual (which is the most important part of the usual purification offering) to the offering upon the altar. In this sense, the variable offering is closer to the guilt offering (which, as we will discuss below, does not purify the Sanctuary). This principle is the key to understanding the more affordable options of the variable offering, which have little or no blood.

A MORE AFFORDABLE OPTION: THE BIRD PURIFICATION OFFERING

While a sheep or goat is the ideal option, the Torah offers the more affordable option of bringing two birds: "If he cannot afford a sheep, he shall bring two doves or two pigeons as his guilt offering to the Lord, one as a purification offering and the other as a burnt offering" (5:7). We have already discussed the leniency the Torah extends to the poor sinner; the surprise here is that alongside a purification offering, another bird must be brought as a burnt offering. There is no mention of a burnt offering alongside a sheep or goat, nor alongside the destitute sinner's purification offering of fine flour. Yet for some reason, in the middle option – the poor-but-not-quite-destitute option – one bird is brought as a burnt offering! Where does this come from?[54]

53. See further options in Sandorfi, "Variable Offering," 58–60.

54. This element is so surprising that Wenham suggests that a burnt offering ought to accompany all purification offerings (Wenham, *Leviticus*, 100–01), but this desperate attempt to solve the mystery has absolutely no basis in the text.

Ibn Ezra proposes two explanations. The first is that the person's inability to afford a "proper" purification offering may lead to problematic thoughts about divine justice and the unfairness of this world. This is consistent with his view of the burnt offering, the ***ola***, as atonement for sinful thoughts that come to mind – "*haoleh al haruaḥ.*" Thus, the accompanying burnt offering is regarded as an atonement for the inevitable problematic thoughts caused by the bird purification offering.

While this reading is sensitive to the workings of the human mind and heart, it is questionable for two reasons: Firstly, the destitute person – who by this logic is even more prone to such thoughts – is not required to bring a burnt offering (although one might argue that a middle-class person is more likely to compare himself to a wealthy person, whereas such thoughts would not even occur to someone who is utterly destitute). Secondly, this recalls the unconvincing argument that a new mother must bring a purification offering to atone for any oaths she might have made during the pain of childbirth (Nidda 31b). If she never says such a thing, isn't her offering redundant? If the burnt offering is for sinful thoughts, this explanation ought to be stated explicitly and unconditionally, as not everyone is guilty of such thoughts. Moreover, we have already discussed how the idea that burnt offerings are brought for sinful thoughts is not consistent with the language of the biblical text.

Ibn Ezra does not seem convinced by his own explanation either, for he raises a second possibility: "I prefer to read that one bird is for the *eimurim*, and the other is a purification offering as the law requires." Assuming that the bird purification offering is inherently inferior, as its flesh is not burned upon the altar,[55] a bird burnt offering is added to compensate. Hizkuni develops this idea further:

> Given that only the bird's blood, which is not edible, is placed upon the altar, one must bring two birds: one for the priests to eat and one as a burnt offering for the altar. But when a wealthy person brings a purification offering, a sheep or goat is enough,

55. In the words of the Mishna: "The altar only receives its blood; it is all for the priests" (Mishna Zevaḥim 6:4).

> for the flesh is given to the priest and the *eimurim* are given to the altar. (Hizkuni on Lev. 5:7)

This certainly explains why a bird purification offering is always accompanied by a bird burnt offering (as in the case of someone who is after purification from a discharge – 15:15, 30; a new mother – 12:8; someone who is poor after purification from skin blight – 14:22; or a *nazir* – Num. 6:10–11). While the text does not explicitly state that the flesh of the purification bird is not burned upon the altar, this can be extrapolated from the distinction between the bird purification and bird burnt offerings. For the purification offering, the bird's head is not separated from its body as it is for the burnt offering (1:15–17). Why is this so?

The simplest explanation is that for the burnt offering, the bird is cut into pieces for the altar in the same way that animals are cut into pieces for the altar (1:6, 12), whereas the bird purification offering is not burnt upon the altar, so its head is not severed from the body. This explanation casts a dramatic light on the sacrificial process of both bird and animal purification offerings. It emerges that there are two crucial components to a purification offering: the purifying blood ritual and the burning of the *eimurim*. The bird purification offering is a reasonable substitute for the blood ritual, but given that the bird has no significant fat to burn on the altar, a second bird is offered for this second component. This confirms our earlier theory that the blood of the purification offering serves to purify, whereas the sacrifice of the flesh symbolizes reconciliation between the worshipper and God. This second bird is offered upon the altar as a "sweet savor to the Lord," not as an act of purification and atonement.[56]

At the same time, this also highlights the unique nature of the variable offering. How can the blood of the lowly bird – created on the fifth day, a lower life form – compare to the blood of a sheep or goat? That the blood of a lowly, barely living bird sufficiently purifies the altar proves that the damage caused by a passive offense is less severe than

56. Thus, I disagree with Milgrom's suggestion that the extra bird is for the sake of enough meat for an honorable offering (*Leviticus*, vol. 1, 304). This is not just for show; it serves a specific purpose.

the damage caused by sins that require full-fledged purification offerings and the fully vital blood of bulls, goats, or sheep.

I will tentatively add that this may also be reflected by a surprising law that the bird's blood is sprinkled on the lower part of the altar, far away from its horns (Mishna Zevaḥim 6:2).[57]

Offering Up the Purification Bird

Two final comments conclude the discussion of the bird purification offering. The first is that the purification bird is offered up before the burnt offering: "He shall bring them to the priest, who will offer the first as a purification offering.... He shall then offer the second bird as a burnt offering in the prescribed way" (5:8–10). This applies to all such offerings: Whenever one brings a pair of birds for both purification and burnt offering, the purification bird is offered first, for as explained in the Talmud, "Once the advocate has appeased, the gift is brought in" (Zevaḥim 7b). Purification must take place before the second bird can be given as a gift to God. Thus, the offering of the first bird corresponds to the blood ritual, whereas the second bird corresponds to the burning of the *eimurim* upon the altar.

A second comment is consistent with the previous observations about bird and blood ritual: "Then he shall sprinkle some of the blood of the purification offering against the side of the altar; the rest of the blood shall be drained out at its base" (5:9). The bird's blood is "sprinkled" rather than "applied" as the blood of the individual's purification offering is (4:30, 34), because there is not sufficient blood to "apply." Just as the blood of the internal purification offering is "sprinkled" so that it will symbolically reach the desired destination (the cherubim in the Holy of Holies), here the blood is "sprinkled" as a symbolic fulfillment of applying the blood to the altar, given that there is not sufficient blood to collect in a bowl and apply.[58] As soon as its neck is severed, the priest

57. Various readings attempt to explain this surprising law. See, for example, Sandorfi, "Variable Offering," 61–62.

58. As mentioned in regard to the bird burnt offering, the biblical text supports Rambam's reading that there is no bringing of the blood (*Hilkhot Pesulei HaMukdashin* 13:5), whereas Tosafot on Zevaḥim 15a state that the bird bleeding until it is placed on the altar constitutes bringing the blood.

shakes the bird to sprinkle its blood over the altar: He "holds its head and body and sprinkles [the blood] on the altar wall" (Zevaḥim 64b) to symbolically reach and purify the entire altar.

He then drains the little blood that remains at the base of the altar – a painstaking act that is considered "the most difficult task in the Sanctuary" (Zevaḥim 64b) – as a symbolic parallel to pouring out the remains of the purification blood at the base of the altar.

AN OPTION FOR THE DESTITUTE: FINE FLOUR

The fine flour purification offering poses a challenging surprise:

> If he cannot afford two doves or two pigeons, he shall bring the purification offering of a tenth of an ephah of fine flour as the sacrifice for his sin. He shall not put any oil on it, nor place on it any incense, for it is a purification offering. He shall bring it to the priest, and the priest shall lift a handful from it – its remembrance – and send it up in smoke upon the altar with the Lord's fire offerings. It is a purification offering. (5:11–13)

If the bird purification option maintains the two basic elements of the regular purification offering – the blood ritual and the flesh burned upon the altar – how is an offering of flour a viable option? How can it purify, and how does it correspond to blood and flesh?

Perhaps the Torah is willing to forgo purification for the destitute so that they can still achieve atonement with a symbolic offering of flour.[59] This further supports the theory that purification is desirable but not essential following an offense that requires a variable offering.

That purification here is not essential is reinforced by the fact that in other situations that take a person's financial means into account, the Torah does not offer an option of bringing a flour offering; their choice is between animal or bird (in the case of the new mother – 12:8; and a person recovered from skin blight – 14:21–22). A flour offering is not

59. Milgrom, *Leviticus*, vol. 1, 307. This is interesting, given that he shows earlier that in the Ancient Near East they ascribed atonement-giving qualities to flour (ibid., 306–07).

usually sufficient when there is need for purification through blood, but it is possible in the case of the variable offering.

We should nevertheless refrain from dismissing the need for purification; the text reiterates that the fine flour offering does serve to purify: "He shall bring the purification offering of a tenth of an ephah of fine flour as the sacrifice for his sin…it is a purification offering…. It is a purification offering." Even if flour does not strictly purify, it still operates as a purification offering on a symbolic level.

A more accurate formulation, perhaps, is that flour can represent life. While blood itself *is* life, food represents life, especially for the destitute person who struggles to survive on their daily bread and must sacrifice a precious portion to God. Perhaps this is reflected in the talmudic comparison between a grain offering and animal offering: "A handful – it is like slaughtering…burning it – it is like dashing the blood" (Zevaḥim 13b). In Rambam's words: "Know that taking a handful of the grain offering is equivalent to slaughtering sacrifices; putting the handful in the service vessel is like collecting the blood…burning the handful with frankincense is like dashing the blood" (Rambam's commentary on Menaḥot 1:3).[60] The Sages perceive the act of burning the handful of the grain offering as corresponding to the act of dashing the blood, not just as parallel to the act of burning flesh or *eimurim* upon the altar. This characterizes the fine flour purification offering as a representation of the animal's lifeblood.

Moreover, the amount of flour brought as a purification offering is also significant.

"A Tenth of an Ephah of Fine Flour" (5:11)

The Sages extend this measurement to the desirable amount for the freewill grain offering as well (*Sifra,* Obligatory Offerings 19:4). It is no coincidence that this measurement first appears in the context of obligatory, rather than freewill, offerings. In the second sacrificial list, the same

60. Rashi writes similarly: "The grain offerings mirror animal offerings in four parts of the service: The handful is like slaughter; putting the handful in the vessel is like collecting the blood; bringing is like bringing; *burning is like dashing the blood*" (Rashi on Zevaḥim 11a and elsewhere).

measurement is specified for the daily grain offering: "One-tenth of an ephah of fine flour as a continual grain offering, half in the morning and half in the evening" (Lev. 6:13). It is also the amount a jealous husband must offer up when he suspects his wife has committed adultery: "Then the man shall bring his wife to the priest together with the prescribed offering for her, one-tenth of an ephah of barley flour" (Num. 5:15).

Why is the measurement specified in these offerings, rather than freewill grain offerings? Ibn Ezra's commentary points to a solution: "A tenth of an ephah is a person's portion of food for a single day" (on Num. 5:11). As discussed above, "a tenth of an ephah" first appears as the amount of manna each Israelite must gather each morning (Ex. 16:36).

The sinner must offer up a portion of their daily bread; this is particularly poignant when they are so destitute that they cannot even afford to bring a pair of birds. There is no blood to purify the altar, but a portion of their daily existence is offered up instead, and this sacrifice is what serves to purify. But this is only possible when the offense does not directly damage the Sanctuary's holiness.[61]

The debate on whether a fine flour purification offering purifies the altar or whether it is possible to forgo purification in the case of someone utterly destitute may be in dialogue with the following strange midrash in which God shows Abraham a vision of the meal offering during the Covenant Between the Pieces:

> "He said to him: Take for Me three calves" – He showed him three types [of atonement] involving bulls, three types involving goats, and three types involving rams: Three types involving bulls – the bull of Yom Kippur; the bull that is brought for the transgression of any of the mitzvot; and the beheaded calf. Three types involving goats – the goats of the festivals; the goats of the New Moon; and the goat offered by the individual. Three types involving rams – the definite guilt offering; the provisional guilt

61. New mothers and people recovered from skin blight are unable to bring a fine flour offering, presumably because their impurity is considered serious; thus, they must bring an offering that truly purifies.

> offering; and the lamb offered by the individual. "And a dove, and a young pigeon."
>
> "He took all these for him" – R. Shimon bar Yoḥai and the Rabbis: R. Shimon bar Yoḥai says: He showed him all the [other] types of atonement, but the tenth of an ephah [grain offering] He did not show him. The Rabbis say: He showed him the tenth of an ephah as well. It is stated here: "He took all these [*elleh*] for Him" and it is stated elsewhere: "You shall bring the grain offering that is prepared of these [*me'elleh*] to the Lord" (Lev. 2:8). (Genesis Rabba 14:4)

The midrash's premise is that during the Covenant Between the Pieces, God reveals the secret of how offerings bring atonement[62] and therefore lists all the effective offerings. The *Tanna'im*, however, argue as to whether the grain purification offering is included in this list or not. R. Shimon b. Yoḥai argues that it is not included, but the others disagree and insist that it is included.

What does this curious argument mean? Abraham does not offer up any grain along with the animals he brings for the covenant, but this is unlikely to be the crux of the debate. Rather, I tentatively propose that this midrash in fact explores the true nature of the "tenth of the ephah" in question. Does the variable grain offering indeed have atoning and purifying power like other offerings do (as the Rabbis contend), or does the Torah give a serious discount to destitute offenders and overlook the damage done to the Sanctuary's purity (as R. Shimon claims)?

Either way, the fact that the Torah offers various substitutions for the purification offering – including an option that doesn't even have blood – shows that the variable offering reflects a shift in focus from the purification of the altar to the process that the sinner must undergo. When someone commits an active offense, they must bring a purification offering to cleanse the altar and thus enable atonement. When

62. Modern scholars also question how much the sacrificial world is in dialogue with this covenant. Some point to a strong symbolic connection (e.g., Loewenstamm, "Des Bundes Zwischen Den Stücken"; Rainey, "Sacrifice," 643), while some reject it (e.g., Van Seters, *Abraham*, 258). See further in Grossman, *Abraham*, 80–82.

the offense is a passive non-action, the damage to the altar is indirect and negligible; what must be dealt with is the person's sense of guilt. By confessing, the offender acknowledges their guilt and the need for atonement, and this is the driving force behind the offering brought to the altar. It matters less whether this offering is goat, sheep, birds of little blood, or flour without any blood at all. What matters is that the offender stands before God and confesses before Him.

"As in the Case of a Grain Offering, the Rest Shall Belong to the Priest"

The purification grain offering differs from the freewill grain offering, which includes costly oil and frankincense, which would of course defeat the purpose of an affordable option for the destitute. Yet the text still links the two: "As in the case of a grain offering, the rest shall belong to the priest" (5:13). Are the two also eaten similarly? The Netziv relates to this question: "Even though the priests' eating of this grain offering is not for the sake of remembrance like the freewill grain offering, the actual law is the same, given that the priests eat and the worshipper achieves atonement, as with an animal offering."

The Netziv points out that even if the laws are identical on a practical level, the purpose and nature of the eating is not. This seems to be the basis of a tannaitic dispute about the priest's own flour purification offering. When a priest brings a freewill grain offering, it is not given to the priests but rather offered up like a burnt offering: "Any grain offering from a priest shall be wholly burned; it shall not be eaten" (6:16). Is the same true of the priest's fine flour purification offering? There are three different opinions in the Talmud, but it is worth noting that all unanimously agree about one particular aspect.[63]

The majority of the Sages (and Rashi) hold that, like the grain offering, a priest's purification offering is burnt whole upon the altar. R. Shimon disagrees about the action of the process, but the end result is the same: He argues that the priest must take a handful and burn this "remembrance" by itself before burning the rest of the offering separately.

63. Menaḥot 72b–74a. The Sages' and R. Shimon's positions are also cited in the *Sifra*; the third opinion is mentioned in Tosefta Menaḥot 8:4 and in the Talmud there.

R. Elazar b. R. Shimon believes that only the handful is burned, while the rest is scattered to where the altar ashes are disposed.

What no one raises is the possibility that the priest eats his own purification offering, and rightly so. The priests' consumption of their portion is, in a sense, part of the sacrificial process, as the Netziv says: "The priests eat and the worshipper achieves atonement." It therefore cannot be that the priest will eat of his own offering. R. Elazar draws a distinction between the purification grain offering and the freewill grain offering. Although both consist of fine flour, the sacrificial process is completely different: The freewill offering is burnt upon the altar like a burnt offering, but the altar cannot accept the entire purification offering. The Sages, however, rule that two priestly grain offerings undergo the same sacrificial process. This is surprising and serves to emphasize the substance of the offerings more than their respective purposes. R. Shimon's position is in between: While both offerings ultimately end up on the altar, their different sacrificial processes reflect the worshippers' different mindsets.

In summary, given that the variable offering is brought for offenses of omission that affect the Sanctuary indirectly, the offender must define their failure to act as an offense through the act of *viddui*, confession. Given this lesser degree of damage, an offering of birds is sufficient, even though they have little blood; even a symbolic, bloodless grain offering – a person's portion of daily bread – can serve to purify and atone. The active act of confession and sacrifice will compensate for negligent passivity.

> I admitted my sin to You and did not cover up my guilt;
> I said, "I confess my offenses to the Lord,"
> and You forgave the guilt of my sin – *Selah.* (Ps. 32:5)

Chapter 11

The Guilt Offering (Leviticus 5:14–26): Repaying Lost or Wrongful Holiness

Like the purification and variable offerings, the *asham*, the guilt offering, is an obligatory offering brought for certain offenses, yet it is clearly in a separate category. This is expressed in a new opening: "The Lord spoke to Moses, saying" (5:14). Like the variable offering, the section consists of three cases in which a person is obliged to bring a guilt offering (three other cases appear elsewhere in the Torah), and here, too, we must seek out the common denominator between them, which will characterize the nature of the guilt offering. The challenge is even greater given that out of six cases, four require a mature ram while two specify that the offender must bring a young sheep. Thus, in addition to understanding the common denominator between all offenses that require a guilt offering, we must determine why two cases require a different animal.

Rather than beginning with a discussion of the name "*asham*," "guilt offering," we will first analyze the cases that require such an offering, which will illuminate the particular nature of this "guilt."

CASES THAT REQUIRE A GUILT OFFERING

1. *Asham Me'ilot*

> If a person commits a trespass (*maal*), sinning unintentionally with respect to any of the Lord's sacred objects, he shall bring an unblemished ram from the flock, valued in silver shekel by the Sanctuary weight, as his guilt offering to the Lord; it is a guilt offering. He shall make restitution for his trespass against the sacred object, adding one-fifth to its value and giving it to the priest. The priest shall make his atonement with the ram of the guilt offering, and he will be forgiven. (Lev. 5:15–16)

The Torah briefly describes the first offense: the "*asham me'ilot*" or "trespass guilt offering," as it is known in halakhic literature. The text seems to assume that readers understand the meaning of the word "*maal*," here translated classically as "trespass," meaning that someone accidentally uses something that has been dedicated to God for their own purposes. When this occurs, the offender must pay the object's value plus an additional fifth.[1] After the fine has been paid, they must then seek forgiveness and atonement, and this is the purpose of the guilt offering. (The Sages emphasize that the offering can be brought after the fine has been paid, which certainly illuminates the nature of the process of atonement.)

Note that this is the process of repentance following an accidental offense. In the case of intentional use of sacred objects, the offender is

1. The *Tanna'im* debate whether this "fifth" includes the additional penalty ("*millibar*," "from outside") or is just added to the original value ("*millegav*," "from inside"). For example, if the sacred object is worth 20 *shekalim*, then the *millegav* value is 20 + 4 (a fifth of 20) and the total fine is 24; if it is *millebar*, then it will be 20 + 5 = 25 in total. This assumes that the fine is monetary, whereas the definition in rabbinic literature is far more complicated.

not required to bring an offering; rather, they receive a penalty of lashes. Whereas a sacred object accidentally used for everyday purposes loses its sanctity, an object that has deliberately been used remains sacred.[2] Perhaps this initially seems surprising: If an accidental offender must bring an offering, surely a deliberate offender is in even greater need of atonement. As we will soon see, however, this is in tune with the nature of the guilt offering and its bringer's sense of guilt.

One of the most surprising elements of this offering is the need to assess the animal's value before it is brought to the Sanctuary: "He shall bring an unblemished ram from the flock, *valued* in silver shekel by the Sanctuary weight." What does "valued" – literally, "as your value" – mean in this context? R. Amnon Bazak suggests that this refers to the monetary value of the offender himself – "as *your* value."[3] This works well grammatically but poses a semantic problem: How can one find an animal worth as much as a human being? A proposition that is easier to apply is that of the Sages, who explain that a person must evaluate how much the animal is worth. (We will soon pose another possibility – that the animal's value must be equivalent to the degree of trespass against the Sanctuary.) Whereas there are no such specifications for a burnt offering or purification offering (other than an animal "without blemish"), a guilt offering's worth is significant. Another possible, logical reading of the text is that a person may bring an actual ram *or* the equivalent amount of money, in exchange for which the priests will provide them with a ram.[4]

In any case, unlike previous offerings, when a guilt offering is brought, the animal's value is of utmost importance. This is even more striking given that this chapter does not relate any of the guilt offering's sacrificial

2. This seems strange. When something is accidentally used it loses its sanctity, but not when it is used intentionally! Perhaps this is so that the willful user will not benefit from the object losing its sanctity, as they would then be able to keep it. Another possibility is that the willful offender still treats the object as sacred: They are not denying its sanctity but rather intentionally using it in order to try and defy its sanctity. In contrast, one who accidentally uses a sacred object treats it as a regular object and thus nullifies its sanctity.
3. Bazak, "Purification and Guilt Offerings."
4. Levine, *Before the Lord*, 95–100; Milgrom, *Cult and Conscience*, 13–15; Wenham, *Leviticus*, 107.

laws: "As far as this sacrifice is concerned, the value of the animal presented was more important than the procedure at the altar."[5] We will relate to how this characterizes the guilt offering below.

2. *Asham Talui*

> If a person sins without realizing it, doing any of the things that the Lord commanded not to be done, he incurs guilt and is subject to punishment. He shall bring an unblemished ram from the flock, of the appropriate value, as a guilt offering to the priest. The priest shall atone for him for that unintentional sin, committed unknowingly, and he will be forgiven. This is a guilt offering, for he had incurred guilt before the Lord. (5:17–19)

This describes the "*asham talui*," as it is called in halakhic literature, meaning "conditional guilt offering." The formulation of this second case is complex. How does this differ from an offense that requires a basic purification offering: "If an individual among the people sins unintentionally with regard to any of the Lord's commands, doing what should not be done and thus incurring guilt" (4:27)? Here, too, someone accidentally does one of "the things that the Lord commanded not to be done" and "incurs guilt." Out of various explanations, here are three:

1. Milgrom proposes reading the second case as a continuation of the first, the only difference being that the first offender knows that they have sinned whereas the second is not entirely sure; they suspect that they have trespassed against something sacred and feel guilty.[6] While we will later confirm that there is indeed a connection between the first two cases, this particular formulation is problematic: The second case refers to "any of the things the Lord commanded not to be done," not specifically trespass against sancta.

5. Wenham, *Leviticus*, 105.
6. Milgrom, *Cult*, 74–83; Hartley, *Leviticus*, 82; Wenham, *Leviticus*, 107–08.

2. Shadal argues that whereas both are cases of accidental sin, a purification offering is brought for something the person commits inadvertently: They did not know that that piece of meat was *ḥelev,* forbidden fat; they did not know that it was Shabbat, etc.; whereas a guilt offering is brought for committing a sin that one did not know is a sin: They did not know that *ḥelev* is prohibited; they did not know that one must not plow on Shabbat, etc.[7]

   The verses can indeed be read in this manner, based on the phrase "if one sins without realizing it" – they were not aware that they were doing something that "the Lord commanded not to be done." Moreover, while the first case explicitly states that the person "sinned unintentionally with respect to any of the Lord's sacred objects," the second states that the offender "sinned without realizing it" – that is, they did not realize that what they were doing is a sin.
3. The Sages' reading, which is most widely accepted by medieval commentators, is that one brings a purification offering when they are sure that they accidentally sinned and a guilt offering when they are not entirely certain. The most famous example of the latter is when a person has eaten one of two similar pieces of meat of which one was forbidden *ḥelev,* they are not sure whether they ate the forbidden piece or not, and there is no way to find out. In such a case, they bring an *asham talui,* a conditional guilt offering: "This is referred to as a conditional guilt offering, for it brings atonement when the person is in doubt, tentatively, until he knows with certainty that he sinned inadvertently, at which time, he brings a sin offering" (Rambam, *Hilkhot Shegagot* 8:1). If the person eventually finds out that they are guilty, they must bring a purification offering, but for now, they must bring a guilt offering.[8] The *Sifra* likens this to the law of the unknown

7. Shadal on Lev. 5:18. He also questions whether this is what Ibn Ezra means; I believe that he uses a different division (see his commentary on Lev. 5:17).
8. The Midrash also debates whether an *asham talui* is brought when there was certainly an action but it is not clear whether this action was forbidden or not, or when the person is not sure whether they did an action at all (*Sifra,* Obligatory Offerings, 12:4).

> murderer: A calf's neck is broken in a ritual that absolves the nearest town of the murder, but if the murderer is discovered, that ritual does not absolve them of their guilt.[9]
>
> This reading is also consistent with the text's emphasis on lack of realization rather than accidental sin. The person is plagued by doubt because they are not sure whether they have sinned, but they cannot achieve atonement with a regular purification offering. Note that the verse emphasizes the worshipper's feeling of guilt: "This is a guilt offering, for he had incurred guilt before the Lord."

It is difficult to determine which reading is correct, and as we will soon see, whether a guilt offering is brought because a person accidentally trespassed against something sacred (Milgrom), because they did not realize they were doing something forbidden (Shadal), or whether they are uncertain whether they have sinned (the Sages), it has no bearing on the process of defining the common denominator among the various cases.

3. *Asham Gezelot*

The third case opens with a new command: "The Lord spoke to Moses saying" (5:20), which is puzzling: Why is a list of three offenses that require a guilt offering suddenly divided up by a new commandment? Perhaps this new opening reflects that this was related to Moses in real time; perhaps it hints that the cases should be divided into two groups, which will contribute to the determination of the common denominator.

In any case, the "*asham gezelot*," as it is known in halakhic literature, meaning "the guilt offering for theft," is presented thus:

> If a person sins, committing a trespass against the Lord by lying to his neighbor about a deposit or pledge, or by robbery, or by defrauding his neighbor, or by finding lost property and lying about it; if he swears falsely about anything he does in any of the ways a person sins, afterward acknowledging guilt for the sin,

9. *Sifra*, Obligatory Offerings, 22:2.

> he shall return what he took by robbery or fraud, or the deposit left with him for safekeeping, or the lost property that he found, or anything else about which he swore falsely. He shall repay its value and add to that a fifth; he shall pay this to its owner on the day he presents his guilt offering. And as his guilt offering to the Lord he shall bring the priest an unblemished ram from the flock of the appropriate value. The priest shall make his atonement before the Lord, and he will be forgiven for whatever he did to incur this guilt. (5:21–26)

The opening of the third case is similar to the first: "If a person commits a trespass, sinning unintentionally with respect to any of the Lord's sacred objects" (v. 15)/"If a person sins, committing a trespass against the Lord" (v. 21). Yet immediately after, it emerges that this "trespass against the Lord" is in fact an intentional offense against one's neighbor through theft and deceit: "By lying to his neighbor about a deposit or pledge, or by robbery, or by defrauding his neighbor, or by finding lost property and lying about it." This is followed by "If he swears falsely about anything he does in any of the ways a person sins," which Ibn Ezra reads as an additional way to cheat. The Sages, in contrast, read this separately, as an additional stage of the offense: First the offender cheats or steals, and then swears falsely about having done so.[10] This reading is supported by the lack of the word "or" before this phrase:

> by lying to his neighbor about a deposit
> *or* pledge,
> *or* by robbery,
> *or* by defrauding his neighbor,
> *or* by finding lost property and lying about it;
> *if* he swears falsely about anything he does in any of the ways a person sins, afterward acknowledging guilt for the sin.

10. Modern scholars also favor this reading. See Milgrom, *Cult and Conscience*, 21–22; Wenham, *Leviticus*, 108.

The impression is that swearing falsely is not just another offense, but rather an additional stage that follows after one of the initial offenses in the list. This is further supported by the opening phrase – "committing a trespass *against the Lord* by lying to his neighbor." How is stealing from a neighbor an offense against the Lord? R. Akiva suggests in the Midrash that all such crimes deny God's omnipresence, for God is witness to every transaction (*Sifra,* Obligatory Offerings), but this is true of all sins. A more convincing explanation is that after committing such a crime, the offender swears falsely in God's name, and this explains why the offense is also a "trespass *against the Lord.*"

Before we move on to the other cases in which a person must bring a guilt offering (which appear elsewhere, not in this chapter), I wish to point out the difference between the order of the offenses when described in verses 20–21 (deposit/pledge/robbery/fraud/lying about finding lost property) and when the offender makes restitution in verses 23–24 (robbery/fraud/deposit/lost property). The first list seems to be arranged according to the owner's awareness of their property being in the offender's possession. When someone deposits something into another's keeping, they are obviously aware that it is in that person's possession. When someone pledges something (the second offense on the list), this refers to money that was given voluntarily (as an investment or loan), but the owner obviously expects their money back. In the third case – robbery – the possession was seized violently, against the owner's will. The fourth – fraud – may have been achieved with or without the owner's knowledge of the offenses committed against them. Finally, in the case of someone finding a lost object and then lying about it, the owner does not know that the offender has it.

In contrast, the list in verses 23–24 describes the process of making reparation, and it is arranged from the most severe to the least severe crime (with robbery at the top of the list and returning lost property, which may be beyond the letter of the law under certain circumstances, at its end).

The first case, *asham me'ilot,* mentions the offering before monetary restitution, but in the case of the guilt offering for theft, returning the other's possession is referred to before any mention of the actual guilt offering. Milgrom does not ascribe any importance to this order,[11] but it may subtly reflect the Torah's value system. When the trespass is solely against the sacred, the offering is central; but in the case of theft or fraud, there are two "prosecutors" – human and God. Before sanctity can be restored, there is a need to settle the earthly balance. This recalls the famous mishna: "Yom Kippur atones for sins against God, but Yom Kippur does not atone for sins between people, and one must first appease one's friend" (Yoma 8:7).

THREE ADDITIONAL CASES

In order to fully understand the nature of the guilt offering, we must take into account the three other instances in which a person must bring a guilt offering, which appear in different contexts.

4. *Asham Metzora*

When someone becomes purified from skin blight (*tzaraat*), they undergo a double process for rejoining the camp. The two-bird ritual allows them to return to the camp itself, but before they are allowed back into their own tent and the Sanctuary, they must undergo further purification rituals and then bring certain offerings. In addition to the burnt and purification offerings that are always brought on the eighth day of the purification ritual after severe impurity,[12] the previously blighted person must also bring a lamb for a guilt offering:

> On the eighth day he shall take two unblemished male lambs and one unblemished ewe lamb in its first year.... The priest shall take one of the male lambs and offer it as a guilt offering. (Lev. 12:10–12)

Milgrom suggests that the guilt offering serves to atone for the sins that caused the offender's skin blight in the first place, which may have

11. Milgrom, *Cult and Conscience*, 80–82; Milgrom, *Leviticus*, vol. 1, 330.
12. Death impurity is the only kind that requires one to wait for seven days before purification, yet those with this type of impurity are exempt from bringing offerings; it seems that the ashes of the red heifer serve as a substitution.

included trespass against sancta, similarly to *asham me'ilot*.[13] But this is a problematic reading, given that the text does not explain why a person is struck with skin blight; in Leviticus, it is not at all clear that this disease is inflicted as a punishment.

On the one hand, the state of the *metzora* presumably has something in common with other offenders who require guilt offerings. On the other hand, the fact that this guilt offering must be a young male lamb rather than a mature ram indicates that this guilt offering somehow differs from regular guilt offerings.

5. *Asham Shifḥa Ḥarufa*

> If a man has carnal relations with a woman who is a slave designated for another man, and who has not been redeemed or given her freedom, there shall be punishment but they shall not be put to death since she has not been freed. The man shall bring his guilt offering to the Lord at the entrance of the Tent of Meeting: a ram for a guilt offering. The priest shall make his atonement before the Lord with the ram of the guilt offering for the sin that he committed, and the sin he committed shall be forgiven. (Lev. 19:20–22)

A man who sleeps with a maidservant intended (*shifḥa ḥarufa*) for another man must bring a guilt offering.[14] The word "*ḥarufa*" in this context seems to mean "intended/designated:"[15] The maidservant (either Israelite, as Ibn Ezra believes, or Canaanite, according to most other *Rishonim*) is intended for a certain man, but another man "steals" her. This is even more problematic given her status: She is not a free woman, subject to punishment by death as a betrothed girl would be (Deut. 22:23–27); nor is she a complete slave, in which case the man would have to pay her master compensation. Under these liminal

13. Milgrom, *Leviticus*, vol. 1, 856.
14. Rashi, based on the Sages: "A Canaanite who is half-slave and half-free, betrothed to a Hebrew slave, who may marry a maidservant."
15. The precise meaning of "*neḥerefet*" is unclear; see De-Paris, "Early Form."

circumstances – where she has not been given her freedom, yet the laws of betrothal still apply – the solution is to bring a guilt offering, which, as Milgrom posits, serves to repair the damage to sanctity caused by this affair.[16]

6. *Asham Nazir*

> If someone dies suddenly beside him, defiling his consecrated head, he shall shave his head on the day of his purification; on the seventh day he shall shave it. Then, on the eighth day, he shall bring two turtledoves or two young pigeons to the priest, to the entrance of the Tent of Meeting. The priest will offer one as a purification offering and the other as a burnt offering, and make atonement for him for the guilt he incurred through contact with the dead body. He shall consecrate his head anew on that day. He must rededicate himself to the Lord for the full term of his vow, and bring a yearling lamb as a guilt offering. The former days are discounted because his separation was defiled. (Num. 6:9–12)

A Nazirite who completes the terms of their vow does not bring a guilt offering; they are still required to bring a whole array of offerings, but this does not include a guilt offering. If, however, they become impure before their term has ended, they must begin their count anew and bring a guilt offering in addition to the burnt and purification offerings that are always brought after a period of severe impurity. Like the *metzora*'s guilt offering, the Nazirite's is also a lamb, not a ram.

THE COMMON DENOMINATOR ACCORDING TO RAMBAM

Commentators have attempted to find the common denominator between all the cases that require a guilt offering. Some do so explicitly and systematically, while others do so as they go along, and their theory can be gleaned from their commentary. Ramban's approach is one of the first and most salient, although it poses a special challenge due to two ostensibly contradictory aspects in his commentary:

16. Milgrom, *Leviticus*, vol. 2, p. 165; also Hartley, *Leviticus*, 913.

> This offering is called *asham*, as the verse states, "After the shekel of the Santuary, for a guilt offering." But "he shall bring '*ashamo*' unto the Eternal" (5:6), mentioned above in the case of the variable offering, means "He shall bring his offering unto the Eternal," for that offering was a purification offering, as it says: "A female from the flock, a lamb or a goat, for a purification offering."
>
> Now it has not been explained why the name of one offering is "a purification offering" and that of the other "a guilt offering," since they both come to effect atonement for sin! We cannot say that the reason is because the purification offering is a female, for there are sin offerings which are male, goats and bulls; nor can we day that this is on account of the severity of the sin, for behold, the leper brings both a purification and a guilt offering. (Ramban on Lev. 5:15)

Ramban begins with a semantic observation: The word "*asham*" does not always refer to the actual *asham* offering, as we saw in the variable offering, where the word "*asham*" appears repeatedly even though the variable offering is actually a purification offering. He therefore goes on to contemplate the difference between the *ḥattat*, purification offering, and the *asham*, guilt offering.

He immediately rules out the idea that a *ḥattat*, which is a feminine word, is brought from female animals, because this is not always the case. (I do not know of any such reading, but as I will explain below, it is characteristic of Ramban's kabbalistic leanings, and he presumably raises and rejects it to express his thought process.)

Another possibility he rejects is that the difference between the two offerings stems from the severity of the sin;[17] he rules this out based on the fact that the *metzora* brings one of each. Rather, the two offerings address two different needs. (Both the *metzora* and the Nazirite who becomes impure bring purification and guilt offerings).

---

17. Here it is not clear which he considers more severe, but he probably considers the *asham* the more severe in this context because it is brought for some deliberate sins; even so, he concludes that the purification offering is more severe.

After rejecting these two hypothetical possibilities, Ramban presents his theory:

> It appears to me that the term "*asham*" denotes some serious deed for which the person who did it deserves to be *shameim* (ruined) and destroyed because of it, similar to the expressions "*haashimem* (destroy them), O God" (Ps. 5:11); "the pastures of the wilderness waste away"[18]...
>
> The word "*ḥattat*" (sin) denotes something which has turned aside off the way, like the expression "Every one could sling stones at a hair-breadth and not miss" (Judges 20:16).

Ramban links the word "*asham*" to "*shamem*," "ruin,"[19] and the word "*ḥattat*" to "*yaḥati*," "miss," "astray," arguing that the punishment for offenses that require an *asham* is complete annihilation and thus far more severe than for offenses that require a *ḥattat*.[20] Why is this so?

> Now the guilt offering for robberies and the guilt offering for lying with a promised handmaid are called "*asham*," because they are for deliberate offenses, and so too the *asham* of the Nazirite. But *asham me'ilot* is called "*asham*," even though it was committed in error, because it concerns God's sacred objects, because the great sin that he did makes him deserve to be *shamem* (ruined) because of it; accordingly, it is called "*me'ila*" (treachery).

Ramban surveys the different offenses that require an *asham* and deems them severe. This is especially striking in the case of the *asham gezelot* and the *asham shifḥa ḥarufa*, given that both are deliberate sins; most offerings provide atonement only for accidental sin. (Withholding testimony is an exception in the variable offering; as we saw above, an

---

18. Ramban cites a verse with similar language from Jeremiah 23:10, but the verse does not actually mention "*asham*."
19. Some point to an etymological connection between "*asham*" and "*shamem*" (Zimmerli, *Ezechiel*, 508) but others reject it (Kellerman, "Asham," 430).
20. Similarly Milgrom, *Leviticus*, vol. 1, 339. He compares also "*avon*," meaning both crime and punishment; see also Ibn Ezra on Gen. 4:13.

offering can atone in this case because withholding testimony is a sin of omission.) In these two cases, however, an *asham* does serve to atone. Ramban then adds: "And so too the *asham* of the Nazirite." This comment requires clarification, given that the Nazirite presumably becomes impure against their will. Perhaps Ramban is implying that because the Nazirite chose to enter a state of higher purity, whatever happens from the moment they enter this state is considered their own responsibility, such that becoming impure is considered "intentional." Another possible reading is that the Nazirite may have intentionally become impure, but the Torah does not distinguish between whether they became impure accidentally or on purpose.

The greater challenge that Ramban's reading poses concerns the other cases that require a guilt offering, which do not seem especially severe. Ramban justifies this in the case of *asham me'ilot*, given that desecrating sacred objects brings ruin whether it is one's fault or not. In this case, it is worth mentioning that the Hammurabi Laws also exact severe punishment – the death penalty – for stealing from the temple (section 6). While biblical law is obviously not identical to Babylonian law,[21] this nonetheless supports the reading that theft and desecration of sanctity is more severe than usual theft, so even if this happens accidentally, the offender must bring a more serious offering – a guilt offering. As Ramban concludes, the term "*me'ila*," "trespass," has severe connotations, and it is no coincidence that the Torah employs this terminology.

Ramban continues his explanation with *asham metzora*:

> As for the *metzora*, because the *metzora* is considered dead, he is like someone *shamem*, ruined and annihilated, so the *asham* protects him from ruination, whereas the *ḥattat* atones for his accidental sin.

Even though the *metzora*'s sin is not especially grave, their impurity is the worst, most severe kind of impurity. To be a *metzora* is like being

21. Neither philosophically nor pragmatically, as shown by Greenberg, *Studies*, pp. 25–41.

dead, and this is reflected in the laws of one afflicted with skin blight,[22] white as a corpse. The *metzora* brings an *asham* to reflect their return from this terrible death-like state.

The greatest challenge, however, is explaining why the *asham talui* is so severe. It is offered when someone is not even certain that they indeed sinned, for an offense that would require the lesser purification offering if the person could confirm that they indeed sinned!

> The reason for the *asham talui* is because the owner thinks that he is not liable to be punished [since his sin has not been confirmed]; therefore, Scripture was more severe with him in the case of his doubt than in that of certainty.

Counterintuitively, Ramban argues that the Torah is far stricter in cases of doubt to prevent liminal situations, which are the most problematic of all. In order to prevent people taking situations of *safek*, doubt, lightly, one must bring a more serious offering to ensure that people avoid such uncertainty in the first place. This recalls halakhic rationale in relation to prohibitions on festivals versus on Shabbat. While certain actions and leniencies are allowed on festivals, certain stringencies are set in place on festivals (but not on Shabbat) to ensure that people do not start taking festivals lightly in general; this is evident in halakhic models that are repeated throughout Tractate Beitza (see, e.g., Beitza 2b).

Thus, according to Ramban, the guilt offering is a powerful offering potent enough to save the offender from ruin and annihilation. This reading is possible but problematic. There are many other grave offenses – especially intentional ones. Why doesn't a guilt offering enable atonement in other cases?

The sense is that rather than answering why these particular cases require an offering, Ramban is addressing why the offering in question is a guilt offering rather than a purification offering. This brings us back to the first question: Do all offenses that require a guilt offering have

---

22. See further in Grossman, "Mourns for Himself." Rocker likens the *metzora*'s expulsion from the camp to the expulsion from Eden (Rocker, *Leviticus*, 191); there, too, expulsion is linked to mortality.

something in common, something that illuminates the nature of this offering?

As stated, Ramban's approach is problematic in itself. In this context, Ramban claims that the guilt offering is more serious than a purification offering, but elsewhere he asserts the opposite:

> The guilt offering is from a male animal; the purification offering is from a female animal, because for offenses that deserve *karet* [the female animal] can bring the soul back to God who bestowed it, but the guilt offering does not atone for *karet* offenses, for it is like a sweet savor to the Lord. (Ramban on Lev. 3:1)

Ramban seeks to explain why some offerings are male and others are female. In the context of this discussion, he addresses the difference between the (female) *ḥattat* and the (male) *asham,* and explains that because the *ḥattat* atones for offenses that would result in *karet* if done intentionally, this offering presumably brings "the soul back to God who bestowed it." In contrast, he likens the male *asham* to a burnt offering, implying that it is for much lesser offenses – to the extent that it is practically a freewill offering that produces a sweet savor!

The question of the difference between male and female animal offerings is notable in itself. In this context, I wish to point out that the premise behind Ramban's claim here that the *ḥattat* is for more serious offenses than the *asham* contradicts his commentary on the *asham.*

Perhaps it can be argued that these are two separate discussions: When it comes to whether the animal is male or female, Ramban focuses on the severity of the offense, whereas when comparing the *ḥattat* to the *asham,* he underscores the future punishment. Yet this is problematic; beyond the illogic of severing the crime from its punishment, Ramban himself (justifiably) perceives the punishment as an indication of the offense's severity.

It is therefore more likely that in the context of discussing the animal's sex, Ramban considers the severity of sin on a formal level: Offenses that require a *ḥattat* are more severe than those that require an *asham.* But in the context of the *asham* in Leviticus 5, he considers the severity of the offense on a practical level: *Ḥattat* is only brought in the case of an accidental sin, so it is less severe than a deliberate offense that requires an *asham*.[23]

Even if we concur with this reading, I believe that there is a more specific common denominator between offenses that require an *asham*.

WRONGFUL USE OF SACRED PROPERTY

The following idea is based on a short but crucial insight of R. Baruch Kehat.[24] Our discussion springs from a particular expression introduced here: "*be'erkekha*," its monetary value. For some reason, the concept of an offering's monetary value appears for the first time in the context of the *asham*; moreover, the offender may bring the equivalent of an offering in silver and the priests will provide a ram.[25]

Some scholars propose that the meaning of "value" is that the offender must bring an offering proportionate to the degree of *me'ila*, trespass or violation.[26] Even if one claims that it is difficult to evaluate the exact fine,[27] the requirement may be more general: an expensive, premium animal for a more severe trespass and a cheaper animal for a lesser offense.

Whether we adopt the Sages' evaluation that the verse demands two silver *sela'im* for a ram, the modern reading that the value of the animal is proportionate to the severity of the trespass, or the alternative theory that the offender must always bring the equivalent amount of silver, the consensus is that this offering combines two areas that are usually completely separate. In most cases, monetary compensation – repaying what one has wrongfully taken from the Sanctuary or another person – is entirely distinct from the sacrificial service. Here, however, the value of the offering itself seems to be directly related to the person's offense.

This reflects much about the nature of the *asham*, which is linked to the offenses of theft, wrongful possession, and trespass of sacred property. Even the act of theft from another person is introduced as a

23. Based on one of my conversations with R. Eli Hadad and R. Baruch Kehat.
24. Kehat, "Guilt Offering," in a slightly different formulation than my own reading.
25. Ehrlich emphasizes this (*Mikrâ ki-Pheschutô*, 215–16).
26. Jackson, *Theft*, 272; Fishbane, "Colophons," 250–51.
27. Milgrom rejects the aforementioned theory with this claim (*Leviticus*, vol. , 326).

trespass against God: "If a person sins, committing a trespass against the Lord by lying to his neighbor…" (5:21). The *asham*, it seems, atones for a more serious form of theft – for trespass against God. The animal must be of a certain value because this offering is profoundly related to compensation and repayment. This principle underlies all instances that require an *asham*; it also explains why lambs and not rams are brought in certain cases.

This, perhaps, is related to the word "*asham*." As mentioned, the term is ambiguous. One meaning is "repayment" (especially in I Samuel 6). Some *asham* offerings require compensation alongside the offering itself – repayment for something that was taken without permission – and it makes sense to name the offering for this element. An alternative claim is that semantically, the *asham* is brought for "*ashma*," "guilt." For now, we will leave both possibilities in abeyance, as both are fitting theories.

We will now consider how the theory that the *asham* is brought for theft against God illuminates each individual case.

For the first case, *asham me'ilot*, no further explanation is necessary, as it outlines the fundamental principle of the *asham*. The second case, *asham talui*, is intriguing in this context. Given that it is followed by a new introduction, it may be that the cases of *asham* can be divided into two subcategories corresponding to the two different openings – the first set comprising *asham me'ilot* and *asham talui*, and the second *asham gezelot*. Reading *asham talui* as a continuation of *asham me'ilot* is supported by R. Akiva in the *Sifra*: "'If' – This adds to the first issue, that is *asham talui* is a possible case of *asham me'ilot*, as R. Akiva says" (*Sifra*, Obligatory Offerings 12:1; similarly Milgrom, as mentioned). R. Akiva bases this connection on the combination of the words "*im*" and "*ki*": "*If* (*im*) a person *should* (*ki*) sin" (5:17). As mentioned, whereas "*im*" usually refers to different options of a certain offering and "*ki*" refers to a new category, the use of both words hints that the *asham talui* is both independent ("*ki*") yet an appendix to or continuation of the previous case ("*im*").

This connection is crucial for understanding the nature of the *asham talui*. The *asham* does not atone for a sin that may or may not have occurred; if the sin is later confirmed, the sinner must still bring a *ḥattat*.

Thus,the *asham* does not atone for the offense, but for some other elusive issue. What is it?

An *asham talui* is brought when someone is concerned that they owe the Sanctuary a *ḥattat,* but they are not certain if they actually sinned. This state of doubt generates a different legal situation that requires a different kind of atonement. Based on the division of this chapter, the *asham talui* is an appendix to the *asham me'ilot,* and this clarifies that a person's concern is that they accidentally kept something sacred in their own possession – for example, that they failed to offer up an animal that should have been sacrificed. Note that the *asham talui* is based on the possible offender's sense that they may have sinned: "This is a guilt offering, for he had incurred guilt before the Lord" (5:19). Similar to the variable offering, in which a person implicates himself through *viddui,* confession, here too the requirement of an *asham* stems from a person's own sense of guilt and concern that they owe something to the Sanctuary.[28]

This illuminates the connection the Sages drew between the *ḥattat* and the *asham talui.* Although these are two different offerings, there is a halakhic ruling that if someone transgresses a negative commandment that does not require a *ḥattat,* they are also exempt from bringing an *asham talui* if they are not sure if they indeed transgressed that commandment. For example, one who accidentally blasphemes is exempt from bringing a *ḥattat,* so if they are not certain whether they actually blasphemed they are also exempt from bringing an *asham talui* (Mishna Keritot 1:2). This is perfectly logical: An *asham talui* is required when there is a concern that someone owes a *ḥattat* to the Sanctuary and cannot bring it; if a certain violation does not require a *ḥattat,* there is no need to bring an *asham* when one is not certain whether they have transgressed or not.

Rambam counts the *asham* as two separate commandments: the *asham talui* (commandment 70) and the regular guilt offering (which he calls "*asham vadai,*" meaning "certain," commandment 71). It is certainly possible to count the *asham talui* as an independent offering, even

28. This conclusion also emphasizes that even accidental sin incurs *ashma,* guilt; moreover, trespass of sanctity is even more severe (Goldenberg, *Exegesis,* 13).

though, ironically, it is presented as an appendix to *asham me'ilot*. Every uncertain sin generates a situation in which someone may or may not owe a *ḥattat* to the Sanctuary, which is a kind of possible *me'ila*. This is the sense of uncertain guilt that lies at the heart of this offering.

This is also supported by Shadal's reading that one brings an *asham talui* when they did not realize that what they were doing was a sin. He explains that a person is only required to bring a *ḥattat* when they accidentally sin, but not if they did not realize that their action was forbidden. (Note that this is his reading, not the accepted halakhic ruling.) Thus, although they are not required to bring a *ḥattat*, they must still bring an *asham talui* to compensate for the offering "owed" to the Sanctuary that they are not bringing because of their lack of knowledge.

The third case – *asham gezelot* – brings us explicitly back to the semantic distinctions between theft, compensation, and questionable ownership. Here, theft or wrongful ownership of another's property is considered trespass against God. Note, however, that most cases of theft do not require an offering: Classic theft demands repayment and compensation alone. Rather, an *asham gezelot* is required when the act of theft is accompanied by an oath, but this does not mean that the *asham* compensates for the false oath (which requires a variable offering – 5:4). Rather, the *asham gezelot* comes into play when a person exploits God's name in order to acquire what is not rightfully theirs – when the offender "steals" God's name to increase their wealth. The value and additional fifth must be repaid to the rightful owner, whereas the *asham* is paid to God for the unlawful use of God's name.

These are the three guilt offerings listed in this section, and all are related to unlawful ownership and trespass against the Sanctuary – either literal, doubtful, or abstract. There are clear connections between the first offering – *asham me'ilot* – and the third – *asham gezelot*: Both mention trespass against God; both require restitution of the sum and an additional fifth; and both, of course, comprise both payment and guilt offering. The *asham talui* between them is characterized as a kind of appendix to the first offering – if someone is uncertain as to whether they have trespassed against the Sanctuary, they bring a guilt offering.

This brings us to the three types of guilt offerings that appear elsewhere in the Torah.

SHIFḤA ḤARUFA

The guilt offering required for having relations with a maidservant intended for another is somewhere along the elusive line between monetary law and the laws of forbidden relationships. When someone steals something, they must make reparation, not bring an offering; when a man and woman have forbidden relations, their penalty is death, not an offering. Yet a maidservant promised (in Hebrew "*mekuddeshet*," literally, "sanctified") to another in marriage is a liminal situation in which she is neither strictly property nor an independent woman, so neither penalty applies.[29] This is reflected in the Sages' ruling: The maidservant herself is punished with lashes, whereas the man who has relations with her must bring an offering (Keritot 11a), so effectively the offense is an instance of wrongful possession – of the maidservant herself.

Yet this is not a form of mere wrongful possession, but rather wrongful possession of something sacred. In the biblical world, a betrothed woman was considered "*mekuddeshet*," "sanctified," since marriage is a holy covenant; as Rashi writes (on Lev. 19:1): "You shall be holy – Separate yourselves from sexual immorality." In the words of Milgrom: "Adultery was considered a violation of the Covenant at Sinai,"[30] or in other words: God is a witness to every marriage ceremony, and adultery denies this. Under the specific, liminal circumstances of a man having relations with a promised maidservant, they are not penalized with death, but the man must still express remorse for his act of taking wrongful possession of a maidservant bound by a holy covenant witnessed by God.

Although, unlike the guilt offerings in Leviticus 5, there is no mention of "value" in this context, the Sages nevertheless rule that all ram (but not lamb) guilt offerings must undergo evaluation:

---

29. Modern scholarship assumes that the maidservant is a girl who was sold for the purpose of marriage in the first place (as in *Parashat Mishpatim*); the Sages largely assume that she is a Canaanite slave. Radatz Hoffmann (*Leviticus*, vol. 2, 39) understands that R. Akiva believes it refers to a Canaanite, whereas Milgrom states that he believes she is a Hebrew (Milgrom, *Leviticus*, vol. 2, 1666). One justification of the term "*shifḥa*" as opposed to the usual "*ama*" is that "*shifḥa*" generates a wordplay with the rest of the verse (Schwartz, *Sanctity*, 153).
30. Milgrom, *Leviticus*, vol. 2, 1674–77; see also Schwartz's reservations.

> Whence is it derived that the *asham shifḥa ḥarufa* should be bought only with silver *shekalim*? From "*ashom asham*" (Lev. 19:20). I might think that I also include the guilt offering of a Nazirite and of a leper. It is, therefore, written [to negate this]: "It [is a guilt offering]" (7:5). Why is the *asham shifḥa ḥarufa* included and that of a Nazirite and of a leper excluded? The *asham shifḥa ḥarufa* is a ram, but that of the Nazirite and the leper is not a ram.

The reason that value is not mentioned in the context of the promised maidservant can also be understood based on our reading. If emphasis on monetary value is linked to wrongful use of sacred property, then the value of an animal offering can be estimated, but the sanctity of a marriage is far more elusive. In the case of this particular guilt offering, there is no mention of the offering's *value* and how it is *given* to the priest, details which are specified for the three guilt offerings in Leviticus 5 (5:16, 18, 25). When the animal's value is emphasized, there is also emphasis on its transferal to the priest.[31]

As mentioned, the two other cases require even further explanation: Are they also related to wrongful use of something sacred, and secondly, why do they require a lamb instead of the default ram? In the sacrificial world, the bird offering is the lowest-ranking offering (due to its low price or the small amount of its flesh and blood), followed by the young lamb, then the mature ram, and finally the bull, which is the largest and most expensive offering. A reasonable estimation is that the two lamb guilt offerings are also linked to the misuse of something sacred, but perhaps to a lesser extent.

ASHAM NAZIR

> If someone dies suddenly beside him, defiling his consecrated head, he shall shave his head on the day of his purification; on the seventh day he shall shave it. Then, on the eighth day, he shall bring two turtledoves or two young pigeons to the priest, to the

31. Compare to Milgrom, *Leviticus*, vol. 2, 1671.

> entrance of the Tent of Meeting. The priest will offer one as a purification offering and the other as a burnt offering, and make atonement for him for the guilt he incurred through contact with the dead body. He shall consecrate his head anew on that day. He must rededicate himself to the Lord for the full term of his vow, and bring a yearling lamb as a guilt offering. The former days are discounted because his separation was defiled. (Num. 6:9–12)

In order to understand the purpose of the Nazirite's guilt offering, we must note its place within the atonement and purification process.[32] The Nazirite first offers two birds, the usual practice for severe impurity; one is offered as a purification offering and the other for a burnt offering, after which the Nazirite's purity and sanctity is restored. They must then complete the full term of their vow, and only afterward do they offer up a guilt offering. This implies that the guilt offering is not a necessary requirement for their atonement, which is achieved through the pair of birds.

Rather, the guilt offering seems to be related to the lost days of the Nazirite's vow; only after they have been completed is a lamb brought as a guilt offering. Like the *asham me'ilot,* which is brought after the wrongful use of sacred *property,* the *asham nazir* is brought after the loss of sacred *time* – a period of particular holiness that was tainted and lost.

This, perhaps, explains why a lamb is brought instead of a mature ram. The use/loss of something sacred is not quite tangible; rather than a concrete, quantifiable object, the value of a sacred period of time is less quantifiable and warrants a different animal.

ASHAM METZORA

This brings us to the other lamb guilt offering, brought by someone who has purified themselves from *tzaraat,* skin blight. The former *metzora* also brings the usual pair of a purification and a burnt offering:

> On the eighth day he shall take two unblemished male lambs and one unblemished ewe lamb in its first year, with three-tenths

32. See also Kehat, "The Guilt Offering."

> of an ephah of fine flour mixed with oil as a grain offering, and one *log* of oil. The priest who purifies shall present the one to be purified, together with these, to the Lord at the entrance to the Tent of Meeting. The priest shall take one of the male lambs and offer it as a guilt offering, along with the *log* of oil; he shall display these, this way and that, as a wave offering before the Lord.[33] He shall slaughter the lamb in the place where purification offerings and burnt offerings are slaughtered within the holy place. For the guilt offering, like the purification offering, belongs to the priest and is holy of holies.
>
> The priest shall take some of the blood of the guilt offering and apply it to the ridge of the right ear, to the right thumb, and to the right big toe of the one who is to be purified. The priest shall pour some of the *log* of oil into his own left palm, dip his right finger into the oil in his left hand, and sprinkle of the oil with his finger seven times before the Lord.
>
> The priest shall apply some of the remaining oil in his hand to the ridge of the right ear, to the right thumb, and to the right big toe of the one who is to be purified, over the guilt offering blood. What remains of the oil in his hand the priest shall pour on the head of the one to be purified. Thus,shall the priest make his atonement before the Lord.
>
> Then the priest shall offer the purification offering to make atonement for the one to be purified of his defilement. Then he shall slaughter the burnt offering. The priest shall offer the burnt offering and the grain offering on the altar. Thus,shall the priest make his atonement, and he shall be purified. (Lev. 14:10–20)

A full analysis of the *metzora*'s return to the camp and Sanctuary exceeds the scope of this discussion; I will focus, rather, on the extensive

---

33. The act of waving the guilt offering (and not the burnt or purification offerings) symbolizes its transferral to a higher sphere (see Milgrom, "Waving," 41–45); see the discussion of waving part of the peace offering in Leviticus 7. There are also biblical instances of waving live creatures, such as the Levites and various lambs (see, e.g., Num. 8:11).

description of the guilt offering. Unlike the Nazirite's purification, the *metzora*'s guilt offering is offered at the beginning of the entire process, and it is central to purification; only after extensive ritual concerning the guilt offering are the other two offerings presented. Beyond its slaughter, the blood of the guilt offering is used in an elaborate ritual of anointing, applied to the subject's right thumb and big toe instead of the altar! Even more surprising, oil is then applied "over the guilt offering blood." What is the meaning of this unusual ceremony?

Many point out the similarities between the *metzora*'s purification process and that of the priests during the days of consecration. As we will discuss below, there, too, Moses takes the blood of the ordination ram and applies it to their right thumb and big toe (Lev. 8:23–24); there, too, the priests (or at least the High Priest) are anointed with oil.[34] These striking similarities reveal the objective of the *metzora* ritual. Both rituals serve to bring the subject into a more exclusive circle and change their status of purity. The priests are sanctified and brought in to serve inside the Tabernacle; the *metzora,* who has been excluded from the camp of Israel, is brought back inside in purity. This is crucial for understanding the purpose of the *asham.*

Like the Nazirite, the *metzora* does not achieve purification and atonement through the guilt offering, but through the purification and burnt offerings, as emerges from the end of the description:

> Then the priest shall offer the purification offering *to make atonement* for the one to be purified of his defilement. Then he shall slaughter the burnt offering. The priest shall offer the burnt offering and the grain offering on the altar. Thus,shall the priest make *his atonement, and he shall be purified.*

The guilt offering is not part of this description. Rather, it seems that the guilt offering allows the *metzora,* who was cut off from the camp, to return to God's presence. Excluded from the camp, the *metzora* was unable to participate in the daily sacrifices or any other kind of

34. Ramban already debates and argues both sides; see his commentary on Lev. 8:12, and see further in the discussion of the consecration days below.

communal worship. Thus, the lamb guilt offering atones for this lost time, for the period in which they were cut off from holy worship, and thus they are able to rejoin the people in whose midst the Divine Presence resides.[35]

Once again, this lost time is symbolized through the offering of a lamb, not a mature ram, given that the sanctity "owed" is more abstract than a tangible animal or other holy object. As the mishna rules, for the two-lamb guilt offerings, "their worth is not brought" (Mishna Zevaḥim 10:5). An offering's equivalent value is only brought when the offense is quantifiable; lost sacred time is too abstract for a monetary assessment.

In summary, the guilt offering is profoundly linked to the sense of guilt that stirs within someone when they make wrongful use of sanctity. Trespass and misuse of sanctity is a grave offense, and a guilt offering helps achieve atonement and repentance and restores balance.

Sforno may have perceived this, as is reflected in his comparison of the purification and guilt offerings in *Parashat Tzav*: "The guilt offering follows the same law as the purification offering: It belongs to the priest who makes atonement with it" (on Lev. 7:7). He writes: "Even though the guilt offering is not brought for offenses that are punished with *karet* as the purification offering is brought, because the offense is trespass against sanctity, they have 'the same law.'" Though the verse discusses all guilt offerings and not just *asham me'ilot*, Sforno defines all guilt offerings as atonement for "trespass against sanctity."[36]

I sense that Rambam also perceives the guilt offering as one of restitution and compensation, as he expresses in his introduction to the laws of *me'ila*, "trespass": "The laws of trespass comprise three commandments: The first is a positive commandment and the other two are negative: (1) The trespasser must pay for his offense, including an additional fifth and an offering..." (in his introduction to *Hilkhot Me'ila*). Rambam refers to the offering as part of the offender's payment.[37] This

35. Some connect the guilt offering lamb to the *metzora*'s alienation from the Sanctuary service; see Wenham, *Leviticus*, 210, and Hartley, *Leviticus*, 197.

36. R. Yehuda Copperman suggests that Sforno is giving an example, not defining all of these terms, but I am not convinced by his reading (Cooperman, *Sforno*, vol. 2, 22).

37. Compare also to his formulation in *Hilkhot Gezela VaAveda* 7:1 about *asham gezelot*.

implies that the offering is characterized by repayment and restitution, although it cannot be confirmed.

This common denominator between all guilt offerings may also illuminate why the laws of its sacrifice are detailed only in *Parashat Tzav* – which is highly unusual, as the sacrifice of all other offerings is described in the first list in *Vayikra*, whereas the laws of their eating are listed in *Parashat Tzav*. As defined above, the first list describes the sacrificial process until the offering reaches the altar, and the second list describes how each sacrifice is shared with the priests and the worshipper. The guilt offering is the only one that deviates from this model.[38] The omission of the description of its sacrifice makes room for focus on how the ram is brought to the Tabernacle.

As Wenham rightly notes: "The value of the animal presented was more important than the procedure at the altar."[39] Compensating for the trespass or wrongful use through and in addition to the ram is an integral part of the sacrificial process. While ultimately, the ram is of course offered up on the altar, what matters is that it is restored to the Sanctuary. We might even say that the guilt offering achieves atonement and equilibrium when the ram is brought "back" to the Tabernacle, even before its slaughter and sacrifice.

PURIFICATION OR GUILT OFFERING?

There are obvious similarities between the two obligatory offerings – *ḥattat* and *asham*. Both are "obligatory" – that is, they are brought as atonement for sin.[40] Moreover, the biblical language blurs the boundaries between them, using the word "*asham*," "guilt," for the purification offering (4:3, 13, 22, 27), the variable purification offering (5:4, 6), and of course the guilt offering itself: "*Asham hu ashom asham laHashem*" (5:19).

This common language is echoed by the Sages, who derive from the mention of "*asham*" in the context of the individual's *ḥattat* that this is

38. Radatz Hoffmann (*Leviticus*, vol. 1, 22) claims that this is because the guilt offering was the only offering not offered during the days of consecration, so it is not an organic part of that section and is therefore included in detail in *Parashat Tzav*.
39. Wenham, *Leviticus*, 105.
40. One of the six demands is that it be "*lishmah*": "Purification and guilt offering for the sake of sin" (*Sifra*, Obligatory Offerings, 14:2).

sometimes accompanied by an *asham talui:* "'Doing what must not be done and thus incurring guilt' (4:22, 27) shows that he must bring an *asham talui*" (*Sifra*, Obligatory Offerings, 7:11).

Both are obligatory offerings, and descriptions of both refer to atonement and forgiveness. What they have in common is reflected in R. Eliezer's position in various disputes in Tractate Zevaḥim; here are two central examples:

1. The Sages rule that offerings must be done *lishmah*; the ritual service involved must be done specifically for that offering, brought by that worshipper. The beginning of Tractate Zevaḥim explores these laws in depth. Basically, if most offerings are not slaughtered *lishmah*, they are not invalidated, but the worshipper does not fulfill his obligation through them – except for the purification offering, which *is* invalidated unless it was slaughtered for that specific purpose (and the Passover lamb, which exceeds the scope of this discussion). R. Eliezer, however, rules that the same is true of the guilt offering – that a guilt offering that is not slaughtered *lishmah* cannot be offered on the altar (Mishna Zevaḥim 1:1).[41]
2. There is an even more surprising instance in which R. Eliezer treats the guilt offering as a kind of purification offering: When the Sages rule that when the blood of an offering intended for the regular altar is accidentally brought inside, most offerings remain valid – with the exception of external purification offerings, about which it is specifically stated that if their blood is brought inside, they must be burnt instead of sacrificed (Lev. 6:23). However, R. Eliezer adds that the same is true of the guilt offering – if its blood is accidentally brought inside, the offering becomes invalid, even though there is no such thing as internal or external guilt offerings.

41. The Talmud questions R. Eliezer's source (Zevaḥim 10b; see also Tosefta Zevaḥim 1). One approach is that he bases this on the phrase, "It is a guilt offering" (Lev. 7:5), which implies that obligatory offerings must be "*lishmah*," whereas another opinion is that he bases this on "The guilt offering follows the same law as the purification offering" (7:7), which implies that R. Eliezer extends some laws of the purification offering to the guilt offering as well.

R. Eliezer thus points to a deeper connection between the two offerings, suggesting that unique aspects of the *ḥattat* also apply to the *asham*. Nonetheless, the Torah clearly draws a distinction between them, from both halakhic (especially the different animals and blood ritual)[42] and literary perspective: They are listed in separate sections, and the guilt offering is only brought for specific offenses. As Ramban writes, that the two are distinct is obvious given that in certain circumstances, the worshipper must bring both offerings (like the *metzora* and the Nazirite who became impure).

What, then, is the actual difference between the *ḥattat* and the *asham*? In this context, what characterizes each individual offering is of lesser importance than the function each one serves and how it brings atonement.

Various opinions have been offered; many emphasize the difficulty more than they offer a viable solution. Among the whole range of (unconvincing) options is Philo's suggestion that the *ḥattat* atones for offenses against people, while the *asham* atones for offenses against God; Josephus's theory that the *ḥattat* is for offenses that were not witnessed, while the *asham* is for offenses that were witnessed (although the *asham talui* certainly does not have any witnesses!); that the *ḥattat* is for sins that warrant the death penalty and the *asham* is brought for less severe sins (although it makes little sense that a ram is brought for less serious offenses than the lamb or goat of the *ḥattat*); and so on and so forth.[43] Others despair of distinguishing between the two and suggest that the two are synonymous terms (although this does not explain why both offerings are sometimes required).[44]

I wish to further this discussion by raising Matan Barzilai's suggestion,[45] which focuses on the "awareness" repeatedly mentioned in the *ḥattat* offering. This is evident in the biblical text and further developed by the

42. I do not understand why the author of *Maaseh HaKorbanot* writes that the ritual process of the *asham talui* is like that of the purification offering (p. 169). While their slaughter and burning on the altar are indeed identical, the blood ritual is significantly different.

43. See Weinberg, "Purification and Guilt Offerings," who also rejects this theory.

44. De Vaux, *Ancient Israel,* vol. 2, 420–21.

45. Barzilai, "Guilt Offering."

Sages. Realization/acknowledgment (*yedia*) of sin is a crucial part of the sacrificial process of the *ḥattat* (except for the High Priest's *ḥattat*), and is mentioned each time (4:14, 23, 28); it is also mentioned in the description of the variable offering (5:3, 4), but not in the context of the guilt offering. The *asham me'ilot* describes a person's accidental sin, but the text does not mention this stage of the atonement process: "If a person commits a trespass, sinning unintentionally with respect to any of the Lord's sacred objects, he shall bring an unblemished ram" (5:15). Moreover, the *asham talui* proves that realization of sin is inherently *not* part of the sacrificial process for the guilt offering: "If a person sins *without realizing it*, doing any of the things that the Lord commanded not to be done, he incurs guilt and is subject to punishment" (5:17). Barzilai uses this as the basis of his definition of each offering's nature:

> When someone knows for certain how they have sinned, they can bring a *ḥattat* and atone... Knowledge paves the way to achieving complete atonement through the offering. However, when someone is not entirely certain of their offense... this uncertainty prevents them from achieving atonement through an offering and they are left with a sense of sin.[46]

Note his extraordinary claim: Barzilai holds that the essence of the guilt offering is contained in the *asham talui* – that all guilt offerings stem not from knowledge and atonement for sin, but from a sense of guilt. He supports this further with Abarbanel's reading that the essence of the guilt offering is indeed the guilt that comes from a sense of doubt.

I wish to take this idea in a different direction. While I believe it is problematic to define the *asham talui* as the quintessential guilt offering (it is more of an appendix to the *asham me'ilot*, and moreover, for most kinds of guilt offering, the bringer is certainly aware of their sin or state of impurity), Barzilai is correct that purification offerings indeed emphasize the acknowledgment of sin, whereas guilt offerings do not.

This can be linked to an even deeper disparity: Purification offerings are brought for cases of accidental sin (or impurity), whereas guilt

46. Ibid., 46.

offerings are brought for accidental and deliberate cases, and even cases beyond a person's control (*asham nazir*). Because the purification offering is brought for accidental sin, a person must become aware of this offense before they can achieve atonement. How they become aware of this sin is irrelevant; what matters is that they realize that they have sinned, even though it was by mistake.

This element of acknowledgment is absent in the guilt offering process because it is not essential to the offering's nature: The bringer of the guilt offering knows that they have sinned (either because they have already learned of it or because they sinned on purpose).

This difference exposes the fundamental nature of the two obligatory offerings. The purification offering focuses on the damage done to the Sanctuary. The offering atones not just for sin but for the impurity it casts. Whatever the degree of impurity, it is a stain that must be scrubbed out and purified, even though it occurred through an unintentional offense, and this purification is achieved through applying (or sprinkling) sacrificial, purifying blood.

In contrast, the guilt offering does not purify the altar; this is not its purpose. The name "*asham*" reveals its nature: The worshipper brings a sacrifice to repay their *ashma*, their guilt or debt. Thus, the true difference between the two offerings is reflected through their blood ritual: Unlike the purification offering, the guilt offering does not serve to purity the Sanctuary or altar; it is the gift of the sinner seeking atonement, seeking to dispel their lingering sense of guilt. The guilt offering focuses on the misuse of holiness, not upon the damage done to holiness; its purpose is to repay what was wrongfully used or taken. The guilt offering serves to repair the breach of trust that was created when the offender used what was not theirs to use: holy objects or God's name.

Barzilai argues that the guilt offering is less severe because it is brought for doubtful offenses,[47] but this is not at all the case: "This is a guilt offering, for he had incurred guilt before the Lord!" (5:19), as Ramban holds. One who misuses God's sacred name or property is cut off from holiness itself, and just like the *metzora* who must undergo

47. At the end of his article, Barzilai indeed has to justify why for the guilt offering a more expensive animal is used than for the purification offering.

purification in order to rejoin the camp of Israel, all bringers of a guilt offering seek to rejoin the sacred system whose trust they violated through their desecration; they must bring an offering to repay this guilt.

> There are more who hate me without cause than there are hairs on my head,
> so many treacherous foes who long to destroy me.
> Must I return what I have not stolen?
> God, You know my folly;
> my guilt is not hidden from You. (Ps. 69:5–6)

Chapter 12

The Second Sacrificial List

In the introduction we have already discussed the relationship between the two sacrificial lists. In *Parashat Tzav*, the discussion of each offering begins with "*Zot **Torat** ha-x*" – "This is the *law* of the x offering"; the laws of the consumption of each offering is the main subject of the second list. Above, we concluded that each list focuses on a different purpose offerings serve: In *Parashat Vayikra*, offerings are a form of human expression to God, either a particular religious expression or a means of atonement or correction. In contrast, in *Parashat Tzav* offerings are a prelude to the description of the days of consecration (Lev. 8–10) and a form of the Divine Presence's manifestation in Israel. The focus is not the human worshipper but the holiness of the Sanctuary and its priests and the eternal fire upon the altar.

This is especially salient in the description of the burnt offering, the first of both lists. In *Parashat Vayikra*, the *ola* is characterized as a freewill offering, while *Parashat Tzav* seems to focus on the *olat tamid*, the daily burnt offering that burns upon the altar all night long.[1] There is no mention of the individual worshipper in this chapter; the text's focus is the altar fire that blazes down to consume the offering.

This focus forms an interesting tension with the fact that the laws of eating the peace offering are also described in this section. Thus, the first list describes the offering until its sacrifice upon the altar, and the second list describes what happens from when it is placed upon the altar, until it is eaten or burnt. This is not a merely chronological division; it reflects two different aspects of the offerings and their purpose.

Why, then, are the laws of eating the peace offering postponed until *Parashat Tzav*? Especially considering that the eating of the sacrifice reflects the nature of the offering, one might expect these laws to be introduced in *Vayikra*. In this second list, the peace offering is divided into thanksgiving offering and the fulfillment of a vow, and the third-person impersonal subject refers to the Israelite worshipper – anomalous to *Parashat Tzav*, where in all other offerings, the impersonal subject (such as "shall send up in smoke" – 6:8) refers to the priest.

To understand this anomaly, we must modify the division of the sacrificial lists: The focus of the second list is on how the offering is consumed. Thus, the laws of the first offering apply to the altar fire that consumes; most of the laws of the offerings concern the priests who consume; and finally, the laws of the peace offering refer to the Israelite who consumes their portion.

This premise will accompany us throughout our analysis. For now, I will note the characterization of the altar in the description of lifting out the ashes: "He shall lift the ashes of the burnt offering *that the fire consumed* on the altar" (6:3). Throughout *Parashat Vayikra*, the priest "sends the offering up in smoke" (*hiktir*); here, however, the altar fire "consumes" the offering. While the two descriptions refer to the same action, each has its own symbolic associations.

1. Hartley, *Leviticus*, 96; Bekhor Shor notes that this specifically refers to the evening daily offering. The demand for a constant flame assumes that other offerings are laid upon the burnt offering, and these are indeed described soon after (see especially Koch, *Priesterschrift*, 62). It is worth noting that the second list also mentions the daily grain offering (*minḥat tamid* – 6:13), and we will discuss the relationship between the two offerings below.

As mentioned, "*lehaktir*" means "to send up in smoke," which describes the transformation of flesh into smoke/spirit as a "sweet savor." In *Parashat Vayikra, aroma* is key; in *Tzav*, the altar *consumes*.

The consuming fire described in *Parashat Tzav*'s burnt offering is profoundly connected to the days of consecration. During these days, the altar fire is described as a consuming fire: "And from before the Lord, fire came forth. It consumed the burnt offering and the fat pieces on the altar" (9:24); in the second sacrificial list the tending and stoking this divine fire is presented (as will be discussed below). In fact, the consuming fire of the days of consecration is the second act of a broader story. This is the same fire that blazed down from the heavens at Mount Sinai: "To the Israelites the appearance of the Lord's glory on the mountaintop was like consuming fire" (Ex. 24:17). The Tabernacle, built to maintain and continue the power of the Sinai revelation, keeps this divine fire burning; in the words of Ramban (on Ex. 25:1): "The glory revealed to Israel at Mount Sinai was always in the Tabernacle."

This is the context of *Parashat Tzav*: The consuming fire is divine revelation, and this is the main objective of the narrative. Thus, how the offering is consumed is not merely a report of what happens after the offering has been sacrificed upon the altar, but a presentation of its main purpose. The priest's holy portion and the people's share of the peace offering is the second list's main objective, for consuming the offering is a profound part of its purpose.

The priests' preparation and purification during the days of consecration, therefore, is essentially the act of sanctifying their mouths and bodies so that they are fit to eat offerings, qualified to place holy flesh and grain between their lips. The second sacrificial list is deeply connected to the days of consecration: The consuming altar fire is the fire of divine revelation; the priests fulfill their role as "offering eaters" as the altar's human representatives.

This paradigm is reflected in several halakhot. One illustrative example is that if a priest attempts to consecrate a woman to him in marriage using a priestly share of the offerings, no matter its level of holiness, she is not considered *mekuddeshet*, consecrated to him (Mishna Kiddushin 2:8), although R. Yehuda disagrees. The question at the heart of this mishna is one of ownership, because one can only consecrate a woman to him with something he truly owns. Does a priest's share of an offering become "his," or is he merely eating a portion that essentially belongs to the altar? This law implies that a priest's share is not truly "his."[2]

A slightly different formulation can be based on the Talmud's focus on the purpose of the meat the priests receive (regardless of the question of ownership): "This shall be for you from the holies of holies, from the fire – R. Yehuda argues: For you and all your needs; R. Yossi argues: As fire: Just like fire consumes, so too it is only for consumption" (Kiddushin 52b). R. Yossi states that just like the altar fire only consumes, so too the priests may only consume their share, not use it for any other purpose. Whether the halakhic prohibition against consecrating a woman with a priestly share reflects limited ownership or the parameters of permitted use,[3] these shares of consecrated meat are not usual "priestly gifts," but portions that must be eaten. This principle will inform the rest of our discussion of this sacrificial list.

"ANYTHING THAT TOUCHES ITS FLESH IS SANCTIFIED": THE CONTAGIOUS HOLINESS OF THE HOLY OF HOLIES

An offering's definition as "holy of holies" forms the backbone of these chapters; *Parashat Tzav* is arranged according to the level of holiness. How are offerings categorized? Why is a particular offering considered of higher or lesser holiness? This is certainly in dialogue with the Torah's definition of the grain offering: "Anything that touches it is sanctified" (6:11).

Rishonim argue about what this statement means. Is this holiness "contagious"? Thanks to the laws of impurity, we are accustomed to the idea that touching something impure can contaminate. Can it be that holiness similarly spreads its status to those who touch it? This idea is related to one of the most fundamental questions of the world of biblical holiness.

---

2. This is the approach of the *Rishonim*. One representative example is Rambam: "The items a priest takes of higher and lesser holiness is considered the property of on high.... God only gave them these portions for eating and for no other purpose" (Rambam's commentary on Mishna Kiddushin 2:8).
3. See also Rapaport, *Mikdash David*, 198–203; also Cherlow, "Mekaddesh BeḤelko."

Rashbam argues that holiness is not "contagious," and that "anything it touches is sanctified" is a condition: One may only touch the offering in a state of purity. Rashbam is consistent, and presents a similar reading in two other places – when the altar is consecrated in Exodus: "For seven days, make atonement for the altar and consecrate it, so that the altar becomes holy of holies – and anything that touches it will become holy" (Ex. 29:37);[4] and when the Tabernacle vessels are anointed with oil: "You shall consecrate them and they will become holy of holies, and whatever touches them will become holy" (Ex. 30:29). According to Rashbam, all three statements are instructions that the vessels may only be touched by someone pure; there is no concept of contagious holiness. The disadvantage of this reading is that all three verses use the future tense, *yikdash*, "will *become* holy," implying that this is a consequence of touching them and not a precondition, parallel to verses about becoming impure, such as: "Whoever touches them – will *become* impure" (Lev. 11:26). Moreover, a similar verse about the purification offering clearly shows that "*yikdash*" refers to the consequence of touching the offering's flesh: "*Anything that touches its flesh is sanctified* (*yikdash*); if any of its blood splashes on a garment, you shall wash that part in a holy place. An earthen vessel in which it was cooked shall be broken, but if it was cooked in a bronze vessel, that shall be scoured and rinsed with water" (Lev. 6:20–21).

The Sages' prevalent approach is that the concept of contagious purity indeed exists. Given that this may have potentially odd results, the Sages qualified this idea by defining that only something fit to be an offering upon the altar can acquire sanctity through contact. A dog or person that touches the offering will not become sanctified, as Rashi writes:

> Henceforth the altar shall be holy – Now what was [the altar's] sanctity? "Whatever touches the altar will be holy." Even an invalid sacrifice that was placed upon it – the altar sanctified it to render it fit so that it would not be taken off [the altar]. Since it is said: "Whatever touches the altar will be holy," I understand it to mean whether it is fit or whether it is unfit, such as something

4. Compare also to Rashbam on Lev. 11:8.

> whose disqualification did not occur in the Sanctuary, such as a male animal or a female animal that was intimate with a human, [or] an animal set aside for a sacrifice to idols, [or] an animal that was worshipped as a god, or an animal that suffered a mortal wound or terminal illness, or [any other disqualification] like them. Therefore, the Torah states: "And this is what you shall offer upon the altar," immediately following it [this verse]. Just as the burnt offering is fit, so is it with anything that was already fit and became disqualified after entering the courtyard, such as a sacrifice that was left overnight, a sacrifice that was taken out of the courtyard, a sacrifice that was ritually unclean, [a sacrifice] that was slaughtered with an intention of [offering it up or eating its flesh] outside the time allotted for it or outside the proper place, and [any other disqualification] like them. (Rashi on Ex. 29:37)[5]

Ibn Ezra debates between the two approaches. He seems to lean toward Rashbam's reading concerning the *altar*: "Whoever touches the altar must be sanctified – so that a foreigner will not touch it; only a consecrated priest. Although many explain: Anything that touches it becomes holy to the Lord" (Ibn Ezra's concise commentary on Ex. 29:37). In the context of *offerings*, however, he does seem to favor the idea of contagious holiness – even, apparently, without the Sages' qualification: "*Anything* that touches the grain, purification, or guilt offering is holy to the Lord" (on Lev. 6:11). Even if something is not fit to be an offering, it still becomes the Tabernacle's consecrated property.

Indeed, the verses that follow the description of the Tabernacle vessels show no indication that only certain items became holy through contact:

> With it, anoint the Tent of Meeting and the Ark of the Testimony, the table and all its utensils, the candelabrum and its utensils, the incense altar, the sacrificial altar with all its utensils, and the laver and its base. You shall consecrate them and they will become holy

5. See also Rashi (on Lev. 6:11) on the grain offering: "Items of lesser holiness or no holiness that touch it will 'become sanctified.'"

> of holies, and *whatever touches them will become holy*. You shall anoint Aaron and his sons and consecrate them to serve Me as priests. (Ex. 30:26–30)

Here it is more problematic to say that the vessels consecrate only entities that are fit to be consecrated. Only certain animals make worthy sacrifices, but these definitions are not relevant when it comes to the Ark or the laver,[6] and Ibn Ezra's reading seems to be the verse's plain meaning.

It thus emerges that like impurity, holiness can also be contagious – but not all holiness. Only holiness considered "holy of holies" can spread through contact.

What, then, defines this level of holiness? Ibn Ezra does not interpret the phrase as indicating a distinction: "Holy of holies – Holy like any of the holy things" (on Ex. 29:37; see also Hizkuni). While not impossible, it makes more sense to read this as a term that does distinguish between different levels of holiness, like the name "Song of Songs" – the highest possible form of song, as R. Akiva expounds: "For the whole world is not as worthy as the day on which the Song of Songs was given to Israel; for all the writings are holy, but the Song of Songs is the holy of holies" (Mishna Yadayim 3:5). One implication of this definition has a direct bearing on our discussion. It is no coincidence that all instances of the Torah's definition of "holy of holies" appear in this particular formulation: "all/whatever/anything (*kol*) + form of the verb root *naga*, "touch" + *yikdash*:

- **The altar**: "So that the altar becomes holy of holies – and anything that touches it will become holy." (Ex. 29:37)
- **The altar vessels anointed with oil**: "You shall consecrate them and they will become holy of holies, and whatever touches them will become holy." (Ex. 30:29)

6. However, see Rashi (on Ex. 30:29), based on the Sages, that these verses can also be read to mean that only certain items can be sanctified, although this reading seems contrived.

- **The grain offering**: "It is holy of holies, like the purification offering and the guilt offering… anything that touches it is sanctified." (Lev. 6:11)
- **The purification offering**: "It is holy of holies…. Anything that touches its flesh is sanctified." (Lev. 6:18–20)

Entities defined as "holy of holies" sanctify others; those defined merely as "holy" do not. Ibn Ezra's aforementioned commentary, "Anything that touches the grain, purification, or guilt offering is holy to the Lord," is accurate: These three offerings are defined as "holy of holies," whereas the peace offering is not. As we will see, the second sacrificial list is shaped by this axis of contagious holiness and its implications for the sacrificial world. Before we delve into this chapter, however, we will first consider prophecies from Haggai and Ezekiel, whose similar portrayal of holiness will hone our conception of biblical contagious holiness.[7]

Haggai 2:11–13

> So says the Lord of Hosts: "Now ask the priests for a ruling of Law: 'If a man carries consecrated meat in the fold of his garment and with that fold touches bread, or a cooked dish, or wine, or oil, or any other food, does it become sanctified?'"
> The priests answered and said: "No."
> Haggai said: "And if someone who has become impure through contact with the dead touches any one of these things, does it become impure?"
> The priests answered and said: "It becomes impure."

On the twenty-fourth of Kislev (the day of the Second Temple's foundation), God commands His prophets to ask the priests for a "*torah*" ("a ruling of law"): If someone is holding a piece of holy meat in his garment, and that garment touches other food, does that other food become sanctified (*hayikdash*)? They reply that it does not. As for impurity, however, the priests answer that someone impure does contaminate

7. See Milgrom, *Leviticus*, vol. 1, 443–56.

others. Haggai then declares that the people are impure (presumably referring to the people of Samaria who want to help rebuild the Temple, but who are still worshipping idols) and therefore must not participate in the Temple's rebuilding.

What is relevant for our discussion, of course, is Haggai's question to the priests. The narrative's premise is that the prophet is asking rhetorical questions whose answer is clear to all: Of course the food does not become holy! Of course the impurity contaminates! And he then uses these obvious answers in order to impart a moral message. Two conclusions can be derived from the priests' answers:

1. Impurity is easily transmitted from object to object; even touching the garment of someone impure is contaminating. In contrast, when holy food is wrapped in a garment, the garment does not transmit this holiness through contact.
2. The prophet's question is whether touching the garment wrapped around the holy food sanctifies other foods; this implies that if the holy food touches other foods directly, they *would* be sanctified. Some exegetes find this difficult and thus read "sanctified" in the sense of "impure food" (such as Rashi's "contamination by a carcass or creeping thing") – as if Haggai is comparing this kind of impurity and *tumat met,* impurity of the dead, the most severe kind of impurity. But the more straightforward reading is that the prophet is contrasting the world of sanctity with the world of impurity. Ibn Ezra, for example, points out that "*yikdash*" (become sanctified) is contrasted with "*yitma*" (become impure).

Thus, this prophecy implies that direct contact with holiness is sanctifying; it seems to affect all foods, not just those fit for sacrifice upon the altar. Given that Haggai's question only concerns food, however, it is unclear whether holiness can also spread to people.

Ezekiel 44:15–19

> But the priests who are Levites descended from Zadok ... are the ones who may draw near Me in order to serve Me, and they shall

> stand before Me to offer Me fat and blood: this is the word of the Lord God. They are the ones who will enter My Sanctuary, and they shall approach My table to serve Me; they shall dutifully protect My precious things. This is how it shall be when they approach the gates of the inner courtyard: they will wear linen garments, and no wool shall be upon them when they serve at the gates of the inner courtyard and within. There will be linen turbans on their heads and linen trousers on their loins; they shall not gird themselves in a way that causes perspiration. And when they leave to go to the outer courtyard – to the outer courtyard to the people – they shall remove the garments in which they serve, leaving them in the holy chambers, and put on other clothing, so that they will not sanctify the people through their garments.

This prophecy also gives the impression that holiness can spread beyond the boundaries of the Temple. For this reason, the prophet warns the priests not to wear their linen garments outside of the Temple courtyard – so that they won't accidentally "sanctify the people" through contact with their holy vestments.

This prophecy may or may not extend the boundaries of holiness. Milgrom claims that Ezekiel extends the concept of sanctity to clothing, beyond offerings and holy vessels,[8] but it is worth pointing out that priestly vestments are a kind of vessel and that they too were consecrated (Ex. 29:21).[9] Moreover, their purpose is expressly defined as to sanctify the priests (Ex. 28:41), and they are further defined as "sacred vestments" (Ex. 29:29–30). Ezekiel is concerned about sanctity spreading beyond the borders of the Temple. This reading seems to be supported by another of his prophecies:

---

8. Milgrom, *Leviticus*, vol. 1, 446.
9. The prevalent halakhic view is that garments are defined as "service vessels" and thus have holiness (see *Encyclopedia Talmudit*, "*Bigdei Kehunna*," vol. 2, 335). The Tosafot point out that the garments are only considered service vessels once they have been worn in service (Kiddushin 54a, s.v. "*kotnot*"). Ritva has a unique opinion that they have no bodily holiness, only *kedushat damim*.

> Then he said to me: "The northern chambers and the southern chambers which face the main enclosure are holy chambers where the priests who approach the Lord may eat the holiest of sacrifices. There shall they place the holiest of sacrifices, the grain offering and the purification offering and the guilt offering, for the place is holy. Once the priests enter, they may not leave the holy area to go to the outer courtyard; first they shall leave the garments in which they minister there, for they are holy. They are to put on other clothes and after that may approach the area designated for the nation." (Ezek. 42:13–14)

While Rashi reads this, too, as related to fear of contamination from impurity outside the Temple grounds, another possible interpretation is the prophet's concern that these sacred vestments will inadvertently sanctify the people.[10] Ezekiel emphasizes that what is holy should remain in its rightful place.

This is in line with Ezekiel's broader perception of maintaining distance between the Temple and the masses; this is even reflected in the redistribution of the tribal portions. In Ezekiel's messianic vision, the Temple has its own special portion; it is not right in the midst of the bustling city that is so accessible to all. Isaiah's vision of the future is universal; Ezekiel dreams of a redemption that "is not for your sake that I do this, House of Israel, but for My holy name that you desecrated among the nations to which you came" (Ezek. 36:22). Ezekiel's view is that redemption is intended to prevent the desecration of God's holy name (similarly to the perception in *Parashat Haazinu,* Moses's final song); the vision in his book creates clear barriers between the Temple and the masses, lest they contaminate God's holy dwelling place. Ezekiel's repeated warning to the priests against wearing their vestments outside the Temple grounds is consistent with his messianic vision.[11]

To summarize the issue of contagious holiness: While there is no such thing according to Rashbam, the Sages (and Rashi in their wake)

---

10. E.g., Kasher, *Ezekiel,* 820.
11. For a broader discussion of the nature of Ezekiel's messianic visions, see Kasher, *Ezekiel,* 125–32; Greenberg, "Ezekiel's Program"; Ganzel, "Ezekiel's Redemption."

believe that holiness can spread (to a certain extent); the same emerges from the prophecies of Haggai and Ezekiel. Like impurity, holiness can be transmitted through touch. In this sense, "the holy of holies" is parallel to "*av tum'a*," a primary source of impurity.

This has broad, crucial implications for the sacrificial list in *Parashat Tzav*. The first is that only the priests may eat from the offering; since the meat can transmit holiness to others, only those who have already been consecrated (i.e., the priests) may partake of it. The verse emphasizes that only male priests may eat from what is "holy of holies" because of this contagious holiness (in contrast to priestly gifts of lesser holiness, which the priest's family may eat as well). As we will soon clarify, the offerings' contagious holiness forms the backbone of the second sacrificial list.

Chapter 13

The Law of the Burnt Offering (Leviticus 6:1–6): Stability and Change

> The Lord spoke to Moses: Instruct Aaron and his sons: This is the law of the burnt offering. The burnt offering shall remain on the altar hearth all night until the morning, and the altar fire shall be kept alight upon it. The priest shall dress in his linen vestments, with linen undergarments against his skin. He shall lift the ashes of the burnt offering that the fire consumed on the altar, and place them by the altar's side. Then he shall take off his vestments, put on other garments, and take the ashes to a ritually pure place outside the camp. The altar fire shall be kept alight; it shall not go out. Every morning the priest shall add wood to it, lay out the burnt offering upon it, and send the fat parts of the peace offering up in smoke upon it. A perpetual fire shall be kept alight on the altar; it shall not go out. (6:1–6)

Unlike the individual's freewill burnt offering of the first list, this "*torah*" (law) seems to refer to the famous daily burnt offering of the evening:

He shall lift the ashes of the burnt offering that the fire consumed on the altar	and take out the ashes
and place them by the altar's side.	to a ritually pure place outside the camp.

The two verses follow the same structure: They begin with describing the priest's vestments; then his action concerning the ashes; and finally, their new place. The Sages perceive these parts as two separate commandments, as Rashi writes:

> "He shall take out the ashes" – which were heaped up in a rounded pile. When this pile became so large that there was no longer any room on the wood pile, he would take it out of there. Now, this was not a daily obligation (Tamid 28b), but lifting out [the ashes from the altar] was a daily obligation. (Rashi on Lev. 6:4)

According to this reading, lifting the ashes off the altar and taking them outside the camp are two distinct commandments; the first is a daily obligation, whereas taking them outside the camp is only necessary when the mound of ashes becomes too large.[3] Given that this process concerns the altar, the priest must be wearing his ritual vestments. The clothing he dons for taking out the ashes are not regular clothes but rather priestly work clothes so as not to ruin the finer linen vestments.[4] As Rashi explains:

> This is not an obligation, but etiquette, that, by taking out the ashes, he should not soil the garments in which he constantly officiates. The clothes worn [by a servant] while cooking for his master are not those he wears when serving his master. Hence he must "put on other" inferior "garments."

3. Rambam's language implies that this was performed every day (*Hilkhot Temidin UMusafin* 2:13) but that taking out the ashes is not actually part of the service, whereas lifting them off the altar is.
4. Note that the *Sifra* is aware of the straightforward reading and rejects it (*Sifra, Tzav,* 2:6).

Another, more straightforward reading is offered by Bekhor Shor: These verses do not refer to two separate commandments, but to one process with two stages: For the stage directly involving the altar, the priest wears proper vestments, but he changes into regular clothing to remove these ashes; the whole process was performed daily.[5] Abarbanel explains that placing the ashes by the altar's side after removing them from the altar is necessary in order to allow the priest to change his clothes.[6] Ramban also rejects Rashi's reading that the priest changes into an inferior form of vestments when he takes out the ashes; like Bekhor Shor and Abarbanel, he explains that the priest changes into regular work clothes.

Thus, the first focal point of these verses is that each day, the priest must clear out the ashes from the previous day. All the ashes from the offerings the altar consumed all night must be cleared out each morning. The Talmud perceives this as "taking out the garbage" and not as the "priestly service." This is reflected in R. Eliezer's claim that even priests with deformities that render them unfit to serve may take out the ashes (Yoma 23b) because it is not really part of the "service," and it is reinforced by Resh Lakish's observation that the priest dons only two of the priestly garments in order to lift the ashes from the altar, which implies that it is not actual service.

In contrast, Rambam's formulation in *Mishneh Torah* is interesting in this context and refers back to the Sages' reading of this commandment:

> The priestly garments [worn] when removing the ashes should be less valuable than those [worn] when performing the other aspects of Temple service, as "he shall remove his garments and put on other garments and remove the ashes." The term "other" does not imply ordinary garments, but rather [priestly garments] that are less valuable than the first. The rationale is that it is not proper conduct to serve a cup [of wine] to one's master in the

5. Rambam combines both readings: that they are two different actions, but also two consecutive stages.
6. The custom of reciting the verses about clearing the ashes before Shaḥarit each morning reflects the Sages' reading that both acts were performed daily. (It could also reflect Rambam's reading above.)

> same clothes as one cooked food for him. (*Hilkhot Temidin UMusafin* 2:10)[7]

The two garments worn for the removal of ashes from the altar are the two most basic vestments. They bring no glory or honor to their wearer, but being vestments of service, they nonetheless allow the priest to approach the altar.

Is Removing the Ashes Really Just Taking Out the Garbage?

Thus, there are two different perceptions of the act of removing the ashes. Is it merely taking out the garbage, in regular work clothes, an act that even priests with deformities may perform? My friend Dr. Hillel Mali (Department of Bible, Bar-Ilan University) pointed out to me that use of the verb "lift" (*herim*) has certain ritual connotations that recall the act of *teruma*, ritual waving, which hints to consecration.

Moreover, referring to the ashes as "*deshen*" alludes to their deeper meaning. The biblical word "*deshen*" connotes richness, fertility, and ever-flowing abundance: "They feast on the *rich plenty* (*deshen*) of Your House; You quench their thirst with Your river of delights" (Ps. 36:9); "Listen – listen to Me: let goodness nourish you, and let your souls delight in *plenty* (*deshen*)" (Is. 55:2); and many others. While the term means simply "ashes" in the context of the altar (e.g., Ex. 27:3; Num. 4:13), the fact that these ashes are referred to as "*deshen*" and not a more neutral or negative term associated solely with refuse or waste hints to a deeper symbolic significance.

The tension between understanding *terumat hadeshen* as waste disposal and as part of the sacrificial service is expressed in halakhic literature. One such example relates to what happens if a non-priest removes the ashes: R. Yoḥanan believes that he deserves the death penalty, as when a non-priest performs any other act of Temple service; Resh Lakish exempts, explaining that "it is waste removal, not an act of bringing" (Yerushalmi Yoma 2:1). Is this indeed merely waste disposal, or something more?

The best path, perhaps, is to hold the rope at both ends. "Lifting up" the *deshen* is a technical, daily chore, but it also symbolizes the encounter

7. See also Rambam's commentary on Mishna Tamid 5:3.

between God and human. This *deshen* is the result of God's revelation upon the altar in the form of a consuming fire. The encounter between flesh and spirit generates *deshen*.[8] Each morning the priest "lifts up" these ashes, recalling anew the covenant between God and humanity and the loving-kindness that God even deigns to allow such an encounter. We will soon come back to this idea when analyzing the connection between the removal of the ashes and the commandment to keep the fire perpetually burning.

THE ALTAR FIRE

The second focal point of the "law of the burnt offering" is the fire that must be kept alight upon the altar: "The altar fire shall be kept alight upon it." For the reader's convenience, the text repeats this at the beginning of the second part. Note the repetition that creates a clear literary framework for this commandment:

> *The altar fire shall be kept alight; it shall not go out.*
> Every morning the priest shall add wood to it,
> lay out the burnt offering upon it,
> and send the fat parts of the peace offering up in smoke upon it.
> *A perpetual fire shall be kept alight on the altar; it shall not go out.*

The refrain reflects a subtle development: The passage opens with "the altar fire shall be kept alight upon it" (6:2); the opening of the second half has an addition: "The altar fire shall be kept alight, *it shall not go out* (6:5); and the final verse expresses: "*A perpetual* fire shall be kept alight on the altar; it shall not go out" (6:6). Thus, the verses themselves give the sense of a perpetual fire that never goes out and burns ever stronger. While regular fire gradually dwindles down as its fuel burns out, the fire upon the altar burns steady and bright. The word "*tamid*" here clearly implies "perpetual," rather than the meaning "daily," as in the "*korban tamid*," the "daily offering."

Beyond the poetic lilt of these verses, each line follows the same structure, so that a literal translation reads:

8. See also R. Samson Raphael Hirsch on Lev. 6:3.

verb + "upon it" + a direct object:

the priest adds /	upon it /	wood
he lays out /	upon it /	the burnt offering
he sends to smoke /	upon it /	the fat parts of the peace offering

Beyond its poetic harmony, this repetition also serves to emphasize the verses' objective: The echo of "upon it" (*aleha*) recalls the fire *upon* the altar. This is embedded within the crucial commandment that the flame must not go out; the wood must be replenished each morning,[9] and all offerings are sacrificed upon this steady, perpetual flame.[10] Given that the focus is the fire upon the altar, the firewood and the peace offering can be mentioned in this law even though the verses are introduced as "the law of the burnt offering."

This emphasis already draws an affinity – albeit technical – between the two halves of the "law of the burnt offering": clearing the ashes and keeping the fire alight. Even when clearing the ashes, one must take care not to let the fire go out;[11] in fact, this is when wood must be added to the fire.

---

9. Rendtorff is correct that the phrase "every morning, in the morning" generates a sense of urgency to add wood before the fire burns out (Rendtorff, *Leviticus*, 234).
10. One prevalent approach by the Sages is that the firewood is a kind of offering in itself (Menaḥot 106b). Some even hold that one who donates wood to the altar must sleep in Jerusalem that night, like those who offer actual sacrifices (Zevaḥim 99b). I believe that this stems from these verses and their repetition of the importance of the wood. Another source is the description in Nehemiah: "We cast lots for the wood offering that the priests, the Levites, and the people would bring to the House of our God at fixed times each and every year, to be burned on the altar of the Lord our God, as is written in the Torah" (Neh. 10:35). The phrase "as is written in the Torah" probably alludes to our passage in Leviticus 6. Even so, what counts as sacred is not the wood itself but its equivalent value (see Rappaport, *Mikdash David*, 171–74).
11. The biblical text mentions only adding wood in the morning, although halakha rules that wood should be added together with the daily evening offering as well (Rambam, *Hilkhot Temidin UMusafin* 2:2). The Sages rule that these verses apply to the morning offering and evening offering alike.

However, we can propose a deeper connection between these two aspects. In a certain sense, the two halves of the commandment impart two opposite themes. Clearing away the previous night's ashes reflects that each new day marks a new beginning; yesterday's offering cannot burn upon the altar of today. In contrast, emphasis on keeping the fire alight expresses the opposite. The same fire must keep burning; it must never go out. From the day God's revelation comes down from heaven in the form of a consuming fire, the priests must keep this same fire burning upon the altar.[12] New daily offerings are brought each new day, but the fire must never go out.

Grouping these two commandments together under the same heading creates a delicate dialogue between stability and change, between continuity and renewal. The two opposites are intertwined upon the altar day after day. God's revelation through fire is perpetual and eternal. But for the transient human worshipper, each new day begins a new journey, new opportunity. The worshipper's stance before God changes every day. Sometimes their emotional and spiritual state will be expressed through a burnt offering, sometimes through a peace offering. The ashes from each day's offerings are cleared away the next morning, while the altar fire burns brightly to receive the new day.[13]

The ashes upon the altar represent the encounter between the fleeting, temporary, changing human and God's stable, constant presence. The ashes are ceremonially "lifted up" as testimony to this complex encounter before they are cleared to make room for the new day's worship.

In this context, the "Song of the Day" the Levites sang each day of the week is an interesting foil to the identical daily sacrifice of each

12. For this reason, Rambam's formulation of the commandment, "It is a positive commandment for the fire to be burning on the altar perpetually" (*Hilkhot Temidin UMusafin* 2:1), is more faithful to the biblical presentation than that of the *Sefer HaḤinnukh*: "It is a mitzva to light the fire on the altar every single day" (commandment 132). Lighting the fire is not the important part so much as keeping the fire burning.

13. According to the Sages, there are different fires upon the altar (see various tannaitic opinions in Mishna Yoma 4:6) – one that keeps burning for the perpetual fire, and a separate fire that consumes the offerings. Here I interpret the plain meaning of the verses: that the consuming fire is the same as the perpetual fire.

morning and evening. Each day of the week has a different psalm. If the daily sacrifice is always the same, why is there a different daily song? Perhaps this variety reflects the new opportunity offered by each new day and its own special quality, tune, and rhythm.

How Does the Perpetual Fire Keep Burning?

Until now, our assumption has been that the fire the priests add wood to each morning is the heavenly fire that descended to the altar on the eighth day of consecration (Lev. 9:24). Yet how can this be? How can the priests keep this same fire burning if they have to pack up the Tabernacle each time the Israelites move camp? When they pack up the camp, the priests must "remove the ashes from the altar and spread a scarlet cloth over it" (Num. 4:13). This presumably means that the altar is cleared of all remaining sacrifices and ashes; moreover, one cannot spread a cloth over a burning fire! The Sages indeed address this question:

1. The Midrash explains that the fire was kept burning, even during travel. "It must not go out – even on journeys. What would they do? They would keep it in a tall jar, according to R. Yehuda. R. Shimon says: Even on Shabbat and journeys they would keep clearing the ashes, as it says: 'They shall remove the ashes and spread a scarlet cloth over it'" (*Sifra, Tzav,* 2:10). Rashi (on Num. 4:13) adopts R. Yehuda's reading: "The fire that descended from heaven crouched under the cloth like a lion during their travels, but it did not burn it because they covered it with a large copper pot." The altar fire was miraculously kept on a low flame throughout their travels, waiting to flare up and blaze brightly when the altar was set up in their new location.[14]
2. The more straightforward reading is R. Shimon's – that they would indeed let the fire go out and clear away the ashes each time they packed up. Thus, the fire was only perpetual from a

14. R. Yehuda's opinion that the fire remained burning may be related to his perception that there were only two altar fires (for offerings and for incense), and not three, as R. Yossi holds (a third for keeping the perpetual fire burning). The Talmud itself links R. Yossi's and R. Shimon's positions (Yoma 45b).

> symbolic perspective. Perhaps this is why the altar was covered with a scarlet cloth (instead of the more typical light blue) – to symbolize the perpetual fire burning upon the altar.

But the question of keeping the fire alight goes beyond what happened when Israel moved camp. The first sacrificial list gives the impression that the priests would light a new fire each day: "The sons of Aaron the priest shall make a fire upon the altar and arrange wood upon the fire" (Lev. 1:6). If they must make a fire, this implies that the fire was not already burning! How can we reconcile these two pictures?

The Sages (and Rashi) explain that the priests add their own fire to the perpetual fire: "Even though the fire already descended from heaven, it is a commandment to add regular fire" (Rashi on Lev. 1:7). Even so, why does the first chapter command the Levites to put on such a show, as if there would be no fire without the priests to light it?

I believe that the two different descriptions of the altar fire are consistent with the objectives of each sacrificial list.

Parashat Vayikra focuses on the Israelite worshipper and their sacrifice. Each individual needs to feel as if the altar fire is lit especially for them, especially for their encounter with God. In contrast, *Parashat Tzav* focuses on how the offerings are functions of God's revelation. The altar fire keeps the fire of God's revelation at Sinai burning. In the first sacrificial list, the fire is lit to consume the offering; in the second list, the offerings are brought to keep the fire burning. *Parshat Vayikra* all but ignores the perpetual fire already on the altar; *Parashat Tzav* does not mention the commandment to light a fire each morning.

Thus, it is clear why *Parashat Tzav* begins with the perpetual fire: This is essential for the objective of the second sacrificial list. The consuming fire of the altar represents God's revelation in the camp of Israel. In order for the Divine Presence to rest among the people, the fire of revelation must be fed with offerings.

THE LAW OF THE BURNT OFFERING?

What remains is to determine why these laws of the altar – clearing the ashes and keeping the fire alight – are listed under the title "the law of the burnt offering," even though they are relevant to all offerings.

The answer touches upon two essential facets of this brief passage, one that characterizes the burnt offering and the other the second sacrificial list. As noted, this second half focuses not on the individual's freewill burnt offering, but on the collective daily offering – specifically, the evening burnt offering that gradually burns into a heap of ashes over the course of the night, ashes that are then cleared the next morning.

The daily burnt offering has a unique role in the sacrificial world. In addition to individual offerings of gift or atonement, some offerings are part of routine. The daily burnt offerings define the altar as the consumer of offerings: The morning burnt offering opens up the altar each morning, while the evening offering is the closing offering of each day. Together, they define the altar as the place of revelation. This is especially striking as depicted in Exodus, where its commandment is juxtaposed with the description of the days of consecration of the Tabernacle and priests. This description ends with the consecration of the altar: "For seven days, make atonement for the altar and consecrate it, so that the altar becomes holy of holies – and anything that touches it will become holy" (Ex. 29:37), which is immediately followed by the commandment of the daily burnt offering: "This is what you shall offer on the altar: two yearling lambs each day, with constancy…" (29:38). These two lambs are an integral part of the altar's definition; their function is to enable revelation, as hinted in the description's conclusion: "This shall be the regular burnt offering throughout your generations at the entrance of the Tent of Meeting before the Lord. There I will meet with you, there I will speak to you, and there I will meet with the Israelites. It will be sanctified by My glory" (29:42–43). The burnt offering is mentioned alongside the fact that it is here that God meets with Israel and speaks to Moses; here is where the Divine Presence rests, kept in Israel's midst through the perpetually burning flame of revelation.[15] This is why the encounter between human and Divine encapsulated in the altar fire is introduced through the law of the burnt offering.

---

15. See further Lichtenstein, *Zevaḥim*, 9–12; Eldar, "Incense." In a slightly different formulation: "The focus of our *parasha* (*Tetzaveh* – Ex. 29) is not the commandment of the daily offering, but an explanation of how to use the brand new altar" (Bick, "Tamid").

In addition to characterizing the nature of the burnt offering, this presentation also affects the interpretation of the second sacrificial list. As mentioned, the focal point of this list is the offering's consumption: most by the priests, the peace offering by the worshipper, and the burnt offering by the altar alone. Just as the Torah gives a measure of time in which the worshipper may eat the peace offering (7:15–18), so too may the burnt offering be "eaten" "until each morning." As the Sages state more than once: "The text speaks of two kinds of eating: by people and by the altar" (Zevaḥim 13b).

This reading is supported by several intriguing parallels between the description of the altar's consumption of the burnt and the laws of the priestly portions. The ashes are taken out to "a pure place" (6:4), similarly to where other offerings must be eaten: the grain, purification, and guilt offerings in a "holy place" (6:9, 19; 7:6), and the peace offering in "a pure place" (10:14).

This is further underscored by the anthropomorphic use of the verb "eating" to describe the altar fire's consumption of the burnt offering: Like the priests, the altar consumes the offering.

Thus, the law of the burnt offering is the lore of the consuming fire of revelation. Each morning, the sacrificial service begins anew, clearing away the remains of the day before to make way for a new song. God's glory – in the form of unchanging, perpetual flame – receives these new offerings. If the first sacrificial list characterizes the burnt offering as the human apology for having the audacity to stand before the Eternal, Divine Maker, this second depiction reinforces that idea with complementary imagery: The encounter of the human and the Divine results in a mound of ashes piling up at the foot of the ever-blazing perpetual fire of revelation. Before the people can reach out to God in love and devotion, each morning must begin with acknowledgment of the unbridgeable chasm between the human and Divine. It is only once the burnt offering is laid upon the flames that the Levites burst into song.

Chapter 14

The Law of the Grain Offering (Leviticus 6:7–16): Opening the Priestly Mouths

This is the law of the grain offering. Aaron's sons shall bring these before the Lord in front of the altar. The priest shall lift a handful of the fine flour and oil from the grain offering, and all the incense on it, and send this remembrance up in smoke upon the altar as a sweet savor to the Lord. Aaron and his sons shall eat what is left of it. It shall be eaten as unleavened bread in a holy place; in the courtyard of the Tent of Meeting shall they eat it. It shall not be baked with any leaven. I have given it as their portion of My fire offerings; it is holy of holies, like the purification offering and the guilt offering. Any male among Aaron's descendants may eat it as their eternal share of the Lord's fire offerings throughout their generations; anything that touches it is sanctified.

THE FINE FLOUR OFFERING?

The most salient aspect of the "law of the grain offering" is not what is written but what is not. There is no mention of the various types of grain offering described in the first sacrificial list. The verses seem to refer only to the fine flour offering: "The priest shall lift a handful of the fine flour and oil from the grain offering." In chapter 2, the verb "to lift a handful" (*likmotz*) indeed only refers to the fine flour offering. Moreover, as noted by R. Meir Spiegelman, the instruction to eat the rest "as unleavened bread," not as leaven (6:9), implies that the priest receives it as flour that he may bake (or prepare) as he pleases, assuming it does not become leaven, whereas cooked grain offerings are already baked before being offered, so giving instructions about their preparation would be irrelevant.[1] In fact, the instructions about the fine flour offering in Leviticus 2:2–23 are extremely similar to the "law of the grain offering" (6:7–8).

A more apt question, therefore, is why *Parashat Tzav* does not mention other variations of the grain offering. This led some modern scholars to surmise that the "law of the grain offering" refers to the communal daily grain offering that accompanies the daily burnt offering (Ex. 29:40) and not to the individual freewill grain offering.[2] Given that the "law of the burnt offering" refers to the daily burnt offering, the argument that the second sacrificial list describes the regular communal offerings is very reasonable; this also explains why there is no mention of any cooked grain offerings.

While this reading is compelling, however, it is still problematic. The priests are given "what is left" of this offering, but the Sages (based on the biblical text) explain that the daily grain offering was entirely burnt upon the altar like a burnt offering, with no part set aside for the priests: "The grain offerings of the priest, the High Priest, and the libation are all for the altar, with nothing for the priests" (Mishna Menaḥot, 6:2).[3]

If so, this brings us back to the understanding that these verses refer to the individual's grain offering, and perhaps these laws can be extended to cooked grain offerings as well. Further analysis reveals that

1. Spiegelman, "Vayikra and Tzav," 73.
2. For example, Hartley, *Leviticus*, 97.
3. As suggested by Milgrom, *Leviticus*, vol. 1, 389–90.

the instruction "Aaron's sons shall bring these before the Lord in front of the altar" (6:7), the law of presentation, which in Leviticus 2 is mentioned only in relation to cooked grain offering,[4] here applies to all grain offerings. Similarly, the addition of frankincense, which in Leviticus 2 applies only to the fine flour offering, is also mentioned here without qualification. Why does this chapter fail to draw any distinction between different types of grain offerings?

Once again, different perspectives of the two lists come into play. The first sacrificial list focuses on the encounter between worshipper and God, and thus places emphasis on different models that convey different expressions of worship. The fine flour offering is similar to the burnt offering; the processed grain offering is more like a peace offering. But the worshipper's mode of expression does not concern the priests so much as the offering's level of holiness and its implications. Regardless of the type of grain offering, the priest receives "what is left," and *Parashat Tzav* has no need to dwell on these differences.

The law of the grain offering in *Parashat Tzav* includes the laws of its sacrifice upon the altar – unlike the laws of the burnt, purification, and peace offerings, which do not mention its sacrifice. This initially seems strange, given that these laws have already been discussed in *Parashat Vayikra,* and one might think it logical for this list to focus on how the grain offering is eaten. While this is unique, it effectively mirrors the description of the grain offering in *Parashat Vayikra,* which – unlike other offerings – is the only one that describes how the grain offering is eaten. That is, both sacrificial lists discuss the grain offering's sacrifice and consumption (whereas the sacrifice of all other offerings is discussed only in *Vayikra,* and their consumption only in *Tzav*). This is due to the unique nature of the grain offering. As discussed, the priests' consumption of the grain offering is considered part of the sacrificial process itself; the altar "gives up" part of its share for the priests. Thus,*Parashat Vayikra* mentions its consumption, and *Parashat Tzav* mentions its sacrifice, for it is an integral part of its consumption. For this reason, the phrase "sweet

4. This is the accepted reading. Hizkuni, who believes that only cooked grain offerings are presented, disagrees.

savor" (6:8, 14) appears only in *Parashat Tzav* in the context of the grain offering, for this phrase focuses on the act of sacrifice, not consumption.

Nonetheless, the different focus of each section is clear. In *Vayikra,* the fact that the priests eat "what is left over" is mentioned only briefly; similarly, in *Tzav,* the sacrifice of the grain offering is described briefly, whereas the laws of eating comprise most of the discussion.

The law that most reflects the grain offering's unique nature is the prohibition against leaven. Leviticus 2 already warns against leaven touching the altar: "No grain offering that you bring to the Lord shall be made with leaven, for no leaven or honey may be used in a fire offering to the Lord" (2:11). Now it emerges that the priests may not consume the rest as leaven either: "It shall be eaten as unleavened bread in a holy place; in the courtyard of the Tent of Meeting shall they eat it. It shall not be baked with any leaven" (6:9–10). This is openly attributed to the perception that the priest's share of the grain offering is a gift from the altar: "I have given it as their portion of My fire offerings" (6:10). The altar receives the entire offering, but then transfers part of it to the priests, who must eat it subject to the same laws that apply to the altar.[5]

IT IS HOLY OF HOLIES, LIKE THE PURIFICATION OFFERING AND THE GUILT OFFERING" (6:10)

Surprisingly, the Torah compares the grain offering's holiness to that of the purification and guilt offerings *before* we hear that these two offerings are indeed holy. The surprises derives not from a halakhic perspective – we already know that these offerings are holy – so much as a literary one; it is odd to compare the grain offering to offerings that have not yet been discussed. In *Parashat Tzav,* the grain offering is the first to be defined as "holy of holies" (and it is the only one defined as such in *Parashat Vayikra*!); it would make more sense to compare the purification and guilt offering to the grain offering. Why is the comparison presented in such a strange order?

5. The Talmud debates whether the priest's share of the grain offering must be baked as matzot, or if what matters that it is not prepared with leaven; the conclusion is the former (Menaḥot 53a), based on the phrase, "It shall be matza" (Lev. 2:5).

Radatz Hoffmann raises the possibility that the comparison of the grain offering to the purification and guilt offerings pertains not to their holiness, but to the laws of their eating.[6] However, beyond the fact that the cantillation marks discourage this reading, it does not even solve the problem: The laws of eating the grain offering are also presented before the laws of eating the purification and guilt offerings, so the order of the comparison is still problematic.

This strange order is justified through the premise that the purification and guilt offerings are the ultimate models of offerings that are "holy of holies." Thus, the grain offering is compared to them even before they are actually mentioned in this sequence. This is clarified by the fact that the grain offering is not compared to the first offering in the list – the burnt offering. While the burnt offering is not of lesser importance, there can be no concept of "contagious holiness" when the offering in question is not eaten by anyone but the altar.[7] The grain offering cannot be considered the paradigm of a "holy of holies" offering either, because even without this definition, the priest's share is considered a continuation of the altar's consumption, so there would still be a need to qualify who may eat it and where. The two offerings whose flesh is shared between the altar and priests from the outset and that are defined as "holy of holies" are the purification and guilt offerings. For this reason, they are considered the archetypes of the "holy of holies" offering.

If the priestly share of the grain offering is considered a continuation of the sacrificial service, perhaps there is subtle wordplay in the instruction, "Any male among Aaron's descendants may eat it as their eternal *share* (*ḥok*) of the Lord's fire offerings throughout their generations; anything that touches it is sanctified." The primary definition of the word "*ḥok*" is "law," "custom," but a secondary meaning in biblical Hebrew is "allotment from the king," as Pharaoh grants to his priests in Genesis: "The only land he did not acquire was that of the priests, because they received an *allotment* of food from Pharaoh; they were able to live on the *allotment* that Pharaoh gave them" (Gen. 47:22). Thus, there seems to be an intentional wordplay in this verse: The priests are allotted their

---

6. Hoffmann, *Leviticus*, vol. 1, 161; also Milgrom, *Leviticus*, vol. 1, 395.
7. See also Milgrom, *Leviticus*, vol. 1, 395.

share "from the King."[8] To claim that this is the primary meaning in this verse is misguided,[9] but it certainly adds to its depth and meaning.

Assuming that the second sacrificial list is indeed read after the first, there may be further wordplay in these verses. The syntax of the introductory verse is strange: The subject of the verse is not clear in the biblical Hebrew – "*Hakrev otah*." Whom does this address? On the one hand, the bringer of the grain offering is not allowed to approach the altar; on the other hand, if this refers to the priests, why is the singular form used when "Aaron's sons" appears in the plural form? Ibn Ezra justifies this by positing that "*Hakrev otah*" is in fact in the infinitive form, but this fails to explain why there is a strange shift from infinitive to plural to singular in these verses.[10]

This strange formulation perhaps can be explained as an allusion to the worshipper's "presentation" of the grain offering to the priests before its sacrifice in *Parashat Vayikra*: "You shall bring the grain offering made in one of these ways to the Lord, presenting it to the priest, who will bring it to the altar" (2:8). Given that the thematic focus of *Tzav* is the offering's consumption, the worshipper's presentation to the priest is not mentioned in the second sacrificial list, but perhaps the odd syntax of the introductory verse hints to this stage – to the Israelite worshipper who anxiously awaits their offering's acceptance by the ever-burning, ever-consuming altar.

MINḤAT ḤINNUKH OR *MINḤAT ḤAVITTIN*?

The "law of the grain offering" is followed by another kind of grain offering that "Aaron and his sons" must offer each day:

> The Lord spoke to Moses: "This is the offering of Aaron and his sons that each shall present to the Lord on the day when he is anointed: one-tenth of an ephah of fine flour as a continual grain

8. This also seems to be the meaning of Ezekiel's prophecy: "So I stretched out My hand against you, reduced your portion and gave you over to the will of your enemies" (Ezek. 16:27); see also Prov. 31:8; Prov. 31:15; Ex. 5:14; Prov. 5:13. On the various meanings of "*ḥok*," see Ringgren, "Ḥ-K-K"; Kaddari, *Dictionary*, 340–41.
9. Ehrlich, *Mikrâ ki-Pheschutô*, 217.
10. The Samarian text changes the verb to plural, presumably for this reason.

> offering, half in the morning and half in the evening. It shall be made on a griddle with oil. You shall bring it well mixed, and offer it in pieces like a crumbled grain offering, as a sweet savor to the Lord. The priest among his sons who is anointed to succeed him shall prepare it; it is the Lord's perpetual share, to be sent up in smoke in its entirety. Any grain offering from a priest shall be wholly burned; it shall not be eaten." (6:12–16)

Before we delve into the nature of this commandment, note that the verses allude to all three kinds of cooked grain offering: "on a griddle with oil"; "well mixed" like a pan offering; "in pieces like a crumbled" baked grain offering. This is no coincidence; it already hints that the priestly grain offering is a symbolic combination of all grain offerings.

The text presents two different views as to the purpose of the offering: "That each shall present to the Lord on the day when he is anointed," which points to its nature as an initiation offering – on his first day of priestly service,[11] the new priest offers up this grain offering. Yet this is difficult to reconcile with its characterization as a daily offering in the second part of the verse: "As a daily grain offering, half in the morning and half in the evening."

The tension between these two opinions led the Sages to interpret that these verses allude to two different kinds of grain offerings – to the *minḥat ḥinnukh*, the ordination grain offering each priest brings on his first day of service, and to the *minḥat ḥavittin* that the High Priest offers each day, half in the morning and half in the evening, right after the daily grain libation offering that accompanied the daily burnt offering, followed by the libation itself.[12] According to the Sages, the *minḥat ḥavittin* consists of twelve loaves; the *Rishonim* discuss how these loaves

11. This could theoretically apply to priests from the age of thirteen, but as Rambam explains (*Hilkhot Klei HaMikdash* 5:15), the priests would prevent anyone from joining the service until aged twenty.

12. There is room to discuss the relationship between the two halves of this offering. Halakhic literature explores this, including when each half becomes holy, what happens if a priest dies after offering the first half, and other instances. We will discuss some aspects below.

are prepared and sacrificed.[13] The obvious advantage of this reading is that it explains the word "*tamid*" and the fact that half is offered in the morning and half in the evening.

R. David Hillel Weiner explains the relationship between the two kinds of grain offering: The first is the regular priest's initiation offering, and the second is part of the High Priest's daily Temple service. This, he explains, is why the regular priest's offering is not brought on Shabbat, but the High Priest's is; this also explains why Rambam does not count the former as an actual commandment, for it is only a means of initiation to the priestly service, whereas the High Priest's grain offering is a mitzva in itself.[14]

Unlike the Sages' reading, however, commentators throughout the generations have proposed that this refers only to the daily *minḥat ḥavittin*. Philo of Alexandria had already written:

> An offering worthy of the priests is not the animal offering, but the purest form of human food: Fine flour is their daily offering. A tenth of a holy measure is offered each day...fried in oil, nothing of it remains for eating, for it is a law that the priestly grain offering shall be offered in its entirety.[15]

This formulation implies that this offering is from all the priests, not just from the High Priest; if so, the clause "the priest anointed among his sons who is to succeed him" does not refer to the High Priest, but to all priests.

We must admit that the fact that there is no mention of this initiation offering during the days of consecration (where the grain offering serves a different function) encourages the reading that this refers to

---

13. The *minḥat ḥavittin* is a tenth of an ephah of flour, which is about 2.28 liters. It is baked into twelve loaves; there is a dispute as to whether six loaves are offered in the morning and six in the evening, or if twelve halves of each loaf are offered each time (see Rambam, *Hilkhot Maaseh HaKorbanot* 13:4, and Raavad there).
14. Weiner, *Priestly Kingdom*, 79.
15. Philo, *Writings of Philo, Laws*, vol. 1, part 255.

the daily *minḥat ḥavittin*.[16] Still, Philo's interpretation (also adopted by others) does not explain the phrase "on the day when he is anointed." If this is a daily offering, what does "on the day he is anointed" mean?

Avraham Shammah suggested to me that the verb "anointed" does not refer to the priest himself, but to the Tabernacle – from the day of its consecration, the *minḥat ḥavittin* was sacrificed every day. This is supported by the description of the altar's consecration by the tribal princes: "The princes presented their dedication offering for the altar at the time *when it was anointed*" (Num. 7:10, 84). Here, too, the anointing may refer to the Tabernacle itself, not to the newly anointed priest. While compelling, this argument is problematic, considering that the "anointed priest" is mentioned again in the same passage: "The priest among his sons who is anointed to succeed him" (6:15). This repetition implies that this "anointing" refers to the priest, not the Tabernacle.

I favor Ibn Ezra's solution: "The prepositional *bet* should be a *mem* – that is, *from* the day of his anointing, he is required to offer a daily grain offering" (on Lev. 6:13).[17] From the day he joins the priestly service, the priest must bring (or is part of) the priestly *minḥat ḥavittin*. This seems to be the grain offering mentioned as part of Elazar son of Aaron's priestly duties when moving camp: "The responsibility of Elazar son of Aaron the priest is for the lighting oil, the fragrant incense, the daily grain offering, and the anointing oil. He is also responsible for the whole Tabernacle and all that is in it, for the Sanctuary and all its utensils" (Num. 4:16).

Yet there is still room to explore the significance of this particular wording. Why is there emphasis on the fact that the priest must bring this offering starting from the day he is anointed? What else would we possibly think – that sons of priests must start offering this from earliest childhood? And why is there no similar emphasis in the context of other

16. Levine, who favors the approach that these verses are about both kinds of priestly grain offering, explains that the basket of matzot brought during the days of consecration (8:26–28) is a fulfillment of this grain offering (Levine, *Leviticus*, 39; see also Hartley, *Leviticus*, 98). The laws of the basket of matzot, however, are not like the laws of this grain offering.
17. This is also adopted by R. Saadia Gaon, Ibn Janah, Radak, Hizkuni, and by modern scholars including Wenham, *Leviticus*, 122; Rocker, *Leviticus*, 130.

priestly duties – that the priest must dash the blood or light the Menora from the day of his anointment? This unusual formulation perhaps hints to the deeper nature of the priestly grain offering and its purpose.

Many explain that this grain offering is an expression of the priests' servitude to God: "The priests, led by the High Priest, are bound to "eternal law" (*ḥok olam*), that is, permanent income from God. Therefore, they must offer up *ḥok olam* to God so that they will be constantly aware that they are dining at God's table."[18]

This idea can be honed further based on the idea that the grain offering is linked to their *consumption* of the offerings, as emerges from comparing the description of the *minḥat ḥavittin* with the similar daily burnt offering. Why is the people's daily burnt offering a sheep and the priests' "daily offering" of fine flour? As discussed, the grain offering is related to food, sustenance, and livelihood; its message does not pertain to life and existence itself, but to life's necessities.

The morning and evening daily offerings constitute a sacrificial framework for all offerings. The day's offerings open and close with the daily offerings.[19] A more specific framework within this sacrificial framework is the opening and closing of the priests' daily sustenance from each day's offerings. Just as each day of service begins with the morning burnt offering and ends with the evening burnt offering, the priests' shares begin with the morning's *minḥat ḥavittin* and end with the evening's *minḥat ḥavittin*. While the priests may continue eating at night – just as the evening daily burnt offering remains upon the altar all night long – they do not receive new portions from that day after the final offering.

Thus, *minḥat ḥavittin* is not just the priests' daily due. This offering allows them to eat from what has been consecrated; it defines their consumption as the continuation of the altar's consumption. This is why their daily offering is a grain offering; it symbolizes their sustenance and livelihood, their dependence on God for this sustenance. Their daily *minḥat ḥavittin* expresses that the priests are not gluttons, eating for the sake of eating; they do not fish around in the sacrificial pots to pick out the

18. Hoffmann, *Leviticus*, vol. 1, 161–62.
19. Except for the Passover offering, which is brought at a time that is neither day nor night.

best pieces (as Eli's sons do in 1 Samuel 2). Rather, their rightful shares are granted within the framework of their daily *minḥat ḥavittin*, which gives them permission to partake of the holy bread and meat.[20]

This explains why there is emphasis on the priest's "anointing." Like the rest of the Tabernacle vessels, the priests themselves are anointed and consecrated during the days of consecration. From the moment of their anointing, they are initiated into the Temple service as God's servants and vessels, entirely devoted to God's service.

This perception has several implications, both halakhic and interpretative.

Regular or High Priest?

As mentioned, Ibn Ezra and others read the Hebrew phrase "on the day that he is anointed" as meaning "*from* the day that he is anointed." Does this refer to the regular priest or the High Priest? The verses themselves are not clear:

> This is the offering of Aaron and his sons that *each* shall present to the Lord on the day *when he is anointed*: one-tenth of an ephah of fine flour as a continual grain offering, half in the morning and half in the evening.... *The priest among Aaron's sons who is anointed to succeed him* shall prepare it; it is the Lord's perpetual share, to be sent up in smoke in its entirety. (6:13–15)

Elsewhere, the phrase "Aaron and his sons" refers to all priests, not just the High Priest. (See Ex. 30:18–19, Lev. 6:9, as just two of many examples.) This supports Philo's reading that the *minḥat ḥavittin* was brought on behalf of all the priests, twice each day.

In contrast, many exegetes explain that this refers to the High Priest alone. One is Rashbam: "According to the plain meaning of the verse, this means the sons of Aaron who served as High Priest under him." He supports this with the phrase "from the day that he is anointed [as High

20. The claim of Rocker (and others) that the daily grain offering was for daily atonement for the High Priest is not convincing; the grain offering has nothing to do with sin or atonement.

Priest]." Even if we claim that all priests were anointed and not just the High Priest (as we will discuss in the context of the days of consecration), regular priests are not characterized as "anointed." For example, the "anointed priest" who must bring an internal purification offering is unanimously interpreted as the High Priest. If so, the "anointed priest" here is the High Priest, the anointed one who brings the *minḥat ḥavittin.*[21]

R. Judah Loew ben Bezalel (Maharal of Prague) attempts to resolve this tension by going back to the idea that there are two different grain offerings in this section (*Gur Aryeh* on Lev. 6:13). It is indeed difficult to read the later verse, the "priest among Aaron's sons who is anointed to succeed him," as referring to a regular priest.

Why, then, is the opening verse so confusing? Why does it give the impression that all priests are required to bring the *minḥat ḥavittin,* and not just the High Priest? The answer is related to the nature of this offering. Unlike the High Priest's purification offering, he does not offer the *minḥat ḥavittin* on his own behalf alone, but on behalf of all the priests. Sometimes the High Priest is Israel's representative; sometimes, like here, he is the representative of all the priests in God's service – of all those who eat of that day's offerings, Israel's purification and guilt offerings. The tension within this opening verse is linked to the unique nature of this grain offering brought on behalf of all the priests. The High Priest is their rightful representative, but because he usually serves as Israel's representative, the special nature of the priests he represents and their consecrated status is emphasized here.

This explains why this particular offering appears here, in *Parashat Tzav*. Its focus on the priestly consecration and consumption – on why, when, and how they are allowed to partake of the altar's offerings – presents the priestly framework that emphasizes that the priests receive their share because they are God's servants, devoted and consecrated to God's service.

In this sense, the *minḥat ḥavittin* recalls all the different variations of the grain offering. All the different kinds of grain offering – whatever aspects and preferences they represent – are ultimately expressions of the human dependence on God for sustenance. Similarly, the *minḥat*

21. As many assume, such as Hartley, *Leviticus*, 98; Rocker, *Leviticus*, 130.

ḥavittin represents the priests receiving their share of different kinds of offerings, and therefore different expressions are used in relation to it.

This brings us back to the Sages' reading that these verses depict two kinds of grain offering – the *minḥat ḥavittin,* but first the *minḥat ḥinnukh,* the initiation grain offering. If the *minḥat ḥavittin* is the offering that allows the priest to eat of the holy offerings, this is indeed a suitable offering to bring as an initiation offering. Moreover, the instruction "on the day when he is anointed," unlike Ibn Ezra's reading, can indeed mean that the priests must bring the *minḥat ḥavittin* on the day they are anointed – for essentially, the priests are consecrated anew each day for God's service.

A similar model can be found in the daily burnt offering. The mitzva of the daily burnt offering is introduced at the end of the days of consecration, so its repetition each day anew reenacts the altar's consecration each and every day. This is how the *minḥat ḥinnukh* can be understood according to the Sages. Even if the commandment ultimately refers to the *minḥat ḥavittin,* it effectively concerns the priests' daily consecration, so the extension of this law to the *minḥat ḥinnukh* is consistent with the theme and context of these verses.[22]

Priests' Mouths, Not Pantheon's Mouths

If I dare venture into more pagan waters, I will cautiously propose that the "opening of the priests' mouths" through the *minḥat ḥavittin* is a covert polemic – or a theological substitution – for a well-known Mesopotamian ritual. A new idol was celebrated with an elaborate initiation ceremony that "enabled its mouth to eat of the temple offerings," thus consecrating it as a new god. Scholars have noted that this ceremony transforms the idol from a mere representation of a particular god into

22. The Jerusalem Talmud, Shekalim 2:4, presents an amoraic dispute about what a High Priest may do with the change of the money he brought for the daily *minḥat ḥavittin.* R. Shlomo Sirilio, who was part of the Spanish expulsion and then settled in Tzefat at the beginning of the sixteenth century, writes that even though the *minḥat ḥinnukh* is not explicitly mentioned, the talmudic discussion also applies to it, as the two offerings are essentially the same.

a manifest form of the god.[23] The ceremony generally consisted of two stages: First its mouth was "washed" (*mīs pî*) – purified from the profanity and impurity that contaminated it during its preparation; and then its mouth was "opened" (*pīt pî*), which enabled it to serve as an actual deity that consumed the offerings it was served.[24]

It goes without saying that there is no need for any ceremony to open the mouth of the God of Israel. However, contrasting the sacrificial process that consecrated the priests anew each day and allowed them to partake of Israel's offerings with these ancient ceremonies perhaps smacks of a certain polemic dialogue with these pagan rituals. There is no need to purify or open God's mouth – the very idea is ridiculous – but His priests' mouths do require a certain purification and consecration in order to receive sacred offerings.

Morning and Evening

This brings us back to the similarities between the daily burnt offering and the priestly daily grain offering. Why does the daily offering consist of two lambs, offered at different times, whereas the priestly offering is one grain offering, half offered in the morning and half in the evening? A simple technical explanation is that a tenth of an ephah of grain is divisible into two parts more easily than is a single lamb. We can, however, cautiously surmise that this points to a deeper difference between the two kinds of daily offerings. We have already suggested that the two kinds of daily offerings open and conclude the sacrificial service: The daily burnt offering opens and closes the altar, and the daily *minḥat ḥavittin* opens and closes the priestly mouths (their shares of that day's offerings). Another paradigm, however, is that the morning burnt offering opens each day's sacrificial service, whereas the evening burnt offering *opens* the sacrificial service of each *night*.

The opening verses of *Parashat Tzav* ("The law of the burnt offering") describe how "the burnt offering shall remain on the altar hearth

---

23. Borger, *Die Inschriften Asarhaddons*, 89. Compare also to Walker and Dick, *Induction*, 4–19.
24. See further about these texts and their importance in Linssen, *Uruk*, 143–54; and see below, in the discussion of the days of consecration.

all night until the morning." Thus, the evening burnt offering does not just mark the end of that day's sacrifices; it marks the beginning of the altar's night. Perhaps we can propose that the evening burnt offering is what fuels the perpetual fire each night. While the altar does not accept any new offerings after the evening offering, this is not because the altar is unable to receive new offerings, but because people – bringers of offerings – sleep at night. If the altar is the place of encounter between human and God, nighttime is not a time of human activity; it is when humans garner new strength for the next day so that they can stand before God anew. Therefore, no encounter between human and Divine takes place at night. The altar, however, continues burning all night long, its consuming fire a reflection of God's eternal presence.

If so, there is a real difference between the daily burnt offering and the daily grain offering. The burnt offering consists of two separate lambs because they open two separate periods of worship: The morning offering opens the new day of sacrificial activity, and the evening offering marks the beginning of that day's night, when human worshippers sleep and God's presence burns upon the altar uninterrupted. In contrast, the priests' two daily grain offerings mark the beginning and end of that day's worship and its offerings, for priests also sleep at night, and their two grain offerings are bookends for that day's sacrificial activity and the priestly shares they receive from Israel's offerings.

Burning the *Minḥat Ḥavittin*

The *minḥat ḥavittin* is burned in its entirety upon the altar; the priest does not take a handful, as with other grain offerings. At the same time, the Torah extends this law to all grain offerings offered by priests, including individual freewill offerings: "The priest among Aaron's sons who is anointed to succeed him shall prepare it; it is the Lord's perpetual share, to be sent up in smoke in its entirety. Any grain offering from a priest shall be wholly burned; it shall not be eaten" (Lev. 6:15–16).

Why can't the priests eat of their own grain offerings? Ramban quotes Rambam:

> The text adds: "Any grain offering from a priest shall be wholly burned; it shall not be eaten." The Rabbi said in *Guide for the*

> *Perplexed* (III:46) that the reason is that if a priest eats from an offering he himself has offered up, it appears as if he has not offered anything at all, for nothing was offered of an ordinary individual's meal offering except the frankincense and the handful of the flour. If then, in addition to the fact that the whole offering was small, he who offered it were to eat it himself, he would imagine that he had brought no offering at all. Therefore [the Torah required] that it be entirely burnt. (Ramban on Lev. 6:11)

This approach is widely accepted: A priest cannot both offer up and eat from that same sacrifice. In the case of a grain offering, given that all that is offered up is a handful, it would seem as if "he had brought no offering at all" (see also *Sefer HaḤinnukh*, commandment 137).

Another possible theory why this is more problematic when it comes to the grain offering (in contrast with, say, the purification or guilt offering) is related to the fact that this law is conveyed about the *minḥat ḥavittin* and then extended to all grain offerings through this offering. It is clear why the priests cannot possibly eat from the *minḥat ḥavittin*: This is the very offering that allows them to partake of the altar's own fare; this is the offering through which the priests declare that all is from God's hand. If the priests dare eat from this sacrificial declaration, their right to eat from the altar's offerings is impaired. This offering is essentially what consecrates their mouths each day; they cannot eat from this act of consecration.

The prohibition against priests eating from the *minḥat ḥavittin* is then extended to all grain offerings from priests, and this presents an insight into the essential character of the grain offering. As stated above, unlike other offerings, which are divided into the altar's share and the priestly share from the outset, the priestly portion of the grain offering is first consecrated to the altar, and then the altar "shares" its portion with the priests. Only of the grain offering is it said: "I have given it as their portion of My fire offerings" (6:10). The priests do receive a share, but it is taken from the altar itself, because the entire grain offering is first offered to the altar and only then shared with the priests. The concept of a priest offering a grain offering to the altar and then taking back a portion is absurd. This is not the case with other offerings, where the priest's share does not reach the altar; a priest who offers a purification offering or guilt offering is usually able to keep the priestly portion for himself. With the grain offering, however, the boundaries between worshipper, altar, and priestly share are all too blurry; instead, the entire grain offering is burnt upon the altar.[25]

25. Herlich argued that this law also applies to the hide of an *ola* (burnt offering), which normally goes to the priests, because it is written: "And the priest who offers a man's burnt offering – the hide of the burnt offering that he has offered – shall belong to that priest" (Lev. 7:8). From this, he inferred: "To exclude a priest who offers his own burnt offering, whose hide does not belong to him" (*Mikra KePeshuto*, 218). He maintained this view also with regard to the priests' burnt offering during the days of inauguration (*milu'im*), stating there: "And from the fact that we do not find mention of its being flayed, we learn that it was offered on the altar with its hide" (Ibid., 220). It is difficult, however, to reach such a far-reaching conclusion solely on the basis of the expression "a man's burnt offering."

Chapter 15

The Law of the Purification Offering (Leviticus 6:17–23): The Boundaries of Holiness

> The Lord spoke to Moses: Tell Aaron and his sons: This is the law of the purification offering. The purification offering shall be slaughtered before the Lord at the place where burnt offerings are slaughtered; it is holy of holies. The priest who offers it as a purification offering shall eat of it. It shall be eaten in a holy place, in the courtyard of the Tent of Meeting. Anything that touches its flesh is sanctified; if any of its blood splashes on a garment, you shall wash that part in a holy place. An earthen vessel in which it was cooked shall be broken, but if it was cooked in a bronze vessel, that shall be scoured and rinsed with water. Any male among the priests may eat of it; it is holy of holies. But no purification offering shall be eaten from which blood is brought inside the Tent of Meeting to make atonement within the Sanctuary; that shall be burned with fire. (Lev. 6:17–23)

It is surprising to find a new commandment in the middle of the second sacrificial list: "The Lord spoke to Moses" (6:17). This is the only offering in the middle of the list that starts with a new commandment.

Radatz Hoffmann surmises that this is because the *minḥat ḥavittin* (6:12–16) interrupts the sequence of the regular offerings, so this new commandment directs the reader back to the list; to use the modern term, this is "connective repetition."[1]

Note that not only does the Torah repeat God's command to Moses; the instruction to speak to Aaron and the priests is also repeated: "Tell Aaron and his sons." Radatz Hoffmann's theory is still possible, but so is another reading: This new opening – like the new command in the first list – serves to divide the second sacrificial list into two, the burnt and grain offerings in one section, and the purification, guilt, and peace offerings in another.

The new section may mark the transition from communal offerings (the daily burnt offering, the priestly grain offering) to individual offerings, especially given the focus on the *minḥat ḥavittin*. The purification, guilt, and peace offerings in this second list are all brought by individuals.

Another important division will be made later through a different literary technique before the peace offering, thus dividing the second sacrificial list between offerings that are "holy of holies" and the peace offering, which is of lesser holiness.

Intriguingly, like in "the law of the grain offering," the "law of the purification offering" also omits the first sacrificial list's division into different kinds of offerings. This list clearly comprises external purification offerings that are shared with the priests, whereas internal purification offerings are mentioned briefly at the end of the section: "But no purification offering shall be eaten from which blood is brought inside the Tent of Meeting to make atonement within the Sanctuary; that shall be burned with fire" (6:23). But no distinction is drawn between the two types of both offerings listed in Leviticus 4; there is no hint to the leader's purification offering. This is consistent with the second list's

1. Hoffmann, *Leviticus*, vol. 1, 166. Similarly Milgrom, *Leviticus*, vol. 1, 396. On biblical "connective repetition," see Seligmann, "Hebrew Fiction," 53–60; Talmon, "Synchroneity"; Berlin, *Poetics*, 126–29.

theme: Regardless of whether the offering is brought by king, leader, or lowly commoner, it is holy of holies; the offering must be slaughtered to the altar's north, and only male priests may eat of it in a holy place. Another notable feature is that there is no mention of the blood ritual or burning of the organs on the altar; these acts are not affected by the offering's status as "holy of holies."

SLAUGHTERING "HOLY OF HOLIES" ON THE ALTAR'S NORTHERN SIDE

The first law in this section concerns the site of slaughter: "The purification offering shall be slaughtered before the Lord at the place where burnt offerings are slaughtered; it is holy of holies" (6:18). The determination of the site is apparently based on the offering's degree of holiness: burnt, purification, and guilt offerings are all sacrificed in the same place.

Some question why this detail is repeated here when it has already been discussed in *Parashat Vayikra*, in the very same way (4:24, 29, 33). Milgrom suggests that this repetition hints that the priests are responsible for slaughtering the offering in the appropriate place, according to the appropriate laws.[2] This is certainly possible, but there may be a more specific reason, related to the offering's degree of holiness.

Why, in fact, are offerings of highest holiness slaughtered to the altar's north? When discussing the first list, we proposed that certain kinds of animal (sheep) have a special connection to the altar and are accordingly slaughtered right next to it. Here, however, the placement seems to be related to its degree of holiness. What does the northern side symbolize? Rabbeinu Yaakov bar Asher explains: "For protection, as is written: 'From the north the evil will embark'" (*Baal HaTurim* on Lev. 1:11). If the northern side is symbolically perceived as a source of particular evil, this ritual is calculated to balance this out. I have already mentioned Yoel Elitzur's fascinating theory that this is a polemic against the Ugaritic belief that the gods live on the "northern mountain." The text is establishing that the Divine Presence rests here, not in the northern mountains revered by ancient pagans.[3]

---

2. Milgrom, *Leviticus*, vol. 1, 401.
3. Elitzur, *Place*, 173–76.

A more likely direction, however, is a technical one, as we will explore through sources of the Oral Law. In Tractate Zevaḥim, the *Tanna'im* disagree whether holy offerings that were slaughtered on the altar itself (and not its northern side) are still valid:

> Holy of holies slaughtered upon the altar itself: R. Yossi says: As if they were slaughtered on the northern side [and are therefore valid]. R. Yossi bar Yehuda says: From the halfway point of the altar to the north – as if the north [therefore valid]; from the halfway point to the south – as if the south [therefore invalid]. (Mishna Zevaḥim 6:1)

The logic is clear, but how can we understand the approach that offerings slaughtered on the altar "are as if they were slaughtered on the northern side"? This curious phrase may reveal the reason for this particular site of offering. Given that the second sacrificial list revolves around the offering's degree of holiness – that is, whether this holiness is "contagious" – this law may be part of the same system. Perhaps the animal is slaughtered in this particular place to avoid its holiness spreading inappropriately. "Holy of holies" offerings must be slaughtered as close to the altar as possible to avoid their blood or other parts coming into contact with objects of lesser holiness.[4] The peace offering, of lesser holiness, may be slaughtered anywhere in the courtyard.

The northern side was presumably chosen because it is closest to the inner Sanctuary: "The one making the sacrifice shall have it slaughtered on the north side of the altar *before the Lord*" (Lev. 1:11).[5] If so, this

4. It may be that slaughtering to the south of the altar was problematic because there was a lot of foot traffic in that area; the north likely had much less movement, which meant that contact with holy blood was less likely.
5. There is room to debate whether R. Yossi means that slaughter directly on the altar is considered fulfillment of "slaughter to the altar's north" (as implied by his language) or whether slaughtering on the altar means that there is no need to slaughter the animal on the northern side in this case (which is more consistent with the above explanation, and as is perhaps implied by Rambam, who writes in his commentary on the Mishna that R. Yossi says that the whole altar is a valid place for the slaughter of all offerings).

explains why according to R. Yossi, an offering slaughtered on the altar itself is still valid; there is even less of a chance that its holiness will spread problematically.

The advantage of this explanation is that it links the law of slaughtering to the other laws in this list that are also based on the offerings' "holy of holies" status and the fear of contagious holiness.

EATING THE PURIFICATION OFFERING AND PREVENTING THE SPREAD OF HOLINESS

The second law of the purification offering is: "The priest who offers it as a purification offering shall eat of it" (6:19). The Hebrew verb for "who offers it as a purification offering" is *meḥatteh,* from the root Ḥ-T-A, like the offering's name, and, accordingly, may mean "the one who purifies" or "the one who cleanses the offender of their offense," as Ibn Ezra explains. This reading is supported by the description of the guilt offering, which is compared to the purification offering: "The guilt offering follows the same law as the purification offering: *It belongs to the priest who makes atonement with it*" (Lev. 7:7). This implies that "*meḥatteh*" means "make atonement." The later verse may prove the opposite, however. The verbs are different because they have different meanings – "atone" applies to both offerings, whereas "*meḥatteh*" applies only to the purification offering (we will clarify this below).

Rashi, in contrast, suggests that the verb "*meḥatteh*" relates to the offering itself: "Who offers it as a purification offering: Who does the specific actions that make it into a purification offering" (on Lev. 6:19).[6] This fascinating reading can theoretically apply to different offerings as well: "*Lehaalot ola*" – to offer up a burnt offering – or "*lizbo'aḥ zevaḥ* – to offer up a peace offering – can be read as "the act of preparing the offering in a specific way that makes it into that particular offering."

I believe that the simplest, most straightforward reading is that the verb, like the name of the offering, means "to purify." Ibn Ezra also adds: "Many exegetes say that this means 'purify' – to wash or cleanse – as in,

6. Similarly Bula, *Leviticus,* 104; Levine, *Leviticus,* 40.

'Cleanse me with hyssop and I shall be purified.'" If so, the verse reads: "The priest who purifies him shall eat of it."[7]

Regardless of the specific meaning of the verb, the ministering priest is the one who receives the priestly portion of the meat. We will yet discuss below how the meat is distributed (7:7–10), but it is already worth questioning whether the share of meat is considered the ministering priest's "wage" or whether this reveals a more fundamental principle about how offerings must be consumed.[8]

If the second sacrificial list indeed perceives the priests' eating of their share as part of the sacrificial process, it makes sense that the ministering priest is the one who must eat its meat. The priest who purifies is the one who placed the offering upon the altar, acting as its hand; thus he must now act as its mouth as well.[9]

Stopping the Spread

The third law in the "law of the purification offering" is inherently related to the issue of contagious holiness. The language clearly recalls the laws of how impurity spreads: "Anything that touches its flesh is sanctified; if any of its blood splashes on a garment, you shall wash that part in a holy place. An earthen vessel in which it was cooked shall be broken, but if it was cooked in a bronze vessel, that shall be scoured and rinsed with water" (6:20–21).

The problem these laws address is generally defined as what to do with the remains – *notar* – or what happens when the holiness is brought outside the Tabernacle (according to the Sages and Rashi, and Rashbam and Ramban in their wake). The garment splattered with holy blood might be worn outside the Tabernacle; the vessels the meat was

7. The preposition *otah* works better with Rashi's reading; in any case, given that the offering's name is derived from "purification," it makes sense that the verb continues this meaning.
8. One possible theory is that the ministering priest is the one who eats the offering to keep the chance of contagious holiness to an absolute minimum. But I think this is problematic, given that the same law applies to the peace offering, where there is no chance of contagious holiness, as the peace offering is of lesser holiness.
9. The Sages view this differently, as we will find in the discussion of how the priestly shares were distributed.

cooked in might contain traces of meat after the permitted time passes. Rashi, for example, writes about an earthen pot: "An earthen vessel in which it was cooked must be broken – because what was absorbed by the pot becomes *notar*, left over, and this applies to all holy offerings." Thus, from a halakhic perspective, a garment needs washing only if it was stained with the offering's blood, not if the garment touched the offering (see especially Ralbag).[10]

However, it seems more likely that the concern that informs these laws is that the offering's holiness will spread to receptacles that are inappropriate for this holiness. All traces of the offering's blood or flesh must be removed for this reason – to stop the spread.

This helps us read the laws in a subtly different light. The first law concerns contact with the offering's flesh ("Anything that touches its flesh is sanctified"); and then its blood (a bloodstained garment must be washed in a holy place); finally, any pots that might have absorbed traces of its flesh must be dealt with. Sanctified vessels are treated similarly to vessels that have become impure. The *Sifra* questions whether "rinsing with water" means that at least forty *se'a* of water are needed, as with cleansing vessels of their impurity (*Sifra, Tzav*, 7:3). Obvious similarities between the systems of holiness and impurity are found in both halakha and the biblical text itself.

The law "If any of its blood sprays (*yizzeh*) on a garment,[11] you shall wash that part in a holy place" deserves attention. Firstly, the phrase "that part" implies that only the bloodstain itself needs washing, and there is no need to wash the entire garment.[12] This is somewhat surprising: If part of a garment becomes impure, the entire garment becomes impure and must be washed. If the concern is that the blood will become *notar*, past the time in which an offering must be eaten, this explains why only

10. See the discussion in the *Talmudic Encyclopedia*, "Dam HaḤattat," vol. 7, 471.

11. There is surprising use of the feminine form referring to the word "garment." While some read this as an instance of a general object (compare Lev. 16:3; Num. 23:19), as Genesius points out (*Hebrew Grammer*, part 135), this is less likely given that the word "garment" actually appears and not a pronoun. Rather, this seems to indicate that Ibn Ezra is correct that the word "*begged*" can be either masculine or feminine (as in Prov. 6:27; see also Malbim on Lev. 6:20).

12. Milgrom, *Leviticus*, vol. 1, 403.

the bloodstain itself must be washed off; the garment's status does not actually change. If, however, the concern is that the blood does sanctify the garment, we might posit that the concern is not that the garment will spread holiness, but rather that the blood itself upon the garment will do so.

Why is there no concern that the offering's holiness will sanctify the priest's garment? A likely theory is that the priestly garments are already holy: "Make sacred vestments for your brother Aaron, for glory and for splendor" (Ex. 28:2). Thus, the only concern is that the blood itself will spread the offering's holiness to others.[13] As Ibn Ezra points out, the fact that the instruction is in the second person, "*You* shall wash that part in a holy place," hints that it addresses the priest, who is by far the most likely to be splattered with blood.

Additionally, the verb used for the blood staining the garment may seem like a surprising choice: "If any of its blood *sprays* (*yizzeh*) on a garment." Since the same root is used to describe the ritual sprinkling of blood that is an integral part of the internal purification offering service, wouldn't it make more sense to use a different verb to describe the accidental splattering and staining of blood? Rabba notes this use and explains that it hints that this law is most relevant to blood that stains garments during the sacrifice of internal purification offerings, when the priest *sprinkles* blood toward the curtain (Zevaḥim 92b).[14] While the verb root also refers to blood in non-sacrificial contexts (such as "They threw her down, and her blood spattered [*vayiz*] the walls" – II Kings 9:33), Rabba is certainly correct that in these chapters, the verb "*lehazzot*" recalls the internal purification offering. In fact, the Sages rule that

13. The Talmud debates whether there is need to wash a garment if it becomes stained from purification blood smeared on another garment (Zevaḥim 92b). We have already seen how Ezekiel is concerned that the priestly vestments may spread holiness; we see here that it is not necessarily because the vestment itself will spread holiness, but that the blood on these vestments might.

14. The Sages rule that the blood needs laundering only if the blood has already been collected in a service vessel and is therefore worthy of being sprinkled (*Sifra*), and only if the garment is stained with an amount that is sufficient to sprinkle (Rambam, *Pesulei HaMukdashin* 1:6). These laws are both more convincing given the use of this verb.

bloodstains from other offerings do not even require washing: "The stringency applies only to internal purification offerings" (Mishna Zevaḥim 11:4). Given that out of all regular offerings, blood is "sprinkled" only in the purification offerings, it is reasonable to posit that any reference to "sprinkling blood" automatically evokes the internal purification offering.

As mentioned in our analysis of Leviticus 4, the blood of the internal purification offering serves a different purpose from that of other offerings; rather than serving as a gift, it purifies. More potent than the blood of other offerings, perhaps its sanctity spreads more easily than the blood of other offerings.[15]

When the Blood Is Brought Inside

The end of the "law of the purification offerings" does distinguish between different kinds of purification offerings: "But no purification offering shall be eaten from which blood is brought inside the Tent of Meeting to make atonement within the Sanctuary; that shall be burned with fire" (6:23). This implies that the laws of eating the purification offering mentioned so far apply only to external offerings, whereas internal purification offerings are burned, not eaten (as explained by Rashbam, Ibn Ezra, and Ramban).

Despite this straightforward reading, some *Tanna'im* read the verse differently, as does Rashi in their wake: "If blood from the external purification offering was accidentally brought inside, it is rendered invalid." According to this reading, this verse does not refer to the internal purification offering, but to the blood of an external purification offering that was accidentally brought inside. If this happens, then its flesh may not be eaten and it must be burned instead. As mentioned, the *Tanna'im* disagree about whether this rule applies to all offerings (R. Akiva) or just to external purification offerings (the Sages).[16] The Sages seem to perceive this law as a concern that the priest is liable to confuse internal and external offerings, so extra stringency is needed. As mentioned

15. Moreover, this explains why the Sages hold that this does not apply to bird blood. Its blood is not potent or "alive" enough to transmit holiness.

16. *Sifra, Tzav,* 8:1; Zevaḥim 81b. See also R. Eliezer's compromise that this applies to the guilt and purification offerings but not to freewill offerings.

above (in the context of the similarities between purification and guilt offerings), this seems to be related to the requirement that the purification offering must be *lishmah*, which to the Sages is crucial.

In any case, the most straightforward reading is that this verse emphasizes that only external purification offerings may be eaten (as per Rashbam et al., and the *Tanna* R. Yossi HaGelili).[17] Nonetheless, the Sages' reading of this verse reveals a fundamental aspect of the burning of internal purification offerings. The Midrash Halakha seems to be based on the text's focus on the blood brought inside; instead of, say, "the anointed priest's offering and the communal purification offering," the verse focuses on the offerings "from which blood is brought inside the Tent of Meeting." Bringing the blood inside is not just a distinguishing marker between internal and external purification offerings; it is what renders the flesh prohibited for eating.[18] This is why, according to the Sages, if the blood of an external purification offering is brought inside, its flesh becomes forbidden to the priests.[19]

In our discussion of the difference between internal and external purification offerings in Leviticus 4, we proposed that the internal purification offerings are burned because priests cannot eat from an offering they themselves bring. This applies to both the anointed priest's offering and to the communal offering, as priests are part of the community. This explanation is consistent with *Parashat Vayikra*'s focus on the bringers of each offering.

Here, however, the emphasis on the place of the blood ritual is related to *Parashat Tzav*'s focus on the offering's level of holiness. Once blood is brought inside the Sanctuary, its holiness transcends the level of holiness

---

17. R. Yossi does not disagree that the external offering whose blood is brought inside may not be eaten, but he believes that this law is not based on this verse, but rather on Leviticus 10:18.
18. The Sages maintain that because bringing the blood inside makes the meat forbidden for eating, the meat must only be burned after it is no longer fit for eating, and it is therefore burned only the day after. In contrast, R. Yossi, who bases his opinion on another verse, says that the meat must be burnt as soon as the blood is brought inside (see Pesaḥim 83a).
19. Thus, R. Shimon's opinion that if the blood is brought inside but is not yet sprinkled the meat can still be eaten is convincing (Zevaḥim 83a; R. Eliezer disagrees).

of the offerings from which priests may eat. This reiterates the fundamental connection between the offering's level of sanctity and where its sacrifice takes place. An offering that is "holy of holies" must be eaten in a holy place. This is not merely a halakhic technicality; it reflects that the priest's consumption continues the altar's consumption. The grain, external purification, and guilt offerings are all eaten next to the altar by the priests who serve as its agents (see especially Lev. 8:30 below). But the blood of the internal purification offering is brought inside the Sanctuary, and thus becomes too holy for the priests to eat. They can serve as agents of the altar, but not of the Holy of Holies itself.

The Law of the Purification Offering and the Spread of Holiness

As stated, the second sacrificial list focuses on the laws of eating the offering and its level of holiness, and the "law of the purification offering" is no exception. All the laws in this section pertain to different issues related to the offering's status as "holy of holies," how this affects how the offering is eaten, and what happens when other objects come into contact with it:

1. The purification offering is slaughtered where the burnt offering is: "It is holy of holies."
2. The ministering priest is the one who eats its meat.
3. The priestly share must be eaten in a "holy place" – the "courtyard of the Tent of Meeting."
4. Anything (or anyone?) that touches its flesh "is sanctified."
5. If the purification blood sprays on a garment, it must be laundered.
6. Vessels that the purification offering is cooked in must be treated accordingly.
7. Only male priests may eat of the offering: "It is holy of holies."
8. A purification offering whose blood is brought into the Tent of Meeting must be burned, not eaten.

The repetition of "It is holy of holies" serves as a literary framework for these laws. Accordingly, component 8 is an appendix; it applies only to internal purification offerings (or external offerings whose blood is accidentally brought inside), whereas the first seven components apply to external purification offerings. Component 4, in contrast, is a central, fundamental principle that underlies all these laws: "Anything that touches its flesh is sanctified." This is the primary principle from which all the laws of contagious holiness extend.

We have already seen that the place of slaughter is affected by the offering's definition as "holy of holies"; the ministering priest is the one who eats it. These laws seem to be intended to keep the spread of holiness to an absolute minimum, as is the law of where the offering must be eaten: "In a holy place – the courtyard of the Tent of Meeting." Of course, the holy meat must be eaten in a holy place, but the other side of the coin is true as well: The holy meat must be confined to a holy place so it will not come into contact with non-holy meat.

Given that these laws recall the laws of purity and impurity, many interpret them as if they refer to the laws of impurity rather than as laws designed to stop the spread of holiness,[20] as if when sacred blood stains a garment, the blood contaminates rather than makes it holy.[21] Yet there is no mention of impurity in this section, so it is preferable to formulate the relationship between holiness and impurity thus: The world of holiness mirrors the world of impurity. A garment must be cleansed of any holiness so that the holiness will not spread beyond the appropriate boundaries. The same is true of contact itself: "Anything that touches its flesh is sanctified."[22] Holiness can spread through contact just as impurity can spread through contact; just as a vessel must be cleansed of its impurity, all traces of holiness must be carefully removed so that the vessel may continue to be used for everyday purposes.

PURIFICATION: A PRECONDITION FOR HOLINESS

There is, perhaps, an intriguing, intricate dialogue between the reason one must bring a purification offering, as suggested in the discussion

20. See *Sifra, Tzav,* 6:6; the discussion clearly applies terms of sanctity to the world of purity and impurity.
21. Similarly, see Milgrom, *Leviticus,* vol. 1, 403. According to his approach, the purification blood absorbs impurity during the purification process, and thus is liable to contaminate others.
22. For a different reading, see Hoffmann, *Leviticus,* vol. 1, 168.

of *Parashat Vayikra,* and the laws of "contagious holiness." Given that burnt offerings, grain offerings, purification offerings, and guilt offerings are all "holy of holies," why are the laws that apply to all "holy of holies" offerings presented in the context of the purification offering? This could be purely technical: The burnt offering is not eaten (by anyone but the altar itself), and the grain offering does not involve messy slaughter or the sprinkling of blood; the purification offering is the first animal offering that is eaten by the priests. Yet given that these laws apply to all holy offerings, they could have been listed together with the laws of distribution of the offerings (7:7–10). Perhaps its placement in the context of the purification offering offers a deeper look into the relationship between purity and holiness.

Our discussion of the laws of the purification offering in *Parashat Vayikra* led to the conclusion that a purification offering is required when unnecessary, avoidable impurity compromises the potential of the Divine Presence resting in the camp of Israel. The camp's default, basic state must be one of purity; this is so important that a variable offering is available even in the case of compromised purity through passive offenses of omission.

Purity is a necessary precursor to the state of holiness. Even offerings of lesser holiness that are eaten by Israelites (the peace offering) must be eaten when the bringer is in a state of purity, in a pure place. If the world of purity and impurity is mirrored by the world of holiness, this relationship is subtly conveyed through the definition of the laws of spreading holiness within the "law of the purification offering." The camp of Israel must be fit for the Divine Presence at all times – first through purity, which can then, through the right conditions, be elevated to a state of holiness. This is conveyed through the broader structure of the book of Leviticus itself: Only after a thorough exploration of the laws of impurity and purification does the Lord finally bid Moses: "Speak to all the community of Israel. Say: Be holy, for I am holy."

Chapter 16

The Law of the Guilt Offering (Leviticus 7:1–6): Repaying What Is Due

> And this is the law of the guilt offering; it is holy of holies. The guilt offering shall be slaughtered at the place where burnt offerings are slaughtered, and its blood dashed against each side of the altar. All its fat shall be offered: the broad tail, the fat covering the entrails, the two kidneys and the fat around them at the loins, and the diaphragm of the liver, which shall be removed with the kidneys. The priest shall turn these into smoke on the altar as a fire offering for the Lord; it is a guilt offering. Any male priest may eat of it and it shall be eaten in a holy place; it is holy of holies. (Lev. 7:1–6).

Like the law of the purification offering, the law of the guilt offering is framed by its holy status. It begins: "This is the law of the guilt offering; it is holy of holies" (7:1), and ends: "It shall be eaten in a holy place; it is holy of holies" (7:6). This framework is more salient than that of the purification offering, given that the phrase "holy of holies" is not presented as the rationale for a certain law, as Malbim notes:

> "This is the law of the guilt offering; it is holy of holies" – It is a fundamental principle that whenever it is given as an explanation – "It is holy of holies," "It is a grain offering," etc., the law is followed with the reason – "It is holy of holies," and so on. As it says of the grain offering: "I have given it as their portion of My fire offerings; it is holy of holies" or: "It must be eaten in a holy place – it is holy of holies." It is unusual for the reason to come before the law... For this reason, the fact that it says "It is holy of holies" at the very beginning is very difficult. (Malbim on Lev. 7:1)[1]

How can this anomaly be explained? Milgrom may be correct that this opening description explains the offering's place of slaughter,[2] but beginning the section with this phrase characterizes it more as a general heading. In the law of the purification offering, the definition "holy of holies" is juxtaposed with the laws of its consumption. In contrast, the law of the guilt offering delves into the laws of slaughter in detail, recalling *Parashat Vayikra*, yet the definition "holy of holies" does not seem to have any bearing on these laws; the blood ritual is identical for the guilt offering and the peace offering, which is of lesser holiness. Thus, the description "holy of holies" here seems to serve as a general heading that sets the appropriate tone for its wider context.[3]

This section defines four laws:

1. The priests must slaughter the guilt offering "at the place where they slaughter the burnt offerings" – that is, on the altar's

---

1. Malbim himself derives halakhic aspects from this unusual language concerning the law of holy blood that is accidentally mixed with blood of lesser holiness before being dashed upon the altar.
2. Milgrom, *Leviticus*, vol. 1, 408.
3. The Netziv refuses to accept that there is no practical implication for the offering's status, and therefore adds on Lev. 7:1: "Holy of holies – The law of *me'ila* applies even when the offering is still alive, like the burnt offering."

northern side, as in the case of holy offerings. Moreover, as the guilt offering is a sheep, it makes sense that the place of slaughter is linked to the altar. Even so, the verse's formulation is unique. The slaughter of the purification offering is described thus: "Where the burnt offerings are slaughtered, the purification offering shall be slaughtered" (6:18), whereas the guilt offering focuses on the ones who slaughter the offering: "Where *they* slaughter the burnt offering, *they* shall slaughter the guilt offering." The sharp-eyed Netziv explains that this implies that the priests are the ones who actually slaughter the animal, whereas freewill offerings may be slaughtered by the Israelite worshippers themselves (see *Haamek Davar* on Lev. 7:2).[4]

Ultimately, the halakhic ruling is that the Israelite worshippers may slaughter their own guilt offerings; for this reason, Menachem Bula proposes that "they shall slaughter" is an impersonal subject that refers to whoever slaughters the animal, be they priests or Israelites.[5] Regardless of the actual halakha, this formulation still demands explanation; the Netziv is correct to point out that it diverts attention away from the offering bringer.[6] To explain that this is consistent with the priests' centrality in this *parasha* is only a partial answer; rather, this seems to be directly related to the nature of the guilt offering. As mentioned, bringing the ram to the Sanctuary is the most important part of the sacrificial process in *Parashat Vayikra*, to the extent that the laws of the guilt offering's slaughter do not even appear in the first sacrificial list. For this reason, the priests – rather than the worshipper – deal with the animal for the guilt offering. (We will

---

4. Interestingly, the *Sifra*'s conclusion is the exact opposite: "Even the foreigners, women, and even slaves may slaughter" (*Sifra, Tzav*, 4:3).
5. Bula, *Leviticus*, 108.
6. Radatz Hoffmann adopts the aforementioned position of the Sages that the plural form implies that the worshippers may also slaughter (*Leviticus*, vol. 1, 169; see also Rashi, as well as *Meshekh Ḥokhma*, who concludes the exact opposite). Even if so, however, the unusual language underscores that the offering is already in the care of the priests, so there is no mention of the worshippers in this section at all.

soon discuss why the guilt offering's sacrificial laws are postponed to the second sacrificial list.)

2. The verb that describes the blood ritual is "*lizrok*," "to dash": "Its blood dashed at each side of the altar," like the burnt and peace offerings.
3. Like the purification and peace offerings, the *eimurim* are offered on the altar while most of the flesh is reserved for the priests.
4. The law of the guilt offering concludes with who may eat its meat: only male priests, in a holy place, like the purification and grain offerings.

These laws are a fascinating combination of different aspects of both obligatory and freewill offerings. Like the burnt and peace offerings, the blood of the guilt offering is dashed; like the purification and peace offerings, only the *eimurim* are offered on the altar; like the purification and grain offerings, only the male priests may eat it, and only in a holy place. The different blood rituals reveal that the two offerings brought for sin are inherently different from each other.

Beyond these details, we must address why the sacrificial laws of the guilt offering appear in this list at all, instead of in *Parashat Vayikra*. Ibn Ezra suggests that these laws also fill in the purification offering's sacrificial laws, which are missing from *Parashat Tzav*. Given that the latter do appear in *Parashat Vayikra*, however, it seems more likely that the mention of the guilt offering's sacrificial laws here compensates for their absence in the first sacrificial list.

Radatz Hoffmann solves the issue of the placement of the guilt offering's sacrificial laws by positing that the second sacrificial list was conveyed to Moses as part of the laws of the days of consecration, before the first sacrificial list was transmitted. All the offerings except for the guilt offering were sacrificed during the days of consecration, so the others are mentioned then, and only the guilt offering is described at length here.[7]

Although creative, this analysis is not quite convincing: ultimately, the second sacrificial list appears after the first chapters of Leviticus,

7. Hoffmann, *Leviticus*, vol. 1, 169.

which do mention the guilt offering, so its sacrificial laws could have been incorporated there.

Like the lack of emphasis on the Israelite worshipper's slaughter of the guilt offering, the inclusion of its sacrificial laws in this list seems to reflect the guilt offering's unique nature. The sacrificial laws of the first list focus on the worshipper who brings the offering in question, whereas the second list, as repeatedly stated, refers to the priests who serve as the altar's consuming mouth. In most offerings, the identity of the sacrifice bringer is fundamental to the sacrificial service; hence its inclusion in the first sacrificial list.

But the most important element of the guilt offering is the bringing of the animal to the Sanctuary in order to repay for what was wrongly used, in order to compensate for the trespass against the Sanctuary. Without paying back for what was wrongfully used, the offender cannot achieve atonement; the additional payment is indeed described in the first sacrificial list (Lev. 5:18, 25). In a certain sense, this is where the worshipper's role ends.[8] Once what was due has been repaid, the priests take over the sacrificial rites, and that is why they are mentioned only in *Parashat Tzav*. As noted, the text implies that the guilt offering is slaughtered not by the sacrifice bringer, but by the ministering priests.

This is further reinforced by Milgrom's aforementioned theory that for the guilt offering, the offender does not bring an actual animal but rather pays its value in silver, while the Sanctuary provides the ram. This further reduces the offender's role in the sacrificial service; he pays his dues and backs away, and the priests take over.[9]

R. Meir Simcha of Dvinsk reaches a similar conclusion from a different direction:

> Out of all descriptions of sacrificial slaughter, only that of the guilt offering is written in the plural form. Usually, the ritual slaughter is performed by the bringer of the offering, as Rashi writes on Pesaḥim 7b: "He shall lay his hands and slaughter." For the guilt offering, however, which is often brought for intentional sin... it

8. See further in Barzilai, "Guilt Offering."
9. Milgrom, *Leviticus*, vol. 1, 409.

> makes more sense for others to perform the slaughtering, and not the worshippers themselves. (*Meshekh Ḥokhma* on Lev. 7:2)

It emerges that whereas the priest usually serves as the Israelite worshipper's agent to offer up a gift from below to above, from the Israelite to the Sanctuary, the main purpose of the guilt offering is to restore what was wrongfully taken from the Sanctuary. For this reason, the priest steps in as early as possible. The guilt offering is but a repayment, compensation for what already belongs to the Sanctuary.

Chapter 17

Dividing the Offerings Among the Priests (Leviticus 7:7–10)

After "the law of the guilt offering," a few verses discuss how the offerings are distributed among the priests:

> The guilt offering follows the same law as the purification offering: it belongs to the priest who makes atonement with it. The priest who offers any person's burnt offering shall keep the skin of the burnt offering that he has offered. Any grain offering baked in an oven or prepared in a pan or griddle also belongs to the priest who offers it, while every other grain offering, whether mixed with oil or dry, shall belong equally to all of Aaron's sons. (Lev. 7:7–10)

This discussion logically flows from the law of the guilt offering, but it actually goes beyond the boundaries of this particular offering and refers to all the offerings listed thus far in this *parasha*. Why do these verses appear here, at the end of the law of the guilt offering? We might expect either that each offering would conclude with the law of who receives it, or that these verses would come at the end of the entire section – that is, after the peace offering. Why do they appear here, between the law of the guilt offering and the peace offering?

Ramban questions why the law that the ministering priest receives the skin of the burnt offering is mentioned here, especially considering that the Sages teach that this rule applies to all "holy of holies" offerings:

> "The priest who offers any person's burnt offering" – This law applies to all holy offerings. The text says "burnt offering," but the law is the same for the aforementioned purification and guilt offerings, but not for peace offerings, and that is why the laws of the distribution to the priests appears here in the middle of the sacrificial section, before the peace offering is mentioned. (Ramban on Lev. 7:8)

Ramban proposes that since the law of the animal's skin does not apply to the peace offering,[1] it is mentioned before, together with the rest of the laws of the priestly distribution. A more fundamental formulation of this idea is that the laws of the priestly distribution are intentionally incorporated here to create a logical barrier between offerings that are "holy of holies" and the peace offering, which is of lesser holiness. In a neat dialogue between form and content, the text itself presents a protective barrier between what is holy of holies and the law of the peace offering, whose meat can be shared with the priestly families and even the Israelite worshippers themselves.

This division may reflect an even more fundamental difference: The priest's consumption of the holy offerings is considered an extension of the altar's own "consumption," whereas the consumption of lesser

1. The rule is that the skin goes together with the flesh. In the peace offering, the bringer of the offering receives the skin together with the meat; in purification and guilt offerings the priests do (*Sifra, Tzav*, 9:4).

offerings is simply eating; although its consumers must be pure, they need not be "holy" like the priests themselves.

THE STATUS OF THE SKIN OF OFFERINGS

Given that the priests' consumption is so significant in *Parashat Tzav*, what status does the skin of the burnt offering have? What is the relationship in this brief section between this particular priestly gift – which is not eaten – and the rest of the priestly portions?

The law that the ministering priest receives the offering's skin is stated as relating to the burnt offering: "The priest who offers any person's burnt offering shall keep the skin of the burnt offering that he has offered" (7:8). While the verb used about the offering of the purification and guilt offerings is "atone" (7:7), the verb for the burnt offering is simply "offer," "*hikriv*."

Even if we adopt the reading that the "law of the burnt offering" in the second sacrificial list refers to the daily burnt offering, the law that the ministering priest receives the burnt offering's skin refers to the individual's freewill offering, as is evident from the phrase "any person's burnt offering."[2]

As mentioned, the Midrash Halakha extends this rule to the skin of all offerings (except the peace offering);[3] what is interesting is that the law is based on the burnt offering. This can be solved with the technical claim that from other offerings, the priests receive more significant portions – meat or flour – whereas the skin of the burnt offering is the only part that is not burned upon the altar. Similarly, the stripping of the animal's skin is mentioned only in the context of the burnt offering: "The burnt offering shall then be skinned and cut into pieces" (1:6) and no other offerings. Hizkuni explains that skinning is only mentioned in context of the burnt offering because we would otherwise assume that the skin was also burnt upon the altar. In other offerings, only the *eimurim* are burnt upon the altar; the assumption is that the skin is considered part of the flesh and is therefore not burned.

---

2. See also Zevaḥim 103a–b.
3. Similarly Dillmann, *Leviticus*, 488.

Yet we can still point to a more fundamental idea: The skin of the burnt offering has a different status than the skin of all other offerings. The two laws about the skin of the burnt offering are presumably related: The skin that must be stripped is then given to the priest. The *Sifra* already notes this connection:

> The purification offering and the guilt offering and the communal peace offerings are given as gifts to the priests. If they wish to flay them, they flay them. If they wish to eat them together with their skins, they do so. But in the case of the burnt offerings, because it is written "And he shall flay the burnt offerings," the Scripture is constrained to state: "the priest shall have to himself the skin of the burnt-offering which he has offered." (*Sifra, Tzav*, 9:5)

When the skin is simply part of the meat, the priest may do with it as he wishes; when it is flayed, there is need to discuss what becomes of it.

In order to clarify the text's focus on the offering's skin, I will briefly turn to a disturbing contradiction in halakhic literature about precisely when the priest receives this holy skin. According to the Talmud (Bava Kama 111a), if someone brings a guilt offering – specifically, *asham gezelot* – but has not yet returned the money they stole, the offering is invalid, and another must be brought *after* the stolen money is returned. The text adds that the priests still get to keep the offering's skin, even though the offering is invalidated even before it has been slaughtered.

However, Mishna Zevaḥim states: "If the altar does not receive the meat the priests may not receive its skin, as it says: 'A person's burnt offering,' that is a burnt offering that was burnt on a person's behalf" (Zevaḥim 12:2).[4] This asserts that the priests may receive the animal's skin only if the altar receives its due portion. If so, if the offering becomes invalid after the blood was dashed (which is the moment the altar "receives the meat" according to Rashi), the priests may receive the skin, but if the

4. The Mishna extends this law to all invalidated offerings except for those invalidated because of requirement of *lishmah*. In such a case, the priests receive the skin of the burnt offering even though the offering does not count. This important aspect of *lishmah* is beyond the scope of this study.

offering becomes invalid before its blood is dashed – which is the case if the stolen money is not repaid before the guilt offering is brought to the Sanctuary – then the priests are not supposed to receive its skin. The *Baalei Tosafot* note this contradiction (on Bava Kama 111a, s.v. "*amar*"), but do not offer any solution.[5]

Shimon Garti addresses this contradiction in a fascinating article about consecrated skins. I will briefly summarize his main argument before applying it to the text. Garti proposes that the priest's reception of the consecrated skin fulfills two different laws or aspects. The verse in *Parashat Tzav* links this law to other sacrificial laws, from which Garti derives that the priests' reception of this share is "part of the sacrificial process." In parallel, the skin of the burnt offering is one of the twenty-four priestly gifts (Bava Kama 110b), based on the list of gifts in Numbers 18.[6] This, Garti suggests, presents a different perspective of the burnt offering's skin: "It is part of the system of priestly gifts."[7]

This brings Garti to a dramatic next step:

> According to the first law (*Parashat Tzav*), the burnt offering's skin is considered part of the offering. It is also consecrated (*kedushat haguf*), because the act of consecration (*kedushat hapeh*) includes it. After and as a result of its sacrifice, the skin is received by the priests.... According to the second law (*Parashat Koraḥ*), the skin is distinguished from the rest of the offering from the outset. The skin is not consecrated to God in the first place, because in a certain sense it already belongs to the priests.[8]

---

5. The tension between the two *sugyot* is also expressed in Mishna Zevaḥim: On the one hand it seems that the priests receive the skin only when the blood is dashed, but after the aforementioned mishnayot it continues: "All consecrated offerings that became invalid before they were flayed – their skin is not given to the priests; if they were already flayed – their skins are for the priests" (Zevaḥim 12:4).
6. Unlike holy meat, the skin may be taken out of the Sanctuary. However, Rambam determines that the consecrated skin has an intermediate status: It may be taken out of the Sanctuary but must remain in Jerusalem (like first fruits) – unlike other priestly gifts that may be taken anywhere in the land of Israel. See Rambam's commentary on Mishna Ḥalla 4:9; we will discuss this further below.
7. Garti, *Consecrated Skins.*
8. Ibid., 96.

There are two different perspectives regarding when the skin is given over to the priests. According to Leviticus, the skin is consecrated together with the entire animal, and therefore the priests only receive it after a successful sacrifice, "similarly to receiving the meat in some sacrifices."[9] In contrast, if the skin is considered a priestly gift from the outset, like tithes, the sanctity of the animal itself does not extend to the animal's skin, which is set aside for the priests regardless of the sacrificial process.

Were Garti to stop here, his observation of this tension would be novel, albeit irrelevant for our question regarding the unique status of the burnt offering's skin. But he then continues with the claim that the Sages perceive the skin as an inseparable part of the animal. Because the burnt offering is completely burnt, it is also completely consecrated, flesh and skin together. Practically, the skin is not burned and it is then given to the priest, but it is initially consecrated as part of the animal's body. In contrast, in other holy offerings, only the *eimurim* are intended for the altar, while the skin has a different status: It is an outer layer on the animal and a gift from the worshipper to the priest. Garti summarizes his analysis thus: The mishna that perceives the dashing of the blood as the moment when the skin is considered the priest's property is based on the burnt offering in *Parashat Tzav*, whereas the talmudic discussion in Bava Kama refers to the guilt offering, when the skin is considered a priestly gift at the outset as soon as it is flayed, before the blood is dashed.[10]

This careful distinction brings us back to the two laws concerning the skin of the burnt offering. The burnt offering is indeed (almost!) entirely offered on the altar, and the animal is consecrated in its entirety, so the skin initially belongs to the altar. Because the skin is not food, the altar fire does not consume it, but it is still considered part of the offering. This is true only about the burnt offering, and for this reason, there are two separate instructions regarding the skin's fate: It is to be flayed and then given over to the priest. This is not a monetary gift, but something that fundamentally belongs to the altar, and for this reason it is the ministering priest who receives the skin. In this respect it is no

9. Ibid., 97.
10. The second mishna in Zevaḥim, which rules that the priest receives the skin as soon as it has been removed from the flesh, applies to all holy offerings (Garti, Ibid., 102).

different than the flesh of the purification or guilt offering that the priest consumes as a continuation of the altar's consumption. The skin of the burnt offering is not eaten, but its status is identical to the priestly share of other holy offerings.[11]

It is for this reason that the skin of the burnt offering appears as part of the series of laws mandating how the priestly shares are distributed: Placed in between the law of the distribution of the purification and guilt offerings and that of the grain offerings, it has a similar status to them all and is thus part of the list. A general overview of this list will charge this discussion with further meaning.

DIVIDING THE MEAT FROM THE OFFERINGS AMONG THE PRIESTS

Even before the law of the burnt offering's skin, the purification and guilt offerings are mentioned together: "The guilt offering follows the same law as the purification offering: it belongs to the priest who makes atonement with it" (7:7). This conveys new information about the guilt offering, as this is already known about the purification offering ("The priest who offers it as a purification offering shall eat of it" – 6:19). In relation to the purification offering, the verb "*meḥatteh*" is used; as discussed, this is the same root as "*ḥattat*" – purification offering – while a different verb, "*mekhapper*," "atone," is used for both purification and guilt offerings together. This may reflect a deeper affinity between how the priests receive these two offerings. From the sinner's perspective, the two offerings function differently, but for the priests on the receiving end, the two are similar, and their consumption of what the altar gives them completes the sinner's process of atonement.

We have already seen R. Eliezer's perception that the purification and guilt offerings have much in common: "The guilt offering follows the same law as the purification offering" (7:7), far beyond the distribution of their meat to the priests. He extends certain laws of the purification

11. As mentioned, the priests receive the skin in Jerusalem and not the rest of the land, which shows that the skins have a different status from that of other priestly gifts.

offering to the guilt offering as well.[12] While the Sages disagree with some of his claims, they still view this verse as the basis of a deep connection between the two offerings. This is especially true of the act of laying of the hands: The Sages apply this law from the purification offering to the guilt offering, based on this verse.[13] Once again, this is only presented in Midrash Halakha; there is no evidence of such an association in the biblical text, which gives the impression that the sinner's part in the guilt offering ends as soon as the animal (or its value in silver) is brought (that is, returned!) to the Sanctuary.

DISTRIBUTING THE GRAIN OFFERING

The greatest challenge in this brief section is posed by the grain offering, which differs from the other offerings; perhaps it is postponed to the end for this reason. There seems to be a distinction between two different kinds of grain offering:

> Any grain offering baked in an oven or prepared in a pan or griddle also belongs to the priest who offers it,
> while every other grain offering, whether mixed with oil or dry, shall belong equally to all of Aaron's sons. (7:9–10)

What is the relationship between these two clauses?

12. See further in R. Lichtenstein's discussion in *Zevaḥim*, 252–63. (As for the laws R. Eliezer derives from the affinity between purification and guilt offerings, see 254–55.)
13. It makes sense that the Sages point to a similarity between the two offerings in relation to the laying of the hands. Whereas R. Eliezer points to similarities *during* the actual sacrificial process, the Sages disagree with this but do point out similarities between the two *before* and *after* the sacrificial process. As discussed, the act of laying the hands creates an affinity between worshipper and their offering. Similarly, in both purification and guilt offering, the ministering priest receives the meat of that offering after. This points to an affinity similar to that of the laying of the hands, so it makes sense that the Sages extend this verse to include the laying of the hands in the guilt offering as well.

The Sages

The Sages – and some *Rishonim* – read both clauses as relating to the same grain offering, and therefore regarded them as contradictory: Is the grain offering given to the "priest who offers it" or "to all of Aaron's sons"?[14]

Rashi explains:

> One might think that it belongs to him alone. The text therefore states: "[And any meal offering...] shall belong to all the sons of Aaron." One might think, then, that it belongs to all of them. The text therefore states: "Belongs to the priest who offers it up." How can this be? [It belongs] to the family of the day when they offer it up.

Rashi, based on the Sages, offers a compromise: The grain offering belongs to the priestly clan of whoever offers up the grain offering that day. The priests were divided according to their clan, and a different clan was on duty each week. Rashi extends this conclusion to all other offerings as well: They go to the family of priests on duty, excluding those who are impure or in mourning. This also addresses a similar tension that can be detected in other offerings, such as the guilt offering: "Any male priest may eat of it... it belongs to the priest who makes atonement with it" (7:6–7). These verses can indeed be read as a contradiction of sorts: Who gets to eat the offering, "any male priest" or "the priest who makes atonement with it"? This seems easy enough to reconcile, especially given the change in verb: The meat "belongs to" the ministering priest, and he may share it with his family, but only the males may "eat" of it. Even though the same verb, "eat," is used for both such statements about the purification offering, this can be similarly explained.

After all, it cannot be that a single priest receives so much meat for himself, especially when the meat in question must be eaten within

14. Rendtorff (*Leviticus*, 248) points out that the phrase "all of Aaron's sons" – "*ish ke'aḥiv*," literally, "each man as his brother" – appears once more in Tanakh, in Ezekiel 47:14, when the prophet describes how all of Israel will receive an equal share of the land. If so, the law of dividing up the offerings among the priests is a model for the equal division of the land to all of Israel. See also Kasher, *Ezekiel*, vol. 2, 914.

a single day. Thus, a more accurate question is: Is the meat (or grain) divided among all the priests on duty, or is the portion given only to the ministering priest for him to share with his own clan?

As mentioned, this contradiction stems from the fact that the Sages (and many *Rishonim* in their wake) assume that these verses refer to the same grain offering.[15] In a more literal reading, however, different kinds of grain offering are given to different recipients. The first kind seems to refer to cooked grain offerings: "Any grain offering baked in an oven or prepared in a pan or griddle"; the second half concerns the fine flour and sinner's grain offering: "Every other grain offering, whether mixed with oil [i.e., the fine flour offering] or dry [i.e., the sinner's grain offering]." The former are given to the priest who offers them, as in the law of the burnt offering's skin and the purification and guilt offering's share, whereas the fine flour and sinner's grain offering are subject to a unique law: They are distributed evenly among all the priests.[16]

Attentive to the *peshat* of the text, the Netziv argues that despite the halakhic ruling that the offerings are distributed among all the priests, it is *always* preferable that the ministering priest is the one who eats the offering as well, for this achieves optimal atonement for the worshipper who brings the offering.[17]

This premise is crucial for understanding the nature and significance of the priestly consumption in this section. It is a fundamental part of achieving atonement. In the Netziv's words: "When a priest begins a mitzva, he ought to finish it." If so, there is a profound connection between the priest who offers and the priest who eats – as mentioned

---

15. Radatz Hoffmann suggests that the phrase "mixed with oil" applies to cooked grain offerings and not just to the fine flour offering, and this supports the Sages' reading. Even so, there is no such division between the priests in Leviticus 2, just a general statement that "what is leftover is for Aaron and his sons" (Hoffmann, *Leviticus*, vol. 1, 173).

16. *Haamek Davar* on Lev. 6:19. He also notes that the *Ḥatam Sofer* (*Oraḥ Ḥayim, siman* 49) writes that it is the ministering priest who must eat the offering in order to properly fulfil the mitzva.

17. The Netziv notes that the *Ḥatam Sofer* (ibid.) also writes that the mitzva of eating the offerings is fulfilled by the ministering priest himself.

repeatedly, the priest's act of consumption effectively serves as an extension of the altar's consumption. There is power in continuity.

In this respect, the Torah's requirement that the ministering priest receives the priestly share reveals a fundamental principle. The priest eats his share in a holy space, beside the altar, at the same time as the altar is consuming the same offering's *eimurim*; he cannot eat the offering with leaven, just as leaven is forbidden upon the altar;[18] and the same priest who lays the offering upon the altar is the one who eats its priestly share. This illuminates the unique opinion of R. Aharon HaLevi (Raah) that the priestly portion must also be salted.[19] If the priest's consumption is an extension of the altar's, it too is part of the "covenant of salt."

But if so, how are we to understand the division of different kinds of grain offerings? Why doesn't the Netziv's reading apply to the fine flour offering, which, according to *peshat*, is divided among all the priests?

The division of the grain offerings is so strange that Shadal proposes that there is no real division between different grain offerings in the biblical text, and the two verses are parallel formulations of the same rule. Biblical parallelism is a well-known phenomenon, and the reading certainly resolves all tension regarding the priestly distribution of the grain offering.

But this reading is contrived: It is no coincidence that the grain offering appears at the end of the list, and the division of the grain offerings into different types indicates that they indeed have different laws. The Torah could have easily maintained the lack of division into different types of grain offering that appears in *Parashat Tzav*, but it does not; moreover, biblical parallelism is less common in passages that are not poetry.

Given that the halakhic ruling differs from the biblical *peshat*, not all *Rishonim* address this division – but Ramban and Rambam do.

---

18. The Talmud relates to whether the priests may eat the grain offering with honey and extra oil (Sota 14b). The reason for the *hava amina* is clear – if honey may not be offered upon the altar, it makes sense to think that this is forbidden to the priests as well.
19. Rashba's *Bedek HaBayit,* vol. 3, on Menaḥot 21a.

Ramban: For the Priest's Efforts

Ramban believes that the difference between the two sets of grain offerings relates to the efforts the priest must invest in the cooked grain offerings.[20] Due to its importance, I will cite his extensive comment on this verse; note especially how he interprets the Sages' explanation:

> The *peshat* reading is obvious: The text commands that if one makes a vow to bring one of three kinds of grain offerings – baked, in a griddle, or in a pan – they should be given exclusively to the ministering priest. It then says that all other grain offerings… should be divided among all of Aaron's descendants – that is, given to their whole clan. The clause "every other grain offering, whether mixed with oil or dry" means a grain offering of fine flour, mixed with oil or dry – but not one of the three aforementioned cooked grain offerings. *The reason for the difference between them is that the priest must take pains to prepare [these three], and he thus deserves greater reward.*
>
> But the Sages did not accept this, because it says: "*All* grain offerings, mixed with oil or dry," which includes all kinds of grain offering, given that all are either mixed with oil or dry. They therefore read "for the priest who offers it" as referring to all pure priests on duty there.
>
> Similarly, when it says: "The priest who offers any person's burnt offering," and "It belongs to the priest who makes atonement with it," both statements mean that it does not belong to the worshippers who bring the offering, but that it is payment given to all the pure priests on duty, whether physically or by command. For any individual or two or three are offering on behalf of all of them, acting as their emissaries, and all were standing by the offering, as is stated: "For the share of those who remain with the baggage should be the same as the share of those who go down to battle; they will share together."
>
> And after the text states that the priests should receive this as payment for their labor, it reiterates: "All grain offerings, whether

20. Similarly, Bekhor Shor on Lev. 7:10.

> mixed with oil or dry," which means that all grain offerings should be shared among all of Aaron's sons alike – that is, given to all the pure members of the clan on duty, for all are considered ministering priests.... The text states this about grain offerings, and it certainly applies to more costly offerings as well. [Despite what the *peshat* of the text implies,] this practice is based on tradition, *and this is what is best for the sake of peace in the Sanctuary*. (Ramban on Lev. 7:9)

This explanation is a paradigm of Ramban's attitude toward the Midrash Halakha in general. While this is not the place to elaborate,[21] I still wish to note several important principles found in this reading. Firstly, Ramban perceives the Sages' interpretation as a departure from *peshat*: "The *peshat* reading is obvious.... But the Sages did not accept this." Even so, he takes care to explain that their reading is still in harmony with the text, even if it is not *peshat*. That is, their interpretation does not pose a contradiction between the Oral and Written Torah.

A third interesting observation is that Ramban explains that the Sages understand the verses as they do on the basis of extra-interpretative factors.[22] In this case, they deviate from the *peshat* "for the sake of peace in the Sanctuary." In other words, in order to prevent conflict regarding which priests get to offer which offerings in order to receive a larger share, the Sages determine that the norm was for all offerings to be shared equally among all the priests on duty each day, no matter which offerings they actually offered up.

Ramban himself suggests that the *peshat* implies that because of the extra effort involved in offering these first three cooked grain offerings, the ministering priest received a special portion, whereas the fine flour offering – which demands little effort on the priest's part – was divided up equally among the priests.

---

21. See Ramban on Rambam in *Sefer HaMitzvot*, root 2:27. On Ramban's approach in this context, see Licht, "Ramban." On Ramban's various methodologies of reconciling Midrash Halakha with *peshat*, see Sklarz, "Disparity."
22. Moshe Halbertal demonstrates this principle in various halakhic episodes (Halbertal, *Revolutions*).

This approach also explains why the fine flour offering is divided up equally, while all other offerings go to the ministering priest. The fine flour offering is the only one that does not demand any special effort from the priest; animal offerings are even more labor intensive. This theory is important because it implies that Ramban believes that the ministering priest earns his share because he works for it.

The problem with Ramban's approach is that it assumes that the priest is the one who prepares the cooked grain offering from the raw materials brought by the Israelite worshipper. However, as discussed in our analysis of Leviticus 2, the most likely reading – that of Abarbanel – is that the Israelite worshipper prepares the cooked grain offering at home and brings it to the Sanctuary ready for the sacrificial process. If so, Ramban's interpretation is unconvincing. On the contrary, the cooked grain offering requires very little work on the priest's part. Furthermore, it undermines Ramban's premise that the priests receive their portion as payment for their work and effort.

Rambam: The Grain Offerings' Size

Before presenting Rambam's approach, we must point out a certain tension in this context between two of his greatest works – his commentary on the Mishna and *Mishneh Torah*. In the former, he draws a distinction between different kinds of offerings. Mishna Ḥalla lists the priestly gifts that can be given to "any priest," and Rambam explains that these can be given to a "common, unlearned" priest – that is, to anyone the person wants. One of the gifts listed in the Mishna is "holy of holies" – the priestly portions of one's offering. In his commentary, Rambam reviews the entire list of priestly gifts and explains that the Mishna intentionally states only "holy of holies" and ignores offerings of lesser holiness that are given to the ministering priest and not to "any priest": "Likewise, consecrated skins are not given to any priest; rather, *the priest who offers that offering receives them*" (Rambam on Ḥalla 4:9). He explains that the same is true of the priestly portions from the Nazirite ram and the peace offering, which are both of lesser holiness; they are also given to the ministering priest.

This reading ignores the Midrash Halakha's interpretation that gifts of lesser holiness are also divided up equally among the clan of the priests on duty that day;[23] like the *peshat,* Rambam rules that the ministering priest receives those portions. He does not discuss the purification, guilt, and grain offerings – that is, those that are "holy of holies." (The skin of the burnt offering is "holy of holies," but it can still be considered a monetary gift, as it is not the offering's actual flesh.)

On the other hand, in *Mishneh Torah,* Rambam fully adopts the Midrash Halakha – that all portions are divided equally among the priests on duty, even portions of lesser holiness. He explains that the two different verses about dividing the grain offerings in fact aim to emphasize that even fine flour offerings are divided equally among the priests:

> Why did the verse draw a distinction between cooked grain offerings and fine flour offerings?… When cooked grain offerings are divided among the members of the clan, whenever a person receives a portion, even if it is [merely] an olive-sized portion of bread, it is worth eating, for it is already ready to eat. However, when it comes to flour, one may receive only a handful of flour or less. This is not fit either to be kneaded into dough or to be baked. Hence, one might think that the fine flour offering should not be divided up among all the priests of the clan… For this reason the Torah emphasizes that every single offering must be divided among "all the sons of Aaron." (*Hilkhot Maaseh HaKorbanot* 10:14–15)

Here Rambam concurs with the Sages that all priestly shares – even those of lesser holiness – are shared among the priests on duty. He then explains the two different verses about grain offerings: When the fine flour offering is divided up among all the priests, they may each receive a small amount that isn't worth preparing. Because of this, one might think that it makes more sense for the priests to take turns in receiving the full share of the fine flour offering instead of dividing it up. To prevent this wrongful conclusion, the Torah emphasizes that every single grain offering should be shared among all the priests.[24]

---

23. *Sifra, Tzav,* 10:8; the same applies to gifts of higher and lesser holiness.
24. Similarly Ralbag on Lev. 7:10.

This indicates that Rambam perceives the priests' consumption of their share as a direct continuation of the altar's consumption. It does not matter if each priest receives just a small amount; what matters is that their consumption continues what began upon the altar, thus completing the sacrificial process.[25]

A Gift from the Worshipper or a Gift from the Altar?

If so, then why does the Torah distinguish between the fine flour offering and cooked grain offerings? Radatz Hoffmann adopts the Sages' reading, but not before surveying various suggestions from scholars (which he rejects).[26] The main theories proposed in scholarly research can be divided into four, or, more precisely, into two that are four:

1. Knohl suggests that that the "grain offering mixed with oil" refers to the libation offering that accompanies every animal offering, not to the independent freewill offering. He claims that the flour from these libations can be collected to divide up among the priests, but the cooked grain offerings had to be eaten immediately, so it was given to the ministering priest.[27] This suggestion is problematic not just because it seems that this libation offering was not actually eaten, but also because it is not even mentioned until the book of Numbers. It is unlikely that the verse refers to an offering that has not been mentioned yet. I am also skeptical about the claim that cooked grain offerings could not be collected and divided up among the priests.

25. This reflects that Rambam's halakhic opinion is that the eating of holy food does not require a minimal amount (similarly *Mikdash David, siman* 14:6, contra *Shaagat Aryeh, siman* 96, and *Minḥat Ḥinnukh*, commandment 134). It is not an act of "eating" that does require a minimal amount. (For example, one only makes a blessing after food if one eats a certain minimal amount.) Rather, it constitutes a different mitzva – that of eating a holy offering to continue the consuming altar fire. This is consistent with the reading of R. Aryeh Leib ben Asher Ginsburg (the *Shaagat Aryeh*) that there is a separate mitzva in eating from every offering, even if one eats more than an olive-sized portion.
26. See further in Hoffmann, *Leviticus*, vol. 1, 172–73.
27. Knobel, *Leviticus*, 406.

2. Similarly, Rendtorff suggests that the grain offering in question is the communal grain offering, while the cooked grain offerings are from individuals. Accordingly, the communal grain offering is eaten by all the priests, and each individual offering by the individual priest.[28]

The above theories suggest that the grain offering divided among all the priests is not the standard freewill fine flour offering. In contrast, the following readings do relate to the individual freewill offering and they explain why fine flour and cooked grain offerings are divided differently.

3. Keil claims that cooked grain offerings are relatively rare compared to fine flour offerings; for this reason, the ministering priest is able to eat it by himself, whereas the large amount of fine flour offerings is far too much for one priest. He adds that not only are they much less common, but they are also smaller, so a single person is able to eat that amount.[29] This is unconvincing, given that the priest's share of the purification and guilt offerings is much, much larger than their share of the grain offering, yet the text still demands that "it belongs to the priest who makes atonement with it."
4. Milgrom surmises that the different laws relate to two different kinds of temple service: Cooked grain offerings were offered at local temples (such as Beit El, Shiloh, or Nob), whereas the fine flour offering was the standard offering at the Temple. Local temples had just a few priests who received these cooked offerings, but the fine flour offering was divided up among the many priests in service at the Temple.[30]

   This theory is absurd; after all, in most offerings the meat or skin is given to the ministering priest, whereas the fine flour offering is the only one that is explicitly divided up among all the priests. Moreover, there is no hint as to any geographical or

28. Rendtorff, *Leviticus*, 248.
29. Keil, *Pentateuch*, vol. 2, 323.
30. Milgrom, *Leviticus*, vol. 1, 412.

> historical distinction between these two verses, so Milgrom's theory is problematic even before considering the improbability that the Torah would legitimize worship at local temples instead of the central "place that the Lord your God will choose."

I have devoted considerable space to the above theories, even though I find none of them convincing, to show the great confusion the description generates. It is fairly common that the Torah decrees certain laws without explanation, and it is up to the reader to determine the rationale behind them. Here, I believe, the answer is already planted in the earlier characterization of the various grain offerings in the first sacrificial list.

Not without hesitation, we can propose that the key to this puzzle is already tucked away in our analysis of Leviticus 2, where the unique, anomalous nature of the grain offering is first presented. As mentioned, even though the laws of its consumption are not listed there, the verses do state: "What remains of the grain offering shall belong to Aaron and his sons; it is holy of holies among the fire offerings to the Lord" (2:3, 10). This unique expression is related to the unclear identity of its recipients. Once again, the priests' eating of the grain offering is perceived as a continuation of the altar's consumption: The priests partake of the "fire offerings to the Lord" – it is a gift directly from the altar. While *Parashat Tzav* characterizes all the "holy of holies" offerings as the priest's continuation of the altar's consumption, the grain offering is still anomalous in that the entire fine flour offering is first offered to the altar, and then a portion of that is given to the priests. (We already discussed its similarity to the burnt offering in this respect.) From the worshipper's perspective, the altar receives the entire offering, even if the altar then transfers some of its gift to the priests.

This has a significant bearing on how the priest's consumption of this gift is characterized, as well as its timing. In most offerings, the worshipper gives part of their offering to the altar while part is inherently designated for the priests, who are its emissaries for the consumption of the portion that is not sent up in smoke. (We will yet see that this model is also used for the peace offering – 7:32–33.) Here, however, the worshipper devotes the entire offering to the altar.

When the priest offers up a burnt, purification, or guilt offering, he receives the animal and divides it up; he sends a portion up in smoke upon the altar, and a certain portion remains in his possession. He is the one who offers up the animal; he is the one who therefore receives the other portion. In regard to the grain offering, however, once he offers up the "remembrance" upon the altar, his task is done. It is now that "what remains" is divided up among the priests. In this case, the ministering priest has no special status among his priestly brethren; all of them are equal representatives of the altar. In fact, dividing "what remains" among the priests equally is an important indication that the priest is receiving a portion not as a gift from the worshipper, but because of his consecrated status, because he is a representative of the altar. What matters here is the status of priesthood, his state of consecration; all Aaron's sons are equally worthy agents of the altar.

Yet it still remains to be understood why the text states that the ministering priest is the one who receives the remaining portion of the cooked grain offering, when Leviticus 2 applies the same phrase to cooked grain offerings as well: "It is holy of holies among the fire offerings to the Lord" (2:10).

One of the differences between the cooked grain offering and the fine flour offering is that only cooked grain offerings are subject to a special law of *haggasha*, "presentation": "You shall bring the grain offering made in one of these ways to the Lord, presenting it to the priest, who will bring it to the altar" (2:8). The worshipper transfers the offering to the priest by presenting it; through this transferral, the priest takes over from the Israelite worshipper. Perhaps through this act the priest already receives his portion at the beginning of the sacrificial process. The priestly portion of the cooked grain offering is still considered "of the fire offerings to the Lord," but in these offerings the altar singles out the priest who initially receives and consecrates the offering through the act of presentation, and thus the altar gives him "what remains."

In this context, it is worth mentioning the Netziv's explanation for the distinction between cooked and fine flour offerings. Though he accepts the Sages' reading, he still relates to the text's presentation of their distribution:

> The different language used for these three grain offerings and the fine flour offering must be explained. There are two reasons for the priest's consumption of the holy of holies: One has nothing to do with their service; it is rather a privilege for priests, as written in *Parashat Koraḥ*, and for this reason all clans and their priests are equal. The second is that they deserve payment for their labor, as the prophet Malachi says: "Oh, who is there among you who would close the doors so that you might not light My altar for naught?" (Mal. 1:10). If so, when effort is exerted, it is fitting that its reward is granted to the ministering priest. (*Haamek Davar* on Lev. 7:9)

The Netziv – like Ramban – believes that special effort is expended by the priest in preparing the cooked grain offerings, and for this reason the ministering priest deserves that portion. At the same time, he also points out another reason the priests deserve a share – it is because they are priests. "The Lord spoke to Aaron: 'I place in your charge the offerings made to Me, all the sacred gifts of the Israelites. I give them to you and your sons as an anointed right; this is an everlasting decree'" (Num. 18:8).

This brings us back to the different natures of the grain offerings already presented in Leviticus 2. The grain offering is an expression of gratitude for God's provision of human sustenance, of thanking (or praying to) God for basic necessities. The fine flour offering is a daily portion of one's most basic staple – flour. It is offered up to the altar whole, like a burnt offering, and then divided up equally among the priests, who are all equal representatives of the altar by merit of their status as priests. As the altar's emissaries, all priests receive their daily bread from God's hand.

In contrast, the cooked grain offering expresses a significant element of the worshipper's personal relationship with God. We have suggested that perhaps it reflects gratitude for abundance; it is the offering with the most room for personal preferences and individual expression. It is in relation to this personal offering that the priest, too, is recognized as an individual in God's service. The worshipper's personal, individualized offering is given to the individual priest who personally handles this offering, and this, perhaps, is conveyed through the law of presentation.

The cooked grain offering acknowledges that each priest is a working man who lives and toils and receives his daily bread directly from God's hand, through the altar. There are certainly prices and heavy obligations for being God's consecrated servants; the reception of the cooked grain offering and the work entailed in its preparation perhaps subtly acknowledge the priest's efforts as an individual who receives his daily bread from God's hand.

Chapter 18

The Law of the Peace Offering (Leviticus 7:11–34): Extending the Altar's Reach

The last of the sacrificial "laws" is "the law of the peace offering." Its length already testifies to its prominence in this list: The twenty-four verses in which this law is presented are at least four times as many as those that mandate the other offerings in this section. Perhaps some may be surprised that the most space is devoted to an offering of lesser holiness, but given that the second sacrificial list focuses on how each offering is eaten, this is no surprise at all. When non-priests are allowed to partake in the eating of a sacred offering, there is much need for laws and regulations that dictate precisely how it may be eaten, as well as warnings against eating the offering when impure. Most offerings are eaten by consecrated priests in the Temple courtyard, where utmost purity is already taken for granted. But the consumption of consecrated meat by regular Israelites poses special challenges and the need for extensive guidelines.

WHAT DOES "LESSER HOLINESS" MEAN?

The most striking element of these verses is what is missing: While the definition "holy of holies" appears in relation to every other offering, this phrase is noticeably absent from the law of the peace offering. Accordingly, the Sages refer to the peace offering as *kodashim kallim*, an offering of lesser holiness ("*kal*" meaning "light" or "lesser"). Yet the word "holiness" is not used in relation to this offering at all! In fact, a cursory reading of this section might lead to the conclusion that this offering is not actually holy. Even if we ultimately determine that the offering does have a certain level of holiness (and for this reason, it may not be eaten when in a state of impurity), the absence of the term "holiness" is striking.

The omission of this term is especially striking if we compare the laws of *piggul* in this context with those in *Parashat Kedoshim*:[1] If one eats the meat of the peace offering beyond the permitted time, *Parashat Tzav* states: "It is offensive, and anyone who eats of it is liable to punishment" (7:18), whereas *Parashat Kedoshim*'s conclusion is far more severe: "Anyone who eats it shall bear his guilt, for he has desecrated what is *holy* to the Lord; *he shall be severed from his people*" (19:18). It is the desecration of the offering's holiness that results in serious punishment, *karet*. The similarity between the two descriptions of the peace offering underscores their different conclusions. For some reason, *Parashat Tzav* refrains from defining the peace offering as "holy" and its improper consumption as the desecration of this holiness. This omission distinguishes the peace offering from the rest of the offerings in the second sacrificial

1. A full comparison would include the passage in Leviticus 22:29–30, which exceeds the scope of this discussion. I will just note that Knohl believes that the peace offering in *Parashat Tzav* refers to both the regular and thanksgiving peace offering; that Leviticus 19 refers only to the vow fulfillment or freewill peace offering; and that Leviticus 22 refers to the thanksgiving peace offering (Knohl, *Temple of Silence*, 113–15).

list. The complete absence of the term implies that rather than different levels of holiness, there are two entirely different sacrificial processes.

What Is Holiness?

In order to consider the absence of the term "holiness," we must first define what that term means within the sacrificial world. Rudolph Otto justifiably points out that "the fact is we have come to use the words 'holy', 'sacred' (*heilig*), in an entirely derivative sense, quite different from that which they originally bore. We generally take 'holy' as meaning 'completely good'; it is the absolute moral attribute, denoting the consummation of moral goodness.... But this common usage of the term is inaccurate."[2] This metaphoric extension of its meaning may already occur in the Torah itself, with the clause "Be holy, for I am holy; I, the Lord your God" (Lev. 19:2)[3] expressing that one who fulfills God's will is essentially aspiring to be worthy of the world of holiness. Yet there remains a distinction between its borrowed meaning and the legal definition of holiness.

A full discussion of all its aspects, complexities, and diverse perspectives as to its meaning (especially of those in Exodus-Leviticus-Numbers versus in Deuteronomy) are beyond the scope of this book,[4] but we may present a basic biblical definition of holiness:

> What God has distinguished, designated, or set aside; from this a similar designation is derived by humanity. God Himself is holy, for He Himself is set aside from the world; those who set themselves aside from the profane or from various prohibitions and grow close to God (such as the Nazirite) similarly become holy. The adjective "holy" designates the divine realm or what is set aside or designated for God. Thus, when an object is given over

2. Otto, *Idea of the Holy*, 5.
3. It may be that Rashi's reading of this verse extends its basic meaning: "Be holy – Abstain from forbidden relations and sin."
4. See further in Weinfeld, "Change in the Conception"; Weinfeld, *Deuteronomy*, 179–243.

> to the possession of God or His emissaries, such as for ritual use, it becomes consecrated, holy.[5]

The biblical concept of holiness (certainly the one relevant to the sacrificial world of Leviticus) is profoundly related to what belongs to the divine realm by virtue of its distinction from the human sphere. This affiliation has diverse legal, moral, and social implications. If holiness means that it belongs to God, what is holy inherently exists with surrounding barriers that offer layers of protection and segregation from the human and the profane: "To distinguish between sacred and profane, and between impure and pure" (Lev. 10:10). R. Soloveitchik translates the term "*kedusha*" as both a mysterious transcendence into the midst of a concrete world and an invitation for humanity to strive to reach beyond their own ephemeral world.[6] In this he exposes a fundamental dichotomy that characterizes the divine sphere: The sublime creates a consciousness of distance, in the spirit of the prophet's words: "Whom can you compare Me to – so speaks the Holy One – and find them equal?" (Is. 40:25), yet it also invites humanity to expand its consciousness beyond its own fleeting existence. Otto expresses similar ideas about the dual nature of holiness – how it simultaneously draws and threatens the believer, whose world is by definition differentiated from the world of holiness. A fundamental aspect of holiness is its distinction from the profane human world; this is especially relevant in the context of the sacrificial world.[7]

The biblical text does not support the prevalent assumption that "holiness is not an immanent quality of objects, but an aspect of how

5. Regev, "Holiness," 53. It is worth noting that the word's etymology is not clear, although some argue for a connection to the root Ḥ-D-SH, "new," for both point to something distinguished, separate: The new is distinct from the old, the holy from the profane; see further in Ringgren, "Kadesh."
6. Soloveitchik, *Lonely Man of Faith*, 48–50. R. Chaim Navon explains that R. Soloveitchik links the ambivalence that accompanies holiness to historical aspects as well, such as to the times Isaiah and Ezekiel, which is uncharacteristic of him (Navon, "Historical Consciousness").
7. Shadal proposes that the term "*kadosh*" is a combination "*kd-esh*," meaning "fire burning" for God's glory (on Ex. 15:11). If so, the whole world of sanctity is rooted in the sacrificial world.

one relates to them."[8] Tanakh describes events that transcend human perception that ostensibly serve as the basis of such a definition of holiness. According to this definition, a Nazirite becomes holy because he separates himself from the profane and from various prohibitions and becomes close to God. But is holiness merely a matter of distance from the profane and closeness to God? It seems that this can be taken much further.

An appropriate test case is God's revelation to Moses at the Burning Bush. There, God explains that Moses must not come too close and he must take off his shoes because the place itself is "holy": "Do not come close. Remove the shoes from your feet, for the place where you stand is holy ground" (Ex. 3:5). Why is the site of the Burning Bush defined as a holy place, and why can't Moses walk around there? After God's revelation ends, the place will revert back to its usual status and be holy no longer.[9] Thus,the logical reading of these directives is that God's presence there makes the place holy: It is elevated above the regular human realm to the realm of the Divine Presence. For this reason, Moses must remove his shoes to show that he has no authority there.[10] The earth is usually human territory, but when God's presence is manifest, certain times, places, or objects are elevated above human dominion – to become holy. The moment the Burning Bush becomes a site of revelation, it immediately generates barriers and boundaries.

Defining holiness as resulting from divine revelation makes both signifier and signified elusive. God Himself is the essence of holiness; God is holiness and the source of holiness: "There is no holy being like the Lord, for there are none besides You" (I Sam. 2:2). This is how God's angels define their Master: "And they called out one to another, 'Holy, holy, holy – the Lord of Hosts – all the world's fullness His glory'" (Is.

8. Cohen, "Kedusha," 208.
9. This example has a further scene: The site of the Burning Bush will become holy once more at the Sinai revelation.
10. Removing shoes as a symbol of submitting or removing authority is also found in legal systems, such as removing the shoe during the *ḥalitza* ceremony. (See Grossman, *Ruth*, 289–92, and references to further sources there.)

6:3);[11] "The Lord is truly the Holy One of Israel" (Is. 10:20). Thus,a precise definition of "holy" is to define God Himself, which is impossible in human terms.

> The "sacred" is what has been placed within boundaries, the exceptional (Latin *sanctus*); its powerfulness creates for it a place of its own. "Sacred" therefore means neither completely moral nor, without further qualification, even desirable or praiseworthy.... Power has its own specific quality... which cannot be evoked from something else but which is "*sui generis*" [unique] and *sui juris* [independent], and can be designated only by religious terms such as "sacred" and "'numinous."[12]

Yet despite the uncertainty surrounding the precise definition of "holiness," the manifestation of holiness in the real world can be explained as derived from God's holy reality. God is holy; holiness spreads; so the place where God's presence rests becomes holy and what belongs to Him becomes holy. If so, the Nazirite is not holy because he becomes close to God, but because he defines himself as "belonging to God" for a certain period of time. The Nazirite's restrictions do not make him holy; they emanate from his state of holiness.

I am aware that this is but a cursory definition, but it suffices to clarify the unique nature of the peace offering. It is evident why offerings belong to the world of holiness; they are by definition dedicated to God and then consumed by the altar fire. When offerings are transferred from human ownership to the Sanctuary, they become "holy of holies," so only priests may deal with them and eat their flesh, for priests are also "holy" – they have also been set aside, anointed and consecrated to God and the Sanctuary. The Israelite worshipper, bringer of the offering, stands at the threshold of the world of holiness, outside looking in. They reach out, bearing their gift to God, but they cannot enter; they need the consecrated priest to mediate between them and the world of

11. This is the prevalent reading; Radak (and others) proposes that the epithet "*Kadosh*" is referring to the angels hurrying each other up ("Hurry up, holy one!").
12. Van der Leeuw, *Religion*, 47–48.

holiness. So it is with the burnt and grain offerings, the guilt and purification offerings. But with the peace offering, this clear order is challenged. These chapters do not define it as "holy," which discloses the simple yet revolutionary fact that the offering is not entirely given over to the Sanctuary. Certain parts are offered up upon the altar, but it still remains in the worshipper's possession; it is still tethered to the human world.

It therefore comes as little surprise that the flesh and *eimurim* of "holy of holies" offerings may not be used for any other purpose (to do so is considered *me'ila*, "trespass") even before the dashing of the blood, whereas the prohibition against *me'ila* does not apply to the flesh of the peace offering (or any offering of lesser holiness) at all, and even the *eimurim* are not considered holy until the blood has been dashed.[13] Before the blood is dashed, the offering is not considered holy at all.[14]

A fitting metaphor, perhaps, is the difference between two people who are invited for a meal. One brings a gift for their hosts; this gift is given over to the hosts' ownership ("holy of holies"). The other brings a dish that will be served and shared by host and guest at the meal ("the peace offering"). The status of the latter offering is far less clear; it is a gesture of gratitude and mutuality, but whether it is considered the guest's or the host's is not fully certain.

The metaphor is certainly an oversimplification (especially in relation to the offerings' halakhic status!), and even though the word "holiness" is not used for the peace offering in this list, this does not preclude a palpable fear of contamination. In a section entirely devoted to the question of holiness, however, the absence of the actual word is a dramatic manifestation.

The peace offering can be eaten by the Israelite worshipper because it is not explicitly defined as "holy." It is inconceivable that an unconsecrated non-priest would be allowed to partake of something that has been consecrated to God; thus, the peace offering must still belong to its

13. Mishna Me'ila 1:4. Tosafot state that there is no such thing as *me'ila* with peace offerings, but there is a basic level of *issur* (see Nedarim 10a, s.v. "*adam mevi kivsato*").
14. I sense that this is why some *Aḥaronim* claim that the worshippers may eat of the peace offering as soon as the blood has been dashed, before the *eimurim* are burned (unlike holier offerings). See Tzelaḥ on Beitza 20b; *Haamek Davar* on Num. 6:20.

bringer, at least to some degree. The barriers erected by the usual sacrificial process are not designed for the peace offering – only the *eimurim* are passed on, while the rest of the flesh remains within the profane human sphere. Even the *eimurim* offered upon the altar must undergo a special ritual before they are fit to be sent up in smoke upon the altar; they must be waved (7:30), because as part of a non-holy offering, there is need for a special act of consecration before they are worthy of the holy altar (as we will explore further below).

Thus, the peace offering – a fitting symbol of the covenant between the human and the Divine – remains partially within human ownership, while part is elevated to the altar. From this perspective, the difference between the peace offering and the rest of the offerings in this section is dramatic. All the previous offerings are entirely offered up to the altar, to become holy of holies; even the priestly portions are considered an extension of the altar's own consumption. Yet the peace offering brought to the Sanctuary is shared between the altar and the Israelite worshipper, whose portion is also shared with the priests. This is a new sacrificial style, paved with its own unique halakhic and spiritual implications.

TWO DIFFERENT PEACE OFFERINGS

There is no such distinction in the first sacrificial list in *Vayikra*, but this section offers two variations of the peace offering:

> This is the law of the peace sacrifice that one may offer to the Lord:
>
> *If it is offered for thanksgiving*, one offers unleavened loaves mixed with oil with the thanksgiving sacrifice, and unleavened wafers spread with oil, and loaves of fine flour mixed with oil. This offering, together with loaves of leavened bread, he shall present with the peace sacrifice of thanksgiving. Of these he shall offer one of each kind as a gift raised up to the Lord. This shall belong to the priest who dashed the blood of the peace offering. The flesh of the peace sacrifice of thanksgiving shall be eaten on the day it is offered; you may not leave any of it to the morning.
>
> *If the sacrifice is to fulfill a vow*, however, or is a freewill offering, it shall be eaten on the day when one offers the sacrifice, while what is left over may be eaten the next day. Whatever of the flesh

> of the sacrifice is left over on the third day shall be burned with fire. If any of the flesh of the peace sacrifice is eaten on the third day, it shall not be accepted, nor shall it be credited to the one who offered it. It is offensive, and anyone who eats of it is liable to punishment. (7:11–19)

For the first time, we learn of two different models of the peace offering. The difference is entirely based on the worshipper's motivation: "If it is offered for thanksgiving" / "If the sacrifice is to fulfill a vow" – and the fact that this is mentioned for the first time in *Parashat Tzav* anticipates that this motivation has a direct bearing on the laws of how the offering will be eaten.

The opening verse is considerably long:[15] "This is the law of the peace sacrifice that one may offer to the Lord," is far longer than "This is the law of the burnt offering"; "This is the law of the grain/purification/guilt offering." The refrain "that one may offer to the Lord" will appear in this section again and again, emphasizing the worshipper's personal, direct connection to God expressed through this particular offering.

The Thanksgiving Offering

The first kind of peace offering is for "thanksgiving" – as an expression of particular gratitude. Some read "*toda*" in the sense of "confession," as in the book of Ezra: "But now, make your confession (*tenu* ***toda***) to the Lord, God of your ancestors, and perform His will by separating yourselves from the peoples of the land and from the foreign women" (Ezra 10:11).[16] However, even if there is some kind of semantic relationship between the two distinct senses of the noun, a clear distinction should be drawn between them.[17] In the book of Psalms, the *toda* offering is

15. Milgrom's claim that the long heading points to a later redaction is unconvincing (*Leviticus*, vol. 1, 408); a later redactor would have been more careful to aim for a similar style.
16. Kiuchi, "Peace Offering," 25: "It is agreed that '*toda*' means not 'thanks' but 'confession.'"
17. Semantically, Kiuchi is correct that the word "*toda*" means both thanksgiving and confession because both are human utterances that follow a certain action or event, but the two still have distinct meanings. Usually, Y-D-H in the *hif'il* stem denotes

characterized as an offering accompanied by praise, thanksgiving, and gratitude to God, not one of confession and regret. This implies that the prevalent translation, "thanksgiving offering," is correct.

The bringer of the thanksgiving offering must also bring different kinds of matzot: "Unleavened loaves mixed with oil with the thanksgiving sacrifice / and unleavened wafers spread with oil / and loaves of fine flour mixed with oil," as well as "loaves of leavened bread."[18]

The instruction to bring "loaves of leavened bread" is surprising – leaven is strictly forbidden upon the altar! Not only is this bread part of the offering, it is even presented as the main accompaniment to the offering: The first three additions are brought "with the thanksgiving sacrifice," whereas "with loaves of leavened bread he shall present the peace offering of thanksgiving"! While Ibn Ezra is correct that the preposition "*al*" in this verse means "with," the syntax gives the sense that the offering is served on the leavened loaves, or to use the Netziv's extreme formulation:

> The text here implies that the offering of the leaven loaves is the offering's ultimate purpose. For this reason, the text explains further: "Upon loaves of leavened bread he shall present the peace offering of thanksgiving" – for the leavened loaves are the main part. (*Haamek Davar* on Lev. 7:13)[19]

We will discuss the purpose of the accompanying leavened and unleavened bread below, but I will first point out the generous amounts

---

praise and expressions of acclaim, whereas in the *hitpa'el* stem it signifies confession. There are, however, instances in the Bible where the context does not clearly refer to one of the two meanings (Prov. 28:13; Ps. 32:5; II Chr. 30:22).

18. The accepted reading (beginning with the Sages) is that these are four different kinds of breads; it is not entirely clear if they refer to three or four kinds. The third kind – "loaves of fine flour mixed with oil" – may be referring to the fourth kind, the leavened bread. Regardless, the main sense is that the peace offering is brought together with both matzot and leavened loaves.

19. That the leavened loaves are the main part is also expressed through the large amount of flour used to prepare the loaves, compared to the smaller amount used for the matzot (Mishna Menaḥot 7:1). According to the Sages, the amount of leavened bread was as much as all three kinds of matzot combined.

of oil referred to, which, as mentioned, symbolize wealth and abundance – "unleavened loaves *mixed with oil* with the thanksgiving sacrifice / and unleavened wafers *spread with oil* / and loaves of fine flour *mixed with oil*." These lavish amounts of oil are a fitting expression of gratitude to God for all His blessing and abundance.

According to the text, the priest is to receive one of each kind of bread: "Of these he shall offer one of each kind as a gift raised up to the Lord."[20] Use of the verb "*lehakriv*," "to offer up," in relation to the matzot is slightly grating; the language implies that the basket of matzot is an offering that will be offered up upon the altar. This verb is presumably used to characterize this addition as an integral part of the offering itself. It is not a mere side dish, but a vital element of the offering itself; it is as important to share the matzot with the priest as it is to offer up the *eimurim* upon the altar.[21] When we discuss the significance of these matzot, we are discussing an integral component of the offering, even if it is not actually offered up on the altar.

The second law of the thanksgiving offering concerns the time allotted for its eating: "The flesh of the peace sacrifice of thanksgiving shall be eaten on the day it is offered; you may not leave any of it to the morning" (7:15). This law is a distinctive feature of the thanksgiving offering, repeated in Leviticus 22: "It shall be eaten on the same day – leave none of it to the morning" (22:30). While the priests are usually allotted the same time period for most offerings, this law is addressed to the Israelite worshipper, and it serves as one of the crucial differences between the two types of peace offering, as we will discuss below.

The Vow Fulfillment or Freewill Offering

The second kind of peace offering may be brought for one of two different motives: "Vow fulfillment or freewill." Its description is shorter

20. The Sages compared this law to the law of tithes and thus inferred the same amount here: ten loaves of each, one of each for the priests – thirty-six for the worshipper and four for the priest altogether.
21. This may be hinted at through the reference in the singular: "And of this he shall present" (*vehikriv mimmenu* – 7:14), which seems to relate to the thanksgiving peace offering, whereas the matzot are referred to in the plural (7:12); the use of the singular gives the sense of the different components forming one cohesive unit.

than the description of thanksgiving offerings; there is no mention of any accompanying loaves, and the bringer is given two days to eat it: "It shall be eaten on the day when one offers the sacrifice, while what is left over may be eaten the next day. Whatever of the flesh of the sacrifice is left over on the third day shall be burned with fire."

Characterizing the Different Kinds of Peace Offering

As stated, the different models are based on the motive for their offering, which is unique in itself. The text does not specify why the worshipper is moved to bring a burnt or grain offering, and the reader must glean their motivation from hints in the verses. Yet the kind of peace offering is explicitly defined by the worshipper's motivation, which even defines the appropriate laws. Why is the difference between a peace offering brought for thanksgiving or another purpose so significant?

The thanksgiving offering is brought as an expression of gratitude to God. The Sages codify this expression almost to the point of obligation: "R. Yehuda said that Rav said: Four must give thanks: seafarers, those who cross the wilderness, those who recovered after sickness, and those who were freed from imprisonment" (Berakhot 54b). These four instances, which Rav bases largely on Psalm 107, are examples, not an exhaustive list of the only cases in which people must give thanks, as Rashi states: "People give thanks for miracles that happened to them, *such as* those seafarers..." (on Lev. 7:12).[22] It is no coincidence that Rambam does not mention these four cases – to show that this offering is brought by "*anyone* who feels a need to give thanks to the Lord."[23] This is also supported by simple logic, given that the offering is by definition "freewill"; it seems that the Sages sought to emphasize the importance of gratitude by institutionalizing it into a formal requirement.[24]

In contrast, the peace offering brought as the fulfillment of a vow or as a freewill offering is based purely on human motivation – not as a

22. For a different reading, see Sandorfi, "Who Brings," 75–76.
23. Sandorfi, "Who Brings," 83.
24. R. Saadia Gaon included "the mitzva of blessing" as a positive commandment that encompasses all blessings (positive commandment 27). In this commandment he includes the *Gomel* blessing as an obligation for these four events.

response to something God has done for them, but as the worshipper's desire to express the human aspect of their relationship with the Divine, as a desire to initiate an interaction with God. This is especially salient when one is making a vow, so we will first draw a distinction between peace offerings brought for vow fulfillment and the freewill offering.

Indeed, what is the difference between them? The Sages point to a halakhic distinction:

> What is a vow? When someone says: "I hereby must bring an offering."
> What is a freewill offering? When someone says: "This is hereby an offering."
> What is the difference between vow and freewill offerings? If the vow offering died or was stolen [before being offered], one must bring a replacement; if the freewill offering died or was stolen, one does not have to replace it. (Mishna Kinnim 1:1)

According to the Mishna, the vow offering is a person's commitment to bring an offering, whereas the freewill offering is designating a specific animal for that purpose. Beyond the legal nature of this definition, there may be a psychological difference between these two variations of peace offering.

The biblical vow is made when individuals are under certain duress and they seek God's help. In these cases, the person proclaims that if God helps them, they will bring a certain offering or perform a certain act of thanksgiving. For this reason, the vow is often conditional: "If God does such-and-such, I will do such-and-such." Several classic examples are Jacob's vow when he flees from Esau: "Then Jacob made a vow. 'If God will be with me, protecting me on this journey I am taking… then the Lord will be my God… of all that You give me I will dedicate a tenth to You'" (Gen. 28:20–22); when they set out for war, the Israelites promise to destroy Arad's cities as an act of dedication similar to an offering:[25]

25. *Ḥerem* especially appears in the context of war; see further in Lohfink, "Ḥerem." See both meanings (consecration and obliteration) in Bin-Nun, *Mikrat – Mishpatim*, 363–64.

"And the Israelites vowed to the Lord: 'If You give this people over into our hands, we will utterly destroy their towns'" (Num. 21:2); and, of course, Jephthah's infamously tragic vow: "Then Jephthah swore a vow to the Lord. He said, 'If You deliver the Ammonites into my hand, then whatever comes out of the doors of my home to meet me when I return safely from the Ammonites shall be for the Lord, and I shall offer it up as a burnt offering'" (Judges 11:30–31).

These examples sufficiently paint the tone of the biblical vow: A person is in dire straits, calls out to God for help, and makes a promise that will be fulfilled if God helps them to overcome the difficulty. Thus,the fulfillment of that vow is inherently expressed with gratitude and thanksgiving, for their prayers have been answered; this explains the common biblical parallelisms of vow fulfillment and thanksgiving: "Offer to God a thanksgiving sacrifice / pay your vows to the Most High" (Ps. 50:14; see also Jonah 2:10; Ps. 56:13, among others).[26] This pairing, of course, raises the question as to the difference between peace offerings of thanksgiving and vow fulfillment, which we will address below.

While the vow fulfillment offering is conditional, the freewill offering is a free, unconditional expression of love and friendship initiated by the human toward the Divine: "The element of free will is determinative. The act of giving, the gift, and the decision are all free and voluntary."[27] The bringer of the freewill offering expects nothing in return; their gift is not a response to something God has done or a debt they owe, but a free expression of emotion. A certain animal is set aside for the Sanctuary, securing the bringer and their family a chance to dine at God's table. A vow fulfillment offering is conditional; a freewill offering is unconditional.[28]

If so, what is the fundamental difference between thanksgiving peace offerings and vow fulfillment and freewill offerings? A different division could theoretically have been possible – with one variation

26. The same pair, "vow" and "*zevaḥ*," is found in Ugaritic, with a similar meaning.

27. Conrad, "N-D-B," 220.

28. Similarly Kiuchi, "Peace Offering," 25 (and unlike Conrad, "N-D-B," 221–22, who claims the two have the same underlying motivation). The same two ways of commitment apply to all non-obligatory offerings; see Lev. 22:18; Num 15:3; Ezek. 46:12.

being thanksgiving and vow fulfillment offerings, and the other freewill offerings – given that the first two are both human responses to help or kindness from God, whereas the freewill offering is a spontaneous, unconditional form of expression. Some do interpret the types of offering thus, such as, for example, Menahem Haran:

> Vow fulfillment and thanksgiving peace offerings are similar but not identical. What distinguishes between them is that the vow fulfillment was undertaken out of prior commitment while there is no such commitment for the thanksgiving offering. In this respect both differ from the freewill offering, which has neither prior obligation and the expectation of its fulfillment, nor the feeling of gratitude for something important.[29]

Haran's reading is admittedly tempting: Vow fulfillment and thanksgiving offerings indeed have a sense of "prior commitment" that the freewill offering does not. Moreover, the sense of commitment seems to have practical expression in halakha: There are certain leniencies in the peace offering that do not apply to the vow fulfillment peace offering. All animal offerings must be *tamim*, "without blemish": "When someone presents a peace sacrifice to the Lord from the herd or flock – whether because of a spoken vow or as a freewill offering – it must be unblemished to be acceptable; there shall be no blemish on it. Do not present to the Lord anything blind, injured, or maimed, or with warts, a severe rash, or scabs. Do not place any of these on the altar as a fire offering to the Lord" (Lev. 22:21–22). Surprisingly, however, there are two exceptions. Animals with very specific deformities may be offered up as peace offerings: "You may offer as a freewill offering an ox or sheep with a limb deformed (*sarua*) or uncloven (*kalut*)," but only as a freewill offering and not a vow fulfillment offering – "but they will not be accepted in fulfillment of a vow" (22:23)!

According to the Midrash Halakha on these verses, it is difficult to accept that an imperfect animal can serve as an offering, and the Sages read "*nedava*" in the sense of "donation" rather than as a freewill offering.

29. Haran, "Vow," 786.

As Rashi explains, the animal may be sold and the money donated to the Sanctuary. Bekhor Shor debates whether this can be read as a rhetorical question: "Shall it be a freewill offering??! It will not be accepted as a vow fulfillment offering!" But this is difficult to justify, especially since a connecting *vav* joins the two halves of the verse. Ramban attempts to adapt the verses' grammar to the Midrash Halakha, but his reading is somewhat contrived, and the *peshat* implies that animals with very specific deformities can be offered as freewill offerings but not as vow fulfillment offerings.

Why are these blemishes less problematic than all others? Rashi explains that "*sarua*" means that one hoof is bigger than the other and "*kalut*" means that its hooves are not split but are joined together, like horses' hooves. This implies that the deformity is a subtle aesthetic issue rather than a significant blemish. If so, the level of perfection required of a vow fulfillment offering is higher than that of a freewill offering. When one owes a debt to God, the offering must be without blemish; a free expression of love, however, can be of slightly lower caliber. Abarbanel follows this direction, although his focus is on the different period of time that elapses between the dedication of and the offering of a peace offering:

> You may offer as a freewill offering an ox or sheep with a limb deformed or uncloven, but they will not be accepted in fulfillment of a vow. This means that he can make it into a freewill offering, if he has nothing else to give. But for a vow fulfillment offering, for which during a time of crisis he vowed that he would bring an ox or lamb, he must provide a perfect male specimen, for he has time to look for one and offer it up to fulfill the vow he made.

Since the vow was uttered during a crisis, the vow maker should take as long as they need to pay the vow properly, with a perfect, flawless offering. In contrast, a person commits to bringing a freewill offering – which is not brought for a specific event, neither positive nor negative – as soon as the commitment is made, so they bring the best animal they can as soon as possible, even if the animal has slight imperfections. Some modern scholars also favor this reading.[30] I am not sure that the issue is a question of time; rather, perhaps, an offering that derives from pure human initiative is still perfect in God's eyes even if it is less than perfect, but a debt owed to God must meet the highest of requirements, even if the vow was made from a person's free will.[31] This indeed seems to bring us back to Haran's logical division: that the vow and thanksgiving offerings are similar, as they are both brought as a response to something God has done for the bringer.

Logical as it is, this fails to explain why the vow fulfillment and freewill offering are grouped together, separately from the thanksgiving offering. I believe that the key to this division lies in the worshipper's stirring of religious emotion that moves them to offer a peace offering in the first place. Peace offerings are a reaction to a divine kindness. God bestows a certain gift or salvation, and the human responds; in a certain sense, this almost characterizes the thanksgiving offering as an obligatory offering, as reflected in the Talmud. A person who is granted such divine benevolence is expected to respond, expected to express thanks: "Four *must* give thanks." In contrast, vow fulfillment and freewill offerings are the result of human initiative. A person in distress *chooses* to turn to God as the source of their salvation; it is a choice to reach out to God as much as it is a choice to offer a peace offering in better times and not just times of crisis. A vow to God, like a freewill offering, is not a response, but an act of human initiative.

This brings us to the different laws of each peace offering. Abarbanel's interpretation of the differences is a fruitful starting point for discussion.

Abarbanel: "The Crowd Shall Exalt Him"

> We can suggest further that thanksgiving peace offerings come with much bread so that when the bringer of the peace offerings

30. Milgrom, *Leviticus*, vol. 2, 1878–79. See also Bekhor Shor's first suggestion: "It is not a blemish, so it may be used as a freewill offering. But if it was a vow fulfillment offering it is not valid, for you make a vow on a regular animal, not an imperfect one."
31. Similarly Noth, *Leviticus*, 162; Hartley, *Leviticus*, 361.

> invites guests, they shall not lack for bread. For if he does not have a sufficient amount of bread, he will refrain from inviting guests to share his peace offering, for meat is not eaten without bread.... Similarly, this explains the difference between allowing one day and night for eating thanksgiving offerings, whereas other peace offerings may be eaten within two days and one night... This is to publicize the miracle.
>
> For when the host sees that the offering must be eaten within a day until midnight, he will invite many family members and friends to eat and celebrate with him. And they will ask each other what he is giving thanks for, and he will share the miracles and wonders God has done for him. Then the crowd shall exalt Him and they shall praise Him among the elders. If two days were allowed for eating the thanksgiving offering, as with other peace offerings, the host would not invite anyone else, for a single household is able to eat it within two days and a night. But when considering the meat and all the bread that must be eaten within a single day and night, he has no choice but to invite many friends and acquaintances. Otherwise he will feel ashamed the next day when people see him burning a large amount of leftover meat from his peace offering because he failed to invite family and friends. (Abarbanel on Lev. 7)

According to Abarbanel,[32] the two unique laws of the thanksgiving peace offering – the extra bread and the brief period in which the offering may be eaten – are calculated to ensure that the worshipper will invite a whole crowd to celebrate with him. Publicizing one's gratitude is an integral part of the thanksgiving offering: "I will praise the Lord with all my heart in the gathered assembly of the upright" (Ps. 111:1).

This approach has far-reaching implications: To this day, the *Gomel* blessing – the post-Temple alternative to the thanksgiving offering – must be recited before a *minyan*, a quorum of at least ten men, preferably during the public Torah reading (*Shulḥan Arukh, Oraḥ Ḥayim* 219:3). This also seems to be what Rambam means when he adds that the reciter of

32. Similarly Netziv, *Haamek Davar* on Lev. 7:13.

the blessing must "stand among ten men" (*Hilkhot Berakhot* 10:8). Many question the meaning of "stand among," and some even explain that Rambam does not actually mean "among," but that this actually refers to being part of a *minyan*. However, the *Tzitz Eliezer* rightly explains that "'to stand among' certainly means actually standing among them, as the greatest of *posekim* confirm" (*Tzitz Eliezer* 13:19). Rambam seems to recognize the value of literally standing among a crowd to publicize God's miracles.

This idea certainly explains the addition of large amounts of bread as well as the limited time allotted for eating the thanksgiving offering. Moreover, the addition of bread (rather than more meat, such as at an additional celebration offering) gives the sense of an actual meal – not a mere celebration toast with snacks and sweets, but a proper festive meal, with meat and bread. God and Moses, seeking to reassure the hungry Israelites, promise: "In the evening, the Lord will give you meat to eat, and in the morning bread to fill you…. Tell them: At twilight you shall eat meat, and in the morning your fill of bread. Then you will know that I am the Lord your God" (Ex. 16:8–12).[33]

As for the allotted time for the thanksgiving offering, note that Abarbanel's premise is that time for the thanksgiving offering should ideally have been two full days like other peace offerings, but the text reduces it to one day. I will address this curious premise below.

Does this reading explain why leavened bread is an integral part of this offering? Given that the priestly share of most offerings is considered an extension of the altar's consumption, the priests may not eat the meat with leaven bread, because leaven is forbidden to the altar. This is not the case with the thanksgiving offering, but that only explains why leaven *may* be eaten with the offering, not why it *must* be eaten.

R. Yoel Bin-Nun gives a general overview of leaven and unleavened bread in the sacrificial world:[34] Leaven bread represents the culmination of a process – the satisfaction and delight of completion – while matza

33. The Hebrew word "*leḥem*" means both "bread" and "food," and sometimes even "meat," like the Arabic. Here, however, since the context is the provision of the manna, it presumably refers to grain bread; see the discussion in Cassuto, *Exodus*, 133.
34. Bin-Nun, "Leaven and Matza."

represents the beginning of a process and the humility of contemplating what the future may yet bring. Thus, for example, Passover – the beginning of the harvest season – is the season of matzot, whereas Shavuot, the end of the harvest season, is celebrated with leaven loaves. If so, the bringer of the thanksgiving offering is giving thanks for the successful end of a process: "Give thanks to the Lord for He is good," rather than "Please, Lord, bring salvation now."[35]

While this idea is certainly possible, it does not explain why leavened bread is not added to the vow fulfillment offering, which also marks the culmination of a process – the fulfillment of a vow. To present a further explanation, I will first take a step back and question the assumption that bread is added only to the thanksgiving offering.

Is Bread Added Only to the Thanksgiving Offering?

The addition of matzot and bread is mentioned only in conjunction with the thanksgiving offering; this results in the reasonable assumption that there is no such addition to the other two peace offerings. Cautiously, however, I wish to reexamine this premise: It may well be that the main difference between the two kinds of peace offerings is only the time allotted for their eating, and that both offerings are actually accompanied by baskets of bread.

There are two main reasons to allow such a reading. The first can be derived from the structure and design of the verses; the second is based on the description of various peace offerings throughout the Torah.

Throughout this specific unit, the Torah refers to this offering as "*zevaḥ toda*" or "*zevaḥ todat shelemav.*" This name includes the word "*toda,*" meaning "thanksgiving," although some claim that the thanksgiving offering is an independent offering appended here to peace offerings.[36] However, the latter reading can be refuted by the description of the

35. In answer to the question of why one must bring matzot with the thanksgiving offering, R. Yoel Bin-Nun replies: "The matzot are for the *metzuka,* distress, that one was in, to symbolize how they cried out" (ibid. 28).

36. Similarly Milgrom (*Leviticus,* vol. 1, 413). The Mishna has other names for these offerings ("*shelamim*"; "*toda*" – see especially Nedarim 1:4; Zevaḥim 5:5–6); also Rambam. Based on this semantics, it is difficult to know that the thanksgiving offering is actually a peace offering.

bread's distribution to the priest: "This shall belong to the priest who dashed the blood of the peace offering (*shelamim*)" (Lev. 7:14) – here the offering is referred to merely as the "peace offering," with no mention of the element of thanksgiving. This general term may imply that all individual peace offerings include bread, not just "thanksgiving offerings."

Yet this cannot serve as irrefutable proof; this verse may simply be using an abbreviated form of the name "thanksgiving peace offering." There is another reason to argue that the loaves accompany all types of *shelamim* offerings. Even in *shelamim* sacrifices that are not thanksgiving offerings, we find the accompanying basket of matzot. True, the Torah explicitly testifies to this only in exceptional cases, but it is clear that we should not expect that every time a *shelamim* offering is mentioned the Torah will also mention the loaves brought with it, since they are not offered on the altar and are merely an additional detail within the laws of how the offering is brought. In exceptional places, where something distinctive is done with these loaves, they suddenly come to light.

The Peace Offerings of the Days of Consecration

One striking example of non-thanksgiving peace offerings accompanied by a basket of matzot is the ram of ordination, which is a kind of individual peace offering:

> Moses then drew close the second ram, the ram of ordination. Aaron and his sons laid their hands upon its head.... Then he took the fat, the broad tail, all the fat around the entrails, the diaphragm of the liver, and the two kidneys with their fat, as well as the right thigh. He took a loaf of unleavened bread from the basket, before the Lord, and also one loaf of oil bread, and one wafer, and placed them on the fat and on the right thigh. (Lev. 8:22–26)

The three kinds of bread that accompany this offering are clearly parallel to those offered together with the thanksgiving peace offering: "Of these he shall offer one of each kind as a gift raised up to the Lord" (7:14). Here, too, one wafer, one matza, and one loaf of bread are waved as the priest's share; on both occasions one kind of bread is "mixed with oil" and the other "wafers spread with oil."

A straightforward reading draws a parallel between the loaves of the thanksgiving offering and those of the ram of ordination, as the Tosefta explains: "The ram of ordination came with the same matzot as the thanksgiving offering: loaves, wafers, and oil loaves. Its oil was as the thanksgiving oil; it was waved as thanksgiving waved" (Tosefta Menaḥot 8:9).[37]

This is surprising: How is the ram of ordination a thanksgiving offering? One answer might be to to point out an aspect of thanksgiving in the ordination offering. Perhaps the priests are thanking God for their special status? A more likely reading, however, is that similar loaves accompany all peace offerings: "Then Moses said to Aaron and his sons: 'Cook the meat at the entrance to the Tent of Meeting and eat it there together with the bread in the basket of the ordination offering, as I have charged you'" (8:31).

This reading clarifies a further textual difficulty: The ram of ordination brought during the seven days is accompanied by a basket of matzot, but there is no mention of matzot accompanying the peace offerings brought on the eighth day of consecration. It is difficult to assume that this is an instance of brevity, because the entire sacrificial service and the priests' consumption of the various sacrifices is described in detail. If there is no mention of a basket of matzot, it presumably means that it was not brought. If the sacrifice of the ram of ordination does include a basket of matzot, why isn't one included on the eighth day?[38]

I believe that this can be explained by differentiating between the individual's peace offering, which constitutes a full meal through the addition of bread to it,[39] and a collective ceremonial peace offering, which is not eaten and therefore does not require the addition of bread.

---

37. The addition of the word "thanksgiving" ("*toda*") at the end of the sentence is according to the *Or HaGanuz* and *Minḥat HaBikkurim* there.
38. R. Baruch Kehat once suggested to me that Abarbanel's theory can be extended to all festive offerings, not just peace offerings; bread is always a must, such as the Nazirite offering and during the days of consecration. But he explains that only peace offerings with a specific purpose include a basket of matzot. (For this reason, the peace offering on the eighth day of consecration is not said to include this.)
39. As explained, for example, by Stuart: "All these represent the components of a special feast."

The Nazirite's Peace Offering

The Nazirite who has completed the full term of his vow must bring a peace offering and a basket of matzot. This can hardly be considered a thanksgiving offering.

> He shall present his offering to the Lord ... one ram without blemish for a peace offering, and a basket of unleavened bread, loaves of fine flour mixed with olive oil, and unleavened wafers smeared with olive oil, along with their grain offering and libations. The priest shall present these before the Lord and offer up his purification offering and his burnt offering. He shall then offer the ram as a sacrifice, a peace offering to the Lord, together with the basket of unleavened bread. The priest shall also offer his grain offering and his libation. (Num. 6:14–17)

Once again, three types of loaves accompany the peace offering; these loaves are clearly not a separate grain offering or libation, which is especially evident given that both grain offerings and libations are offered as well.[40] This provides further support for the idea that loaves accompany all individual peace offerings.

A careful comparison of the thanksgiving, ram of ordination, and Nazirite peace offerings shows that all include a similar combination of matzot, loaves, and wafers. The Nazirite offering, however, comes with only two kinds of matzot, according to the Mishna: "The ordination ram is accompanied by the same kinds of matza as the thanksgiving offering: loaves, wafers, and loaves poached in water; the Nazirite offering came with only two kinds of the matzot brought with the thanksgiving offering: loaves and wafers, but not with poached loaves" (Menaḥot 7:2).

Notably, even though there is an additional matzot component in the thanksgiving *shelamim* offering, in the ram of ordination, and in the nazir's *shelamim*, for some reason, the term "basket of matzot" is stated

40. Milgrom posits that the text needs to emphasize the addition of libations to the Nazirite offering because usual thanksgiving offerings do not include libations (Milgrom, *Numbers*, 48). On the issues accompanying the libations mentioned in the verse, see Ashley, *Numbers*, 146–48.

explicitly only for the ordination and for the nazir, and not for the matzot that are added to the thanksgiving *shelamim.*

I would like to suggest that the reason is that within the basket of matzot accompanying the thanksgiving *shelamim* there is also leavened bread, and therefore the entire basket cannot be called a "basket of matzot." In the ordination and in the nazir's offering, where there is no leavening but only matzot, the basket can be given a single, inclusive name: "basket of matzot."

The reason for the absence of leaven from the ordination offering is clear: The accompanying matzot were offered up on the altar, which cannot come into contact with leaven. Given the profound affinity between the Nazirite's offering and the days of consecration, it makes sense that the Nazirite's offering cannot contain any leaven as well. (An examination of this affinity goes beyond the scope of this analysis, but put briefly, at the end of his period of abstention, the Nazirite undergoes his own personal process of consecration, similar to the priestly status, for a certain period of time.)[41]

Even so, the description of the ram of ordination still hints to the thanksgiving offering's leaven bread: "Unleavened bread, and unleavened loaves" (Ex. 2:29); similarly, "Loaves of oil bread" (Lev. 8:26). These descriptions echo those of the loaves that accompany the thanksgiving peace offering: "Loaves of leavened bread" (Lev. 7:14), as a tribute to the leaven loaves that cannot be offered up on the altar.[42]

In addition to these two kinds of peace offering, a similar model of meat and bread is worth mentioning: the Passover offering.

The Passover Offering

The Passover lamb is not a peace offering but a family offering of lesser holiness that is also eaten together with matzot: "They shall eat the meat that night, roasted over a fire; with unleavened bread and bitter herbs

41. Prof. Eli Hadad once suggested to me that the consecration of the Nazirite is just before he burns his hair, and this is effectively the purpose of his consecration – to consecrate his hair.

42. I have already noted that there may be three kinds of loaves for all peace offerings, that the expression "leavened loaves" is what "oil loaves" means, and oil loaves are always leaven whether this is explicitly stated or not.

they shall eat it" (Ex. 12:8). These matzot are not counted as part of those eaten for the Festival of Matzot, but rather an obligatory accompaniment to the Passover lamb, on that first Passover and Pesaḥ Sheni as well: "With unleavened bread and bitter herbs they shall eat it" (Num. 9:11). This is not the full array of matzot, but nor is the Passover lamb a typical sacrifice. The Sages, however, justifiably perceive it as a certain form of peace offering, so perhaps the addition of matzot represents the basket of matzot that always accompanies the peace offering.[43]

This brings us back to Leviticus 7:11–34. If a basket of bread and matzot indeed always accompanies the peace offering, why isn't it explicitly mentioned with vow fulfillment or freewill peace offerings? The answer is that this follows biblical convention: The full sacrificial process is often presented in the context of the first type of the offering in question, while subsequent variations of the offering focus mainly on differences. This is already true of the first sacrifice in Leviticus 1. The burnt offering from the herd is described in full, whereas the burnt offering from the flock omits certain details, such as the laying of the hands and skinning the animal, even though all agree that these laws also apply to the burnt offering from the flock. The Torah clearly omits certain details that apply to all variations of a certain offering, as R. Haim ben Atar notes about the text's briefer description of the goat peace offering after a lengthier description of the sheep peace offering:

> ...to teach that *all the laws pertaining to the peace offerings outlined in the first section also apply to the goat peace offering,* the only reason the Torah mentions the goat peace offering separately is because of the different law of the [sheep's] fat tail. (*Or HaḤayim* on Lev. 3:12)

43. For example, Propp, *Exodus I*, 393. I am disregarding whether the Passover offering is considered a communal offering; it is eaten like an individual offering. R. Menachem Leibtag concludes that the matzot make it a kind of thanksgiving offering (Leibtag, "Passover and Thanksgiving"). This issue is irrelevant if we accept the idea that all peace offerings include matzot.

He explains that both male and female goats may be brought as peace offerings, even though this is only specified about sheep peace offerings.[44]

This biblical model also occurs elsewhere, not just in relation to the sacrificial world. One clear example is the law of the new mother's impurity:

> If a woman conceives and gives birth to a son, she shall be impure for seven days, as she is during her menstrual period. On the eighth day, the child's foreskin shall be circumcised.
> For thirty-three days she shall wait, bleeding pure blood, but until her time of purification is completed, she must not touch anything holy or enter the Sanctuary.
> If she gives birth to a daughter, she shall be impure – as she is during her menstrual period – for two weeks, and bleeds in purity for sixty-six days.
> When the days of her purification are complete, whether for a son or a daughter, she shall bring a yearling sheep as a burnt offering and a pigeon or dove as a purification offering. (Lev. 12:2–6)

The discussion of the new mother of a baby boy has two components: the duration of her impurity (forty days) and the prohibition against her coming to the Sanctuary during this time. The law of the new mother of a baby girl mentions the duration of her impurity (eighty days) but not the prohibition against coming to the Temple. The obvious conclusion is not that the mother of a daughter is allowed to come to the Temple in her impurity, but rather that the same law that applies after the birth of a son applies after the birth of a daughter.

This seems to be the case with peace offerings as well. The loaves brought with the thanksgiving offering are also presumably brought with

44. It is worth noting that this example is not strictly like those in the discussion at hand, because the possibility to offer either male or female animals is already mentioned before the distinction is made between goat and sheep (3:6), so the law obviously applies to both options. I mention this here for his broader argument.

vow fulfillment and freewill peace offerings as well; this is not repeated, because the laws are the same.[45]

This shifts the question from "Why does bread accompany the thanksgiving offering?" to "Why does bread accompany all peace offerings?" – a question that is far easier to answer. The peace offering is a covenant feast, so bread is an obvious addition, especially considering that loaves of bread are symbolically associated with covenants of peace.[46]

Moreover, the required combination of leavened and unleavened bread evokes the theme of covenant between human and God even more strongly. Leaven bread alone does not accurately reflect the nature of a peace offering. Perhaps thanksgiving or vow fulfillment marks the successful conclusion of a process, but a freewill offering may be brought as a symbol of continuing, renewed, or even the beginning of closeness with God. Nor would unleavened matza alone symbolize the covenant between human and God. Only unleavened bread may touch the altar; it is a symbol of holiness and consecration, whereas leavened bread symbolizes the human and their home, such as the bread that is brought "from your dwelling place" (Lev. 23:17) for the two-loaf offering of Shavuot. The requisite combination of both matzot and leavened bread represents the encounter between the human and the Divine that is manifest through the peace offering and its combination of earthly bread and bread of Heaven.[47]

45. This law may or may not be supported by a passage in one of the Qumran scrolls found in Cave 4 (the scroll is one of the most ancient of the Dead Sea Scrolls and is generally dated to the second century BCE), discussing that the grain offering that accompanies the peace offering must be eaten the same day (B:9–13). As shown by Eyal Regev, if this relates to the accompanying libation, it contradicts a basic halakha, given that the libation is completely burned. For this and other reasons, therefore, Regev proposes that the text is actually referring to the bread that always accompanies the peace offering (Regev, "Eating the Grain Offering").

46. As shown by Mazor, *Bread in the Bible.*

47. The *Amora'im* argue whether the thanksgiving loaves must be in the proximity of the offering's slaughter to have the same sanctity of the offering itself, or if they are still consecrated even if they are outside Jerusalem (Menaḥot 78b). It is clear that both must be actually present to create the required "feast."

THE TIME ALLOTTED FOR EATING THE PEACE OFFERING

While bringing bread therefore seems to apply to all kinds of peace offering, there is one inarguable difference: The thanksgiving offering must be eaten within a single day and night, whereas the vow fulfillment and freewill offering must be eaten within two days. (The precise definition of "two days" will be discussed below.) These different time periods offer a glimpse into the subtle difference between the nature of these two variations.

In addition to Abarbanel's aforementioned suggestion that the thanksgiving offering must be eaten within a single day to make sure that the worshipper invites a crowd to celebrate with, there are other explanations. Radatz Hoffmann comments on the general prohibition against eating offerings after the permitted time period: "*Notar*" – "What is left over."

> The reason for the prohibition against *notar* is not to compel the worshipper to include poor people... nor is it out of fear of the meat spoiling... This reason does not apply to grain offerings or the thanksgiving bread. Rather, the rationale is that one dining at God's table must not hoard, but must instead express their confidence in God by eating it all within a day and trusting that God will provide for them the next day as well.[48]

Radatz Hoffmann believes that the consumption of offerings is limited to a single day as an expression of the worshipper's and priest's complete faith in God as their Provider. This recalls the story of the manna: The Israelites would gather a single portion of manna each day as an expression of their utter belief in and dependence on God (see also Yoma 76a).[49] If so, the peace offering is anomalous in this respect, as he explains:

48. Hoffmann, *Leviticus*, vol. 1, 176.

49. Radatz Hoffmann also compares this to eating the manna; see also Propp, *Exodus I*, 397. Note that the story of the manna is also in dialogue with the Passover offering in Egypt (see further in Grossman, "Manna and Passover"). See also our discussion of the manna in the context of grain offerings.

> The only exception is the peace offering, which is brought during times of great success, and the bestowal of God's abundant blessing is expressed through this offering. For this reason, what is left over may be eaten the next day as well.

Radatz Hoffmann's premise about the difference between the two kinds of peace offering is the opposite of Abrabanel's. The former assumes that all offerings must be eaten within a day except for the vow fulfillment and freewill offerings. In contrast, the Netziv posits that the single day allowed for eating the thanksgiving offering is the exception. As paradoxical as this may seem, I believe that both readings are correct, as I will now explain.

The Time Allotted for Each Peace Offering

In order to explain the different time periods allowed for each kind of peace offering, we must first consider the concept of limiting eating to a single day. Even if Radatz Hoffmann is correct that this prevents hoarding the meat, why is the allotted time specifically until daybreak of the next day? Intriguingly, in the book of Leviticus, this time limit is only mentioned in regard to the difference between the two kinds of peace offering; there is no explicit reference to the time allotted for the eating of other offerings. The book of Exodus does state: "Do not offer the blood of My sacrifice together with anything leavened. Do not let the fat of My festive offering remain until morning" (Ex. 23:18), but even regardless of whether this alludes specifically to the Passover offering (based on a comparison to Ex. 34:25), the context refers to festival – pilgrimage – offerings. If so, why do the Sages and all halakhic authorities extend this time limit to the priestly shares of all offerings?[50]

The text's absolute silence about this time limit implies that the given time of a single day is obvious, so obvious that it only needs to be specified in the case of the peace offering that is the exception to this rule. If the priests' consumption is parallel to the altar's consumption, then the priests may only eat their portion while the altar fire still eats the

50. See Radatz Hoffmann's proofs in *Leviticus*, vol. 1, 175.

offerings of that day.[51] As soon as the ashes of the previous day's offerings are cleared away, the priests may no longer eat the meat of that day.

This idea is explored in the *Mekhilta DeRashbi* on Exodus 23:18:

> "Do not let the fat of My festive offering remain until morning" – From this we learn that the fats burned all night. We found that with holy of holies offerings, *the time of their eating is the time they burn*. Is the same true of offerings of lesser holiness? The text teaches: "Do not let the fat of My festive offerings remain until morning."

This midrash expresses the same idea from a different angle: If the time allotted for eating offerings is the time they burn, are offerings that may be eaten over two days also allowed to burn on the altar for two days? The midrash answers: No, "do not let the fat… remain until morning."

The correlation between the time permitted for eating and burning the *eimurim* upon the altar can also be formulated thus: The description of removing the ashes at the beginning of *Parashat Tzav* reverberates throughout these sacrificial chapters and defines the Sanctuary day – from the clearing of the ashes until the next morning, when the clearing of the day's ashes marks the start of the new day. Each day is a new beginning with its own new song; the remains of the previous day's sacrifices are no longer relevant.

The very first mishna alludes to this correlation in its juxtaposition of the altar fire's consumption and the priests' consumption:

> The offering of the fats and *eimurim* upon the altar – The mitzva of burning them may be performed until the dawn. All that may be eaten during that day [by the priests] may be eaten until dawn. If so, why do the Sages say [they may be eaten] until midnight? To prevent them from sinning. (Mishna Berakhot 1:1)

51. Rambam perceives the priestly eating of holy offerings as a separate mitzva from offering them (*Hilkhot Maaseh HaKorbanot* 10:1–2). See further in Wiener, *Kingdom of Priests*, 67–75. Kahan ("Berakha") discusses the relationship between Rambam's reading and the Tosefta in Berakhot 5:22, which describes two separate blessings.

According to the Torah, the *eimurim* may be burned and the priests may eat their portions until dawn, although the Sages decreed an earlier time – midnight – to prevent them from sinning.[52] Tractate Berakhot – the very first tractate of the Oral Law – shapes the laws of prayer based on the Temple day, particularly the *Shema*, to create a profound connection between prayer and the Temple service.[53] For our purposes, the Mishna's opening certainly emphasizes the connection between the altar fire's consumption of the offerings and the priests' consumption of their share.

Thus,Radatz Hoffmann's premise seems more apt than that of the Abrabanel. The main question is why vow fulfillment and freewill offerings are an exception to this rule, with two days allowed for the consumption of their meat.[54] The key to the difference seems to be that unlike most offerings, the worshipper's eating of the meat does *not* represent the continuation of the altar fire's consumption. The meat is of lesser holiness, the Israelite worshipper eats of it, and the bread and meat are a meal of companionship shared by the altar, priests, and worshipper. For this reason, there are two full days for eating its meat: The first is compatible with the altar fire's consumption of the offering's *eimurim*, whereas the second is a day of human celebration. The two days symbolize the convergence of human time and Godly time, the domain of the human and the world of the Temple.[55]

This principle is fundamental to the peace offering, which is eaten in a pure – but not holy – place; both consecrated priests and Israelites eat of it, in purity; it is not "holy of holies" and can therefore come into contact with a non-holy (but pure!) sphere. If for some reason a certain

52. According to the Tosafot, the offering may not intentionally be offered up at night in order to prevent sin, but if the priests did not have time to offer the sacrifice or eat it before midnight they may retroactively do so (on Pesaḥim 120b; see also *Beit HaLevi*, part 1, *siman* 34).

53. Safrai ("Blessings," 45) explains that the Mishnah's determination of the proper time for the recitation of the *Shema* reflects the view that this recitation is analogous to the priests' service of God in their consumption of *terumah*.

54. Indeed, to answer this anomaly we will need to ask the Netziv's question: Why doesn't this apply to the thanksgiving offering?

55. Compare to Cherlow, "Peace Offerings."

peace offering becomes consecrated, it must then be eaten within the usual sacrificial day: "If any of the meat of the ordination ram or any of the bread is left over until morning, you shall burn what remains with fire" (Ex. 29:34).

If so, however, why must the thanksgiving offering be eaten within a single day?[56] This can be answered by going back to the source of each kind of peace offering: What motivated each one? Once again, the vow fulfillment and freewill offering is born of human initiative. It is the human who makes a vow or freely brings an offering to God; it is the worshipper who initiates a religious dialogue. For this reason, they have an extra day – a day of human time – in which to eat their offering. In contrast, the thanksgiving offering is a response to a great kindness or miracle that God bestows upon the human. To offer thanksgiving in kind is not quite a legal or halakhic obligation, but it represents a profound moral obligation. Gratitude, while voluntary, is nonetheless expected from the moral, ethical person. Thus, the thanksgiving offering is a worthy response to an act of God. For this reason, the thanksgiving offering straddles the boundary between freewill and obligatory offering, and as the response to a gift from God, it must be eaten within the regular sacrificial day. I am not suggesting that thanksgiving offerings are holy of holies. They are still eaten by the Israelites who offer them up,[57] but the extra day that symbolizes human initiative is not granted to the bringer of the thanksgiving offering. The bringer of the thanksgiving offering recognizes God's hand and eats their sacrifice within God's time.[58]

---

56. Abarbanel perceives vow fulfillment offerings as a request for the future and thanksgiving offerings as a thank you after salvation, and he explains that this is why the two have different time frames: "One spends more time praying for the future than giving thanks and praise for the past" (in his introduction to Leviticus, 19).
57. R. Yehuda Copperman, however, perceives the thanksgiving offering as a fusion of holy components and those of lesser holiness (Cooperman, *Peshuto, Tzav*, 247).
58. Avraham Shammah proposed to me that this can be taken a step further: The regular workday represents a person's confidence in their own power; they make plans and are certain that everything will indeed come to pass as planned. A thanksgiving offering expresses that they have been through a crisis that teaches them that they are not in control, but that everything is in God's hands – like saying, "Please God" when discussing the future.

If so, the two days allotted for eating the vow fulfillment or freewill peace offering are not one unit of time but rather two separate "days." This is subtly reflected in the language of the verse:

> If the sacrifice is to fulfill a vow, however, or is a freewill offering, it shall be eaten on the day when one offers the sacrifice, while *what is left over may be eaten the next day*. Whatever of the flesh of the sacrifice is left over on the third day shall be burned with fire. (Lev. 7:16–18)

The clause "What is left over may be eaten," the usually prohibited *notar*, is strange. If there are two days in which to eat the offering, then why is the meat that has not been eaten by the end of the first day considered "left over"? The phrase "left over" implies that the meat was not eaten within the expected time, but in this case there were two days allowed for eating in the first place. Usually "what is left over" must be burned, as is any meat that remains of the peace offering on the third day: "What is left over on the third day shall be burned with fire."

This oddity is reflected in the Septuagint, which omits the phrase "left over" in relation to the second day: "When you offer a peace offering to the Lord of your own free will, it may be eaten on that day and the next day, and what is left over on the third day shall be burned with fire."[59]

Ramban notes this surprising phrase and explains that it conveys that there is no obligation to intentionally save meat for the second day – in fact, it is forbidden to save it all for the second day – and therefore, what remains on the second day is still considered "left over."[60]

This curious phrase is easily illuminated through the reading that the time period allowed for eating the peace offering is in fact one day plus a bonus day. If these two days were one continuous time period, the phrase "what is left over on the second day" would indeed be problematic. If, however, the time period is actually one Godly day followed by

59. Milgrom, *Leviticus*, vol. 1, 420.
60. Compare to Rabbeinu Bahya on Leviticus 19: "It is a mitzva to eat it on the first day, and what is left over may be eaten on the next day." This is based on the *Sifra*, *Tzav*, 12:11.

an extra human day – one Sanctuary day that ends with dawn, followed by a day of human celebration – then what is not eaten within the regular time period allowed for most sacrifices can be considered "what is left over." In fact, it is more significant to perceive the offering through this lens, because it expresses that the second day is an extra day, granted for the human perspective and initiative that motivated these offerings.

If so, there is room to consider the halakhic differences between how the meat is eaten on each day. The only hint to this difference in the biblical text is "what is left over," but the Sages develop this further.

The Two Days of the Peace Offering and the Sacrificial Day

The Sages interpret the two days allowed for eating the vow fulfillment and freewill peace offering in the unexpected form of "a day and night, and day," or, in the words of the Mishna, as "two days and one night" (Zevaḥim 5:7). How do the Sages reach this conclusion? The language of the verse does not imply that the second day ends at nightfall instead of the usual dawn of the following day.[61]

Whether or not this is based on the text, it is worth pointing out that the Midrash Halakha seems to integrate two different definitions of "day" – the Temple day and the regular definition of the full rotation of the earth with respect to the sun. The Temple day begins at daybreak with the clearing of the ashes,[62] but the regular Hebrew day outside the Temple starts at nightfall and ends when the sun sets the following day. For example, Shabbat and the festivals all begin at sundown and end when the stars come out the following day. In light of this distinction, R. Samson Raphael Hirsch proposes reading the time allotted for eating the peace offering as a fusion of these two paradigms: The first "day" ends when the Temple day ends at daybreak, and the second "day" – the extra day granted in honor of human initiative – ends at nightfall, when

61. Binyamin Frankel pointed out to me that this possibility is present in Tosafot on Pesaḥim 71b, about the issue of eating the festival offering of the fourteenth of Nisan.
62. For the spiritual significance of this division, see R. Tzadok HaKohen of Lublin, *Tzidkat HaTzaddik*, 3.

the regular working day ends.[63] This is a perfect reflection of the nature of the peace offering, as R. Yuval Cherlow indicates:

> The allotted time marries two distinct concepts: the day and night of the Sanctuary, and the night and day of the regular workday. Because of the connection between the workday and the Sanctuary day that is the heart of the peace offering, the time allotted for its eating combines the laws of the holy and the mundane together.[64]

It thus emerges that the first "day" retains the nature of the Sanctuary day and the second "day" the regular workday that ends at nightfall. This complex idea invites a closer look: Is this distinction indeed reflected in the biblical text? We will explore this through various sources that touch upon this issue.[65]

The New Day Begins at Daybreak

Some biblical passages imply that the day begins at daybreak:[66]

1. Leviticus 7:15–16: When defining what part of the peace offering is "left over": "The flesh of the peace sacrifice of thanksgiving shall be eaten on the day it is offered; you may not leave any of it to the morning." This implies that the transition occurs at daybreak and not nightfall.
2. Genesis 19:33–34: "That night they gave their father wine to drink. Then the elder daughter went in and slept with him. He was

---

63. Hirsch, *Leviticus*, 121.
64. Cherlow, "Peace Offerings," 10–18.
65. McGuire explores this throughout Tanakh and concludes that both perspectives are present ("Evening or Morning").
66. Meir Rotenberg suggests that the biblical expression "*kayom*" – "today" – means "first." For example, when Jacob says to Esau: "Sell me *kayom* your birthright" (Gen. 25:31), he means: "I will give you this stew if you *first* sell me your birthright." Rotenberg gives further examples and claims that this meaning is borrowed from the world of time, where day comes first, before nightfall. This is arguable, but certainly supports the idea that daylight comes first and a new day begins with new daylight. Rotenberg, "Kayom," 60; see Talshir's response in "Comment"; also Dotan, "Kayom."

unaware when she lay down and when she arose. The next day, the elder said to the younger…" Here, too, the "next day" seems to refer to the morning after.

3. Numbers 9:11–12: "They shall offer it in the afternoon of the fourteenth day of the second month; then shall they eat it with unleavened bread and bitter herbs. They shall not leave any of it over until morning, nor shall they break any of its bones." Given that the Passover offering must be eaten within that same day – that is, from the afternoon of its slaughter and all night long "until morning" – the "day" here follows the Temple day, which ends at daybreak.
4. Numbers 33:3: "They set out from Ramesses on the fifteenth day of the first month. On the day after the Passover the Israelites went out defiantly, before all the Egyptians' eyes, while the Egyptians were burying their firstborns." Here, too, the new day ("the fifteenth day") seems to begin at daybreak, the morning after the devastation that strikes Egypt at midnight.
5. I Samuel 19:11: "Saul sent messengers to David's house to keep watch over him so that they could kill him in the morning. Michal, David's wife, told him, 'If you do not run for your life tonight, tomorrow you will be killed.'" If David does not flee that night, the next day – "tomorrow" – Saul will kill him.

The New Day Begins at Nightfall

Other passages imply that the new day begins when daylight ends:

1. Leviticus 22:6–7: "The one who touches these things shall be impure until the evening, and shall not eat of the sacred offerings until he has washed his body in water. When the sun sets, he shall become pure again and may eat of the sacred offerings, for they are his food." Assuming that a day is a set time period, so if a person becomes impure they are impure all that day, this impurity passes with sunset – which implies that a new day then begins. (As mentioned, the priests begin eating their *terumot* when the stars come out – Mishna Berakhot 1:1.)

2. Exodus 12:18: "From the fourteenth day of the first month in the evening until the twenty-first day of the month in the evening, you may eat only unleavened bread." The Festival of Matzot begins at nightfall and ends seven days later, again with nightfall. This is perhaps less convincing, given that the exodus from Egypt takes place at night and thus reverses the natural order, so commemoration of this day does not prove that this is the default transition between days.[67]
3. Leviticus 23:32: "It is a Sabbath of complete rest for you, and you shall afflict yourselves from the evening of the ninth day of the month: from evening to evening shall you observe your Sabbath." Here, too, Yom Kippur is from evening to evening; perhaps the definition of this evening as "the ninth day of the month" and not the tenth shows that this is the exception, not the rule, but ultimately, the Torah defines Yom Kippur as a day that begins at night.[68]
4. Exodus 16:6–8: "So Moses and Aaron told all the Israelites, 'At evening you will know that it was the Lord who brought you out of Egypt, and by morning you shall see the Lord's glory.... In the evening, the Lord will give you meat to eat, and in the morning bread to fill you, for He has heard you railing against Him." Here, the evening comes before the morning, which may reflect their perception of the passing of time. Alternatively, however, this may support the idea that morning marks the new day; a double portion of manna falls on the sixth morning.
5. Nehemiah 13:19: "Then, when the shadows darkened the gates of Jerusalem before the Sabbath, I ordered the doors shut, declaring that they should not be opened until after the Sabbath. And I stationed some of my men at the gates so that no loads could be

67. As claimed by Milgrom, *Leviticus*, vol. 3, 1967.
68. This verse in itself contains tension between whether the day begins at nightfall or dawn; because Yom Kippur is inherently connected to the Temple, there is a possibility that it will follow the Temple day. (See further in Grossman, "The Atonement of the Tabernacle.")

> brought in on the Sabbath." In this description, the lengthening shadows of dusk marks the beginning of Shabbat.

There are conflicting descriptions of when the new day begins throughout Tanakh. Even the seemingly obvious primordial verses of Creation are not as straightforward as they first appear:

> When God began creating heaven and earth, the earth was void and desolate, there was darkness...
> God said, "Let there be light." And there was light...
> And God called the light "day," and the darkness He called "night."
> There was evening, and there was morning – one day. (Gen. 1:1–5)

From the very beginning, time starts with darkness – evening – and shifts to light – daytime – and this is the biblical day; this is the Sages' perception (e.g., Berakhot 2a, 26a). Yet Rashbam proposes that verse 5 is not a summary, but a description of the passage of time – how the first day came to an end and the second day began:

> "There was evening and there was morning" – The Torah does not state, "There was night and then day," but rather "evening" – that the first day turned into evening when the light grew dark... and then the second day began.... The text does not mean that evening and morning are one day... rather that one day ended and the second day began. (Rashbam on Gen. 1:5)

According to this reading, the verse is a continuous description of God's continuous creation during the first six days: After God calls the light "day" and the darkness "night," the day darkens, and when the new morning comes, the first day is complete – that is, the biblical "day" is the daytime followed by the night. God works for six days. He works during the day, but each night He waits for the new day to break before continuing His acts of creation. This characterization is important, given that humans must strive to emulate God and His ways; they too must work during the day, rest at night,[69] and refrain from work the entire seventh day.

The Darkness of Night

A third approach is capable of solving the ambiguity that confuses any attempt to define the biblical day: The night does not mark the beginning or end of the day; rather, it does not count as part of the day at all. To grasp this idea, let us return to Rashbam's reading of the opening lines of Genesis.

In the account of Creation, God is not active at night, like the humans of the ancient world. Creation occurs during daylight; during the night, it seems that God waits for the dawn to break before continuing His acts of creation.[70]

If so, God's revelation in Egypt "at midnight" transcends the law of nature and reality. In the ancient world, when light sources were not readily obtainable or even available, the dark of night was a time of silence and inactivity. This was sometimes used to an advantage, as Abraham does when he overpowers the four kings at night (Gen. 14:15), the first of various biblical heroes who exploit the dark of night to ambush the enemy.[71]

The onset of Shabbat in the evening is anomalous but logical: Shabbat begins at dusk when the day's work comes to an end; the sanctity of Shabbat bursts out at the moment rest begins. The "Shabbat day," however, begins the next morning and has its own special holiness. Accordingly, Kiddush is recited both night and day, sanctifying each part of Shabbat.[72]

---

69. See further in Grossman, *Creation*, 51–69.
70. A similar model can be found in the Hebrew calendar: The "first month" is Nisan, the spring, and the year seems to end with the "seventh month," Tishrei, with autumn. There is no biblical mention of festivals that take place during the eighth to twelfth months; there is almost a kind of winter hibernation, which indeed reflects the agricultural year. (Compare Granot, *Sukkot*, 43–44.) The biblical text pays little regard to times of inactivity – both night and winter.
71. See Ben-Shem, "Nocturnal Warfare," 362–64.
72. In a certain sense, the Shabbat model occurs elsewhere: When something happens at night, it is worth considering whether this already began at the end of the previous day.

How is this significant in regard to the time allotted for eating the peace offering? We should read the verse again with the premise that night is a time of inactivity: "If the sacrifice is to fulfill a vow, however, or is a freewill offering, it shall be eaten on the *day* when one offers the sacrifice, while what is left over may be eaten the next *day*. Whatever of the flesh of the sacrifice is left over on the third *day* shall be burned with fire" (7:16–18). There is no mention of eating the peace offering during the night; the dark ancient night was a time for resting, not feasting. Thus, the halakha is unclear: May one eat after nightfall on the second day, before the dawn of the third day breaks?

The Sages fill in the biblical silence and rule that the peace offering may be eaten after the first day, but not after the second day, even though any leftovers from the second day will only be burned on the morning of the third day. The Torah intentionally overlooks the nights; this reflects a religious and pragmatic rhythm of active days and quiet nights.

This has dramatic significance for other offerings, which, as stated, are eaten by the priests on the day they are offered up and the following night. The law of the burnt offering focuses on the clearing of the ashes, which is not done at the end of the day but rather on the following morning, after the evening burnt offering has been burning away all night long. This marks the difference between the human world and the Temple world: Divine revelation never ceases, and the altar is active all day and all night.[73] In contrast, the regular human world bustles with activity during the day but rests at night.

All "holy of holies" offerings may be eaten at night as well, but the peace offering that is related to the altar from a human perspective is not eaten on the second night. It may be eaten on the first night, in parallel to the altar's consumption, but the eating permitted on the second day takes place in human time and therefore ends when the sun sets on the human workday.

---

73. Yet the offering itself must be brought during the day, during the human working day; see Rambam, *Hilkhot Maaseh HaKorbanot* 4:1.

The Third Day: The Law of *Piggul*

What is left over on the third day is forbidden. The law of *notar*, of what must be done with the "leftover" sacrificial meat, relates to all offerings that must be eaten within a certain time, but it is applied here for the first time, because regular Israelites are more likely to make mistakes than the priests, who are used to eating offerings. Moreover, although this applies to all offerings, we will soon see that essentially, for the peace offering the third day poses more of a threat than does the forbidden "second day" for all other offerings:

> If any of the flesh of the peace sacrifice is eaten on the third day, it shall not be accepted, nor shall it be credited to the one who offered it. It is *offensive* (*piggul*), and anyone who eats of it is liable to punishment. (Lev. 7:18)

It emerges that if the remains are eaten on the third day, then not only is the offender subject to punishment, but the entire offering is retroactively invalidated – "it shall not be accepted," and the worshipper must bring a new offering.[74]

What is the meaning of the term "*piggul*"? Some explain it as "desecrated," or "the opposite of holiness."[75] While these definitions certainly make sense in context, the word's appearance in other places points to a different meaning. The term "*piggul*" appears twice elsewhere. Ezekiel is commanded to eat bread baked over human excrement as a symbolic act:

> "You will eat it as though it were a barley cake, and you will bake it over dung – human excrement – before their eyes." And the Lord said: "This is how the children of Israel will eat their bread, impure, among the nations that I will banish them to." And I said, "Ah, my Lord God! Never before has my throat been defiled; I have never eaten flesh from a carcass or mauled animal even as

74. The Sages rightly understand the phrase "*lo yeiratzeh*" as referring to the offering and not the worshipper, for there is no indirect object after the verb; thus, this presumably refers to the offering itself (compare Milgrom, *Leviticus*, vol. 1, 421).
75. Wright, *The Disposal of Impurity*.

> a youth, never until now, and *piggul* meat has never entered my mouth." (Ezek. 4:12–14)

The prophet objects to the revolting food he has just been commanded to eat, protesting that he has never eaten impure food, including "*piggul* meat."

The prophet Isaiah speaks on God's behalf against the people:

> The people anger Me, always there before Me sacrificing in gardens, burning incense on the slabs, sitting among the graves and passing the nights in caverns, eating the meat of pigs and filling their bowls with a broth of *foulness* (*piggul*). (Is. 65:3–4)

These prophecies both imply that "*piggul*" means something foul or repulsive. This points to an etymological connection between the biblical word "*piggul*" and the Arabic word "*pagala*," meaning "rotten," as suggested by Gesenius and many other translators who used various terms expressing revulsion and disgust.[76]

Why is the leftover meat considered so repulsive after the permitted time for eating, and why is this disgust emphasized in relation to the peace offering in particular? The most straightforward explanation may be a technical one: In the ancient world, after three days without refrigeration, meat began to decay. Rotten meat is certainly antithetical to the idea of holiness. The natural aversion to rotten meat explains the use of the term "*piggul*" beyond the mere technical, halakhic reservation. Moreover, it is most appropriate in relation to the peace offering: While most offerings are already forbidden by the second day, when the meat is still edible, the vow fulfillment and freewill peace offering is only forbidden on the third day, when the meat is no longer appetizing, so the term "*piggul*" is most apt.[77]

---

76. See a summary of various views in Kellerman, "Piggul," 468–69.
77. Hadad, "Piggul," 117. Therefore there is no need to adopt Milgrom's reading that there is no fear of eating *piggul* in the Sanctuary because the offerings were eaten in the courtyard under the priests' scrutiny (Milgrom, *Leviticus*, vol. 1, 419). The warning is stated in regard to eating vow fulfillment and freewill offerings on the third day, whereas thanksgiving offerings are forbidden on the second day.

The biggest challenge is how to understand why an offering eaten past its permitted time is invalidated retroactively. The Sages, troubled by this idea, suggest that the term "*piggul*" does not actually apply to an instance in which a person eats the offering on the third day, but to the priest's problematic intentions when he offers up the offering. As Rashi explains:

> "If any of the flesh is eaten" – The text refers to the thought of eating it on the third day. For how can it be that if one eats of it on the third day it will be retroactively forbidden? Rather, the text says: "Nor shall it be credited to the *one who offered it*" – meaning, it can only be invalidated while offering it, but not on the third day. This means that if one merely thinks about [eating the offering past its time] while offering the sacrifice, it then becomes *piggul*. (Rashi on Lev. 7:18)

According to the Sages, if the priest or worshipper thinks about eating the offering past the permitted time during one of the four main sacrificial stages (slaughter, collecting the blood, bringing the blood to the altar, dashing the blood), it becomes *piggul*. This is a bold reading, which simultaneously presents a significant stringency (forbidden thoughts have potent implications) and an equally significant leniency (in contrast to what is stated in the text, actually eating from the offering on the third day does *not* invalidate it!).

Endless ink has been spilled in the attempt to reconcile the biblical text with this reading,[78] whose main objective is evident in Rashi's explanation: "For how can it be that if one eats of it on the third day it will be retroactively forbidden?" Halakhic thought is averse to retroactive invalidation, especially in the sacrificial world. Because retroactive invalidation renders the dashing of the blood and the burning of the *eimurim* utterly superfluous, it is thus best to keep it to the absolute minimum. Rashi therefore does his best to reconcile the Sages' reading with the biblical text: "This means that if one merely thinks about

78. See, for example, R. Samson Raphael Hirsch on Lev. 7:18; Hoffmann, *Leviticus*, vol. 1, 176–77.

[eating the offering past its time] while offering the sacrifice, it then becomes *piggul*." Other exegetes, however, explicitly state that the Sages' reading deviates from *peshat*. Rashbam, for example, writes: "The Sages deviate from the *peshat* by explaining that *piggul* means thinking about eating the offering on the third day during one of the four main acts of the sacrificial service."[79]

It makes sense that the Sages attempt to reinterpret the biblical text: How is it logical to invalidate an offering three days after its blood is dashed and its fats are sent up as smoke upon the altar? While the four main sacrificial acts constitute the main fulfillment of the offering in the first sacrificial list, eating is a crucial part of the sacrificial process in the second list in *Parashat Tzav*. Not merely the aftermath of the sacrificial process, eating the offering is the culmination of the process itself.

The second sacrificial list opens with the altar's consumption of the burnt offering ("He shall lift the ashes of the burnt offering that the fire *consumed* on the altar – 6:3). The burnt offering is the ultimate offering, entirely consumed by the altar itself. Thereafter, the offerings are eaten by the priests (or the Israelite worshippers) as an integral part of the sacrificial process – whose purpose is to perpetuate the Divine Presence within the Sanctuary.

Thus, the eating of the offering is not something that takes place after the completion of the sacrificial process; it is the culmination of the process itself. Incorrect eating of the offering is tantamount to dashing the blood incorrectly. If the blood is dashed incorrectly, the acts of slaughtering and collecting the blood are retroactively meaningless.

---

79. Compare to Shadal, who claims that it is extreme leniency to think that if someone eats of the sacrifice within the permitted time it is retroactively a sin if the meat is then eaten on the third day; the Torah means that the offering is invalid and must be offered again. Yet Shadal's reading is prevalent among *Rishonim*. Ibn Ezra, for example, asks how something that rose up in a sweet savor to the Lord can then be considered invalid, and answers that *piggul* desecrates what is holy, so it cannot count as vow fulfillment and it is as if he has failed to fulfill his vow. R. Amnon Bazak convincingly suggests that the Sages' emphasis on the power of thought and intention is part of the objective to shift the gravity of the sacrificial world to intentions rather than actions in a post-sacrificial world (Bazak, "Piggul").

According to *Parashat Tzav*, the same is true if the offering is eaten after the permitted time.

Yet the question remains: Why is this law specified in the context of the peace offering? Symbolically, it is the peace offering that challenges the proper boundaries of sacrificial time: The layperson's participation in the consumption of sacrifices – even those of lesser holiness – threatens the balance of holiness. The worshipper is already allotted an extra day to eat the peace offering; to upset the delicate balance between the mundane and the divine world by eating the leftover meat on the third day must be prevented by emphasis on the threat of *piggul*. The layperson is allowed to participate, but they must be keenly aware of their proper place. To eat the leftover meat on the third day is the profane's violation of the sacred; it is the human's improper appropriation of the Divine. It causes the whole system to collapse, which of course invalidates the offering.

EATING IN PURITY (7:19–21)

After the time frame for eating the peace offering is laid out, the Torah presents the laws of its eating – or, to be more precise, the required state of purity for everyone who comes into contact with this offering. While purity is mandatory in relation to all offerings, once again it is no coincidence that these laws are presented in the context of the peace offering,[80] which is eaten outside the Sanctuary itself (7:19–21):

- Flesh that touches any impure thing shall not be eaten; it shall be burned with fire.
- As for other flesh, any ritually pure person may eat it, but one who eats the flesh of a peace sacrifice to the Lord in a state

80. This is the example brought in the *Baraita DeRabbi Yishmael* (the thirteen principles of interpreting the Torah): "When a particular case, already included in the general statement, is expressly mentioned to teach something new, that special provision applies to all other cases included in the general statement." Because the peace offering is included as part of all offerings, the law governing it applies to all offerings. The Talmud and its exegetes (e.g., R. Meir Abulafia – Ramah) perceive that this verse is superfluous, as the law is taught elsewhere (Lev. 22:3).

> of impurity shall be severed from his people. When anyone touches any impure thing – human impurity, or an impure animal, or any impure, detested creature – and then eats flesh from the Lord's peace sacrifice, that person shall be severed from his people.

This section presents two different focal points: subject and object – "*ḥeftza*" and "*gavra*" in talmudic terms. The first statement is that impure flesh may not be eaten and must be burned with fire; the second is that only a person in a state of purity may eat the meat of the peace offering.[81] Both statements anaphorically open with the word "flesh" (*basar*), which simultaneously underscores their differences and similarities.[82]

The second statement presents a causal connection: *If* someone touches the meat in a state of impurity, *then* they will be punished. Given that there are two separate offenses (eating impure sacrificial meat and eating sacrificial meat while impure), we might expect two separate penalties:

> One (*nefesh*) who eats the flesh of a peace sacrifice to the Lord in a state of impurity shall be severed from his people.
>
> One (*nefesh*) who touches any impure thing – human impurity, or an impure animal, or any impure, detested creature – and then eats flesh from the Lord's peace sacrifice, that person shall be severed from his people.

What is the relationship between these two sentences? The second clearly focuses on the person who becomes impure and then eats sacrificial meat, but does the first focus on the person or the flesh? What does "in a state of impurity" refer to, the flesh or the person?

---

81. Nonetheless, for some reason the Sages do not regard the second as a warning against eating sacred meat, even though that is the plain meaning of the verse. See Rashi; see also Pesaḥim 24b.

82. Some Sages link the prohibitions on impure meat with the prohibitions on human impurity, stating that if one kind is, for some reason, canceled out, then the second is also automatically canceled out as well (Pesaḥim 79a; 95b).

Commentators generally agree that the punishment of *karet* is imposed on someone who eats sacrificial flesh in a state of impurity, not to someone who eats impure sacrificial flesh. The phrase "in a state of impurity" is more appropriate for a person than an object, especially in light of a parallel verse that forbids priests to work "in a state of impurity" (Lev. 22:3).[83]

If so, however, why is the punishment of *karet* for one who eats the peace offering in a state of impurity repeated twice in succession? A careful comparison of the two sentences reveals a subtle difference:

One (*nefesh*)	**One** (*nefesh*)
who eats the flesh of a peace sacrifice to the Lord in a state of impurity	who touches any impure thing – human impurity, or an impure animal, or any impure, detested creature – and then eats flesh from the Lord's peace sacrifice,
that person shall be severed from his people.	that person shall be severed from his people.

The components are in slightly different order, but both verses describe someone who eats the peace offering when in a state of impurity, and the punishment is identical in both cases.[84] The difference is that the first kind of impurity seems to refer to someone in a state of bodily impurity such as *zav* or *metzora* (see Ibn Ezra) whereas the second verse lists different kinds of impurity that comes from contact with something impure. From a halakhic perspective, the source of impurity seems immaterial, but from a biblical perspective, there is a substantial difference between different kinds of impurity, some of which are considered more severe than others. Thus, there is need to point out that both kinds of impurity prevent the worshipper from eating the peace offering, for they will be punished with *karet* if they do so. The *Sifra* seems to note this as well and includes all different kinds of severe impurities:

83. Compare Lev. 5:3; 15:24.

84. For a survey of various understandings of this punishment (by divine or human hand), see Hartley, *Leviticus*, 100.

"Impurity from the dead and from one who lies with a *nidda* and everything that contaminates someone – from where? From the verse 'any impure thing'" (*Sifra, Tzav*, 9:2).

This raises the question of whether there is such a thing as lesser impurity that does not result in such a harsh punishment. The list of impurities includes one who touches an impure animal or carcass, but what about someone who touches the carcass of a pure animal that may be eaten? Ramban noted its absence from the list but rules that even one who touches a pure carcass and then eats from the peace offering is punished by *karet* (see Ramban on Lev. 7:21). However, it is possible to argue that certain omissions are not merely for the sake of brevity in the text, but that people who have a lesser degree of impurity and then eat of the peace offering deserve a less severe punishment.

Moreover, the question remains unresolved: Why does the Torah devote so much space to how a person becomes impure, but fail to discuss the punishment of one who eats of a peace offering that has become impure? It is certainly possible that the punishment is much less severe. After all, one who eats the peace offering when in a state of impurity makes the holy meat impure as well, which is especially severe, whereas one who eats meat that has already been contaminated is not actually desecrating their sanctity.

Milgrom takes this a step further and sees the lack of punishment for eating the contaminated flesh of the peace offering as part of the unique biblical perspective of animal impurity:

> The implication is fundamental. Contrary to the rule in the pagan world, Israel holds that impure animals – even if they are brought into contact with sancta (e.g., by being sacrificed) – offer no threat to society. Danger resides in impurity only if it emanates from the human being.[85]

Milgrom's position requires analysis that is beyond the scope of this discussion. If, however, we accept it as a premise, it is clear why there is no punishment for eating the meat of a peace offering that has been

85. Milgrom, *Leviticus*, vol. 1, 426.

tainted with impurity: It is not considered severe from a biblical perspective, nowhere near as severe as an impure person who eats of the peace offering. The latter is punishable with *karet*; according to the Sages, the former receives only lashes (Tosefta Zevaḥim 5:6).

Until now, the discussion has been based on the accepted premise that both statements of punishment apply to the impure person. But can they be paired with the two different offenses instead? This would mean that the phrase "in a state of impurity" (7:20) applies to the meat, not the person, with two punishments corresponding to two offenses.[86] If so, then the Torah does not differentiate between different ways in which a person becomes impure (bodily impurity and contact impurity, as suggested above); rather, the distinction is more basic – between eating impure meat and an impure person eating meat.

If so, this emphasizes the repetition of the phrase "and the flesh" in verse 19. The meaning of this phrase at the beginning of the second half is not clear; the verse reads more easily without it. (It is indeed omitted in the Septuagint, *Peshitta,* and Vulgate translations.) This omission, however, fails to emphasize that the prohibition against impurity applies to both *ḥeftza* and *gavra,* both object and subject: The offering must be eaten in purity, and only when it is pure. And just as there are two focal points of prohibition, both are punished by *karet*. Even so, given that there is no basis for this reading in traditional exegesis, it remains with a question mark.

There is room to debate whether there is special significance to the fact that the punishment applies only to *eating* the peace offering in impurity and not to touching it. Merely touching the offering while in a state of impurity is also forbidden, as is learned from a parallel passage:

> Tell Aaron and his sons to take great care with the sacred offerings that the Israelites consecrate to Me, so that they do not profane My holy name: I am the Lord. Tell them: If any descendant of yours throughout the generations comes near the sacred offerings

86. This can arguably be supported by the masculine language, which is more easily applicable to the masculine word "flesh" than the feminine word "*nefesh*." However, it seems that the word "*nefesh*" is sometimes masculine and sometimes feminine.

> that the Israelites have consecrated to the Lord while in an impure state, he shall be severed from My presence. (Lev. 22:2–3)

Parashat Tzav generally focuses on eating, but these laws presumably apply to any contact with holy offerings.

Why is there emphasis on purity laws in the context of the peace offering in particular, when they clearly apply to all offerings, and priests are punished equally for contact with any offering while in a state of impurity? The answer comes as no surprise: The priests are familiar with the stringencies that are an integral part of the sacrificial world, but the common Israelite is not. The law is addressed to the Israelite, even though the priest receives his own share of the peace offering at the same time. This recalls how in the book of Samuel, Samuel makes sure that Yishai and his family purify themselves before they eat of the sacrifice: "'I have come to sacrifice to the Lord. Sanctify yourselves and come with me to the sacrifice.' Then he sanctified Yishai and his sons and summoned them to the sacrifice" (I Sam. 16:5).[87]

Between the lines, however, we realize something even more important. Where do the Israelite worshippers eat their peace offering? It turns out that the requirement to eat the offering "in purity," "in a pure place" (not "a holy place"!), is repeated again and again because the worshipper is allowed to eat the offering in their own home! A "holy place" refers to the Sanctuary or Temple, but a "pure place" may refer to anywhere where there is no impurity. The Sages read the verses similarly and allow the worshipper to eat the offering anywhere in Jerusalem (but not outside that city). The holiness of the camp during Israel's years in the wilderness is transferred to the entire city of Jerusalem during the Temple period. This is evident in various halakhot (such as sending impure people outside the "camp"). Jerusalem symbolizes the camp where the Divine Presence rests.[88]

Proof that the peace offering may be eaten in one's own home is found in the book of Proverbs – ironically, in the temptress's attempt to lure the

87. Samuel's words, "He said, 'Peace. I have come to sacrifice,'" echo the full name of the peace offering, "*zevaḥ shelamim*."
88. This idea is already discussed in the context of biblical impurity; see especially Rambam, *Hilkhot Beit HaBeḥira* 7:11.

young man into her home to lie with her: "I owed a sacrificial peace offering; today I fulfilled my vow. That is why I went out toward you, to search for you, and I found you!" (Prov. 7:10–15). The wanton woman appeals to the young man to enter her home. Why does she refer to a peace offering in her attempt to seduce him? Rashi explains that she has prepared a feast in honor of the day's event: "A feast that I have prepared, for today I sacrificed a vow fulfillment peace offering." Ralbag's reading is even more straightforward: "I have my peace offering here, for today I fulfilled my vow in the Temple and I have a lot of that meat in my house."[89] While a harlot is hardly a role model, her seduction attempt reflects a certain reality; it emerges that the meat of peace offerings was eaten at home.

This has tremendous implications for the religious experience of the peace offering. A person makes a pilgrimage to the Temple and brings back the meat of his sacrifice and loaves of bread to feast with his family and friends, a celebration for his whole neighborhood. God's table reaches far beyond the boundaries of the Sanctuary, with a place set for anyone pure who seeks Him out.

THE PROHIBITION AGAINST SUET

After discussing the prohibition against eating the peace offering when impure, the Torah addresses another prohibition that applies to all offerings, but must be emphasized for the Israelites who have less experience with eating offerings:

> The Lord spoke to Moses:
> Tell the Israelites: Do not eat the suet of any ox, sheep, or goat. The suet of one of these that died naturally or was killed by another animal may be put to other use, but you may not eat it. For anyone who eats the suet of an animal of which a fire offering could be offered to the Lord – he is severed from his people. Do not eat any blood, whether that of a bird or of an animal, in any of your dwellings.

89. The language of this verse contains strong irony that contrasts how she is attempting to seduce the young man with the sanctity of offering sacrifices in the Sanctuary (see Prov. 7:11).

> Anyone who eats any blood shall be cut off from his people." (Lev. 7:23–27)

The double opening ("The Lord spoke to Moses: Tell the Israelites:") teaches that this was conveyed to Moses at one point in time and incorporated here in the context of the peace offering. One of the most burning questions based on these verses is whether suet (a particular kind of fat) is always forbidden whenever eating meat – for every animal that could potentially become an offering – or if this prohibition applies only to animals that have actually been designated as offerings.

The Sages explain that the suet of any animal is prohibited, because it inherently belongs to the altar.[90] Suet represents the world of holiness, so even when the animal is not consecrated as an offering, its suet may not be eaten.[91] This is indeed implied by the language: "Do not eat the suet of any ox, sheep, or goat." Moreover, this prohibition is juxtaposed with the prohibition against eating blood, which applies to any blood from any animal.

Nonetheless, Ibn Ezra boldly sketches out a different reading of these verses, arguing that the suet is forbidden only from animals that are offered up as sacrifices. His main proof is that the verb provides a reason for this prohibition: "For anyone who eats the suet of an animal *of which a fire offering could be offered to the Lord.*" Only suet from an animal designated as a fire offering is prohibited, whereas the suet from regular animals is not. He explains:

---

90. I adopt the obvious premise that this applies only to animals that are mentioned as sacrifices in the Torah (from the herd, flock, and birds). Resh Lakish has a surprising opinion that other, non-kosher, animals may also be sacrificed (Zevaḥim 34a). This surprising opinion has sparked many a debate (see *Lekaḥ Tov*, rule 4), and the discussion goes beyond the scope of this book.
91. The connection between ritual slaughter of offerings and non-offerings is clear: Even though the Torah does not specify that all animals must be ritually slaughtered to make them kosher for eating, the Sages clearly rule that they must. Ramban, for example, derives this from the laws of ritual slaughter (see his commentary on Deut. 12:21). Others suggest that the laws of ritual slaughter are not derived from sacrificial law; see, e.g., Garti, "Halakhic Aspects," 159–68, who concludes that there are two aspects to the ritual slaughter of regular meat.

> A Sadducee once came to me and asked: "Does the Torah prohibit the fat tail?" I answered that it is true that the fat tail is called "fat" (*ḥelev*), for the Torah states: "The fat thereof, the fat tail entire." However, while our Sages prohibited all fat, they permitted the fat tail. The Sadducee then replied: "Does not the Torah prohibit all fat? Indeed it is written, 'You shall eat neither fat nor blood' (Lev. 3:17). The latter is preceded by Scripture's statement, 'It shall be a perpetual statute throughout your generations.'" *I once again answered him that this verse relates to the peace offering….* He, on his part, replied: "You shall eat no fat, of ox, or sheep, or goat." *I again answered that this verse too refers to a peace offering….* This section was written in order to explain *the punishment incurred by one who eats the fat of sacred flesh.* The verse relating to "any blood" (7:27) was similarly written to add that the blood of fowl is prohibited. The fat of fowl is therefore permitted…. The Sadducee's eyes opened and he uttered an oath to the effect that he will never rely on his judgment when it comes to explaining the commandments. He will rely only on the tradition transmitted by the Pharisees. (Ibn Ezra on Lev. 7:20)

Ibn Ezra's story is surprising. He rejects the Sadducee's claim that it is forbidden to eat the fat tail by proving that only consecrated suet is forbidden, not that of regular meat.[92] Though this contradicts the Sages' ruling, he still persuades the Sadducee to adhere to the Sages' tradition of Torah interpretation.

Ibn Ezra bases his proof on the law in Deuteronomy:

> Whenever you desire, you may slaughter and eat meat in any of your towns, according to the blessing that the Lord your God gives you. People both impure and pure may eat of it, as they would of gazelle or of deer. The blood, however, you must not eat. Pour it out on the ground like water. (Deut. 12:15–17; see also 23–25)

92. Ḥullin 117a; Rambam *Hilkhot Maakhalot Asurot* 7:6. On various approaches to what the *Amora'im* and *Rishonim* define as the "fat tail," see *Encyclopedia Talmudit*, "*Ḥelev*," vol. 2, 7–8.

Eating blood is always forbidden, but in this context there is no prohibition against eating the suet of regular, non-consecrated animals. If Ibn Ezra is correct that suet is not universally forbidden, it is clear why the suet is not mentioned along with blood in this context.[93]

Ramban fiercely rejects Ibn Ezra's reading:

> It is impossible that the explanation of the phrase "of the animal that can be sacrificed" is that this animal is itself an offering, so that an unconsecrated animal be excluded from this prohibition, since in the section of *Vayikra*, Scripture has already prohibited all suet in an unqualified manner, without any condition or exception. (Ramban on Lev. 7:25)[94]

As strange as it may seem, both Ibn Ezra and Ramban may be correct.[95] The plain meaning of the verse may be that all suet from all animals is forbidden. Given that in every single offering, the suet is the part offered up upon the altar, it makes little sense to specify that the suet of offerings may not be eaten. Because that part is always offered up on the altar, there is not even any possibility of eating it. Thus, it is far more logical that this prohibition applies to the suet of all animals.[96] At the same time, Ibn Ezra is correct that the language seems to refer to the suet of offerings in particular.

In Moses's time, however, there would belittle dispute between Ibn Ezra and Ramban. These laws are conveyed to a generation in which there was no such thing as non-consecrated meat: It was forbidden to slaughter an animal outside of the Tabernacle (Lev. 17). In the wilderness, the only way to eat meat was to offer a peace offering. Thus,there

93. See also Milgrom, *Leviticus*, vol. 1, 427.
94. Ramban adds a disparaging remark that presumably hints to Ibn Ezra's conclusion of his argument with the Sadducee.
95. I sense that even the Sages, who extended this prohibition to the suet of all animals, perceive the suet of sacrificial animals as the main prohibition, for there are two separate sources: Leviticus 7:23–24, which refers specifically to sacrificial animals, and a separate prohibition for all animals (Lev. 3:17). See Keritot 4b.
96. As Ramban notes, the prohibition against eating suet is already mentioned in Leviticus 3, and it refers to all suet, not just of offerings.

was no such thing as eating the suet from non-consecrated animals (as Ramban), but all meat came from offerings whose suet was offered upon the altar (as Ibn Ezra).

For our purposes, what matters is that the prohibition assumes that certain parts are inherently consecrated, and for that reason they are forbidden for human consumption. This was an integral part of life in the wilderness, but the concept is supposed to be maintained for all generations: Certain parts ought to be kept for God, and people do not have the authority to eat them.

This brings us to the prohibition against eating blood. There are various biblical reasons for this prohibition; this context (and that of Leviticus 3:17) implies that because the blood is reserved for the altar, it is too holy for human consumption.[97] While the verb associated with blood is sometimes "drinking," as in, "A people – see – rises like a lioness, lifts itself up like a lion. It will not lie down until it eats its meat and drinks the blood of the slain" (Num. 23:24, and others),[98] in this context the verb "eat" is used. This connects the prohibition against consuming blood to that of consuming suet:[99]

The Prohibition Against Eating Suet	The Prohibition Against Eating Blood
Do not eat the suet of any ox, sheep, or goat....	Do not eat any blood....
For anyone who eats the suet of an animal of which a fire offering could be offered to the Lord	Anyone who eats any blood
shall be severed from his people.	shall be severed from his people.

The similar form points to similar content. As mentioned, there are various biblical reasons for prohibiting the consumption of blood. First and

97. See further in Granot, "Prohibitions of Blood."

98. R. Samuel Strashon (Rashash) writes that the prohibition deserves punishment only if a whole *kezayit* is consumed. This is a measure for solid food, not the *revi'it* of liquids (see Rashash on Yevamot 114b).

99. Milgrom writes that the verb "eat" refers to eating meat before the blood has been properly drained out of it, hence "eat" (see *Leviticus*, vol. 1, 429). Compare also Schwartz, "Eating Blood," 44.

foremost is the idea that the essence of life is contained in the blood, as Ramban comments on the clause, "But flesh with its lifeblood still in it you may not eat" (Gen. 9:4). The same reason is presented in the prohibition against slaughtering animals outside the camp: "For the life of all flesh – its blood is its life. That is why I have said to the Israelites: You must not eat any creature's blood, because the life of every creature is bound up with its blood" (Lev. 17:14). Ramban again explains that "something that has a spirit must not eat another spirit, for all spirits belong to God."[100]

However, in that context a further reason is given for the prohibition against consuming blood – one which seems to be the rationale for the prohibition in *Parashat Tzav* as well:

> Anyone of the House of Israel, or any migrant living among you, who eats blood – I will set My face against that person who eats blood and will sever him from his people, for the life of a creature is in its blood. I have given it to you to make atonement for your lives on the altar, for blood, which is bound up with life, atones. That is why I have told the Israelites: None of you may eat blood, nor may any migrant living among you eat blood. (Lev. 17:10–12)

The essence of life is contained within the blood; for this reason, blood is used to achieve atonement. Thus, eating an animal's blood is effectively wrongful use of something that belongs to God and the Sanctuary. Because the blood is intended for the altar for the purpose of atonement, it is considered consecrated, and a person must not consume it.

This seems to be the basis for the prohibition in our chapter: Blood and suet are off-limits for human consumption because they are meant for the altar, used for atonement, consecrated to the Sanctuary. Milgrom wrongly argues that suet is forbidden because it belongs to the altar while the prohibition against blood is far more extensive and includes

---

100. Baruch Schwartz ("Eating the Blood," 40–41) notes that while most laws of Leviticus 17 open with "*Ish ish* – each man" (17:3, 8, 10, 13), the prohibition against eating blood has "*nefesh*" (17:12). This presumably links the law to the idea that the blood is in the *nefesh*.

all animals, not just those that may be offered upon the altar.[101] While it is true that people may not eat the blood of any animal, in *Parashat Tzav* the focus is on the blood of animals and birds that are sacrificed upon the altar, and the prohibition is based on the fact that the blood is designated for the altar.

This also explains the relationship between the prohibition in *Tzav* and the brief reduction of these verses in Leviticus 3: "All the fatty parts belong to the Lord: this is an everlasting statute throughout your generations in all your dwellings: you shall not eat any suet or any blood" (3:16–17). While these prohibitions seem to be general, all-inclusive prohibitions that go beyond the sacrificial world, they are clearly based on the idea that this is so because suet and blood belongs to God and the Sanctuary: "All the fatty parts belong to the Lord." Moreover, the Torah intentionally integrates this with the usual formula: "A fire offering for a sweet savor [all suet] is for the Lord." This variation on the usual formula confirms that the prohibition against consuming suet and fat derives from the fact that these parts belong to the Lord.

But if the prohibition is profoundly linked to the sacrificial world, why does it include "all suet and all blood," "throughout your generations in all your dwellings"? Why isn't the prohibition limited to consecrated animals, as Ibn Ezra holds? It emerges that this formulation refers to Israel in the wilderness, when the only meat they ate was the meat of peace offerings. Thus, under these circumstances, "all suet and all blood" refers exclusively to animals offered up as sacrifices.

THE WAVE OFFERING AND PRIESTLY GIFT

The order of laws within "the law of the peace offering" is significant. Unlike "the laws" of other offerings, *Parashat Tzav*'s "law of the peace offering" is a compilation of various laws that seem to have been issued at various times, especially the prohibitions against eating in impurity and eating the blood and suet. After these interruptions, the text repeats the classic opening: "And the Lord spoke to Moses: Tell the Israelites"

---

101. Milgrom, *Leviticus*, vol. 1, 428.

(7:28), which serves as connective repetition, bringing the reader back to the specific laws of the peace offering.[102]

The unexpected order of the laws indicates that they have been arranged in an intentional design with a particular objective. Surprisingly, the laws of the peace offering do not follow the chronological order of the sacrificial process. Only after the laws of the Israelite worshipper's portion are presented – including various appendixes and the law of *notar*, that leftovers must not be eaten on the third day – does the text go back to how the actual offering is brought to the Sanctuary; ritually waved (7:29–30), the suet burned on the altar (v. 31), and especially, what gifts are given to the priest (vv. 31–34).

This sequence shows that the Israelite worshipper's consumption of their portion is central to this offering: Only after all the relevant laws about their portion are listed does the text go back to the rest of the sacrificial process. This may also reflect the other side of the coin: that the priests' consumption of their portion (the breast and thigh) is different from their eating of the priestly share of the guilt and purification offerings. The consumption of these parts is not a continuation of the altar's consumption; rather, they are gifts to the priests themselves.[103] If so, the sequence of the "law of the peace offering" essentially follows the same order as other "laws of offerings": It first mentions the laws of eating (in all other offerings – by the altar and priests; in peace offerings – by the Israelite worshipper); afterward, as a kind of appendix, it is announced which priest is to receive his share. In parallel, the sacrificial laws and distribution of the peace offering are also listed. This order will be clarified below.

> And the Lord spoke to Moses: Tell the Israelites: One who brings a peace sacrifice to the Lord is to bring the offering of his peace sacrifice before the Lord himself; with his own hands he shall

102. Milgrom, *Leviticus*, vol. 1, 429. See also Dillmann, *Leviticus*, 994, who draws diachronic conclusions.

103. As mentioned, according to Rambam, eating holy offerings is a separate mitzva, while eating offerings of lesser holiness – such as the peace offering – is included in the mitzva of sacrificing.

> present the Lord's fire offerings. He shall bring the animal's fat and breast so that the breast can be displayed, this way and that, as a wave offering before the Lord. The priest shall send the fat up in smoke upon the altar, but the breast shall go to Aaron and his sons. The right thigh of your peace offering you shall give as an upraised gift to the priest. The one among the sons of Aaron who offers the blood and fat of the peace offering shall receive the right thigh as his portion. For I have taken from the peace sacrifices of the Israelites the breast of the wave offering and the thigh of the upraised gift, and given them to Aaron the priest and to his sons as their perpetual share from the Israelites. (7:28–34)

This passage opens with special emphasis on the worshipper's active participation in this offering: "One who brings a peace sacrifice to the Lord is *to bring the offering* of his peace sacrifice before the Lord *himself; with his own hands he shall present* the Lord's fire offerings." Here, it is not the priest who presents the suet and priestly portion to God but the worshipper himself. The worshipper is an active participant in the sacrificial process. As Malbim states: "The owner of the offering who brings a peace offering to the Sanctuary must himself offer up the part that is offered up to Heaven" (on Lev. 7:29).

It is the Israelite worshipper's active participation in this offering that makes it necessary to perform a ritual that is not part of other offerings: The parts designated for the altar and the priest are *waved* in order to symbolically transfer them to a higher authority. No part of the burnt, grain, purification, or guilt offering is similarly waved; there is no need to wave something that is already considered holy property. The act of waving submits the waved object to a higher authority.[104] The peace offering, which is of lesser holiness, remains in the worshipper's possession; in order to sanctify certain parts, they must be waved.

After the offering is brought to the Sanctuary, all the suet is laid upon the animal's breast and they are waved together – this transfers them to the Sanctuary's possession. Afterward, the suet is burned upon the altar, while the breast is given to the priests.

104. Milgrom, "Tenufa."

Nor does this mark the end of the offering's distribution. The right thigh is then given to the priests as a gift: "The right thigh of your peace offering you shall give as an upraised gift to the priest. The one among the sons of Aaron who offers the blood and fat of the peace offering shall receive the right thigh as his portion" (7:32).[105]

There is, of course, a significant difference between the breast, which is waved, and the thigh, which is not: The former is consecrated to the Sanctuary, "before the Lord," while the latter is a gift, given from one person to another; the phrase "before the Lord" is not used. Milgrom suggests that this indicates that the breast is waved in the Sanctuary courtyard while the thigh can be gifted in any pure place.[106]

If so, then the peace offering is divided into three different levels of sanctity. The suet is consecrated and burnt upon the altar; the breast is also waved in consecration but then given to the priest; the thigh is not waved but is still given to the priest as a gift. This is supported by the text's different epithets for the different parts: "For I have taken from the peace sacrifices of the Israelites the *breast of the wave offering* and the *thigh of the upraised gift,* and given them to Aaron the priest and to his sons as their perpetual share from the Israelites" (7:34). The breast is a wave offering; the thigh is a gift. As Ramban explains: "The *peshat* seems to be that the breast is waved together with the suet, but not the thigh" (on Lev. 7:30).

Nonetheless, the Sages explain the verses differently, and many follow suit. As Rashi writes: "*Tenufa,* waving, is back and forth; *teruma* means up and down – [the priest would move them both] back and forth, up and down" (on 7:34)!

This reading is revolutionary. If the thigh is indeed waved like the breast, then it effectively becomes part of the consecrated offering,

105. The gift of the *right* thigh is presumably linked to the symbolic superiority of the right side. This may also have been a polemic against the Ancient Egyptian custom of sacrificing one thigh to the dead (see Junker, *Gîza,* 229). The biblical custom is to give this part to the priests. The *Epic of Gilgamesh* also emphasizes the right side's symbolic dominance when Enkidu tears off the Bull of Heaven's "right thigh" and flings it at the furious goddess Ishtar (*Gilgamesh,* Tablet XI, lines 151–53).

106. Milgrom, *Leviticus,* vol. 1, 474–81; he devotes a separate study to the topic: Milgrom, "The Thigh of *Teruma.*"

whereas if the breast is raised like the thigh, it becomes similar to a priestly gift, not to a consecrated share. The Sages' and Rashi's reading can be justified: The term "waving," "*tenufa*," is also used to refer to monetary donations to the Sanctuary (as when gold and bronze is donated in Exodus 38:24–29).[107] Thus, as proposed by Menachem Bula, the physical act of waving may well be a secondary meaning of the word's primary definition, which is "dedication to the sacred."[108] Yet the distinction between the two parts as "the breast of *tenufa*" and "the thigh of *teruma*" indicates a significant difference between them.

Ramban continues with an explanation of the Sages' reading:

> But our Rabbis have said that the priest placed the fats upon the hand of the owner of the offering, with the breast and thigh above them [and waved them – Menaḥot 62a). The reason they hold that waving is mentioned only in regard to the breast is to show that even if one of the two parts becomes impure, the remaining pure part should still be waved.

He explains that the verses mean that both parts should be waved, but if one of them becomes impure or is somehow misplaced, the remaining part should be waved on its own. They are not an inseparable gift to the altar.

In order to understand the complex relationship between the breast and thigh, we will zoom out to other biblical passages to see what led the Sages to explain that both portions were waved together, despite the *peshat* of the verse.

Firstly, in this section, the different natures of the two parts are expressed not only through the epithets of *tenufa* and *teruma,* but also through their different laws. While the breast is given to "Aaron and his sons" (7:31), a generic term meaning "all priests," the thigh is given to the ministering priest: "The one among the sons of Aaron who offers the blood and fat of the peace offering" (7:33). As Ibn Ezra explains: "The

---

107. See further in Dotan, "The *Tenufa* of Gold."

108. Bula, *Leviticus,* 122; see further about the definitions of the two terms (in light of Akkadian and Arabic) in Anderson, *Sacrifices and Offerings,* vol. 2, 133–44.

right thigh to the one who dashes the blood, the breast to all the priests." This is a similar division to that of the grain offering: The fine flour (and purification) grain offering is divided among all the priests, while the cooked grain offerings are given to the ministering priest.

A similar division presumably applies here: While both portions are initially in the worshipper's possession and end up in possession of the priests, their respective paths are different. When the worshipper waves the breast together with the suet, it is transferred to the altar's possession. The altar consumes only the suet, however, while the breast is given over to the priests, to be shared among them like the fine flour offering. In contrast, the thigh is transferred directly from the worshipper to the priests, like the cooked grain offering. This is supported by the biblical language: The suet and breast are called "the Lord's fire offerings" (7:30), as the grain offering is (six times!). Only the grain offering and the suet and breast of the peace offering are referred to as "the Lord's fire offerings"; the priests receive them as gifts from the altar.[109]

For this reason, Milgrom's reading of "the Lord's fire offerings" as "food gifts" is inaccurate.[110] These parts are indeed eventually given to the priest as gifts, but they are gifts from the altar, while the worshipper offers them to God. It is deeply symbolic that the priest – the mediator between the Israelite and the altar – receives portions of the peace offering from both. The *Sifra*'s words can be read in this light: "*Shelamim*: For all is *shalom*, 'peace,' through them: The blood and *eimurim* are for the altar; the breast and thigh – for the priests; the skin and meat – for the worshippers" (*Freewill Offerings*, 16:2).

The distribution of the peace offering is not merely a technical sharing among the worshipper, priest, and altar: The priest's portion is a gift from both the human and the Divine, which sheds light on the different names for each portion: "The breast of *tenufa*" is the altar's gift to the priests and the "thigh of *teruma*" is from the worshipper.[111] In order to

109. Whether the phrase "the fire offerings of the Lord" (7:35) refers specifically to the peace offering or all offerings will be explored extensively below.

110. Milgrom, *Leviticus*, vol. 1, 430; his claim is discussed further in my introduction.

111. In a certain sense, this division concurs with Vincent's claim that *tenufa* is a gift to the Sanctuary whereas *teruma* is a regular gift (Vincent, "*Tenouphah* et *Teroumah*,"

reconcile this distinction with the Sages' reading, we will look to other passages that mention the breast and thigh.

The Eighth Day of Consecration

For now we will skip over the mention of the breast and thigh given to the priests during the seven days of consecration and begin with the eighth day of consecration:

> He slaughtered the ox and the ram: the people's peace sacrifice. Aaron's sons presented him with the blood, and he dashed it against each side of the altar, and the fat parts of the ox and ram: the broad tail, the covering fat, the kidneys, and the diaphragm of the liver. They laid the fat parts over the breasts, and he sent them up in smoke upon the altar. But the breasts and right thigh Aaron displayed, this way and that, as a wave offering before the Lord, as Moses had commanded. (Lev. 9:18–21)

The phrase "as Moses had commanded" belies the disparity between the commandment and its execution. In Leviticus 7, Moses instructs that the breast be waved; for some reason, Aaron waves both breast and thigh together. The suet is laid upon the breast on its way to the altar, but after the suet is burned, the two parts are suddenly waved together.

The excuse that this was a unique process during the eighth day of consecration is challenged by the fact that this becomes a commandment for all generations:

> Moses told Aaron, and Elazar and Itamar, the two sons left to him, "…You and your sons and daughters may eat the breast of the wave offering and the thigh of the upraised gift in any ritually pure place, for these have been given to you from the peace sacrifices of Israel as your portion and the portion of your children. *The thigh for the upraised gift and the breast for the wave offering are to be brought, with the fat of the fire offering, to be waved as a wave*

267–72). Some modern scholars believe, like the Sages, that there is no difference between the two (Driver, "Technical Terms," 100–05).

> *offering before the Lord.* These are to be your share and that of your children forever, as the Lord has commanded." (Lev. 10:12–15)

Waving the breast and thigh together has suddenly been instituted as their share "forever." Moreover, the verse implies that the suet is waved at the same time, as in Leviticus 7. For some reason, however, the verse maintains the distinction between "the thigh of *teruma*" and the "breast of *tenufa*." Why is this so, given that the two are waved together?

Before we attempt to solve this mystery, it is worth noting that these verses clearly informed the Sages' interpretation in Leviticus 7 that the two parts are waved together. Yet the question remains: What is the relationship between the first commandment, which distinguishes between the breast (that is waved) and the thigh (that is not), and the later commandment in Leviticus 10, which maintains the different epithets for the two parts even though the eternal law is to wave them both together?

In order to understand this process, let us return to the chapter we skipped: Between the sacrificial laws of Leviticus 7 and the description of the eighth day of consecration are the seven days of consecration in Leviticus 8. The ordination ram is a peace offering:

> Moses then drew close the second ram, the ram of ordination. Aaron and his sons laid their hands upon its head.... He took a loaf of unleavened bread from the basket, before the Lord, and also one loaf of oil bread, and one wafer, and placed them on the fat and on the right thigh. All of this he placed on the palms of Aaron and of his sons, and displayed them this way and that as a wave offering before the Lord. Then Moses took them from their hands and burnt them upon the altar with the burnt offering. This was the ordination offering, a sweet savor, a fire offering to the Lord. Moses then took the breast and waved it as a wave offering before the Lord. This was Moses's portion of the ordination ram, as the Lord had commanded him. (Lev. 8:22–29)

These verses describe two acts of waving. The first is: "All of this he placed on the palms of Aaron and of his sons, and displayed them this way and that as a wave offering before the Lord." Ibn Ezra interprets that Moses waves "Aaron and his sons, as Aaron waves the Levites" (!), but the more logical, prevalent reading is that Moses waves the bread, fat, and thigh that "he placed on the palms of Aaron."[112] Then, after the above is burnt upon the altar as an "ordination offering," Moses then takes the breast separately and waves it "as a wave offering before the Lord." This is then given to Moses as his own personal share.

The question of what "all of this" means is fascinating. Usually, "one matza" of each kind is given to the priest along with the right thigh, but during the seven days of consecration, these items are burned on the altar along with the suet! Unlike the usual peace offering, this time the three loaves are all of unleavened bread, because leaven may not touch the altar. Thus, the peace offering of the seven days of consecration is anomalous in several ways: All three kinds of loaves are unleavened; the breast is not waved with the suet, but by itself; and, even more surprising, the right thigh *is* waved, together with the suet and loaves, and all are burned upon the altar!

These deviations are all presumably related: Because the thigh is burned upon the altar, it must first be waved. Milgrom believes that this resolves all the issues:

> This text is not difficult because it discusses the thigh of ordination, not that of the peace offering. The difference between them is that the thigh of ordination is not given to the priests – it is offered on the altar. It requires waving for the sake of consecration, to signify its transferal from the worshipper's possession to the Sanctuary's possession. It is the consecration of the thigh of ordination to God that makes waving requisite.[113]

Milgrom is correct that waving and burning the thigh upon the altar are profoundly linked, but this does not fully solve this offering's anomalous nature. Rather, the question shifts: Why is the right thigh burnt on the

112. As waving serves to transfer something from the profane sphere to the sacred sphere, the Levites are waved, but there is no need to wave priests who have been consecrated by sacred oil.
113. Milgrom, "The Thigh of *Teruma*," 5.

altar during the seven days of consecration, and what does this teach us about the thigh of the peace offering? I will address this below; for now, I wish to focus on Moses's status during the week of consecration.

The prevalent reading is that during the week of consecration, Moses acts as the High Priest. The priests themselves are undergoing a process of consecration and are thus not yet fit to serve, so Moses takes their place: "Rav said: Our teacher Moses is the High Priest and received a portion of consecrated offerings, as it says: 'This was Moses's portion of the ordination ram'" (Zevaḥim 101b).[114]

Yet this does not explain the sacrificial process either: If the peace offering thigh is given to the priest as a gift, why is the thigh of ordination burned on the altar, rather than given to Moses? Moreover, the breast of the regular peace offering is usually given to the priest as a portion *from the altar* – yet the breast of the ordination ram is given to Moses. Effectively, the ordination offering is the opposite of the usual peace offering; instead of waving the breast with the suet, the thigh is waved with the suet and the selection of matzot.

This raises the question as to whether Moses indeed acts as High Priest during the seven days of consecration. He does not receive the usual priestly gift, nor does he wear the priestly vestments,[115] as the talmudic discussion shows:

> R. Akiva came to Ginzak, and they asked him: What did Moses wear during the seven days of consecration? He did not know. He went and asked in the *beit midrash*...What did Moses wear?.... A white cloak. R. Kahana said: A white cloak without a hem. (Avoda Zara 34a)

Why does Moses wear special white clothes instead of the usual priestly vestments? Rashi and Tosafot present two different perspectives:

114. See also Weinel, "M-SH-Ḥ," 37. The Midrash states that Moses served as High Priest during all forty years in the wilderness (*Pesikta Rabbati* 14).

115. Note that sacrifices made before the Tabernacle is ready are not offered up by Moses, as is evident from the offerings at Mount Sinai (Ex. 19:24; 24:5). (Moses does dash the blood, but this is an act of covenant and is hard to use as proof for anything else.) See also Milgrom, *Leviticus*, vol. 1, 566.

Tosafot's position is the prevalent reading that Moses served as an alternative priest and thus wore unique service robes, because the usual garments were not yet consecrated.[116] This is not detrimental to Moses's status; rather, it simply means that the garments were not yet ready. Rashi, however, explains: "Moses did not wear priestly vestments … he was considered an outsider. Thus, although he ministers by God's word, there is no mention of the garments." According to Rashi, the regular priestly laws do not apply to Moses; he acts similarly, but he is not defined as an actual priest.[117] His position is thus unique.

Milgrom proposes that Moses's position is that of a leader, a king. He oversees the construction of the Tabernacle; he consecrates it and its priests.[118] Thus,the gifts he receives are not the usual priestly gifts: "Moses, then, according to P, was the interim priest only by necessity and divine dispensation."[119] Yet this does not explain why Moses receives the breast that is usually consecrated to the altar, rather than the usual priestly gift of the right thigh. This subtle reversal hints that Moses's role during the week of consecration does not conform to the prevalent reading.

The week of consecration indeed poses a unique challenge: The priests have not yet been consecrated, so they cannot approach the altar yet. However, rather than Moses being perceived as an alternative priest, he can be regarded as an alternative representative of the *altar itself*. Since Aaron is not yet able to serve as ritual slaughterer, the altar appoints a representative – not because Moses is a temporary priest, but because there is no available priest, so he acts as the altar's emissary.

---

116. The Tosafot go on to offer a different explanation for the lack of priestly garments: The Tabernacle was considered a *bama* ("high shrine") during the week of consecration, and the priestly garments are not worn in a *bama*.

117. R. Haim ben Attar offers a bold reading: Moses wears a special white cloak because he has a unique status. The priests must wear the priestly garments for "glory and for splendor" (Ex. 28:2), but Moses himself is of a different status.

118. Milgrom (*Leviticus*, vol. 1, 556–57) shows that throughout Tanakh, kings offer sacrifices and have a similar status to the priests: Saul (I Sam. 13:9–10); David (II Sam. 6:13); Solomon (I Kings 3:4, 15); Jeroboam (I Kings 12:32–33). Some of these sacrifices are from the king, but it is not clear if the king himself is actually offering it up; in the case of Jeroboam, he is clearly acting as actual priest.

119. Milgrom, ibid., 558.

A careful reading of these verses reveals that Moses indeed has the authority to consecrate the priests, the vessels, and the garments. He is not merely a priest, but a human agent of the Divine: "Take the anointing oil, pour it on his head, and anoint him. Then bring his sons forward and dress them with the tunics. Gird Aaron and his sons with the sashes and fasten their headdresses. The priesthood shall be theirs as a law for all time. *Thus, you shall ordain* Aaron and his sons" (Ex. 29:7–9).

At first glance, perhaps, this definition may seem like a mere technicality: Why is it significant if Moses is defined as an alternative priest or as the altar's emissary? Yet it has profound implications for the subject at hand: If Moses is the altar's emissary, it is clear why he receives the breast, while the thigh usually reserved for the priests is burned upon the altar because Moses is not a priest, and there are not yet consecrated priests to receive it. Thus, Moses receives the altar's portion, whereas the priestly portion – the right thigh and the matzot – is burned together with the suet.

This also explains why these two portions are referred to as "the breast of *tenufa*" and "the thigh of *teruma*" even though both portions are waved. The verses in Leviticus 7 define their essence: The breast is inherently waved; it becomes the altar's property along with the suet, and the priest receives the breast as a gift from the altar. In contrast, the thigh is not consecrated to the altar; rather, the worshipper gifts it directly to the priest. During the week of consecration, however, the thigh is also consecrated to the altar since there are no priests to receive it, and the altar is therefore also able to receive the thigh. For this reason, the commandment for all generations is to wave both the breast and the thigh, even if their initial definitions are "the breast of *tenufa*" and "the thigh of *teruma*."

It thus emerges that Leviticus 7–10 presents the halakhic development of the status of the peace offering thigh. This explains why the Sages' ruling deviates from the *peshat* in Leviticus 7 and why the respective epithets for thigh and breast remain in Leviticus 10 even though both parts are waved. Once both parts are waved in Leviticus 8, the altar's sanctity forever clings to the thigh of the peace offering, and the priests must wave it forever after, for all generations.

The Netziv expresses this similarly:

> "You shall give the right thigh as a gift, etc." – Even though it is also waved for all generations, as below in Leviticus 10:15... it does not have the same status as the breast, which is waved together with the suet, but God gave it to the priests as a gift from Heaven. The thigh, however, belongs to the worshipper, as does the rest of the meat, but they give it as a gift to the priests. And for this reason, the waving is not the same action: The breast is brought together with the suet, but the thigh is only placed on top of the suet while it is waved. (*Haamek Davar* on Lev. 7:32)

The Netziv explains that the difference between the breast and thigh is not just manifest in their adjectives, but at the end of the sacrificial process as well: The breast, which belongs to the altar, is brought together with the consecrated suet, whereas the thigh, which is waved only due to its affinity with the altar during the seven days of consecration, is added to the suet only when the two are waved, not before.[120]

An alternative formulation is that the difference between the peace offering's breast and thigh reflects the difference between nature and nurture, between whether Israel are the chosen nation because they are special or because God has chosen them. The breast innately belongs to the altar; like the suet, it is inherently designated for God. In contrast, during the seven days of consecration, the thigh's encounter with the altar forever alters its nature; thus, the thigh of the peace offering must be waved forever after.

---

120. See further (including other related ideas) in Kahan, "Priests."

Chapter 19

Conclusions (Leviticus 7:35–38)

The final four verses that end the sacrificial chapters in *Parashat Tzav* present two conclusions (7:35–38):

- *This* is the anointed right of Aaron and his sons from the Lord's fire offerings from the day they are presented to serve the Lord as priests;*which the Lord commanded when* He anointed them as priests – that these be given them by the Israelites as their perpetual share throughout the generations.
- *This*, then, is the law for the burnt offering, the grain offering, the purification offering, the guilt offering, the ordination offering, and the peace offering, *which the Lord commanded* Moses at Mount Sinai *when* he commanded the Israelites to bring their offerings to the Lord, in the Wilderness of Sinai.

Even before we delve into these verses, their parallel structure is evident: Both open with "*Zot*" – "This" – and both continue with "which the Lord commanded when…" This presents a double challenge: What is each concluding, and what is the meaning of this similar pattern?

Radatz Hoffmann shows that these verses serve to conclude the second sacrificial list, for it follows the same order as *Parashat Tzav*: Beginning with "This is the law," as all offerings are introduced in the second list,[1] it lists "the burnt offering (6:2), the grain offering (6:7), the purification offering (6:18), the guilt offering (7:1)… and the peace offering (7:11)." Moreover, given that this signature mentions that these laws were transmitted to Moses "at Mount Sinai," Radatz Hoffmann explains that this second list is given over before the first list, which is conveyed to Moses after the Tabernacle is erected (Lev. 1:1).

We will yet come back to precisely where these lists were transmitted; for now we will begin with the first conclusion, which presents a particular exegetical challenge. The word "this," "*zot*," implies that the reader knows what "this" refers to, yet it may be referring to one of two possibilities. The first is that "this" refers to the priestly gifts from all the various offerings; alternatively, it might be referring more specifically to the priestly portion of the peace offering, the breast and thigh.

There are differing opinions among the *Rishonim*. Rashbam believes that it serves as a conclusion to the entire sacrificial list: "To the skin of the burnt offering, the meat of the purification and guilt offering, the thanksgiving bread, the peace offering breast and thigh, and what is left over of the grain offering" (on Lev. 7:35).[2]

There are two good reasons to interpret in this way, as most commentators do. Firstly, there is the use of the plural form: "The fire *offerings* of the Lord."[3] Secondly, the festive, dramatic mention of the day of

1. See further in Shammah, "Two Objectives"; Milgrom, *Leviticus*, vol. 1, 436–37.
2. See also Dillmann, *Leviticus*, 494. It is interesting that Rashbam's order is not the same as the verses. There is a certain logic to mentioning the grain offering last, as plant offerings are certainly different than animal offerings; even so, in both lists the Torah lists the grain offering in the middle of the animal offerings.
3. Most translations preserve this plural form for "fire offerings"; sometimes it is lost in translation, such as the New Jerusalem Bible's "Such was the portion of Aaron and his descendants in the food burnt for the Lord."

consecration seems incongruous if it refers to the peace offering alone, and is far more suitable for the conclusion of the entire sacrificial list.

If so, there are two conclusions for the second sacrificial list, the "law for the offerings": The first focuses on the priestly gifts, while the second concludes the law of the offerings that Moses teaches Israel.

Milgrom, however, argues that the first conclusion refers exclusively to the peace offering.[4] He points out that the description of the peace offering also uses the plural form – "the Lord's fire offerings" – in reference to the suet: "With his own hands he shall present the Lord's fire offerings" (7:30). Milgrom supports his assertion with two arguments. Firstly, one offering in this list cannot be defined as a "fire offering"; the purification offering is never defined as such, so the phrase "fire offerings" in the conclusion must be referring to the peace offering. Secondly, the verse describes the gifts the Israelites give to the priests: "When the Lord anointed them as priests He commanded that *these* be given them by the Israelites as their perpetual share throughout the generations." This is an apt description of the breast and thigh from the peace offering (and the same phrase, "from the Israelites," appears three verses earlier in relation to these particular gifts), but it is strange to refer to the priestly shares of the purification and guilt offerings as gifts "from the Israelites."

A third approach may be adopted – namely, to argue that both readings are justified, but with respect to different parts of the verse. Let us begin with Milgrom's proofs, the first of which concerns the absence of the definition of the purification offering (*ḥattat*) as a "fire offering" (*isheh*). At first glance, he is correct that the purification offering is not described as an *isheh,* and this in particular highlights the distinctive nature of the offering and the unique role of its blood, which is conceived as purgative blood rather than blood intended for the fire. However, this does not preclude the possibility of also regarding the purification offering as "the Lord's fire offering" when attention is directed to the burning of the suet. In this respect, the purification offering is consumed on the altar like other sacrifices, and it is destined for the divine fire. Therefore, in so general a concluding formula, I do not consider it problematic to include the purification offering as well. Milgrom is correct, however,

4. Milgrom, *Leviticus,* vol. 1, 433–34.

that it is strange to define all priestly portions from the offerings as a gift from Israel to the priests. The law of the grain offering, in particular, emphasizes that the priest's share is a gift from the altar, not from the Israelites: "What remains of the grain offering shall belong to Aaron and his sons; it is holy of holies among the fire offerings" (2:3; see also 2:10, 8:10–11). The Israelites bring their grain offerings to the altar; the priests receive nothing directly from their hands.

Nonetheless, the beginning of the conclusion strongly evokes the grain offering: "This is the anointed right of Aaron and his sons from the Lord's fire offerings." "From the Lord's fire offerings" is the same phrase used in reference to the grain offering. How can the gifts from the altar be considered gifts "from the Israelites"?

The solution is that the first conclusion (7:35–36) combines two different kinds of priestly gifts, in the same order as they appear in the sacrificial list itself: gifts that are "holy of holies" and gifts that are of lesser holiness – the peace offering:

> (v. 35) This is the anointed right of Aaron and his sons *from the Lord's fire offerings* from the day they are presented to serve the Lord as priests;
>
> (v. 36) when the Lord anointed them as priests He commanded that these be given them *by the Israelites* as their perpetual share throughout the generations.

The two statements describe two separate priestly privileges. The anointed priests are to receive gifts from both the altar and the people. The altar's gifts are "holy of holies"; the people's gifts are of lesser holiness. Note the precise language: God does not actually give the priests the Israelites' gifts; rather, He commands that they be given *by* the Israelites.

The culmination is that Rashbam is correct that the first conclusion refers to all the priestly gifts, but to be more precise, it refers to all priestly gifts that are "holy of holies" – that is, from the altar. Milgrom is also correct that the second verse refers specifically to the peace offering – but not because, as he claims, the verse is an organic part of the peace offering section, but rather because the division between different degrees of holiness is so central in *Parashat Tzav* that the conclusion itself is divided into two distinct degrees of holiness. The first conclusion refers to shares from the altar, gifts that are "holy of holies." The second conclusion refers to gifts of lesser holiness – the peace offering.

Note that to adopt Rashbam's reading means that the priests' role in the sacrificial service is centralized. This makes sense, given that the priests' share in the offerings is not merely payment for their service, but the continuation of the altar's consumption. The priests' eating of the offering is an essential part of the sacrificial journey.

SINAI AND THE DAYS OF CONSECRATION

This brings us to the deeper connection between the two conclusions of the second sacrificial list. The repetition and similar language of the two conclusions invites comparison. Of special interest is the event each conclusion refers to. The first conclusion repeatedly mentions the days of the Tabernacle's consecration: "This is the anointed right of Aaron and his sons from the Lord's fire offerings *from the day they are presented to serve* the Lord as priests; *when the Lord anointed them as priests*" (vv. 35–36). These verses anticipate the very next chapter of Leviticus, which describes the days of consecration themselves.

In contrast, the second conclusion transports the reader from the world of the Tabernacle to the foot of Mount Sinai: "This, then, is the law…which the Lord commanded Moses at Mount Sinai when he commanded the Israelites to bring their offerings to the Lord, in the Wilderness of Sinai" (7:35–38). God commands Moses to consecrate the Tabernacle at Sinai, so there is no contradiction; yet this juxtaposition points to a deeper connection between the two sites. God's presence at Sinai takes the form of a consuming fire – represented by the perpetual consuming flame of the altar. Thus, the two conclusions of the second sacrificial list remind the reader of these two forms of divine revelation and the manifestation of God's presence within the camp of Israel. The altar fire keeps the fire of revelation burning.

As mentioned, the priests are already commanded to purify themselves and (partially) ascend the consecrated mountain: "Even priests who come near to the Lord must first consecrate themselves, or the Lord will break out against them" (Ex. 19:22); "Then He said to Moses,

'Ascend to the Lord, you and Aaron, Nadav and Avihu, and seventy of Israel's elders and bow down from afar'" (Ex. 24:1).[5]

Even at Sinai, the priests' role was to eat the offerings: "They looked upon God and they ate and they drank" (Ex. 24:11). Thus, the detailed laws of the priests' consumption of the offerings in our chapter ends with an allusion to Mount Sinai, where the priests ate and drank of the offerings as they gazed upon God.

The priests receive their share of God's fire offerings, "holy of holies," at God's command (the peace offering, which is of lesser holiness); their consumption is "their perpetual share throughout the generations," like the perpetual fire of God, the consuming flames of the altar.

5. On the relationship between these two commandments (the first mentioned before the Ten Commandments and the second at the end of *Parashat Mishpatim*), see especially the analysis of R. Itamar Eldar, who claims that they should be read together (Eldar, "Revelation at Sinai").

Chapter 20

The Days of Consecration (Leviticus 8): A Rite of Passage

THE BEGINNING OF A NEW SECTION?

Is the description of the days of consecration in Leviticus 8–10 a continuation of the sacrificial chapters 1–7 or a new section? One can justifiably argue that it begins a new unit that presents the execution of the commandments given to Moses at Mount Sinai (in Exodus 29 and 40). Given that this question touches upon the chapter's objective and purpose, we will discuss its characterization before delving into the verses themselves.

John Hartley argues for distinguishing between the sacrificial chapters in Leviticus 1–7 and the days of consecration (8–10), pointing out that the two sections have markedly different language and laws:

> There are many indications that chaps. 8–10 stand apart from chaps. 1–7. The liturgical vocabulary of chaps. 8 and 9 varies from that found in chaps. 1–7: niggash, "bring near" (8:14), for hikriv, "present,

bring near" (e.g., 1:2–3);[1] the use of the general term *shafakh*, "pour out" (4:7) instead of the liturgical term *yatzak*, "pour out," as in 8:15; 9:9; and the absence of the phrases *lifnei Hashem*, "before the Lord," except with the elevated offering (8:26, 27, 29), and *Ohel Moed*, "the Tent of Meeting," in the sacrificial descriptions.

Furthermore, there are variations in ritual procedure. In chaps. 8 and 9, the burning of the whole offering takes place in two stages (8:18–25; 9:12–14),[2] whereas in the basic regulation it is done in a single step (1:9). The *ḥattat*, "purification offering," presented on the first day of public sacrifices is a general purification offering, not the one presented for a specific sin committed by the high priest, as described in 4:3–12. That there is a significant difference between these two kinds of purification offerings is evident in the way the blood is handled. In the general ritual, blood is put on the horns of the main altar (v. 15), not taken into the Holy Place to be sprinkled on the curtain and then put on the horns of the altar of incense as with a purification offering for a specific sin (4:6, 7).

Moreover, in the list of the parts of the bull to be burned outside the camp, there is no mention of the bull's head (9:17) as there is in 4:11. The distinction between *tenufa*, "the elevated offering," and *teruma*, "the contribution," has disappeared (9:21; 10:14–15; cf. 7:30–34). Furthermore, the description of the grain offering in 8:26–28 differs significantly from the regulation for grain offerings to be offered on the day of Aaron's anointing found in 6:13–14 (20–21).[3]

1. In the days of consecration there is use of the term "*vayaggesh*, "bring forward" the purification bull (8:14), while the verb used to describe the burnt offering at the beginning of the book is "*yakriv*" (1:3).
2. He is referring to the description of the burning of the head, pieces, and suet (8:20); only after stating how they are washed does the text go back to how they are sent up in smoke (8:21).
3. Hartley, *Leviticus*, 104.

Some of the differences he notes fail to invalidate the connection between the chapters. For example, while the "Tent of Meeting" is indeed not mentioned in the description of where the consecration offerings are slaughtered, it is mentioned twice at the beginning of the chapter (8:3–4) and three times at its end (31–35); its omission seems to be an instance of brevity. Similarly, the omission of the bull's head in Leviticus 9:11 makes sense, as "He burned the flesh and skin with fire outside the camp" includes the entire body including the head.

Other differences that Hartley points out are more convincing, however, and do indicate that Leviticus 1–7 and 8–10 are two separate units.

Yet even so, Hartley's conclusion cannot be adopted. As mentioned, the conclusion of Leviticus 7 points to a profound connection between the sacrifices listed in *Parashat Tzav* with the ordination offerings (7:37), and, as discussed, it is likely that the second sacrificial list is part of God's instruction to Moses regarding the days of consecration, when many offerings were brought.[4] Thus, while Hartley is correct to point out distinct aspects of the ordination offerings, this is not an indication that the two sections are completely divorced from each other. Rather, the unique aspects of the ordination offerings point to the objective and purpose of the days of ordination.

Some of the differences Hartley points out are merely technical. Some of his claims are also misguided. While he asserts that the verb "*vayaggesh*" for bringing the purification bull (8:14) would be "*hikriv*" in Leviticus 1–7, this is not correct; the parallel verb for bringing the bull to the Tabernacle is actually "*hevi*" (4:4, 23, 28); it *is hikriv* in 4:14, but the three different verbs show that the act of bringing the animal to the courtyard can be described with equally appropriate synonyms. Perhaps the use of "*vayaggesh*" during the days of consecration indicates that it is Moses, and not the regular worshipper, who brings the animal to the courtyard. The same phenomenon occurs elsewhere throughout the sacrificial corpus. When a person brought to a designated place an offering that was not his own, the verb *higgish* ("to present") is employed: "When you bring

4. The *Sifra* can also be read similarly: "Just as the ordination offerings was given at Sinai with all its details, so all of them were given at Sinai with their rules and their details" (*Sifra, Tzav*, 18:3).

the grain offering that is made of these things to the Lord, it shall be presented to the priest, and he shall bring it to the altar" (Lev. 2:8). The owner "brings"(*mevi*) the grain offering and "offers" (*makriv*) it to the priest, but the priest, who is not the owner of the sacrifice, "presents" (*maggish*) it to the altar. Similarly, in the account of the ordination (Lev 8), the verb chosen to describe the presentation of the bull before the priests – "and he presented" (*vayaggish*) – is consistent with this usage and conveys Moses' presentation of a sin offering that was not his own.

Other differences can also easily be explained as deriving from the unique sacrificial process of the days of consecration.[5] Yet others cannot be ascribed to technicalities – in particular, the purification offering of Aaron and his sons. Hartley is correct to point out the fundamental disparity between the purification offering described in the first seven chapters of Leviticus and the purification offering of the days of consecration. Though this is clearly the anointed priest's offering, its blood is not brought inside, but rather applied to the external altar; and though this makes it an external purification offering, its flesh is not eaten but is burned outside the camp. Rashi already notes: "We have no other cases of an external purification offering being burnt besides this one and the ordination offering [of the seven days of consecration]" (on Lev. 9:11). This anomaly indeed demands explanation, and we will address it below. Even so, this discrepancy fails to justify the claim that this is a wholly new section.

The juxtaposition of the days of consecration (Leviticus 8–10) with the opening sacrificial chapters (1–7) is not a technical issue; it touches upon the deeper nature and purpose of these days. We will soon explore this further. For now, the fact that the sacrificial chapters end with the Tabernacle dedication and the consecration of the priests is worthy of contemplation. The days of consecration are depicted in a similar narrative style to that found at the end of Exodus, but the integration of sacrificial laws into biblical narrative is seminal. The offerings are not

5. It is also worth pointing out that the verb "*yatzak*" instead of "*shafakh*" does not indicate that the two sections are distinct either. The verb "*shafakh*" is used in Exodus 29:12, which is definitely connected to the days of consecration. The use of "*yatzak*" serves a particular function that I will discuss below.

merely laws – they are part of the story of how God's presence comes to rest within the camp of Israel.[6] Biblical law is always presented within a narrative context that conveys where the Israelites are when they receive a certain law. As Wenham aptly expresses:

> It is not just that the narrative explains when and why certain laws were given. It does that. But the events are often as important as the laws. God's saving action is just as significant as His word. Biblical revelation is more than the bare communication of truths about God and His will. The Bible affirms that God directed the course of history in order to create a holy people who knew and did His will.[7]

The seven days of consecration, which culminate in the eighth day, tell the story of the Tabernacle's consecration and the revelation of God's glory upon the altar. This event is the narrative framework that gives validation and significance to the sacrificial laws while, on the other side of the coin, the offerings offered up each day on the altar perpetuate the revelation of the eighth day – the revelation of God's glorious presence as an ever-consuming, ever-blazing fire.

WHEN AND HOW MUCH

It is fascinating that the seven days of consecration (that take place around Rosh Ḥodesh Nisan, about a year after the exodus from Egypt)[8] are presumed to be a vehicle to transform and transport human and place from profane to sacred. As discussed, the ultimate holiness is God, and it takes more than mere proximity for a space or entity to be defined as holy. In order to become holy, a person (the priest) or place (the Tabernacle) must transcend human reality and ascend to the divine

---

6. See especially Bibb, *Ritual Words,* 100–32. Various disparities in the days of consecration narrative lead him to the conclusion that it is selective and presented with certain theological and literary objectives in mind (ibid, 107).
7. Wenham, *Leviticus,* 129.
8. This is subject of dispute: One prevalent approach is that the first of Nisan was the eighth day; Ibn Ezra claims that the seven days began on the first of Nisan. See Shammah, *The Mekhiltot,,* 174–81, who tends toward the latter.

sphere. The importance the Bible ascribes to this process and its legal-halakhic implications cannot be exaggerated; these days are characterized as a model of a rite of passage.[9]

Rites of passage usually comprise three stages: separation from the past; a mediary stage in which the participant must leave the bounds of time and society; and finally, the return to receive the new status. "Taking" Aaron and his sons and cleansing them symbolizes their separation from society; during the seven days of consecration they are forbidden to leave the bounds of the Tabernacle; and finally, after these symbolic "seven days" that represent their re-creation,[10] they receive their new garments and are anointed with sacred oil, which is of course symbolic of their new sacred role.

At the same time, the Israelites have their own role in the process. The people's assembly is of special interest:

> "Take Aaron, and his sons with him, the vestments, the anointing oil, a bull for the purification offering, two rams, and a basket of unleavened bread, and assemble the whole community at the entrance to the Tent of Meeting."
> Moses did as the Lord commanded him; and the community was assembled at the entrance to the Tent of Meeting.
> And Moses told the community, "This is what the Lord has commanded us to do."
> (8:2–5)

9. Gorman, *Ideology*, 103–30; Milgrom, *Leviticus*, vol. 1, 566–69. Milgrom compares these days to other rites of passage in the Ancient Near East. One salient element of these ceremonies is the humiliation of those leaving the old sphere and moving into the new. Milgrom argues that there are certain echoes of the priests' silence and submission (they do not respond to any of the commandments), but this seems contrived. See also Jürgens, "Wiederherstel," who explores the relationship between these days and Yom Kippur (the former is a rite of passage, the latter serves to restore order).
10. On these seven days as as a rite of passage (against the background of other seven-day references in the Bible, both legal and narrative), see Klingbeil, "Ritual Time."

Moses is commanded to "take" Aaron and his sons but to "assemble" the people, who then "assemble." Everything and everyone Moses "takes" will undergo transformation, while those who "assemble" are to play the important role of spectating.

The significance of Israel as spectators and eyewitnesses is also evident in Moses's address to the assembly: "This is what the Lord has commanded us to do" (8:5). The reader would not notice if this statement was omitted. The people themselves do not take an active part in the consecration of the priests or Tabernacle; they bring no offerings during the first seven days. Nor will the consecration of the priests bear any similarity to the appointment of the Levites, when Israel played a part and laid their hands upon the heads of the Levites (Num. 8:9–10).

The Netziv indeed questions what Israel are actually doing at the beginning of the consecration scene, and he creatively suggests that due to the differences between God's instructions in Exodus 29 and their imminent execution, Moses is taking advantage of the opportunity to teach the Israelites in a public forum about the nuances of the Oral Law. Certain premises regarding the nature of the Oral Law are necessary in order to adopt this bold reading. The Netziv does not attempt to bridge the disparities between commandment and execution; rather, he perceives them as the inevitable difference between what is written and the oral instructions Moses receives from God.[11]

The Netziv develops the idea of the Midrash that the people assemble for educational purposes – to witness the sanctity of the priesthood and the sacrificial service. Not only is it important for them to revere the priests for their sanctity, it is also crucial for the people to understand how central the Tabernacle is in their own lives and religious sphere. The priests are not a secret, inaccessible sect – as they were in Egypt, for example – but rather the people's emissaries for the altar, their bridges to the Divine. The great assembly reflects that the priests are consecrated

11. Milgrom proposes that the literary purpose of the people's assembly is to generate a dialogue with Solomon's inauguration of the Temple (1 Kings 8:1–2; Milgrom, *Leviticus*, vol. 1, 499). There is certainly a dialogue between the two scenes, but surely the later Temple scene is based on this Tabernacle scene, so the assembly here ought to be explained without mention of the later scene.

for the people's sake, with the people's consent. The people may not take an active part in the consecration process, but their presence is essential.[12]

Moreover, the people's assembly that is so central to Leviticus 8 is not even mentioned in the instructions in Exodus 29, which is strange indeed, considering how significant their participation is. This is just one of the differences between the instructions given in Exodus 29 and their execution in Leviticus, which we will soon address. For now, I wish to take advantage of this disparity to give Leviticus 8 its proper context. The book of Exodus contains multiple passages pertaining to the priests' consecration and ordination. For example, the description of the priestly garments ends thus: "Put these on your brother Aaron and his sons; then anoint, ordain, and consecrate them to serve Me as priests" (28:41); the description of the anointing oil includes: "With it, anoint the Tent of Meeting and the Ark of the Testimony…. You shall consecrate them and they will become holy of holies, and whatever touches them will become holy. You shall anoint Aaron and his sons and consecrate them to serve Me as priests" (Ex. 30:26–30). Exodus 40, especially, contains an extensive description of the consecration of the Tabernacle, its vessels, and its priests. All these descriptions are streams that flow into the stormy sea of Leviticus 8, which vividly depicts the actual process of how the Sanctuary and its priests are consecrated. Thus, some components found in Leviticus 8 are not mentioned in the instructions in Exodus 29 because they are manifestations of commandments given in different contexts.[13]

The people's assembly is a convenient window into this phenomenon. That there is no mention of this assembly in Exodus 29, which focuses

12. From a slightly different direction, see Watts, *Leviticus*, 453, and Dillmann, who argues that the people had to assemble to participate in the priests' consecration (*Leviticus*, 505).
13. See Hauge, *Descent from the Mountain*, 190–96; he believes that Leviticus 1–10 repeats the basic model of Exodus 19–40, which also begins with instructions to Moses and ends with divine revelation (see especially 191). Moreover, he correctly points out that on one hand, Leviticus 8 seems to parallel God's glory in Exodus 40, but on the other, the sacrificial chapters are based on the end of Exodus and the days of consecration continue these chapters, so the days of consecration are essentially both a parallel and a continuous account (194–95).

on the priests' ordination, indicates that the assembly is presumably not essential to their actual ordination. Rather, it is probably related to the consecration of the Tabernacle and altar, which is a crucial element of other sections. As R. Baruch Kehat states:

> In addition to the instructions in *Parashat Tzav,* the mitzva of assembly at the entrance to the Tent of Meeting is added here… It seems that this difference can be explained by stating that the command only appears in *Parashat Tetzaveh* to show how the garments are used, for the command to make them is introduced there, for the purpose of the priestly consecration. For this purpose, the presence of the Israelite assembly was not necessary. Rather, their assembly was needed for the days of the Tabernacle dedication, which include the seven days of consecration followed by the eighth, for which the entire congregation's participation was appropriate. Thus, only at the climax of this process do they receive the glory of God's revelation (Lev. 9:23–24). Therefore, the command to assemble the congregation appears only during the process itself.[14]

R. Kehat believes that the commandment of the days of consecration in Exodus 29 is mentioned only in the context of making the holy garments, so there is no mention of the assembly. This can be formulated differently – and I will do so below – but for now, I wish to adopt a principle based on his explanation. The absence of the assembly in Exodus 29 shows that its objective is related to the consecration of the Tabernacle and its vessels (which are not mentioned in Exodus 29) – that is, to the laws given in Exodus 40.

As noted, this is just an example of the exegetical challenge posed by the days of consecration: The intense rite of passage of Leviticus 8 is a bold, vivid tapestry of themes woven from passages throughout the book of Exodus.

14. Kehat, "Days of Consecration," 22.

Tables Set for Seven Days

A fundamental preliminary question pertaining to the days of consecration is how to interpret the relationship between the first day of consecration, which is described in great detail, and the six days that follow. Are the same offerings and their accompanying ceremony repeated on each of the seven days of consecration, or do the priests remain at the entrance to the Tent of Meeting for six days without bringing any further offerings as they complete the process of ordination?

Medieval commentators generally agree that the same offerings and anointing of the altar take place each day, as emerges from the end of Leviticus 8: "Do not leave the entrance to the Tent of Meeting for seven days, until the days of your ordination are complete, for your ordination will take seven days, each like today. This is what the Lord has commanded to be done to make your atonement" (8:33–34). The phrase "each like today" is interpreted as referring to the entire ceremony that the chapter describes in great detail: "The meaning of 'each like today' is that Moses does what 'the Lord has commanded to be done' – for all seven days of consecration" (Ibn Ezra on 8:34). Milgrom supports this reading by citing the instructions in Exodus: "This is what you must do for Aaron and his sons, just as I have commanded you. Their ordination shall take seven days" (Ex. 29:35).[15]

This reading is widely accepted, but I believe that the question of repeating each day's proceedings is more complex. If the entire elaborate ritual of sacrificing multiple offerings and sprinkling the priests and dressing them in their garments is indeed repeated for seven days ("to reinforce the process"),[16] why is the repetition of such an extensive ceremony reduced to a subtle phrase, "each day like today"? The impression one gets of the opening ritual is that this took place just once. Does it even make sense that Moses re-dresses the priests each day anew? Does it make sense that Moses reapplies the blood of the ordination ram to the priests' ears, thumbs, and big toes each day? (Is there any indication that the priests wash it off each day, or is the blood reapplied over what remains of yesterday's blood?) If one claims that only some of the

15. Milgrom, *Leviticus*, vol. 1, 540–41.

16. As formulated in Baentsch, *Leviticus*.

first day's ritual was repeated, but, say, Moses does not dress the priests anew each day, then why is there no indication of any such a distinction in the text?

Moreover, whereas Exodus 29 specifies that the priests must wear their garments for seven days in order to achieve ordination (29:29–30), and that a purification bull must be offered up each day for seven days as well (29:36), there is no such commandment about the other ritual elements described in Leviticus 8, which implies that they do not need to be repeated all seven days.

The concluding verses only add to the confusion: The language is ambiguous, and it is not certain what "each day like today" actually means.

We will begin with the instructions in Exodus. The text first focuses on the priests: "This is what you must do for Aaron and his sons / just as I have commanded you. / Their ordination shall take seven days" (29:35). The phrase "just as I have commanded you" is a classic convention for a concluding formula. But what does "Their ordination shall take seven days" mean? Are the same offerings to be repeated for seven days, and this is what will achieve their ordination (as Milgrom claims), or, in addition to the above instructions, is it the priests' seven-day stay at the entrance to the Tent of Meeting that fulfills their ordination? In comparison, someone who has an impure bodily emission (*zav* or *zava*) must wait for seven days before they can be purified, but they do not need to immerse themselves each day – only on the seventh day. The *metzora* must wait outside the camp for seven days before reentering the camp and offering the requisite offerings, but the offerings are only sacrificed once, after the seven days of waiting (Lev. 14:8–20).

"Their ordination shall take seven days" seems to have a similar meaning. Moses offers the requisite sacrifices and performs certain rituals just once, on the first day, but in order to complete the process, the priests must wait at the entrance to the Tent of Meeting for seven full days in order to become ordained and serve as priests.[17] It does *not* mean that

17. R. Baruch Kehat offers a different explanation: The priests are commanded to wait seven days, as in the law of the succeeding High Priest (Leviticus 21); it does not effect their consecration, but is rather the result of it ("Days of Consecration," 30).

they must wash themselves anew, be dressed by Moses each day, and be sprinkled with blood and oil on all seven days.

The same idea emerges from the execution of these instructions in Leviticus 8:

> "Do not leave the entrance to the Tent of Meeting for seven days, until the days of your ordination are complete, for your ordination will take seven days, each like today. This is what the Lord has commanded to be done to make your atonement. Stay, then, at the entrance to the Tent of Meeting for seven days, day and night, keeping the Lord's charge – and you will not die. This is what I have been commanded." Aaron and his sons did everything that the Lord had commanded through Moses. (Lev. 8:33–36)

While the phrase "seven days – each like today" can be read as an abridged version of the full ritual instructions, which is the view of Rashi and other *Rishonim*, it is even simpler to read the text literally: that the main ritual has been completed, Moses declares to the priests that he has done exactly what God commanded,[18] and now the priests must wait for seven days in order for the process to be complete.[19]

For these seven days (and nights), the priests may not leave the sacred area: "Keeping the Lord's charge – and you will not die." "Keeping the Lord's charge" may generally mean to keep all God's laws (as in Genesis 26:5), but in the context of the Sanctuary, this phrase is in dialogue with the instructions to the Levites in Numbers:

---

18. On the use of the third person rather than "I did," see Ibn Ezra: "Such is the holy tongue." Milgrom may be correct that this apparently active verb is in fact passive: "As was done on this day, the Lord commanded to do" (Milgrom, *Leviticus*, vol. 1, 540).
19. See, similarly, Wenham, *Leviticus*, 144; Hartley, *Leviticus*, 115 (although he debates whether it makes sense that certain offerings were offered repeatedly). Martin Noth believes that the concluding verses show that it was in fact seven days of ritual, although he debates if the entire chapter is consistent with the conclusion (Noth, *Leviticus*, 73).

> They shall keep his charge and that of the whole community at the Tent of Meeting, carrying out the service of the Tabernacle. Theirs shall be the charge of all the utensils of the Tent of Meeting, and they shall keep, too, the charge of the Israelites by performing the service of the Tabernacle. Give the Levites over to Aaron and his sons; they among the Israelites are to be dedicated wholly to him. Appoint Aaron and his sons to attend to the priestly duties; any outsider who draws close will die.
> (Num. 7–10).

The Levites' duty is not merely technical, physical guarding of the Sanctuary. As Rashi explains: "They shall keep his charge – Any office to which a person is appointed and [the duty] he is bound to carry out is called 'keeping charge' in Scripture and the Mishna" (on Num. 3:7).

Applying this reading to our verse clarifies its plain meaning. Moses tells the priests that they must fulfill what they were instructed in the previous verse – to remain at the entrance to the Tent of Meeting for seven full days to complete their ordination.[20] This is the meaning of "keeping the Lord's charge"; the verse is not referring to the extensive rituals of the first day, but merely to staying in the sacred area for seven days to complete their ordination.[21]

This should come as no surprise. Counting for seven days to complete the process of a change in status is a classic biblical model. There are no other instances of people counting seven days and repeating certain actions on each of the seven days (compare also to the Nazirite's fulfillment of their term – Num. 6:13–20).[22]

---

20. As claimed by Rendtorff, *Leviticus*, 288.
21. The concluding verse warns that if the priests leave the entrance to the Tent of Meeting they will die; this has a certain tragic irony, given that Aaron's sons die inside the Tent of Meeting itself. This is the danger of holiness: Its precise measure is crucial. To leave the holy area means death; to enter an even holier area also means death.
22. Milgrom compares our verse to the seven days of offerings to consecrate Ezekiel's Temple (Ezek. 43:25–26 – see Milgrom, *Leviticus*, vol. 1, 537). But the purpose of Ezekiel's offerings here is to purify the Temple, not to consecrate it, and note that the purification bull *is* offered on all seven days of consecration as well.

Yet the discussion does not end with this conclusion. In the final verses of the instructions in Exodus 29, the laws of the purification bull introduce a different perspective:

> This is what you must do for Aaron and his sons, just as I have commanded you. Their ordination shall take seven days. Each day, offer a bull as a purification offering for atonement. Purify the altar by making atonement for it, and consecrate it by anointing it. For seven days, make atonement for the altar and consecrate it, so that the altar becomes holy of holies – and anything that touches it will become holy. (Ex. 29:35–37)

The purification bull *is* offered on all seven days in order to purify and consecrate the altar. It thus emerges that special offerings are brought during the seven days of consecration after all, not just on the first day. This makes sense of the mysterious ambiguity. The first day of consecration indeed requires special offerings and rituals, after which the priests must remain in the holy place for all seven days until their ordination is complete. During this week, however, the purification bull (which seems unrelated in Exodus) *is* offered up every single day.[23]

As we will clarify below, in the book of Leviticus, the priests' purification offering and the altar's purification offering converge into the same offering, so in this respect the priests' ordination does have a repeated, active component during the seven days; we will explore this further below.

THE ANOINTING OF THE PRIESTS

The refrain throughout the chapters of consecration, "as the Lord had commanded Moses," can be read as a positive report of Moses's loyalty to the instructions given in Exodus 29. Some even interpret this devotion as reparation for the sin of the Golden Calf and the people's

23. I will discuss this in depth below and thus be brief here: The purification bull mentioned in Exodus 29 is presumably the same purification bull (see, e.g., Kehat, "Days of Consecration," 23), but even if so, this commandment's division into two different parts demands explanation.

complaints about hunger and thirst on their way to Mount Sinai (Ex. 15–17).[24] Others point out that the phrase appears seven times, in a symbolic parallel between the creation of the world and the building of the Tabernacle.[25] I am not sure that this symbolism is so heavily loaded, but it certainly helps divide the rites and rituals of the seven days into smaller subunits. When the section based on the phrase "as the Lord commanded Moses" is divided, the resulting division is not necessarily intuitive:

1. Taking the day's required components and the people's assembly (8:1–5)
2. Washing Aaron and his sons; dressing Aaron in his garments (6–9)[26]
3. Anointing the Tabernacle, its vessels, and Aaron himself with oil; dressing the sons of Aaron in the priestly vestments (10–13)[27]
4. The purification bull (14–17)
5. The burnt offering ram (18–21)
6. The ordination ram (22–29)
7. Sprinkling blood and oil on Aaron and his sons; eating the ordination ram (30–36)

This division is surprising in two main respects. Firstly, Aaron and his sons are washed together but dressed separately; while Aaron has more sacred garments than his sons, it still comes as a surprise that after Aaron is dressed, the Tabernacle, its vessels, and Aaron are anointed with oil

---

24. Hartley, *Leviticus*, 104. See also Wenham, *Leviticus*, 131–32; Watts, "Ritual," 106–18; who emphasize the obedience to God as the chapter's guiding theme.
25. Gorman, *Ideology*, 49–50.
26. It is interesting that the Hittites had a detailed order for the process of sacrifices offered by the king or queen, which began with dressing the king, then cleansing his hands (Weinberg, *Sacrifice in Israel*, 115).
27. Nor should we ignore the fact that there was no special ceremony for bringing the Ark into the Tabernacle; this is surprising given such biblical ceremonies (II Sam. 6; I Kings 8:1–11) and extrabiblical ceremonies (Hundley, *Keeping Heaven on Earth*, 57–58). This draws a sharp distinction between the Ark itself and the Divine Presence; it also emphasizes that the main focus of the days of consecration was the altar, where the Divine Presence would soon appear.

before the sons are also dressed.[28] The second surprise is that anointing the Tabernacle with oil is grouped with the same scene as the dressing of Aaron's sons.

Both surprises come from the same source: In this chapter, the priests are essentially objectified into vessels of the Tabernacle, sanctified as part of "the Tabernacle and everything in it" (v. 10). Both the High Priest and his sons are service vessels, waiting to be anointed.[29] This is reflected in Rambam's *Mishneh Torah*: The laws of the priest are grouped together with the laws of the anointing oil and the preparation of the incense as "*Hilkhot Klei HaMikdash VeHaOvdim Bo*" – "Laws of the Temple Vessels and its Workers."

This, however, raises the question as to why Aaron is dressed before the Tabernacle is anointed. This sequence compels us to conclude that Aaron indeed has a separate status from that of his sons. On the one hand, all the priests are essentially service vessels; on the other, Aaron does have a special, distinct role. And indeed, the High Priest has duties beyond the world of the Sanctuary, not only because he addresses Israel's warriors before they set out for battle (Deut. 20:2), but because he is considered Israel's emissary to God, as emerges from the case of the anointed priest's purification offering (Lev. 4:3–12). His sin reflects upon the entire congregation; for this reason, he brings an internal purification offering. His array of garments reflects not mere seniority, but a different, more diplomatic role.

The disparity between Aaron and his sons is also expressed through their respective anointing ceremonies. Ramban debates whether all of Aaron's sons are anointed with oil, or just their father. There are verses that present apparently contradictory views.[30]

---

28. Aaron is not treated separately from his sons in the whole chapter: Moses applies the blood of the ordination ram to them all together (Ex. 29:20–21). In the words of the Tosefta: "The ordination ram – Aaron and his sons at once" (Tosefta Menaḥot 10:4).
29. See further in Levine, "Tabernacle."
30. See further in Weinel, "M-SH-Ḥ." Some descriptions of priests who are anointed with oil seem to depict his future successors (see, e.g., Stuart, *Exodus*, 622, n. 438). In other cases, all the priests are anointed with oil: see especially Ex. 28:41; Ex. 40:15.

As is evident in this chapter, the text clearly specifies that Aaron is anointed with the anointing oil: "Some of the anointing oil he poured on Aaron's head, anointing him, consecrating him" (8:12). There is no description, however, of his sons being anointed. This is consistent with Exodus 29, where Moses is commanded to dress and anoint Aaron: "Take the anointing oil, pour it on his head, and anoint him" (Ex. 29:7). There are instructions to dress Aaron's sons, but none to anoint them. Moreover, the synonym for the High Priest in Leviticus 4 – "the anointed priest" – implies that he is the only priest who is actually anointed with oil.

Yet, as mentioned, Exodus 28 issues instructions for the anointing of all the priests: "Put these on your brother Aaron and his sons; then *anoint*, ordain, and consecrate them to serve Me as priests" (28:41). This is also evident from the instructions relating to the oil itself: "Take the finest spices.... Make from these a sacred anointing oil...with it, you shall anoint Aaron *and his sons* and consecrate them to serve Me as priests" (Ex. 30:22–31). An even more explicit description is found at the very end of Exodus: "Then bring his sons forward...*anoint them as you anointed their father*, that they may serve Me as priests. Through this anointing, theirs will become an everlasting priesthood throughout the generations" (Ex. 40:14–15; see also Lev. 7:35).

Ramban offers a brilliant solution to the contradictions in these verses. In his commentary to Lev 8:12, he proposes that only the High Priest is anointed by oil poured on his head, whereas the other priests are anointed through just the sprinkling of oil: "Moses took some of the anointing oil and some of the blood from the altar and sprinkled it on Aaron and on his vestments, and on his sons and theirs. Thus,Moses consecrated Aaron and his vestments, and his sons and their vestments" (8:30). This justifies the command "Anoint them as you anointed their father"; the verse certainly implies that the act of sprinkling serves to consecrate.[31] Ramban's inclusion of both traditional anointing and sprinkling under the category of "anointing" serves to reconcile what may initially seem to be contradictions.

31. Similarly Hartley, *Leviticus*, 110; Watts, *Leviticus*, 466.

This offers a further glimpse into the disparity between the "anointed priest" and his sons. Aaron's head is drizzled with oil, consecrating him personally as a sacred entity. In contrast, when Aaron's sons are sprinkled with oil, their garments are also sprayed in the process, creating the sense that the priests are inseparable from their garments: "He sprinkled it on Aaron and on his vestments, and on his sons and theirs. Thus,he consecrated Aaron and his vestments, and his sons and their vestments" (8:30). This clarifies how central the priestly vestments are to their role and sanctity.

Aaron has already undergone an initial, individual anointing ceremony; now he undergoes another ritual together with his sons, all of them together with their garments. This is a different kind of consecration: The first anointing marks him as Israel's emissary to God; now he is sprinkled with oil together with his sons, consecrating them all to God's service in the Tabernacle.[32]

That the priests are essentially service vessels is evident in the instructions of how to consecrate them in Exodus 40, while their consecration as a distinct group is depicted in Exodus 29. Both aspects are fulfilled in the days of consecration in Leviticus; different descriptions are in dialogue with the two chapters in Exodus.

In addition to the priests being mentioned as part of "the Tabernacle and everything in it," one vessel receives special attention, the burnt offering altar: "He sprinkled some of the oil on the altar seven times. He anointed the altar and all its vessels, and the laver and its base, thus consecrating them" (8:11). No other vessel is sprinkled a symbolic seven times. Avigdor Horowitz proposes that the altar always has an independent status that transcends its role and place in the Sanctuary; there are many mentions of *bamot,* and altars were built before, during, and after the time of the Sanctuary. Each altar was presumably consecrated

32. Milgrom proposes that because priests are born priests, there is no need to consecrate them; only the High Priest requires anointing, because his status changes, just like a king is anointed (Milgrom, *Leviticus,* vol. 1, 554–55). He is correct, although other parts of the chapter show that this is a more fundamental change to his role.

before use; thus, the altar within the Sanctuary is granted special ceremonial status.[33]

Milgrom offers an alternative reading. Unlike other Temple vessels, the altar remains exposed in the Sanctuary courtyard, more vulnerable to outside impurities than any other vessel. For this reason, its consecration ceremony is far more comprehensive than that of any other vessel.[34]

I believe that the seven symbolic sprinklings of the altar are related to this chapter's objective, which is focused on consecrating the entities that consume the offerings. The priests undergo intense rites of passage because it is their mouths that consume God's offerings; the altar, of course, is the first and foremost consumer of all offerings, hence its special ritual of consecration.

THE PURIFICATION BULL

How is the purification bull related to the priests' consecration? The offering of the purification bull daily during the days of consecration does not conform to any usual purification offering. A comparison of the instructions given in Exodus 29 and their execution in Leviticus 8 hints to its unique nature and purpose:

Commandment: Exodus 29:10–14	**Execution: Leviticus 8:14–17**
Then bring the young bull in front of the Tent of Meeting,	Moses drew close the bull for the purification offering,
and have Aaron and his sons lay their hands on its head.	and Aaron and his sons laid their hands on its head.
Slaughter the bull before the Lord at the entrance of the Tent of Meeting.	It was slaughtered,
Take some of the bull's blood and put it on the horns of the altar with your finger.	and Moses took the blood and applied it with his finger to all the altar's horns, purifying the altar.

33. Horowitz, *Temples*, 115–16.
34. Milgrom, *Leviticus*, vol. 1, 516–17. He adds that out of all the Temple vessels, the altar is the only one defined as "holy of holies," which perhaps requires extra oil.

Pour out the rest of the blood at the base of the altar.	The rest of the blood he poured out at the altar's base. Thus,he consecrated it so that, upon it, atonement could be made.
Take all the fat that covers the entrails, the diaphragm of the liver, and the two kidneys with the fat around them, and send them up in smoke on the altar.	Moses removed all the fat around the entrails, the diaphragm of the liver, the two kidneys and their fat, and sent them up in smoke upon the altar.
Burn the bull's flesh, its hide, and its waste outside the camp; it is a purification offering.	But the rest of the bull, its skin, its flesh, and its waste, he burned with fire outside the camp as the Lord had commanded him.
Exodus 29:36 Each day, offer a bull as a purification offering for atonement. Purify the altar by making atonement for it and consecrate it by anointing it.	

The instructions are carried out almost word for word, with the exception of certain synonyms (for example, "drew close," "*vayaggesh,*" instead of "bring," "*hikravta,*" as discussed). Yet there are two dramatic additions to the blood ritual in Leviticus 8: "Purifying the altar" and "Thus,he consecrated it so that, upon it, atonement could be made."

In order to discuss these additions, I will begin with the most unusual aspect of the particular purification bull offering mentioned in both Exodus and Leviticus: burning the bull outside the camp. This detail is surprising, given that only internal purification offerings – those whose blood is sprinkled inside the Sanctuary – are usually burned outside, whereas external purification offerings are usually eaten by the priests. The purification bull of the days of consecration is an external purification offering, yet for some reason its flesh is burned outside the camp instead of shared with the priests. Various solutions are proposed; I wish to note two central ideas.

The Priests' Own Purification Offering

Some argue that during the days of consecration, the priests cannot eat the offerings, because they are not yet fully consecrated. Moses offers the sacrifices up in their place (or as the altar's emissary, as noted above, in the context of the discussion of the breast and thigh), but he cannot eat of the offerings either, because he is not strictly a priest, so the purification offering is burned even though its blood is not brought inside the Tent of Meeting.[35] This is a compelling approach, but the fact that the priests do eat of the purification on the eighth day of consecration challenges this idea.

It thus makes more sense that the priests' status affects the sacrificial process of the purification offering from a different angle. As Hizkuni writes: "Some explain why the consecration purification bulls of the days of consecration are burned: because they are the priests' own offerings; similar to the priest's own grain offering, "they must be entirely burned" (on Ex. 29:14).

If the priest is not supposed to eat his own offerings (and this applies to all offerings, not just grain offerings), it is obvious why the priests do not eat their own purification offering during the days of consecration; this has already been discussed in the context of the internal purification offerings of Leviticus 4.[36]

External as Internal

In order to present the alternative approach, we must first articulate the issue: Is the purification bull of the days of consecration offered as "an external purification offering" – i.e., one whose blood is burned on the outer altar – that is nonetheless burned outside the camp? Rashi notes: "There is no other case of an external purification offering burnt except for this one." Or, alternatively, should it be perceived as an internal purification offering whose blood is, for some reason, not sprinkled inside the Sanctuary?

35. Dillmann, *Leviticus*, 508. As mentioned, the Sages agree that Moses acts as a priest during the days of consecration; their only debate is for how long and in which contexts (see the *Encyclopedia Talmudit*, "*Kohen*," vol. 27, 168). However, even so, he is still not strictly defined as a priest: He does not wear the priestly vestments, and he presumably did not fulfill all the usual priestly roles, such as examining blemishes (see further in Zevaḥim 101b–102a).

36. Similarly Milgrom, *Leviticus*, vol. 1, 525.

Ramban favors the second approach; thus, his question is not why the bull is burned outside the camp, but rather why its blood is not sprinkled inside the Sanctuary:

> The reason is that this purification bull was for atonement for the Golden Calf and offered up by the anointed priest, and [in Leviticus] he was commanded to bring the blood inside the curtain, but he did not yet wish to bring it inside, given that [God says to bring it] "in front of My holy curtain" (Lev. 4:6). However, it had not yet been sanctified and the Divine Presence did not yet rest there for it to be called a "holy curtain," so this external purification offering was essentially an internal purification offering. (Ramban on Ex. 29:14)

Setting aside (for now) Ramban's premise that the purification offering's purpose was to atone for the Golden Calf (which did not yet happen if the chapters are read in chronological order),[37] Ramban's theory is important: Since it is the priests' offering, it is essentially considered an internal purification offering, but because God's presence has not yet settled inside the Sanctuary, the blood is not yet sprinkled inside, and is instead applied to the outer altar.[38]

Perhaps Rashi's reading seems more intuitive, as where the blood is applied characterizes the offering's nature, but a closer analysis favors Ramban's direction. This is evident, given that the purification animal is a bull and not a goat or sheep. In Leviticus 4, internal purification offerings are bulls, whereas external purification offerings are from the flock.

If so, why isn't its blood sprinkled inside? Beyond Ramban's view that God's presence has not yet sanctified the Sanctuary, this may reflect the place of revelation. The internal purification offering purifies the place where the blood is sprinkled. The usual place of revelation is inside the Holy of Holies, but given that on the eighth day of consecration God's

---

37. As implied from his commentary here; elsewhere Ramban seems to have a different view.
38. Although if so, it is still not explained why the altar is already considered holy (and able to receive blood) before the Tent of Meeting is.

glory appears on the outer altar, this is the site that must be purified in preparation for God's revelation. In the words of Ramban, "So this external purification offering was essentially an internal purification offering."[39]

God's blazing revelation upon the outer altar is fundamental to the objective of the days of consecration, which culminate in the eighth day's divine revelation. This brings us back to our opening question: What role does the purification offering play in the priests' consecration and atonement? Ramban indeed perceives this as an offering of specific atonement for the anointed priest (and for his sons as well, who did not actively participate in the sin of the Golden Calf).

In fact, the instructions in Exodus 29 and the execution of Leviticus 8 seem to conflict with regard to this question. Exodus 29 seems to present two separate purification bulls: the priests' purification bulls (29:10–14), and another bull whose purpose is to purify the altar (29:36–39). The latter concluding verses seem distinct from those describing the seven days of consecration – to the extent that some commentators read them as a commandment to purify the altar that has nothing to do with the days of consecration:

> Although it is certainly possible that the same week was originally used for the consecration of the altar as for the consecration/ordination of Aaron and his sons, these verses almost surely address a separate and distinct ceremony, in which seven bulls, other than those used for the ordination of the priests, were sacrificed, once each day, "as a sin offering to make atonement."[40]

As mentioned, it may be that the rest of the priests' offerings were only brought on the first day, whereas the purification bull was offered on each of the seven days. If so, based on the two separate commandments in Exodus, the priestly purification bull can indeed be perceived as a

39. R. Yoel Bin-Nun shows that there is an affinity between the eighth day of consecration and Yom Kippur. The difference is that on the eighth day, the drama of revelation is focused on the outer altar – reflecting the nature of the day – whereas on Yom Kippur, the High Priest goes deep inside (Bin-Nun, "The Eighth Day"). Compare also to Jürgens, "Wiederherstellung."
40. Stuart, *Exodus*, 628.

separate offering, unrelated to the purification bull whose purpose is the altar's purification.

In fact, this is almost explicit in the second commandment in Exodus; the text emphasizes that this purification offering is brought in addition to the atonement offerings: "Each day, offer a bull as a purification offering for atonement. Purify the altar by making atonement for it and consecrate it by anointing it" (Ex. 29:36). Most commentators interpret the "purification offering for atonement" as the burnt offering ram and the priestly ordination ram, and do not include the priestly purification bull in this category. These include Ramban: "The correct interpretation of '*al hakippurim*' is, however, [that he is to bring the purification bull] in addition to the two rams which were an atonement for Aaron and his sons" (on Ex. 29:36). Clearly uncomfortable with excluding the purification bull from the priestly atonement, Ramban adds: "And surely the purification offering was for the purpose of atonement." The verse reads more easily, however, if it indeed hints to all the priestly offerings – the burnt offering, the ordination ram, and the purification bull. Thus, according to Exodus 29, the bull brought for the altar's purification is an additional offering.

In Leviticus 8, however, only one purification bull is brought to perform both purposes: Its explicit role is to purify the altar. As shown, both acts of the priests' purification bull's blood ritual are followed with a description of the purification and atonement of the altar: "Purifying the altar" and "Thus,he consecrated it so that, upon it, atonement could be made." These two additions are not mentioned in the instructions for the priestly purification bull (Ex. 29:10–14). Rather, they are a fulfillment of the separate instructions Moses receives at the end of the chapter: "Each day, offer a bull as a purification offering for atonement. Purify the altar by making atonement for it and consecrate it by anointing it" (Ex. 29:36). In Leviticus 8, the priests and altar are purified and atoned for by the same bull.

Two Different Verbs for "Pouring"

The new meaning that applies to the priestly purification bull is reflected in the change of verb from the root SH-P-KH, "*tishpokh,*" to Y-TZ-K, "*yatzak*." Both verbs mean "pour,"[41] but the term "*shafakh*" is more commonly used in the sacrificial chapters. Is there any significance – even if only literary – to the less common word "*yatzak*" in Leviticus 8?

The verb "*shafakh*" is appropriate for the priestly purification offering: After the main blood ritual, what remains is "poured out" at the altar's base (Lev. 4:7, 18, 25, 30), which implies that "the leftover blood has no ceremonial purpose."[42] Given that the purification bull serves a dual purpose in Leviticus 8, however, the pouring of the remaining blood is more aptly described with the verb "*yatzak*," which has ritual connotations. For example, when Jacob wakes from his dream of revelation, he "rose early the next morning, took the stone he had placed under his head, set it up as a pillar, and *poured* (*vayitzok*) oil on top of it" (Gen. 28:18). Similarly, when he returns from Haran to Beit El to fulfill his vow, "Jacob set up a stone pillar at the place where God had talked with him, and on it he offered a libation and *poured* (*vayitzok*) oil" (Gen. 35:14). "*Yatzak*," then, connotes ritual, intentional pouring, rather than the "pouring out" of excess. Jacob's ritual pouring of oil is comparable to Aaron's anointing in Leviticus 8: "Some of the anointing oil he *poured* (*vayitzok*) on Aaron's head, anointing him, consecrating him" (8:12).[43] The purpose of the pouring of oil is to consecrate the object of the anointment.[44] Similarly, pouring the "excess" blood at the base of the altar in this ritual is not an act of pouring *out* the leftover blood, but an intentional act of ritual pouring that effects purification and

41. Kaddari, *Dictionary*, 452.
42. Rendtorff, *Leviticus*, 280.
43. Compare also to the pouring of oil to anoint the king: "And Samuel took the juglet of oil and *poured it* (*vayitzak*) over his head and kissed him. And he said, 'The Lord hereby *anoints* you as ruler over His estate" (I Sam. 10:1); "Then take the flask of oil and *pour* it on his head and say, 'Thus,says the Lord: I have *anointed* you as king of Israel'" (II Kings 9:3).
44. Warning (*Literary Artistry*, 137) shows that the term "*yatzak*" appears in Leviticus a symbolic seven times, creating a chiastic structure: three pourings of oil, then two of blood, then three more of oil (Lev. 2:1, 6; 8:12, 15; 9:9; 14:15, 26; 21:10). This brilliant observation may or may not show that the use of the verb is intentional, given that the verbs appear across different chapters; however, he also shows similar connections throughout Leviticus and its priestly sections and holy laws, which makes his work an important study for the question of the cohesion of Leviticus.

consecration: "The rest of the blood he *poured* out at the altar's base. *Thus,*he consecrated it so that, upon it, atonement could be made."[45]

The purification bull brought in Leviticus 8 is thus an offering for both the priests and the altar itself. What is usually "leftover" blood here serves to purify, anoint, and consecrate the altar so that it can become a vehicle for God's glory before the eyes of all Israel.

THE ANOINTING OIL, VESTMENTS, AND THE ORDINATION RAM[46]

Various sections describe the process of the priests' ordination. All contain three main components to this process: (1) dressing the priests in their garments; (2) anointing them with oil; and (3) the days of the consecration ceremony.[47] The instructions regarding the priestly garments, for example, end thus: "Make tunics, sashes, and caps for Aaron's sons, for glory and for splendor. Put these on your brother Aaron and his sons; then *anoint, ordain,* and *consecrate them* to serve Me as priests" (Ex. 28:40–41). The final goal of both ordination and consecration can only be achieved through all three components: dressing the priests in their vestments for glory and for splendor, anointing them, and ordaining them.

---

45. There is room in this context to consider the meaning of applying blood to the altar "all around." In the sacrificial chapters, blood is dashed "all around the altar" for the burnt, peace, and guilt offerings, but applied to the horns for the purification offering, with no mention of the phrase "all around." The instructions in Exodus 29 are consistent with these semantics, using "apply," but in Leviticus, the term "all around" also appears. This is also presumably due to the complex nature of the purification offering that purifies both the priests and the altar.
46. The following discussion is the result of extensive debates with R. Dr. Eli Hadad. See further in Grossman and Hadad, "Ram of Ordination."
47. Weinel believes that the description of the days of consecration is structured according to the five components of the priests' qualification: purification, dressing in vestments, atonement, consecration, and ordination (Weinel, "M-SH-Ḥ," 42–43). He is correct that both purification and purifying the altar appear in this chapter, but not in relation to the priests' preparation. Pruification is often a requirement, such as the Levites' purification, for example (Num. 8:6–7); nor is the purification offering what qualifies them.

These three components also feature elsewhere, and not just in passages that focus on the priesthood. For example, when the Tabernacle's purification ritual is complete, "the priest who is *anointed* and *ordained* to succeed his father and serve as priest shall perform the atonement, *wearing* the sacred linen vestments" (Lev. 16:32). Even though the topic at hand is the Tabernacle's purification, all three components appear. Similarly, in the context of the prohibition on the High Priest to mourn for family members: "The priest, the highest among his brothers, on whose head the *anointing oil* has been poured and who has been *ordained* to *wear the vestments*, shall not dishevel his hair or tear his clothes" (Lev. 21:10).[48]

What constitutes each component? Michael Hundley is correct that "whether or not they consecrate, the priestly attire forms an integral part of the consecration process, one which, if extracted, would ruin the whole. To say that one element alone consecrates is to misunderstand both the complexity and interconnectedness of the ritual."[49]

All three components are indeed necessary, and none can be omitted. Yet the fact that various components are emphasized in different contexts shows that each makes its own unique contribution to the priesthood of Aaron and his sons. The present challenge is to characterize each of the three.

Exploring the passages devoted to the garments, the oil, and the days of consecration reveals what each contributes to the nature of priesthood. The text uses three different expressions to describe the purpose of each action that serves to qualify the priests: "to consecrate" (*lekaddesh*); "to serve as priests" (*lekhahen*); "to ordain" (literally, "to fill their hands" – *lemallei yad*). Each expression can be linked to one of the three components, although all three are used for different components as well.

48. We will soon posit that the verb "to serve as priest" (*lekhahen*) is associated with the priestly garments; thus, the genealogy of Aaron in Numbers also hints to the three components (3:3): "These were the names of Aaron's sons, the *anointed* priests, *ordained* for *priestly service* (*lekhahen*)."

49. Hundley, *Keeping Heaven*, 74.

The Anointing Oil

The anointing oil "consecrates" whatever it is poured on – objects or people.[50] Why oil is the chosen means for this purpose is debatable,[51] but it is explicitly stated in the description of the method used to prepare the oil in Exodus 30:22–33. Moses is commanded to make "a sacred anointing oil" to anoint the Tabernacle and its vessels to consecrate them: "You shall consecrate them and they will become holy of holies" (Ex. 30:26–29). In this section, Aaron and his sons are mentioned as part of the Tabernacle vessels that require consecration: "You shall anoint Aaron and his sons and *consecrate* them to serve Me as priests" (Ex. 30:30). This implies that the act of anointing consecrates the priests and sets them apart as entities that belong to the Tabernacle, just like its other vessels. Moreover, the text warns against using the oil on any non-priest, to avoid any wrongly applied consecration (30:32–33).

The sacred oil's capacity to consecrate is also evident in Exodus 40: "Take the anointing oil and anoint the Tabernacle and everything in it. *Consecrate* it and all its furnishings so that it becomes *holy*. Anoint the sacrificial altar and all its utensils, *consecrating* it so that it becomes *holy of holies*. Anoint the laver with its base, making it *holy*" (Ex. 40:9–11). The oil's consecrating properties are reiterated in the execution of Leviticus 8: "Then Moses took the anointing oil and anointed the Tabernacle and everything in it; thus he consecrated them.... He anointed the altar and all its vessels, and the laver and its base, thus consecrating them. Some of the anointing oil he poured on Aaron's head, anointing him, consecrating him" (Lev. 8:10–12).

---

50. Klingbeil points out the parallels between the consecration of the biblical High Priest and other acts of anointing in the Ancient Near East (chiefly Syria) in the fourteenth century BCE. This leads him to conclude that there is no reason to date this ritual to later than Moses's time (Klingbeil, "Anointing of Aaron").

51. See, for example, Houtman, "Sacred Anointing Oil"; Viberg, *Symbols of Law*, 89–119. See also Magness's discussion of the lack of mention of the anointing oil in the Qumran and Josephus (Magness, "Impurity of Oil"). Given that oil was widely used for anointing in the ancient world (see Lam, "Reassessment"), the question is what makes the biblical oil unique.

Even if there is an affinity between the anointing of priests and the anointing of the Israelite king,[52] it is worth emphasizing that the act of anointing kings is not an act of consecration, just appointment. Kings Saul, David, Absalom, Joash, Jehoahaz, and Hazael of Aram are all anointed with oil,[53] yet none is considered "holy."[54] Rather, the act of anointing the chosen king is presumably designed to evoke connotations of divine appointment (such as David's anointment in I Samuel 16:1–13; Psalms 45:8),[55] but this does *not* constitute consecration. The priests' anointment as part of the sacred vessels proves that the anointment of the priests is not merely appointment, but consecration as well.

The Priestly Vestments

The description of preparing the priestly garments in Exodus 28 implies that the garments are designed to allow the priests to serve in the Tabernacle:

> From among the Israelites, draw your brother Aaron and his sons close to you to *serve Me as priests* (*lekhahano Li*).... Make sacred vestments for your brother Aaron, for glory and for splendor... Have them make Aaron's vestments; these will consecrate him *to serve Me as priest* (*lekhahano Li*)... Sacred vestments shall they make, for your brother Aaron and his sons to *serve Me* in (*lekhahano Li*). (Ex. 28:1–4)

52. North attempts to prove that biblical kings have a special connection with God (North, "Religious Aspects"). I find Berman's perception of kingship more convincing (Berman, *Created Equal*), but the common act of anointing with oil does point to a certain affinity between kings and priests. But as North also emphasizes, anointing a king does not bestow the same eternal status as priests receive.
53. Compare also Judges 9:8; see also Seybold, "M-SH-Ḥ," 45–46. On whether all kings were anointed, see Weinel, "M-SH-Ḥ," 21–23.
54. Dommershausen states that ancient Israel is the only culture in the Ancient Near East in which the king never claims that he is a priest ("Kohen," 73). However, this was only true of ancient Israel before the schism between Judea and Israel.
55. This is also salient given that a prophet or priest anoints the king (Weinel, "M-SH-Ḥ," 23–25). The Septuagint implies that all the people anoint Saul (the MT is "crown as king," the Septuagint has "anoint" in I Sam. 11:15).

The root of "priest" as a verb (*lekhahen*) appears three times in this introduction, and this points to the purpose of these vestments.[56] These garments are to single the priests out from the people as God's chosen servants – the priests.

This section contains no hint of the priests being serving vessels; rather, they are the servants. In other words, while anointing the priests with oil makes them into sacred vessels, dressing them in the priestly garments makes them into servants. Oil can be poured on anything, but garments are for humans, and they lend their wearers glory and splendor. Like any uniform, these vestments define the priests as being in their Master's service. It emphasizes their purpose rather than their names.[57]

The same verb, "*lekhahen*," is used in the instructions to Betzalel: "The sacred vestments for Aaron the priest and the vestments for his sons for when they serve as priests" (Ex. 31:10). This verse draws a subtle distinction between the sacred nature of Aaron's garments compared to the service nature of his sons' garments (which we will explore further below), but sacred or non-sacred, they all "served as priests": "Then bring his sons forward and dress them with the tunics. Gird Aaron and his sons with the sashes and fasten their headdresses. The *priesthood* (*kehunna*) shall be theirs as a law for all time" (Ex. 29:8–9).[58]

We can point to a more specific purpose these garments serve, beyond marking them as God's servants. These garments grant their wearer passage into the sacred sphere of the Sanctuary courtyard. The outsider who enters the courtyard must be put to death, but those wearing the priestly garments are not considered "outsiders." To enter the sacred sphere, one must wear the proper vestments. Various ideas in the text support this.

---

56. Cassuto, *Exodus*, 259.
57. Wenham, *Leviticus*, 138.
58. The end of the verse also states: "You shall ordain Aaron and his sons," but this serves as the transition to the next unit, which describes the priestly offerings. The phrase "*ḥukkat olam*" ("a law for all time/eternal law") is a common concluding formula for a legal passage (e.g., Lev. 7:36). This also seems to conclude the section about the priestly vestments. After this, the narrator begins to describe the offerings of the days of consecration, beginning with the phrase "to ordain Aaron and his sons," as we will explore below.

Firstly, there is an intriguing similarity between Aaron's vestments and the materials of the Tabernacle itself (Ex. 26:1, 31, 36):

> One notes immediately that the fabrics and colors of the materials for the garments (v. 5) were the same as those also used for the lovely inner curtains and entrance curtain of the tabernacle itself. The description given clearly makes the vestments similar to and reflective of the "dignity and honor" of the tabernacle.[59]

Assuming this is not merely the result of the biblical perception of what expresses glory and beauty, the similarities may hint that only one wearing such vehicles of glory and beauty is granted access to the sphere of glory and beauty.[60]

Secondly, while Aaron's garments are not consecrating, they are still referred to as "holy garments," "*bigdei kodesh*" (Ex. 28:2, 4). The word "*kodesh*" also means "Sanctuary," so this phrase can also be read as "garments of the Sanctuary," meaning "garments in which one may enter the Sanctuary." This is evident from the purification of the Sanctuary ceremony in Leviticus 16, where in order to enter the Holy of Holies Aaron must don special vestments:

> This is how Aaron is to enter *the holy place* (*kodesh*): with a young bull as a purification offering and a ram as a burnt offering; he shall put on the *holy* (*kodesh*) linen tunic with linen undergarments covering his body. He shall bind the linen sash around himself and wrap a linen turban about his head. These are *holy* (*kodesh*) vestments; he shall immerse himself in water and only then put them on. (Lev. 16:3–4).

The phrase "these are holy vestments" can also literally mean "these are the vestments of the holy place." Only when wearing these "vestments of the holy place" may Aaron enter "the holy place."

---

59. Stuart, *Exodus*, 605. This idea is developed by Haran, *Temples*, 165–74.
60. Although the regular priests are not granted entry into the Sanctuary itself – only the High Priest is – they must still wear appropriate clothing to enter the compound.

Thirdly, the definition "*bigdei kodesh*" leads to a distinction between the High Priest's vestments and those of the regular priest. While this is generally regarded as an expression of status, "garments that specify their rank of holiness,"[61] it can also be read as a reflection of where each priest is allowed to enter. The *peshat* of the verses implies that Aaron is the one who serves within the Tent of Meeting itself.[62] According to the text, it is Aaron who burns the incense: "Aaron should burn incense on it every morning when he tends the lamps, and before evening when he lights the lamps.... Once a year Aaron shall make atonement on its horns" (Ex. 30:7–10); he also lights the lamp: "Speak to Aaron; say to him: When you raise up the lamps.... Aaron did so" (Num. 8:2). The same is true of lighting the perpetual fire and setting the showbread upon the table (Lev. 23:3–8) – all tasks are given specifically to Aaron. In this context, the description of transferring the High Priesthood to the next generation is particularly interesting: "Aaron's sacred vestments shall pass on to his sons after him. In them they shall be anointed and ordained. The son who succeeds him as priest, entering the Tent of Meeting to minister in the Sanctuary, shall wear them for seven days" (Ex. 29:29–30). The transferral of priesthood from one generation to the next is manifested by the son wearing the vestments and entering the Tent of Meeting in them.

Thus, Aaron's vestments, designed for serving inside the *kodesh*, are referred to as "*bigdei kodesh*," whereas the regular priest serves in the courtyard wearing garments that are for "glory and splendor," but

61. Cassuto, *Exodus*, 259.

62. Compare: Milgrom, *Leviticus*, vol. 1, 232–33; vol. 3, 2088.. In light of this, he questions why for the anointed priest's purification offering, the High Priest himself sprinkles the blood even though he is the sinner. He explains that the regular priests served in the entrance to the Sanctuary, whereas only Aaron himself was allowed inside. He attempts to justify the verses that say "Aaron and his sons" entering the Tent of Meeting, but I believe that "and his sons" refers to his successors. Nonetheless, Leviticus 16:17 implies that regular priests were not allowed to actually serve inside the Sanctuary, but were allowed inside for other purposes, such as helping the High Priest and cleaning, etc.

nowhere are these vestments referred to as "*bigdei kodesh*."[63] This distinction is apparent whenever the regular priest's garments are mentioned:

- Exodus 31:10: "The service vestments, the *sacred* vestments for Aaron the priest and the vestments for his sons for when they serve as priests."
- Exodus 35:19: "The service vestments for ministering in the Sanctuary, and the *sacred* vestments for Aaron the priest and for his sons for their priestly service."
- Exodus 39:41: "And the service vestments for ministering in the Sanctuary, both the *sacred* vestments for Aaron the priest and the vestments for his sons to wear when serving as priests."

One of the most important examples is the preparation of Aaron's vestments: "From the sky-blue, purple, and scarlet wool they made woven garments for ministering in the Sanctuary. They also made *sacred* vestments for Aaron" (Ex. 39:1).

All these verses maintain the distinction between Aaron's *sacred* vestments and those of the regular priests; Aaron serves in the Sanctuary itself, whereas his sons "serve as priests." However, the meaning of the phrase "service vestments" – "*bigdei serad*" – is not clear. Some *Rishonim* (Rashi, Ibn Ezra, and Rashbam) take them to mean the woven garments that covered the service vessels, but Ramban vehemently opposes this reading. His main objection is that it makes no sense to suddenly mention coverings that have not hitherto been mentioned at all; moreover, the phrase "to serve in the Sanctuary" seems to refer to people, not coverings. Ramban ultimately explains that these "*bigdei serad*" refer

63. The Netziv already points out this principle: "The regular priests' garments are not commanded to be made to be sanctified, but to serve Me as priests" (on Ex. 28:4).

to Aaron's special garments.[64] This makes sense;[65] accordingly, these garments are defined as those worn for service in the Sanctuary itself."[66]

If so, the sons mentioned in Exodus 28:4, "Sacred vestments shall they make, for your brother Aaron and *his sons* to serve Me in," are the heirs to the High Priesthood.[67] This is already evident from the fact that regular priests do not wear "a breast piece, an ephod, a robe, a quilted tunic, a miter."

One further proof that the priestly vestments are the vehicle that allows their wearers passage to a holy place is that the instructions about Aaron's clothing in Exodus 28 reveal that the vestments are fundamentally linked to his entrance into a sacred site. The precious stones upon the ephod are worn by Aaron "on his shoulders as a remembrance *before the Lord*" (28:12). The phrase "before the Lord" may be metaphoric, but in the context of the Sanctuary, it makes sense to read it as a spatial expression for entering the Tent of Meeting. This is even more

64. As shown by Ofer and Jacobs, this was a later addition by Ramban after his arrival in Israel. He initially concurred with Rashi that these were coverings for service vessels, but after further study he arrived at this conclusion (Ofer and Jacobs, *Ramban*, 347–50).

65. Many modern translations rendered the phrase "*bigdei serad*" as a heading to the priestly vestments, including the vestments of both Aaron and his sons. For example: "The service cloths, the sacred vestments for Aaron the priest, the vestments for his sons in their ministry" (New American Bible); "And also the woven garments, both the sacred garments for Aaron the priest and the garments for his sons when they serve as priests" (New International Version).

66. There might be a semantic connection between "*serad*" and "*sarat*," "service," as is documented in Ugaritic (Held, "Biblical Mystery"). Cassuto refrained from adopting this interpretation, arguing that there is no need for the verse to repeat mention of the priests' garments if the term *bigdei haserad* already refers to them. He therefore suggested that the verse refers to garments "which the priests would wear in the winter, underneath the tunic, during the service, to protect themselves from the cold. Their wearing was not obligatory but optional, and therefore they were not mentioned earlier" (*Exodus*, 282).

However, aside from the fact that this explanation contradicts the rulings of the Sages, who were careful that nothing intervene between the garments and the priests' bodies, it also remains no more than a conjecture. Nowhere in Scripture do we find even a hint of such garments being worn.

67. As proposed by Stuart in relation to the anointing of Aaron's sons (*Exodus*, 622, n. 438).

explicit in relation to the breastplate: "Thus,will Aaron carry the names of Israel's sons on the breast piece of judgment at his heart *whenever he enters the Sanctuary*, as a remembrance *before the Lord* at all times ... they too will be at Aaron's heart *when he comes before the Lord*. Aaron will then always be carrying at his heart Israel's means of judgment, *before the Lord*" (Ex. 28:29–30). The same is true of his robe: "Aaron shall wear this robe whenever he ministers, and its sound will be heard *when he enters the Sanctuary before the Lord* and when he leaves, so that he will not die" (28:35), and his headplate: "It shall be on his forehead always, that they may find favor *before the Lord*" (28:38).

In contrast with this emphasis on Aaron's entrance into the Sanctuary, there is no mention whatsoever that the regular priests ever went into it. The vestments they wear – which are not described as "sacred" – allow them entry only into the courtyard. Thus, the verse presenting the requirement to wear linen trousers: "They must be worn by Aaron / and his sons / whenever they enter the Tent of Meeting /or approach the altar to minister in the Sanctuary so that they do not incur guilt and die" (28:43), has a split structure; the trousers must be "worn by Aaron" when he "enters the Tent of Meeting" and worn by "his sons" whenever they "approach the altar."

If so, the introduction to the chapter about the priestly garments already hints to the spatial connection between the priests, their clothing, and their place of service: "From among the Israelites, *draw your brother Aaron and his sons close* to you to serve Me as priests.... Make sacred vestments for your brother Aaron, for glory and for splendor" (28:1). This is certainly true metaphorically, for the priests are singled out among the Israelites to serve God in the Sanctuary, but it also has a material connotation: Moses physically brings the priests to serve at the heart of the camp, and this proximity requires special clothing.

This recalls Mordechai being unable to enter the king's gate when wearing sackcloth (Est. 4:2) and Ruth asking Boaz to spread his garment over her to signify that she belonged to him (Ruth 3:9; see also Ezek. 16:8). Clothing symbolizes belonging. One may not enter God's dwelling place in regular clothing, and at the same time, the sacred vestments express that the priests belong to God and His house.

Given that the vestments serve to mark the priests as God's servants, this clarifies the order of the three components that define priesthood: The priests are first dressed in their priestly vestments, then consecrated with oil, and finally, "ordained." This is logical, since it is only appropriate to anoint the priests after they are dressed, and only once they are consecrated can they be ordained.[68] But more profoundly, this sequence reflects that the priests may only enter the sacred sphere while wearing the appropriate garments; that the anointing oil "consecrates" the priests themselves and allows them to approach the altar, which is "holy of holies"; and finally, that the act of ordination, "filling their hands," qualifies them for the unique, specific third stage of service.

The Ordination Ram

The unique contribution of the days of consecration to the priestly training is especially salient in light of the absence of the ordination offerings in the description of establishing the Tabernacle in Exodus 40. This chapter describes the priestly garments and anointing, but there is no mention of the ordination offerings that the priests must bring:

> Then bring Aaron and his sons to the entrance of the Tent of Meeting, and cleanse them with water. Robe Aaron with the sacred vestments, anoint him, and consecrate him that he may serve Me as priest. Then bring his sons forward, robe them with tunics, and anoint them as you anointed their father, that they may serve Me as priests. Through this anointing, theirs will become an everlasting priesthood throughout the generations. (Ex. 40:12–15)[69]

These instructions are similar to the process laid down for the days of ordination, but this similarity only serves to underscore the absence of

68. Compare Stuart, *Exodus*, 617.
69. Compare to Shammah, *The Mekhiltot*, 180–81; he also pointed out the connection between these verses and the instructions in Exodus 29. In his opinion, this is their main objective – to integrate the instructions given in this chapter with the instructions in Exodus 29.

the ordination offerings described in depth in Exodus 28 and Leviticus 8. The verse is arranged in a chiastic order:

> Robe Aaron with the sacred vestments
> anoint him
> and consecrate him
> that he may serve Me as priest.

The priestly vestments allow their wearers to "serve Me as priests";[70] the anointing oil "consecrates them," but there is no mention of the ordination offerings that "ordain them." What is the meaning of this ordination, and why is it an integral part of the days of consecration?

The Main Focus of the Days of Consecration

To determine the purpose of the days of consecration, we must first ascertain the ritual focus. All three components that define the priestly status feature in Leviticus 8: the vestments (8:7–9, 13), the anointing oil (8:12, 30), and, of course, the ordination offerings. A closer look reveals that these offerings are the chapter's main focus,[71] especially the ordination ram.

This is evident from a comparison between the days of ordination as described in Leviticus 8 and the instructions given in Exodus 29. Leviticus 8 opens with a list of things Moses must "take" (8:1–3):

Take:

1. Aaron and his sons with him
2. The vestments
3. The anointing oil
4. A bull for the purification offering
5. Two rams
6. A basket of matzot

---

70. A slightly different picture emerges with Aaron's sons; once again, there is no mention of holiness.

71. Weinel, however, claims that all three components are of equal importance in this chapter, whereas Exodus 29 focuses on the anointing oil (Weinel, "M-SH-Ḥ," 34).

The instructions in Exodus 29 also list the things Moses must take, but this list only includes offerings (Ex. 29:1–3):

Take:

4. A young bull
5. Two unblemished rams
6. Matzot... in a basket

The omission of the priestly vestments and the anointing oil shows that these two are of secondary importance at this time. Given that the description of the days of ordination in Leviticus 8 is presenting the culmination of different chapters (especially Exodus 29, but Exodus 40 as well),[72] the priestly vestments and the anointing oil are mentioned, but in the context of the ordination itself they are only secondary to the ordination ram.

The instructions about the days of consecration in the book of Exodus do mention the oil and the vestments, but they are clearly secondary. Moses is commanded to "take" the priests and wash them, thus beginning the day's rituals, but the clothing and oil are mentioned only afterward (Ex. 29:5, 7). Their absence from the chapter's opening verses reveals that they are of lesser importance. Of primary significance is the ordination ram that ordains the priests:[73] The Hebrew phrase for the accomplishment of ordination is "*milluim*" and "*millui yadayim*" – literally, "filling," "the filling of the hands."

Unlike the vestments that allow the priests to "serve as priests" (*lekhahen*) and the oil that "consecrates," the ordination offerings – chiefly the ram of ordination – are the focus of these chapters: The one who offers

72. This is true not just of the priests, but also in relation to the anointment of the Sanctuary and its vessels (as described in Leviticus 8:10–11) and not at all in the instructions in Exodus 29, although it fulfills what Moses is instructed in Exodus 40:9–11 (see especially Fleming, "Priests," 411–13).

73. Weinel, "M-SH-Ḥ," 46. Snijders ("M-L-A," 303) writes that the term "*milluim*" defines the *milluim* ram, the flesh (Ex. 29:34), the burnt offering (Lev. 8:28), the basket of matzot (Lev. 8:31), and the seven days (Lev. 8:33). This, however, depends on various exegetical positions. The ram and its accompanying basket are indeed "*milluim*," as are the seven days, but there is less certainty regarding the burnt offering.

them up "fills his hands" – is ordained.[74] This is certainly supported by the approach that Leviticus 8 has a concentric structure, with the ordination offerings at its center.[75] If so, what is the significance of "filling the hands" – ordination – and how it is achieved through offering sacrifices? What does this component of the priesthood mean?

The phrase "to fill the [priestly] hands" appears sixteen times in Tanakh, and it is associated with assignment to a certain task, such as the appointment of the Levites after the sin of the Golden Calf: "Moses said, 'Ordain yourselves (*mil'u yedkhem*) to the Lord today. You have been willing to act even against your son or brother. May He bestow a blessing on you this day'" (Ex. 32:29); or Micah's ordination of the Levite lad in the story of Micah's image: "Micah ordained the Levite, and the lad became a priest to him" (Judges 17:12).[76] Some attempt to find a concrete origin related to literally filling the priest's hands, but even if there is one, by the time of the writing of Leviticus the term had already been reduced to an abstract concept, as Joüon writes:

> In both texts (Ex. 29:35; Lev. 8:33), the ordination takes seven days. What kind of concrete action can go on for seven days straight?... Whoever is looking for a physical action – the actual filling of the hands – in these texts may refer to Exodus 29:24, where the loaves and suet are laid upon two hands: "You shall place all these on Aaron's hands." But on the contrary, this only proves the opposite, for if this physical filling of the hands constitutes the act of ordination, it is difficult to understand why these very words are not used – it should have been stated: "You shall fill Aaron's hands with all these." Rather, completely different words are used that do not describe the act of filling the hands, but rather refer to other parts of the offering that are placed on Aaron's open hands.[77]

74. Bula explains that the plural form refers to the word "*milluim*" (*Leviticus*, 139).

75. Klingbeil, "Semantic Structure," 510.

76. Compare also I Kings 13:33; II Chr. 39:31. Various scholars view the Akkadian phrase "*mullü qātā*," meaning "to anoint to a position," as the basis of this phrase (see further in Sniders, "M-L-A," 302).

77. Joüon, "Locutions Hébraïques," 64.

Joüon is correct, but even if the term is entirely abstract, meaning "ordination," there is still a specific priestly role that accompanies the ordination that is central to these chapters.

Is the Ordination Ram a Peace Offering?

In order to understand what the ordination ram contributes to the ordination process, we must ask a more fundamental question: What kind of offering is it? The answer, it seems, is that the ordination ram is a kind of peace offering: "This teaches that the ordination is a peace offering for Aaron and his sons" (*Mekhilta DeMilluim, Tzav*, 20). Some even claim that the ordination ram in Exodus 29 is the etiological basis for the breast and thigh given to the priests in all peace offerings.[78] It indeed seems that the right thigh and basket of matzot (vv. 22–23) are sanctified through this process to become the priestly share forever (vv. 27–28). The sacrificial process of the ordination ram is identical to the regular peace offering: its blood ritual, the burning of its suet, its accompaniment by a basket of matzot, and, above all, its cooking and eating by the priests, without the breast and thigh.

Rashi claims that there are semantic connections between the word "*milluim*," "filling," and "*shelamim*," "full, complete" (on Ex. 29:22). Maharal explains Rashi's comment further:

> For the ordination ram is a peace offering – *shelamim* in the sense of "perfect, complete"... meaning that *milluim* expresses perfection, completion, for what is full is complete, so the meaning of *milluim* is a peace offering, *shelamim*. (*Gur Aryeh* on Ex. 29:22)

This approach, which is widely held, is certainly correct, but the definition of the ordination ram as a peace offering is more complex. Firstly, the ordination ram is not explicitly defined as a peace offering anywhere in the text; rather, it is always referred to as "*milluim*": "This was the ordination offering, a sweet savor, a fire offering to the Lord" (Lev. 8:28). This is how it is referred to even when its laws are explicated on the basis of its sacrificial definition, and use of the term "*shelamim*" would

78. Hyatt, *Exodus*, 247; Kahan, "Priests."

have been appropriate: "From the ram take its fat parts – the broad tail, the fat that covers the entrails, the diaphragm of the liver, and the two kidneys with the fat on them – and the right thigh, for *this is the ram of ordination*" (Ex. 29:22). Furthermore, the list of offerings that concludes the second sacrificial list surprisingly includes the ordination ram, thus distinguishing it from the peace offering: "This, then, is the law for the burnt offering, the grain offering, the purification offering, the guilt offering, the ordination offering, and the peace offering" (Lev. 7:37). R. Abraham Saba takes note of this: "It says here 'the ordination offering,' as we said, that even though it is a kind of peace offering, it is its own unique offering, and this hints to the offerings of the eight days of consecration" (*Tzeror HaMor* on Lev. 8:2).

Moreover, from a halakhic perspective there are clear differences between the ordination and peace offerings, especially regarding how they are eaten. The vow fulfillment and freewill offerings may be eaten within two days, whereas "if any of the meat of the ordination ram or any of the bread is left over until morning, you shall burn what remains with fire. It must not be eaten, for it is consecrated" (Ex. 29:34). Given that the ordination ram is probably not considered a thanksgiving offering, we might expect that there would be two days allotted for its eating. If the only difference were its limited period for eating, perhaps this could be ascribed to the fact that the ordination offering is obligatory,[79] but there are additional restrictions compared to the normal peace offering. One is that it must be cooked and eaten in a *holy* (and not just pure) place, at the entrance to the Tent of Meeting (Ex. 29:31–34). Even more surprising is the fact that only male priests (not even their families) may eat of it: "Because they are consecrated no layman may eat of them" (Ex. 29:33). Regular peace offerings, of course, may be eaten by "laymen" in purity.

Its unique laws, as well as the significant absence of the term "peace offering," lead to the central issue that requires our attention, which revolves around its unique blood ritual: "Slaughter the ram, take some of its blood and put it on the ridges of the right ears of Aaron and his sons, and on the thumbs of their right hands and on the big toes of their right feet. Sprinkle the rest of the blood on the sides of the altar" (Ex. 29:20).

79. As claimed, for example, by Anderson, "Offerings," 878.

In addition to the usual blood ritual of sprinkling the blood on the sides of the altar, the blood is applied to the priests' right ears, thumbs, and toes.[80] Since this is similar to the purification of the *metzora* rite (Lev. 14:14–18), some claim that the ordination ritual achieves purification, not ordination.[81] Yet it is this similarity that implies that the purpose of this ritual is not to achieve purification, because the *metzora* does not achieve purification through the blood of the guilt offering, but rather through the purification and burnt offerings he brings on the eighth day of the purification process. The procedures associated with the other bodily impurities – childbirth, *zav*, and *zava* – prove that the sacrificial pair of burnt and purification offerings achieve purification. The mixture of blood and oil applied to the *metzora*'s body are instead related to his readmittance to the camp of Israel after he has already been purified. The priests in the process of ordination undergo a similar experience, and the difference between their blood ritual and that of the *metzora* reveals the difference between their spheres of action. The ordination blood is applied to the priests twice. The second time, blood is taken from the altar and sprinkled on the priests (Lev. 8:30). The blood applied to the *metzora* readmits them to the camp of Israel; the second sprinkling of blood upon the priests represents their admission into an inner circle within the camp of Israel – into the sacred sphere of Israel's altar.

The process of the ordination ram can be compared to the process of the purification bull during the days of consecration. The Tabernacle and its vessels are consecrated through two different actions: The Tabernacle and its vessels are consecrated by the anointing oil (Lev. 8:10), but the altar requires two levels of consecration through the anointing oil (Lev. 8:10) as well as the blood of the purification offering upon its horns. This blood serves to purify and consecrate: "Moses took the blood and applied it with his finger to all the altar's horns, purifying the altar....

80. This model also recalls the Covenant at Sinai, where Moses dashes some blood on the altar, and dashes the rest at the people: "Then Moses took the blood, sprinkled it on the people, and said, 'This is the blood of the covenant that the Lord is making with you regarding all these words'" (Ex. 24:8). Perhaps the ordination rite also alludes to a covenant with the priests. See further in Weinel, "M-SH-Ḥ," 39.

81. Eberhart, *Verbrennungsriten*, 222–88.

Thus, he consecrated it so that, upon it, atonement could be made" (Lev. 8:15).

Like the altar itself, the priests require two stages of consecration, through the oil and the ordination blood. The altar is "purified... consecrated so that upon it, atonement could be made." Similarly, the priests "eat these things, through which atonement will be made, to be ordained and consecrated" (Ex. 29:33). We will analyze this further below; for now, we note that the similarity between the processes is striking, including the common language: The blood is "taken... and applied" to both priest and altar. It is more problematic to argue that the ordination blood "purifies" the priests, given that what they are bringing is essentially a peace offering rather than a purification offering,[82] but in most respects, the similarity between the two models is irrefutable.

Moreover, the similarity between the ordination ram and the purification offering reveals a fundamental aspect of the nature of the ordination blood. When sacrificial blood is "dashed" upon the altar, it is like an offering sent up in smoke; when the blood is "applied," it effects purification. Similarly, when the ordination blood is "applied" to different parts of the priests' bodies, it effects ordination.[83]

What does this mean? What does this application of blood achieve, instead of the anointing oil alone? Some propose that "filling the priests' hands" refers to the sacrificial portions handed over to them.[84] This can be honed further: Their ordination does not qualify them to receive sacrificial portions so much as it ordains them to *eat* these portions as the altar's emissaries. Like the altar, the priests are consecrated in two separate stages because they are to continue the altar's function.

---

82. See Milgrom, *Leviticus*, vol. 1, 528–29; he refers to Driver's proposal that applying blood to the ear, thumb, and toe prepares their ears to listen, their hands to serve, and their feet to walk to fulfill God's service.

83. There is an interesting dialogue between these two applications of blood and the application of the Passover blood to the doorposts in Egypt. Perhaps it can be stated that this blood serves to identify the home as an "Israelite" home within Egypt, just as the ordination blood identifies the priests as priests within Israel.

84. For a survey of approaches that support and oppose this position, see Snyders, "M-L-A," 302–03. Some regard the priestly gifts as what literally "fills their hand."

This idea is substantiated by the fact that eating is the first and only actual action that the priests perform during the seven days of consecration. They are passively anointed with oil and blood (Lev. 8:30); then Moses commands Aaron and his sons to cook and eat the ordination ram together with its accompanying matzot at the entrance to the Tent of Meeting: "Cook the meat at the entrance to the Tent of Meeting and eat it there together with the bread in the basket of the ordination offering, as I have charged you: Aaron and his sons shall eat it" (8:31). The end of the verse is of special interest: "As I have charged you: Aaron and his sons shall eat it." Why is God's commandment emphasized in regard to eating the offering, when all the rest of the chapter is also the fulfillment of God's command? This is calculated to direct the reader's attention to the climax of this process.[85] The entire day has been leading up toward this moment – to Aaron and his sons' consumption of the ordination offering, at God's command.

In other words, the priestly ordination focuses on qualifying the priests' mouths to eat of God's offerings. This is achieved through the eating of the ordination ram after its blood is sprinkled over the priests. The profound connection between "filling their hands" and eating is evident in the instructions given in Exodus 29:

> Take the ram of ordination
> and, in the sacred precinct, cook its flesh.
> Aaron and his sons shall *eat* the meat of the ram, and the bread in the basket, near the entrance of the Tent of Meeting.
> They shall *eat* these things, through which atonement will be made, to be ordained and consecrated.
> Because they are consecrated no layman may *eat* of them.
> If any of the meat of the ordination ram or any of the bread is left over until morning,
> you shall burn what remains with fire.
> It must not be *eaten*, for it is consecrated. (Ex. 29:31–34)

85. Some perceive the eating of the ram an appendix to the ordination process (such as Levine, *Leviticus*, 54), but Moses's emphasis on eating being a fulfillment of the commandment indicates that the eating is a fundamental part of the process.

The verb "eat" appears four times: where it must be eaten; who must eat it; who must not eat it; and what must not be eaten.

The most obscure verse in this section is "They shall eat these things, through which atonement will be made, to be ordained and consecrated" (33). The result of what does the phrase "to be ordained and consecrated" represent? Is their ordination and consecration achieved through the sacrifice of the offering, as Rashi explains,[86] or is it through the eating itself, as the Netziv explains: "They shall eat the sacrificial meat and matzot – after they have been atoned – and now they must eat for the purpose of ordination and consecration"?[87] According to the latter reading, it is the act of eating the ordination ram that ordains and consecrates the priests.[88]

I am strongly inclined toward this understanding – that the act of eating the offering is what ordains the priests for service. It is perhaps difficult to conceive that offering up the ram and applying its blood to the priests' bodies "consecrates" them; the blood of the *metzora*'s offering is also applied to his body but does not serve to "consecrate."[89] What seems to be the key to consecration, rather, is the repeated sprinkling of blood taken from the altar *combined with the sacred anointing oil* (Ex. 29:21). If we indeed adopt this reading, the text is explicitly stating that eating the offering is a vital component of the priestly ordination.

This can also explain the surprising act of applying blood to the priests' "horns"/"corners" – to the outermost edges of their bodies. Effectively, applying blood that otherwise would be consumed by the altar marks

---

86. Mizraḥi was aware of the alternative reading, and in his commentary on Rashi points out that this is the reading Rashi is attempting to negate: "Not by their eating of it" (Mizraḥi on Rashi on Ex. 29:33).
87. "'To ordain' – thanks to this eating, they were not tired, but rather their hands were ready to serve. 'To consecrate them' – to help them become consecrated" (*Haamek Davar* on Ex. 29:33).
88. Compare to *Meshekh Ḥokhma*: "The whole purpose of the ordination was that from this they were consecrated for generations and granted the privilege of the breast and thigh from the peace offering, through which, when the priests eat it, the worshippers achieve atonement."
89. See Milgrom, *Leviticus*, vol. 1, 529, who proves from this verse that the purpose of applying blood is atonement – contrasted with sprinkling, which consecrates.

them as an extension of the altar itself, their mouths serving as an extension of the altar's own consuming fire.

To some extent, the definition of the priests as another of the altar's "horns" is also expressed through the sacrifice of the ordination ram's *eimurim*. We have already mentioned Moses's waving of the *eimurim* upon the priests' hands before burning them on the altar:

> Then he took the fat, the broad tail, all the fat around the entrails, the diaphragm of the liver, and the two kidneys with their fat, as well as the right thigh. He took a loaf of unleavened bread from the basket, before the Lord, and also one loaf of oil bread, and one wafer, and placed them on the fat and on the right thigh. All of this he placed on the palms of Aaron and of his sons, and displayed them this way and that as a wave offering before the Lord. Then Moses took them from their hands and burnt them upon the altar with the burnt offering. This was the ordination offering, a sweet savor, a fire offering to the Lord. (8:25–28)

The unique nature of this process is especially salient in comparison to the waving of the usual peace offering, where only the breast and thigh of the priestly share is waved. Here, Moses waves the *eimurim* resting upon the priests' hands – the parts that are designated for the altar! Later on, he also waves the breast he will receive for his own share – as is done in the usual ritual. But why does he wave the ordination ram's *eimurim*, which are not usually waved?[90] It is worth repeating what has already been discussed – that what is usually waved is what belongs to the offering bringer, who seeks to consecrate it.

This enigma can be explained by pointing out what distinguishes this act of waving from other biblical waving rituals: The *eimurim* are waved together with the parts that are waved in the usual peace offering – the right thigh and one of each kind of matzot. The ram is not waved in its entirety (as the *metzora*'s lamb is, for example – Lev. 14:21); just the parts designated for the priest are waved.

90. Milgrom is aware of this anomaly, but writes that he is not able to explain it (*Leviticus*, vol. 1, 531).

This is presumably related to the surprising anomaly that the parts usually reserved for priests are burnt upon the altar, so they must be waved so that they may be transferred from the human sphere to the sacred sphere. This forms an intriguing merging of the ordination suet (which is always burned on the altar) and the right thigh and matzot (which are always given to the priest) in a ceremonial declaration that all these belong to God, granting the priests permission to eat of what has been consecrated.

This brings us back to the distinction between Aaron and his sons that results from the different purposes their vestments serve, and to the surprising instruction that Aaron's successors must wear his vestments for a whole week (Ex. 29:29–30), an instruction that is interpolated between the description of the ordination ram's offering upon the altar and the command to cook it and eat it. For some reason, the reference to Aaron's successor interrupts this sequence about the ordination ram, rather than appearing (more logically) after it.

The vestments are first mentioned earlier – therein, it seems, lies the solution. It is first stated that the priests in their vestments are to be sprinkled with the ordination blood together with the sacred anointing oil: "Collect some of the blood on the altar and some of the anointing oil and sprinkle it on Aaron and his vestments, and on his sons and his sons' vestments. Then he, and his sons with him, and their vestments, will be consecrated" (Ex. 29:21). It is no coincidence that the text juxtaposes each wearer with their garments (Aaron and his vestments/his sons and his sons' vestments), rather than "Aaron and his sons/and their vestments." The vestments are consecrated along with their wearers and according to the degree of their wearer's sanctity: Aaron, the sacred High Priest, is dressed in scared vestments – that is, vestments that will grant him access to the Sanctuary, whereas his sons' vestments only allow them access to the courtyard entrance to the Tent of Meeting.

For this reason, after the ordination ram is sacrificed, the text diverges into two different descriptions. The first is how Aaron and his successors are consecrated. He must wear the blood- and oil-spattered garments for a full week in order to gain access to the Inner Sanctuary: "Aaron's sacred vestments shall pass on to his sons after him. In them they shall be anointed and ordained. The son who succeeds him as priest, entering the Tent of Meeting to minister in the Sanctuary, shall wear them for seven days" (29:29–30). The plain meaning of this verse is that each new High Priest does not require actual anointing with oil; rather, a full week of wearing his garments serves for them to "be anointed and ordained." This procedure does not apply to the consecration process of the regular priests, only to the High Priest who enters the Sanctuary itself.

The text then continues with the ordination process of the regular priests. How is this achieved? The answer lies in a surprisingly wordy description: "They shall eat these things, through which atonement will be made, to be ordained and consecrated" (29:33). As well as being eaten by Aaron himself, the offering is also eaten by his sons, who will also have to serve at the altar; they must all eat of the ordination ram to ordain their mouths to eat of the altar's offerings.

This explains the puzzling absence of ceremonial laying of the hands during the priestly appointment. When the Levites are appointed, the Israelites lay their hands upon them (Num. 8:10); the same occurs when Moses appoints Joshua as his successor: "And he laid his hands upon him and commissioned him" (Num. 27:23). Daube claims that these verses became the basis for the traditional way to appoint new Rabbis in Israel, continuing this symbol of authority from generation to generation (compare Mishna Avot 1:1).[91] For some reason, this classic symbolic act is absent from the priestly consecration.[92]

This is a case in which a component's absence is as meaningful as its presence. No one lays their hands upon the priests because the authority they are being granted is not human but divine; only the altar or God's glory is the fitting party for this gesture. Unlike the Levites, who are Israel's emissaries to serve the priests, and unlike Joshua, who succeeds Moses, the priests are consecrated by God, and their chief role will be to serve as the altar's hand and mouth.

Instead of laying hands on the priests, the altar's blood and the sacred oil is applied and sprinkled on their bodies, a physical act that

91. Daube, "Laying of the Hands," 232.

92. Some even claim that because of the absence of laying the hands, accounts of other appointment are based on the Levite appointment ritual rather than this one (Watts, *Leviticus*, 450).

represents the altar taking them under its wing. This may be hinted to in the missing subject of the verse that literally reads "Do not leave the entrance to the Tent of Meeting for seven days, until x completes the days of your ordination" (Lev. 8:33). This verse is generally translated in the passive form instead, "Do not leave the entrance to the Tent of Meeting for seven days, until the days of your ordination are complete,"[93] but this subtle ambiguity hints that it is God Himself who ordains the priests and symbolically "lays hands" upon them.

Thus, the eating of the ordination ram has complex symbolism. It is both a peace offering of which the priests are the bringers (and for this reason they eat the rest of the meat, not the traditional priestly portion), but it is also the first time they eat from an offering as priests.[94] This is especially salient in the requirement that they must eat their share in a holy place, within the entrance to the Tent of Meeting. Such an instruction may represent a technicality, namely that they are not allowed to leave that area for seven days, but the latter requirement is only specified a few verses later (33–35); moreover, there is emphasis that it must be eaten specifically "at the entrance to the Tent of Meeting" (8:31).

The Ordination Ram and *pīt pî*

If the focus of the days of consecration is indeed related to the priests eating of the ordination ram, there is reason to compare this ritual to that of the Mesopotamian "opening of the gods' mouths" ritual (already mentioned in the context of the *minḥat ḥavittin*).[95] Various Ancient Near Eastern texts document a complex ceremony in which new idols are initiated as gods into the Temple.[96] As Oppenheim describes:

> They had to undergo an elaborate and highly secret ritual of consecration to transform the lifeless matter into a receptacle of the divine presence. During these nocturnal ceremonies they were

93. Similarly NIV, JPS, NIB, NAB.

94. Wenham, *Leviticus*, 143–44.

95. Most evidence is from Mesopotamia. However, Anne Roth shows that it was also prevalent in ancient Egypt (Roth, "Opening of the Mouth").

96. There is much research devoted to this ceremony and its meaning.

> endowed with "life," their eyes and mouths were "opened" so that the images could see and eat, and they were subject to the "washing of the mouth," a ritual thought to impart special sanctity.[97]

This ceremony was of utmost importance in the pagan world, for, as Horowitz explains, "the main purpose of this ceremony was a magical, symbolic denial – in speech and action – of man's part in the creation of the idol and its transformation into a new god that has just descended from the birthing stone of the mother of the pantheon."[98] The ceremonial climax, however, centered on the opening of the god's mouth:

> The statue of a god was made, i.e., given birth to, with great care. In order to endow the statue with life it was subjected to rituals and incantations. Two of these were the "washing of the mouth" (*mīs pî*) and the "opening of the mouth" (*pīt pî*), which together enabled the statue to eat the foodstuffs and drink the liquids served during the divine meal.[99]

Who was responsible for the first stage, the washing of the "newborn" deity's mouth? This was (at least sometimes) the king, as is evident from the cuneiform testimony of King Nabu-Apla-Iddina: "He [i.e., the king] washed the mouth of the statue before Shamash through the purification rites of Aa."[100]

If the ordination ram serves to consecrate the priests so that they may eat of the altar's offerings, it is possible to regard this ritual as a polemic against the pagan "washing/opening of the gods' mouth." The same two stages can be found in the days of consecration: First Moses washes and purifies the priests (Lev. 8:6); then he dresses them in splendid

97. Oppenheim, *Mesopotamia*, 186. See an extensive survey in Horowitz, "Impure Lips"; for the texts themselves, see Walker and Dick, "Induction"; Dietrich and Loretz, "*Jahwe und seine Aschera*," 5–38.
98. Horowitz, "Image."
99. Linssen, *Uruk*, 153–54.
100. As quoted in Horowitz, "Image," 345. He explains that the perception was that the gods are the ones who open the new idols' mouths.

vestments;[101] finally, he carries out the instructions for the ordination ram. This "washing" is followed by the (literal!) opening of the priests' mouths (to eat).

This reveals a profound disparity between the Israelite Sanctuary and the ancient pagan world.[102] Humans do not have the power to consecrate God or His "mouth"; only the altar and its representatives' mouths can be consecrated. By eating the ordination ram, their mouths are opened in holiness; now they must remain at the entrance to the Tent of Meeting for seven days to become "Tabernacle vessels," in their new vestments, so that they may serve as extensions of the altar.

This reading illuminates the end of the eighth day of consecration. We will explore it in depth below, but for the sake of this discussion, I will already point out that the entire consecration process culminates in God's revelation in the blazing, consuming fire upon the altar (Lev. 9:23–24). In this sense, the eighth day is a climactic fulfillment of the perspective the second sacrificial list presents, as well as that of the consecration of the priests who are to embody this consuming fire.

The end of the scene also reveals that eating is the focal point of the entire chapter, as Moses chastises Aaron and his sons for not eating the purification offering:

> Why did you not eat the purification offering in the holy area? It is holy of holies, and it has been given to you to remove the guilt of the community and atone for them before the Lord. Because its blood was not to be brought into the inner Sanctuary, you should have eaten it in the Sanctuary, as I commanded. (Lev. 10:17–18)

101. On the ritual of dressing the idols in garments (*lubuštu* – not necessarily at their "birth" but at some point during their "lives," probably once a week), see Linssen, *Uruk*, 51–56. On the special vestment storage in the temples (*bit pirišti*), see Falkenstein, *Sumerische Götterlieder*, 40–44.

102. If McDowell is correct that these chapters are in dialogue with the first chapter of Genesis and the Eden narrative (McDowell, *The Image of God*), then the polemic already begins there.

Aaron answers him well, as we will see below, but it is no coincidence that this marks the end of the days of consecration narrative. The priests' eating of the offerings is the underlying theme of these days; now that their mouths have been consecrated with the altar's sanctity, they must fulfill their roles by eating the offerings to bring atonement for Israel.

Chapter 21

The Eighth Day of Consecration (Leviticus 9–10): Revelation and Concealment

WHO COMMANDED THIS DAY, AND WHEN?

That the eighth day of consecration happens at all is somewhat surprising. The commandment about the seven days of consecration in Exodus 29 does not mention an additional day with its own array of offerings; the commandment mandates only that the priests must remain in the Tabernacle courtyard for seven days in order to become ordained. Why is there no mention of the eighth day?

Ramban, in whose opinion chapters 9 and 10 appear in the correct chronological order, perceives the additional eighth day as atonement for the sin of the Golden Calf, which takes place in between the instructions for and the execution of building the Tabernacle and the days of consecration:

> It seems probable that these offerings were added to atone for the sin of the Calf, for when He commanded, "This is what you must do to consecrate them," the calf had not yet been made, so it is not yet mentioned...The calf offered on the eighth day is to atone for the sin. (Ramban on Lev. 9:3)

Ramban supports his theory with strong evidence: On the eighth day, Aaron is told to take a bull calf for his own purification offering (Lev. 9:2, 8), whereas Israel must bring "a goat for a purification offering, and a calf and a lamb, both yearlings without blemish, for a burnt offering" (9:3). Perhaps the choice of a calf represents something new, but it is still a curious alternative to the usual purification bull (that is brought during the seven days of consecration – the appropriate option for the anointed priest). It indeed makes sense that this anomaly is in dialogue with the sin of the Golden Calf.[1]

But this explanation is not sufficient. On the eighth day, most of the offerings are brought by Israel and not the priests, and their purification offering is a goat, not a calf (9:3–4). Moreover, the purification offering is overshadowed by the double burnt and peace offerings, which seem to play a more central role. Moses himself explicitly defines the purpose of the day: "For on this day the Lord will be revealed to you" (9:4); thus, the offerings presumably serve to facilitate this revelation. Therefore, even if Ramban's explanation clarifies certain aspects of the day, it does not sufficiently justify an unexpected, hitherto unmentioned extra day of consecration.

---

1. There are striking analogies between the revelation at Sinai and the revelation of the eighth day. Both depict God's appearance as a consuming fire (Ex. 24:16–17/Lev. 9:24). Both revelations are followed by a sin with fire: The people throw their gold into the fire to make the calf (Ex. 32:25) and Aaron's sons offer a "strange fire" (Lev. 10:1–2). Both sins are followed by lament. These corresponding events perhaps raise concerns that the Divine Presence will not remain in Israel, but in the end only the sinners are punished. Ramban's reading demonstrates that he attributes immense significance to this analogy by suggesting that God's revelation on the eighth day marks full forgiveness for Israel's sin of the Golden Calf. He also notes that the close parallels between the two events are already found in the Midrash. See Shammah, *The Mekhiltot*, 154–62.

Before the eighth day begins, the Tabernacle and its vessels have already been purified and consecrated; its priests are ready to serve. This explains why the eighth day is not included as part of the instructions about building and preparing the Sanctuary and its vessels.[2] The eighth day, rather, is a reception for the new occupants of this Sanctuary. One may instruct the architect and designers precisely how to build the house, what furniture to create and where to put it. One may even give precise instructions to the cleaning crew. The reception party for the new, completed house, however, is a separate affair. Nor can this particular house's builders be guaranteed that the Occupant will indeed take up residence there; God's presence is granted only if God wills it. For this reason, no instructions are given in advance; only God will determine whether the Divine Presence indeed settles in the resting place Israel builds for it.[3]

This can be taken a step further. The absence of reference to the eighth day in the book of Exodus is consistent with the surprising language in this chapter. For some reason, the chapter does not open with God's instructions to Moses, but rather with Moses's instructions to Aaron: "On the eighth day, Moses called to Aaron and his sons, and to the elders of Israel. 'Take a bull calf for yourself as a purification offering.... Then tell the Israelites: Take a goat for a purification offering... for on this day the Lord will be revealed to you'" (Lev. 10:1–4). It is as if God is absent for this scene because He is staying backstage, waiting to make a climatic appearance. This is especially apparent in Moses's command to Aaron to speak to the Israelites: "Then tell the Israelites." It is usually God who tells Moses to speak to them.

Ramban argues that Aaron is asked to give instructions to the people for educational purposes: "[Moses] wanted Aaron to be the one who commands the people in God's name, for he is the one who offers the sacrifices, to make him esteemed in the eyes of the people" (on Lev. 9:3;

2. Ramban's aforementioned commentary continues: "[In Exodus 29] Israel were only commanded about the days of consecration, but now on the eighth day they themselves offer up dedication offerings to commemorate the day" (on 9:3).
3. Compare to R. Avia Hacohen, *Sanctuary*, 51–54. Several midrashim characterize the eighth day as one with an element of uncertainty and surprise (like throwing a party for someone who may or may not show up). See Leviticus Rabba 11:6; *Sifra, Mekhilta DeMilluim, Shemini,* 11).

but see also his later discussion with Ibn Ezra). Yet even if so, it does not explain why God does not give Moses the initial command, as usual.

The ambiguity about these instructions' origins continues with their execution: "They brought *what Moses had commanded* to the space before the Tent of Meeting, and all the community drew near and stood before the Lord" (9:5). The narrator implies that these instructions are from Moses, not God.[4] It is only once all the people have gathered before the Lord that Moses explicitly states that he is passing on God's own command: "Moses said, 'This is what the Lord has commanded you to do so that the Lord's glory be revealed to you'" (v. 6). God's unusual absence from the beginning of the scene maintains the impression that the eighth day is the people's initiative rather than God's; they are the ones who seek His presence.

This is the perception even after Moses reveals that this is all at God's command. While the phrase "as the Lord commanded Moses" is a refrain throughout the seven days of consecration, it is almost completely absent on the eighth day: It only appears before the sacrificial service (9:7) and once more after the priests' purification calf is offered up (9:10). More dominant is Moses's instruction: "But the breasts and right thigh Aaron displayed, this way and that, as a wave offering before the Lord, *as Moses had commanded*" (9:21).

All this creates the impression that the eighth day is the fruit of human initiative, that Moses and the people are the ones who choose to bring the offerings that ultimately result in divine revelation. Israel throng to greet their King as He arrives to settle in the new dwelling place they have built for him, and the absence of divine instruction allows for the sense of a mutual covenant. Moses and Israel take a devout, widespread initiative to invoke God's presence, and He rewards these efforts with divine revelation.

---

4. R. Eli Hadad tentatively suggested to me that it may well be that Moses begins the proceedings of the eighth day on his own initiative, based on God's command about the seven days of consecration. Even though I find this doubtful, given that Moses explicitly states that this is at God's command (9:6), this idea still reflects the striking departure from the unusual opening of most such scenes.

GIVE OF WHAT IS YOURS TO SEVEN, TO EIGHT

Although the eighth day of consecration is of a different nature than the week preceding it, it is still referred to as "the eighth day of consecration," which implies an inextricable connection with the previous week: "On the eighth day, Moses called to Aaron and his sons, and to the elders of Israel" (9:1). After the priests have remained in the Tabernacle courtyard for seven days, they are now fully ordained and ready to serve. Now it is time for God's glory to descend upon the altar in fiery revelation.[5] This follows a classic biblical convention of seven + one = eight:

1. When an animal becomes fit for an offering: "Likewise with your oxen and sheep; let them stay with their mothers for seven days, and on the eighth, give them over to Me" (Ex. 22:29).[6]
2. Impurity: Three forms of bodily impurity – the *metzora, zav,* and *zava* – wait for seven days and come to the Sanctuary on the eighth day with their purification and burnt offerings to become pure (in the *metzora*'s case, with a guilt offering as well).[7]
3. The grain offering of first produce: The two-loaf offering is brought after counting seven weeks, and on the morrow the new grain is brought as a grain offering. (Here, the fiftieth day is parallel to the eighth day.)
4. Circumcision: This is not mentioned in the original command to Abraham in Genesis 17, but the law of the new mother does follow this model: "If a woman conceives and gives birth to a son, she shall be impure for seven days, as she is during her menstrual period. On the eighth day, the child's foreskin shall be circumcised" (Lev. 12:2–3).[8]

---

5. The Hanukka miracle – which revolves around the re-dedication of the Sanctuary/Temple – reflects how, from a Maccabean perspective, consecrating the Temple is an eight-day process, not seven. See, for example, Regev, "Hanukkah."
6. On the unlikelihood of the theory that this includes the prohibition against "cooking a kid in its mother's milk" (Ex. 23:19; 34:26), see Haran, "Kid in Its Mother's Milk."
7. The eighth day of the *metzora*'s purification process allows him to return to the Sanctuary, and to his home as well (Lev. 14:8).
8. The Septuagint adds the "eight days" before circumcision to the original command (in Gen. 17:14), thus emphasizing the importance of the eighth day, more than the

In all of the above, the eighth day marks a change in status in relation to God: After seven days (a sense of new creation?) those not yet fit to stand before God become worthy on the eighth. The covenant of circumcision also hints that a new baby is able to join God's covenant only once the mother who bore him and nurses him becomes pure as well.[9] Seven days represent a full cycle, a certain stability of presence in the world, only after which the subject is worthy to come into contact with the Divine.

It is possible to develop this model much further, but the above list suffices to illustrate how the eighth day is both the culmination of a process and a new stage. The eighth day of consecration sees a new level of God's presence within reality; all the people witness God's glory descending to the altar in a blazing, consuming fire, and they fall to their faces (*panim*) before God's presence (*panim*).

On the other hand, this is only achievable after seven full days of waiting: The newborn child, newborn animal, new produce, or newly ordained priest are fit to enter into God's service, to come to the Sanctuary, only after seven days of stabilization. Yet on the eighth day of consecration, it is not the human but God's glory that enters the Sanctuary. The priests await God's presence for seven days and wait for the Owner of the House to reveal Himself.

PRIESTS AND ISRAELITES

Only the priests offer sacrifices during the seven days of consecration, but on the eighth day, Israel do as well; moreover, their sacrifices are the day's central ritual. While the priests bring burnt and purification offerings on the eighth day, Israel must bring burnt, purification, peace,

---

MT (see Thiessen, "Genesis 17"). Propp seeks textual proof that the baby must be circumcised on the eighth day and not later; he claims that until eight days, an uncircumcised baby is taboo, but afterward, the child is in a state of danger until he is circumcised (Propp, "Origins of Infant Circumcision").

9. Richard Hess notes a connection between the mother's impurity and the baby's, but inverts it: that the mother cannot become pure until the baby is circumcised (Hess, *Leviticus*, 687). This is a bizarre reading, given that she cannot go to the Sanctuary a full thirty-three days after the circumcision and must first bring offerings to become pure.

and grain offerings. The peace offering and the covenant with God it symbolizes is the most important of all. If the ordination ram was the focus of the seven days of consecration, on the eighth day the communal peace offering takes center stage.

That the priests themselves are of secondary importance on this day is evident through the fact that what they provide is technical support for their father Aaron:

- The priests' purification offering: "Aaron drew close to the altar and slaughtered the calf of his purification offering. *Aaron's sons presented him with the blood,* and he dipped his finger into it and applied the blood to the horns of the altar.... Then he sent the fat...up in smoke upon the altar...and he burned the flesh and skin with fire outside the camp."
- The priestly burnt offering: "Then he slaughtered the burnt offering. *Aaron's sons presented him with the blood,* and he dashed it on each side of the altar. *Then they presented him with the burnt offering in its pieces,* with its head, and he sent them up in smoke upon the altar."
- The people's offerings: Aaron performs the entire service with two exceptions: "Aaron's sons presented him with the blood" and "They laid the fat parts over the breasts" (Lev. 9:8–20).

Aaron's sons are included, but Aaron himself performs all the actual sacrificial acts;[10] his sons merely hand him the blood or the parts for sacrifice, like a surgeon's assistant. Given that the Israelites are the focus of this day, it makes sense that all rites are performed by Aaron, their main representative.

This leads to the main objective of the eighth day: "For on this day the Lord will be revealed to you.... This is what the Lord has commanded you to do so that the Lord's glory be revealed to you" (9:4–6). That God's revelation descends and settles in the camp of Israel – and that all Israel witnesses this – is crucial. After months of toil to build and consecrate the Tabernacle, the entire assembly must see that God

10. Compare Hundley, *Keeping Heaven,* 62.

chooses to dwell in this house and that God's fire accepts and consumes their offerings. God's glory descends upon the altar in the form of a consuming fire. In biblical perception, this fire is not merely symbolic. This divine fire literally consumes Israel's offerings, and it never goes out: "Daily fire shall be kept alight on the altar; it shall not go out" (Lev. 6:6). In Hizkuni's words: "The fire that descended in the days of Moses did not leave the bronze altar until the Eternal Temple was built; then the fire that descended in the days of Solomon did not leave the burnt offering altar until it departed in the days of Menashe" (on Lev. 9:24, based on *Sifra*, Freewill Offerings 5:10).[11]

A DOUBLE BLESSING

After the sacrificial service of the priests' and Israel's offerings, the narrative reaches its climax: God's revelation before the eyes of all the people.

The verses leading up to the actual revelation describe a double blessing: "Then Aaron raised his hands to the people and *blessed them*. And, having presented the purification offering, the burnt offering, and the peace sacrifice, he stepped down. Moses and Aaron entered the Tent of Meeting; when they came out, *they blessed* the people" (9:22–23). Immediately after this second blessing, "the glory of the Lord was revealed to all the people" (v. 23).

Why are there two consecutive blessings? What purpose do they serve? Based on the Midrash, cited by Rashi, some perceive the first blessing as a first, unsuccessful attempt to bring down the Divine Presence:

> Because Aaron saw that all the offerings had been offered and all the rites had been performed but the Divine Presence did not yet descend to Israel, he was regretful, and said: I know that the Holy One, blessed be He, is angry at me, and the Divine Presence

11. Rabbeinu Bahya takes this a step further and writes that the same fire was transferred from the bronze altar to the altar of Solomon's Temple. The inauguration of Solomon's Temple sees a cloud descending and filling the House of God, but there is no mention of fire (I Kings 18:10–11). The parallel account in Chronicles does mention fire (II Chr. 7:3), and there is also divine fire that descends to Ornan's threshing floor (I Chr. 21:26), which is also absent in the original account in I Samuel 24.

> did not descend to Israel because of me. He said to Moses: My brother Moses, how could you do this to me, to let me go in and be ashamed? Moses immediately went in with him and asked for mercy, and the Divine Presence descended to Israel. (Rashi on Lev. 9:23)

This midrash attempts to explain why Moses and Aaron go into the Tent of Meeting together before the second blessing, and at the same time, the reason for the two blessing emerges: The second blessing is a successful second attempt after the first blessing fails.

The disadvantage of this reading is the revelation's dependence on the blessing. Why should the Divine Presence descend due to a blessing from Moses and Aaron? It makes more sense to interpret both blessings as necessary, perhaps as related to the revelation but not its direct cause. Three differences between the two blessings reveal their respective purposes:

1. The blesser: The first blessing is from Aaron, the High Priest ("He blessed them"); the second is from both Moses and Aaron together ("They blessed the people").
2. The place of blessing: Aaron pronounces the first blessing next to the altar; only after this blessing does the verse state: "Having presented the purification offering, the burnt offering, and the peace sacrifice, he stepped down." Some commentators read "he stepped down" as a past participle, "having stepped down," meaning he blessed the people after descending from the altar and not before,[12] but the plain meaning is: "In the place where he offered his sacrifices and his service was accepted while upon the altar, he blessed the people, and then went down" (Abarbanel on Lev. 9). In contrast, the second blessing is associated with the Tent of Meeting. Why do Moses and Aaron enter the Tent of Meeting, especially as there is no indication of what they do inside? "Moses and Aaron entered the Tent of Meeting; when they came

12. As in the *Sifra, Mekhilta DeMilluim, Shemini*, 29; see also R. Saadia Gaon, Ibn Janah, and Hizkuni.

out, they blessed the people."[13] Moses and Aaron's entry into the Tent of Meeting is indeed dramatic in itself, regardless of what they did inside; it is not to be taken for granted, as is evident from the end of Exodus: "Moses could not now enter the Tent of Meeting, because the cloud had settled on it, and the glory of the Lord filled the Tabernacle" (Ex. 40:25). Only after God calls Moses is he able to enter the Tent of Meeting. Now, when Moses takes Aaron by the hand and leads him inside, Aaron is also granted official permission to enter the Sanctuary.[14] As discussed, it is not at all clear that regular priests were allowed to enter the Sanctuary itself; it seems more likely that this privilege was only granted to the High Priest. If so, then the first time Aaron goes inside is a momentous occasion, even if this entry served no other purpose. The description gives the sense that Moses and Aaron emerge from the Tent of Meeting imbued with the blessing of this first entry and spread it outward to the people.

3. The Act of Blessing: Another subtle difference is that the first time, "Aaron raised his hands to the people and blessed them," but there is no such gesture the second time.

These disparities reveal the fundamental difference between the two blessings and the need for both. The first blessing is part of the sacrificial service, bestowed by the High Priest as part of his role, recited next to the altar, fueled by the altar (compare to I Kings 8:54–55). Therefore, as the Talmud, the *Sifra*, and Rashi surmise, this blessing was likely the priestly blessing. One of the priestly duties was to bless the people with the priestly blessing: "May the Lord bless you and watch over you. May the Lord make His face shine upon you and be gracious to you. May the

13. Rashi refers to the Midrash and explains that Moses was teaching him about the incense (on Lev. 9:23); Milgrom assumes that they prayed inside (*Leviticus*, vol. 1, 588) and bases this on Solomon's focus on the importance of prayer at the Temple's inauguration (I Kings 8). However, the text's silence and failure to mention prayer shows that this is not the objective of their unexplained entrance to the Tent of Meeting.

14. Rocker explains that Moses and Aaron's entrance symbolizes Moses passing on the role of mediator on behalf of the people to Aaron (Rocker, *Leviticus*, 154).

Lord raise His face toward you and grant you peace" (Num. 6:24–27). It makes sense that this was the first time that this blessing burst out with all the purity, holiness, and celebration of the occasion. As Ramban writes:

> I have already mentioned in the *parasha* of "On the Eighth Day" that He commanded Aaron to lift up his hands toward the people and bless them on that day, and here He commanded Aaron and his sons to do so throughout the generations, and He explained what the blessing was with which they are to bless them. He mentioned this blessing in connection with the setting up of the Tabernacle, for there the Eternal commanded the blessing, even life forever.
> (Ramban on Num. 6:23)

Aaron's raising up of his hands hints to the connection between the eighth day of consecration and the priestly blessing. It is not unreasonable to surmise that the word "raise" alludes to the blessing itself: "May the Lord raise His face toward you and grant you peace" (Num. 6:26).[15]

What, then, is the purpose of the second blessing? The fact that Moses joins Aaron shows that this has nothing to do with the priestly blessing. Some may suggest that this is a spontaneous act of love that is unconnected with the formal rituals of the day. No one, of course, asks parents why they spontaneously bless their children right before they stand under the ḥuppa even though they are about to recite the seven formal blessings of the marriage service. The parents' impulsive blessing is a personal, intimate expression of the love and the emotion of that day.

Nonetheless, we can still point to an additional role this second blessing fulfills, one hinted at through the place where Moses and Aaron

15. See especially Geiger, "Handeln im Aaronitischen Segen" (who sees this as an intentional merging of human action and divine blessing). Ibn Ezra proves that Aaron's priestly blessing is communal, not individual, which is the accepted halakhic perception (Ibn Ezra on Num 6:21). But Haran might also be correct that even if the priestly blessing on the eighth day was communal, it is possible to read the *peshat* as applying to the priestly blessings for each individual bringer of offerings (Haran, "The Priestly Blessing," 79–81); this is also hinted at in Psalms 118:26.

recite it. While the first, priestly blessing is recited next to the altar, the second is related to the Inner Sanctuary.

As mentioned, the days of consecration are described in the book of Leviticus, but they come full circle with the book of Exodus – and each book describes a dramatic, unique account of divine revelation.[16] In the book of Exodus, the Tabernacle is built as a dwelling place for the Divine Presence, and the entire camp of Israel is arranged around it. The book of Exodus concludes with the Divine Presence resting in God's new home – thereby preventing Moses from entering. The book of Leviticus, however, opens with God inviting Moses to come in, and with detailed instructions on how to sacrifice offerings. The Israelite worshipper is invited to come and serve their Maker at the place where God's glory blazes upon the altar. Therefore, the focal point in Leviticus is the divine revelation upon the altar, where God's fire consumes the offerings and from where Aaron's blessing to Israel emanates.

The second blessing, however, has a different background – one that transports the reader back to Exodus and the Divine Presence inside the Tent of Meeting. Moses's presence hints to Exodus's perspective; he and his brother enter the divine resting place and come out bearing a blessing for the people.

REVELATION AS CONSUMING FIRE

After these two blessings, the chapter reaches its narrative climax:

> And the glory of the Lord was revealed to all the people.
> And from before the Lord, fire came forth. It consumed the burnt offering and the fat pieces on the altar; and all the people saw it, and cried out for joy, and threw themselves facedown upon the ground. (9:23–24)

We will first consider a straightforward reading of this description. The prevalent, logical view is that of R. Saadia Gaon, Rashbam, and others. The first line, "The glory of the Lord was revealed to all the people," is

16. See especially Shammah, *Two Objectives*. As mentioned, there is a third perspective in addition to these two, found in the book of Numbers. See Kehat, *Sanctuary*.

a heading, followed by its explication: In what form did God's glory appear? "Fire came forth."[17] The revelation of the eighth day takes the form of a blazing, consuming fire – not an obscuring cloud that veils God's true glory as it enters the Tent of Meeting, but a public revelation for all to see upon the altar.

Thus, the books of Exodus and Leviticus depict divine revelation in three acts. The first, upon Mount Sinai, is a double revelation of fire sheathed in cloud: "As Moses climbed the mountain, it was covered in a cloud. The glory of the Lord rested on Mount Sinai, and the cloud covered it for six days. On the seventh, He called to Moses from within the cloud. To the Israelites the appearance of the Lord's glory on the mountaintop was like consuming fire" (Ex. 24:15–17). God's fiery glory is covered by clouds, and only Moses is invited inside the cloud, although the Israelites can see still its blazing glory.[18]

As Ramban explains, this glory descends to the Tabernacle, and two separate scenes reflect the two separate aspects of God's revelation. The end of Exodus depicts the revelation of cloud: "Then the cloud covered the Tent of Meeting, and the glory of the Lord filled the Tabernacle. Moses could not now enter the Tent of Meeting, because the cloud had settled on it, and the glory of the Lord filled the Tabernacle" (Ex. 40:34–35). In contrast, the revelation in Leviticus depicts God's glory as a consuming fire: "The glory of the Lord was revealed to all the people. And from before the Lord, fire came forth. It consumed the burnt offering and the fat pieces on the altar" (Lev. 9:24).[19]

Not only do these separate scenes portray the two aspects of God's revelation, they also take place in different settings: God's cloud "fills

---

17. For an alternative reading, see Bula, *Leviticus*, 151. He believes that the "God's glory" they saw were the clouds of glory descending upon the Tabernacle, and then fire came forth out of these clouds.
18. Compare to Weinfeld, "Glory," 31. He writes that Israel were granted a proper view of the divine fire only on the eighth day, and that at Sinai this fire was veiled within cloud. This is open to interpretation, however.
19. "Thus,it was of no unusual significance that the Israelites could behold the Lord's *kabod*; it was 'a pillar of fire by night' (Ex. 40:38; Num. 14:14). What was unusual, indeed unprecedented, in the theophany was that the fire emerged from the adytum without its cloud cover and consumed the sacrifices upon the altar" (Milgrom, *Leviticus,* vol. 1, 589–90).

the Tabernacle," while on the eighth day of consecration, God's fire appears upon the altar.

It is not clear from where exactly this "fire" descends to the altar. In other scenes of revelation, the fire appears to *descend* from above, such as at Mount Carmel: "And fire from the Lord *flared down* and consumed the offering.... And all the people saw, and they fell on their faces and cried, 'The Lord – He is God! The Lord – He is God!'" (I Kings 18:38–39). Similarly, at the Temple inauguration: "As Solomon concluded his prayer, fire flared down from the heavens.... When all the Israelites saw the fire and the Lord's glory descending to the House, they kneeled down on the floor with their faces to the ground, bowed down, and gave thanks to the Lord" (I Chr. 7:1–3). Furthermore, when David purchases the threshing floor: "David built an altar there for the Lord and sacrificed burnt offerings and peace offerings. He called out to the Lord, and He answered him with fire from heaven upon the altar of burnt offerings" (I Chr. 21:26). This common trope may lead us to assume that the fire of the eighth day also comes down from heaven – but the verb "came out" at the place "before the Lord" may favor Rashbam's reading that the fire flared out from the Tent of Meeting to the altar.[20]

The People's Reaction

The people are clearly elated by the revelation, and their reaction is moving and dramatic: "And all the people saw it, *vayaronnu*, and threw themselves facedown upon the ground" (9:24). The combination of "saw" and "they threw themselves facedown"/"fell on their faces" is a classic reaction, as at Mount Carmel: "And all the people saw, and they fell on their faces" (I Kings 18:39). The same appears in our scene, with the exception of one word – *vayaronnu*.

The verb "*ron*," which appears for the first time in this verse, has several different meanings, and what it means in a particular context is

20. Similarly, Milgrom (*Leviticus*, vol. 1, 590). The verb "came out" often functions metaphorically, however, and does not necessarily point to a physical "coming out" from one place to another (e.g., Gen. 19:23). Others assume that the fire "came out" of heaven, as in most cases of fiery revelation; see Rocker, *Leviticus*, 158.

not always clear.[21] Ibn Ezra reads it as "raising the voice," as in the verse "Wisdom will *ring out* (*taronna*) in public and give forth her voice in the squares" (Prov. 1:20). Rashi and Onkelos read it as an expression of praise: "Clap your hands together, all peoples; shout out joyfully to God" (Ps. 47:2). Some even associate it with religious joy in particular.[22]

Either way, the verb reflects the excitement that grips the people, moving them to cry out in joyful song, to awe and joy and fear as one, as is reflected in the combination of "*yaronnu*" and "threw themselves facedown." While some, such as Malbim, question how joy and fear can coexist, this is in fact the heart of every revelation, as in Rudolph Otto's definition of holiness – "*mysterium tremendum*."[23] The people rejoice at God's revelation in the form of consuming fire; they cry out in glad song at His acceptance of their offerings and His presence among them. But at the same time, they fall to the ground in awe and reverence: "Serve the Lord with reverence and tremble as you exalt" (Ps. 2:11).

It is against this background of religious reverence and ecstasy that the tragedy of Nadav and Avihu takes place.

NADAV AND AVIHU'S SIN

Needless to say, the eighth day of consecration is one of the most momentous, joyful days of Israel's time in the wilderness. Yet as the people celebrate in reverence and awe, the newly ordained priestly family is struck with grave tragedy. R. Aḥa bar Ze'eira links this tragedy to the verse from Job: "At this my heart quakes and falters in its place" (Job 37:1).[24]

No other sin in Tanakh is subject to as much dispute as the mysterious offense of Nadav and Avihu. A broad range of suggestions exist that attempt to explain the severity of their actions and why they result in so grave a punishment; indeed, the brief, cryptic scene lends itself to

21. The root R-N-N appears in other ancient languages, such as Ancient Egyptian, in both verb and noun form; and Ugaritic, always in a positive context of joy.
22. Hausmann, "R-N-N," 516.
23. Otto, *The Idea of Holy*, 12–24
24. Leviticus Rabba 20:5.

many different readings.[25] A brief survey of various midrashic explanations suffices to illustrate this confusion:[26]

1. Before the fire of revelation lit the altar, they lit their own fire.
2. They brought fire from a profane source.
3. They entered the Holy of Holies.
4. They entered drunk.
5. They entered naked.[27]
6. They entered without cleansing and consecrating their hands and feet.
7. They entered bareheaded.[28]
8. They contradicted Moses's teachings.
9. They had no children or were not married.
10. They died on account of their father's sin of the Golden Calf.

Some of these propositions are based on hints in the text or context; others are creative interpretations that have no direct connection to the eighth day of consecration. Some of these explanations stray from the *peshat* and are fueled by moral rather than interpretive objectives.[29] The brief incident is oblique indeed, inviting this plethora of

25. Various plot holes make it difficult to piece the story together:
    1. When did they offer up this "unauthorized fire"? Before the fiery revelation (*Mekhilta DeMilluim, Shemini,* 22) or after (the same source, *halakha* 32)?
    2. Where was the fire offered? In the Holy of Holies (ibid.); on the incense altar (Raavad ad loc.); or on the burnt offering altar (Tosafot on Eiruvin 63a)?
    3. What does "*esh zara*" mean? A fire lit by men (*Mekhilta,* ibid.); a fire from a profane source (R. Akiva ibid.); a fire lit at the wrong time (R. Yishmael, ibid.); or "unauthorized fire" they brought of their own volition (R. Eliezer, ibid.)?

    There are far too many questions to explore in this context; I will address certain aspects in my discussion below.
26. For a broad survey of different approaches of the Sages, see Hakham, "Nadav and Avihu"; Shinan, "Nadav and Avihu"; Kirshner, "Rabbinic and Philonic Exegeses."
27. On the reading that they were naked like pagan priests in the Ancient Near East, see Hepner, "The Naked Truth."
28. Tosafot, Yoma 53a, quoting the *Sifra*. This does not appear in our current version of the *Sifra*, but Amos Hakham ("Nadav and Avihu," 106) notes that a similar style in found in Leviticus Rabba 20:10 about their behavior on Mount Sinai.
29. See especially Shinan, "Nadav and Avihu"; Bibb, "Nadav and Avihu."

interpretations; the list above is solely from tanna'itic sources, to say nothing of the endless suggestions by *Rishonim*, *Aḥaronim*, and modern research. In fact, the incident is so enigmatic that certain commentators (chiefly kabbalistic) reject the notion that Nadav and Avihu's action was a sin, and rather perceive it as a holy, mystical union with God's own fire of revelation; in fact, they praise them for the high spiritual level that the two manage to attain![30]

This episode is a case that might fall under one of several contradictory categories: Either the sheer variety of interpretations raises the suspicion that the narrator intentionally obscures their actual offense,[31] or they did not, in fact, sin at all, and their death serves a different purpose;[32] or, alternatively, that their offense is hiding in plain sight, and in order to perceive it, the reader must look to a different place. We will take the latter path below.

Two different events may shed light on the nature of their offense: the description of the actions that led to their death and Moses's words to Aaron immediately after. Combining these two scenes reveals their sin, which is profoundly linked to the nature of the eighth day of consecration.

Nadav and Avihu's *Death* by Fire

> Aaron's sons Nadav and Avihu took their fire pans,
> put fire in them, and placed incense upon it,
> and they offered unauthorized fire before the Lord:

30. See Keniel, *Burning with Love.*
31. See Greenstein, "Deconstruction"; Anderson, "Nadab and Abihu." Binyamin Sommer ("Expulsion as Initiation") suggests that this episode is part of a common biblical model of problematic beginning narratives. I favor James Watt's reading that even if we cannot determine the actual sin, we must examine the premises of the communication between "author" and "reader" and thus seek to understand the intentions of the text (Watts, *Ritual*, 101–03). He concludes that after the focus on the consecration and prestige of the priests, this episode reveals the danger that comes with such privilege (ibid., 113).
32. Levine even proposes that this was a tragic accident and not a punishment (Levine, "Sense and Incense"), while Greenberg suggests that their punishment is a response to their part in the sin of the Golden Calf, for unlike their father, they failed to atone (Greenberg, "The True Sin").

> fire He had not commanded.
> And fire came forth from before the Lord and consumed them.
> They died before the Lord. (10:1–2).

Rashbam's interpretation of the fire that "came forth before the Lord" advances our discussion:

> "And fire came forth from before the Lord and consumed them" – This is the fire of the earlier verse... when the fire came forth and consumed [the burnt offering] and peace offerings of the outer altar. As Aaron's sons offered an unauthorized fire on the inner altar – the fire came forth from before the Lord to first burn the incense, and went through Aaron's sons there and they died, and the fire continued on to the outer altar and consumed the burnt offering. (Rashbam on Lev. 10:1)

Rashbam connects the two mentions of fire at the end of chapter 9 and in this verse, explaining that they are the same fire: "And fire came forth from before the Lord" (9:24 and 10:2). The same divine fire comes from within the Sanctuary itself and burns up Nadav and Avihu as it blazes toward the outer altar. This is characteristic of biblical narrative: Rather than interrupt the description of one part, the narrative then goes back to the same point in time and describes another aspect that occurred at the same time. As Israel stood, waiting for divine revelation, Nadav and Avihu were already offering up their unauthorized fire, but the text first describes God's glorious fire blazing toward the altar before the assembly, and then goes back to describe how this same fire burned up Nadav and Avihu before it reached the outer altar.

It is not necessary to adopt Rashbam's (and others') suggestion that Nadav and Avihu were offering up incense on the incense altar (of which there is no explicit mention in the text).[33] Indeed, from the fact that there is no indication of any need for decontamination and purification due

33. For support of Rashbam's approach that Nadav and Avihu burned incense inside, see Eldar, "Incense." His theory is based on the connection to the Korah rebellion and the Yom Kippur service.

to their deaths, it seems that they died outside, probably in the courtyard.[34] But his theory that they died in the same flames that appeared before all of Israel is crucial to our understanding of what Nadav and Avihu were trying to achieve.

In order to clarify what transpires in this brief scene, we must study the description of their actions carefully. Many exegetes focus on the phrase "*esh zara*," "strange/foreign/unauthorized fire." Yet I believe that a different component is key: Nadav and Avihu took firepans, "put fire in them, and placed incense upon it." They brought fire in order to burn incense,[35] but they are not in the usual place for burning incense (as is evident from the fact that they seem to be in the courtyard, as mentioned).[36] Why are they offering incense? In order to understand this, we must first consider the purpose of the incense.

Incense as a Cover

A full exploration of the meaning, role, and significance of the incense is beyond the scope of this discussion; for our purposes, I wish to focus on one direction that can illuminate Nadav and Avihu's actions. Incense is most famous for its scent, but here, this aspect of the incense leads to a false trail that obscures the true intentions of Aaron's sons.[37] The biblical incense's other purpose is to create smoke – a cloud of smoke

---

34. Ehrlich proposes that one who dies by God's hand (like Nadav and Avihu and those burned in the Korah rebellion) is not impure in death (Ehrlich, *Mikrâ ki-Pheschutô*, 221). This does not seem to be the case based on Moses's reaction – having other Levites take them out the camp by their clothing (10:4).
35. According to Haran, the problem was that they burned the incense on a fire that was not from the altar (Haran, "Incense Firepans"). As we will see below, the incense burning and producing smoke is the problem.
36. Haran (ibid.) explains that there are two ways to offer incense: upon pans and upon the altar (compare to Wellhausen, *Prolegomena*, 64–66). Ariel Stollman similarly claims that there are two different aspects of divine revelation in the Sanctuary: The first takes place within the Holy of Holies, which is veiled and does not require the smoke-veiled incense, as it is already covered; it is the Divine Presence in the Tent of Meeting that relies on the incense altar to create a concealing veil of smoke (Stollman, *Search of Lost Meaning*, 276–77).
37. As Rambam, *Guide to the Perplexed*, III:45. For a broader survey of how incense was used in Israel and other ancient peoples, see Nielsen, *Incense.*

that veils and screens the Divine Presence and thus allows Aaron to enter the Sanctuary and perform his priestly duties.[38] This is true of the everyday incense, and is true sevenfold of the Yom Kippur service, whose opening (Lev. 16:1) is explicitly linked to Nadav and Avihu's deed and their resulting death.[39]

This aspect of the incense is already evident in the commandment to build the Tabernacle vessels in Exodus 25–31:[40]

1. The Ark and the cherubim (which are in the Holy of Holies)
2. The table and the candelabra (in the Sanctuary)
3. The Tabernacle sheets and boards
4. The burnt offering altar (in the courtyard)
5. The courtyard hangings and posts
6. The commandment about keeping the perpetual lamp lit and making the priestly garments
7. The commandment about ordaining the priests and consecrating the altar
8. The concluding verses: "There I will meet with the Israelites. It will be sanctified by My glory. I will consecrate the Tent of Meeting and the altar. I will also consecrate Aaron and his sons to serve Me as priests. I will have My Presence dwell among the Israelites and I shall be their God. Then they will know that I am the Lord their God, who brought them out of Egypt to dwell among them. I am the Lord their God" (Ex. 29:43–46)
9. Additions: *the incense altar*; the half-shekel; the basin; the preparation of the incense and anointing oil; appointing Betzalel and Oholiav; the commandment about Shabbat

38. The motif of covering and concealment is fundamental in the Tabernacle. This is the main function of the screen (*parokhet*) around the Ark. The word "*kapporet*" is also related to "covering," and its main purpose is to cover the broken tablets inside the Ark (Grintz, "Munaḥim," 163–167).
39. On the connections between Leviticus 16 and Nadav and Avihu's sin, see especially Rendtorff, "Nadav and Avihu"; Eldar, "Incense."
40. See Herzog Bible Center, *Genesis and Exodus*, 76–77.

The order of the vessels follows their placement – beginning at the center and moving outward. But given this clear pattern, the incense altar, which should be mentioned along with the other vessels in the Sanctuary, and the basin, which ought to be listed with the other vessels in the courtyard, are obviously out of place. The suggestion that this order forms an *inclusio* is not convincing;[41] this would only make sense if these two vessels were mentioned before the general conclusion, but they appear after the clearly defined opening and conclusion, which form a tight, closed unit: "I will dwell among them (25:8) / "I will dwell among the Israelites" (29:45). This marks the incense altar and basin as anomalous appendixes to the entire section.

That these two vessels are mentioned after the obvious conclusion of the Tabernacle vessels indicates that they are considered part of the description of supplementary Temple activity and preparation. In other words, certain vessels define the Tabernacle as God's house; without the candelabra, table, or altar, the Tabernacle is not a Tabernacle. The incense altar and the basin, however, are secondary, auxiliary vessels that facilitate the priestly service. This is explicitly stated about the basin: "Put water in it, for Aaron and his sons to wash their hands and feet. When they enter the Tent of Meeting or approach the altar... they must wash with water, so that they do not die. They must wash their hands and feet so that they do not die; it shall be an eternal law for them" (Ex. 30:19–21). The priests must wash their hands and feet in order to approach the altar. The Tabernacle is still defined as God's house without the basin, but the priests cannot serve in this house without using the basin.

It emerges that the incense altar performs a similar function: God dwells in the Tent of Meeting regardless of whether the altar is there or not, but the priests are unable to work where God's presence rests without the incense altar's smokescreen. In the words of Sforno:

41. Muchiki, "Altar of Incense." Carol Meyers proposes that since incense was offered inside the Holy of Holies on Yom Kippur, the incense altar was actually a "wandering altar." Its textual placement at the end of the list reflects its movement (Meyers, "Realms of Sanctity," 33–46).

> This altar is not mentioned together with the other vessels in *Parashat Teruma,* because it did not bring down God's presence as the other vessels did: "They shall make Me a Sanctuary and I will dwell in their midst. Form the Tabernacle and form all of its furnishings following the patterns that I show you." Nor was its purpose to bring down God's glory to the House, as the rite of the offerings did. (Sforno on Ex. 30:1)[42]

For this reason, "unlike the descriptions in chapter 25, the content of this section is not just a description of the object itself. The main purpose of this section, from verse 7 and on, is to describe the service it was used for, the service performed each and every day."[43]

How, then, did the incense contribute to the daily priestly service? Sforno suggests that it is an expression of God's glory: "To honor God after He accepts the morning and evening offerings with favor." It seems, however, that the incense has a more specific purpose. This is evident through the Yom Kipper service: "He shall place the incense on the fire before the Lord *so that the cloud of incense conceals* the cover on top of the Ark of the Testimony, so that he does not die" (Lev. 16:13). The smoke raised by the incense conceals the Divine Presence and thus allows the priest to serve alongside God's glory. Just as the priests must wash their hands "so they will not die," the incense conceals God's glory so the priest "will not die." I believe that the same is reflected at the beginning of the Yom Kippur service as well: "Tell your brother Aaron that he may not come at any time into the holy place inside the inner curtain in front of the cover on the Ark, or he will die – for in a cloud above the cover I appear" (Lev. 16:2). This cloud is the same cloud of incense that Aaron creates when he brings a burning pan of incense into the Holy of Holies with him: "As these are the only mentions of the word 'cloud' in

42. Compare to Cassuto: "The incense altar is not a vessel that belongs to God's dwelling place, but to human worship of God. Thus,it is not mentioned in Exodus 25 as part of the vessels in the Divine Abode, but here, at the beginning of the sections about the Tabernacle service" (Cassuto, *Exodus,* 273).
43. Cassuto, *Exodus,* 273.

the book of Leviticus, and they are all within the same section, it makes sense that they refer to the same cloud."[44]

If so, the purpose of the incense is to conceal the Divine Presence, thus allowing the priests to serve in the midst of this powerful divine manifestation. God's revelation to the Israelites in the wilderness always occurs within a cloud, so that they may survive this encounter; within the Tabernacle as well, His presence is always veiled in a protective layer of incense smoke. When revelation is the result of divine initiative, it takes place within a cloud; when the people seek to create the right setting for revelation, they burn incense to create a similar, cloud-like screen of smoke.

This reading is consistent with the placement of the incense altar and its timing within the daily Tabernacle service. In our discussion of the internal purification offering, we already mentioned that the incense altar's placement is emphasized as being in front of the Ark and the cherubim: "Put it in front of the screen that veils the Ark of the Testimony, in front of the cover above the Ark, where I will meet with you" (Ex. 30:6). The incense altar's placement in front of the Ark puts it in line with the cherubim, where the Divine Presence rests.[45] While the candelabra's purpose is to illuminate and the table's purpose is for the placement of the showbread, the incense altar is related to the Divine Presence. Its purpose is to create a smokescreen that enables the priest to serve alongside the Divine Presence itself.

This is also consistent with the daily Temple service schedule: "Aaron should burn incense on it every morning when he tends the lamps, and before evening when he lights the lamps" (Ex. 30:7–8). Why are the lamps mentioned in relation to the incense altar? Cassuto's suggestion that the incense masked the smell of the wicks and burning oil is not convincing;[46] burning olive oil does not have an unpleasant smell (nor is it nearly as strong as the smell of burning fat and meat!). The incense

44. Stav, *Beyond the Curtain*, 195; his conclusion is different.

45. Cassuto's suggestion that both the incense altar and the cover above the Ark are part of the Yom Kippur service and are therefore aligned is less convincing (*Exodus*, 274).

46. Cassuto, *Exodus*, 274.

altar and the lamps are much more logically connected through the incense's smoke-raising capacities. The veiling smoke of the incense must be renewed whenever the lamps are lit to achieve the necessary balance between revelation and concealment.

Even if this aspect of the incense's purpose is arguable all year long, the incense smoke as a screen is explicitly described on Yom Kippur itself. As R. Avraham Stav aptly points out, on Yom Kippur the incense is not "burned" (*haktara*) but rather "placed/given" (*netina*): "He shall *place* the incense on the fire before the Lord so that the cloud of incense conceals the cover on top of the Ark of the Testimony" (Lev. 16:13). On Yom Kippur, the incense itself is not an offering, but a smokescreen. This is further indicated by the fact that it is not burned on the incense altar, but rather on a pan: "The verses of the Yom Kippur service focus on the consequence of the incense burning, unlike the daily incense which is considered a regular offering whose main purpose is the burning of the incense itself."[47]

When the encounter with God's glory occurs somewhere besides the usual place in the Sanctuary – where most of the priestly service takes place – the cloud of incense must be brought along. The firepan is like a portable incense altar. This is what Nadav and Avihu use when they burn incense: "Aaron's sons Nadav and Avihu took their fire pans, put fire in them, and placed incense upon it" (Lev. 10:1). As mentioned, Rashbam's suggestion that they offered incense on the regular incense altar is not convincing. It makes more sense that they raised incense smoke on their firepans next to the special site of revelation on the eighth day, next to the outer burnt offering altar.

This implies that Nadav and Avihu attempt to veil the revelation of God's glory in a cloud of incense smoke – which is wholy antithetical to the nature of this unique day: "For on this day the Lord will be revealed

47. Stav, *Beyond the Curtain*, 192–93. The *Tzofnat Paneaḥ* disagrees (*Letters of Torah*, 144) – he argues that the opposite is true, and that only on Yom Kippur is the incense considered an actual offering. R. Stav shows that all year long a certain amount is offered twice daily, whereas on Yom Kippur the amount is a question of the priest's own hand – implying the amount needed to create the proper amount of smoke (Mishna Yoma 5:1). This also shows that the incense serves a different role than usual on Yom Kippur.

to you" (9:4). Why do Aaron's sons attempt to conceal this revelation from the people?

Once again, the revelation of God's glory in the form of a blazing, consuming fire upon the altar is a direct continuation of God's revelation as a consuming fire at the top of Mount Sinai. There, too, Israel are granted a similar revelation to that of the eighth day of consecration: "To the Israelites the appearance of the Lord's glory on the mountaintop was like consuming fire" (Ex. 24:17). Some read this to mean that the Israelites only perceived glimpses and sparks of this fire gleaming through the veil of cloud,[48] but this is not the plain meaning of the verse. The cloud is mentioned as well, but what the Israelites see is intense fire, not fire covered by cloud.

The connection between the eighth day and the Sinai revelation sheds dramatic light on the significance of the eighth day, reinforcing Ramban's theory that the Tabernacle "continues" the Sinai revelation: God's glory descends to the mountain and from there continues to the new dwelling place Israel builds so that the Divine Presence may rest in their midst. The affinity between the two scenes is also related to the cast of characters in each: Moses ascends to the top of the mountain, while the highest of Israel's ranks begin to follow, then stop along the way: "Then He said to Moses, 'Ascend to the Lord, you and Aaron, Nadav and Avihu, and seventy of Israel's elders and bow down from afar. Moses alone shall approach the Lord. The others must not come close, nor shall the people come up with him'" (Ex. 24:1–2). This is indeed what comes to pass: "Then Moses went up with Aaron, Nadav, Avihu, and seventy of Israel's elders. They saw a vision of the God of Israel, and beneath His feet what looked like a lapis lazuli pavement as clear as the sky itself. And He did the leaders of Israel no harm – and they looked upon God and they ate and they drank" (24:9–11).

The verse emphasizes that God does not harm or punish them for gazing upon this vision, which colors this event as a rare, unique encounter indeed, as no human is usually able to withstand and survive such a close encounter with the Divine. At Mount Sinai, "Aaron, Nadav, Avihu, and seventy of Israel's elders" are granted the privilege of being "beneath

48. Weinfeld, "Glory," 31.

His feet," while at the foot of the mountain below, the rest of Israel see "the Lord's glory on the mountaintop like consuming fire." This account, then, describes three different levels of revelation.[49]

Given the clear connection between the scenes, the fact that Nadav and Avihu appear by name in both episodes of God's revelation in the form of consuming fire is unlikely to be coincidental. Some of the Sages perceive the two scenes as crime and punishment: Although "He did the leaders of Israel no harm" there upon the mountain, Nadav and Avihu were punished on the eighth day of consecration instead:

> "And He did the leaders of Israel no harm." R. Pinḥas said: From here [it may be derived] that they were deserving of harm... [because] they feasted their eyes on the Divine Presence.... This is analogous to a king who was marrying off his daughter and found in one of the members of the wedding party a matter of infamy. The king said: "If I kill him now, I will compromise my daughter's celebration. Tomorrow, my celebration will come. It is preferable during my celebration and not during my daughter's celebration." So too, the Holy One, blessed be He, said: "If I kill them now, I will compromise the celebration of My daughter. Tomorrow, My celebration will come." His daughter, this is the Torah. That is what is written: "On the day of his wedding and on the day of the rejoicing of his heart" (Song. 3:11). "On the day of his wedding," this is Mount Sinai, "and on the day of the rejoicing of his heart," this is the Tent of Meeting. (Leviticus Rabba 20:10)[50]

This is a problematic reading for two reasons. Firstly, there is no hint of criticism toward the leaders of Israel who look upon the vision of God; on the contrary, they are instructed to go partway up the mountain together with Moses, which implies that they are privy to a higher degree of revelation than the rest of the people. Secondly, it makes no

49. George Savran shows that Tanakh favors listening over sight, but Exodus 24 is an exception, and the focus is on seeing God's glory (*Savran,* "Seeing is Believing").
50. See further approaches that support this in Bin-Nun, *Mikraot – Mishpatim*, 463–68. On reading "Israel's leaders" not as the priests, see ibid., 483–84.

sense that Nadav and Avihu are the only ones punished at a later stage, since there is no distinction between Nadav and Avihu's actions at Mount Sinai and those of Aaron and the seventy elders who stood with them.

The connection between their appearance in both scenes can be understood differently. At Mount Sinai, the priests are privileged to witness a higher degree of revelation than the rest of Israel. This is already hinted at in the instructions given before the Ten Commandments: "The Lord told Moses, 'Go back down – warn the people not to force their way through to look at the Lord, or many will die. *Even priests who come near to the Lord must first consecrate themselves,* or the Lord will break out against them'" (Ex. 19:21–22). Herein lies the difference: The people must not touch the mountain, but the priests may "come near to the Lord" if they "first consecrate themselves."[51]

We can certainly imagine Nadav and Avihu's exultation when they return to the camp at the end of the Sinai revelation. As Israel's emissaries, they have gazed upon God in His crystal-blue heavens. Just as their mouths are later ordained to eat from His own altar, already up on Sinai they have been privileged to taste the peace offerings sacrificed on the mountain of revelation (Ex. 24:5; see Ibn Ezra's commentary there). Ramban even adds that they eat from the peace offering by the altar at the foot of the mountain before they return to the camp, just as peace offerings must be eaten in Jerusalem (on Ex. 24:11).

This sense of exclusive privilege illuminates Nadav and Avihu's behavior on the eighth day of consecration. When their Israelite friends tell them they have witnessed God's heavenly consuming fire upon the mountaintop, they know that they themselves have seen a far more powerful vision of divine revelation. Consecrated, they sat beneath God's own feet and feasted on the offerings of His very covenant. In their minds, only the priests ought to witness such a high level of revelation; Israel may stand at a distance to see His glorious consuming fire, but the entrance to the Tent of Meeting is far too close for them to experience such a degree of revelation. The priests are fully consecrated, but Israel must not gaze upon God's fire upon the altar in the courtyard. Out of

51. On linking this commandment (Ex. 19) to the covenant in Exodus 24, see Eldar, *Revelation at Sinai.*

burning jealousy for the glory of God, out of a fierce passion for the priesthood, they take up firepans and fill them with incense, rushing to create a screen of smoke to obscure the fire of revelation that blazes toward the altar. Essentially, they seek to reenact the revelation as they imagine Israel witnessed it at Sinai: sparks of veiled fire gleaming through a protective sheath of smoke.

Once again, this reading began with Rashbam's theory that the fire that burned up Nadav and Avihu is the same consuming fire that lights up the altar and its offerings. As the divine flames flared up, the two priests ran out with their firepans burning, trying to fill the space around the altar with a screen of smoke. But on the eighth day of revelation, God wishes to reveal and not conceal His glory. At Mount Sinai, the priests were granted a special degree of revelation, but the people, too, were able to see God's fiery glory crowning the mountain.[52]

God's revelation is the main objective of this day, and Nadav and Avihu's attempt to hold back this sight from the people is a grave miscalculation. Venturing forth with their unauthorized pans of fire, they are burned up in the consuming flames of revelation. Nothing will stop the Divine Presence from appearing in a blaze of glory before the eyes of all the assembly.[53]

Moses's Explanation

As mentioned, the nature of Nadav and Avihu's offense can also be clarified through Moses's explanation to Aaron immediately after their death, which further supports the reading that Nadav and Avihu's miscalculation was to conceal the fiery Divine Revelation with smoke: "Moses

52. Nadav and Avihu are overlooking the fact that at Mount Sinai all of Israel are sprinkled with ritual blood in a similar act to what happens to the priests during the days of consecration: "Then he sent young men of Israel, and they sacrificed bulls as burnt offerings and peace offerings to the Lord. Moses took half the blood and put it in bowls. The other half he sprinkled on the altar.... Then Moses took the blood, sprinkled it on the people, and said, 'This is the blood of the covenant that the Lord is making with you regarding all these words'" (Ex. 24:5–8).
53. Milgrom's understanding is that the fire came out of the Tabernacle while Nadav and Avihu were at the entrance to the Tent of Meeting (*Leviticus*, vol. 1, 600). This is a reasonable reading, but it is not explicit in the text; they may have been next to the outer altar, nor did the fire necessarily come out of the Tabernacle.

said to Aaron, 'Of this the Lord spoke when He said: I will be sanctified through those close to Me, and before all the people I will be honored'" (Lev. 10:3). Some interpret this as a consolation in the sense that Moses is saying that Nadav and Avihu are those close to God through whom He is sanctified (Rashi, Ibn Ezra, Ramban),[54] while others explain that Moses is telling Aaron and his remaining sons that they are the close ones, so there is no need for mourning and impurity right now (Rashbam, Bekhor Shor). Yet from a perspective of the plot, given that Moses speaks up immediately after the tragedy, the reader expects Moses's words to serve as some kind of explanation. When read as a statement that expresses a contrast, they indeed do explain what has just taken place:

> Moses said to Aaron, "Of this the Lord spoke when He said: I will be sanctified through those close to Me / but before all the people I will be honored."

Some read the phrase "Of this the Lord spoke when He said" as a heading, like "Thus,said the Lord" (Shadal and Milgrom). Others look for a specific statement God has already uttered (Rashi, Bekhor Shor, Rabbeinu Bahya, Abarbanel – each suggest a different statement). Ramban, however, logically points out that "spoke" (*dibber*) can often refer to general thoughts and intentions: "For by way of *peshat,* the expression 'God spoke' refers to His decrees, His thought, and the manner of His ways, and the term 'speaking' is used with reference to all these.... Thus, Moses said here: This incident is that which God decreed, 'saying to His heart'" (Ramban on Lev. 10:3).

According to Ramban, Moses is referring to God's intentions, explaining to Aaron that God is indeed sanctified through those closest to Him (i.e., the priests – see Ezek. 42:13: "The priests who are closest to the Lord"), but today, God's plan was to show His glory to *all the people.*[55]

---

54. The most prevalent reading in modern research is that Nadav and Avihu are the ones who sanctify God's name, because through their deaths, the whole people are warned of the dangers of proximity to holiness and of entering the Sanctuary unbidden (Hartley, *Leviticus,* 134; Wenham, *Leviticus,* 156–57).

55. Elsewhere the roots K-V-D/K-D-SH are regular parallels, as in Ezekiel 28:22. However, given the centrality of God's *kavod* in this chapter, Moses's words cannot be

Thus, the most logical reading of these verses is that Moses is contrasting the priests, through whom God "is sanctified," and the people, before whom God wishes to show His glory. With this contrast, Moses is explaining to his brother that Nadav and Avihu die due to their attempt to conceal God's glory from the people in order to maintain the priesthood's exclusivity. Your sons are indeed especially close to God, and they sanctify Him through their service, but the purpose of this day was for God's glory to be revealed to all the people.

Esh Zara – What Kind of Fire?

Another enigmatic description that is clarified through this reading is the phrase "*esh zara*": "Aaron's sons Nadav and Avihu took their fire pans, put fire in them, and placed incense upon it, and they offered *zara* fire before the Lord: fire He had not commanded" (10:1). The word "*zar*" has several meanings – "foreign," "other," "strange." What does the word *zara* mean here?

> A list of the major theories will suffice to demonstrate the difficulty of knowing the exact nature of this phrase. They may have offered at the wrong time of day, or from the wrong motive, or in an over-zealous manner because of the shouts of the people. Maybe they used the wrong procedure by not purifying themselves properly, by daring to enter the adytum, or by taking fire from a profane source. Perhaps they were bringing in foreign incense used in pagan cults, or maybe they were not even priests at all![56]

But even if we cannot determine the precise meaning of this phrase, we can sketch out its parameters. A helpful verse in this context is the prohibition against offering foreign incense upon the golden altar: "Offer no *zara* incense on it, or any burnt offering, grain offering, or libation" (Ex. 30:9). Some explain that "*zara*" here means that the incense was not properly prepared according to the strict sacrificial guidelines (see Ibn

detached from their context.

56. Bibb, *Ritual*, 118.

Ezra).[57] The verse before this prohibition, however, does not address the preparation process, but rather *when* the incense is to be offered: "Aaron should burn incense on it every morning when he tends the lamps, and before evening when he lights the lamps. It shall be a perpetual incense offering before the Lord throughout your generations" (30:7–8). Thus, Rashi's reading that the incense should never be offered at any other time as a freewill offering seems more likely. It may also be that both interpretations are correct: Any incense that does not follow the precise guidelines – either because it is offered at the wrong time or because it is improperly prepared – is considered "*zara*" to the altar. An appropriate translation would be "unauthorized," that is, offered without the proper authorization.

If so, it is clear why Nadav and Avihu's fire is considered an "unauthorized fire": It is offered up without any divine command or authorized instruction.

Aaron accepts Moses's explanation with a humble, poignant, deafening silence that still reverberates to this day: "And Aaron was silent" (10:3). Every moment of silence in the midst of lament and loss recalls Aaron's silent acceptance: "He should sit alone and be silent: this was inflicted on him" (Lam 3:28). As soon as Aaron accepts this decree, Moses forbids the priestly family to mourn for the two sons who died.

"YOU AND YOUR SONS MUST NOT DRINK WINE OR STRONG DRINK"

The tragedy of the eighth day is suddenly interrupted by an unexpected commandment – the prohibition against priests drinking alcohol while in service:

> And the Lord spoke to Aaron: "You and your sons must not drink wine or strong drink when you enter the Tent of Meeting, so that you do not die. This is an everlasting statute throughout your generations, to enable you to distinguish between sacred and profane, and between impure and pure, and to teach the

57. In parallel to this reading, Milgrom proposes that *esh zara* shows that the fire they took was not from the altar (*Leviticus*, vol. 1, 598).

> Israelites all the statutes that the Lord has spoken to them through Moses." (Lev. 10:8–11)

Since these verses are interpolated in the middle of the events of the eighth day, they are presumably related to the verses before or the verses after this unexpected passage. In this case, it seems to make the most sense that this prohibition is a reaction to the tragedy of the death of Aaron's sons. There are already midrashic commentaries that explain that Nadav and Avihu's sin was to "enter the Sanctuary drunk" (as cited by Rashi on Lev. 10:2),[58] while others propose that this is inserted here "because the custom was to give wine and strong drink to those who were suffering or in mourning. For this reason, this prohibition is mentioned here for the priests in mourning."[59]

There is another way, however, to interpret this prohibition. Not only is the placement of these verses in the middle of those relating to the eighth day somewhat surprising, but their "correct" placement is evident elsewhere. Given that the reason that active priests must remain sober is so that they can "distinguish between sacred and profane, and between impure and pure," these verses would have been aptly placed at the beginning of the chapters of purity and impurity that follow the chapters about the eighth day, Leviticus 11–16. These chapters encompass detailed descriptions of all kinds of impurity (11–15) and conclude with an account of the purification of the Tabernacle itself (16). These chapters are interspersed with formulaic phrases that recall the stray verses in Leviticus 10: "To distinguish between impure and pure" (11:47); "To determine when they are impure and when they are pure" (14:57). Given that the first time that this priestly role is defined is in juxtaposition with the prohibition against drinking alcohol,[60] it would have made sense to begin the chapters of purity and impurity with this prohibition.

58. And modern scholars as well; see Gispen, *Leviticus,* 166; Hartley, *Leviticus,* 135.

59. See also Bekhor Shor, Hizkuni, *Keli Yakar,* and Bula (*Leviticus,* 157) on this verse.

60. This implies that the *peshat* of these verses is not to generally teach about purity and impurity, as the Sages explain, but rather to specifically determine whether problematic *nega'im* (sores, suspicious patches that may be *tzaraat,* etc.) are pure or impure.

If so, why are these verses inserted here in the middle of the description of the eighth day, after the death of Aaron's sons, instead of at the beginning of the next unit?

Rashi already comments on the special revelation Aaron is granted following his unfathomable silence in the wake of his sons' sudden death: "And Aaron was silent – He is rewarded for his silence. What was his reward? That he alone then received God's word: He alone was told the law that priests may not drink wine" (on Lev. 10:3). Ibn Ezra debates whether Aaron is granted his own prophecy or if Moses still serves as prophetic mediator, even though his name is not mentioned in this verse (see also the *Sifri* on Num. 18:1). Either way, God speaking only to Aaron gives the impression that Aaron is indeed granted a personal revelation.[61]

These verses' contribution can be understood differently from Rashi's interpretation: They do express a gift, but one that helps restore the priests' status that Nadav and Avihu's death so severely damaged. After all, Aaron's two sons have just been consecrated and ordained with the oil and blood of the ordination ram; they have spent the last seven days at the entrance to the Tent of Meeting. Dressed in their new priestly vestments of glory and honor, on the most important day of their lives, they are burned to death. Tragically, they are dragged out for burial in their brand-new, consecrated garments: "They carried Nadav and Avihu out by their tunics to a place outside the camp" (10:5).

This catastrophe – especially one that points to the dangers of arrogance and elitism that the priesthood may engender – damages the priestly status in the eyes of the people, of Aaron himself, of his two remaining sons, and of the reader as well. The reference to the priests' roles of determining purity and impurity for the people, however, helps restore the priesthood's dignity. They are still of utmost importance: The responsibility to distinguish between the pure and the impure, between

61. Wenham writes that this is testimony to the importance of priestly abstinence from alcohol (*Leviticus*, 158). He also notes the importance of this law for Aaron and his sons' personal feelings, similar to my own argument below. Besides this law, there are two other laws which Aaron is commanded without mention of Moses (Num. 18:1; 18:8).

the sacred and the profane, still rests upon their shoulders, and to this end they must remain sober at all times to keep their faculties sharp and ready for duty.[62]

The priests' status and responsibility is further explored in the second half of the chapter, when after this brief interlude the text goes back to the eighth day of consecration.

A FURTHER INFRINGEMENT: BURNING THE PURIFICATION OFFERING

In the second half of the chapter – which is also the second half of the eighth day of consecration, after God's revelation and the death of Nadav and Avihu – Aaron's two remaining sons also violate the law. The parallel between the two halves of the chapter is clear, but for some reason, the decision made by Aaron's two other sons is accepted, not punished.

The second half of the day is devoted to the priests' eating of the offerings, which comes as no surprise. As mentioned, the priests' consumption of the offerings is perceived as a continuation of the altar's consumption in the second sacrificial list and during the days of consecration; it is the act of eating that ordains them as priests. Moses explicitly emphasizes the importance of this act: "It is holy of holies, and it has been given to you to remove the guilt of the community and atone for them before the Lord" (10:17). We will explore this further below; what is relevant for now is that the priests' act of eating effects atonement for the people.

Moses then goes on to instruct the priests about the laws of how each offering of the eighth day is to be eaten. He begins with the grain offering, and commands Aaron, Elazar, and Itamar – "his *remaining* sons" – to eat "the *remaining* grain offering of the Lord's fire offerings" (10:12–13).[63] The instruction to eat the matzot "by the altar" once again

---

62. On whether they must always refrain from drinking (Rambam in *Sefer HaMitzvot*, negative commandment 73; *Hilkhot Biat HaMikdash* 1:1) or only when on priestly duty (Ramban, based on the Sages), see Milgrom, *Leviticus*, vol. 1, 612–14.

63. It is difficult to know if the word "remaining" is intentional and significant. Are they, in a sense, an offering, with the same divine fire consuming them and the offerings together? Perhaps Ehrlich is correct that this expresses the acute, indescribable pain (Ehrlich, "Notes," 36). See further below.

confirms that the priestly portion of the grain offering is a gift from the altar, and they must eat it unleavened by the altar, just as the altar consumes its portion of the grain offering.

After the commandment about the grain offering, Moses mentions the priestly portion of the people's peace offering: "The breast of the wave offering and the thigh of the upraised gift in any ritually pure place, for these have been given to you from the peace sacrifices of Israel as your portion and the portion of your children" (10:14–15). "Any ritually pure place" subtly defines that the peace offering does not possess the same holiness as other offerings, although the priests are still confined to the Tabernacle entrance (10:7), so they effectively eat their share in a holy place anyway.[64] Some suggest that the people's share of the peace offering is eaten by the elders (mentioned in 9:1), so this instruction is still necessary,[65] but given that this is a communal offering, it was probably not shared with the people. (According to Zevaḥim 97b, communal peace offerings were only eaten by the priests, not the people.) For this reason, there is no mention of the accompanying loaves.

This is followed by a dramatic conflict about the purification offering. It emerges that Aaron and his sons burned the purification offering instead of eating their share. It seems that the purification offering is delayed to the end of the list because of this drama; otherwise, it would have presumably been listed after the grain offering and before the peace offering, following the usual sacrificial order in the first chapters of Leviticus.[66]

> Moses inquired about the goat for the purification offering, and discovered that it had been burned.
> He was furious with Elazar and Itamar, the two sons left to Aaron.
> "Why did you not eat the purification offering in the holy area?" he asked.

---

64. See further in Kasher, *Torah Shelema*, vol. 27, 205–06. In contrast to the above reading, Bula proposes that the specification of a pure place teaches that the priests were allowed to leave when they were not working, even on the eighth day itself (Bula, *Leviticus*, 160).
65. Milgrom, *Leviticus*, vol. 1, 619.
66. For the first instance of this model, see Gen. 31:33–35.

> "It is holy of holies, and it has been given to you to remove the guilt of the community and atone for them before the Lord. Because its blood was not to be brought into the inner Sanctuary, you should have eaten it in the Sanctuary, as I commanded." (10:16–18)

What purification offering is Moses talking about? Rashi, following the Sages, explains that this is a purification offering that has not yet been mentioned: the New Moon purification offering. According to Rashi, the eighth day of consecration took place on the first of Nisan, and the purification goat is part of the sacrifices brought each new month (Num. 28:15). While this is theoretically possible, it is difficult to reconcile this idea with the *peshat*. It makes little sense that the purification offering in question is mentioned without prior introduction, without any prior mention of the special sacrifices of the New Moon. Moreover, Hizkuni is correct that the emphasis on atonement in this particular purification offering seems to be referring to one of the people's offerings mentioned at the beginning of the eighth day: "Then prepare the people's offering to make atonement for them, as the Lord has commanded" (9:7).[67] A further problem with Rashi's reading is that the eighth day of consecration did not necessarily fall on the first day of Nisan (see Ibn Ezra and others).

The simpler reading is that because Aaron burned the priestly purification offering outside the camp as instructed (9:10), the offering in question is the people's purification goat brought on the eighth day. To his dismay, Moses discovers that the priests have burned that offering outside the camp as well, and he is "furious." His long speech reveals exactly why: "It is holy of holies, and it has been given to you to remove the guilt of the community and atone for them before the Lord." Moses is concerned that the people will not achieve atonement if the priests do not eat their portion.[68]

---

67. "'And the purification goat' – According to the *peshat* this is of what it says: 'Take a goat for purification,' for in both places it says "atonement" (Hizkuni on Lev. 10:16).
68. Thus, there is no need to adopt Milgrom's claim that Moses's concern is due to the fact that in the ancient world, remains of offerings were used for black magic (Milgrom, *Leviticus*, 635–40). This is his general approach to the eating of purification

This background information is necessary in order to understand the priests' response. Note that Moses – with subtle sensitivity – directs his anger toward Aaron's sons, not to their newly bereaved father: "He was furious with Elazar and Itamar, the two sons left to Aaron" (10:16). Yet Aaron, who is equally responsible, knows that Moses is just as angry at him, so he is the one who responds and explains their actions:

> It was Aaron who replied to Moses,
> "They offered their purification offering and their burnt offerings before the Lord today – but such things have happened to me. Would it really have been right in the Lord's eyes if I had eaten a purification offering today?"
> Moses listened; and it was right in his eyes. (10:19–20)

Aaron explains that this was not a mistake; they intentionally burned the purification offering that the priests were supposed to eat. His actual explanation, however, is enigmatic. A broad range of suggestions attempt to interpret how Aaron's response quells Moses's anger.[69] Ibn Ezra even adds that Aaron ate a tiny piece of the offering before he burned it to make sure he first fulfilled the priestly obligation:

> "But such things have happened to me" – meaning, my troubles and grief at the death of my sons, and for this reason I could not eat all the purification offering, so I just ate enough to please God, enough to fulfill my obligation. (Ibn Ezra on Lev. 10:19)

Ibn Ezra famously favors the *peshat*, yet Aaron's vague reply pushes him over the edge. The logic indeed seems contrived: Can it really be that

---

offerings; see ibid., 261–64. Here, however, Moses is explicitly concerned that this will affect the people's atonement.

69. The simplest reading is that Aaron asks a hypothetical question (as in the current translation: "Would it really have been right in the Lord's eyes if I had eaten a purification offering today?"). Bula suggests a different reading: that the *vav* of "*ve'akhalti*" ("I had eaten") is the *vav* of contrast: "Even with all that happened to me, *even so I ate.*" According to Bula, only Aaron's sons fail to eat the purification offering, but Aaron does (Bula, *Leviticus,* 163). This is difficult to accept.

Aaron changes the law based on personal conjecture? Moreover, Moses is satisfied with this conjecture! It must be, surmises Ibn Ezra, that Aaron ate just enough to fulfill his obligation, and Moses must have thought that he burned the offering without eating it at all.

Does Aaron indeed explain that he wasn't able to finish eating the purification offering due to his sorrow? The real problem with this interpretation is that there is no mention of him burning the grain offering or peace offering instead of eating it. Why does the initial misunderstanding between Aaron and Moses revolve around the purification offering?

Rashbam takes a slightly different approach: "But such things have happened to me – How can I eat the holy of holies purification offering on this day, when our joy has been tainted? 'Insolent is the bride who is promiscuous under her wedding canopy!'" Rashbam, like Ibn Ezra, points out that the joy of the day has become tainted, but his talmudic quote proceeds in a different direction. The parable of the promiscuous bride refers to Israel's sin of the Golden Calf while Moses is still on Mount Sinai (Shabbat 88b; Gittin 36b). Aaron is not merely too distressed to eat;[70] rather, he feels that it is immoral and ineffective for him to effect atonement for Israel's sin when the altar has just rejected his own sons from serving as priests. After what has just happened to the priestly family, are Aaron and his remaining sons worthy to serve as the emissaries of the altar to atone for Israel?

Aaron's concern is profoundly linked to the nature of the purification offering. There is no aspect of atonement in eating the priestly share of the grain or peace offering, so Aaron eats of them without any issue.

This charges the verb "consume" – "And from before the Lord, fire came forth. It consumed the burnt offering and the fat pieces on the altar" / "And fire came forth from before the Lord and consumed them" – with its full significance. God's fire consumed those who attempted to stop this fire consuming the offerings before the eyes of all Israel, and for this

70. This direction is developed further by Kiuchi, *Purification Offering*, 77–85. Wenham proposes that Aaron's speech should be understood as an expression of fear of God; after his sons die, Aaron refrains from eating holy of holies offerings and keeps his distance from the Sanctuary (Wenham, *Leviticus*, 160). This is strange, given that they eat the grain offering, which is also holy of holies.

reason the priests refrain from "consuming" the offerings as the altar's representatives.

This affinity continues to reverberate throughout the rest of the scene: As mentioned, whether the narrative intentionally generates a connection between the offerings themselves and Aaron's sons is questionable: "Moses told Aaron, and Elazar and Itamar, his two *remaining* sons, 'Take the *remaining* grain offering of the fire offerings to the Lord and eat it unleavened beside the altar" (10:12). Moses also refers to Elazar and Itamar as Aaron's "remaining sons" when he discovers they have not eaten the purification offering: "He was furious with Elazar and Itamar, Aaron's two *remaining* sons" (10:16). This points to a connection between the priests who remained after the consuming fire has burned their brothers and the remaining portions of the offerings, the part they must eat.[71] Moreover, this affinity is the basis of Aaron's explanation: Because the consuming fire consumed his sons as well, the priests cannot eat from the purification offering that Israel's atonement depends on. On this day they bow their heads in need of their own atonement; they are not able to effect atonement for others.

This response mollifies Moses. Aaron asks: "Would it really have been right in the Lord's eyes if I had eaten a purification offering today?" (10:19), and although there is no explicit answer as to whether God deems it right, it is certainly right in Moses's eyes (10:20).

Overreaching, Pulling Back

This brings us to the parallels between the two priestly violations that occur during the eighth day of consecration. Any religious violation – even a violation "for the sake of Heaven" – sends shockwaves through the religious world, which is fundamentally based on the keeping of God's word.[72] This is true sevenfold of the sacred realm of the Sanctuary. So how can it be that on the eighth day of consecration, during the sacred climax of the Divine Presence's revelation upon the

71. See further in Waxman, "Firepan," who writes that the parallel language between consuming the offerings upon the altar and burning Nadav and Avihu characterizes them as offerings.
72. See further in Lichtenstein, "Aveira Lishmah."

altar, at the very beginning of the institutionalized sacrificial service to God, the priests themselves – the sacred mediators between the people and God – commit not one but two violations?

The two violations are evaluated very differently in the text. Nadav and Avihu, who burn incense on an unauthorized fire, are burned to death; Elazar and Itamar, who do not eat the purification offering, manage to offer an explanation, and their answer is accepted. Why are these two violations treated so differently?[73]

In both cases, Aaron's sons' violations are directly related to their priesthood, but in opposite directions: Nadav and Avihu attempt to maintain the priesthood's exclusive access to divine revelation, whereas Elazar and Itamar's violation stems from concern that they are unworthy to serve as priests who effect atonement for others. These are two opposite psychological motions: One overreaches in violation, and the other shrinks back.

If so, these are not two independent violations that happen to take place on the eighth day. Both of them touch upon fundamental themes of consecration and priesthood: the nature of revelation; the consuming fire of the altar; the priestly capacity to serve as extensions of the altar fire's consumption. Nadav and Avihu overreach and overestimate the priestly role as mediators between the people and God through the altar's consuming flames, and when they offer "unauthorized fire" in an attempt to restrict the people's access to divine revelation, they are burned up. The priest must accept his role as the altar's hand – placing the correct parts upon the flames – and its mouth – eating his due share. "The altar fire shall be kept alight; it shall not go out" (Lev. 6:5). He must maintain but never censure God's consuming fire.

In contrast, Elazar, Itamar, and even Aaron are concerned that they are not worthy to be the altar's mouth and effect the people's atonement. In light of Nadav and Avihu's overreach, they hold back. They

73. Wenham writes that God is apparently more forgiving of those who make mistakes out of fear of Him than those who are negligent or disrespectful, as he surmises Nadav and Avihu are (Wenham, *Leviticus*, 160). I do not believe it is accurate to say that they are disrespectful, nor that Elazar and Itamar refrain from eating the purification offering out of fear of God.

must perceive themselves as the altar's human representatives, and this is a delicate balance to achieve. Moses's acceptance of Aaron's explanation shows that the withdrawal by Aaron and his remaining sons rightly balances out the first two sons' crossing of boundaries. This is a worthy lesson on the day when the sacrificial service truly begins: The priests' mediation between the people and God through the consuming flames of the altar is a delicate, dangerous balancing act.

This tension is an inherent part of the sacrificial world. The sweet savor and simple pleasure of eating meat carries an intrinsic danger that unworthy priests will crave and feel entitled to the meat of purification and guilt offerings, that they will abuse their role as the consuming mouths of the altar. The story of Eli's sons at the beginning of the book of Samuel is an apt illustration of this danger:

> Eli's sons were depraved men who would not acknowledge the Lord. This was how the priests would deal with the people: Whenever someone offered a sacrifice, the priest's boy would come along as the meat was boiling, a three-pronged fork in his hand. He would stab it into the cauldron, kettle, pot, or vat, and the priest would snatch whatever came up on the fork. This was how they treated every Israelite who came there to Shilo. Even before they burned off the fat, the priest's boy would come and say to the person who was sacrificing, "Hand over some meat to roast for the priest – he won't accept boiled meat from you, only raw." And if the man would say to him, "Let them first burn off the fat, then take as much as you want," he would reply, "No, hand it over at once – if not, I will take it by force." The young men's offense was very grave before the Lord, for the men showed contempt for the Lord's offerings. (I Sam. 2:12–17)

The wickedness of these priests is portrayed very harshly in this scene – "depraved men who would not acknowledge the Lord"; "the men showed contempt for the Lord's offerings." This frame has a subtle tragic irony, for "everyone in Israel must know the Lord, but this obligation is especially incumbent upon the priests."[74] Yet it is the sons of Eli who do not know God. Their insistence on grabbing their share before the fats are burned upon the altar is fundamentally perverse: Instead of the priests eating what the altar leaves over for them, this corrupt form of sacrifice leaves the altar with the leftovers of the meat the priests have greedily appropriated. Greed has compromised the sanctity of the people's offerings.

The humbling dialogue between Moses and Aaron marks the end of the days of consecration, as well as the end of the sacrificial chapters. This exchange clarifies the significance of the priestly role and the priests' consumption of the offerings, emphasizing that this is not a technical act of magical significance. Israel bring their offerings to God, seeking closeness and forgiveness; the priests are their emissaries who place their offerings upon the altar. The priests also eat part of these offerings as the altar's emissaries, but ultimately, they are but vessels who must maintain perfect purity and humility to act as sacred mediators for both sides.

The overreach of Nadav and Avihu and the humility of the remaining father and sons is a fitting end to the sacrificial chapters of the book of Leviticus, known as *Torat HaKohanim* – "The Law of the Priests." At the beginning of this study, we asked why the two lists of sacrifices are presented in reverse chronological order: The list of laws in *Parashat Tzav* was given over to Moses at Mount Sinai, whereas the list in *Vayikra* was transmitted at the Tent of Meeting after the Tabernacle's consecration. Yet the earlier list – which focuses on the priest's role in the sacrificial service – is presented in the book only after the later list, which focuses on the Israelite worshipper's role. Our conclusion was that this order conveys the Torah's message that even though the consecrated priests

74. Bar Efrat, *Samuel*, 68. Later on in the chapter: "The young men's offense was very grave before the Lord, for the men showed contempt for the Lord's offerings" (I Sam. 2:17); while in contrast, "Now Samuel was serving before the Lord" (v. 18). In the Korah rebellion, Datan and Aviram are characterized similarly to Eli's sons (Num. 16:30). In the Samuel story, the tables turn: The non-priest is chosen above the born priests, which is the opposite of what happened in the Korah rebellion, where the non-priests do not replace the rightful priests. This opposite analogy has special significance considering that Samuel is descended from Korah (I Chr. 6:7–8, and as Ibn Ezra emphasizes more than once in his commentary).

are in charge of the Sanctuary and its offerings, they are but mediators between the people and God, for the highest purpose of the sacrificial service is to bring down God's presence into the camp of Israel. After the second sacrificial list and its focus on the consuming flames of the altar and the consuming mouths of the priests, and after extensive descriptions of the seven days of consecration and the priests' purification, consecration, and ordination, the sacrificial chapters end with a warning that the priests must not overstep their boundaries. Their service must bring the people closer to God; it is not their place to keep the full glory of God's revelation from the people. Ultimately, they are but Tabernacle vessels, and their duty is to act as the people's emissaries to the altar and as the altar's hand and mouth. They are, after all, the consecrated representatives of "a kingdom of priests and a holy nation."

Bibliography

Abarbanel, commentary on the Torah: פירוש אברבנאל על התורה, מהדורת בני ארבאל, ירושלים תשל"ט.

Abba, R., "The Origin and Significance of Hebrew Sacrifice," *Biblical Theology Bulletin* 7 (1977), pp. 123–138.

Ahuviah, *As Written*: א' אהוביה, ככל הכתוב: הארות על כתובים במקרא, תל אביב תשל"ז.

Albright, W. F., *Archaelogy and the Relgion of Israel*, Baltimore, 1942.

Amar, "Bird Sacrifice": ז' עמר, "קרבן העוף – ביאור ריאלי בשולי גופי ההלכות", מעלין בקדש ד (תשס"ב), עמ' 117-144.

Anderson, G. A., "'Through Those Who Are Near to Me I Will Show Myself Holy': Nadab and Abihu and Apophatic Theology," CBQ 77 (2015), pp. 1–19.

Anderson, G. A., "Sacrifice and Sacrificial Offerings," *ABD*, vol. 5, pp. 870–886.

Anderson, G. A., *Sacrifices and Offerings in Ancient Israel: Studies in Their Social and Political Importance*, Atlanta, 1987.

Ariel, "Blessing of the Commandments": הרב ע' אריאל, "ברכת המצוות בהולכת הדם", אמונת עתיך 113 (תשע"ז), עמ' 30-31.

Ashley, T. R., *The Book of Numbers*, NICOT, Grand Rapids, 1993.

Averbeck, R. E., "K-T-R," *NIDOTTE*, vol. 3, pp. 913–916.

Avnery, "Sin Offerings": נ' אבנרי, "חטאות שגגה – חטאי פרט והנהגה", מגדים כד (תשנ"ה), עמ' 27-38.

Bach, D., "Rites et paroles dans l'Ancien Testament: Nouveaux elements apportés par l'étude de Tôdâh," *VT* 28 (1978), pp. 10–19.

Baden, J. S., "The Structure and Substance of Numbers 15," *VT* 63 (2013), pp. 351–367.

Baentsch, B., *Exodus, Leviticus un Numeri*, Göttingen, 1903.

Baer, *Studies*: י' בעה, מחקרים ומסות בתולדות עם ישראל, ירושלים תשמ"ו.

Bailey, L. R., *Leviticus-Numbers*, Smyth & Helwys Bible Commentary (ed. R. Scott Nash et al.), Macon, GA, 2005.

Bar Efrat, *Samuel*: ש' בר־אפרת, שמואל א, מקרא לישראל, ירושלים ותל אביב תשנ"ו.

Barstad, H. M., "Ratza, Ratzon," *TDOT*, vol. 13, pp. 618–630.

Barur, *Blessing*: א"י ברוה, "לשונות ברכה וקללה במקרא", בית מקרא טו (תש"ל), עמ' 449–455.

Barzilai, "Guilt Offering": מ' ברזילי, "מה בין חטאת לאשם? על תפקידם של קרבנות החובה בספר ויקרא", משלב מ (תשס"ו), עמ' 31-50.

Bazak, "Ḥodesh BeḤodsho": הרב א' בזק, "מידי חודש בחודשו ומדי שבת בשבתו", בתוך: הרב ע' ביק וי' פיינטוך (עורכים), תורת עציון - במדבר, ירושלים תשע"ו, עמ' 401-406.

Bazak, "Piggul": הרב א' בזק, "דין פיגול בפשוטו של מקרא ובמדרש ההלכה", בתוך: י' קלמנוביץ, א' בן־דוד וא' מושקוביץ (עורכים), מאמר הזבח, אלון שבות תש"ע, עמ' 209-215.

Bazak, "Purification and Guilt Offerings": הרב א' בזק, "מה בין חטאת לאשם", בית המדרש הוירטואלי, ישיבת הר עציון:
hatanakh.com/lessons/מה-בין-חטאת-לאשם

Beal, T. K., and T. Linafelt, "Sifting for Cinders: Strange Fire in Leviticus 10:1–5," *Semeia* 69/70 (1995), pp. 19–32.

Benish, *Middot*: ח"פ בניש, מדות ושיעורי תורה, בני ברק תשמ"ז (מהד' שניה).

Benmelech, “Baked”: מ׳ בנמלך, ״מאפה אנטי־תרבותי״, מוסף שבת של מקור ראשון, י״א בניסן תשע״ז, עמ׳ 4.

Ben-Shem, “Nocturnal Warfare”: י׳ בן־שם, ״מלחמת לילה״, בית מקרא יז (תשל״ב), עמ׳ 362-364.

Bergman, J., “Kohen,” *TDOT*, vol. 7, pp. 61–63.

Berlin, A., *Poetics and the Interpretation of Biblical Narrative*, Sheffield, 1983.

Berman, *Created Equal: How the Bible Broke with Ancient Political Thought*, Oxford, 2008.

Bibb, B. D., “Nadab and Abihu Attempt to Fill a Gap: Law and Narrative in Leviticus 10.1–7,” *JSOT* 96 (2001), pp. 83–99.

Bibb, B. D., *Ritual Words and Narrative Worlds in the Book of Leviticus*, New York and London, 2009.

Bick, “Haktara”: הרב ע׳ ביק, ״הקטרה״, בתוך: הרב ע׳ ביק וי׳ פיינטוך (עורכים), תורת עציון – ויקרא, אלון שבות תשע״ה, עמ׳ 33-38.

Bick, “Tamid”: הרב ע׳ ביק, ״עולת התמיד״, בתוך: הרב ע׳ ביק וי׳ פיינטוך (עורכים), תורת עציון – שמות, ירושלים תשע״ה, עמ׳ 345-350.

Bin-Nun, “Ḥametz and Matza”: הרב י׳ בן־נון, ״חמץ ומצה בפסח, בשבועות ובקרבנות הלחם״, מגדים יג (תשנ״א), עמ׳ 25-45.

Bin-Nun, “The Eighth Day”: הרב י׳ בן־נון, ״היום השמיני ויום הכיפורים״, מגדים ח (תשמ״ט), עמ׳ 9-34.

Bin-Nun, “Unintentional Congregation”: הרב י׳ בן־נון, ״קהל שוגג ומי שחזקתו שוגג או טועה: חילוניים וחילוניות בהלכה״, אקדמות י (תשס״א), עמ׳ 225-267.

Bin-Nun, *Mikraot – Mishpatim*: הרב י׳ בן־נון וש׳ ברוכי, מקראות: עיון רב תחומי בתורה – כרך משפטים, ראשון לציון 2018.

Boileau, G., “Some Ritual Elaborations on Cooking and Sacrifices in Late Zhou and Western Han Texts,” *Early China* 23/24 (1998–99), pp. 89–123.

Borger, R., *Die Inschriften Asarhaddons. Königs von Assyrien* (Archiv für Orientforschung 9), Osnabrück, 1956.

Bravman, M. M., *Studies in Semitic Languages and Linguistics,* Leiden, 1977.

Breuer, "Impurity": י' ברויאר, "איסור טומאה בתורה", מגדים ב (תשמ"ז), עמ' 53-45.

Breuer, *Acts of Creation*: הרב מ' ברויאר, "מעשי בראשית", מגדים יב (תשנ"א), עמ' 9-15.

Breuer, *Pirkei Bereshit*: הרב מ' ברויאר, פרקי בראשית (שני חלקים), אלון שבות תשנ"ט.

Büchler, A., *Studies in Sin and Atonement in the Rabbinic Literature of the First Century,* London, 1928.

Budd, P. J., *Leviticus,* NCBC, Grand Rapids, 1996.

Bula, *Leviticus*: מ' בולה, ויקרא, דעת מקרא, כרך א, ירושלים תשנ"ב.

Caquot, A., "Devash," *TDOT,* vol. 3, pp. 128–131.

Cassuto, *Exodus*: מ"ד קאסוטו, פירוש על ספר שמות, ירושלים תשמ"ח.

Cherlow, "Mekaddesh BeḤelko": הרב י' שרלו, "המקדש בחלקו", קול ברמה יז (תשנ"ז), עמ' 14-27.

Cherlow, "Peace Offerings": הרב י' שרלו, "זבחי שלמים עלי", עלון שבות 82 (תש"ם), עמ' 10-18.

Chisholm, R. B., "דלש," *NIDOTTE,* vol. 4, pp. 127–128.

Cohen, "Kedusha": א' כהן, "קדושה", אנציקלופדיה למדעי החברה, כרך ה, עמ' 207-208.

Cohen, *Impurity and Purity*: מ' כהן, "דיני טומאה וטהרה במקרא וזיקתם לדיני איסור והיתר בספרות חז"ל", דברי הקונגרס העולמי למדעי היהדות יא (תשנ"ג), חטיבה א, עמ' 107-114.

Cohen, S., "The Pastoral Idea of *Hesed* and the Symbolism of *Matzo* and *Hamets,*" in: S. Yonah et al. (eds.), *Marbeh Ḥokmah: Studies in the Bible and the Ancient Near East in Loving Memory of Victor Avigdor Hurowitz,* Winona Lake, 2015, pp. 111–137.

Conrad, J., "N-D-B," *TDOT,* vol. 4, pp. 219–226.

Cooperman, *Peshuto*: הרב י' קופרמן, קדושת פשוטו של מקרא, ירושלים תשס"ט.

Cooperman, *Sforno*: הרב י' קופרמן, פירוש ספורנו על התורה – מנוקד ומבואר (שני כרכים), ירושלים תשנ"ב.

Cothey, A., "Ethics and Holiness in the Theology of Leviticus," *JSOT* 30 (2005), pp. 131–151.

Curtis, A. H. W., "Some Observations on 'Bull' Terminology in the Ugaritic Texts and the Old Testament," *Oudtestamentische Studiën* 26 (1990), pp. 17–31.

Damrosch, D., "Leviticus," in: R. Alter and F. Kermode (eds.), *The Literary Guide to the Bible*, Cambridge, 1987, pp. 66–77.

Daube, D., "The Laying on of Hands," in: *The New Testament and Rabbinic Judaism*, London, 1956, pp. 224–246.

Davidson, R. M., "The Genesis Flood Narrative: Crucial Issues in the Current Debate," Andrews University Seminary Studies 42 (2004), pp. 49–77.

De Vaux, R., *Ancient Israel*, New York, 1961.

De Vaux, R: ר' דה־וו, חיי יום־יום בישראל בימי המקרא (שני כרכים; תרגם א' אמיר), תל אביב תשכ"ט.

De-Paris, "Early Form": ב' דה־פריס, "לצורתן הקדומה של הלכות והשתלשלותן", תרביץ לג (תשכ"ד), עמ' 8-19.

Dietrich, M., and O. Loretz, *"Jahwe und seine Aschera": Anthropomorphes Kultbild in Mesopotamien Ugarit und Israel: Das biblische Bilderverbot*, Münster, 1992.

Dillmann, A., *Das Bucher Exodus und Leviticus*, Leipzig, 1880.

Dommershausen, W., "Kohen," *TDOT*, vol. 7, pp. 60–75.

Dotan, "Kayom": א' דותן, "לעניין 'כיום' = תחילה", לשוננו מח-מט (תשמ"ה), עמ' 220-221.

Dotan, "The *Tenufa* of Gold": א' דותן, "זהב התנופה", מחקרי מורשתנו ב-ג (תשס"ד), עמ' 225-231.

Douglas, M., *Leviticus as Literature*, Oxford, 2000.

Driver, G. R., "Three Technical Terms in the Pentateuch," *JSS* 1 (1956), pp. 97–105.

Dussaud, R., *Les Origines cananeennes du sacrifice Israelite* (second edition), Paris, 1941.

Eberhart, C., "A Neglected Feature of Sacrifice in the Hebrew Bible: Remarks on the Burning Rite on the Altar," *HTR* 97 (2004), pp. 485–493.

Eberhart, C., *Studien zur Bedeutung der Opfer im Alten Testament: die Signifikanz von Blut – und Verbrennungsriten im kultischen Rahmen*, Neukirchener Verlag, 2002.

Efrati: י"א אפרתי, "עיון בפרשת מנחת הבכורים ובפרשת העומר", ספר בר־אילן ג (תשנ"ח), עמ' 13–20.

Ehrlich, "Dwelling Place": א' ארליך, "שאלת מקום השכינה בנוסח התפילה הקדום", סידרא יג (תשנ"ז), עמ' 5–23.

Ehrlich, A. B., *Randglossen zur Hebräischen Bible, Zweiter Band: Leviticus, Numeri, Deuteronomium*, Leipzig, 1909.

Ehrlich, *Mikrâ ki-Pheschutô*: א"ב אהרליך, מקרא כפשוטו, כרך א (דברי תורה), ברלין תרנ"ט.

Eldar, "Incense": א' אלדה, "הקטורת, נדב ואביהוא ויום הכיפורים", עלון שבות 158 (תשס"א), עמ' 81–95.

Eldar, "Revelation at Sinai": א' אלדה, "מעמד הר סיני והגבלותיו", מגדים לו (תשס"ג), עמ' 9–23.

Elitzur, "Early Benedictions": ש' אליצור, "לדמותן של הברכות הקדומות: כמה קווי יסוד", סידרא לב (תשע"ז), עמ' 7–33.

Elitzur, *Place*: י' אליצור, מקום בפרשה: גיאוגרפיה ומשמעות במקרא, תל אביב תשע"ד.

Elliger, K., *Leviticus*, HAT, Tübingen, 1966.

Even-Shoshan, *Dictionary*: א' אבן שושן, המלון החדש (המהדורה המשולבת בחמישה כרכים), ירושלים תשנ"ז.

Fabry, H. J., "Korban," *TDOT*, vol. 13, pp. 152–158.

Fabry, H. J., "Minḥa," *TDOT*, vol. 8, pp. 407–417.

Falkenstein, A., *Sumerische Götterlieder*, vol. 1, Heidelberg, 1959.

Fishbane, M., "Biblical Colophons, Textual Criticism and Legal Analogies," *CBQ* 42 (1980), pp. 438–449.

Fisher, L. R., (ed.), *The Claremont Ras Shamra Tablets*, Roma, 1971.

Fleischer, "Prayers": ע׳ פליישר, "לנוסח ברכת העבודה", בתוך ספרו: תפילות הקבע בישראל בהתהוותן ובהתגבשותן, ירושלים תשע"ב, כרך א, עמ׳ 245-252.

Fleischer: ע׳ פליישר, "תפילת שמונה־עשרה – עיונים באופיה, סדרה, תוכנה ומגמותיה", תרביץ (תשנ"ג), עמ׳ 179-223.

Fleming, D., "The Biblical Tradition of Anointing Priests," *JBL* 117 (1998), pp. 401–414.

Frymer-Kensky, T., "What the Babylonian Flood Stories Can and Cannot Teach Us About the Genesis Flood," *Biblical Archaeology Review* 4 (1978), pp. 32–41.

Fuller, R., "Ephah," *NIDOTTE*, vol. 1, pp. 382–388.

Gane, R., "'Bread of the Presence' and Creator-in-residence," *VT* 42 (1992), pp. 179–203.

Gane, R., *Ritual Dynamic Structure*, Piscataway, 2004.

Ganzel, T., "The Descriptions of the Restoration of Israel in Ezekiel," *VT* 60 (2010), pp. 197–211.

Garti, "Halachic Aspects": ש׳ גרטי, היבטים הלכתיים נוספים בשיטת הבחינות (ללא מקום ושנת הוצאה).

Garti, *Consecrated Skins*: ש׳ גרטי, "בעניין עורות קודשים", מעלין בקדש ד (תשס"ב), עמ׳ 91-103.

Geiger, M., "Synergie zwischen priesterlichen und gÖttlichem Handeln im Aaronitischen Segen (Num 6,22–27). Ein Beitrag zum Verständnis der Wendung *yiśa' yehṿah panaṿ 'elekha*," *VT* 68 (2018), pp. 51–72.

Gese, H., *Zur biblischen Theologie: Alttestamentliche Vorträge* (2nd ed.), Tübingen, 1983.

Gesenius, W., *Hebräische Grammatik*, Leipzig, 1889.

Girard, R., *La violence et le sacré*, Paris, 1972.

Gispen, W. H., *Het Boek Leviticus*, Kampen, 1950.

Goetze, A., "The Hittite Laws," in: *ANET*, pp. 188–197.

Goldenberg, *Biblical Exegesis*: א׳ גולדנברג, מחברות לפרשנות המקרא: ספרי ויקרא ובמדבר, תל אביב תשל"ז.

Gordon, *Leviticus*: ש"ל גורדון, ויקרא, בתוך: פירוש חדש לתנ"ך, כרך חמישה חומשי תורה, תל אביב.

Gordon, *Malachi*: ש"ל גורדון, "מבוא לספר מלאכי" בתוך: פירוש חדש לתנ"ך, כרך תרי עשר ב, תל אביב.

Gorman, F. H., Jr., *Ideology of Ritual Space Time and Status in the Priestly Theology* (JSOTsup 91), Sheffield, 1990.

Granot, "Prohibitions of Blood": הרב ת' גרנות, "איסורי הדם בספר ויקרא", בתוך: הרב ע' ביק וי' פיינטוך (עורכים), תורת עציון – ויקרא, ירושלים תשע"ה, עמ' 239–248.

Granot, *Sukkot*: הרב ת' גרנות, "חג הסוכות כחג ה' וכגולת הכותרת של חגי תשרי", בתוך: א' בזק (עורך), ובחג הסוכות: קובץ מאמרים על חג הסוכות, אלון שבות תשע"א, עמ' 33–71.

Gray, J., *The Legacy of Canaan*, Leiden, 1957.

Greenberg, M., "The Design and Themes of Ezekiel's Program of Restoration," *Interpretation* 38 (1984), pp. 181–208.

Greenberg, M., "The True Sin of Nadab and Abihu," *JBQ* 26 (1998), pp. 263–267.

Greenberg, M., *Studies in the Bible and Jewish Thought*, Philadelphia, 1995, pp. 25–41.

Greenstein, E. L., "Deconstruction and Biblical Narrative," *Prooftexts* 9 (1989), pp. 43–71.

Greenstein, E. L., *Job: A New Translation*, New Haven and London, 2019.

Grintz, "Munaḥim": י"מ גרינץ, "מונחים קדומים בתורת כהנים", לשוננו לט (תשל"ה), עמ' 163–181.

Grintz, *Genesis*: י"מ גרינץ, ייחודו וקדמותו של ספר בראשית, ירושלים תשמ"ג.

Grossman, "Mourns for Himself": י' גרוסמן, "אדם המתאבל על עצמו", בתוך: הרב ע' ביק וי' פיינטוך (עורכים), תורת עציון – ויקרא, ירושלים תשע"ה, עמ' 179–184.

Grossman, "Binding of Isaac": י' גרוסמן, "'וירא את המקום מרחוק' – עקידת יצחק כסיפור רקע לברית האגנות ולסיפורים נוספים", מגדים כה (תשנ"ו), עמ' 79–90.

Grossman, "Covenant at Sinai": י׳ גרוסמן, ״עקדת יצחק וברית סיני״, בתוך ב׳ לאו וי׳ רוזנסון (עורכים), עקדת יצחק לזרעו: מבט בעין ישראלית, תל אביב תשס״ג, עמ׳ 355–364.

Grossman, "Egla Arufa": י׳ גרוסמן, ״עגלה ערופה״, בתוך: הרב ע׳ ביק וי׳ פיינטוך (עורכים), תורת עציון – דברים, אלון שבות תשע״ה, עמ׳ 227–232.

Grossman, "Exile and Redemption": א׳ גרוסמן, ״גלות וגאולה במשנתו של רש״י״, בתוך: י׳ ברוכי, ח׳ הלפרין וי׳ מילוא (עורכים), משעבוד לגאולה: מפסח עד שבועות, אסופת מאמרים לזכרו של משה ברי הי״ד, אור עציון תשנ״ו, עמ׳ 239–266.

Grossman, "Manna and Passover": י׳ גרוסמן, ״המן וקרבן פסח״, עלון שבות 153 (תשנ״ט), עמ׳ 115–136.

Grossman, "Minḥa": י׳ גרוסמן, ״קרבן המנחה״, מגדים לו (תשס״ג), עמ׳ 25–40.

Grossman, "Postponing Prayer": א׳ גרוסמן, ״ראשיותיו ויסודותיו של מנהג 'עיכוב התפילה'״, מלאת א (תשמ״ג), עמ׳ 199–219.

Grossman, "The Atonement of the Tabernacle": י׳ גרוסמן, ״מכפרת המשכן אל כפרת הגבולין (ויקרא כ״ג, כו-לב)״, בתוך: א׳ בזק (עורך), וביום צום כיפור יחתמון, אלון שבות תשס״ה, עמ׳ 11–24.

Grossman, "Wings Spread": י׳ גרוסמן, ״פורשי כנפיים למעלה – איש אל אחיו״, עלון שבות 145 (תשנ״ה), עמ׳ 134–147.

Grossman, *Abraham*: י׳ גרוסמן, אברהם: סיפורו של מסע, תל אביב תשע״ה.

Grossman, *Creation*: י׳ גרוסמן, בראשית: סיפורן של התחלות, ראשון לציון ואלון שבות תשע״ז.

Grossman, J., "The Significance of Frankincense in Grain Offerings," *JBL* 138 (2019), pp. 285–296.

Grossman, *Jacob*: י׳ גרוסמן, יעקב: סיפורה של משפחה, ראשון לציון תשע״ט.

Grossman, *Rashi*: א׳ גרוסמן, אמונות ודעות בעולמו של רש״י, אלון שבות תשס״ח.

Grossman, *Ruth*: י׳ גרוסמן, מגילת רות: גשרים וגבולות, אלון שבות תשע״ו.

Grossman: י׳ גרוסמן, גלוי ומוצפן: על כמה מדרכי העיצוב של הסיפור המקראי, תל אביב ואלון שבות תשע״ו.

Grossman: י׳ גרוסמן, ״יום ולילה: על מלכות שמים משתנה – עיון בצדקת

הצדיק, תורה ג'", בתוך: ד' עזריאל (עורך), אשרי האיש – פרקי לימוד בחסידות (גולות יב), עתניאל תשס"ג, עמ' 155–166.

Hacohen, *Leviticus*: א' הכהן, אל מול מקדש ספר ויקרא: מילות הקדמה לספר ויקרא, תקוע תשע"ט.

Hadad, "Piggul": א' חדד, "דין פיגול במקרא ובהלכה", מגדים נח (תש"פ), עמ' 117–129.

Hadad, E., and J. Grossman, "The Ram of Ordination and Qualifying the Priests to Eat Sacrifices," JSOT 45 (2021), pp. 476–492.

Hakham, "Nadav and Avihu": ע' חכם, "נדב ואביהוא", מעינות יא (תשמ"ו), עמ' 96–137.

Halbertal, M., *On Sacrifice*, Princeton and Oxford, 2012.

Halbertal, *Revolutions*: מ' הלברטל, מהפכות פרשניות בהתהוותן: ערכים כשיקולים פרשניים במדרשי הלכה, ירושלים תשס"ד.

Halevi, *Oaths*: א"א הלוי, "על השבועה (פרק בתולדות ההלכה)", תרביץ לז (תשכ"ח), עמ' 24–29.

Hallo, W. W. (ed.), *The Context of Scripture: Canonical Compositions, Monumental Inscriptions, and Archival Documents from the Biblical World*, vol. 1, Leiden, 2003.

Hamori, E. J., *Women's Divination in Biblical Literature: Prophecy, Necromancy, and Other Arts of Knowledge*, New Haven and London, 2015.

Haran, "Incense Firepans": מ' הרן, "קטורת מחתות וקטורת תמיד", תרביץ כו (תשי"ז), עמ' 115–125.

Haran, "Kid in Its Mother's Milk": מ' הרן, "גדי בחלב אמו", ארץ־ישראל: מחקרים בידיעת הארץ ועתיקותיה יד (תשל"ח), עמ' 12–18.

Haran, "Minḥa": מ' הרן, "מנחה", אנציקלופדיה מקראית, כרך ה, עמ' 23–30.

Haran, "The Priestly Blessing": מ' הרן, "ברכת כוהנים מכתף הינום המשמעות המקראית של התגלית", קתדרה 52 (תשמ"ט), עמ' 77–89.

Haran, "Vow": מ' הרן, "נדר", אנציקלופדיה מקראית, כרך ה, עמ' 786–790.

Haran, M., "'Incense Altars' – Are They?," in: A. Biran and J. Aviram (eds.), *Biblical Archaeology Today – 1990*, Jerusalem, 1993, pp. 237–247.

Haran, M., "Altar-ed States: Incense Theory Goes Up in Smoke," *Bible Review* 11 (1995), pp. 30–37, 48.

Haran, M., "Uses of Incense in the Ancient Israelite Ritual," *VT* 10 (1960), pp. 113–129.

Haran, M., *Temples and Temple-Service in Ancient Israel,* Oxford, 1978.

Hartley, J. E., *Leviticus,* WBC, Texas, 1992.

Hauge, M. R., *The Descent from the Mountain Narrative Patterns in Exodus 19–40,* Sheffield, 2001.

Hausmann, J., "*R-N-N*," *TDOT,* vol. 13, pp. 515–522.

Held, "Biblical Mystery": מ' הלד, "סתומה מקראית ומקבילתה באוגריתית (שורש "שרד" במקרא ובכתבי אוגרית)", ארץ ישראל ג (תשי"ד), עמ' 101–103.

Helfgot, *Holidays and Blessings*: הרב נ' הלפגוט, דברי ברכה ומועד: עיונים בנושאי ברכות ומועדים, אלון שבות תשס"ב.

Hendel: נ' הנדל, "חוק לא תעמוד על דם רעך, התשנ"ח-1998: השראה ומציאות", מחקרי משפט טז (תשס"א), עמ' 229–275.

Henshke, "Amida": ד' הנשקה, "לתולדות תפילת העמידה: בין ברכה לתפילה", תרביץ פד (תשע"ו), עמ' 345–395.

Hepner, G., "Jacob's Oath Causes Rachel's Death, Reflecting the Law in Lev. 5:4–6," *Zeitschrift für Altorientalische und Biblische Rechtsgeschichte* 8 (2002), pp. 131–165.

Hepner, G., "The Naked Truth Concerning the Deaths of Nadab and Abihu," *Revue biblique* 121 (2014), pp. 108–111.

Herodotus, *History*: הרודוטוס, היסטוריה, תרגמו: ב' שימרון ור' צלניק-אברמוביץ, תל אביב תשנ"ח.

Hess, R., *Leviticus,* EBC, Grand Rapids, 2008.

Hieke, T., "Priestly Leadership in the Book of Leviticus: A Hidden Agenda," in: K. Pyschny and S. Schulz (eds.), *Debating Authority: Concepts of Leadership in the Pentateuch and the Former Prophets,* Berlin and Boston, 2018, pp. 68–88.

Hirshman, M., "A House of Prayer for All Peoples: Isaiah 56:7 in Rabbinic Thought," in: G. A. Anderson and J. S. Kaminsky (eds.),

The Call of Abraham: Essays on the Election of Israel in Honor of Jon D. Levenson, Notre Dame, IN, 2013, pp. 199–209.

Hoffmann, *Leviticus*: רד"צ הופמן, ספר ויקרא (שני כרכים), ירושלים תשי"ג.

Hoffner, H. A., "Second Millenium Antecedents to the Hebrew *'ob*," JBL 86 (1967), pp. 385–401.

Horowitz, "Image": ו' הורוויץ, "עשה לך פסל", בית מקרא מ (תשנ"ה), עמ' 337-347.

Horowitz, *Temples*: א' הורוויץ, טכסי חנוכת מקדשים במקרא (והשוואה לחומר חוץ מקראי), עבודת מוסמך, האוניברסיטה העברית, ירושלים תשל"ד.

Houtman, C., "On the Function of the Holy Incense (Exodus xxx 34–8) and the Sacred Anointing Oil (Exodus xxx 22–33)," *VT* 42 (1992), pp. 458–465.

Hundley, M. B., *Keeping Heaven on Earth: Safeguarding the Divine Presence in the Priestly Tabernacle*, Tübingen, 2011.

Hurowitz, "Isaiah's Impure Lips and Their Purification in Light of Mouth Purification and Mouth Purity in Akkadian Sources," HUCA 60 (1989), pp. 39–89.

Hyatt, J. P., *Exodus*, NCBC, London., 1971.

Jackson, B. S., *Theft in Early Jewish Law*, Oxford, 1972.

Jacob, A.: א' יעקב, "אפקטיביות החובה להציל – ניתוח פסיכולוגי", עיוני משפט כד (תשס"א), עמ' 605-661.

Janowski, B., *Sühne als Heilsgeschehen*, Neukirchen-Vluyn, 1982.

Janzen, J. G., "The Character of the Calf and Its Cult in Exodus 32," CBQ 52 (1990), pp. 597–607.

Jenson, P. P., "The Levitical Sacrificial System," in: R. T. Beckwith and M. J. Selman (eds.), *Sacrifice in the Bible*, Grand Rapids, 1995, pp. 25–40.

Joüon, P., "Locutions hébraïques," *Biblica* 3 (1922), pp. 53–74.

Junker, H., *Gîza 3: Die Mastabas der Vorgeschrittenen V. Dynastie auf dem Westfriedhof*, Vienna and Leipzig, 1938.

Jürgens, B., "Wiederherstellung der SchÖpfungsordnung: Levitikus.

Teil 2, Rituelle Kommunikation," *Bibel und Liturgie* 75 (2002), pp. 133–137.

Kaddari, *Dictionary*: מ"צ קדרי, מילון העברית המקראית, רמת גן תשס"ו.

Kahan, "Berakha": הרב י' קאהן, "ברכה על אכילת שלמים", בתוך: י' קלמנוביץ, א' בן־דוד וא' מושקוביץ (עורכים), מאמר הזבח, אלון שבות תש"ע, עמ' 37-50.

Kahan, "Priests": הרב י' קאהן, "כוהנים ובני אהרן", בתוך: הרב ע' ביק וי' פיינטוך (עורכים), תורת עציון – ויקרא, אלון שבות תשע"ה, עמ' 83-90.

Kam, A. Y., and L. Kwun-Cheung, "Incense Burning: A Far Eastern Chapter on Biblical Customs," *Jian Dao* 13 (1999), pp. 25–68.

Kasher, *Ezekiel*: ר' כשר, יחזקאל (מקרא לישראל), שני כרכים, ירושלים ותל אביב תשס"ד.

Kasher, *Torah Shelema*: הרב מ"מ כשר, חומש תורה שלימה, ירושלים תשנ"ב (מהדורה שנייה).

Kaufmann, *The Religion of Israel*: י' קויפמן, תולדות האמונה הישראלית (שמונה כרכים), ירושלים ותל אביב תשי"ד.

Kehat, "Bikkurim Offering": הרב ב' קהת, "מנחת הביכורים וקרבן העומר", מגדים נז (תשע"ח), עמ' 7-19.

Kehat, "Days of Consecration": הרב ב' קהת, "ימי המילואים – הציווי וקיומו", מגדים לח (תשס"ג), עמ' 17-31.

Kehat, "Guilt Offering": הרב ב' קץ (קהת), "קורבן האשם", דף קשר 328 (תשנ"ב), עמ' 2-3 [= ספר דף קשר, כרך 4, אלון שבות תשנ"ה, עמ' 60-61].

Kehat, "Sacrificial Laws": הרב ב' קהת, "חוקי הקרבנות – פרשת ויקרא לעומת פרשת צו", מגדים נד (תשע"ג), עמ' 63-73.

Kehat, "Sanctuary": הרב ב' קהת (קץ), "ועשו לי מקדש ושכנתי בתוכם", מגדים ו (תשמ"ח), עמ' 17-21.

Keil, C. F., *The Pentateuch*, BCOT, Grand Rapids, 1968 (reprint).

Kellerman, D., "Asham," *TDOT*, vol. 1, pp. 429–437.

Kellerman, D., "Frankincense," *TDOT*, vol. 7, pp. 441–447.

Kellermann, D., "Piggul," *TDOT*, vol. 11, pp. 468–470.

Keniel, *Burning with Love*: ר' קרא־איוונוב קניאל, "לבעור מאהבה", תעודה כו (תשע"ד), עמ' 585-654.

Kidner, D., "Sacrifice: Metaphors and Meaning," *Tyndale Bulletin* 33 (1982), pp. 119–136.

Kirschner, R., "The Rabbinic and Philonic Exegeses of the Nadab and Abihu Incident (Lev. 10:1–6)," *JQR* 73 (1983), pp. 375–393.

Kiuchi, N., "Spirituality in Offering a Peace Offering," *Tyndale Bulletin* 50 (1999), pp. 23–31.

Kiuchi, N., "Translating *selamîm*," *Exegetica* 15 (2004), pp. 29–41.

Kiuchi, N., *A Study of Hata and Hattat in Leviticus 4–5*, Tübingen, 2003.

Kiuchi, N., *The Purification Offering in the Priestly Literature: Its Meaning and Function*, Sheffield, 1987.

Klingbeil, G. A., "Ritual Time in Leviticus 8 with Special Reference to the Seven Day Period in the Old Testament," ZAW 109 (1997), pp. 500–513.

Klingbeil, G. A., "The Anointing of Aaron: A Study of Leviticus 8:12 in Its OT and ANE Context," *Andrews University Seminary Studies* 38 (2000), pp. 231–243.

Klingbeil, G. A., "The Syntactic Structure of the Ritual of Ordination (Lev. 8)," *Biblica* 77 (1996), pp. 509–519.

Knierim, R. P., *Text and Concept in Leviticus 1:1–1: A Case in Exegetical Method* (FAT 2), Tübingen, 1992.

Knobel, A. W., *Die Bücher Exodus und Leviticus*, Leipzig, 1857.

Knohl, "The Law of the Purification Offering": י' קנוהל, "חוק החטאת של 'אסכולת הקדושה' (במדבר טו, כב-לא)", תרביץ נט (תש"ן), עמ' 1-9.

Knohl, *Biblical Beliefs*: י' קנוהל, אמונות המקרא: גבולות המהפכה המקראית, ירושלים תשס"ז.

Knohl, *How Was the Bible Born*: י' קנוהל, איך נולד התנ"ך, מודיעין תשע"ח.

Knohl, *Temple of Silence*: י' קנוהל, מקדש הדממה, ירושלים תשנ"ג.

Koch, K., *Die Priesterschrift van Exodus 25 bis Leviticus 16: Eine überlieferungsgeschichtliche und literarkritische Untersuchung* (FRLANT 71), Göttingen, 1959.

Kochman, *Leviticus*: מ' קוכמן, ויקרא, עולם התנ"ך, תל אביב 1993.

Kornfeld, K., (and H. Ringgren), "Holy," *TDOT*, vol. 12, pp. 521–545.

Kosman, "Salt": א' קוסמן, "לטעמי צירופו של המלח לעבודת המקדש פרקטיקה, סימבוליקה, מיתוס, מאגיה ואנתרופולוגיה", דרך אגדה יב (תשע"ג), עמ' 75-28.

Krüger, A., "Annette Salbungsrituale im Begräbniskontext," in: *Menschenbilder und Körperkonzepte im Alten Israel, in Ägypten und im Alten Orient*, Tübingen, 2012, pp. 345–363

Kuenen, A., *An Historico-Critical Inquiry into the Origin and Composition of the Hexateuch* (translated by P. H. Wicksteed), London, 1886.

Kurtz, J. H., *Sacrificial Worship of the Old Testament* (translated by J. Martin), Grand Rapids, 1980.

Kutsch, E., *Salbung als Rechtsakt im alten Testament und im alten Orient* (BZAW 87), Berlin, 1963.

Lam, J., "A Reassessment of the Alphabetic Hurrian Text RS 1.004 (KTU 1.42): A Ritual Anointing of Deities?," *JANER* 11 (2011); pp. 148–169.

Lambert, W. G., *Babylonian Wisdom Literature*, Oxford, 1960.

Landes, *Development of Birkat HaAvoda*: י' לנדיס, ברכת העבודה בתפילת העמידה: עיונים בנוסחיה ובתולדותיה, ירושלים תשע"ח.

Lang, B., "K-P-R," *TDOT*, vol. 7, pp. 288–303.

Latham, E. J., *The Religious Symbolism of Salt*, Paris, 1982.

Latoundji, D., "יתר," *NIDOTTE*, vol. 2, pp. 571–574.

Leibowitz, "Kilya": יהושע ליבוביץ וישעיהו ליבוביץ, "כליה", האנציקלופדיה העברית, כרך כ, עמ' 854-838.

Leibowitz, *Leviticus*: נחמה ליבוביץ, עיונים חדשים בספר ויקרא, ירושלים תשמ"ג.

Leibtag, "Passover and Thanksgiving": מ' ליבטאג, "קרבן פסח וקרבן תודה", ספר דף קשר ז (תשנ"ח-תשנ"ט), עמ' 504-506.

Leslie, E. A., *Religion in the Light of its Canaanite Background*, Cincinnati, 1936.

Levin, S., "Sense and Incense," *JBQ* 21 (1993), pp. 242–247.

Levine, B. A., "The Descriptive Tabernacle Texts of the Pentateuch," *JAOS* 85 (1965), pp. 307–318.

Levine, B. A., *In Pursuit of Meaning: Collected Studies* (Volume 1: Religion; Edited by A. D. Gross), Winona Lake, 2011.

Levine, B. A., *In the Presence of the Lord*, Leiden, 1974.

Levine, B. A., *Leviticus*, JPS, Philadelphia, 1989.

Levine, *The World of the Bible*: ב"א לוין, ויקרא, עולם התנ"ך, תל אביב 1993.

Licht and Milgrom, "Sacrifice": י"ש ליכט וי' מילגרום, "קרבן", אנציקלופדיה מקראית, כרך ז, ירושלים תשל"ו, עמ' 222–251.

Licht, "Omer": י"ש ליכט, "עמר", אנציקלופדיה מקראית, כרך ו, ירושלים תשל"ב, עמ' 303–300.

Licht, "Ramban": י' ליכט, "רמב"ן", בתוך: מ' גרינברג (עורך), פרשנות המקרא היהודית – פרקי מבוא, ירושלים תשמ"ג, עמ' 68–60.

Licht, "Zevaḥ": י"ש ליכט, "זבח", אנציקלופדיה מקראית, כרך ב, עמ' 904–901.

Lichtenstein, "Aveira Lishmah": הרב א' ליכטנשטיין, "עבירה לשמה – הרהורים בהלכה ובמחשבה", בתוך: ח' דויטש ומ' בן־ששון (עורכים), האחר: בין אדם לעצמו ולזולתו (לזכר דודי דויטש ז"ל), עמ' 125–99.

Lichtenstein, *Taharot*: שיעורי הרב אהרן ליכטנשטיין – טהרות, אלון שבות תשנ"ח.

Lichtenstein, *Torat HaKorbanot*: הרב מ' ליכטנשטיין, "זאת תורת הקרבנות", בתוך: י' קלמנוביץ, א' בן־דוד וא' מושקוביץ (עורכים), מאמר הזבח, אלון שבות תש"ע, עמ' 136–95.

Lichtenstein, *Zevaḥim*: שיעורי הרב אהרן ליכטנשטיין – זבחים, אלון שבות תשנ"ט.

Linssen, M. J. H., *The Cults of Uruk and Babylon: The Temple Ritual Texts As Evidence for Hellenistic Cult Practices*, Leiden and Boston, 2004.

Loewenstamm, S. E., "Zur Traditionsgeschichte Des Bundes Zwischen Den Stücken," *VT* 18 (1968), pp. 500–506.

Lohfink, N., "Ḥerem," *TDOT*, vol. 5, pp. 180–199.

Luciani, D., "Structure et théologie en Lv 1,1–3,17," in: Th. Römer (ed.), *The Books of Leviticus and Numbers* (BETL 215), Leuven, 2008, pp. 319–327.

Luria, "Maaleh Ashan": ב"צ לוריא, "'מעלה עשן' בעבודת יום הכיפורים", בית מקרא כא (תשל"ו), עמ' 198–193.

Maaseh HaKorbanot: ספר מעשה הקרבנות: ענייני המקדש וקדשיו, קרית ספר תשס"ח (ללא ציון שם מחבר).

Magness, J., "The Impurity of Oil and Spit among the Qumran Sectarians," in: A. A. Orlov and D. V. Arbel (eds.), *With Letters of Light: Studies in the Dead Sea Scrolls, Early Jewish Apocalypticism, Magic, and Mysticism*, Berlin and New York, 2010, pp. 223–231.

Marcus, "Salt": י' מרקוס, "מצוות מלח בקרבנות", מעלים בקודש יח (תשס"ט), עמ' 79–88.

Marwil, D. J., "A Soothing Savor," *JBQ* 42 (2014), pp. 169–172.

Marx, A., "Sacrifice de reparation et rites de levee de sanction," *ZAW* 100 (1988), pp. 183–198.

Marx, A., "The Theology of the Sacrifice According to Leviticus 1–7," in: R. Rendtorff (ed.), *The Book of Leviticus: Composition and Reception*, Leiden, 2003, pp. 103–120.

Marx, A., *Les offrandes vegetales dans l'Aneien Testament: du tribute d'hommage au repas esehatologique*, Leiden and New York, 1994.

Mazor, *Bread in the Bible*: ל' מזור, "הלחם במקרא בחיי הפרט והכלל", עת מקרא 3 (תשע"ה).

Mcdowell, C. L., *The Image of God in the Garden of Eden: The Creation of Humankind in Genesis 2:5–3:24 in Light of mis pi pit pi and wpt-r Rituals of Mesopotamia and Ancient Egypt*, Winona Lake, 2015.

McGuire, "Evening or Morning: When Does the Biblical Day Begin?," *Andrews University Seminary Studies* 46 (2008), pp. 201–214.

Mercaz HaHadrakha LeTanakh: מרכז ההדרכה לתנ"ך, בראשית-שמות, דפים למעיין ולמורה, אלון שבות תשנ"ט.

Meshel, N. S., "The Form and Function of a Biblical Blood Ritual," *VT* 63 (2013), pp. 276–289.

Meshel, N. S., "Toward a Grammar of Sacrifice: Hierarchic Patterns in the Israelite Sacrificial System," *JBL* 132 (2013), pp. 543–567.

Meyer, E., "The Particle kî, a Mere Conjunction or Something More?," *Journal of Northwest Semitic Languages* 27 (2001), pp. 39–62.

Meyers, C., "Realms of Sanctity: The Case of the 'Misplaced' Incense Altar in the Tabernacle Texts of Exodus," in: *Texts, Temples and Tradition: A Tribute to Menachem Haran*, Winona Lake, 1996, pp. 33–46.

Meyers, C., "Realms of Sanctity: The Case of the 'Misplaced' Incense Altar in the Tabernacle Texts of Exodus," in: M. V. Fox, et al. (eds.), *Texts, Temples and Tradition: A Tribute to Menachem Haran*, Winona Lake, 1996, pp. 33–46.

Milgrom, "Ḥattat": י' מילגרום, "תפקיד קרבן החטאת", תרביץ מ (תשל"א), עמ' 1-8.

Milgrom, "Tenufa": י' מילגרום, "התנופה", בתוך: ב"צ לוריא (עורך), זר לגבורות: ספר זלמן שז"ר, ירושלים תשל"ג, עמ' 38-55.

Milgrom, "The Thigh of Teruma": י' מילגרום, "שוק התרומה: פרק בתולדות הפולחן", תרביץ מב (תשל"ג), עמ' 1-11.

Milgrom, J., *Cult and Conscience: The Asham and the Priestly Doctrine of Repentance*, Leiden, 1976.

Milgrom, J., "Israel's Sanctuary: The Priestly 'Picture of Dorian Gray,'" *Revue Biblique* 83 (1976), pp. 390–399.

Milgrom, J., "Priestly ('P') Source," *ABD*, vol. 5, pp. 454–461.

Milgrom, J., "The Hattat: A Rite of Passage?," *Revue biblique* 98 (1991), pp. 120–124.

Milgrom, J., "Two Kinds of *ḥaṭṭāʾt*," *VT* 26 (1976), pp. 333–337.

Milgrom, J., *Leviticus 1–16* (AB), New York, 1991.

Milgrom, J., *Leviticus 17–22* (AB), New York, 2000.

Milgrom, J., *Leviticus 23–27* (AB), New York, 2001.

Milgrom, J., *Numbers*, JPS, Philadelphia and New York, 1990.

Milgrom, J., *Studies in Cultic Theology and Terminology*, Leiden, 1983.

Milgrom: י' מילגרום, "החטאת המודרגת של ויקרא ה', א-יג", בית מקרא כט (תשמ"ד), עמ' 139-148.

Mitcham, "Suggestion of Linguistic Explanation": ת' מיטשם, "הצעת פירוש לשוני בדין ימי טומאה וטהרה ליולדת נקבה", שנתון למקרא ולחקר המזרח הקדום יא (תשנ"ז), עמ' 153-166.

Moreshet, "Predicate": מ' מורשת, "הנשוא הקודם לשני נושאים בלשון המקרא", לשוננו לא (תשכ"ז), עמ' 251–260.

Muchiki, Y., "Why the Description of the Altar of Incense was Postponed (Exod 30:1–10)," *Exegetica* 10 (1999), pp. 19–31.

Müller, H. P., "Ḥartum," *TDOT*, vol. 5, pp. 176–179.

Myhre, K., "'Måltidsofferet' i Det gamle testamente: En undersøkelse av offertypen šĕlamim/zœbaḥ šĕlamim," *Tidsskrift for Teologi og Kirke* 52 (1981), pp. 107–210.

Naeh, "Structure and Division": ש' נאה, "מבנהו וחלוקתו של מדרש תורת כוהנים. א: מגילות (לקודיקולוגיה התלמודית הקדומה)", תרביץ סו (תשנ"ז), עמ' 483–515.

Navon, "Historical Consciousness": ח' נבון, "גישתו של הרב סולובייצ'יק לתודעה ההיסטורית", סיני קמא (תשס"ח), עמ' קסז–קפד.

Neusner, J., *The Idea of Purity in Ancient Judaism*, Leiden, 1973.

Niehr, H., "Nasi," *TDOT*, vol. 10, pp. 44–53.

Nielsen, K., *Incense in Ancient Israel* (SVT 38), Leiden, 1986.

Nihan, C., "The Templization of Israel in Leviticus: Some Remarks on Blood Disposal and *Kipper* in Leviticus 4," in: F. Landy, L. M. Trevaskis and B. D. Bibb (eds.), *Text, Time, and Temple: Literary, Historical and Ritual Studies in Leviticus*, Sheffield, 2015, pp. 94–130.

Nissinen, M., *Prophets and Prophecy in the Ancient Near East*, Atlanta, 2003.

Noam, "Purity Laws": ו' נעם, "שוב לתחומן של הלכות טהרה", ציון עב (תשס"ז), עמ' 127–160.

Noam, *Qumran*: ו' נעם, מקומראן למהפכה התנאית: היבטים בתפיסת הטומאה, ירושלים תש"ע.

Nolland, J., "Does the Cultic *shm* Make Reparation to God?," *Ephemerides Theologicae Lovanienses* 91 (2015), pp. 87–110.

Noordtzij, A., *Leviticus* (Bible Student's Commentary; translated by R. Togtman), Grand Rapids, 1982.

North, C. R., "The Religious Aspects of Hebrew Kingship," ZAW 50 (1932), pp. 8–38.

Noth, M., *Leviticus*, OTL (translated by J. E. Anderson), London, 1965.

Odes: מ' אודס, "לטעמי דיני החטאת והאשם", מעלין בקודש ז (תשס"ג), עמ' 117-142; מעלין בקודש ח (תשס"ד), עמ' 13-30.

Oppenheim, A. L., *Ancient Mesopotamia: Portrait of a Dear Civilization* (revised edition), Chicago, 1977.

Otto, *The Idea of Holy*: ר' אוטו, הקדושה: על הלא רציונלי באידאת האל ויחסו לרציונלי (בתרגום מרים רון), ירושלים תשנ"ט.

Paran, "Laying the Hands": מ' פארן, "שני סוגים של 'סמיכת ידיים' במקור הכהני", באר שבע ב (תשמ"ה), עמ' 115-119.

Paran, *Leviticus*: מ' פארן, ויקרא, עולם התנ"ך, תל אביב 1993.

Philo, *Writings*: כתבי פילון האלכסנדרוני (תירגמו וערכו: י' עמיה, מ' ניהוף וס' דניאל־נטף), חמישה כרכים, ירושלים תשנ"א-תשע"ב.

Pilch, J. J., "House and Hearth," *Bible Today* 31 (1993), pp. 292–299.

Porter, J. P., *Leviticus*, CBC, Cambridge, 1976.

Propp, W. H. C., *Exodus 1–18*, AB, New York, 1999.

Propp, W. H. C., *Exodus 19–40*, AB, New York, 2006.

Propp, W. H., "The Origins of Infant Circumcision in Israel," *Hebrew Annual Review* 11 (1987), pp. 355–370.

Rabinovitz, *Blessing*: ח"ר רבינוביץ, "הברכה והקללה במקרא", בית מקרא יח (תשל"ג), עמ' 370-374.

Rainey, A., "Sacrifice," *Encyclopedia Judaica* (Second edition) vol. 17, pp. 639–644.

Rappaport, *Mikdash David*: הרב דוד הכהן ראפאפרט, מקדש דוד, ירושלים תשנ"ו (מהדורה חדשה).

Regev, "Eating the Grain Offering": א' רגב, "המחלוקות על אכילת מנחת זבח השלמים ולחמי התודה על-פי 'מגילת מקצת מעשה התורה', 'מגילת המקדש' והסכוליון ל'מגילת תענית'", תרביץ סה (תשנ"ו), עמ' 375-388.

Regev, "Hanukkah": א' רגב, "חנוכה, סוכות וימי המילואים בספר מקבים ב'", בית מקרא מו (תשס"א), עמ' 227-243.

Regev, "Holiness": א' רגב, "קדושה דינמית או קדושה סטטית?", שנתון למקרא ולחקר המזרח הקדום יד (תשס"ד), עמ' 51-74.

Reizel, *Introduction to Midrashic Literature*: ע' רייזל, מבוא למדרשים, אלון שבות תשע"א.

Rendtorff, R., "Nadab and Abihu," in: J. C. Exum and H. G. M. Williamson (eds.), *Reading from Right to Left: Essays on the Hebrew Bible in Honour of David J. A. Clines*, London 2003, pp. 359–363.

Rendtorff, R., *Leviticus*, BKAT, Neukirchen-Vluyn, 1985.

Rendtorff, R., *Studien zur Geschichte des Opfers im Alten Israel*, Neukirchen-Vluyn, 1967.

Ringgren, H., *Israelite Religion*, Philadelphia, 1966.

Ringgren, U., "Ḥ-K-K," *TDOT*, vol. 5, pp. 139–147.

Ringgren, U., "Kohen (Mesopotamia and Western Semites)," *TDOT*, vol. 7, pp. 63–65.

Rooker, M. F., *Leviticus*, NAC, Nashville, 2000.

Rosenson, "Concerning the Binding": י' רוזנסון, "על העקדה ובעקבותיה – שני עיונים מקראיים", בתוך: י' רוזנסון וב' לאו (עורכים), עקדת יצחק לזרעו – מבט בעין ישראלית: לזכרו של יצחק הירשברג הי"ד, תשס"ג, עמ' 321-335.

Rotenberg, "Kayom": מ' רוטנברג, "להוראת המלה כיום בשמונה ממקומותיה במקרא", לשוננו מח-מט (תשמ"ד-תשמ"ה), עמ' 60-62.

Roth, A. M., "Fingers, Stars, and the 'Opening of the Mouth': the Nature and Function of the Ntrwj-Blades," *Journal of Egyptian Archaeology* 79 (1993), pp. 57–79.

Sabato, "Freewill Offerings": הרב מ' סבתו, "קרבנות הנדבה", בתוך: הרב ע' ביק וי' פיינטוך (עורכים), תורת עציון – ויקרא, ירושלים תשע"ה, עמ' 19-25.

Safrai, "Blessings": ש' ספראי וז' ספראי, מסכת ברכות, משנת ארץ ישראל, ירושלים תשע"א.

Samet: הרב א' סמט, עיונים בפרשות השבוע: סדרה ראשונה (שני כרכים), ירושלים תשס"ב.

Sandorfi, "Sin Offering": א' שנדורפי, "פרשת קרבן חטאת", מעלין בקדש ט (תשס"ה), עמ' 13-33.

Sandorfi, "Variable Offering": א' שנדורפי, "פרשת קרבן עולה ויורד", שמעתין 146 (תשס"ו), עמ' 48-66.

Sandorfi, "Who Brings": א' שנדורפי, "מי מביא קרבן תודה?", מעלין בקודש ד (תשס"ב), עמ' 75-89.

Sansom, M. C., "Laying On of Hands in the Old Testament," *Expository Times* 94 (1983), pp. 323–326.

Sarna, N. M., *Understanding Genesis,* New York, 1966.

Savran, G., "Seeing Is Believing: On the Relative Priority of Visual and Verbal Perception of the Divine," *Biblical Interpretation* 17 (2009), pp. 320–361.

Schötz, D., *Schuld- und Sündopfer im Alten Testament,* Breslau, 1930.

Schunk, K. D., "Tuaḥ," *TDOT,* vol. 5, pp. 318–319.

Schwartz, "Nosei avon": ב"י שורץ, "מה בין מונח למטפורה? נשא עון/פשע/חטא במקרא", תרביץ סג (תשנ"ד), עמ' 149-171.

Schwartz, B. J., "The Prohibitions Concerning the 'Eating' of Blood in Leviticus 17," in: G. A. Anderson and S. M. Olyan (eds.), *Priesthood and Cult in Ancient Israel,* Sheffield, 1991, pp. 34–66.

Schwartz, *Sanctity*: ב' שורץ, שלושה פרקים מספר הקדושה, עבודת דוקטור, האוניברסיטה העברית, ירושלים תשמ"ז.

Seebass, H., "Berit im Buch Numeri," in: C. Dohmen and C. Frevel (eds.) *Für immer verbündet: Studien zur Bundestheologie der Bibel: Festgabe für Frank-Lothar Hossfeld zum 65,* Stuttgart, 2007, pp. 219–230.

Seebass, H., "Nefesh," *TDOT,* vol. 9, pp. 497–519.

Segal, P., "The 'Divine Penalty' in the Harna Inscriptions and the Mishnah," *JJS* 40 (1989), pp. 46–52.

Seligmann, "Hebrew Fiction": י"א זליגמן, "סיפורת עברית והיסטוריוגרפיה מקראית", בתוך: א' הורביץ, ש' יפת וע' טוב (עורכים), מחקרים בספרות המקרא, ירושלים תשנ"ב, עמ' 46-61.

Seybold, K., "M-SH-Ḥ," *TDOT,* vol. 9, pp. 43–54.

Shadal: פירוש ר' שמואל דוד לוצאטו על חמשה חומשי תורה, תל אביב תשכ"ו.

Shammah, "Two Objectives": א' שמאע, "שתי מגמות בחנוכת המשכן והשתקפותן בתורת הקורבנות", מגדים ב (תשמ"ז), עמ' 32-44.

Shammah, *The Mekhiltot*: א' שמאע, המכילתות הנספחות לספרא: מכילתא דמילואים ומכילתא דעריות, עבודת דוקטור, האוניברסיטה העברית, ירושלים תשס"ט.

Shinan, "Nadav and Avihu": א' שנאן, "חטאיהם של נדב ואביהוא באגדת חז"ל: לבעיית הסיפור המקראי המורחב באגדת חז"ל", תרביץ מח (תשל"ט), עמ' 201-214.

Sklarz, "Disparity": מ' סקלרץ, "התמודדות עם הפער בין הפשט לדרש – רמב"ן בעקבות ראב"ע", שנתון למקרא ולחקר המזרח הקדום כב (תשע"ג), עמ' 189-222.

Smith, W. R., *Lectures on the Religion of the Semites: The Fundamental Institutions*, London, 1927.

Snijders, L. A., "M-L-A," *TDOT*, vol. 8, pp. 297–307.

Soloveitchik, *Lonely Man of Faith*: הרב י"ד סולובייצ'יק, איש האמונה הבודד, ירושלים תשכ"ח.

Soloveitchik, *Yom HaKippurim*: i:- הרב י"ד סולובייצ'יק, שיעורי הגרי"ד עבודת יום הכיפורים, ירושלים תשס"ה.

Sommer, B. D., "Expulsion as Initiation: Displacement, Divine Presence, and Divine Exile in the Torah," in: A. Cohen and S. Magid (eds.), *Beginning/Again: Toward a Hermeneutics of Jewish Texts*, New York and London, 2001, pp. 23–48.

Speiser, E. A., "Background and Function of the Biblical *Nasi*," *CBQ* 25 (1963), pp. 111–117.

Spiegelman, "Vayikra and Tzav": הרב מ' שפיגלמן, "בין ויקרא לצו", בתוך: הרב ע' ביק וי' פיינטוך (עורכים), תורת עציון – ויקרא, אלון שבות תשע"ה, עמ' 69-75.

Spiro, A., "A Law on the Sharing of Information," *PAAJR* 28 (1959), pp. 95–101.

Statman, "Thou Shalt Not Stand Against": ד' סטטמן, "לא תעמוד על דם רעך – מחובת הזהירות לחובת השומרוני הטוב", מחקרי משפט טו (תשנ"ט), עמ' 89-116.

Stav, *Beyond the Curtain*: הרב א׳ סתיו, מבית לפרוכת: פשט, עיון ומשמעות בעבודת יום הכיפורים, אלון שבות תשע״ו (מהדורה שנייה).

Steinberg, "Kelayot": א׳ שטיינברג, ״כליות ודרכי השתן״, אנציקלופדיה הלכתית רפואית, כרך ה, ירושלים תשס״ו, עמ׳ 110–133.

Steinberg, *Biblical Dictionary*: י׳ שטיינברג, מלון התנ״ך, תל אביב תשכ״ב (מהדורה שלישית).

Stollman, *Search of Lost Meaning*: א׳ סטולמן, בעקבות הפשט האבוד: קריאה חדשה בפרקי התורה, ירושלים תשע״ט.

Stuart, D. K., *Exodus*, NAC, Nashville, 2006.

Talmon, S., "The Presentation of Synchroneity and Simultaneity in Biblical Narratives," *Scripta Hierosolymitana* 27 (1978), pp. 9–26.

Talshir, "Comment": ד׳ טלשיר, ״הערה על מ׳ רוטנברג, ׳כיום׳״, לשוננו מח-מט (תשמ״ה), עמ׳ 220.

Thiessen, M., "The Text of Genesis 17:14," *JBL* 128 (2009), pp. 625–642.

Thompson, R. J., *Penitence and Sacrifice in early Israel outside the Levitical law: An examination of the Fellowship Theory of Early Israelite Sacrifice*, Leiden, 1963.

Urbach, *Pillars of Jewish Thought*: ש״ב אורבאך, עמודי המחשבה הישראלית, ירושלים תשל״א.

Urbach, *The Sages*: א״א אורבך, חז״ל: פרקי אמונות ודעות, ירושלים תשל״א (מהדורה שנייה).

Van den Branden, A., "Lévitique 1–7 et le tarif de Marseille, CIS I. 165," *RSO* 40 (1965), p 107–130.

Van der Leeuw, G., *Religion in Essence and Manifestation* (Translated by J. E. Turner), vol. 1, Princeton, 1986.

Van Seters, J., *Abraham in History and Tradition*, New Haven, 1975.

Vancil, J. W., "Goat, Goatherd," *ABD*, vol. 2, pp. 1040–1041.

Vancil, J. W., "Sheep, Shepherd," *ABD*, vol. 5, pp. 1187–1190.

Viberg, A., *Symbols of Law: A Contextual Analysis of Legal Symbolic Acts in the Old Testament*, Stockholm, 1992.

Vincent, A., "Les rites du balancement (*Tenouphah*) et du prélèvement

(*Teroumah*) dans le Sacrifice de Communion de l'Ancien Testament," *Melanges syriens* 1 (1939), pp. 267–272.

Vinci, L., *Incense: Its Ritual Significance, Use and Preparation*, New York, 1980.

Volz, P., "Die Handauflegen beim Opfer," *ZAW* 21 (1901), pp. 93–100.

Vriezen, T. C., "The Term *Hizza*: Lustration and Consecratio," *OTS* 7 (1950), pp. 201–235.

Walker, C., and M. Dick, *The Induction of the Cult Image in Ancient Mesopotamia: The Mesopotamian Mīs Pî Ritual: Transliteration, Translation, and Commentary*, Helsinki, 2001.

Warning, W., "Terminologische Verknüpfungen und Leviticus 11," *Biblische Zeitschrift* 46 (2002), pp. 97–102.

Warning, W., *Literary Artistry in Leviticus* (BIS 35), Leiden, 1999.

Wasser, "Laying of the Hands": א' ווסר, "מצוות הסמיכה בקורבנות", מעלין בקודש לו (תשע"ח), עמ' 85-116.

Watts, J. W., "Olah: The Rhetoric of Burnt Offerings," *VT* 56 (2006), pp. 125–137.

Watts, J. W., "The Historical and Literary Contexts of the Sin and Guilt Offerings," in: F. Landy, L. M. Trevaskis, and B. Bibb (eds.), *Text, Time, and Temple: Literary, Historical and Ritual Studies in Leviticus*, Sheffield, 2015, pp. 85–93.

Watts, J. W., *Leviticus 1–10 (HCOT)*, Leuven, 2013.

Watts, J. W., *Ritual and Rhetoric in Leviticus: From Sacrifice to Scripture*, Cambridge, 2007.

Waxman, "Firepan": ח' וקסמן, "איש מחתתו: מות נדב ואביהוא", בתוך: הרב ע' ביק וי' פיינטוך (עורכים), תורת עציון – ויקרא, ירושלים תשע"ה, עמ' 109-115.

Weinberg, "Purification and Guilt Offerings": צ' וינברג, "חטאת ואשם", בית מקרא יח (תשל"ג), עמ' 524-530.

Weinberg, *Sacrifice in Israel*: צ' וינברג, הקרבן בישראל על פי המקרא והמנהגים של העמים השכנים, עבודת דוקטור, אוניברסיטת תל אביב תשל"א.

Weinel, H., "M-SH-Ḥ und seine Derivate: Linguistisch-archäologische Studie," ZAW 18 (1898), 1–82.

Weiner, *Priestly Kingdom*: ד"ה וינר, ממלכת כהנים: עיון במצוות הכהונה, עכו תשס"ו.

Weinfeld, "Afternoon Prayer": מ' ויינפלד, "תפילת מנחה – משמעה והתפתחותה", בתוך: ז' פלק (עורך), גבורות הרמח: מוגש לר' משה חיים ויילר, ירושלים תשמ"ז, עמ' 77-81.

Weinfeld, "Change in the Conception": מ' ויינפלד, "המפנה בתפיסת האלהות והפולחן בספר דברים", תרביץ לא (תשכ"ב), עמ' 1-17.

Weinfeld, M., "Glory," TDOT, vol. 7, pp. 22–38.

Weinfeld, M., "Minḥa," TDOT, vol. 8, pp. 407–420.

Weinfeld, M., *Deuteronomy and the Deuteronomic School*, Oxford, 1972, pp. 179–243.

Wellhausen, J., *Prolegomena zur Geschichte Israels: Mit einem Stellenregister*, Berlin and New York, 2001.

Wenham, G. J., "The Theology of Old Testament Sacrifice," in: R. T. Beckwith and M. Selman (eds.), *Sacrifice in the Bible*, Oregon, 1995, pp. 75–87.

Wenham, G. J., *The Book of Leviticus*, NICOT, Grand Rapids, 1979.

Werblowsky, "Sacrifice": צ' ורבלובסקי, "קרבן", האנציקלופדיה העברית, כרך ל, עמ' 58-59.

Whitekettle, R., "A Study in Scarlet: The Physiology and Treatment of Blood, Breath, and Fish in Ancient Israel," *JBL* 135 (2016), pp. 685–704.

Wolf, "Pure Bird Carcass": הרב ד' וולף, "נבלת עוף טהור", עלון שבות 149 (תשנ"ז), עמ' 11-16.

Wolff, H. W., *Anthropology of the OT* (translated to English), Philadelphia, 1974.

Wright, D. P., "The Spectrum of Priestly Impurity," in: G. A. Anderson and S. M. Olyan (eds.), *Priesthood and Cult in Ancient Israel*, Sheffield, 1991, pp. 150–181.

Wright, D. P., *The Disposal of Impurity: Elimination Rites in the Bible and in Hittite and Mesopotamian Literature*, Atlanta, 1987.

Yeivin, "Tabernacle": ש' ייבין, "מקדש, מקדשים במזרח הקדמון", אנציקלופדיה מקראית, כרך ה, עמ' 322-304.

Zimmerli, W., *Ezechiel*, BKAT, 2 vols., Neukirchen-Vluyn, 1979 (second edition).

The fonts used in this book are from the Arno family

Maggid Books
The best of contemporary Jewish thought from
Koren Publishers Jerusalem Ltd.